Men and Sex

Bernard Zilbergeld graduated from Ohio University and

by

...xuality Program in the University of California in San Francisco. There he has developed many successful group and individual treatment schemes for men, and has worked with men who simply wanted to enhance their sexual functioning and enjoyment without having any specific problems. He has organized and conducted workshops for men to explore various male sexual roles, family planning, etc., and, as well as teaching at several local colleges, has also maintained a private practice.

BERNARD ZILBERGELD
With the assistance of John Ullman

MEN AND SEX
A Guide to Sexual Fulfilment

HarperCollins*Publishers*

HarperCollins*Publishers*
77–85 Fulham Palace Road,
Hammersmith, London W6 8JB

This paperback edition 1995
1 3 5 7 9 8 6 4 2

Previously published in paperback by Fontana 1980
Reprinted ten times

First published in Great Britain by
Souvenir Press Ltd 1979

ISBN 0 00 638323 8

Set in Meridien

Printed in Great Britain by
HarperCollinsManufacturing Glasgow

The excerpt from *The Betsy* by Harold Robbins is reprinted by permission
of Simon & Schuster. Copyright © by Harold Robbins. The author is
grateful for the permission to reprint the drawing on page 257 from *Pediatrics
and Adolescent Gynecology* by S. Jean Herrior Emans, M.D. and Donald Peter
Goldstein, M.D. Copyright © 1977 by Little, Brown and Company. The
author is also grateful for the permission to reprint the
illustrations on pages 299 and 302 from *Human Sexual Inadequacy* by
William H. Masters and Virginia E. Johnson. Copyright © 1966 by
Little, Brown and Company, and by the same authors the diagram,
modified with permission, on page 132 from *Human Sexual Response*.
Copyright © 1966 by Little, Brown and Company.

For my father,
who was both father and mother
and gave far more than he knew

Contents

CONTENTS

Acknowledgments

This book began as a combined effort by me and John Ullman. We had been working with men at different places in San Francisco – John at Fort Help, I at the Human Sexuality Program, University of California Medical Center, and in private practice – and decided to pool our resources. The book was to have been one of the products of our collaboration. Unfortunately, because of the illness of his wife, John was unable to do as much as he had hoped. As his wife's condition deteriorated, it became clear to both of us that the project could not proceed as anticipated and that I would have to complete it on my own.

The finished work is substantially different from the one John and I envisioned. As new chapters were written and old ones revised, I relied more and more on my own experience and knowledge. Although the final version is my own work, and I assume full responsibility for any errors and stupidities, I want to acknowledge John's contributions. He shared in the original planning of the book, wrote parts of Chapter 9, and contributed some of the material I used in Chapters 1, 5, 7 and 12. He also read my early drafts with care and made many helpful suggestions. I regret that we could not write the book as we had planned and at the same time am grateful for the assistance he gave me.

Many other people gave valuable help.

A few friends and colleagues were there from the beginning, reading the entire manuscript, correcting errors, and giving perspective and support. My thanks to Lonnie Barbach, Jackie Hackel, Bruce Heller, Lillian Rubin, and especially to Carol

Rinkleib, as loving a friend and critical an unofficial editor as I could ever ask for.

My thanks to the following people who read portions of the manuscript and/or made suggestions regarding some of the ideas in it: Bob Badame, Harvey Caplan, Bob Geiger, Seymour Freedman, Linda and Bernard Gore, Jose Gutierrez, Linda Janowitz, Sue Knight, Don Linker, Jay Mann, Kate Mollinoff, Ann Spence, Lynn Stanton, Douglas Wallace and Joyce Welsher.

Everyone in the sex field owes much to three individuals who built the foundation on which the rest of us stand. They fought the battles, cleared the way, and made it easy for those of us who followed. Although I take issue with them in several places, it's an honor to acknowledge my debt to Alfred Kinsey, William Masters and Virginia Johnson.

I was fortunate in having an excellent agent, editor and copy editor. They were all there when I needed them and gave me plenty of help. My thanks to Rhoda Weyr, Bill Phillips and Mike Mattil.

Last, I owe a special debt to the men and women from whom I learned in therapy, workshops, classes, and talks. Though I was their therapist, teacher, or speaker, I probably learned as much from them as they did from me. In sharing their experiences with me, some of which are recounted in the book, they gave me the understanding and knowledge to better help others.

                                                    Bernard Zilbergeld

ONE

Men and Sex

A common myth in our culture deals with the supposed sexual differences between men and women. According to this bit of fantasy, female sexuality is complex, mysterious, and full of problems, while male sexuality is simple, straightforward, and problem-free.

Part of women's complexity – still following the myth – is due to their equipment. In contrast to men, who have only one sexual organ, women have several; moreover, clitorises and vaginas aren't very visible. Then, too, women have some, well, peculiar attitudes about sex. They seem always to be talking about feelings, tenderness, communication, and relating. What these things have to do with sex is often unclear to men. And women want to go about sex in interesting ways. They don't seem to desire it as much as men and, even when they do, they require endless amounts of gentleness and foreplay, and still take forever to reach orgasm. And they have no end of problems in, and requirements for, sex. They need to feel certain ways to get in the mood; they require stimulation done in a very precise manner; they have pain with intercourse; they have difficulties reaching orgasm or the right kind of orgasm; and when it's all over, it's still not over because they need cuddling and talking and relating. On the other hand, however, there is the puzzling situation, one which many men have experienced and most others have at least heard about, where a woman gets totally out of control, wanting more sex than any sensible man could supply and acting like a crazed beast, moaning and shrieking through endless orgasms, mocking her man's inability to keep up.

It's clear, then, that women are a bit strange, and it's a good thing there are so many books and articles coming out on female sexuality. Somewhere in one of them must be the answers to what women are about sexually, and how a man can better understand them.

In contrast, the myth goes, men are very simple creatures when it comes to sex. They have no special requirements, they are almost always ready and willing, and their only problem is how to get enough of it. Men's equipment is the essence of simplicity. A man's sexuality is concentrated in one place and there it is, hanging out for all the world to see. What could be mysterious about anything that obvious and what more would anyone need to know about it? A man's sexual tastes are easy, too. He will, as the old maxim has it, take it any way he can get it, but what he really wants to do is stick it in and hump away until he has an orgasm, with as little tenderness, communication, and relating as possible. Of course, given the fact that few women are willing to put up with this kind of behavior anymore, most men are willing to do some foreplay to get their ladies ready and to try to hold off orgasm until their partners have had one of their own.

According to this myth, then, there is quite a lot to be learned about female sexuality – about why women think and act as they do sexually and how their many, mysterious problems in this area can be dealt with – but little or nothing to be learned or said about men and sex. The males, after all, are so simple and quite content as long as they're getting enough.

The myth may appear ridiculous the way we've stated it, and of course it is, but you'd be surprised how many people believe it. It is erroneous in almost every point it makes. Men are neither so simple nor content as we have been led to believe. Moreover, at this point we know much less about male sexuality than about female sexuality.

We started working with men six years ago in two large clinics in San Francisco. At first, we did sex therapy only with couples but soon developed group and individual formats for men without partners and men whose partners refused to participate in treatment. It was not surprising that all the men who came for therapy were dissatisfied with their sex lives. But two factors about them greatly impressed us. By and large, they were normal, healthy men; only a few could be called neurotic or seriously disturbed. It became clear that you didn't have to be psychologically impaired to have sexual difficulties. The other interesting factor was the rigidity with which the men clung to certain rules as to how sex should be and how a man should act in sex. We began to wonder where they had gotten these rules and why they held to them so tenaciously.

Then we also started working with men who had no sexual problems. We gave talks, classes, and workshops on sex, sensuousness, assertiveness, social skills, communication skills, and forming more meaningful relationships. Even though some of these were not intended to deal specifically with sex, sex always came up and we kept hearing the same things again and again. Most men were not satisfied with their sexuality and most wanted to learn more about it. The real shocker, however, was that those without specific sex problems believed in the same set of sexual rules as those with problems, though perhaps not quite as rigidly.

Our observations regarding male discontent and problems were confirmed by the observations and studies of others. Herbert Hendin, for example, in his excellent study of college students, *The Age of Sensation*, noted that sex problems had become one of the main reasons college men came for therapy. And this was the younger generation, thought by so many of us over thirty to be free of sexual troubles. In a survey of over 52,000 people by *Psychology Today*, 55 per cent of the men said they were dissatisfied with their sex lives and 39 per cent admitted to various problems such as disinterest in sex and premature ejaculation.

We were impressed by both the widespread prevalence of specific sexual problems and the even greater sense of dissatisfaction. All was not as well with men and sex as had been supposed.

If what we are saying is valid, how is it that so many of us believe the opposite, that men are sexually content?

One of the chief reasons is that men have been, and to a large extent still are, extremely secretive about their sexuality. They may joke about sex, talk a lot about this or that woman's characteristics and how they'd like to get her in bed, and make many allusions to their sexual prowess, but, other than these bits of bravado, most men simply don't talk about sex to anyone.

One of the cornerstones of the masculine stereotype in our society is that a man is one who has no doubts, questions, or confusion about sex, and that a real man knows how to have good sex and does so frequently. For a man to ask a question about sex, thereby revealing ignorance, or to express concern, or to admit to a problem is to risk being thought something less than a man.

Almost every man tends to think that all other men are having a better time sexually than he is, with none of the worries or questions that he has (the men in the *Psychology Today* survey guessed that only 1 per cent of their peers were virgins, a bad miscalculation since the actual percentage of virgins in that sample was 22). This reinforces his idea that it's best to keep his mouth shut. How would it look, being the only guy on the block who comes too fast or who isn't having much sex or who isn't enjoying it as much as he thinks he should?

So men learn to fake it. They can't fake erections, but we know of more than a few who fake orgasms. But the main things they fake are their feelings. They pretend to be confident when they're not, to know when they don't, to be comfortable when they're uneasy, to be interested when they couldn't care less, and to enjoy when they feel otherwise. The cost of this deception is horrendous. It keeps men from being honest with either men or women, thus preserving the illusion that men have no doubts or questions or concerns about sex, which in turn makes it harder for any other man to voice misgivings or problems.

Another factor that generates a false picture about male sexuality is the sheer quantitative discrepancy between what has been said and written about female sexuality and growing up female on the one hand, and what has come forth about men on the other. A whole literature has appeared on what it's like to be a girl and woman – physically, socially, sexually, and politically – much of which has sensitively portrayed the trials and tribulations, both major and minor, that any growing up and interacting with humans entails. Since much less has been said and written about men, the impression is conveyed that women have many more problems than men and that it must be very easy to be male in this society, especially when it comes to sex.

But, as we have said, men really do have concerns about sex, even though they may try to pretend that this isn't so. What follows is a presentation of the kinds of sexual interests and attitudes expressed by the men we talk to.

Almost all have questions about their sexuality, about how they feel and function, and how they can make sex better for themselves and their partners. They are not content with the knowledge they have acquired; many have questions about what other men are like and whether their own thoughts and behaviors are all right. They wonder about such things as: 'Do other men do it like I do?' 'Do they also worry if their penises are adequate?' 'Does everyone get as nervous as I do when I make it with a new woman?' 'Are my fantasies really OK?' 'Am I some kind of nut for not wanting sex sometimes or for not liking oral (or anal or group) sex?' They want to know more, to expand and enhance their sexuality, even though they may have only a vague idea of what this might mean.

Other men say they have relatively good sex but wonder if they're missing something. Sex is pleasant, but not quite what it was cracked up to be – the earth doesn't move, bells don't ring, trumpets don't blow – and, when it's over, they still have to walk the dog and pay the bills. Sex just hasn't united them with the cosmos or changed their lives in any way. Is it possible, they ask, that there is some new position, partner, practice, or gimmick that would bring sex up to expectation?

Another attitude is represented by the surprising responses

to a question we frequently ask at talks and workshops: 'How many men have felt, at least at times, that sex was a burden?' In most instances, at least 30 per cent of the men admitted to that feeling, and many times over half of them did. From some of them, as well as from some of the clients we see in sex therapy, come statements that a few years ago were heard only from women: 'It feels like work some of the time, like a duty, but I try my best because I want to keep my wife happy.' 'I often don't enjoy it much but I feel I owe it to her. Besides, if she doesn't get what she wants from me, she might get it somewhere else.'

Sex feels more like work than fun to these men. They have so much to do – initiating, getting their partners turned on, orchestrating the whole event, making sure their partners are satisfied, and, finally, finding their own satisfaction. And theirs is the responsibility; they believe they are accountable if their partners don't have orgasms or if the experience is lacking in any way. All the publicity of the last few years about female sexuality, especially about women's 'need' for sexual fulfillment and multiple orgasms, has served primarily to increase the dimensions of what these men see as their duty and also to increase their concerns about what might happen if they don't perform well. These men wonder if there are ways of making sex more enjoyable, of making it less work and responsibility and more fun.

And some men have problems that trouble them greatly. The types of problems vary considerably: lack of interest; difficulty getting or maintaining erections; ejaculating faster than they or their partners desire; inability to get what they want in sex (a much more common problem among men than has been appreciated); and a lack of feeling, although the ability to function may be unimpaired. Older men, and men with serious illnesses or injuries, are often concerned about the effects of aging or physical disability on their sexual expression.

Men who have any of these concerns or problems spend much time and energy worrying about themselves, wondering if there is any help for them or if their manhood, as they are wont to call it, is slipping away. Some give up sex altogether, so greatly do they fear another failure or finding out that things aren't the way they used to be. Others blame the problem on their partners, thus attempting to find release from the fears that haunt them. And still others play musical beds, vainly searching for the magical woman with whom all will be well.

This book is intended for men in all categories – for those who want to learn more about their sexuality, those who want to get more out of sex, those who are looking for ways to integrate sex into their lives in ways consistent with their own values and feelings, and those who want some specific skills for dealing with problems they are experiencing. These categories are not as disparate as they may sound; the principles and methods for dealing with them are quite similar. Change in one area often also means changes in the other areas.

While the book is primarily intended for heterosexual men and employs a heterosexual idiom, much of the material and most of the techniques have been used with equal success by ourselves and others with homosexual men. Gay readers will, of course, have to translate some of our words into language more appropriate to their own situations.

This book is also for women. Many women have told us of their ignorance of male sexuality and their desire to learn more. Because of their candid conversations with other women and the wealth of reading material on female sexuality, they know a lot about women and sex but not nearly as much as they'd like about men's attitudes and experiences with sex.

Even in a book of this length we could not cover everything, so we chose the topics and techniques that we found to be the most interesting and beneficial to the men we have talked to and worked with in enhancing their sexuality and resolving specific problems.

We begin with a discussion of what men learn about sex.

Our thesis is that the rules and concepts we learn are destructive and a very inadequate preparation for a satisfying and pleasurable sex life. As incredible as it may sound to you now, we believe that men have been duped about sex. They have accepted unrealistic and, in fact, super-human standards by which to measure their equipment, performance, and satisfaction, thus ensuring a perpetual no-win situation. Whatever men do, it's somehow not enough, not when compared to the standards they learned. Without a doubt, this learning is the source of most of our sexual discomforts and problems. It prevents us from resolving whatever problems we encounter and also hinders us in our search for sexual expression that is a true reflection of ourselves.

Having a better sex life is in large measure dependent upon your willingness to examine how the male sexual mythology has trapped you. After coming to grips with your learning and expectations, you are in a position to change, and much of the book is devoted to material and techniques that will give you the opportunity to experience different ways of being and behaving sexually.

There are chapters on discovering and asserting your sexual needs and desires; the physical side of sex; touching; masturbation; relaxation and sex; the uses of sex and sex problems (what at first seems like a problem is sometimes a solution to another problem); dealing with partners; and female sexuality. There is also a chapter on sex and aging and another on sex and medical conditions; these chapters are not as specialized as they sound and are intended for all men. The difficulties that older men and disabled men have with sex are really not so different from the difficulties that the rest of us experience. For men with erection problems, there is a chapter package, and there is a similar unit for men who want to develop better ejaculatory control. Even if you do not have either of these concerns, you may find it interesting to read the first chapter in each of these units.

Series of exercises are presented in most of the chapters. Readers whose interest is only in obtaining information may be content reading and not doing any of the exercises. Those desiring to make changes in their behavior, however, will want to do the exercises. Behavior change is difficult to accomplish without the development of new skills, and the purpose of the exercises is to help you develop new skills and understanding. And many of them can be fun as well.

The material and exercises are presented in the order that has proved most effective in our experiences working with men. The exercises themselves are arranged so that you always start with ones that are relatively simple and easy to do, gradually working up to ones that are more complex. As we discuss throughout the book, going slowly and being comfortable with what you're doing are essential ingredients for a good sex life.

In a workshop, class, or therapy, the leader or therapist tries to tailor his material to the specific requirements of the individuals involved. This is not easily done in a book, however, since the writer can have only a general idea of who his readers will be. Consequently, a much broader approach must be used so that readers can choose from a variety of sources to fashion their own programs. Some men will want to do most of the exercises, some will do fewer, and others will do only those in one or two chapters. The best guide we can offer is to tell you to do what fits your interests and situation. Some of the exercises and suggestions may strike you as irrelevant to your life or too easy. Start where you like. However – and this is an extremely important qualification – if you have difficulty doing what you choose to do or if you do not obtain the results you desire, the reason is probably that you tried to do too much too soon, a very common tendency among men. Instead of giving up, consider going back and doing the exercises you skipped.

Our approach to helping you enjoy sex more is based on the assumption that you are a unique individual with your own sex preferences and style. You are the person best qualified to discover what works for you and gives you pleasure. In other words, you need to learn more about your sexual self, a self that in some ways is similar to those of other men but in other ways is different. Such an exploration is not always easy and, in truth, requires both courage and persistence. Despite the lip service given by both professionals and lay people to the idea that people are unique, we all have strong tendencies to want to be precisely like everyone else, particularly in anxiety-laden areas like sex.

There is no right way to have sex. People are too different for there to be one or two or even a dozen right ways. Since people really are different and since no two people function in exactly the same way – regardless of the attempts of our sexual mythology and many sex manuals to convince you of the opposite – a book cannot tell you what you would enjoy or how to turn yourself or your partner on.

What a book can do, and what we attempt to do, is provide a framework within which you can explore what you are about sexually: your own body, patterns, preferences, and turn-ons. Such explorations fare best if they are relaxed experiences, free from demands that you be such and such a way or that you enjoy such and such an activity. Our suggestions and exercises are only opportunities for you to discover something about yourself. We hope you will give some of them a chance to work for you, but we are aware that what you learn from any given exercise may be different from what other men have learned; and that is fine.

Since many of the men we worked with have enjoyed and profited from hearing other men's feelings and experiences, we include numerous examples. Some of them are from men we have seen in therapy, classes, and workshops, and are so identified. Others are from our own lives or from friends or colleagues who did not wish to be identified. We have tried to present sufficient information so that you could develop a feeling for the man and his situation. We hope that some of these examples will be relevant to you and will give you a sense of how other men relate to their sexuality.

Resist the temptation, so common among men, of assuming that something is wrong with you if your experiences or responses are different from what is portrayed in our examples or text. Your feelings and reactions are right for you, and only by acknowledging, exploring, and building upon them will you develop the kind of sexuality that gives you the most pleasure.

TWO

Learning about sex

Although many people think of sex as something that is natural or instinctive – just doing what comes naturally – human sexuality is basically a learned phenomenon. Very little of our sexual behavior can properly be called instinctive. There are a few exceptions: new-born males, for example, have erections and obviously they have not had the chance to learn anything. It is easy to assume that since we, like all animals, are programmed to continue our species, intercourse would occur without learning. But the issue is much more complex than this, as we shall soon discuss.

Nature would be content and the human species would survive if some men at some time impregnated some women. This could be accomplished through rape, through sex that involved only penetration and quick ejaculation, with no good feelings between the participants and with neither partner enjoying it at all. The only important thing from nature's point of view is that enough births occur to replenish the lives lost through illness, injury, and old age. The ideas that some ways of having sex are better than others, that certain actions are decent while others are indecent, that some partners and places are appropriate while others are not – all these are products of learning. Nature seems to care not a whit about any of it.

Even lower animals, though they have a much larger component of instinctive programming than humans in sexual and other matters, need to learn about sex. Animals that through accident or human intervention miss their 'sex education' have a difficult time of it when they are adults and many never learn to mate. Monkeys who are deprived of certain childhood experiences – touching and being touched by their mothers, playing with and grooming peers, and/or observing adult monkeys engaging in sex – are unable to have sex when they grow up. They may try – the drive seems to be there – but they do it all wrong. Males look puzzled, unsure of what to do. They either physically assault receptive females or clumsily grope them and try to mount in inappropriate ways. The fact that animals whom we think of as more instinctually controlled than ourselves need to learn about sex should alert us to the tremendous importance of learning in our own sexual behavior.

Sex researcher John Gagnon gives this example of the role of learning in human sexuality:

It is common for heterosexually oriented men to be aroused by seeing women's breasts under clothing, by taking off a brassiere, by touching a woman's breasts . . . These activities are often accompanied by dramatic psychological and physiological changes in the man, experienced as appropriate to the sexual things he is doing. It is difficult for him as a participant . . . to recall the amount of learning that had to take place for all of these events to make sense as sexual events. There is no automatic connection between touching a woman's breasts and blood flow into the genitals.

The following personal experience may help make the point clearer.

When 1 went to summer camp, a very naive thirteen year old, I was quite conscious of being the youngest boy in my cabin. I was intrigued by what most of my roommates were doing at night. It was hard to see but it was obvious that they were doing something to themselves – to their penises, I realized as my observations continued – to the accompaniment of moaning and heavy breathing. I decided that whatever it was, it must be good since all the older boys were doing it, and that it would pay me to find out more about this activity. As soon as everyone else went to their swimming lessons, I headed for the bathroom and got to work.

At first my investigations were a flop. I did just about everything I could think of to my penis – squeezing it, petting it, rubbing it between my hands, pushing it against my thigh, waving it around like a flag – and nothing happened. It hadn't occurred to me that it would help if I had an erection. Then, one day as I was absentmindedly stroking my penis and thinking that I would have to retire from such pursuits unless more rewarding results were forthcoming, I became aware of some pleasurable sensations. I kept stroking, my penis got hard, and the sensations felt better and better. Then I was overcome with feelings I had never before felt and, God help me, white stuff came spurting out the end of my cock. I wasn't sure if I had sprung a leak or what. I was afraid but calmed down when I thought that since it was white it couldn't be blood. I kept on stroking and it hurt. l didn't know if the hurt was connected with the white stuff (had I really injured myself?) or if the event was over and my penis needed a rest. But I decided to stop for the moment. Of course I returned the next day and did it again, thus beginning a daily habit that continued for many years.

As I look back at those days, I can see how much I had to learn. The first ejaculations fired my curiosity – they were certainly interesting – but they didn't feel all that great. I wasn't sure what to make of them. Only gradually did I begin to experience them as extremely pleasurable, perhaps more pleasurable than anything else. The most interesting thing, though, is that for many months after I started masturbating, I never connected what I was doing with girls or what little I knew about sex. Masturbation – 'whacking off' is what my roommates called it – was just an enjoyable activity that boys did alone or in darkness.

Only after I heard that one could put his penis in a vagina and experience similar sensations did I begin to put together what I was doing with what I might someday do with a girl and start developing sexual fantasies to accompany my solo ministrations.

In all important areas of life we seek information about how we should act. We are acutely sensitive to information regarding roles and behaviors that are applicable to us, and we pick up relevant information in both conscious and unconscious ways.

The boy interested in becoming a doctor may read a book about medicine. He may also get information about doctors in ways that he is not aware of, so that after a while he may start walking or talking or in some manner imitating his doctor or one he has seen on television. Much of what he learns, especially from the media, is misleading, distorted, and inaccurate. He does not have much ability to differentiate between information that is accurate, that which is basically true but exaggerated, and that which is totally false. He may well build up expectations that will cause frustration and disappointment when he encounters the realities of medical practice. If he is to function well and be content with his career, he will have to unlearn or give up the false information he acquired and replace it with more realistic data.

Learning about sex is similar in many ways but also much more difficult. We all want to learn about sex since it seems like such an important part of being masculine and adult, but, because of all the double messages we get from our parents and other sources, it is a subject loaded with anxiety. Such anxiety is not conducive to clear thinking, viewing things in perspective, or calmly assessing how what we hear or read fits with our own values and experience. And sex is one of the few areas of life where it is almost impossible to observe accurately how others are doing it. It is of course possible to obtain sexual information – we are deluged with it – but much of this information is absurdly exaggerated and inaccurate and the growing boy has no way of knowing this.

A crucial element that motivated our learning and fueled our anxiety was the necessity of proving that we were men. In our society, as in almost every other society that has ever existed, manhood is a conditional attribute. The possession of a penis is necessary but not sufficient; you still had to prove, and keep on proving, that you were worthy. As Norman Mailer put it: 'Nobody was born a man; you earned your manhood provided you were good enough, bold enough.'

From countless sources we learned that our masculinity and therefore our self-esteem was always on the line: from Western and gangster movies where men never back away from a fight, even if it means almost certain death; from endless newspaper and magazine articles announcing that so-and-so had 'become a man' by enduring some terrible ordeal, leading his team to victory, or some other extraordinary task; from the sting, even if experienced only vicariously, of a male being called a 'boy', 'girl', 'fag', or 'sissy' for some supposedly unmasculine trait or act.

The badge of manhood can be won only temporarily; it can be questioned or taken away at any time. One job poorly done, one 'failure', one sign of weakness – that's all it took to lose your membership in the charmed circle. Many of us can remember how our parents, teachers, coaches, and friends used this knowledge to keep us in line.

Most of us experienced no choice: we had to demonstrate our masculinity no matter how ill-equipped and ill-prepared we felt. In his essay 'Being a Boy', Julius Lester captures the agony so many of us felt. Comparing himself to girls, he says:

There was the life, I thought! No constant pressure to prove oneself. No necessity always to be competing. While I humiliated myself on football and baseball fields, the girls stood on the sidelines laughing at me, because they didn't have to do anything except be girls. The rising of each sun brought me to the starting line of yet another day's Olympic decathlon, with no hope of ever winning even a bronze medal.

Through no fault of my own I reached adolescence. While the pressure to prove myself on the athletic field lessened, the overall situation got worse – because now I had to prove myself with girls. Just how I was supposed to go about doing this was beyond me . . . Nonetheless, duty called, and with my ninth-grade gym-class jockstrap flapping between my legs, off I went.

Like Lester, we sooner or later realized that sex was one of the most important areas in which to prove ourselves. But where could one go to find out what sex was about?

Our culture does not assist us much in acquiring accurate sexual information. Ten or more years ago, when many of us learned about sex, reliable information was not readily available. Courses on sex, even in medical and graduate schools, were virtually nonexistent, which meant that the professionals we went to for advice often knew little more than we. There were few factually accurate articles in the popular literature. And whom could you talk to? It was widely accepted that nice people didn't talk about such things and, even if you didn't consider yourself nice, it was difficult to admit ignorance or concern.

In recounting his thinking on the days before what was to have been his first sexual experience, Bill Cosby demonstrates the dilemma many of us experienced.

So, man, Saturday comes, and I've been thinkin' all week about this p-u-s-s-y. You know, and I'm tryin' to ask people questions about how they get some p-u-s-s-y. And I don't want guys to know that I don't know nothin' about gettin' no p-u-s-s-y. But how do you find out how to do it without blowin' the fact that you don't know how to do it ? So I come up to a guy, and I say, Say, man, have you ever had any p-u-s-s-y ? And the guy says, Yeah. And I say, Well, man, what's your favorite way of gettin' it? He says, Well, you know, just the regular way. And I say, Well, do you do it like I do it? And the cat says How's that? And I say, Well, hey, I heard that there was different ways of doin' it, man. He says, Well, there's a lotta ways of doin' it, you know, but I think that . . you know, the *regular* way . . . I say, *Yeah*, good ol' regular way . . . good ol' regular way of gettin' that p-u-s-s-y.

As he continues his ruminations on the way to the girl's house, Cosby – all of eleven years old at the time – neatly illustrates the influence of the idea that a man should be able to do it all on his own, even though he hasn't the faintest notion of what sex is about.

So now, I'm walkin', and I'm trying to figure out how to do it. And when I get there, the most embarrassing thing is gonna be when I have to take my pants down. See, right away, then, I'm buck naked . . . buck naked in front of this girl. Now what happens then? Do you . . . do you just . . . I don't even know what to do . . . I'm gonna just stand there and she's gonna say, You don't know how to do it. And I'm gonna say, Yes I do, but I *forgot*. I never thought of her showing me, because I'm a man and I don't want her to show me – I don't want *nobody* to show me, but I wish somebody would kinda slip me a note . . . I stopped off at a magazine stand to look and see if there were any sexy magazines about it. I mean if I wasn't going to learn how to do it, I figured there might be some pictures in there of somebody *almost* getting ready to do it. But I don't find nothin'.

Cosby arrives at the girl's house in a state of near-hysteria and avoids having sex with her. But on the way home he struts like the world's greatest lover. He brags to his friend Rufus about the 'goooooooooood p-u-s-s-y' he had gotten and when Rufus asks how he did it, he answers 'if you don't know how to do it, I ain't gonna tell you how to do it . . .' And so it goes, with ignorance proliferating at a fantastic pace and everyone thinking that everyone else really knows how to do it.

The anxiety about not knowing, about not being man enough, was so great, as was our need for acceptance from our peers, that we often faked it. Like Cosby, we lied to our friends about how far we had gone with our last date and assumed a mask of confidence and knowledge that had little basis in reality. Better to lie than risk having our fragile egos battered and ridiculed.

I remember trying to smile knowingly whenever my high school friends talked about sex and how much they were getting. I tried to give the impression that I, too, was getting a lot, even though I was very unclear about what it was I was supposed to have gotten. I felt that I had to fake it, for to have admitted my ignorance and virginity would have degraded me in the eyes of those from whom I most wanted and needed respect. It was obvious that the most adult and manly thing one could do was get a lot, so I pretended, always fearing that my deception would be discovered. I was surprised to learn, years later, that many of my friends had been lying just like me.

The last decade has of course brought a much greater availability of sexual knowledge and a greater permission to be interested in it. Stopping at a magazine stand today, you can find pictures not only of people getting ready to have sex, but doing it in every conceivable manner and place. Good reading material can be conveniently purchased; some physicians, therapists, and educators now know about sex; and it is even considered legitimate, in some circles at least, to have sexual questions, concerns, and problems.

But most of us developed our sexual scripts or models (the organized totality of our sexual knowledge) before we had access to accurate information. We grabbed whatever information we could find, from our friends and older boys (many of whom differed from us only in having a larger store of misconceptions), from the media, from sexual humor, and from any other sources at our disposal. Bit by bit we constructed a sexual script for ourselves, something to guide our sexual thoughts and behavior. Such scripts are acquired at a relatively early age and quickly become entrenched and resistant to major change.

That a more permissive attitude now prevails may seem to herald the end of sexual misinformation and ignorance, and the beginning of a state of unprecedented sexual bliss. But such is in fact not the case. Opportunities for obtaining more accurate information have clearly expanded, thus making more possible the development of more appropriate and personally satisfying sexual scripts. But all is still very far from well. Many health professionals are still abysmally ignorant about sex and much of the information disseminated by self-styled experts – like David Reuben and the anonymous authors of *The Sensuous Woman* and *The Sensuous Man* – is misleading, inaccurate and, in some cases, even dangerous. We are inundated with articles, books, courses, and programs about sex, but, because of the anxiety surrounding sexuality, most people are in no position to separate the wheat from the chaff.

And of sexual chaff there is no end. There seems to be no limit to the amount of nonsense people will believe about sex. Old misconceptions are discredited and disappear only to reappear under new labels or to be replaced by new ones at least as absurd. What sounds at first like liberation usually turns out on closer inspection to be a new and sometimes even harsher tyranny.

Because of the cultural uneasiness about sex – which affects us all, virgin and swinger alike – and because of our desperate desire to do sex the 'right way' and not miss anything for fear that we be judged less than men, we tend to distort even information that is accurate. Perspective and personal evaluation ('Does this really fit and feel good for me?') are lost as we frantically attempt to prove our masculinity and sexiness. The fact that some women sometimes have multiple orgasms gets translated into an imperative ('I've got to make my partner have several orgasms every time'). A statistic demonstrating that men in a certain age bracket have sex 2.5 times a week on the average becomes an iron-clad rule. Options like open relationships and bisexuality become necessities or causes for concern.

The problem is cultural rather than personal. Whether we formed our basic sexual scripts in the last five years or forty years ago, we are all victims of the cultural imperative to prove our manhood and the unwillingness of society at large to present us with realistic and meaningful sexual scripts to follow.

The models of sex and masculinity that were and are presented to us are deficient in a great many ways, harmful to both us and our partners, and the main cause of our sexual dissatisfaction and problems. These models have little to do with what is possible or satisfying for human beings.

We had little choice. We tried to get the best possible information. We could not foresee the negative implications of what we were learning. We were too young, too naive, too busy growing and living to have much perspective and to realize what was happening to us. Much of the time we were not even aware that we were learning anything. As we shall see in the next chapter, much of our sex education comes from sources not usually thought of as educational.

Not all of our sex education was negative, however. Although all of us have been influenced to some extent by the myths and fantasies discussed in the next two chapters, some of us were influenced less than others. Some men were fortunate in having understanding parents, teachers, lovers, or others from whom they were able to obtain information and the space to develop in their own way. Others, with little or no outside assistance, had to struggle harder to develop their sexuality in personally satisfying ways. And some of these men were able to replace early, destructive knowledge with models more consistent with their own personalities and values.

While we acknowledge these exceptions and salute the increasing number of men willing to deal with the sex-role stereotypes and sexual mythology that chains them, it is certain that these chains still exert an incredible influence on most of us. The sexual model we will be discussing guides much of our sexual behavior (including thoughts and feelings) even though we are usually unaware of its influence. In a real sense, the model is our problem. It is what prevents us from expressing and enjoying our sexuality in the most satisfying ways.

What has been learned can be unlearned and replaced by more personally appropriate knowledge. Actually, you don't really have to unlearn anything. All you need to do is recognize what is getting in your way and loosen its grip just a little bit. Much of sex therapy, and much of what occurs in workshops and courses on sex, is simply the use of techniques designed to gently unleash you from some of your early sexual learning and give you the opportunity to experience other ways of being sexual.

And that, in essence, is what this book is about.

THREE

It's two feet long, hard as steel, and can go on all night: the fantasy model of sex

In this and the following chapter we discuss the model of sex that is prevalent in our society. The model is rarely encountered in its entirety, but bits and pieces of it are found everywhere. Its purest exemplar is pornography (movies, books, and, more recently, comic books), but it also abounds in sexual humor, popular literature, those works of 'good' fiction that deal explicitly with sex, and even in technical and scientific literature.

We believe that sexual learning takes place all the time. Whenever something happens that affects our subsequent behavior, thoughts, or feelings, learning has occurred. While we don't listen to or tell what used to be called dirty jokes in order to learn anything, the sexual messages are there and, because of our basic insecurity about sex and our sensitivity to anything sexual, the messages get through to us whether we realize it or not. And what is true about humor is also true for all the other sources of the sexual model. The fact that we are unaware of having learned anything is unimportant. In fact, some of the most important learning in our lives happens without our knowledge. Many of the things we believe are not learned but are simply 'the way it is' are in fact learned but, because of our insistence to the contrary, extremely resistant to change.

An interesting fact that ensures that just about all men (and women) will learn the same model of sex is that all the media sources portray essentially the same sexual messages. What is picked up from one is reinforced by the others. Even if we never read a book and never saw a movie, we would still learn the model. It pervades our culture. Our friends learned it, as did our parents, and it would be a mistake of major proportions to assume that the professionals who talk and write about sex have completely escaped its tentacles.

There can be no question regarding the influence of the fantasy model of sex. In their highly regarded study *Pornography and Sexual Deviance*, Michael Goldstein and Harold Kant report that erotic literature and films are 'often the only media' through which the roles of men and women in sex and 'concrete models of the actual "mechanics" of heterosexual relationships' are gained. Erotic literature is the primary source of sex education for many young people, as well as for many not so young. When we add the effects of sexual humor, popular literature, movies, television, and other media, we begin to get an idea of the immensity of the problem.

There has also been, at least up until very recently, a relative paucity of competing models. The variety of possibilities and problems of real sexuality – as opposed to the superhuman sexuality of the model – are detailed only infrequently. With the new openness about sex in the culture there is some hope that this may change in the future, but what we have seen so far gives us little cause for optimism. Which is not surprising since the people who write for and direct the media were brought up on the same sexual script as the rest of us, a fact to which their productions attest.

Enough introduction for now. The following quotation, from Harold Robbins's *The Betsy*, is useful for setting the proper mood for our discussion of the model. Try to keep in mind that this book is not only not pornographic by any of the usual definitions but can be conveniently purchased at many drugstores and supermarkets. It may also be helpful to know that Robbins is the best-selling author of fiction in the world. His works have sold well over 150 million copies. Considering this, he may be the most influential sex educator of our time.

Gently her fingers opened his union suit and he sprang out at her like an angry lion from its cage. Carefully she peeled back his foreskin, exposing his red and angry glans, and took him in both hands, one behind the other as if she were grasping a baseball bat. She stared at it in wonder. '*C'est formidable. Un vrai canon* . . .'

. . . Naked, he looked even more an animal than before. Shoulders, chest and belly covered with hair out of which sprang the massive erection . . .

She almost fainted looking down at him. Slowly he began to lower her on him. Her legs came up . . . as he began to enter her . . . It was as if a giant of white-hot steel were penetrating her vitals. She began to moan as it opened her and climbed higher into her body, past her womb, past her stomach, under her heart, up into her throat. She was panting NOW, like a bitch in heat . . .

[He then flings her onto the bed.] Then he was poised over her . . . His hands reached and grasped each of her heavy breasts as if he wanted to tear them from her body. She moaned in pain and writhed, her pelvis suddenly arching and thrusting toward him. Then he entered her again.

'*Mon Dieu!*' she cried, the tears springing into her eyes. '*Mon Dieu!*' She began to climax almost before he was fully inside her. Then she couldn't stop them, one coming rapidly after the other as he slammed into her with the force of the giant body press she had seen working in his factory . . . Somehow she became confused, the man and the machine they were one and the same and the strength was something else she had never known before. And finally, when orgasm after orgasm had racked her body into a searing sheet of flame and she could bear no more, she cried out to him in French.

'Take your pleasure with me! . . . Quick, before I die!'

A roar came from deep inside his throat and his hands tightened on her breasts. She half screamed and her hands grabbed into the hair of his chest. Then all his weight seemed to fall on her, crushing the breath from her body, and she felt the hot onrushing gusher of his semen turning her insides into viscous, flowing lava. She discovered herself climaxing again.

While this quote was not chosen randomly, there are literally thousands of similar ones that could have been used.

We now examine in greater detail some of the major components of this sexual fantasyland. In the rest of this chapter we deal with the model's prescriptions for male equipment and the sexual partner. In the next chapter, we talk about the process and goals of sex. Although we mainly use quotations from books to demonstrate our points, it is well to remember that the other sources of sexual information convey the same information and that some of those sources may have been more influential than books in your own education.

THE EQUIPMENT

By equipment we mean penises, since the model teaches that they are all men need to have good sex. Presumably that bit of skin between your legs is the only sexual part of you.

It is not much of an exaggeration to say that penises in fantasyland come in only three sizes – large, gigantic, and so big you can barely get them through the doorway. This joke has been around at least since we were in high school: A woman tells the man she has been dating that she would never marry anyone unless he had twelve inches. To which he replies that he refuses to cut off four inches, even for her.

Penis size is frequently mentioned in jokes and literature, and of course bigger is always better. Average or small penises are noted only as objects of derision. A woman in Joyce Elbert's *Crazy Ladies* complains that the men she meets have such small penises that they might as well use their fingers, but then becomes ecstatic when she finds a man with 'an erection a mile long'.

Women, we are given to believe, crave nothing so much as a penis that might be mistaken for a telephone pole. They receive such monstrosities with thanksgiving and complete satisfaction. Who can forget that tender love scene in *The Godfather* where Sonny, the best-hung stud in town, gets together with Lucy, who has hitherto been unable to find a penis large enough to fill her up?

> Her hand closed around an enormous, blood-gorged pole of muscle. It pulsated in her hand like an animal and almost weeping with grateful ecstasy she pointed it into her own wet, turgid flesh. The thrust of its entering, the unbelievable pleasure made her gasp . . . and then like a quiver, her body received the savage arrows of his lightning-like thrusts . . . arching her pelvis higher and higher until for the first time in her life she reached a shattering climax . . .

The fact that the penis is not a muscle and contains no muscular tissue at all is conveniently ignored, a clear example of how far from reality is the model.

Not only are fantasyland penises much larger than life, they also behave peculiarly. They are forever 'pulsating', 'throbbing', and leaping about. The mere sight or touch of a woman is sufficient to set the penis jumping, and whenever a man's fly is unzipped, his penis leaps out. From Harold Robbins's *The Inheritors*: '. . . she pulled open the buttons on his trousers. He sprang swollen into her hand . . .' Nowhere does a penis merely mosey out for a look at what's happening.

The penis should also be unbelievably hard. It is often described as being hard as rock or steel, anything less apparently being inadequate. The fantasy penis is always totally full and firm, always ready to go.

Or to stay. The last characteristic of the idealized penis is its infinite capacity to satisfy, either by lasting for hours on end or by immediately regaining its hardness after ejaculation. Henry Miller gives this example of total control over the ejaculatory process:

> I was in such a cold-blooded state of control that as she

went through her spasms I poked it around inside her like a demon, up, sideways, down, in, out again, plunging, rearing, jabbing, snorting, and absolutely certain that I wouldn't come until I was damned good and ready.

From *The Pearl* comes this example of a penis that never needed to rest: 'I could not exhaust him; he was continually shooting his love juice into my . . . womb . . .'

Wonderful instruments, these penises. Though they be like rock, they just keep rolling along.

The penis is the central figure – the hero, so to speak – of the fantasy model. Not the human penis, to be sure, but an organ of make-believe, conceived of, in the words of Dr Steven Marcus, as 'a magical instrument of infinite powers'. The names given to these penises reflect their inhuman nature – tools, weapons, rods, ramrods, battering rams, shafts, coursers, and formidable machines. Somehow the humanity of the penis has been lost. The model makes it quite clear that the quality of a sexual experience and the measure of the man is a direct function of the size and power of that magical toy between his legs.

Real men with real penises compare themselves to the model and find themselves woefully lacking. Most men believe that their penises are not what they ought to be. They are not long enough or wide enough or hard enough, they do not spring forth with the requisite surging and throbbing, and they do not last long enough or recover fast enough. A recent magazine survey of over a thousand men found that 'all male respondents, with the exception of the most extraordinarily endowed, expressed doubts about their own sexuality based on their penile size'.

Given what we learned, this isn't surprising. The problem is that we think we should measure up to what are basically impossible standards. The penises in the model are products of fantasy and the real always loses when compared to the creations of human imagination.

But, you may be thinking, that isn't the whole story. What

about the huge organs you've seen with your own eyes in pornographic movies and magazines? And in the movies some of those guys seem to last forever or regain their erections immediately after orgasm. Aren't these things for real ? Sure, in a way. There is no question but that some men are more generously endowed than the rest of us and that they are sought after by those whose business it is to titillate the public. There are also all kinds of things that can be and are done to make the huge look even larger than it actually is. There is very little that cannot be accomplished through the magic of photography. And splicing works wonders in films. What looks like a continuous sequence in a movie is often the result of taping together segments filmed at different times. You'd be surprised how much film is wasted because the actors don't get erections, or come before they're supposed to. But the film you see looks perfect. What you see isn't necessarily what is when it comes to sex.

We don't want to gloss over the fact that there are some large penises around. It is also true that some men can last long periods of time or have relatively brief refractory periods. But such phenomena are statistically rare. There is no more reason to try to match them than there is to try to grow to be seven feet tall just because there are a few men of that height, or to try to run a four-minute mile because a few men have accomplished that feat.

Accepting your own merely human penis can be difficult. You know it is somewhat unpredictable and, even when functioning at its best, looks and feels more like a human penis than a battering ram or a mountain of stone. Not much when compared to the fantasies we are brought up on. But you do have one small advantage – you are alive and can enjoy yourself whereas the supermen of the model with their gigantic erections are unreal and feel nothing. Later in the book we give some exercises to assist you in learning more about your penis and enjoying it. For now, it might be helpful if you would look at your penis and ask whether you can live with it. After all, unless you are contemplating a transplant from a horse, it's the only penis you'll ever have and, whatever its characteristics, it can give you much pleasure.

THE PARTNER

The women in fantasyland are all gorgeous and perfectly formed. A glance at the cartoons in any issue of *Playboy* or *Penthouse* makes the point succinctly: the women men desire are beautiful and flawlessly built; women who do not fit this mold are ridiculed.

Average-looking women, women who look older than twenty-two, those whose breasts sag or whose skin is not the model-conforming smooth, creamy, and silky – such women rarely appear in the world of sexual make-believe. It is a world where no one ages and no one wrinkles and no one loses her jutting breasts. In keeping with this notion, many of the women in popular literature keep peering into mirrors and noting that, though they have reached the advanced age of, say, thirty, there's nary a crease or wrinkle marring their charms.

Feminists and other women have long complained that men are too interested in physical appearance, paying more attention to 'tits and ass' than to the personality and intelligence of women and being uninterested in women who do not fit the current standard of physical perfection. There is more than a bit of truth in this, for men have learned that sex is something one has only with young and beautiful women. Given all the brainwashing we have been subjected to, it is understandable that we should pay so much attention to physical attributes and that middle-aged and older men should so often prefer to go out with much younger women. On the other hand, it is a tribute to the resiliency and common sense of men that so many have been able to see through the propaganda and find happiness with women who don't fit the requirements of the fantasy script.

Women in the fantasy model are also portrayed as wanting

sex all the time and wanting to be handled roughly, no matter how much they may request gentleness or protest the male's sexual advances. Such characteristics are regular features in pornography and also occur frequently in other sources of the fantasy model. The maid in Norman Mailer's *American Dream* resists Steven Rojack's sexual advances. But he overpowers her and is later rewarded for 'taking her' by such statements as 'You are absolutely a genius, Mr Rojack', and 'I love you a little bit'.

D. H. Lawrence's Lady Chatterley, though 'it cost her an effort to let him have his way and his will of her', allows her lover to have anal intercourse with her. It is a wonderful experience:

> [S]he had needed this phallic hunting out, she had secretly wanted it, and she had believed that she would never get it . . . What liars poets and everybody were! They made one think one wanted sentiment. When what one supremely wanted was this piercing, consuming, rather awful sensuality. To find a man who dared do it, without shame or sin or final misgiving. If he had been ashamed afterwards . . . how awful !

The message couldn't be clearer if it were written across the sky in neon – never listen to what a woman says when it comes to sex. She means yes even if she says no. She wants to be taken despite her protestations, she wants roughness even when she asks for tenderness.

As the following joke indicates, contempt is the only reward for the man who takes a woman's resistance seriously.

> A traveling salesman found lodging at a farmer's house and was told that he would have to sleep with the farmer's beautiful daughter. The salesman started having fantasies of a sex-filled night and eagerly awaited bedtime. But when it arrived the girl piled a few pillows between them on the bed and told him not to cross over them. He

was disappointed but complied with her request. In the morning the girl was gone, and the salesman dressed and started to leave. As he left the house, he saw the girl doing some chores on the other side of a fence and called to her: 'Wait a minute, I'll jump over this fence and give you a kiss good-bye.' To which she contemptuously replied: 'Hell, if you can't make it over three pillows, you ain't never going to get over the fence.'

Men in the fantasy model are always rewarded for not listening to a woman rather than for taking her seriously. Is it any wonder that men in the real world have trouble knowing what to do when a woman says 'No' or 'Stop' or 'Be more gentle' ?

The idea that women shouldn't be listened to is also learned from, and reinforced by, the social game in which the woman, trying to protect her reputation and not appear 'loose', resists the man's advances even when she is willing to have sex. She resists to comply with the rules of the game and, having satisfied the requirements, lets the man proceed. The understanding the man develops as a result of this game is, don't listen to what she says.

The problem for the man is how to differentiate between sincere rejections and requests on the one hand, and those that are ambivalent or merely façades on the other hand. Since the task is difficult and since the risks in backing off when the rejection is not real are so grave, many men simply give up trying to make the distinction and forge ahead regardless of what the woman says.

Women are caught in a bind because many of them were taught that it is important to put up a show of resistance even when they don't mean it. In rewarding men for not listening to them, they add to the already considerable amount of deafness in the male population. And then they get angry because men don't take them seriously.

This is not to suggest that women are the culprits in this situation. They are doing what they were taught was necessary, while men are doing the same. The point is that our sexual scripts are harmful to both men and women, making it difficult for either to be honest and enjoy sex.

Another important characteristic of women in fantasyland is that they constantly validate their lovers' egos and sexual prowess in particular ways. They behave in a manner calculated to leave no doubt that their men are the greatest sex machines in the world. From James Baldwin's *Another Country*:

> Her hands . . . had their own way and grasped his friendly body, caressing and scratching and burning . . . He felt a tremor in her belly, just beneath him, as though something had broken there, and it rolled tremendously upward, seeming to divide her breasts, as though he had split her all her length. And she moaned . . . He began to gallop her, whinnying a little with delight . . . Her moans gave way to sobs and cries. *Vivaldo. Vivaldo. Vivaldo.* She was over the edge . . . 'It never happened to me before – not like this, never.'

And here is one of Henry Miller's many partners going through her innumerable gyrations:

> Moving with furious abandon, biting my lips, my throat, my ears, repeating like a crazed automaton, 'Go on, give it to me . . . Oh God, give it, give it to me!' She went from one orgasm to another, pushing, thrusting, raising herself, rolling her ass . . . groaning, grunting, squealing like a pig, and then suddenly, thoroughly exhausted, begging me to shoot. 'Shoot it . . . I'll go mad.' . . . I shot a wad into the mouth of her womb that jolted her like an electric charge.

The women in the world of make-believe are always moaning and shrieking in ecstasy, demonstrating time and again what wonderful lovers their men are. In pornography, they frequently lose consciousness as they climax, the ultimate tribute to the potency of their lovers. Pornography sometimes also features women who ejaculate (a physiological impossibility). Torrents of 'love juice' gush from the man and the woman and it is a wonder they both don't drown.

It goes without saying that all women in the fantasy model are multiply orgasmic through intercourse. Nonorgasmic women exist, but only until a man who is big enough and rough enough comes along to open them up to the joys of sex. Women who are orgasmic only through means other than intercourse are unheard of, a very inadequate preparation for the realities of the world.

That is the main problem with the model of the partner – it is not a good preparation for the real world. The model ignores the fact that very few women meet the specified criteria of beauty and that even those who do will deviate further and further from them as they age. The standard of physical perfection influences the types of sexual partners men choose and/or makes them feel deficient if they end up with someone who does not meet all the specifications.

The model also leads men to expect that women will behave in certain ways. But what if she never shrieks and moans in sex? What if her orgasms do not resemble an epileptic seizure? Suppose she doesn't have an orgasm every time they have sex or doesn't have orgasms in intercourse? How is the man to know that he's a good lover? His idea of a good lover is defined by the fantasy script. What is he to think of himself when reality doesn't match the fantasy?

The stage is set for trouble. The man may feel inadequate and put pressure on his partner to live up to the model. Questions are asked or implied: 'How come you don't want sex more often?' 'Why don't you make more noise (or shout obscenities)?' 'Did the earth move for you?' 'Are you *sure* you wouldn't like to have another orgasm?'

A man came to therapy literally dragging his wife along. The problem according to him was that she was multiply orgasmic with masturbation and with stimulation from his hand, but she usually had only one orgasm in intercourse. That she was perfectly content with this state of affairs mattered not at all to him. He didn't know who was at fault but he wanted one or both of them fixed up so that she could have as many orgasms with intercourse as with manual stimulation. Only then would he feel adequate as a lover.

We want to make it clear that we are not saying that anything is wrong with fantasies per se, no matter how unrealistic they are. If you enjoy thinking about how life would be if you had a penis four feet wide and ten feet long, that's fine, as is fantasizing about being the greatest lover in the world, able to satisfy twenty women with a single spurt. Any fantasy is fine so long as you are aware that it is a fantasy and so long as it does not make you feel inadequate when reality does not conform to it.

The problem with the sexual model we are discussing is that it is not just a fantasy, one that can be turned on or off at will and that has little influence on behavior. It is rather the description of how our sexual world 'should be' and it affects our thinking, feeling, and behavior. Many of us are unaware that the model is indeed a fantasy, one that has little to do with what is possible or desirable for human beings. Since we take the script for the way things ought to be, we measure ourselves by it, striving to match its standards and feeling badly when we don't. Instead of asking whether the model is physiologically feasible, personally satisfying, or enhancing of ourselves and our relationships, we ask what is wrong with us for not being able to meet its standards. And that is precisely why this model is so destructive.

FOUR

The fantasy model continued: the process and goals of sex

While most of us learned the same sexual model, the specific myths affect us differently. You may believe in some with a very firm conviction, while others may have little influence on you. We ask you to read carefully, to consider if and how each myth pertains to you and how it affects your sexual functioning and enjoyment.

The first two myths or rules are part of both the fantasy model of sex and the general model of masculinity taught in our culture. Their impact can be felt in all aspects of men's lives but we focus primarily on their influence in the sexual area.

MYTH 1: MEN SHOULD NOT HAVE, OR AT LEAST NOT EXPRESS, CERTAIN FEELINGS

While looking at the boats from a dock on San Francisco Bay, a four-year-old boy fell into the very cold water. After being fished out of the water by his father and others in the party, he was trembling, looking very scared and like he might cry. His father patted him on the back and loudly announced that 'Billy doesn't cry; he's a big boy'.

In ways like this, and from the media, we learn early that only a narrow range of emotion is permitted to us: aggressiveness, competitiveness, anger, joviality, and the feelings associated with being in control. As we grow older, sexual feelings are added to the list. Weakness, confusion, fear, vulnerability, tenderness, compassion, and sensuality are allowed only to girls and women. A boy who exhibits any such traits is likely to be made fun of and called a sissy or girl (and what could be more devastating?).

We learn this lesson well and there is no lack of later reminders lest we be tempted to deviate from the true path. To give but one example, newspapers and commentators throughout the country questioned Edmund Muskie's emotional stability because he had shed some tears during a speech when he was campaigning for the presidency. Other males who have publicly expressed fear, deep sadness, or any other feelings on the prohibited list have sometimes lost the respect of their peers and themselves.

We end up either consistently denying to ourselves that we have any of the taboo feelings or, if we do acknowledge them, we are careful to hide them from others and often worry about the consequences of being found out. We are convinced that others will find us unacceptable if we reveal certain feelings or qualities, and so we go through life blocking out huge portions of our beings.

It is no wonder that close relationships are, at least, very difficult for most men. Looking at the feelings prohibited to us, we can begin to understand why we have so much trouble relating to others. What kinds of relationships can be built on the basis of aggressiveness, competitiveness, anger, sex, and joviality? How can there be closeness without compassion, tenderness, caring, trust, vulnerability – all the emotions not allowed for men?

The point is simple and frightening: the socialization of males provides very little that is of value in the formation of intimate relationships.

Everyone suffers as a result of this. Women constantly complain about the inexpressiveness of their men and how this causes problems in relationships. What women often fail to understand is that it is not a case of stubbornness on the part of men. We simply were not and are not given the permission to be expressive that most women were. We were not allowed to acknowledge even to ourselves all those emotions labeled unmanly, which has resulted in an inability to recognize and differentiate among them. Many times we are aware of feeling something but, because of our lack of experience in dealing with feelings, we don't know exactly what we are feeling or how to find out. And even if we do find out, we aren't sure it would be acceptable to express the emotion.

It is often said that men don't communicate, which is only partly true. Men can communicate very well about certain things, like their jobs, sports, and the state of the world. But this isn't what is meant by those who fault men; they say men don't talk about their feelings and hopes and problems. That is generally true, but given what we have said, how could it be otherwise? Talking about feelings and concerns is itself considered feminine by the models we were raised on. And when it comes to sex, what's there to communicate?

In the fantasy model no one ever has much to say. Doing it is the only thing that matters, and aside from the 'I'm going to do it to you' and 'Do it to me harder and faster' routine, what could there possibly be to say? The superstuds in the model never feel fear or concern or tenderness or warmth, they never have problems, they never need to stop or rest. So where can a boy or man turn for an example of emotional or sexual communication? No place at all.

Our partners sometimes say that there is something machine-like about our sexual behavior and that something seems to be missing. What is usually missing is our human, feeling side: our likes and dislikes, our tenderness and concern, our fears (breathes there a man who has never been fearful in a sexual situation?), and sometimes our excitement and enthusiasm as well.

Because we learned that it is not right or manly for us to be ignorant or scared or tender, we try to hide these feelings under a mask of aggressive sexuality, cool confidence, or stony silence. This often backfires in sex. Our arousal systems and our erections, as we discuss later in greater detail, are extremely sensitive to certain feelings, especially anxiety. What is not expressed in other ways may well be expressed by a lack of interest or by a refusal to become or stay erect, or by a tendency to ejaculate very quickly. The tragedy is that often a simple acknowledgment of the feeling is all that is needed to resolve the difficulty.

Another problem created by this myth is that we tend to label any positive feelings we have toward another person as sexual. All of us – men, women, children – need support, validation, physical affection, tenderness, and the knowledge that we are loved and wanted. Sometimes these needs can best be met through sexual activity; many times they are best fulfilled in other ways. But since men were not taught to differentiate among these needs and since the needs themselves are suspect for us – is it really OK to want to be held or 'just' to snuggle or to want to hear that she cares for me? – whenever one of them presses for expression, we assume that sex is what we want. In sex we can get some of these other needs met without raising any questions about our masculinity.

We often try for sex when that is not really what we want or need. Sometimes a hug or hearing 'I love you' is much more satisfying than sex. It is more satisfying because it is more relevant to our needs at the moment. If, on the other hand, we were to go through a complete sex act just to get that hug, we might well end up feeling disappointed and resentful. After all, the best way to get a hug is to get a hug. But if getting a hug is not legitimate, we may have to try for sex or get nothing at all. We thus often do not get our needs met, or go to ridiculous effort to get very simple things. And in the process, we stay confused about what we really want.

We miss so much by hanging on to this myth. We miss opportunities to let our partners really know us, and as long as we feel that parts of ourselves must never be revealed, we must constantly be on guard lest some of our secret feelings or qualities sneak out. Being on guard all of one's life hardly seems to be the best way to live. We miss the chance to be open about our needs and have them met. So we go without the support, the understanding, the physical affection, and, in a word, the love we all want. And we overburden sex, forcing it to meet needs that really aren't sexual. Since, as we discuss later, our sexual systems are fragile, they may function poorly when too much responsibility is placed on them.

MYTH 2: IN SEX, AS ELSEWHERE, IT'S PERFORMANCE THAT COUNTS

As boys and men we are socialized in what Jay Mann calls the three A's of manhood: Achieve, Achieve, Achieve. We learn that it is by our performances and productions that we will be judged. We are taught to accept or create tasks, to focus on the goals and work doggedly until they are reached. Nothing comes easily or by itself; only by trying and working hard can anything be accomplished. Feelings and any other factors that might get in the way are denied or ignored.

We are good at being achievement machines. Give us a job and we are in business. And it works well in many areas; this orientation has been useful to us in getting through school, winning games, making money, and so forth.

The problem is that the performance ethic becomes the only way of doing things. Rather than a useful approach appropriate to some situations, it becomes our only approach, and, for many of us, our only way of being. We are uncomfortable with time and situations that are unstructured, with just letting things happen. We feel uneasy when we do not have a goal to strive toward. We have to make tasks of everything, since we feel at ease only when we have a job to do.

It is understandable that we should bring this performance orientation to sex. How else could we, given our training, handle such an anxiety-laden experience? And we get plenty of support from the sexual model because, being a predominantly male enterprise, it is about nothing so much as performance.

The goals – usually intercourse and orgasm – are the only

important factors in make-believe sex. One does a minimum amount of what is needed to achieve these goals. You might have to wine and dine the woman, say sweet nothings you don't mean, and perhaps engage in some foreplay – but you keep it to a minimum and never lose sight of the reason you are going through all this uninteresting activity. There is actually little foreplay in most erotic materials, and just playing around with each other's bodies without any particular goals in mind is almost unheard-of.

The point is clearly made in this joke popular during World War II. A soldier on leave finds his wife exposing her breasts provocatively. 'I haven't got time to chew the fat,' he says, 'just time to come and go.'

Throughout his work, Henry Miller offers countless examples of goal-oriented sexuality. He goes immediately for the crotch. The fewer words and other preliminaries, the better. In the following example, he is visiting a woman he hardly knows to console her on the death of her husband. She has asked him to sit beside her on the couch

> Sitting there on the low sofa, the place flooded with soft lights, her big heaving loins rubbing against me, the Malaga pounding in my temples and all this crazy talk about Paul and how good he was, I finally bent over and without saying a word I raised her dress and slipped it into her. And as I got it into her and began to work it around she took to moaning like, a sort of delirious, sorrowful guilt punctuated with gasps and little shrieks of joy and anguish . . .

The preoccupation with reaching goals that is induced by our performance orientation means that we tend to ignore or not fully participate in the process of sex (it is 'only foreplay') and therefore miss out on experiences that might well be stimulating and pleasurable. We miss more than we realize. The willingness and ability to participate and 'get into' the process is precisely what makes possible a full and enjoyable sexual response. Paradoxically, focusing on the goal to the exclusion of what comes before it makes attainment of the goal difficult or impossible.

The result of our goal orientation is an inability to focus on the present, since we have been trained always to attend to what is in the future. The tragedy is that even when we reach our goal – be it intercourse, orgasm, or something nonsexual like a certain status or income – we can't enjoy it because our goal orientation forces us to focus on yet another goal. We can never pay attention to where we are at the moment, which means that it is very difficult for us to enjoy anything.

We make work of sex. It becomes businesslike and mechanical, another job to be done, another goal to be achieved. As Roxie Hart says of her man in *Chicago*, 'When Amos made love it was like he was fixin' a carburetor'. Rather than seeing sex as a way for two people to relate and have fun, and asking how much pleasure and closeness there was, we view it as a performance and ask how hard the erection was, how long we lasted, and how many orgasms she had. When problems develop we look for mechanical aids and advice to help us to do it better, much as we read manuals on how to care for our cars and other machines. The more we do this, the further we get from our feelings, ourselves, and our partners. The more this happens, the better the chances that sex will become boring and grim or that a dysfunction will develop.

Living in an advanced technological age, it is easy to assume that what is needed to make sex more interesting and exciting is a technical solution – a pill or shot, a new position or partner, a better foreplay routine, and so on – when, in fact, in sex and all aspects of human relating what is really needed is the willingness to get to know ourselves and our partners better and to flow with or 'get into' whatever contact there is.

Preoccupation with reaching goals also means high levels of anxiety, for anxiety is simply the fear that the goals will not be reached. The greater the need to achieve them, the greater the anxiety. Since anxiety tends to block sexual interest and response, we are caught in a bad bind: the more concerned we are with performing well and the harder we try, the less well things go. There is no doubt that it is this need to perform, to do it right and reach the goals, that makes sex so difficult for so many of us.

A last consequence of the performance ethic is that we tend to place a high value on work and a much lower value on pleasure. Many of us still believe deep down that it is not quite right to be doing something just for fun. As a result we set aside little time for physical affection and sex. Other things – work, paying bills, taking care of the children, doing maintenance work around the house – all take precedence. Sex is usually squeezed in between these 'more important' matters. Many men engage in sex only when they are tired, in a hurry, or have other things on their minds. Is it surprising that they are not quite satisfied with their sexual experiences?

The alternative to performance orientation is easy to state but it goes against our training and is therefore not so easy to put into practice. Sex need not be a performance. There is no right way to do it and there are no particular goals to achieve. Sex can be whatever you and your partner want it to be at the moment, whatever best expresses and satisfies the two of you. All that is needed in this regard is the expenditure of a little time and energy to find out more about your sexual self. The information and exercises in this book are of course dedicated to this end.

MYTH 3: THE MAN MUST TAKE CHARGE OF AND ORCHESTRATE SEX

I remember the first time a woman told me to relax and do nothing, that she wanted to make love to me. Even as I was agreeing to her proposal, I was busy doing things to her. I wanted to comply with her request but had tremendous difficulty being passive and letting her lead.

Only then did it occur to me how busy I was in sex. I not only conducted the band but played all the instruments as well.

We learned that sex was our responsibility and that we had to do it all. We should initiate (and even if she initiates, we still have to do the rest), we have to turn her on, we have to turn ourselves on, we have to lead all the way (deciding which procedures and positions should be adopted), we have to give her at least one orgasm, and we have to produce our own orgasm. No need for any help from our partner, thank you.

This myth stems from two old ideas about the nature of masculinity: that being a man means being the leader and the active one (and the concomitant fear that not being in charge is a sign of inadequacy); and that a real man needs little or nothing from a woman, either in terms of information or stimulation.

All of this responsibility and activity are often experienced by us as burdens but are nonetheless difficult to relinquish because they exemplify so many of the masculine 'virtues'.

This myth leads to problems in relationships since the partner is denied the opportunity to be the initiating, active one. More and more women want to initiate and take charge, at least some of the time, and battles can develop when their partners refuse to let them do so.

Another problem deriving from this myth is that when we are so busy doing for our partners we often do not get anything for ourselves and do not get aroused or erect.

Jim, a man in his forties who was in a sex therapy group because of erection problems, went on at great length about all the things he had done for his partner – touched her there, kissed her here, rubbed her somewhere else – and was perplexed by his lack of erection. When asked what she had done for him, he was stunned. It simply had not occurred to him that she wasn't the only one who needed to be touched and rubbed.

That it didn't occur to him is understandable since our basic sexual model teaches us that men don't need anything special to get aroused and erect. The thought of having sex or the mere sight of a woman should be all that is required. Only women need special attention to 'get in the mood', or so the model says.

Many men believe that they should produce their own turn-on, that they should come to a sexual situation already excited and erect. This, they think, is the 'normal' way, while getting an erection as a result of direct stimulation from the woman somehow indicates a deficiency.

Because of this conviction many of us, like him, do not get the stimulation we need. Being more passive and allowing our partners to stimulate us is particularly important if we have trouble getting or maintaining erections. For being more passive allows a greater focusing of attention on the incoming stimulation, and it is just such focusing that can often overcome the difficulty, as well as increasing the amount of pleasure that is experienced.

We have also taken total responsibility for satisfying our partners. She *should* have an orgasm, at least one, and we feel guilty if she doesn't. And, since we were taught that being a man means knowing it all, we are reluctant to ask her what we should do to help her reach orgasm. Like Bill Cosby said: 'I never thought of her showing me, because I'm a man and I don't want her to show me – I don't want *nobody* to show me, but I wish somebody would kinda slip me a note . . .'

We look everywhere for that note. We read books, attend speeches, and talk to doctors and therapists to find out how to satisfy a woman. We look everywhere but the one place where we might get the answer – the woman herself. We are afraid to ask what she likes because such an admission of ignorance might raise questions about our manhood. After all, we should know what to do; the men in erotic literature and films don't have to ask their partners what turns them on, they just know.

What we need to learn is that there is no way to know in

advance what will please a partner. All women are different and even the same woman will have different desires at different times. No matter how experienced we are and no matter how many books we have read, we are going to have to learn from her, just as she will need to learn from us what we like. We need to understand that a good lover is not one who already knows what to do (since such knowledge is simply not available beforehand) but one who is open to learning about his partner's needs and desires. If the information we desire is not spontaneously offered, we need to learn to ask for it.

It would also benefit men tremendously to understand that we have taken on too much responsibility in sex. Partner sex by definition is a two-person venture and it is a bit presumptuous for one of the parties to assume that he has to take charge of, and be accountable for, everything that happens. Women want to share in what happens – in fact, one of the major complaints women have about men in sex is their unwillingness to share more of the responsibility and themselves. It's really not true that you have to do it all by yourself.

MYTH 4: A MAN ALWAYS WANTS AND IS ALWAYS READY TO HAVE SEX

Erotic materials portray men as always wanting and always ready to have sex, the only problem being how to get enough of it. We have accepted this rule for ourselves and most of us believe that we should always be capable of responding sexually, regardless of the time and place, our feelings about ourselves and our partners, or any other factors. We have thus accepted the status of machines, performing whenever the right button is pushed.

Most of us have acknowledged a woman's right to say no to sex (even if it made us angry and we tried to change her mind, it was still her right) and to set conditions as to when and how she would have sex with us. But we have been unable to take these rights for ourselves, to recognize that sometimes we are simply not interested in sex, and that sex is better for us under certain conditions than under others. We work very hard to live up to this myth of perpetual readiness and severely berate ourselves and wonder why we are inadequate when we do not function according to plan.

It is not a question of adequacy. We simply are not sex machines and we cannot function as the fantasy model demands we do. Our sexual systems are highly complex, influenced by many factors and vulnerable to many kinds of interference. Just as each of us has a particular constellation of circumstances that allows us to do our best creative or productive work, and sets of conditions under which we carry out such necessary operations as digestion, elimination, and relaxation, we each also have a set of conditions that maximizes the probability of a full and satisfying sexual response. When these conditions are not fulfilled or at least approximated, we function poorly or not at all.

This is a hard pill for most of us to swallow since it runs counter to the deeply held conviction that a man is always capable sexually and that only women need conditions to be right. After all, the men in sexual fantasyland can do it any time, any place, and with anybody. And we were also told that a man is one who is not deterred by adverse conditions; he grits his teeth and pushes on, bowling over or in some other way overcoming obstacles and difficulties. While this procedure may work in some areas, in sex it works not at all, for here the harder one tries, the less enjoyment and arousal there is.

While the idea of sexual conditions takes some getting used to (as does the related idea that sometimes you just aren't going to be interested), it's definitely worth the effort. Acceptance of these ideas is directly related to how much you get out of sex.

MYTH 5: ALL PHYSICAL CONTACT MUST
LEAD TO SEX

Physical contact in the fantasy model serves only as a request or demand for, or a prelude to, sex. Cuddling, hugging, kissing, holding, caressing, and other types of physical affection that do not lead to sex are completely absent in pornography and rarely encountered in any erotic material. Touching is always portrayed as the first step toward sex. It is not seen as something valuable or pleasurable in its own right; it is useful only to the extent that it paves the way to a presumably grander event.

These beliefs about touching affect men much more strongly than women. There is a greater tolerance for females of all ages to touch and want to be touched. A girl or woman can ask for a hug, or to be held, without much hindrance (although some men are likely to get angry if she doesn't want to go further). But can you imagine a man asking 'only' to be held and seriously meaning it? A lot of people would think that very strange. We are taught that only two types of physical contact are appropriate for males. One is aggressive and includes not only the rough contact in sports and fighting but also the mock violence men often display with one another (as when friends greet each other with a playful slap or punch). And the other is sexual. Physical contact that is neither sexual nor aggressive is truly a no-man's-land. According to what we were taught, it really isn't OK for a man to want only a hug or a caress.

The idea that touching is sexual is so deeply ingrained in us that many men refuse to engage in any physical contact whatsoever unless it is going to lead to sex. They think they are being considerate, not wanting to tease or, in the words of one man we worked with, 'not wanting to start something I can't finish'. A common phenomenon in couples where the men are experiencing sexual problems is the complete absence of any touching: no hugging, no kissing, and, often, sleeping at opposite sides of the bed.

As we discuss later, the myth that touching must lead to sex is harmful to everyone, but particularly to men since we have been most powerfully affected by it. It robs us of the joys of 'just' touching, it confuses us as to what we really want at any given time, and it puts pressure on us to be sexual whenever we touch or are touched.

MYTH 6: SEX EQUALS INTERCOURSE

Both men and women learned that the main thing in sex is intercourse, and for most of us the two terms are synonymous. This is hardly surprising since almost all resources that deal with sex-medical books, textbooks, popular books and articles, as well as erotic materials – treat sex and intercourse as if they were the same thing. Kissing, hugging, and manual and oral stimulation of the genitals are all fine, but mainly as preliminaries to the ultimate goal: intercourse. The very term we use to describe these other activities – foreplay – clearly indicates their lowly status relative to intercourse. They are presumably important only as means to that main event.

The extent to which this myth pervades our culture can be measured by its place in the thinking of serious and intelligent sex therapists and researchers. Even Masters and Johnson show little understanding in their three books that real sex can be anything but intercourse.

In the past, when the goal of sex was conception, intercourse was absolutely necessary. You can't make babies without it. But times have changed and these days the goal of most sexual encounters is recreation rather than procreation. There is no longer any good reason why a sexual experience has to end in or include intercourse, unless that is what the participants desire.

This means that there is no 'normal' or 'natural' way for sex to proceed. There are always many choices that can be made regarding what is to be done, when, and how. And this, as the following story demonstrates, can be unnerving.

During the first few years that I was sexually active, I sometimes wondered about how homosexuals decided what to do in sex. I had a reasonably accurate idea of *what* they did, but it was unclear how they went about organizing what was to happen in a given encounter. They had so many possibilities to choose from and no normal or regular way like we heterosexuals did. I knew that heterosexual sex usually more or less followed the same routine: kissing and hugging, playing with her breasts and then between her legs, putting my finger in her vagina (no one seemed to know about the clitoris in those days) and then, either because of a signal from her or because I felt like it, insertion and intercourse. This was just the way it was supposed to be. I occasionally engaged in oral or manual stimulation to orgasm but only when circumstances were not conducive for intercourse. So I knew how the game was to be played and was certain that all other heterosexuals did it just the way I did. But I imagined that each homosexual encounter was preceded by a long negotiating session in which the partners decided who would do what, and in which order. What I didn't realize until years later was that I actually had as many options as they did but, because of the myth of coital primacy (sex must include intercourse), I wasn't able to see them. This realization was less of a thrill than you might imagine because it brought up the possibility of communicating with my partners about what I wanted and what they wanted, something I had little experience with, and that made me somewhat uncomfortable. I was barely secure in doing sex the 'normal way': the last thing I needed was the possibility of making choices and having to talk about my desires.

You may be wondering why we're making such an issue about this myth. Does it really make any difference if you use sex and intercourse synonymously or, in behavioral terms, think that every sexual act should include intercourse? The answer is yes, it makes a great deal of difference.

Belief in this myth can prevent us from discovering what we like.

For many years, while I enjoyed all kinds of sexual stimulation, I always insisted on 'finishing' (coming inside a vagina. I just 'knew' that this was the best way. I was quite surprised when I finally allowed myself to climax with other types of stimulation. I enjoyed a sense of being done to or being taken care of that I rarely got with intercourse, and I found that I have the most explosive orgasms through hand stimulation. Of course, explosive orgasms and being taken care of are not the only things I want from sex, and intercourse is better at providing some of the other things I want. But now that I know what leads to what, I feel I have more options and can better choose one that will fit my wants at the moment.

Even if we know what we want, this myth can prevent us from getting it. Many men wonder what their partners will think if they say they are more interested in manual or oral stimulation than intercourse.

Because this myth defines intercourse as the goal and most important part of sex, it reinforces our performance orientation and makes it difficult for us to enjoy other parts of a sexual experience. Many men, when asked how it felt to touch their partners or be touched by them, have said that they didn't know because they were so busy thinking about getting to intercourse. In this way we rob ourselves of pleasure and of fully experiencing the stimulation necessary for an enjoyable sexual response.

Men are not the only ones hurt by this myth. Women who do not reach orgasm through intercourse but who respond best to manual or oral stimulation – and there are many such women – are put under tremendous pressure by the idea that intercourse is the 'normal' way to have sex. It makes it difficult for them to tell their partners what they need. And we often feel that something must be wrong either with the woman or with us because she doesn't respond the 'right' way.

We hope that what we have said will not be taken as an argument against intercourse. Intercourse can be a wonderful way of having sex. But it is only one way of relating sexually, rather than the only way, and at any given time it may not be the best or most appropriate.

MYTH 7: SEX REQUIRES AN ERECTION

This is a corollary of the preceding myth since intercourse is the one sexual act that is impossible without an erection (this is a bit of an overstatement since it is possible to get a flaccid penis into a vagina, but it's not all that easy to do and it certainly doesn't conform to the usual meaning of intercourse). The fantasy model goes even further, however. It teaches that any kind of sex requires an erection.

The erection is considered by almost all men as the star performer in the drama of sex, and we all know what happens to a show when the star performer doesn't make an appearance. The whole show is cancelled or, to be a bit more accurate, the planned performance gives way to an impromptu tragedy, replete with wailing and self-blaming, usually ending with everyone feeling miserable. The woman may blame herself ('I'm not attractive or sexy enough to turn him on') or be thoroughly confused as to why her partner is so furious with himself. The man, angry and confused, may apologize profusely to no constructive purpose, start a fight with her, or go into a fit of sulking which can last hours or even days.

This myth puts tremendous pressure on the man and places him in an extremely vulnerable position. He thinks he absolutely must have an erection, he knows he can't control his penis, and he's also aware that there's no way to fake an erection or hide the lack of one. A most interesting situation, to say the least. We doubt that there is a man anywhere who has not wondered, right in the middle of some enjoyable sex play, if his penis was going to come through for him this time, and quivered at the prospect of its not doing so.

Of course erections are nice and we have nothing against them. Penises were designed to get hard and they usually do when your conditions are fulfilled. But sometimes they don't and you need to be able to take such situations in stride. The problem with this myth is that it creates too much pressure and it is precisely this desperate need to get an erection that makes erections difficult to get or maintain.

You need to learn that all is not lost when you don't have an erection. The penis is not the only sexual part of your body. You can do wonderful things for your lover with other parts of your body and you can enjoy her touching other parts of your body. A penis that is not hard can still feel very good when stimulated, and you might want to give this a try. Regardless of which particular options you choose, the main point is that lack of erection need not mean a miserable time. The experience can still be close, warm, and fun. Neither erection nor intercourse is necessary. Even if you are unwilling to give up the idea that an erect penis is the star of a sexual performance, we want to remind you that every star has an understudy, and understudies have been known to do very well when given a chance.

And, as you will see, the less important erections become, the less it matters to you whether or not you have one, the more abundant they become. Erections flourish best in a relaxed setting, where there is no pressure for anything in particular to happen.

MYTH 8: GOOD SEX IS A LINEAR PROGRESSION OF INCREASING EXCITEMENT TERMINATED ONLY BY ORGASM (THE MYTH OF THE HARD-DRIVING FUCK)

This myth is actually composed of several different ideas. The first holds that sex should be a process of continuously increasing excitement and passion. Whether the act lasts for minutes or hours, the arousal must continue to build. This notion is typical in erotic materials.

Because of this myth, the idea that sex can be leisurely, with breaks for resting, talking, laughing, or whatever, is foreign to many men. Some of us feel that there is something wrong with a leisurely approach to sex, thinking that it connotes a lack of passion, spontaneity, or masculine vigor.

Here, as with all the myths, there is pressure to perform in ways that may be totally inappropriate to the circumstances. This idea overlooks a basic fact of human psychology, namely that attention and arousal cannot be maintained at very high levels for long periods of time and that as a result there is a natural tendency for them to wax and wane. The same is true of erections: they, too, may wax and wane during a sexual experience, especially as we get further away from our adolescence. But we are not always aware of this, so when we notice our arousal level or our erections subsiding, we panic and try to re-establish the excitement or erection. Such frantic efforts usually end in failure, for neither arousal nor erection can be coerced. How much better if we could just stop and cuddle or rest for a while.

Belief in this myth often gets in the way of developing better ejaculatory control. Such control is relatively easy to develop if the man is willing to stop stimulation when it gets very intense, resuming when the urge to ejaculate has subsided. But this myth makes no provision for stopping during sex.

John, a member of a sex therapy group for men wanting to develop ejaculatory control, had achieved good control with masturbation exercises. When I suggested it was time for him to employ the stop-start method in sex with his partner, he was astonished. He couldn't believe that I wanted him to stop during sex with his partner. Not being able to convince me that the idea was absurd, he turned to the female co-leader and asked indignantly: 'What would you think if a man you were making love to said he wanted to stop . . . right in the middle of things?!'

The outcome of John's story is illuminating. After much hard work by the group leaders, he agreed to use the stop-start method with his partner, but only because it seemed necessary to resolve his long-standing problem of premature ejaculation. He followed through and gradually developed good control with her. To his great surprise, he found that he very much enjoyed this more leisurely approach to sex. Sex became a more relaxing and satisfying experience for him, and what began as a distasteful but necessary solution to a problem became an integral part of his sexual behavior. Other men have reported similar stories. Once they found that sex didn't have to follow any specific progression, they were free to discover the ways that best suited their partners and themselves.

Another part of this myth is that sex is wild and uncontrolled. This process is illustrated by the following selection from Harold Robbins:

I don't know how it happened but she was in my arms. Then it was like an atomic fire searing through us. We couldn't wait to get at each other. Our clothes made a trail up the stairs to the bedroom. We fell naked on the bed, tearing at each other like raging animals. Then we exploded and fell backward on the bed, gasping for breath.

According to this scenario, someone must be out of control but it need not be the man and, in fact, he often is exactly the opposite. This makes sense because men have forever been taught the virtue of keeping their wits about them and not letting their feelings get the best of them. But since the fantasy model demands something or someone wild with passion, the role is often assigned to the woman.

Lust without limits is what the sexual model is about. Desire flows in torrents, sweeping everything in its path, and the exuberance frequently verges on or becomes violent. This is the realm of the hard-driving fuck, where better means harder and rougher. From Joyce Elbert's *Crazy Ladies*: 'He was much bigger than Peter and he rammed it into her with such force that she screamed out in delicious agony . . .' A recurring feature of the model is a situation where the woman tells the man that whatever he's doing hurts and then warms up to it and begs him to continue hurting her.

From the novelized version of the film *The Devil in Miss Jones* comes this sterling example:

'Just hold it there for a minute . . . Yes, put it there . . . Oh god, oh, Jesus, I can't take it – No, do it, it hurts, but do it. Do it now, do it more . . . Ahh, it hurts, hurt me . . . faster . . . hurt me . . . hurt me . . . hurt me . . . HURT ME!'

This is a wonderful world indeed, where pain and pleasure are the same and where being pounded and split apart are delicious.

With all the grinding and slamming and banging portrayed in the media, and with the absence of good examples of more tender lovemaking, it is not surprising that many men think of sex as a rough-and-tough business, and that they will be most appreciated if they pummel the hell out of their partners. Since women in fantasyland are always grateful to the most aggressive and even violent lovers, and since there is a clear implication that a man who cannot brutalize a woman is something less than a man, there is considerable pressure for a man to restrain his more tender expressions of affection and give free rein to his more aggressive tendencies.

Aside from the violent part of things, we should also consider the imperative, driven, and mindless way in which passion is presented. Here is an example from a recent sex manual called *Sexual Loving* by Joseph and Lois Bird:

> Ideally, the husband enters the wife when the sex drive of both is near its peak . . . And at this intensity, sexual actions become very self-centered. They are imperative. His overwhelming desire is to penetrate her fully. Her desire is to be penetrated. At that moment each becomes an almost totally *sensual* being. Nearly all sensations are concentrated in – or related to – the aroused genitals . . . in the flood of sexual sensations we tend to shut out everything else. Even what would be uncomfortable or painful under other circumstances goes unnoticed in those seconds . . . the concern and awareness which were dominant during the preceding lovemaking give way, in large part, to the imperious demands of self-satisfaction.

There is nothing wrong with this kind of sex and most people have probably experienced something like it (although we hope you realized that the business about penetration is only another way of saying that sex equals intercourse). But this is just one kind of sex, though it is usually portrayed as the only kind. Sex need not be so driven, so urgent, so mindless, so focused in the genitals. In fact, it seems that real sex is only rarely this way. Usually it is simply not so imperious or 'spaced out'. Sex can proceed in a more leisurely, gentler fashion, with irrelevant thoughts floating through your mind, with awareness of things other than your genitals, and with no overwhelming desire to do anything at all. And such experiences can be very pleasurable and certainly need not be cause for worry because you were not consumed by passion. What's so wonderful about being consumed anyway?

A universal rule of make-believe sex, and the last part of this myth we're discussing, is that it must end in at least one, but preferably more, orgasms for everyone. And these are no ordinary orgasms. They are raging, exploding, and earth-shaking. From Norman Mailer's *American Dream*:

> I could not hold back, there was an explosion, furious, treacherous and hot as the gates of an icy slalom with the speed at my heels overtaking my nose, I had one of those splittings of a second where the senses fly out and there in that instant the itch reached into me and drew me out and I jammed up her ass and came as if I'd been flung across the room.

We don't understand what he said either, except that it was quite a jolt. Here's a tender thought from Mickey Spillane's *The Last Cop Out*:

> All she wanted was for him to enjoy, to take, to spend, to rise to the heights of screaming physical pleasure where everything becomes blanked out in those nerve-shattering waves of orgiastic abandonment that left the body spasm-wracked and helpless.

One wonders how anyone could survive all this nerve-shattering, crashing violence.

Orgasms need not be explosive or violent to be part of fantasyland. In this passage, D. H. Lawrence provides the romantic version of unrealistic expectations:

> Oh, and far down inside her the deeps parted and rolled asunder, in long, far-travelling billows, and ever, at the quick of her, the depths parted and rolled asunder . . . as the plunger went deeper and deeper, touching lower, and she was deeper and deeper and deeper disclosed, and heavier the billows of her rolled away to some shore, uncovering her . . . and further and further rolled the waves of herself away from herself, leaving her, till

suddenly, in a soft, shuddering convulsion, the quick of all her plasm was touched . . . the consummation was upon her, and she was gone. She was gone, she was not, and she was born: a woman.

There are no ordinary, run-of-the-mill orgasms in most erotic materials. Every orgasm is explosive, body-wrenching and/or mind-blowing, and even better than the one before. Needless to say, such is not the way it is in the real world. But many of us take the fantasy as our goal and spare no effort to achieve the ultimate orgasm for ourselves or our partners. Compared to the fantasy, real orgasms can feel rather humdrum.

But there is much more to the orgasm story than that. Even if we do not believe in the fantasy type of orgasm, most of us are wedded to the idea that every sexual event must culminate in some kind of orgasm for our partners and most definitely for ourselves. Well, maybe not quite as far as she is concerned. We know a woman may not have an orgasm every time. But a man must beyond any doubt have a climax in every sex act. Otherwise, as is well known, he will suffer the painful and crippling conditions known as 'blue balls' and 'lover's nuts'. At least that's what we were taught.

Actually, there is no good reason why a man must have an orgasm every time he has sex. Despite the high school horror stories about blue balls and lover's nuts, they are rare conditions. They can be painful but they usually don't last very long. But because of the influence of those stories and because our sexual model presents almost no cases of men who do not ejaculate every time they have sex, we are convinced that we must come every time, no matter how much we have to work to make it happen.

Sometimes it becomes clear that an orgasm is not going to occur, at least not without great effort. But how many of us have toiled on anyway, frantically grabbing at our partners and every conceivable fantasy in a desperate attempt to come? Why not just stop when we are still feeling good? Orgasms can be wonderful, as can hard-driving fucks, but they are not always necessary or the best way to go. The same can be said of passionate, nonstop sex. It can be nice. But there is also something to be said for a gentler, nonlinear, less lustful approach.

MYTH 9: SEX SHOULD BE NATURAL AND SPONTANEOUS

Most of us believe that good sex should somehow just happen. The following quotation from Peter Benchley's *The Deep* well illustrates this notion. The participants met for the first time only a few hours earlier.

> After lunch, they played tennis . . . After tennis, they swam, had dinner, went for a walk on the beach, and then – as naturally as if the act were the next event in the day's athletic schedule – made noisy, sweaty love in Gail's bungalow.

The fantasy model teaches that sex is natural. There may be a need for initiation with an experienced partner, and we can always learn some new tricks, but basically we need do only what comes naturally. There should be no necessity for learning any skills, talking about sex, or taking any corrective measures, for there is nothing to learn and nothing to correct.

In our complex modern society, where everything seems so difficult and artificial, we yearn for something simple and spontaneous that requires no thought or conscious effort. What is more natural than wanting sex to be natural? One man we worked with echoed the sentiments of many when he said: 'Why do I have to learn about my feelings and conditions? It seems so artificial. I should just be able to do it!' Why can't sex be natural?

Perhaps sex would be more natural and spontaneous if we had not been taught how *not* to be natural and spontaneous.

Perhaps sex would be different for us had we not been bombarded with sexual restrictions, inaccuracies, unrealistic expectations, and double messages all of our lives. We really don't know. But we do know that we were taught about sex from the day we were born. We learned not only from the types of sources cited in this and the preceding chapter, but also from the way our parents touched us; from their reactions to our explorations of our own bodies; from their response to our game of 'doctor' with the girl next door; from the way our parents related to each other; and from the images of men and women in the media.

Unfortunately, our learnings made us confused, conflicted, and nervous about the whole subject. Much of what we learned doesn't work or doesn't satisfy us. Talking about natural sex or 'just doing it' makes little sense when all this is taken into account.

If natural is taken to mean without learning, sex will never be natural for us. As pointed out in Chapter 2, sex in humans and many other animals is largely a product of learning. Learning cannot be eliminated, but inaccurate and unsatisfying knowledge can be replaced by learning better suited to our needs.

'Spontaneity' and 'passion', though having definitions quite different from 'natural', are often used in a similar sense, implying a lack of preparation or learning. People often talk of spontaneous or passionate events as if they came out of nowhere, with absolutely no premeditation, training, or preparation. Although such usage has wide currency, it is in error. All acts of adults – whether the artistry of a Van Gogh, Rubinstein, or Nureyev, the grace and 'naturalness' of great athletes, the ways we relate to one another – all of these are the result of years and years of training and preparation. It is so easy to overlook the tremendous amount of training and learning, of objectification and routine, and of sheer boring effort, that make any 'spontaneous' action possible. Spontaneity and passion are *not* the result of knowing nothing and preparing nothing. Rather, they result from knowing the skills so well that you have forgotten them as skills; they have simply become part of you. Then, when an appropriate situation occurs, they come into play without thought or effort.

The problem with the naturalness myth is that it can get in the way of taking the steps necessary to get the type of sex life you want. Some men find it easier to sit around and bemoan their fate than to do something about it. Your sexual discontent is a product not of what you are but rather of what you learned. That learning can be moved aside to make way for a more satisfying sexual expressiveness.

Our last myth is not a product of the fantasy model. It is a recent idea inspired by the sexual revolution.

MYTH 10: IN THIS ENLIGHTENED AGE, THE PRECEDING MYTHS NO LONGER HAVE ANY INFLUENCE ON US

Surely, many people say, in these days of increased openness about sex and wider availability of accurate information, the old sexual model must be losing its hold on people. It must be in the process of being replaced by saner and more realistic models.

It would give us great pleasure to agree with such statements but, unfortunately, they don't seem to be true. In many ways the pressure on men (and on women as well) is becoming worse.

Much of the explicitness of recent film and fiction serves only to give more detailed presentations of the same old myths, thus creating even more pressure than before to do it right. The old myths die slowly. You need only go to one pornographic film to check this out.

And a lot of nonsense is coming from people whom one might hope would know better. In the old days, the experts were saying that sex, or too much sex, or certain kinds of sex, wasn't healthy. Now, in a complete about-face, many are saying you can't live, or live well, without it. Albert Ellis devotes the entire first chapter of his book *Sex and the Liberated Man* to the disadvantages of sexual abstinence. Ellis, like so many sex educators and therapists, is in the business of selling sex. He tries to make a case that abstinence will impair your physical and emotional health, your future sexual adequacy (presumably you might forget how to do it), and, aside from all this, 'it also has grave social disadvantages'. In support of his views he cites a number of authorities, including that well-known sex expert, Henry Miller. And, lest you still haven't been convinced, Ellis says interesting things like the following:

> But voluntary abstinence remains an *un*necessary evil. Accept *that* misery, and you seem off your rocker. You'd better see a psychologist, fast, than keep afflicting yourself with that kind of nonsense.

That Ellis and others of his kind are for sex rather than against it may seem liberated, but it's only a modern version of tyranny. Their stance in favor of sex is as rigid as that of the people who used to be against sex and, in fact, their arguments and hysterical tone are remarkably similar.

Sex, we are told in many articles and books, is good for you. It's good exercise, a wonderful way of losing weight, the best way to get to know others, and, well, it's just good for you. The result is pressure to get into sex, whether or not you feel ready for it or interested in it. Just so long as you do it. We fail to see how freedom has been increased.

Group sex and open relationships have become chic in recent years, thus following the road paved in erotica where almost everyone has multiple partners and where in each work there is at least one scene in which sex is done in threesomes, foursomes, hordes, or whole villages. This is fine for people who like their sex communally, but many are feeling that they ought to do it even if they don't want to.

While we're on the subject of current fads, we should

mention the resurgence of sado-masochism (S&M), also called bondage and discipline (B&D). Violence and brutality are regular fixtures in erotic material and are currently being peddled as methods for the enhancement of your sexual enjoyment. A recent publication, called *S-M: The Last Taboo*, argues for a repeal of the prohibition. Apparently the authors, and others, feel that there shouldn't be any prohibitions on behavior. That way we could all feel free to punch out anyone we don't like – or do like, as the case may be. In any event, it now appears that you're somewhat square if you haven't at least tied someone to a bed. If you're really with it, of course, you gave them a few smacks while they were helpless. All in the name of pleasure and liberation.

Much of the new pressure on men has to do with the scientific discovery of multiple orgasms in women. The phenomenon of multiple orgasms was a regular feature of pornography for over a hundred years but it became a big issue only after Masters and Johnson reported in 1966 that some women in their laboratory had experienced multiple orgasms with self-stimulation. Their data have been distorted and exaggerated almost beyond recognition. The message most commonly heard now is that all women have this capacity and it should be exercised every time they have sex. Guess who is supposed to produce all these orgasms (that's right: you) and how (right again: through intercourse).

Gail Sheehy, in her book *Passages*, provides a good example of this viewpoint. Although she is aware of the tremendous burden we place on erections, she is so enmeshed in the idea that sex equals intercourse that the best she can do is approvingly cite an example of how a woman can help a man insert a soft or partially erect penis into her vagina. Hard or soft, it just has to go in there. Throughout her chapter on sex, she indicates not the slightest understanding that sex can consist of anything other than penis-in-vagina.

And once it's in there, the man's task is very clear according to Sheehy: to bring his partner 'to ecstasy again and again' or, put slightly differently, 'through an ascending chain of orgasms'. All we can make of this is there is an ascending chain of pressure and responsibility being put on men and women to act in certain ways, all of them rooted in the fantasy model of sex.

Our last example is perhaps the most tragic, for it comes from a therapist who has worked with men and professes sympathy for them. In his *Hazards of Being Male*, Herb Goldberg is appalled by statistics indicating that men in their forties spend more time shaving than having intercourse. 'Surely, the male is cheating himself of a vital joy and is entitled to reclaim his full share of the primal pleasures of sex.' In other words, you *should* spend more time in bed and perhaps less time shaving. The idea that men may be having as much sex as they want seems not to have occurred to him.

But this is only the beginning. Goldberg then goes on to something he calls fusion sex.

The experience of fusion sex is one of an intense, totally unselfconscious sexual coming together during which the male is not focusing on or aware of having sex per se but is simply a part of a wholly spontaneous, ecstatic union or fusion with the female, one that often brings him to tears of joy.

In fusion sex there is the phenomenon of a seemingly endless potency, lasting sometimes for an entire weekend or several days during which time he remains in bed making love continually. Men who have reported fusion sex to me describe the phenomenon of ejaculating and then almost immediately becoming erect again. They may have as many as twelve to fifteen orgasms during a weekend's experience of fusion sex.

You're right if you think this sounds familiar. Aside from the tears of joy, it differs little from the examples of fantasy sex we quoted earlier. But now it is coming under the guise of social science.

Fusion sex is merely old nonsense with a new label. We

don't question the fact that it can happen, but such experiences are rare and cannot be trained for or planned. What's the point of writing about them? Surely we already have enough unrealistic expectations. All that Goldberg and others who write of such things accomplish is to convince many men that they really aren't getting as much out of sex as they should, and they therefore should try harder, or try more things, or else feel bad about all the joy they're supposedly missing.

We trust we have said enough to help you realize that the old model of sex is very much with us today. It may now be called liberation or freedom but it's still the same old junk. What's sadly missing is any sense of perspective on the role of sex in the lives of human beings and any understanding of what freedom means. Sex is not the most important thing in the world and it is not necessarily good for you. Only the individual can decide how and where sex should fit into his life, if at all.

Freedom to be obliged to have sex is no freedom at all and, in fact, is a contradiction. The same is true for having to have sex in certain ways or under conditions set by outside authorities. True freedom means the freedom to do or not do as you please, to not have sex as well as to have it, and to have it in circumstances of your own choosing. Freedom may be a wonderful goal for humans to aspire to, but we seem little closer to it in the sexual area than we were fifty years ago.

The chief difficulty with the fantasy model of sex is that it establishes standards for the way things ought to be, standards that ignore individual differences and that are highly unrealistic, thus setting the stage for disappointment and frustration when reality doesn't match the model. Ralph Keyes, in his excellent study of the influence of high school, *Is There Life After High School?*, makes the point succinctly: 'Adult reality generally can't top our high school fantasies. Or match them. Or even come close. In fact, compared with high school's aspirations, sexual reality can really be a drag.' High school aspirations are, of course, made up primarily of the fantasy model.

So many times, for both men and women, the reaction to their first sexual experience with a partner is: 'Is that all there is to it?' Compared to the fantasies and expectations, it often isn't much. It takes time to adjust to reality and give up the unrealizable expectations. Some of us manage the transition with relative ease, although it is never easy, but many of us have great difficulty letting go of the fantasy.

We strive mightily to play the role we learned. We believe that there is some way of achieving the standards of the model, of having superhuman sex. Somehow, there's got to be a way. And we believe that everyone else knows the secret and is enjoying sexual delights we can barely imagine. So we get angry with ourselves and our partners for not being able to make the magic happen.

Despite our anger and despite whatever remedies we try, the disappointment often remains and even deepens. For in our search for the impossible, we forget the obvious and the important. We forget that in human events there are no right ways, no external scripts that will make us happy. We forget about ourselves, about discovering what we are about, about our own sexuality and the best ways of expressing it. In straining to make reality match our expectations, we lose contact with ourselves and our partners, robbing ourselves of any joyful experience. In our intentness to make sex better, we forget that sex is only a small part of life. We focus on it too much, not putting enough time and energy into other aspects of relating, thus cheating ourselves of opportunities to relate in ways that might bring us much satisfaction.

Are we then saying that there is no way of enhancing your sexuality, of making sex a more comfortable and enjoyable experience than it has been? Not really, but we are suggesting that changing your sex life may not lie in the direction you think. What is needed is not more exotic practices, techniques, or equipment, but rather a willingness to let go of the sexual script you learned and to create new ones that are more relevant to you. Will this, then, lead to passion-filled sex and the ultimate orgasm? Probably not. But it can lead to sex that accurately reflects your values, your body, and your personality – your self. Sex, like everything else, is limited in what it is and what it can produce. The secret, however, is not to try to increase its yield by adding more partners and equipment, but to 'get into' and participate fully in whatever sexual expressions and activities seem appropriate to you. Such experiences are most likely to occur when you are aware of your sexual needs and wants and able to get them.

You may be in a place where 'working on sex' to develop some new ways of thinking and acting seems appropriate. This 'work' will not always be exciting. It may be boring at times and you may find yourself wondering if sex is becoming too mechanical or routine, or if you are being too self-conscious about it. It may be this way for a while.

What you need to keep in mind is that your training or work time need not be long. How long depends on a number of factors, but most of all on how much time you are willing to give each week. For most of the men we've worked with, a few hours a week for seven to ten weeks has been sufficient.

The process of acquiring new sexual skills is similar to learning most other skills. You may remember that when you were learning some skills that you are now proficient in – such as driving a car, playing tennis, talking to women – you were extremely selfconscious. You were continually wondering what to talk about or what to do with your hands or feet. But if you persevered you reached a point where you forgot about your hands and feet and what to say. You could just get into the activity in a way that others called spontaneous. The same thing happens in learning sexual skills. At first there may be some confusion, routine, and self-consciousness. But as you learn the details, you forget them. They become part of you and you become free to get more involved in the activity. Then you are open to real spontaneity and abandon.

FIVE

Where are you now?

Before you can start changing and growing sexually, it is necessary to examine where you are starting from. This may sound so obvious as to not warrant discussion, but it's unfortunately true that many people who want to change have only the foggiest notion of where they are and where they want to go.

One of the most important lessons to be learned from the remarkable success of the behavior therapies, of which sex therapy is the most successful stepchild, is that the probability of producing change is directly related to, first, a detailed assessment of your current situation and, second, the delineation of specific goals to be achieved. It is, of course, much easier to say something vague about wanting to be happy or to have a better sex life, but the chances of reaching such goals are slim indeed. What specifically would have to happen for you to feel happier or have better sex? That is the key question, since specific goals can be worked toward and achieved; vague generalities, on the other hand, do not lend themselves to planning for change.

Another important aspect of producing change involves dealing with the obstacles to change. There are always obstacles. If there were none, you would already be where you want to be and there would be no need for change. As we mentioned several times in the previous chapters, the main obstacles for men are the sexual fables that comprise the fantasy model of sex. It is essential that you recognize the influence these myths exert on your thinking and behavior. Obstacles can be successfully negotiated, but only when you are aware of which ones are doing what to you.

The exercise below will help you take the first step toward change by giving you an opportunity to examine where you are now. Once that step has been taken, you will be in a better position to set some specific goals for yourself.

EXERCISE 5–1: YOUR PRESENT SITUATION
Time Required: 1 to 2 hours

Write a detailed statement of your present sex life. The more detailed the better. Give concrete examples of all major points. Include the following items:

1. **What do you like about your sex life? What parts of it give you pleasure?**
2. **What about it is not satisfying to you? Be specific as to when and how problems occur and how they make you feel.**
3. **Which of the myths in the last two chapters are helping to maintain the problems? How?**
4. **How are you dealing with the problems or unsatisfactory elements (e.g., are you avoiding sex, not asking for what you want, having sex a lot in order to prove that you're really OK)?**

This exercise can be done as a list, essay, or in any other form. It doesn't have to be neat, and spelling and grammar don't count. It is for you alone.

If writing is difficult for you, do the exercise by talking into a tape recorder or by covering the material in a conversation with a friend. If you are in a relationship and communication with your partner is good, you might want to discuss the material with her. Obviously, if you do not feel your partner would be a supportive listener, you shouldn't do the exercise with her. Should you choose to do the exercise in conversation, your friend is to function primarily as a listener, reserving comment until you are finished.

If you read the exercise but did not take the time to do it, perhaps telling yourself that you'll go back and do it later, you might want to rethink that decision, particularly if you wish to make changes in your sexual behavior. Changes rarely come about through reading alone.

We wonder if you paid much attention to the first item in the exercise, the satisfactory aspects of your sex life. Men often skip that part, thinking that they should concentrate on what is not going well. That isn't necessarily the case. Surely there are some satisfactory aspects of your sexual behavior, and it's nice to get them on paper so that you can put everything in perspective. Also, sometimes the pleasurable parts offer the best clue about where to go next, as the following example illustrates.

Robin was fairly well satisfied with his sex life but wondered if there were ways of making it even better. In doing the first part of Exercise 5–1, he remembered an experience that he very much enjoyed: his partner giving him oral sex. This was a bit confusing since Robin and his partner often engaged in oral sex. What made this one experience stand out? It turned out that their usual pattern was simultaneous sex; whatever one did to the other was reciprocated at the same time. During the experience he recalled, however, they had not assumed their usual '69' position but he had just lain there and let her do all the work. And it had been one of the most enjoyable sexual experiences he had ever had. But, though it had occurred about two months before he came to see us, it had never been repeated. As we talked further, it became clear that Robin was interested in further exploration of nonsimultaneous sex but that he was so accustomed to being active in sex that this was unlikely to happen unless a program of exercises was established and followed. With our assistance, this was done. Robin and his partner gradually explored various aspects of being active and passive in sex. The process was not always smooth since Robin, like many men, sometimes found that being passive was uncomfortable (a man is not supposed to just lie there and be dependent on the woman's ministrations), but within a few weeks he and his partner felt that they had considerably increased their sexual options and enjoyment.

This example also underscores the necessity of being specific. Until it was discovered what in particular (his passivity) had made his recalled experience so special, it was impossible to know in which direction to go to help him enhance his sexuality.

We tried to be clever in our wording of the exercise to prevent you from using terms like impotence, premature ejaculation, insufficient enjoyment, and lack of interest. These labels are convenient to use, but they aren't very helpful. As we mentioned earlier it's the specifics that count. When do you get an erection and when don't you? When are you interested or what are you interested in? What do you mean when you call yourself impotent or premature? It can make a lot of difference.

Arthur said in his initial interview that he was a premature ejaculator. When asked if he had any control over when he ejaculated, he answered affirmatively, indicating that he could last for thirty-five to forty minutes in intercourse. But that obviously wasn't sufficient, he maintained, since his wife climaxed only rarely. He thought that if he could last a few minutes longer, his wife would have more orgasms.

Arthur was looking in the wrong place. Teaching him to last for fifty minutes or two hours would probably have been a huge waste of time. Anyone who has some control over when he ejaculates or who can last for thirty minutes can by no stretch of the imagination be called a premature ejaculator.

What Arthur didn't realize is that many women never have orgasms during intercourse and that many others reach orgasm this way only a small percentage of the time unless supplementary manual stimulation is applied simultaneously. Lasting for hours on end doesn't help the situation any and will probably only bore everyone. If you are labeling yourself premature, carefully examine what you mean by that and how realistic your goals are for lasting longer.

The same is true for erection problems. Do you believe you should have erections all the time, that you should get them without any direct stimulation, or that they should be as hard as steel? How realistic are your goals?

A sixty-year-old man came over a thousand miles to see us. His wife of thirty-two years had died less than a year before and, while he had had a few erections by himself since then, he did not get one on the few occasions when he had gone out with a woman. He wanted to get married again but felt it would be impossible until he was capable of having erections with a partner. The man was clearly depressed and we asked who or what turned him on. He couldn't think of anyone or anything. Upon questioning, he admitted that he had not felt sexually aroused since his wife died. We tried some sexual fantasies with him and they failed to evoke any interest. The same was true for erotic literature and movies. Nothing elicited the slightest degree of sexual interest, and yet he was convinced he should be able to get an erection. Needless to say, his goal was somewhat unrealistic. Not until he finished mourning for his wife was he able to get aroused and erect again.

This man did have a problem, but it wasn't sexual.

Since, as we have already discussed, men tend to sexualize everything, you will not be surprised to hear that men tend to make sexual problems out of things that really don't have that much to do with sex. We have seen men who insisted they had a sex problem when what quickly became evident was that they disliked or were angry at their partners. Sure, we can say there was a sex problem of sorts (they couldn't get or stay erect), but the primary problem was in the relationship. Their penises were not being contrary but rather were acting precisely the way they were designed to act. Hostility is not an atmosphere in which erections and good sex flourish. The angry feelings, or the situations that produce them, may have to be dealt with first. Until they are resolved, at least partially, better sex may be impossible.

In looking at the myths or rules that are maintaining your difficulties, perhaps you came up with some that were not discussed by us. That is fine. There are many, many myths that get in the way of good sex, and we discussed only a few. The important thing is to recognize the ones that are getting in your way.

Terry was generally satisfied with sex but there was one aspect that, while not a major problem, was an annoyance. The first few times he had sex with a new partner, even if he was comfortable with her and felt very good about her, he could not have an orgasm. He could live with this situation but preferred not to if a solution was available. Terry knew a lot about what excited him and never had any problem coming through his own efforts. We asked what prevented him from using this knowledge with a partner. It turned out that he had tried telling his partners how to touch him and, while they did what he wanted, it still did not result in orgasm the first few times. We asked about the possibility of his touching himself while he was having sex with a partner (e.g., touching the base of his penis while having intercourse or using his hand as well as her hand or mouth when they were doing something else). It sounded reasonable to him but there was some resistance because one of his rules – a quite common myth in our culture – was that in partner sex you do not touch yourself. The resistance was worked through in a few sessions and the problem was resolved.

What is keeping you where you are is what you need to discover, whether or not we mentioned it or whether or not other people also believe in that rule. It can probably be moved out of the way so that you can get more from sex, but the chances are much improved if you can clearly identify it.

The last aspect of Exercise 5-1 is the role of solutions, how you are dealing with the problem. Home remedies frequently serve to maintain rather than resolve the problem. Trying to will an erection, for example, usually makes an erection impossible. The same is true of gritting your teeth and trying to hold back an ejaculation. Not letting your partner touch your penis because you fear she will find it too small or soft does nothing to resolve those fears and, in fact, often maintains or even increases their power.

Take a close look at how you answered the last item in the exercise. Is it possible that your 'solution' is maintaining the difficulty? If so, what steps can you take to stop applying that solution?

Now that you have determined where you are starting from, you can set some goals you'd like to achieve. You should be aware that you need not achieve all of them right now. Changes can be made in steps, and short-range goals may be considerably less than what you would like in the long run.

Bob had never been able to ejaculate during intercourse and, during his current relationship, found that he rarely could maintain an erection for more than a few minutes. Although he wanted to resolve the ejaculation problem, it seemed logical to deal only with the erection problem first. Once that was resolved and he was able to have intercourse, we could deal with the remaining difficulty.

To put the lesson from that example in other words, don't take on too much at once. That will only serve to disappoint and frustrate you. Go slowly, taking small steps. Be realistic: you can only do so much at a time. Also, be sure your goals are in fact *your* goals, not standards of someone else's choosing.

The following exercise will help you be more specific about your goals.

EXERCISE 5–2: YOUR GOALS FOR A BETTER SEX LIFE
Time Required: 30 to 45 minutes

Write a letter to an imaginary friend telling him or her how you would like your sex life to be. Be wary if it sounds anything like the fantasy material we discussed in Chapters 3 and 4. Discuss the aspects you would like to change, listing how you would like them to be different. If there is a need, separate immediate and long-range goals.

Do not be brief. Discuss your wishes in detail and be very specific about any changes you plan. Note any obstacles that might get in the way of reaching your goals. Mention any concerns you may have about reaching your goals. Is it possible that there would be negative aspects to making the changes? This is not uncommon and, should there be even a slight hint that problems could occur as a result of making changes, read the part of Chapter 22 called 'The Uses of Sex Problems'.

Now that you have set some goals for yourself, you have laid the foundation for change. Keep your answers to the last two exercises; you may wish to refer back to them later.

Before going further, you should consider the following issues.

If you found possible negative consequences for making sexual changes, you should follow the suggestions in Chapter 22. Trying to make changes before you are more comfortable with the probable outcome may be very difficult.

Since whatever can get in the way probably will, pay careful attention to any obstacles to change you noted in Exercise 5–1. Are there any ways of precluding their appearance or at least of mitigating their influence?

If you suffer from a serious illness or injury, have had surgery recently, are taking medication of any sort, or have reason to question your health in any way, get a complete physical examination and read Chapter 21. When you see your doctor, discuss your sexual problem with him and ask him to check for possible physiological causes. If your doctor is not comfortable discussing sexual matters or does not seem knowledgeable in this area (and many doctors fall into these categories), ask him to refer you to one who is. It is up to you to get complete and understandable information about the issues that concern you. Ask questions, ask for clarification when you do not understand; be sure you get what you are paying for. It is important that you try not to be intimidated by the doctor's professionalism or his apparent lack of time. Even if you are intimidated, as most of us are in the presence of physicians, attempt to get the information.

Look at your priorities and time schedule to determine how you can devote the two to five hours a week we'll ask for sexual exercises. You should make sure that you can spend the time leisurely and without interruption.

Many men, although claiming that sex is very important to them, allow very little time for it in their schedules. This usually does not make for enjoyable sex. The time you set aside should be prime time. Be good to yourself.

If you are in a relationship, you might want to discuss your plans for change with your partner. While not absolutely essential, it is preferred, since you will progress much faster if your partner is informed and willing to cooperate when necessary.

If you find that the two of you are unable to agree on the importance or goals of change, or that you have difficulty talking about the subject, read Chapter 12, 'Dealing with a Partner', now. It is important that the two of you agree on the nature of the problem and how it's going to be resolved. If there is substantial disagreement – if, for example, you believe there is a sexual problem but she feels the difficulties lie in other areas – it will be very difficult to make progress in resolving anything. Talk it out and decide where you should put your energy.

SIX

Your conditions for good sex and how to get them

This chapter is one of the most important in the book. It presents a way of looking at sex that is different from the one most of us learned. Having a better sex life very much depends on understanding and being able to apply what is in this chapter.

As we mentioned in Chapter 4, men learned that they should be able to perform on demand. Given a willing partner, we should become aroused and erect, ready and able to have a good sexual experience. While girls and women had all sorts of special requirements (needing to trust us, to feel loved, and so on) we were less complex and didn't need anything 'special'. If she was willing, that was sufficient to get our sexual apparatus working. And if that wasn't sufficient, we tried frantically to kick the machinery into operation by trying harder, by working at it. Then we began to worry. What was wrong with us that it required so much effort to become aroused or erect? Why didn't it happen spontaneously the way it was supposed to?

The truth is that it was never supposed to work the way we were taught. We men are not as simple as we have been led to believe. We are complex human beings, with diverse styles, needs, likes and dislikes. This is as true in sex as in other areas, but because of what we learned about how we were supposed to be sexually most of us don't know this. When sex doesn't work out the way we like, we are all too ready to assume that something is wrong with us for not responding the way we think we should, rather than to look at the situation to discover what about it might be blocking our sexual responses.

Let's look at what is needed for a satisfying sexual response in more detail so you can get a better idea of what facilitates or blocks such a response. The two basic ingredients are arousal and a relatively open nervous system.

Arousal (synonymous with desire, excitement, and turn-on) is not easy to define. It is not the same as erection. Arousal and erection are separate systems. They often go together – you feel excited and get an erection – but not always, and it is crucial to separate them in your thinking.

Arousal refers to feelings, a desire to touch someone and have sex with her. It is often experienced as a pull or surge toward a lover and it can also be more abstract, with the desire or pull being present but without a specific partner in mind. Men have described arousal in these ways: 'a wanting to be with her, to be close to her, to merge with her'; 'a warm tingling sensation in my penis and elsewhere'; 'an overall feeling that I want her'; 'feels like my blood is racing and I can feel my heart beat'; 'my whole body comes alive in a special way'.

Your own experiences of arousal may or may not be similar to these examples. The important thing is that you know when you are sexually excited. What specific sensations or feelings tell you that you're in a sexual mood?

Men often think they are turned-on when they aren't. Because of our training, we frequently look to the situation rather than to our feelings to determine if we're interested in sex. If the situation is one that our education defined as sexy (e.g., having an attractive woman indicating that she wants sex with us) we assume that we are, or should be, aroused, without checking to see if that is indeed the case.

The importance of arousal can hardly be overstated, yet it is commonly overlooked. We are all so caught up in the myth that men (and more recently, women as well) will automatically be turned-on in a situation the fantasy model defines as sexual that we often forget to ask whether we really are interested.

Despite this cultural blindness, however, you need to check

your interest if you desire a better sex life. Before launching into a sexual experience, ask yourself if you *feel* aroused (remembering that feeling is not the same as thinking) or if there is some potential for becoming excited. If not, better do something other than sex. Otherwise, you risk the possibility of not enjoying the sex or not functioning well.

The second ingredient for good sex is an uncluttered nervous system that will allow your arousal to be reflected in your bodily state (e.g., getting an erection) and let you fully experience what is happening.

Let's say a man is looking at something, perhaps his partner's legs, that usually excites him. If his nervous system is obstructed – by concerns about something that happened at work, for example – seeing her legs may not feel sexual and, in fact, her legs may hardly be noticed at all. He's looking at her legs but the perception has no impact on him. This is an example of how a cluttered nervous system can block arousal.

But let's assume that man does experience his partner's legs as sexy and feels turned-on. For this feeling to have an impact on the state of his penis, a message has to be sent to it through his nervous system. The message says, in effect, 'This feels great, so get hard.' As the man continues looking at his partner, or as this is replaced by other types of stimulation – touching, talking, fantasy, and so forth – more and more similar messages are sent and received, producing and maintaining a state of arousal and erection.

Simple enough, but there is a slight hitch. The messages to the penis must be clearly sent and received. If his nervous system is obstructed, the messages to the penis don't get through properly.

There are many things that can clutter the nervous system so that sexual messages don't get through. Alcohol and many other drugs are well-known culprits. Other common factors are guilt about sex, anger at partner, preoccupation with other matters, fatigue, and poor physical health.

The most common obstructor of the nervous system during sex, however, is nervous tension or anxiety. This includes any doubts or concerns about the situation and one's acceptability and performance ('Will the kids walk in?' 'Will she think I'm as good as her other lovers?' 'Can I last long enough for her?').

Such concerns, if they are strong, throw the whole nervous system into a tizzy, obstructing the transmission of sexual messages to the penis and other areas. Regarding the penis, the messages may not get through at all or only a few may get there; you may not get an erection, or it may not be as firm as usual, or you may quickly lose it. Anxiety, anger, and other feelings can also stimulate the processes involved in ejaculation, triggering quick ejaculations. Any efforts to get or keep an erection, or to hold back ejaculation, usually only add another layer of tension to whatever is already there, thus making it even more likely that something will go wrong.

An obstructed nervous system can also block enjoyment. There are men who can function even when they are unaroused and/or their nervous systems are cluttered up with anxiety, concerns, or anger. For reasons we don't understand, they are able to bypass many of the requirements that other men have. They can function no matter how nervous or bored or angry they are. These feelings affect their nervous system in a different way – they function but they don't feel much. They feel little closeness, love, joy, or excitement. Theirs may seem like a wonderful situation, since they can function almost anytime regardless of the situation, but you need only to talk to one or two of them to realize they get very little from their sexual encounters.

Erections, ejaculatory control, and feelings of arousal and enjoyment cannot be directed by force of will. We cannot coerce an erection or force ourselves to get turned-on or to enjoy an experience. This is a crucial point and one that is difficult for many men to accept, since it goes counter to our training. As mentioned in our discussion of the performance orientation, we men learned to get things done by giving direct commands to our minds and bodies. ('Don't get rattled; stay calm.' 'You can do it; push harder.') This system works well enough much of the time, but only with those parts that we can directly control.

For better or worse, our arousal, erection, ejaculation, and feeling systems cannot be controlled in this way. They do not take orders. In fact, attempts to direct them a certain way more often than not result in their doing just the contrary. If you have any doubts about this, it is important that you put the proposition to the test. Whenever you want, try to will arousal, erection, good feelings, or to hold back an ejaculation. Beg, threaten, sweet-talk, issue any kind of command you like, and observe the results. Then perhaps you'll be more open to considering the idea that this isn't the best way to deal with sex.

So what can you do to have better sex? Very simply, you need to discover the conditions under which you are most able to become aroused or erect or experience good feelings. A 'condition' is anything at all that makes a difference to you sexually. It can involve your physical and emotional state, how you feel about your partner, what you think you can expect from her, the type of stimulation you want, the setting you are in, or anything else. A condition is anything that makes you more relaxed, more comfortable, more confident, more sexual, more open to your experience in a sexual situation. Another way of looking at conditions is that they are the factors that clear your nervous system of unnecessary clutter, leaving it open to receive and transmit sexual messages in ways that will result in satisfying sex for you.

We sometimes conveniently ignore the fact that even machines have conditions, requirements that allow them to function at their best. Our highly valued cars, for example, have requirements in terms of type of gas, oil, servicing, and ways and places they should and should not be driven. Yet we seem more tolerant of their needs than of our own. We don't call our car stupid or bad or impotent if it doesn't run with an empty gas tank. We simply accept the fact that it needs gas to run and we meet the requirement. But when it comes to ourselves, we have a different set of standards and don't hesitate to call ourselves inadequate or bad or impotent if we don't function the way we think we should, no matter how poorly the situation meets our requirements.

Mort, a man in his early thirties with erection problems, had no trouble understanding the idea of conditions . . . for his boat. He was very proud of his possession and could talk eloquently about all of its requirements, which he was happy to meet in order to get the best possible performance from it. On the other hand, when it came to his penis, he couldn't understand why it didn't operate the way he wanted. That a boat should have all sorts of special needs he could understand, but a penis, well, it should just work all the time and not need any special attention. It took him a while to understand that a penis is, if anything, more sensitive and more vulnerable than a boat, and that its needs have to be attended to for it to function satisfactorily.

The reason that Mort and so many of the rest of us have trouble accepting our sexual needs as valid is that they run counter to the fantasy model, to the way we were taught 'it ought to be'. There is no tolerance in the model, and therefore very little in ourselves, for individual variations or needs. Which means, when you get right to the essence of it, that our model has little room for individuals at all.

It seems obvious to say that we all have our individual preferences, styles, and needs; they are what make us the unique person that we are. The problem is that, except in those rare cases where our own styles and desires are similar to those glorified in the model, we tend to be ashamed of them. We have been carefully taught to feel guilty for having any special or unusual needs (which means anything that does not fit the model).

We try to hide the parts of ourselves that do not conform to our sexual script in order to spare ourselves and others from seeing how 'inadequate' or 'strange' we are. We try to pretend that we don't need or want what in fact we do, that we aren't who we really are.

It is worth repeating what we said in Chapters 3 and 4. Compared to the sexual model we learned, we are all inadequate and deficient. None of us can measure up to its absurd standards. The problem is not in us, but in the model we compare ourselves to, a model that, to be charitable, is utter nonsense and unfit for human consumption.

It is perfectly acceptable to be yourself, to have your own desires, anxieties, concerns, and style. They need not be viewed as deficiencies or, as one man called them, 'weird-nesses'. They are merely expressions of your uniqueness. Your special requirements or conditions, in sexual and other areas, are a large part of what you call your 'self', and the less of it you feel bad about and want to hide, the easier your life will be.

We realize that at this point some readers may be confused. They will recall times in their lives when arousal, conditions, and feelings didn't have to be considered. They were usually aroused in sexual situations, they functioned well, and they enjoyed themselves. What happened? We can't really answer that question, but the phenomenon is a common one. Many men function automatically – that is, without regard for any particular conditions or, as we mentioned earlier, without even needing to be aroused – for a while. And then the system breaks down. We aren't sure why the automatic functioning ceases, although it is clear that it often involves a trauma of some sort – divorce, infidelity on the part of a partner, loss of job, or one sexual experience that goes poorly. Whatever the cause, it appears from our experience that automatic functioning, once disrupted, cannot be restored, at least not in the same way it existed before the disruption. The man is forced to start paying attention to factors he once could ignore: e.g., whether he is aroused, relaxed, and getting the proper stimulation. Of course, as time goes on and these factors become a regular part of his thinking, his functioning will become less self-conscious and, therefore, more automatic.

But it will now include some elements previously ignored.

Your sexual systems were designed to work for you and allow you to have good sex. All you need to do is determine the conditions under which they can best satisfy you. Here is an example of how one man discovered this.

Jan had never had a sexual dysfunction but both he and his wife of two years felt that they weren't having as much sex as they wanted and that it wasn't as enjoyable as it was in the past. His wife complained that he rarely initiated sex and often turned down her invitations. It turned out that Jan had many times felt interested in sex but had not acted on it and was now trying to quash even the interest. What, we asked, would have to change so that he would feel free to have sex when he felt in the mood? This was his answer: 'I'd just have to know that we wouldn't get locked into the same routine every time. When I think about what sex will be like, I lose all interest. It's always the same routine. I have to spend lots of time getting her ready for intercourse, even when she initiates, and it all goes according to the same ritual. I enjoy it this way sometimes, but it's the thought that it always has to be this way that gets me. I know I probably shouldn't say this, but sometimes I'd like a quick screw, with no foreplay or messing around. Sometimes I'd like just a blowjob, without having to do anything in return right away. I guess I mainly want the feeling of some freedom. I want to know that there are some possibilities other than the same old stuff.'

Jan was stating his conditions for being more interested in sex. It was interesting to watch his wife while he talked. Although they had good communication in most areas of their relationship, sex was something they hadn't been able to talk about. His wife at first looked shocked – she had never heard him say these things – but then started smiling and finally was laughing wildly: she felt precisely the way he did. It rarely works out this quickly, but the important thing was that once his conditions were met, once he knew that sex could go in many different ways, his interest returned and sex became more enjoyable.

Before presenting two exercises that will help you discover your conditions for good sex, we want to mention a difficulty that you may encounter. You may find yourself coming up with things you wish were not true. Some of your conditions may at first strike you as old-fashioned, feminine, strange, or something else that you feel is bad or inappropriate. Whatever your feelings, it is best to write the conditions out and give them serious consideration. We say this because it is our experience that most conditions are easier to accept and fulfill than to change. Unless your conditions involve pain or harm to you or your partner, the chances are very good that, no matter how new or unusual they seem to you now, you can learn to accept them and find effective ways of meeting them.

The two exercises that follow have been very useful to many men for discovering their conditions. Read them both and then do the one that you like best. The first one is stated in general terms. If you have been having a problem in a specific area, e.g., arousal, erection, or enjoyment, you might want to direct the exercise toward it.

EXERCISE 6–1: CONDITIONS ESSAY
Time Required: 45 minutes

Compare the three or four best sexual experiences you have had with an equal number of ones that did not turn out well, and list all the factors that differentiate between the good and bad ones (for example 'In all the good experiences, I knew the woman well; this wasn't true in the bad ones'). The elements that characterize the good experiences and are lacking in the bad ones are your conditions for good sex. Be sure to be as specific as possible. If you have not had any good experiences, or if it is difficult to remember them in sufficient detail, simply use your

**imagination and list those things you think would be
necessary and helpful for you to have good sex.**

**Whether you use comparisons or your imagination,
consider all these areas: your physical health; amount of
anxiety or tension; use of alcohol and other drugs; your
feelings about yourself; the extent to which you were
preoccupied with other matters; fears about performance,
pregnancy, and venereal disease; your feelings about your
partner (how much you are turned-on to her; your
conviction that she cares for you; your confidence that she
will not put you down if you are not a perfect lover; and
any anger or resentment toward her).**

**When you have finished with your list, put it away for a
day or two, then reread it and see if there is anything you
want to change or add. Now go through each item and
reword it so that it is specific enough to put into practice.
Let's assume that one of your conditions is 'knowing it
won't be a disaster if I don't get an erection'. This is too
vague. You need to ask yourself: 'What would have to
happen for me to know that it won't be a disaster if I don't
get an erection?'**

One man we worked with answered that question like
this: 'First, I'd have to know that she was interested in
more of me than just my sexual performance and,
second, that she could take a lack of erection in stride
without getting angry.' This was still too general. We
asked him what he would have to do in order to feel
confident that she was interested in him as a person and
that she wouldn't be angered by a soft penis. He came up
with more specific ideas: 'I'd have to spend some time
with her before we got into sex. If we got along well and
I felt she liked being with me and doing things with me,
then I'd know she was interested in more than just my
cock. I'd also need to talk to her about sex, to tell her
that I don't always get an erection, and also that her
satisfaction is very important to me. I'd want to know if

she would let me take care of her orally if my penis wasn't working. If she reacted well to this, I'd feel comfortable.' His hitherto vague conditions were now workable. He could take his time with his partner before getting into sex and, with a little help from us, was able to have the conversation he wanted. He followed through beautifully, he met his conditions, and his sex life improved rather dramatically.

The importance of being specific cannot be over-emphasized. If your conditions are too general to be put into practice, you obviously will be unable to attain them.

The next exercise may strike you as a bit odd when you first read it. We hope you won't let this put you off. It has worked extremely well for many men – most of whom thought it was strange indeed when they first heard it – and it can also be lots of fun.

EXERCISE 6–2: LETTER FROM YOUR PENIS
Time Required: 60 to 75 minutes

This letter (or list) is to be written from the point of view of your penis. Yes, you read it right, from the point of view of your penis. So before beginning take a minute or two to imagine what it's like to be your penis. Try to put yourself in its place. Imagine yourself dangling there between your owner's legs. What would that be like? Then address yourself to the question given below and let yourself write whatever comes to you. It is important that you write with as little censoring and editing as possible. Just write whatever comes, no matter how messy, ungrammatical, illogical, or silly it seems. As much as possible let your penis do the writing, so to speak.

The question to be answered is: HOW DOES MY OWNER MISTREAT ME? Be as specific as possible, giving examples whenever appropriate. Spend no more than 45 minutes on

this question. When you are done, put your letter away for a day or two. When you come back to the letter, reread it and add anything you want. Then again take the point of view of your penis and spend 15 to 30 minutes answering this question: HOW COULD MY OWNER TREAT ME BETTER?

From these two letters you should be able to come up with a fairly complete list of your conditions for good sex. Spend as much time as you need to make them specific enough to be workable.

There are two conditions that are absolute musts, no matter what your situation or concern. Please add them to your list if you did not come up with them yourself. NEVER TRY TO USE YOUR PENIS IN SEX WHEN YOU ARE NOT AROUSED, and NEVER TRY TO USE YOUR PENIS IN SEX WHEN YOU ARE ANXIOUS. These are other ways of saying that you should involve your penis only when you are turned-on and reasonably relaxed. Flouting these conditions is an excellent way of getting into a war with your penis, a war you cannot possibly win.

Check your list of conditions again. How many of the items are absolutely necessary and how many are not? You probably need to attend to only the most important ones. Most men we've worked with have found that meeting one, two, or three of the most important ones are all they need to improve their sex lives.

The implication of discovering your conditions is simple. You are going to have to learn to deal with sexual situations so that your most important conditions are met or at least approximated. How well you function and how much you enjoy are directly related to the extent to which these conditions are fulfilled.

At this point you may be feeling discouraged. Knowing your conditions sometimes has this effect at first. Do some of the items on your list surprise you, make you wonder if you're weird, or leave you feeling that you'll never be able to meet them? Such reactions are common. We were trained to think that we had no special requirements, so it's no surprise that we get concerned when we find that we do. Here are two typical responses:

> I guess I always sort of knew about these things but I never saw them so clearly or took them seriously. Now I'm worried. Seems like it would take lots of work to get them all set up.

> Some of this sounds so feminine. Trust, closeness, knowing she likes me – those are things I expect to hear from my sister. Do you really think there are women who would go to bed with me with this damn list of stuff?

It can be upsetting to learn that we are quite human and have very human kinds of requirements. It is natural to wish that things were different, that meeting conditions was not necessary. Before you get depressed or throw part of your list away, consider the items carefully. Are you really less of a man because you have such needs? If you answer in the affirmative, you should clearly delineate just what is your image of a man. Is it at all human? Does it make any sense for you to compare yourself to such a standard?

Consider your conditions again. Is it at all conceivable for you to honor them without giving up your membership in the male sex? Do you really believe there are no women who could accept you and your conditions?

While you are thinking about these heavy questions, you may find some comfort in the following story, the source of which we no longer remember:

> A world-famous bullfighter, the epitome of masculinity in his culture, entertained some guests at his villa one evening. After dinner he disappeared and one of the male guests went in search of him. He found the bullfighter in the kitchen, wearing an apron and washing dishes. The

guest was appalled and blurted out, 'How can you be doing such a feminine thing?' To which the bullfighter replied, looking down his nose at the guest: 'Whatever I do is masculine.'

The bullfighter made an important point. Whatever he does, and whatever you do, is an expression of yourself. Since you are both male, how could it be feminine? Wearing an apron and washing dishes, taking care of children, wanting gentleness and emotional closeness in sex, or almost anything else – if it is an expression of a male, how could it be other than masculine?

That the bullfighter's guest or you or anyone else thinks otherwise is only because you have accepted certain social fictions – sex-role stereotypes – as valid. Such fictions may have had some useful functions in the past, but it is painfully clear that the present demands more flexible arrangements. John Wayne, Harold Robbins, Henry Miller, and the rest of their kind are no longer relevant, if indeed they ever were.

And it still isn't easy. It is difficult to admit needing things that contradict the myths and stereotypes we learned so well. It becomes easier, however, when we realize that the myths themselves are what limit our functioning and enjoyment, in sex and elsewhere. It is precisely through our conditions – our needs and desires – that we can express our maleness, our humanness, ourselves. And it may help to know that not one of the men we have worked with felt that he lost any of his masculinity in the process of fulfilling his conditions. Many, in fact, spontaneously reported that once they could accept and express their conditions, they felt more like men than ever before.

Greg never had any problems functioning sexually – he was a swinger by any standard – but he rarely experienced any joy in his activities. He was well versed in the techniques and tricks of sex, he always had erections, he could last forever, and his partners often complimented him on his virtuosity. He got little, however, beyond the knowledge that he was 'a great fuck'. Even his orgasms felt 'only like a few muscle contractions'. Greg thought that conditions were 'dumb' but, since nothing else worked, he reluctantly set about discovering his. He found that he needed to like and care for his partner, feelings he had spent most of his life running away from. He feared getting involved with women and therefore only had sex with those he found attractive but didn't like. It was a long, hard struggle for Greg to overcome some of his fears of caring and involvement, but he made it to the point where he could enjoy sex and relating to his partners on many levels.

Several months after he terminated therapy, Greg asked for an appointment to deal with another issue. In the course of the session, he said the following about his sexuality. 'It's strange looking back at where I was. I thought I was the biggest cocksman in town. But now I know the horrible price I paid for all those performances with women I didn't care for. It's like I buried a big part of me, all my feelings, so I could play the role. Now I've mellowed out and settled down. I love Jenny and we've been thinking about living together. She satisfies all my sexual desires. Sex is great with her. I'm not performing actually, I'm having less sex than ever before in my life – but I enjoy it so much. It's really fine and I feel more of a man than ever. Not the kind of rowdy, show-off I was before, but more quiet, more secure. I like it better this way.'

MEETING YOUR CONDITIONS: BASIC ASSERTIVENESS

Conditions fall into two general categories: those that can be dealt with entirely on your own, and those that require you to deal with a partner. Examples of the first type would include requests from your penis for some nonsexual contact with you (such as talking to it or light touching) or for gentler treatment in masturbation. These and similar goals can be accomplished without anyone else's knowledge or participation. Sometimes these are easily dealt with and sometimes not. It mainly depends on your willingness to take the time and energy to be good to yourself. We give an exercise later in the chapter to help you with this.

The second class of conditions, those requiring a partner's participation, may be more difficult. Let's say that one of your conditions is not to have sex when you are tired. This is easily accomplished if your partner never takes the initiative. But suppose you are tired and she indicates that she wants sex. You now have to deal with her. Many men deal with such a situation either by not dealing with it – that is, by acquiescing to the partner's requests and ignoring their conditions – or by pretending not to notice the partner's advances. Done often enough, the first method can lead to a dysfunction or a dislike of sex, while the second can leave the partner feeling confused and rejected. In neither case is the man honoring both his condition and his partner.

Men have a reputation for being able to get what they want and to stand up for their own interests. That's what being a man is about, isn't it? Sadly, we have found that when it comes to sex, men are rarely able to do what is best for them, rarely able to communicate their needs and feelings to their partners. However assertive they may be at work or in other areas of their lives, most men have difficulty getting their sexual needs met. They are so focused on acting the way they think a 'real man' should or on pleasing their partners that they often do not get what they want.

We have come a long way from the heyday of the 'Slam, bam, thank you, ma'm' performances. Now women are supposed to have orgasms and we feel it is our responsibility to provide them. It is true that there are still some men around who are totally inconsiderate of and insensitive to their partners' needs, but their ranks seem to be dwindling rapidly.

The pendulum has swung far in the opposite direction and most men feel under tremendous pressure to satisfy their partners. If they don't, they feel guilty and label themselves failures.

Because of the pressure to satisfy their partners' needs and live up to the standards of the fantasy model, men often sacrifice their own enjoyment. Thus we find men making love when they don't want to, when they are too tense to fully respond, in ways they don't like, and sometimes even with partners they find unattractive – usually with the excuse that 'she expected it, so what else could I do?' Such self-sacrifices rarely make for good sex.

If you think we are joking or that meeting your conditions will be easy, consider the following questions seriously:

- Could you let your partner know that you are not in the mood for sex even though she is interested?
- Could you tell her that you don't want intercourse but would like some other form of sex?
- Could you indicate in a clear way that you want to stop in the midst of a sexual experience?
- Could you let her know that certain feelings (anger, anxiety, boredom, etc.) are interfering with your sexual feelings and functioning?
- Could you give her directions how to stimulate you in ways you find most pleasurable?
- Could you ask her to tell or show you how she likes to be stimulated?

If you answered yes to some or all of these questions, we have another one for you. Could you tell her these things in such a way that did not leave her feeling humiliated, disliked, or undesirable? If you can honestly answer yes, you are one of the fortunate few. These are generally situations that men find difficult to handle.

The trick is to learn to assert yourself in sex, to learn to get the conditions you need and not go along with situations that make you uncomfortable – and to do so in ways that do not crush your partner. Assertiveness is not rudeness, bullying, or aggression. Being assertive does not mean that you won't consider your partner's needs or satisfy her. It does mean, however, that you are going to pay serious attention to your own needs. It does mean that you will express your desires directly and try to get what you want. Your partner may not always be responsive and compromises will have to be negotiated. This may be new to you but you will find that they can be worked out in ways that honor both of you.

So often in sex today the situation is that each partner is focused primarily on the other's satisfaction. The woman is trying to figure out what the man wants and expects, while he is busily trying to determine how to satisfy her. Each is looking out for the other and neither is taking care of his or her own needs. So much time and effort is spent on the other that both partners are unlikely even to be aware of what they themselves want. A lot of mind reading and guesswork are necessarily involved since neither partner is willing to be direct about what is wanted. That, we have been taught, is selfish and to be avoided. While such altruism may sound lofty and virtuous, the result is usually somewhat less than satisfying for both participants. If both could start paying more attention to getting their own needs met – a little selfishness, if you like – sex would be so much better for both.

Meeting your conditions and asserting yourself sexually are parts of a larger concept: being good to yourself. We men are always so busy doing our tasks – work, studies, chores around the house, taking care of bills, and so on – that we rarely take sufficient time to get what we need and enjoy, and this is directly related to the problems we have in sex.

The following exercise is intended to give you the opportunity to do some of the things that please you. Though important in its own right, it is also good preparation for the exercise that follows it, which deals with asserting yourself with others.

EXERCISE 6–3: DOING SOME THINGS YOU ENJOY
Time Required: Variable

This week do one or two things that you really want to do and that are fun for you. The main criteria are that you enjoy them and they not be work-related. They may or may not involve other people.

Here are some examples of what some men have done with this exercise. Robert, who was working himself to death, took a few hours to lie in bed and watch television. Stan went fishing, an activity he loved as a young man but had 'been too busy to do' in the last twelve years. Lou, always busy doing something 'useful' and 'constructive', allowed himself three hours a week for fun things that were absolutely useless, like reading mysteries and science fiction. And George, who loved animals, spent a relaxed afternoon at the zoo.

Your activities may or may not be similar to these examples. As long as you enjoy them, you're on the right track.

If you have trouble thinking of things you like to do, think back over your past and see if there were any activities you once liked but have given up. You might want to try some of them again. Or ask yourself what you would do if you had a million dollars and didn't have to work.

Do at least one or two enjoyable things per week as long as you follow the programs in this book. We hope you will continue taking time for yourself long after you have forgotten the book.

Now that you've had some practice being good to yourself, it is time to begin asserting yourself with others, which is just another way of being good to yourself. The next exercise was developed by our friend and colleague Lonnie Barbach and is the best we have found to help you learn to assert yourself with others and get your sexual conditions met. It is long and a bit complex, so we suggest you read it and the discussion that follows it carefully before putting it into practice.

EXERCISE 6–4: YES'S AND NO'S
Time Required: Variable, but usually no more than a few minutes a week

---

Yes's: A Yes involves getting or attempting to get something you want from someone, which you ordinarily would not allow yourself to ask for. It can literally be anything at all so long as you really want it and it's something you usually don't ask for. The assignment lies in the request, not the response. Even if your request is rejected, you have done a Yes by asking. Some examples of Yes's are: asking someone to give or ban you something, like a book, record, or money; asking someone to spend time with you or listen to a problem; asking for a certain type of stimulation or sexual activity.

The following example is a good illustration of how one man went from doing enjoyable things for himself to asking others for things he wanted and, finally, to getting his needs met in sex.

Roy had worked hard all his life building up his construction firm, taking very little time off for personal pleasure, and asking little from anyone except for business reasons. While he at first saw no connection between this pattern and his lifelong problem with erections, he agreed to do some things that pleased him. He took off three hours from work on Saturday mornings to do some reading, an activity he had enjoyed in his youth but had not done for years. He was pleasantly surprised at how much pleasure he still derived from reading. Another nice thing for himself involved coming home from work earlier than usual a few days a week so he could do sexual exercises while he still had some energy. He soon found that he could come home at a reasonable hour every evening, with plenty of time for reading, doing sexual exercises, and spending some time with his family. He also found, and this is typical, that his work suffered not at all; if anything, he was getting more done at work than before and in much less time. In therapy we talked about the kinds of things he had once enjoyed, like sailing and fishing, and he used some of his Yes's to ask his wife and friends to join him in some of these longforgotten activities. As he became more confident about asserting himself, Roy started talking to his wife about what he wanted in sex. In time, all of his conditions were met and his sex life showed considerable improvement.

No's: **A No is a refusal to do something that you don't want to do but usually go along with, perhaps to prevent an argument, to preserve your nice-guy image, or for some other reason. If you habitually loan money to a friend not because you want to but because you fear what he will think of you if you refuse, turning him down the next time he asks would be a No. We all do many things we don't want to do. Some of them are necessary since the consequences of not doing them are quite serious (not paying your income taxes, for example). But there are many other things we don't like that we really don't have to put up with. The No's will give you an opportunity to turn some of them down. Being able to say no is very important in sex: going along with things you don't like in sex is one of the best ways not to get turned-on and to lose interest in the whole subject.**

While most No's are in response to direct requests from others, some are not. You probably do some things because of expectations built up long ago. Refusing to continue these behaviors, even though no direct requests are made, is a No.

Maggie and Fred had for years driven thirty miles every Sunday night to have dinner with his parents. This had been going on so long that invitations were no longer extended. It was simply understood by all that Maggie and Fred would show up Sunday at five o'clock. In therapy both said they would prefer to spend their Sunday evenings in other ways, but they were worried how his parents would feel if they stopped coming to dinner every week. It was pointed out to Maggie and Fred that this worry controlled their lives. Most of their time was taken up meeting the needs and expectations of their parents, children, and friends. Even though they didn't like many of the things they were doing, they couldn't change because of their fear of hurting someone's feelings. They were far better at respecting everyone else's feelings than they were at taking care of their own. After some talk, Fred told his parents that although he and Maggie would be happy to consider individual invitations, they would no longer be coming every Sunday. His parents were disappointed and hurt, but Fred stuck to his position. This No turned out to be very important to this couple. After dealing with his parents, they were able to make similar changes in other important relationships and start living their lives more in accordance with their own desires. They learned that you can't satisfy everyone else's needs and that they can live with the occasional disappointment friends and others express toward them. Two years after that first No to his parents, their marriage and sex life are better than ever.

SUGGESTIONS FOR DOING YES'S AND NO'S
1. Do two Yes's and two No's the first week. After that, do three of each a week. As you do them, you will discover what is easy and what is difficult for you. Since there is no benefit in endlessly repeating easy items, gradually include more difficult ones. If, for example, after a week or two you find that Yes's are easy for you but No's are hard, you can do only No's, six a week.

2. Start small. Discouragement is the only reward for trying to change the world in a week. Start with items that

are easy, even trivial, and gradually work up to topics and items that are more difficult. Unless you believe that you are already quite assertive, do not do any sexual Yes's and No's the first few weeks. Wait until you are comfortable doing them in other areas.

3. Use your common sense. There are situations where the consequences for being assertive may be very serious. We suggest you don't say no when the highway patrol pulls you over for speeding or when a thief demands your money unless, of course, you are willing to accept the consequences.

4. Continue doing Yes's and No's until you feel confident of being able to get your sexual conditions fulfilled. This may take anywhere from two to twelve weeks. Since this exercise takes only a few minutes a week, it is simple to do while you continue with other exercises in the book.

POSSIBLE PROBLEMS

1. You don't find anything to say yes or no to. If there is nothing for you to ask for or reject, then your life is precisely the way you want it and you are probably perfectly content. Or maybe you're not looking hard enough. You might find it helpful to take some time every night to review the events of the day and see if there's anything you wanted that you didn't ask for or anything you did that you wish you hadn't.

2. You try to do too much too soon. This is the most common problem in doing this exercise. It cannot be sufficiently emphasized that you should start with relatively easy situations and only slowly work up to more difficult ones. For example, if asking someone to loan you something is difficult, don't start out by asking for $1000 or the use of his car. Start with something you are more comfortable with, perhaps the loan of a book or a dollar. Since this is an extremely important exercise, do it in such a way that will allow you to progress and feel good about it.

3. You feel bad about being rejected. You will undoubtedly get turned down some of the time when doing Yes's. If you are getting rejected almost every time, this either means that you are asking for too much or from the wrong people, or that you are asking in such a way that defeats your aim. You should carefully read the discussion that follows the exercise.

If you are getting rejected some of the time, there's probably nothing to be done about it. It is a basic fact of life that neither you nor anyone else is going to get everything he wants. And it may not feel good. The negative feelings about being rejected will probably diminish as you realize that you are also getting some of the things you wanted, but they will never disappear entirely. The only thing to be concerned about is if your fears of rejection prevent you from asking for what you want. The only way to get what you want is to ask, and this inevitably entails some unfulfilled desires, some hurt and disappointment. The alternative, however, is far worse for most people: less disappointment perhaps, but also far fewer of the things desired. The choice is yours to make.

4. You feel guilty about being assertive. Contrary to popular opinion, women do not have a monopoly on feelings of guilt. Many men feel bad when they start putting their own interests first. In some extreme cases, dealing with this guilt requires professional assistance. For most men, however, these feelings will diminish in frequency and intensity as they get more practice in using their assertive skills. If you are feeling guilty, it may help if you write down what rules you have broken (guilt usually involves a rule that has been violated: something you 'should' have done but didn't or something you 'shouldn't' have done but did). For example, 'I should always put a woman's needs before my own,' or 'It's not nice to try to get what I want; it's selfish, and no one will like me.' Seeing these rules in writing can help you understand the absurdity of the standards you are trying to meet.

Being assertive means expressing yourself directly in appropriate ways. It means avoiding the extreme position of being so compliant and mousy that you don't get your needs met and also avoiding the other extreme of being so overbearing and aggressive that you trample over the rights of others. This middle position of assertiveness, however, is by no means a thin line. There are almost an infinite number of ways to express directly and appropriately what you want and what you don't want, and you can find those that feel most comfortable and work best for you. The Yes's and No's exercise will provide you with many chances to try different approaches and evaluate their effectiveness.

Below are some guidelines that have been helpful to the men with whom we've worked. Try them out and see which are most useful to you. The examples, here and throughout the book, are real. They were reported by men we've talked to and worked with.

1. *Be direct and to the point*. Beating around the bush may be easier, but it's likely to confuse the other person regarding what you are saying, thus making a positive response less likely. Try an approach like these:

(A) John, could you give me a ride home tonight? My car is being fixed and I took a cab here.

(B) I'm sorry but I'm working on something that's very important to me and I just don't have the time to give you a massage tonight.

Not like this:

(C) Gee, Molly, you want me to help you move tomorrow . . . Well . . . that's Saturday and I was thinking of going to the beach to relax . . . Hmmm, I guess I could go to the beach some other time . . . Tomorrow, huh? . . . I'm not sure . . .

The speaker in example C is not giving a clear message. He probably hopes that Molly will notice his ambivalence and withdraw her request. By not directly expressing himself, he's putting himself at Molly's mercy. If she doesn't tell him to forget it, he may well find himself helping with the moving, even though he doesn't want to.

2. *Don't blame, just say what you want or don't want.* You are much more likely to get an affirmative and understanding response when you put your request in the most positive terms possible. For example:

(A) Honey, it's been a long time since you and I spent some time together without the kids or anyone else. I'd like to have a few days just with you, the way we used to before we were married. What about going to Mendocino next weekend and leaving the kids at home?

Calling people names or blaming them is not useful in most cases. Here's a negative version of example A:

(B) Goddamn it, I'm sick and tired of having the kids around the house all the time, along with all your stupid relatives. Why the hell don't you tell them to stay at their own homes sometimes? Another Sunday like this, with twelve people in the house, and you better believe it, I won't be coming home anymore!

The men in examples A and B really wanted the same thing, but they expressed themselves rather differently. While example B looks extreme on paper, we have heard similar speeches too many times to think that they are unusual. You won't be surprised to hear that while one of these men had a lovely weekend with his wife in Mendocino, the other got a battle that raged for almost a month.

And like requests, rejections are more effective (and less painful to all concerned) when they are put in the most positive way possible. For example:

(C) You look wonderful and I'm getting tempted. But I'd rather not make love now. I'm tired and I have to be at work early tomorrow. Tell you what, if you're free tomorrow afternoon, I can come home early and we can stay in bed as long as we want. That way, I'll be rested and can give you the attention you deserve.

Not like this:

(D) I don't know what it is about you, but you're always wanting sex when I'm tired or have to get up early in the morning. The last few weeks I've had lots of free time and could have gotten interested in sex, but did you show any interest? No. Now when I'm tired and up to my neck in worries, now you get interested. I think there's something wrong with you.

Both men are saying no, but the man in example C is doing it in a way that is probably acceptable to his partner and is also working out a compromise. The man in D is clearly headed for trouble with his partner.

3. *Give a reason for your request or rejection.* People tend to respond more positively if they understand the reasons for your yes's and no's. Note, however, that giving a reason is not the same as telling a lie. All of the constructive examples given so far include reasons.

4. *Be firm and persistent.* Many people give up too easily after making a request or giving a rejection, especially when they encounter resistance or do not immediately achieve their goal. Persistence often pays off. Like this:

(A) Touch me there but a little harder . . . That's better but I'd like it still harder . . . I think you might be afraid of hurting me. I'd like it harder and you don't have to worry about hurting me . . . Here, let me show you how hard I want it . . . Wow, that's much better, really feels good.

Not like this:

> (B) Touch me there but a little harder . . . Hmmm . . . is
> that harder? . . . I don't know . . . I guess that's OK . . .
> Could you, well, no, it's OK the way it is . . . yeh, it's fine
> [and, of course, it isn't].

The man in B is settling for less than he wants. He'll feel
dissatisfied, and perhaps angry or resentful as well. The man in
A is being clear, firm, and persistent, and he's getting what he
wants. Being firm, however, does not mean being stupid:

> (C) Touch me there but a little harder . . . Harder, I said!
> . . . That's not harder. Don't you think I know what I
> want? . . . Can't you do anything right?

There's simply no reason to carry on this way.

Being firm is particularly important when doing No's. Some
people will try to sweet-talk you into changing your mind or
make you feel guilty for rejecting their request. Here's an
example:

> (D) I'm sorry, Mary. I'd like to help you out but I have to
> teach a class at eight in the morning and I don't see how I
> could take you to the airport at two am.
>
> (Mary says you're her last hope. No one else can take
> her and there's no other flight she can take. She'll have to
> call off her trip if you don't take her. Besides, she's done
> you some favors.)
>
> I know you've done me some favors, and I'm grateful.
> And I realize you're in a bind. I would like to help you but
> I'm not willing to go at that hour on Tuesday morning. If
> you like, I could take you at midnight and you could wait
> at the airport for the plane, or I could take you on another
> morning, but not Tuesday.

But won't Mary be angry, disappointed, or frustrated?
Probably. And there's nothing you can do about it except to

take her to the airport when she wants to go. But that's going to make you unhappy. This is a clear case of having to decide whose needs come first. You have tried to do what you could for Mary without sacrificing your sleep. You have even offered her some alternatives which leads us to our next guideline.

5. *When doing No's, offer alternatives if you want to.* If you are unwilling to grant a request as it is given but are willing to do something else, say so. The man in example 4D had done this: he offered to take Mary to the airport at two different times that were more convenient to him and that might be of help to her. If nothing else, the offering of alternatives can help ease any guilt you are feeling about rejecting the other person's original request. You are not totally refusing to help but are offering a compromise. If a compromise is not acceptable, if your friend wants what she wants precisely the way she asked for it, you can feel easier about saying no.

Offer alternatives only if you mean them. Otherwise, someone may call your bluff and you'll have to deliver. If you simply don't want to have anything to do with taking Mary to the airport, regardless of the time of day, better say so.

6. *Express your appreciation when your requests are granted.* When you do a Yes and the response is positive, be sure to indicate your appreciation. Long speeches and gushing sentimentality are not needed, just a simple 'I appreciate this' or 'Thank you for taking the time.' Such expressions let the other person know you recognize his or her efforts and are grateful for them, which usually will have the effect of making him or her more open to future requests from you.

These suggestions and examples should be sufficient to help you begin to get your conditions met. We return to this subject in Chapter 12, with further discussion of how to assert yourself in sexual situations and how to communicate with sexual partners.

If after giving the Yes's and No's a fair trial for at least four or five weeks, you are still having great difficulty doing them, you might want to consult one of several good books on assertiveness. *Your Perfect Right, Don't Say Yes When You Mean No,* and *I Can If I Want To* have been helpful to some of our clients.

Before leaving the issue of expressing yourself, we need to give further attention to positive expressiveness. Being able to do Yes's and No's is absolutely necessary for getting your conditions fulfilled and enhancing your sex life. At the same time, it is very important to express approval, praise, appreciation, and caring. Much of what passes for assertiveness training overlooks the necessity for balancing expressions of wants and rejections with expressions of liking and approval.

This is an especially difficult area for men. Our social scripts give us permission to be assertive. We still have difficulty with it, especially in the sexual area, but at least we have the permission. But where is the permission to say, 'I care for you', 'I feel good when I'm with you', or 'I really appreciate your help'? The answer is that there hasn't been much permission or even tolerance. The strong, silent heroes we were given as models didn't say such things.

Expressing approval, support, and liking seems, well, feminine to many men. We know that women express such thoughts and feelings, and we like it when they are directed at us, but we aren't sure it's OK for a man to say such things. And besides, we haven't had much practice doing it.

An exercise we've used for years in group therapy involves the men pairing up and role-playing, asking their 'partner' to stimulate them in ways they like. The 'partners' stimulate the men's arms. We set the situation, which usually involves the 'partners' not doing it quite the way asked for, so the man must keep correcting 'her' with further instructions. Many of the men have trouble getting their 'partners' to do it the way they want, and this is what we expected. What surprised us at first was the reaction we invariably got when we gave this situation:

'She's doing it perfectly now, just the way you want. It feels wonderful. What do you do now?' Their reaction: dead silence. So we try again. 'She's doing exactly what you want. It feels great. Can you somehow express how good it feels or how much you appreciate what she's doing?' At this point, some of them, with difficulty, give some positive feedback. Others continue to have trouble even after we give them specific examples of what they might say or do.

It may be difficult at first but giving positive feedback is well worth the effort. It makes you more balanced and makes it easier for others to hear and respond to your requests and rejections. It can also ease any guilt you have about asserting yourself, since you know that you also express things the other person likes to hear. Other people can understand you better; they get more information about you when you give compliments and praise. And last, expressing yourself in positive ways broadens your ability to express a wide range of emotions, a type of expressiveness most men lack and one that is greatly admired by women.

A few more examples of what we are talking about:

I appreciated your help with this project. It sure eased my burden.
That outfit looks wonderful on you.
It's nice to know I can turn to you when I have a problem.
It feels wonderful when you touch me like that.
You look so beautiful when you come. It makes me feel good.
I'm glad you're in my life.

Sound corny or mushy? Maybe, but only when such responses are not sincere. We are not suggesting you lie in order to gain some advantage with others; rather, we are saying that you must like and approve of some of the things that people around you are doing, particularly those you are closest to, and that you should make sure you are letting them know about it. Do you verbalize the good feelings you have for others as much as you could? Do people know that you like and appreciate them? Do they know you are thankful when they do something for you?

If you think you are not doing as much in this area as you'd like, you can assign yourself the task of giving one or two positive expressions every day. As time goes on, the practice will become automatic, but at first it may be difficult. You may have to spend a bit of time thinking about what you like and are grateful for in particular persons before you go to tell them. And you may find yourself coming up with reasons why you don't have to tell them ('She already knows I care – I'm living with her – so what's the point of telling her?' 'I show my appreciation and love in action, so why should I use words?'). Expressing feelings through nonverbal means is fine, but words can add a lot, too.

The message is: express yourself. Your likes and dislikes, and your approval, support, thanks, and love.

SEVEN

The physical aspects of sex

Any sexual activity is an elaborate combination of physical and psychological factors. Feelings, thoughts (yes, it's really OK to think during sex), and physical changes are all part of sex. Yet it is surprising how often one or the other aspect is ignored. We have heard talks on sex that so focused on the feelings of the participants that one could easily forget that sex has anything to do with the rubbing of bodies. On the other hand, and perhaps more commonly, sex is treated as though getting one set of plumbing fixtures to mesh with another and produce a grand splash is the only thing that matters.

Both the physical and psychological are important. They do not always work together and, indeed, may be at complete odds with one another, but they both need to be considered if you are to understand yourself and have good sex.

This chapter is designed to give you a better understanding of, and appreciation for, your sexual anatomy and physiology. Such knowledge has proved helpful to most of the men with whom we have worked. At the same time, we try to place the physical in a psychological perspective, for one without the other is quite meaningless.

Women are not the only ones concerned about their physical appearance. Many men are dissatisfied with their bodies. They believe that they are too fat, too thin, not muscular enough, too short, or too tall. We have even talked to a few who refused to wear short-sleeve shirts because they felt their biceps were insufficiently developed.

If you are greatly dissatisfied with your body, you might ask yourself how you think it ought to be – i.e., what are the standards to which you are comparing yourself? Are they realistic for you? Are you really willing to put in the time and effort to change the way you look?

You might want to take a careful look at yourself in a mirror, slowly going over each part and seeing how you feel about it. Is there any chance that you can accept yourself the way you are right now? Any chance that you could accept the fact that your waist will never be slimmer, your arms never bigger, your head never hairier? And be sure to ask where you got the idea that you should look different than you do. Whatever the sources, must they run your life? You will not suddenly like all those parts you didn't like before. The question is whether you can accept them the way they are, even if you don't like them. If you can accept yourself the way you are, you can at least stop nagging yourself to do something about it, and get on with your life.

While we are on the subject of bodies, we'd like to ask you to consider yours from another vantage point. We men have been trained to think that our only sexual part is between our legs. When we think of sex, we almost automatically think of our penises and what we want to put them into. There's good reason for us to think this way since it is precisely what the fantasy model of sex teaches, but the truth is that such thinking is unnecessarily narrow. We can give and receive sensual and sexual pleasure with many other parts of our bodies. We haven't had much permission to explore areas other than our crotches, but there are many possibilities. Can you imagine what it might be like to have your face, neck, chest and nipples, stomach, legs, and the areas between your toes touched, stroked, and perhaps kissed and licked by your partner? Any chance you'd be willing to try out some of these activities with her?

It is also true that our mouths, hands, legs, hair, and so on can be exquisite instruments for giving pleasure. You might try running your hair across the sensitive parts of your partner's body. Or sucking her finger or having her suck yours. No, it's not the same as having your penis sucked, but many men who have tried it reported that it was interesting, to say the least. All or most of your body can give and receive pleasure. Your penis doesn't have to carry the whole load. Consider your body and see if this isn't true for you.

Which brings us to the next point we want to discuss, the true nature of the human penis, perhaps the most mis-understood organ in the male body. Penises have had a bad press lately. The popular and scientific literature tells us that impotence is reaching epidemic proportions; and even those penises not so afflicted still don't perform the way they should – they come too fast or not at all, or in some other way they don't measure up to expectations.

The truth is that nothing is wrong with penises. It is our thinking about them, the expectations and goals we have set for them, that is terribly mistaken. Both men and women have absorbed the erroneous notions about penises we discussed in Chapter 3, and berate real penises for not living up to these superhuman standards.

Let us then consider the penis, probably the laziest part of a man. Your heart, lungs, and brain are working all the time, even when you sleep, and you would be in serious trouble if they stopped for even a few minutes. Less impressive parts of you – your liver, kidneys, stomach, knees, and elbows, for example – are busy working for you much of the time. In contrast, most of the time your penis does exactly nothing. While it serves as a tube through which urine passes, it has no active part in the process. And a penis is not necessary for your survival. Even if you didn't have one, or had one that never became erect, you could live a long, healthy, and perhaps happy life. So, despite fashionable ideas of penises being necessary and always active, hopping about with lots of throbbing and crashing, the real penis is much given to rest and relaxation.

The major exception is the adolescent penis, a creature known to act with great peculiarity. It may be in a state of almost constant erection, regardless of the appropriateness of the situation. Teenage penises seem to take a perverse joy in getting hard at the wrong times, causing their owners much embarrassment. But after adolescence, penises revert to form, being more likely to cause embarrassment by their lack of activity than by their exuberance.

Penises are also somewhat mercurial. They sometimes get erect in the absence of any identifiable sexual stimulus or any interest on the part of their owners. They almost always get hard when their owners dream (about four or five times a night) whether or not the dreams have any sexual content. (While we're talking about dreams, we want to mention that morning erections, often called 'piss-hards', are not, as the name implies, due to having a full bladder. The best evidence available indicates that morning erections are simply the erections that accompany the last dream of the night. Why penises get hard when you dream is something that has not been answered with any certainty.) Penises can also become erect during periods of general excitement as, for example, before or during a rock concert or sports event.

The other side of the coin is only too well known. There you are, trembling with lust, feeling passion in every corpuscle . . . and there's old penis, snoring away and feeling not a thing. What we're talking about, of course, is the distinction between arousal and erection. As we said in the last chapter, they are separate systems. Don't confuse them.

The lack of response in your penis usually causes great confusion and frustration. You think you're turned-on and can't figure out what's wrong. Your partner, also having been taught that desire should produce an erection in you, may think that she is not attractive or that you don't like her. Actually, especially if you don't know each other well, the situation may be just the reverse. You may find her particularly attractive and want very much to please her. But this may arouse concerns about whether you are equal to the task, and these concerns are precisely what can cause your penis to go into a deep sleep.

On the other hand, having an erection is no reason to assume you want sex. You may or you may not. You need to check your feelings to find out.

There is nothing wrong with using an erection even if you do not have accompanying feelings of desire, but your penis may not stay erect for long if the feelings do not develop as you get into sex. If that's going to be a problem for you, it's probably best not to have sex until you feel aroused.

Implicit in what we've said is the idea that your penis is a relatively frail instrument. It bears little resemblance to the fantasy model's bars of steel that can be knocked around and handled with impunity. Like any other part of you, it needs attention and consideration.

Here's what one penis (in the penis letter exercise) had to say to its owner, a man who hadn't had a good sexual experience in five years:

> I never feel included. You don't care about me and don't pay any attention to me. Only when you want to fuck do you show any interest, and then it's only to scream and yell that I better come through for you. Usually you pay more attention to your goddamn knees and ankles than to me. Why should I do anything for you? I'd like a little attention and some consideration for my needs. I'd be much more willing to do what you want if I felt that you cared about me. Please pay some attention to me.

Another example:

> A man in one of the first sex therapy groups we did was in the habit of calling his penis 'you little son of a bitch' and threatening it with all sorts of dire consequences when it did not meet his expectations. Needless to say, the more he did this, the less his penis worked. Here is what came out when he did the penis letter exercise:
> 'I'm sick and tired of being called names and threatened. Don't you think I have feelings? I try to do my best and you don't do a damn thing for me or yourself. You get into the weirdest sexual situations that anyone

can imagine and expect me to perform. And when I refuse, you get all huffy and start yelling at me. Christ, you don't even like most of the women you want me to screw! And do you ever ask me how I feel about them? Never! Well, the hell with you, Charlie. I'm putting you on notice right now. Either you start treating me with some respect and get into situations that interest both of us, or I'm never going to do anything for you again. And, despite all your threats, you know there's not a thing you can do about it. If you want to start off on a new track with me, the first thing you can do is apologize for all the insults you've thrown my way.'

If your penis doesn't work the way you want it to, remember that it's trying to tell you something. It's not your enemy. It was made for sex, it likes sex. If it's not working the way you like, it's telling you that there is something wrong with the way you are going about sex. If you want better sex, you need to start deciphering your penis's message.

Now on to sexual anatomy, a department in which men differ as much as they do in other areas like weight, height, color, amount of hair, and proportion of muscular to fatty tissue. Penises come in a variety of shapes and sizes (as do testicles), and about the only thing most penises have in common is that they are the wrong size or shape as far as their owners are concerned. In the many hours we have spent talking to men in and out of therapy, we have heard every conceivable complaint about penises. They are too small (the most common complaint), too large, too thin, too thick, stand up at too small (or great) an angle when erect, bend too much to the right, or left, or in the middle, or don't get hard enough when they erect.

A large portion of our concern about our penises undoubtedly stems from the silliness conveyed in the sources we explored in Chapter 3. Confronted by phalluses of superhuman dimensions, we feel inadequate when we survey our own merely human organs.

It is also true that most of us lack information about what a 'normal' or average penis is like. Almost all of us have seen other penises in locker rooms or similar situations and we somehow come away with the conviction that everyone else's is larger or better formed (forgetting to take into account that we view others' from a very different perspective than when we look down at our own). And, when you think about it, it's clear that most of us have never seen another erect penis, or at least not a typical one. The erections we are likely to have viewed, in pornographic films or pictures, are hardly representative. Given the absence of reasonable models or standards, there is good reason for us to wonder about the adequacy of our own penises.

Figures 1 and 2 (pages 126 and 127) illustrate some of the variability of human penises in the flaccid and erect states. Yours may or may not closely resemble the drawings, but the chances are at least 999 in 1000 that it is perfectly normal and quite capable of giving you and your partner much joy.

Your penis is the right size and shape for your body. It is as it is, and if you can accept it and worry less about how it compares to others (whose owners share the same concerns you have), it will serve you well. We will give you an exercise to help you become more familiar with your penis and see how you feel about it, but first we want to discuss some of the more important features of your sexual anatomy.

Figure 3 (page 128) represents the typical male genital anatomy.

The external sex organs consist of the penis and the scrotum, the latter containing the testes. The penis contains three cylinders of spongy tissue surrounded by a tough fibrous covering.

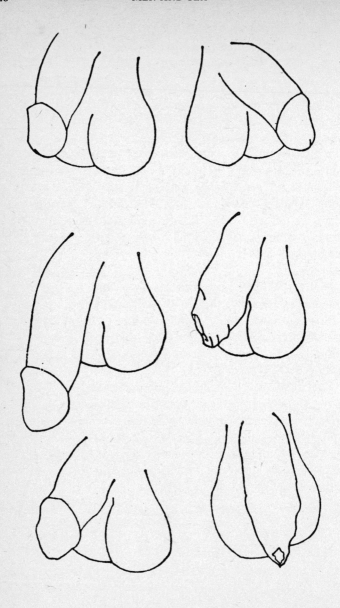

FIGURE 1: FLACCID PENISES

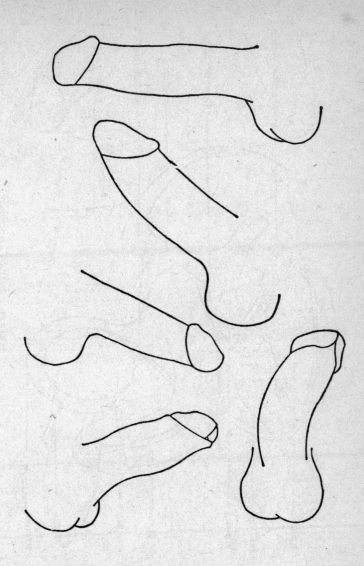

FIGURE 2: ERECT PENISES

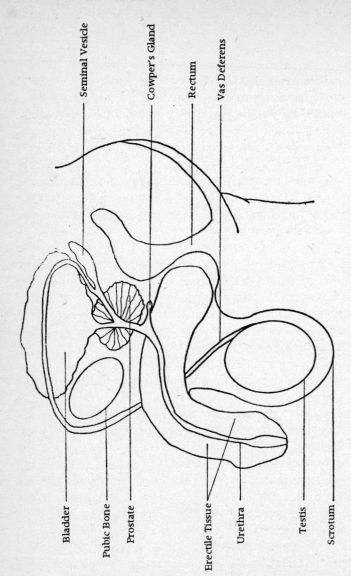

Seminal Vesicle

Cowper's Gland

Rectum

Vas Deferens

Bladder

Pubic Bone

Prostate

Erectile Tissue

Urethra

Testis

Scrotum

FIGURE 3: MALE GENITAL ANATOMY

During sexual excitement, the spongy tissues become engorged with blood, causing the penis to expand. Since the fibrous sheath covering the spongy tissues will expand only so far, as the tissues fill with blood they press against the sheath, making the penis hard. The process is quite similar to what occurs when you fill a bicycle or car tire with air. The tube in the tire (comparable to the spongy tissues in the penis), if not constrained by the tire (comparable to the fibrous sheath in the penis), would keep expanding until it burst. Since it is constrained by the tire, it can only expand so far and becomes hard.

If you study the diagram carefully you will notice that the penis extends far into the body, almost to the rectum. You can feel this portion of your penis if, when you have an erection, you press a finger up into the area behind your scrotum.

The penis has no muscle in it and therefore cannot be enlarged by exercise. However, although not shown in the diagram, the part of the penis inside the body is surrounded by muscles which can be strengthened by exercise. At the end of the chapter we present an exercise that will help you do this; it will not increase the size of your penis, but it does have some benefits which we discuss later.

For many men the head is the most sensitive part of the penis, especially around the ridge that connects it to the shaft of the penis.

The major internal sex organs consist of the testes, vas deferens, seminal vesicles, Cowper's glands, prostate gland, and urethra.

The testes produce sperm and the hormone testosterone. The vas deferens are two firm tubes that extend from the testes to the prostate. The sperm travel through the tubes and are stored at their upper ends until they mix with the secretions of the seminal vesicles and prostate just prior to ejaculation. It used to be thought that sperm was stored in the seminal vesicles, but this idea has been abandoned. The exact purpose of the vesicles is unclear, but it is known that they contribute a portion of the ejaculate. The secretions of the prostate comprise most of the seminal fluid or ejaculate, giving it its whitish color and its odor. The sperm actually account for only a tiny fraction of the seminal fluid or ejaculate, which explains why a man who has had a vasectomy still ejaculates about the same amount of fluid as before the operation.

It is believed that the Cowper's glands secrete a small amount of clear, sticky fluid which is often visible prior to ejaculation. This fluid sometimes contains sperm, making withdrawal of the penis from the vagina prior to ejaculation not a very safe method of contraception.

The urethra is a tube running from the bladder through one of the spongy cylinders in the penis and ending in a slit in the head of the penis. Both urine and seminal fluid travel through it, but not at the same time. The prostate surrounds the urethra where it leaves the bladder, and prostate problems – such as inflammation or enlargement, which are quite common in men over fifty – very often cause urinary difficulties.

Although this description has been somewhat simplified, it is sufficiently detailed for our purposes. Our goal is to help you understand yourself better, not to make you an expert on male anatomy. The following exercise will help you further that knowledge.

EXERCISE 7–1: EXPLORING YOUR GENITALS
Time Required: 30 to 45 minutes

Undress and, using a hand mirror, carefully examine your genitals. Look at your penis and scrotum from different angles. See how everything fits together. Also look at the perineum (the area between the scrotum and the anus) and anything else that interests you. Then determine how you feel about the various parts. Can you accept that perhaps you don't like the size, shape, or color of some of your sexual anatomy? Can you live with them without forever wishing that things were different?

Now explore your genitals with your fingers. You might

want to press in above your penis to feel your pubic bone, and you might also press a finger up between your scrotum and anus to feel the bulb of your penis (although this is easier felt if you have an erection). If you gently squeeze the scrotum above the testes, with one finger in front and another behind the sac, you'll be able to feel the vas deferens; it feels like a cord or piece of wire.

Then gently stroke your penis, scrotum, and the area behind the scrotum, paying close attention to the various sensations produced.

Try different types of touching and be aware of which strokes and which areas are most sensitive and which are least sensitive. Take your time and learn as much as you can.

If you become aroused and/or get an erection, that's fine. Continue with the exercise and be aware of how sensitivities change when you go from the unaroused to the aroused state. Discover as much as possible about how and where you like to be touched.

If you had a lot of trouble accepting the way your genitals look, it would probably be worth your time to ask yourself what makes you think they ought to be different than they are. A fantasy, something you read or heard or saw? Also ask yourself who, aside from yourself, would be happy if they were different. How do you know they would? Consider the sources of your discontent. Are they so important to you that you are willing to continue making yourself miserable over something you can't change? Then go back to the mirror and do the exercise again. Is it possible to accept yourself the way you are? We hope you can gain some self-acceptance because, like it or not, there are no genital transplants and we are all stuck with what we got. Which, if you think about it carefully and identify the expectations that make you wish it were different, really isn't all that bad.

We now go to the changes that usually occur as a man goes through a sexual experience. This is a difficult area to discuss since the popularizations of the research data on this subject have in many ways been confusing and misleading.

In their pioneering work, *Human Sexual Response*, Masters and Johnson described the physiological changes a man goes through during sex in terms of a sexual response cycle arbitrarily divided into four phases: excitement, plateau, orgasm, and resolution. You may have read or heard about this cycle and seen the diagram used to illustrate it, a copy of which is included below.

Masters and Johnson's work in this area has been uncritically accepted by most people in the sex field. Almost all the books and articles that deal with sex merely summarize their description and classification scheme without noting variations or raising questions. The problem is that while Masters and Johnson's research constitutes a milestone in sex research, it suffers from a number of limitations, some of which they noted in their book but which have been neglected by those who summarize their findings. The classification of their findings into a response cycle with four phases is probably the weakest part of their work. Many men's changes do not fit neatly into the phases, and some people have asked us what was wrong with them for not fitting the model.

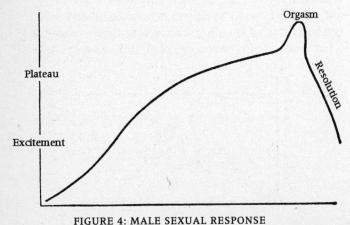

FIGURE 4: MALE SEXUAL RESPONSE
Adapted from Human Sexual Responses, *by William H. Masters and Virginia E. Johnson, 1966*

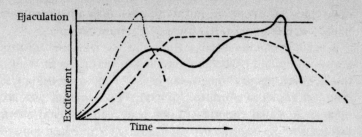

FIGURE 5: OTHER MALE SEXUAL RESPONSE CYCLES

Our ideas about sexual response conform to what Kinsey had to say on the subject: 'There is nothing more characteristic of sexual response than the fact that it is not the same in any two individuals.' There is no right or normal way to have a sexual experience. Your body's responses are the result of a complex interaction among many variables including, for example, your physical and emotional state at the time, what your partner does and how you feel about it, and your feelings about her. In contrast to Masters and Johnson's notion that there is only one type of male sexual response cycle, we believe that there are many possible cycles, a few of which are diagrammed in Figures 5 and 6.

The main changes that occur during a sexual experience are the result of vasocongestion, the accumulation of blood in various parts of the body. Muscular tension increases and other changes also occur. Ejaculation reverses the blood flow

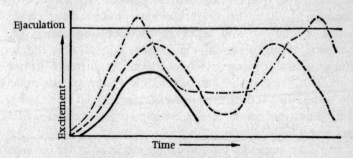

FIGURE 6: MORE MALE SEXUAL RESPONSE CYCLES

and releases the tension, but these phenomena happen even without ejaculation or orgasm, though more slowly.

A sexual response begins when you receive some form of sexual stimulation. The stimulation can be in the form of a touch, smell, sight, thought, fantasy, or almost anything else that has sexual significance for you. Provided that you are open to a sexual experience, that your conditions are met, certain changes begin to occur.

An increased volume of blood is pumped into various parts of your body, increasing their size and often their sensitivity to stimulation. Your penis is not the only area so affected. Your lips, ear lobes, and breasts are other areas that may become engorged with blood.

What happens to your penis deserves further comment. In its soft state, the amounts of blood going into and out of the penis are about equal and the penis stays about the same size. When there is sexual stimulation, an increased amount of blood is pumped into the penis and the outflow is reduced. The spongy tissues in the penis become engorged with blood, getting larger and, as they push against their fibrous covering, harder.

Full erection may or may not occur early in a sexual experience. In many young men, erection is almost instantaneous; they get hard as soon as they get any stimulation. With increasing age, however, it may take the penis longer to get hard, and it may also take more direct stimulation of the penis to reach full erection. There is nothing wrong with either the shorter or longer route to an erection.

The scrotal sac and testes go through some interesting changes during a sexual experience. The skin of the sac thickens and contracts, while the testes increase in size because of the engorgement of blood. The testes are also pulled up within the sac until they press against the wall of the pelvis. This elevation of the testes anticipates ejaculation and is necessary for it to occur.

Increased muscular tension can be observed in various parts of your body. You may notice, for example, that you are tensing your stomach or leg muscles. There may be involuntary contractions or spasms in your pelvis and buttocks, and also in your facial muscles. As the excitement builds, pelvis thrusting begins and becomes involuntary as you approach ejaculation (although some men unconsciously inhibit these movements).

Other bodily changes include increased blood pressure, heartbeat, and breathing rate. Some men have nipple erection; and a sex flush, a reddening of the skin that looks like a rash, may appear on the upper part of the body.

All bodily changes are reversible. You might reach a peak of excitement and erection and then, because you were distracted, stopped to talk, weren't getting the most exciting type of stimulation, or if the experience went on for a long time, you might lose some of your erection and experience other changes that reflect the lowered level of excitement. This is not something to get concerned about. You can probably return to a higher state of excitement when you reinstate the conditions and activities that got you there in the first place.

What you are feeling while all this is going on is another matter. Sometimes you feel extremely excited, very much into all the sensations, and are having a grand time. At other times, it may feel good, but you are also aware that your mind wanders now and again, seeming to be only partially involved in the experience. On other occasions, you may be but little involved in what's happening, perhaps experiencing it as boring or as disconnected from you, as if it were happening to someone else. Sexual experiences do not always feel the same, ranging from wonderful to good-but-not-exceptional to hardly-worth-the-effort. Expecting a mind-blowing experience every time is a sure way of keeping yourself in a state of perpetual frustration. But there is no reason to go through bad experiences. If it doesn't feel good at all, it might be best to stop and see what you really want. Perhaps sex is not for you at the moment, or perhaps a different kind of sexual activity would please you more.

What would happen if you got very excited and did not go on to orgasm? Many men believe that the lack of orgasm would lead to the condition commonly called blue balls or lover's nuts: pain, discomfort, or soreness in the testes. This belief is easy to understand when you realize that the fantasy model of sex almost invariably includes orgasm for the male. The implication seems to be that its absence would be disastrous.

In fact, it is not disastrous. There may be some soreness or pain, but this is rare. You might want to think back over your sexual experiences and see if this is true for you. Be sure to include all instances where, whether with masturbation or with a partner, you got very aroused and did not ejaculate. How many times was there pain? Probably very few, although those are the ones we tend to remember. Try to keep in mind that it's not necessary to ejaculate every time you have sex. It's nice when it happens but there's no reason to try to force it. You and your partner will probably feel better stopping while you are still feeling good. Working at producing an ejaculation has a way of making sex boring or frustrating.

Ejaculation is a spinal reflex which, as we mentioned earlier, reverses the flow of blood in the body, draining it away from the penis and other engorged areas, and releases the muscular tension that has been built up. Two distinct steps are involved in ejaculation. In the first, the prostate, seminal vesicles, and vas deferens contract, pouring their contents into the urethra; the sperm mix with the secretions of the seminal vesicles and the prostate to form the ejaculate. The contractions are the beginning of ejaculation and are often interpreted by the man as 'It's starting' or 'I'm going to come.' Masters and Johnson have called this ejaculatory inevitability. Since the ejaculatory process is already in motion, ejaculation is indeed inevitable. Nothing can stop it once the point of inevitability has been reached.

During the second step of the ejaculatory process, the fluid is propelled through the urethra by strong contractions of the muscles in the pelvis. The semen may spurt several inches or even feet beyond the tip of the penis, or it may just ooze out.

The number of contractions, the amount of ejaculate, and the force with which it is ejaculated are dependent on a number of factors, including age and amount of time since the last ejaculation.

Ejaculation involves more of the body than just the penis and internal genitalia. Respiration, blood pressure, and heartbeat rate increase as the man approaches ejaculation, usually peaking at the moment of ejaculation. Involuntary muscle contractions and spasms may occur in various parts of the body, including the legs, stomach, arms, and back. Ejaculation is a total body response, not just something that happens in the crotch.

Most authorities have accepted the contention of Masters and Johnson that while women have several different patterns of orgasmic response, only one type of ejaculatory response is possible for men. We disagree with this thinking, having ourselves experienced different ejaculatory patterns and having heard from a number of other men that they sometimes have ejaculations substantially different from the Masters and Johnson standard. Sometimes the excitement is so intense before ejaculation that it in itself feels like a long orgasm, and the actual ejaculation not only doesn't add anything to it but is experienced as a letdown. Another variant seems similar in some ways to multiple orgasms in women – a number of peaks that feel like mild orgasms are experienced, with ejaculation occurring only during the last one. Still another pattern involves continued pelvic contractions far beyond the usual number and long after the last of the ejaculate has appeared. Such contractions are accompanied by feelings of intense pleasure, sometimes as pleasurable as those accompanying the ejaculation.

We strongly believe that future research in this area will confirm that there are many different ejaculatory patterns in men. Whichever pattern or patterns you experience are perfectly normal. There is no one right way.

While ejaculation and orgasm are often used synonymously even by some sex experts, we find it useful to distinguish between them. Ejaculation is the physical process involved in propelling the semen through the penis. Orgasm refers to what you feel. Generally the two go together; you ejaculate and enjoy very pleasurable feelings. But one can occur without the other. You can have orgasms without ejaculating. Some men have trained themselves to do this and, according to their reports, have been able to have multiple orgasms like women. And some men, who have trained themselves carefully to tune into their sensations during sex, say that they sometimes notice very high peaks of feeling long before ejaculation. Were they not so indoctrinated in the idea that orgasm occurs only with pelvic contractions and ejaculation, they would be inclined to call these peaks orgasms.

The reverse situation is more common, where the man ejaculates – there's the white stuff to prove it – but feels very little. If this happens infrequently, there's nothing to worry about. But a number of men have consulted us about the possibility of enhancing their orgasms, and this question deserves comment. Even when you get past the unrealistic expectations (orgasms rarely feel like what D. H. Lawrence or other purveyors of fantasy sex lead you to think they'll be like), it is clear that many men do not experience as much feeling with their ejaculations as is possible. Near the end of this chapter we offer some suggestions that have been helpful in increasing orgasmic feeling.

After ejaculation, your body starts to return to where it was before the sexual experience began. As blood flows out of it, your penis returns to its nonerect state. The rate at which this occurs depends on many factors and varies from time to time. Sometimes your erection may go down immediately, while at other times it may stay relatively firm for many minutes after ejaculation.

The scrotal sac and testes descend to their normal position. Blood pressure and pulse and breathing rates gradually return to their prearousal levels. The sex flush disappears and a thin film of perspiration may appear over much of your body.

During this period of resolution many men experience

feelings of lassitude and deep relaxation, and for some this immediately leads to sleep, often to the chagrin of their partners. For some of the men we've worked with, it's been clear that falling asleep directly after orgasm has been an escape from activities – cuddling, relaxed talk, relating without a goal – with which they were uncomfortable. Once they became more comfortable doing these things, they tended to stay awake longer most of the time. And sometimes, of course, sleep is just the best thing to do after sex.

In situations where high levels of stimulation continue after orgasm, some men, particularly younger ones, may not go through a clearly defined resolution period. They may begin to get aroused and erect again fairly quickly. For most men, however, once ejaculation has occurred, a definite period of rest – called a refractory period – is necessary before they can again respond to sexual stimulation. The length of the refractory period varies according to a number of factors, including age and amount of time since last ejaculation.

When there has been excitement and no orgasm, the resolution period usually takes longer. The muscular tension and accumulation of blood are released more slowly than when there has been an ejaculation. Because of this, you may feel a bit congested in the pelvis and perhaps a little tense or jittery. If it's more than this, you might want to consider how much of it is psychological, due to feelings of disappointment or anger because you think you should have come.

We now return to the enhancement of orgasms, but first let us repeat that the bombs-bursting and mind-blowing orgasms of the fantasy model are not what we have in mind. We are simply dealing with methods that are helpful for increasing bodily sensations or the experience of such sensations during ejaculation.

One of the best ways to increase the enjoyment of any experience is to fully participate in it, to really be there when it is occurring. Since many people seem to be someplace else during sex – thinking about other matters, wondering if they are doing it right or if their partner is satisfied – their pleasure can be enhanced by paying more attention to their sensations. Many of the exercises in the book are designed to help you focus on your sensations. Doing them as suggested will increase your awareness of what you are experiencing, making your orgasms, as well as the rest of your sexual experiences, more enjoyable.

Other methods involve relaxing the degree of control that many men exercise on themselves during sex. Men often seem to try to keep their bodies and feelings under control by limiting their movements, breathing, and sound, so much so that a number of women have told us that they usually can't tell if their partners have had an orgasm. Restricting your body in such ways tends to reduce feeling, and therefore pleasure. Check to see if you are controlling your breathing – by slowing it down or even holding your breath during orgasm – or restricting your movements, or suppressing noises. If you are, you might want to allow yourself to do the opposite next time you have sex. Don't try to let go of all your controls at once; just do one thing you've been preventing yourself from doing before. Perhaps there are some moans or grunts or cries that want to come out; let one or two come out the first time you try this. Or perhaps you can allow your body greater leeway in moving the way it wants. And be sure you breathe (good advice under any circumstances). If you notice that your breathing is slow before or during orgasm, experiment with taking quick breaths, panting, during these times. Gradually relax more of your controls and see if you aren't experiencing fuller orgasms.

The last method of increasing the orgasmic experience is the strengthening of the pelvic muscles that produce the ejaculation by their contractions. The exercise we use for this also serves other important functions and has an interesting history. It was developed by a gynecologist, Dr Arnold Kegel, for women who had trouble holding their urine after childbirth. Many of his patients reported greater sexual enjoyment as a result of doing the exercise, and this led Dr

Kegel to consider the importance of the pelvic musculature to female sexual responsiveness. In the years since then, thousands of women have increased their sexual responsiveness by doing the Kegel exercise.

We tried the Kegel exercise ourselves out of curiosity and, since it produced interesting results, started suggesting it to clients. Regular practice strengthens the muscles that surround the penis and improves the circulation of blood in the pelvis, a factor of obvious importance since increased flow of blood to the penis is what makes an erection.

The exercise has been useful for several types of situations and problems. Many men who practiced it report stronger and more pleasurable orgasms. Others have used it to develop better ejaculatory control, a point we discuss further in Chapter 15. And it's also been helpful to men with erection problems and those who didn't experience much feeling in their pelvises.

EXERCISE 7–2: KEGELS
Time Required: A few minutes a day

First you need to get in touch with your pelvic muscles, and there are two ways of doing this. One way is simply to contract your buttocks as you sit or stand. Pretend that you are in danger of having a bowel movement but need to keep it in until you can get to a bathroom. The muscles you squeeze to hold it in are the ones you will use in the exercise. The other way of getting in touch with these muscles is to stop and start the flow several times next time you urinate. The muscles you squeeze to stop the flow are the ones you're interested in.

The exercise itself is quite simple. Start by squeezing and releasing the muscles fifteen times. There is no need to hold the contraction for now; just squeeze and let go. Do one set of fifteen twice a day. At first, you may also be squeezing your stomach and thigh muscles. It will take a few days until you acquire the coordination to squeeze only the pelvic muscles. When this happens, you can do the exercise unobtrusively anywhere – while driving a car, watching television, reading, at a meeting, and so forth.

Do the Kegels every day, gradually increasing the number until you can do at least sixty or seventy twice a day. Build up slowly; we have known a few men who tried to do too many the first few days and developed sore muscles.

When you can do sixty or seventy comfortably, you can also do a slight variation. Instead of immediately releasing the contraction hold it for a count of three, then relax and repeat. Work up to sixty or seventy of these twice a day.

You can do both the long and short Kegels, making two sets of each per day, or alternate between them, doing the long one day and the short the next.

Some men have developed rather extraordinary control over their penises by experimenting with the muscular movements. They can move their penises back and forth and from side to side. We're not sure what good this does, but some people like to experiment.

Continue doing the long and short Kegels for at least six weeks. Results usually aren't noticeable for a month or more. As you continue doing them, they will become automatic and require no conscious attention or effort.

EIGHT

Touching

> To be held is support;
> to be touched is contact;
> to be touched sensitively
> is to be cared for.

Our culture is highly sexual but not very sensual (sensual defined here as body contact that is pleasurable but not erotic). While the manipulation and union of genitals is greatly valued and much discussed, there has been, at least until very recently, an almost wholesale disregard for the uses and pleasures of other kinds of physical contact. For many adults, only two kinds of touching seem acceptable: the superficial and ritualized (shaking hands, a pat on the back, a hug when greeting and leaving) and the sexual (anything that is a prelude to or part of sexual activity). We have sexualized touching to the point where all but the most superficial types of touch are thought to be sexual invitations.

Several astute observers of the American scene have claimed that we suffer from sensory starvation, a lack of nonsexual touching, and worse, that most of us are unaware of how damaging this state of affairs is. Touching is important to us throughout our lives and, strange as it may sound now, the amount and quality of our nonsexual touching experiences are intimately related to how satisfied we are with our sexual activities.

The importance of touching in human life can hardly be overemphasized. The tactile sense is the first to develop: an embryo is sensitive to touch long before it can see and hear, long before it even has eyes and ears. Touching is essential for healthy development. Babies who have not received sufficient tactile stimulation – hugging, cuddling, kissing – do not develop normally and many do not grow at all; the mortality rate for babies deprived of touching is extremely high. In the months after birth, touching can literally mean the difference between life and death. Parents, especially mothers, seem to understand this instinctively and engage in a lot of physical contact with their babies. Unfortunately, this lasts for only a few years, after which there is a sharp decline.

The child's training about touching begins fairly early, as he starts to hear what soon becomes a familiar litany. 'Don't touch this, it'll hurt you.' 'Don't touch that, you'll break it.' 'Don't touch yourself, it's naughty.' 'Don't touch him (or her), it's not nice.' Over and over he hears, 'Don't touch!' Where touching was once a source of pleasure to him, his first knowledge of being cared for and his main way of exploring the world, it now becomes a problem: touching provokes his parents' wrath. So he starts to feel inhibited about touching and guilty about the pleasures derived from it.

The rule not to touch is also taught by an important omission.The child may rarely see anyone else touching. Aside from perfunctory hugs or pecks on the cheek, many children don't see their parents being physically affectionate. While there are many exceptions – with some people reporting lots of physical affection between their parents – we have been astonished by the number of people we have talked to who could barely recall even a few instances of physical affection in their homes. The child also sees that he isn't being touched much either. Perhaps a small peck from his mother before he goes to bed, and being held if he hurts himself, but only in the very early years, and that's about it. He soon learns that when adults talk about getting in touch or keeping in touch, they certainly don't mean it literally.

Another message is also conveyed to the child: touching is sexual. If he does see his parents touching, it is followed by embarrassment (and what is he to make of that?) or by their going off to the bedroom, telling him they don't want to be disturbed. It doesn't take him long to figure out what that means. And the media, from which he learns so much, reinforce the message. People hug, then kiss, then they have sex. Slowly, but very surely, the child acquires the societal understanding about touching: it is sexual.

Although America is a particularly nontouching society and the restrictions we have discussed apply to almost everyone, it is evident that boys fare much worse in this drama than girls. Boys generally get much less touching than girls. Their mothers are likely to stop touching sons at a much earlier age than they stop touching daughters. The reluctance to continue being physically affectionate with sons seems to stem from two reasons. First, some mothers fear that their sons will interpret the touching as sexual and that this may be a cause of later psychological difficulties. Second, mothers as well as fathers know the masculine model and fear that too much 'mothering' may make sissies of their sons. A real man shouldn't need to be hugged or held, so the boy has to be weaned early from such 'feminine' or 'childish' practices.

Fathers, having lived in a culture that is terrified of affectionate physical contact between males, do not touch their sons much after infancy. Since it is the father whom the boy will try to emulate, a very powerful lesson is transmitted by this lack of touching. The boy also does not see other males touching. He sees that men shake hands and pat one another on the back, and nothing else. Again, he learns something about touching. A girl, on the other hand, sees other females touching. She sees her mother hugging and kissing relatives and friends, and this is reinforced by seeing and reading about other women being physically affectionate. The lesson she learns is somewhat different from that learned by boys.

Girls also have far greater permission to experience their own sensuality – not, of course, by touching 'down there', but in many other ways. It's considered normal and acceptable for a girl to derive physical pleasure from wearing frilly clothes, from washing herself or brushing her hair, and from trying out different scents on herself. These concessions may seem small, but they are far more than is permitted for boys.

Boys learn that physical contact is acceptable only in sports and sex. There are no taboos against touching if you are playing football, or wrestling, or boxing, or in some other way being rough. One cause, as well as result, of this notion can be seen in the way fathers handle their sons. They often seem uncomfortable just holding or cuddling their boys, being more at ease when throwing them around or engaging in mock wrestling or boxing bouts. Since roughness is what we learned, it's no surprise that we often show affection by being rough, by wrestling with our lovers and playfully punching our friends. And it's no surprise that we're often rough in sex, less gentle than our partners would like.

The main way for a man to have physical contact is by having sex, and the equating of touching and sex causes no end of problems for us. As discussed earlier, it hinders the expression of physical affection between parents and children, for the parents are concerned about the possible sexual implications. It also gets in the way of physical contact between both same-sex and opposite-sex friends. Men who have been friends for twenty years are often afraid to touch one another because, as one man put it, 'Other people might think I was gay. Hell, even I might begin to wonder.' And to touch a woman friend might be construed as sexual by her, by you, and by God knows whom else. The link between sex and physical affection even works to keep lovers from touching each other. Since touching is seen not so much as a thing in itself but as the first step toward intercourse, many people won't touch unless they feel ready and willing to 'go all the way'.

The taboo on touching except as a part of sex confuses us about what we want and how to get it. Ashley Montagu, a pioneer in the exploration of the importance of touching, says in his book *Touching* that 'it is highly probable that . . . the frenetic preoccupation with sex that characterizes Western culture is in many cases not the expression of a sexual interest at all, but rather a search for the satisfaction of the need for contact.' And this seems to be truer for men than women.

In growing up, girls more so than boys were allowed to express and explore their desire for physical contact. Having the permission, girls learned to differentiate their needs for support, comfort, validation, a sense of connection with another, and similar needs from the need for sex. In fact, given the way girls were brought up, sex was the one need they had trouble noticing and expressing. Boys developed in the opposite direction. Wanting sex was legitimate, even encouraged, while such things as wanting to be held or loved or to know they were not alone were unacceptable.

These needs did not disappear in boys and men. They simply went underground and got reorganized and relabeled. Wanting a hug or to feel close to another sounded too effeminate, but wanting sex was the epitome of masculinity; and in sex you could get some of these other things as well. After years of practice, the man just never felt a need for closeness or comfort or support. All he wanted was – sex. Whenever he felt something that might be called warm or close or loving, he read it as indicating a desire for – sex.

This may seem like a brilliant feat of engineering, but the result too often for too many men has been a frustrating confusion about what they want, and therefore an inability to meet many of their needs. One place where this is especially evident is in the relations between men. Many men are realizing that they want something from other men: closeness, understanding, camaraderie, support, and so forth. But as soon as they start getting any of these things, they very often pull back in fear and sometimes come into therapy to discuss their 'latent homosexual feelings'. This is especially true of men who have engaged in some physical contact with other men and found it pleasurable. Because touching is so closely tied to sex in our thinking, they decide that what they really want from other men is sex and, since that is unacceptable to them, they should just stay away from men. What they fail to see is that touching need not be sexual, any more than feelings of love or closeness or caring need to be sexual. One can hug or cuddle a man or a woman or a child, or animal for that matter, and not have sex. Touching serves many functions, sex being only one and probably not the most important.

But, we have been asked, cannot touching lead to sexual feelings and erections? Of course, it often does, but that in itself doesn't mean a lot nor does it imply a necessary course of action. In the first place, an erection can be caused by lots of things and does not necessarily indicate a desire for sex. Your erections need not run your life. Men often have such limited ideas about what erections mean and what must be done about them. The following story proved very helpful to many of the men we worked with in workshops dealing with male friendships, where there was great concern about what it meant if a man got aroused or erect when touching or being with another man.

> As a teenager, John frequently rode on buses. The vibrations of the bus, sometimes combined with adolescent sex fantasies, often produced an erection. Despite the erection, and despite the fact that it was often accompanied by feelings of arousal, he somehow managed to contain himself and never became a busfucker.

The second point we want to make is that even if your feelings about someone are sometimes clearly sexual you don't have to act on them. It is possible for all of us to be turned-on by many different people and even things. We have talked to men who became aroused and erect while stroking a child or pet, and to a few who have become aroused while listening to music or watching a sunset. And neither they nor you have to do anything about such events except, if you wish, appreciate the good feelings.

It has become clear to us that men need different things from different types of people. They need men as well as women, though perhaps for different reasons, and many feel incomplete unless they can also relate to people much older as well as those much younger than themselves. It seems a great tragedy that we separate ourselves from those we want to be with because of our fears about what being close and touching imply. They need indicate nothing more than what they obviously are, and we don't mean sex.

Even lovers don't seem to touch as much as they want. This is not usually true in the beginning of a relationship where the couple seems unable to keep their hands off each other: they are always holding hands, kissing, hugging, and so on. But when the relationship becomes sexual, the nonsexual touching often declines rather sharply. The following observation by Masters and Johnson in their book *The Pleasure Bond* is consistent with our own:

> Once a sexual relationship has been established, most young couples use touch as little more than a wordless way to communicate a willingness, a wish or a demand to make love. It is functional; beyond that, it seems of limited value and is regarded, especially by men, as a waste of time and effort, an unnecessary postponement of intercourse.

Interestingly, many men and women will admit, the men usually with some embarrassment, that they really would like more nonsexual affection. But the men wonder if it's OK for a man to feel that way and they fear 'leading their partners on'. One man put it this way:

> I've gotten through the thing about men not needing touching. I know I like to be held without wanting to have sex. But I'm afraid that the woman will get turned-on and want to have sex. Then, if I'm not in that space, she'll get mad at me or at least be disappointed. I just don't feel it's right to lead her on.

Now look at what the woman he was seeing at the time said:

I guess I'm just an old-fashioned woman but I just love to be held and touched. It's much more important to me than sex. But I'm almost afraid to touch Ralph. He thinks that I want sex and immediately starts into the foreplay routine. Or else, if he's not in a sexual mood, he runs away . . . Really, he starts making excuses about having to get up early or just happens to remember that he forgot something and gets busy taking out the garbage or doing some other chore. You'd think I was asking for a two-hour screw rather than some snuggling.

The problem was that neither of them was asking for anything, at least not in a way that was clear to the other. They were busily not getting what they wanted even though, as far as touching went, they both wanted the same thing.

And what does touching have to do with the quality of your sexual behavior? Probably quite a bit. For most people, sex is best, and the chances for avoiding sexual problems highest, when they have sex only when their conditions are met and when sex is really what they want. When you use sex as a way of fulfilling nonsexual needs – e.g., the need for support, love, physical contact – you run the risk of disappointment, sex that isn't quite satisfying, and perhaps even the beginning of a sexual problem. Your penis may be uninterested in your desire for some cuddling and may refuse to respond. And, when you think about it, going through a whole sexual experience just to get a hug is a lot of unnecessary exertion.

When physical contact and affection are restricted to your lover, and then only as part of sexual activity, sex takes on an exaggerated importance. You expect and want it to meet all the needs that aren't being met elsewhere. Sex can become weighted down with these expectations. As we have said a number of times, our sexual systems are fragile and do not work well when too great a burden is placed on them. Get your *sexual* needs and desires fulfilled in sex; satisfy your needs for *other* kinds of contact and affection in more appropriate ways.

Ask yourself if you'd like more touching than you are currently getting. If the answer is yes, all you have to do is start touching more. Choose someone you care about – whether a partner, relative, or close friend – and next time you are with that person touch a bit more than you have before. Don't try to do too much too soon. If you haven't touched at all before, a pat on the hand or back or shoulder may be sufficient the first time. When you see that person again, go a bit further. You may wish to talk to your friend about wanting to touch more; if so, do it. If you've already engaged in some touching with the person and simply want to do more, just do it. There may be a specific type of touching you want. It may take some courage, but see if you can try to get it.

A couple told us this story at a men's conference. They had always done lots of touching but the man had wanted something that took him months to ask for. Since he was almost a foot taller than the woman, he always felt like the giver or comforter whenever they hugged, even in bed. He wanted to experience the feeling of being the smaller person, the one being comforted. He finally got up the nerve to deal with this one day when his partner was standing on a chair. He went over and put his arms around her and she hugged back. This was a very pleasant experience for him so he told her about his secret desire. It made a lot of sense to her that he sometimes wanted to be 'mothered' this way and they have since incorporated this into their touching activities. It turned out that she very much enjoys being the taller one and 'mothering' him.

Another thing you can do is to ask yourself what you really want when you think you want sex. Is it closeness to someone you care about? Compassion? Understanding? Support? A feeling of connectedness? Knowing that she cares? Physical contact? Intercourse? Orgasm?

When you have some idea of what you want, ask what is the

best way of getting it now. Would a hug do? Being held? A conversation? Giving or getting a massage?

The results of such questioning can be amusing as well as informative, as indicated by this example.

A few years ago, I taught two three-hour classes one day a week, with an office hour sandwiched in between. I was drained by the end of the day and could barely crawl to my car. But I noticed that about an hour before the end of the second class I started feeling very aroused and thinking how nice it would be to have sex when I got home. One day, when I was feeling particularly tired and having the sexual fantasies, I thought: 'This is crazy. I don't have the energy to stand up or do anything. What makes me think I want sex? I wonder what's going on?' As I started to drive my car home, I got my answer, in the form of another fantasy. When I got home, the fantasy went, a woman greeted me warmly, helped me undress and guided me to a bath she had drawn. Then she lovingly washed and dried me, after which she spoon-fed me supper. When that was over, she tucked me in bed, turned out the lights, and left. The fantasy ended with me falling asleep, feeling very good and well cared for. As soon as I had this fantasy, I realized it expressed my needs far better than the sexual fantasies. I was tired and felt I had put out all day, trying to care for the needs of my students. I now wanted someone to take care of me. Sex was about the last thing I wanted but, even so, my first clue that I wanted anything was a feeling of sexual arousal.

Of course, sometimes you're going to be clear that sex is exactly what you want and, when that's the case, sex is what you should have. But we encourage you to consider these other possibilities since men so often ignore them and think of sex when they would, in fact, be happier with something else.

To help you discover more about what you can get from touching, we offer a few simple exercises. You might want to try them regardless of what specific changes you want to make in your sexual behavior.

A good way of getting back into touching is to start touching yourself. This is the way you learned about yourself as an infant, and there is much to be said for it as a means of giving yourself pleasure. Unfortunately, most adult men touch themselves only when they masturbate, when the touching is confined to a very small portion of their anatomy.

EXERCISE 8–1: SELF BODY-RUB WITH LOTION
Time Required: 30 to 45 minutes

Get undressed, put some kind of lubricant on your hands (hand or body lotion is fine), sit or lie down, and begin to stroke yourself. Touch and stroke all the parts of your body that are readily accessible. Vary the types of strokes and pressures. Try very light touches, circular movements, both long and short strokes, slaps, and so forth. Play around with different types of touches and try to keep your attention on the skin immediately under where your hand is touching. Just be in touch with what it feels like. Go slowly and experience the sensations. Be aware of how and where you most like to be touched.

You may include your genitals in the touching, but do not spend a disproportionate amount of time on them.

Although this exercise is not intended to produce arousal or erection, it sometimes does. Whatever happens in this regard is fine. Should you become aroused, just enjoy it. Do not masturbate while doing the exercise, however.

Do this exercise one or two times. What did you learn about yourself? Did you learn some things you'd like to share with a partner? Are there any types of touching you'd like to continue giving yourself on a more or less regular basis?

There are many ways of including pleasurable self-touching

in your daily life. You may, in fact, already be doing some of the things we suggest, but perhaps you are not taking the time to experience the enjoyable sensations produced. Washing and combing your hair, soaking in a hot bath, taking a shower, and drying yourself are activities that lend themselves to experiencing the sensations of touch, but only if done leisurely and with some awareness of your feelings at the time. Most men simply rush through these activities with little or no awareness of what they feel. Try to take your time.

All of these activities can also be done with a partner. If you've never washed your partner's hair or had her wash yours, or if you've never bathed or showered together, you may want to try it. You may be surprised at how much fun can be derived from such simple experiences.

Another way of getting experience with touching is to get a professional massage. This can be especially valuable if you have trouble being passive; the masseur or masseuse will help you just to receive. A good massage can also be a marvelous means of reducing tension.

Should you decide to get a massage, be careful where you go. Most so-called massage parlors are nothing but houses of prostitution, a fine example of how sex and touching have become confused. Legitimate masseurs and masseuses do not offer sex, and their advertisements do not feature naked women or promises of blowing your mind (or something else).

It is very important in doing touching exercises with your partner that both of you understand that they are not to end in sex. Otherwise, there is a risk that one of you will feel misunderstood or misled. Also, when touching is merely a prelude to sex, there is a tendency not fully to 'get into it' or experience it, since you're looking forward to the 'more important' activity that is to follow. When you're more comfortable with both touching and sex, and with getting your various needs met, you can do whatever you want, sometimes touching for its own sake and sometimes using it as a prelude to sex. But in the beginning, it's best to be clear that touching is not to lead to anything else.

One of our students, Penny Schuchman, gave the name 'nondemand snuggling' to the instructions we gave couples for being physically affectionate without going on to sex. Snuggling refers to any type of physical contact that is pleasurable or comforting, while nondemand means that there is to be no expectation, request, or demand that it lead to sexual activity. Nondemand snuggling is simply touching for its own sake, the type of contact we have been discussing in this chapter. Here is an exercise that will assist you in cultivating it.

EXERCISE 8–2: NONDEMAND SNUGGLING
Time Required: Variable, but usually 5 to 20 minutes

Tell your partner you do not want sex but would like to be close her. Whether you are clothed or not is up to you. Pick a comfortable place – sitting or lying on a sofa, bed, or the floor – and be close in any way that you want. You might want to hold each other with little or no movement or activity, or you may prefer that one or both of you lightly stroke the other (leaving out breasts and genitals).

Use your imagination and try different things. Perhaps putting your head in her lap, or vice versa, doing some back-scratching, toe-pulling, scalp-rubbing, or maybe just lying next to one another. Try whatever you want, but take it slow: give yourself a chance to experience and savor the sensations. Make sure you are passive at least part of the time, just experiencing what is happening.

Continue for as long as you want and stop when you feel like it. Should one or both of you fall asleep during the experience, that is fine.

People sometimes get sexually aroused during the exercise and that can be nice. Do not have sex. Just continue doing what you are doing.

If this experience is new for you, a few minutes is sufficient the first few times you do it. Gradually increase

the amount of time until you are comfortable with ten to twenty minutes of snuggling.

If you don't have a partner, you might want to consider doing the exercise with a friend. In any case, you should think about how you will do it when you are in a relationship. The chances are that sex will be better in a new relationship if you do lots of snuggling before you get to sex.

We wonder if you found yourself being very active during the exercise. Many men find it difficult to be passive, sometimes just to lie still and experience their partners' touching them. If that is true for you, try lying on your hands next time you do the exercise. Being passive may feel very strange to you, so proceed gradually, increasing the amount of passive time as you feel comfortable doing so. You can, of course, do something for your partner before or after. It is very important for both your sensual enjoyment that you develop the capacity to do nothing except experience your partner's touching you.

The next exercise is more formalized and detailed than the preceding one but the general goal remains the same. It is important that it be done as described and that it does not lead to sex. If you do not have a partner, you might want to do it with a friend. If you follow this option, feel free to exclude the genitals if that will make you more comfortable.

EXERCISE 8–3: NONSIMULTANEOUS BODY-RUBS
Time Required: 30 to 60 minutes

In both steps of the exercise, one of you gives a light, stroking body-rub to the other. How light depends on individual preferences, but you should avoid the heavy, kneading type of rubbing usually called massage.

You will need a warm room, a comfortable place for the receiver to lie, and a lubricant (hand lotion, massage oil, or baby powder).

First you must decide who will give and who will receive in a particular session. The nonsimultaneous in the title of the exercise means that the distinction between giver and receiver must be rigidly adhered to. The receiver is not to touch or do anything else to or for the giver, except as specified in the instructions.

Since the receiver may not feel like doing anything active after the session, we suggest you do not plan to have two sessions back to back. It is usually best to wait at least an hour between sessions.

The goal of both steps is to allow you to experience touching and being touched without any other ends in mind. The giver should focus on his touching and the receiver on the sensations produced by being touched.

You may or may not get turned-on, you may or may not enjoy the experience. Whatever happens is fine. Just keep in mind that this exercise is not a prelude to anything. It is simply what it is.

Step A: The giver touches, strokes, and rubs his partner for his own pleasure, doing whatever he wants. The receiver should accept what is done without comment unless there is pain or discomfort, in which case she should ask the giver to discontinue what he is doing.

The giver should use this opportunity to explore his partner's body with different types of touch, pressure, and rhythm. Touch where and how you want to for your own pleasure. Discover what you like to do.

Spend at least thirty minutes per session. When time is up, take a few minutes talking about what the experience was like for each of you. You should both say what you liked most and least about the experience, and also indicate any difficulties you experienced – e.g. in being active or passive or in doing what you wanted. This talking is useful for learning how to communicate better about physical preferences; include it after every session and be as specific as possible. Give and receive at least one rub before going on to the next step.

Step B: Here the receiver is in complete control, giving directions on where and how he wants to be touched, while the giver simply follows the instructions.

The receiver should use this opportunity to discover where and how he likes to be touched. You can ask for anything at all as long as there is not a disproportionate amount of attention given to the genitals. Try new things and places even if you're not sure how they will feel. If you've ever wondered how it would feel to have the areas between your toes touched, or how a light touch would do on your lower back, or anything else, now is the time to find out. Make sure you are getting precisely what you want, no matter how many times you have to give instructions or demonstrate to the giver.

The giver should do everything that is asked so long as it is not obnoxious or uncomfortable for her. She should also feel free to ask for more specific instructions if needed.

Spend at least thirty minutes per session and, as in Step A, take some time afterward to share your feelings about what the experience was like. This may be more complex than in Step A for there are sometimes problems around the giving and following of instructions. If such difficulties are present, use this time to deal with them. The receiver should be as clear as possible about what he wanted and the giver should talk about the difficulties encountered in following the instructions. The better you can resolve these issues now, the easier it will be for you when you do exercises dealing more directly with genital touching.

You should each give and get at least two rubs and be comfortable with both giving and following directions before leaving this exercise.

POSSIBLE PROBLEMS *(IN STEP B)*

1. **Receiver does not give sufficient feedback to giver.** As receiver, you should give as much feedback as you are comfortable with, indicating not only desired changes but

also when the stroking is just as you want it. For example: 'A little higher and a bit lighter . . . that's the right place but lighter yet . . . that's perfect, just like that.'

If you have trouble giving instructions because you feel guilty, see point 2.

2. Receiver feels guilty about getting and tries to take care of the giver. Many people have trouble receiving, feeling that they don't deserve it, that they are being selfish, or that the giver is really bored and doesn't want to give to them. In response to these feelings, they may try to make it easier for the giver by not giving instructions or by cutting the session short, or they may try to repay the giver by doing something for her (e.g., rubbing her or saying nice things when they should just be receiving). Try to resist doing these 'nice' things, as they only hinder progress. It will probably be useful to talk to your partner about what is going on, your feelings about just receiving, your concerns about what she is thinking, and so on.

If you absolutely must pay some dues (i.e. take care of the giver), do so before or after the session, not during it. Some men find it easier to receive if they have already done something for their partner, so you may want to give her a rub in the morning if she is going to do one for you later in the day.

3. Giver has trouble following directions. This can happen for a number of reasons. If you are not clear what your partner is asking for, request clarification. If you are clear but have some trouble complying, talk it out with her; let her know what's getting in your way and see if something can be worked out (and remember that you should not do anything that is distasteful or uncomfortable for you).

A problem encountered by many men is that they try to do what is asked and then get frustrated and angry when they are corrected. Try to remember that the exercise encourages exploration. We want the receiver to ask for many different things, to make corrections, and to feel free

to change her mind. And the giver must therefore be willing to follow the changes and corrections.

Being the giver is often frustrating. You may feel like a child trying your best to do what is asked but somehow being unable to satisfy your partner. This is due in part to the fact that we often touch another the way *we* want, without considering what *they* want. Learning to follow detailed instructions, which may not even be clear to the receiver, is a bit difficult and may be new to you. Like any new experience or skill, it takes time and patience.

You may have experienced more difficulty than anticipated in giving directions on how and where you wanted to be touched. Let's use an example of scratching an itch to see how this can happen. When you scratch your own itch, you make use of an automatic, nonverbal, self-correcting feedback loop. Your nervous system has precise and accurate information on where the itch is and what should be done to relieve it, and it guides your hand accordingly. There is continuous feedback regarding the itch and the efforts to relieve it, causing corrective action as needed, moving the position of your scratching fingers, their pace, pressure, and so on. All this is done without words, without conscious effort, and perhaps even without your knowledge.

The situation is radically changed when your partner is scratching you. Her nervous system gets no information about the itch or her efforts to relieve it other than what you show or tell her. To supply the information to her, you need to make verbal what was automatic and nonverbal when you did it yourself. And this can be frustrating. Practice and learning are required to unscramble the automatic feedback loop so that it is, first, clear to you, and second, so that it is understandable to your partner. It may help to keep in mind that there's no way your partner can know what you want unless you tell her. She simply does not have access to the continuous stream of information that your body is supplying to you. You, of course, may not have much experience in making explicit the nonverbal messages of your nervous system. Continued practice will definitely help and we hope you can learn to enjoy it.

Most of the men we have worked with found the touching exercises enjoyable and real eye-openers. They had forgotten how much fun it can be to touch and be touched.

Jack, a man in his forties who had come for therapy with his wife, agreed to try the touching exercises only after he was convinced that they would help in the treatment of his erection problems. The first time he and his wife snuggled, he became disappointed and then furious because he didn't get an erection. He strongly believed that the purpose of any kind of physical contact was to arouse him so that he could have intercourse. He was then told that the snuggling was to continue and that he should do everything possible to prevent himself from getting an erection. There was to be no genital contact whatever. Jack was at a loss to understand what was going on but agreed to find out what this touching stuff was about. It wasn't easy for him, for he believed in all the male myths more strongly than most men, but he gradually got more comfortable with touching. Within a few weeks, he even admitted that he was enjoying the new physical closeness with his wife. She was overjoyed; for the eighteen years of their married life she had been unable to get any physical contact from him except when he wanted sex, and this was the main cause of her coldness and sarcasm. As she became less critical, he became more aroused, and in less than two months they were having very enjoyable sex. But the real surprise was what Jack said in a phone conversation six months after the end of therapy.

'I owe you a lot. Sex is fine, and that's great. But there's more. This closeness and cuddling stuff is really something. I never would have believed that I, of all

people, would like it. Never even occurred to me to try it.
Our lives are better because of it. I've gotten addicted to
having my feet rubbed and licked and it's great. And this
you'll never believe: it's helped us with our kids. They
were really shocked when I started touching them, but
they've gotten used to it and we all touch more now.
When my boy came home from college, I hugged him at
the door. He must have thought I was nuts but he's
gotten used to the idea and now we always hug when
we see each other. Makes us feel closer.'

If your experiences with touching are different from Jack's,
if they're not enjoyable for you, try to determine what is
standing in your way. Your image of how you should be as a
man? The idea that touching is only for women and children? The myth that touching is only acceptable as the
prelude to intercourse? The notion that touching should be a
mind-blowing experience? Once you've found the obstacle,
determine if there is something you can do to move it out of
the way a little bit, and do it.

We are not prescribing touching as a panacea for all your
ills or as a compulsory ritual that should be followed whether
you like it or not. Rather, we view touching as a very important human need, probably much more basic than the need
for sex, a need you should be free to fulfill in ways and
with people of your own choosing. It won't change the
world and it won't solve all your problems, but it may help
you feel better and bring you a bit closer to the important
people in your world. Men need touching as much as anyone else, and there is no good reason to deprive yourself in
this area.

Touch [say Masters and Johnson] is an end in itself. It is
a primary form of communication, a silent voice that
avoids the pitfall of words while expressing the feelings
of the moment. It bridges the physical separateness from

which no human being is spared, literally establishing a sense of solidarity between two individuals.

Get in touch with those you care for. Stay in touch. Literally.

NINE

The importance of relaxation

Although modern living has benefited us in many ways, it has also had many negative effects. The pace of living has accelerated at an alarming rate. Life has become more hectic, and the pressures of daily living seem considerably greater than in the past. We are tense and distraught much of the time, struggling to keep up with the treadmill of our lives and resorting to a vast array of chemical uppers and downers, including tobacco and alcohol, to help us cope with our tensions. But the tensions and anxieties remain, affecting almost all areas of our lives.

Nervous tension is not compatible with good sex. It can prevent you from becoming aroused, from experiencing the pleasurable sensations that would be available were you not so tense, and it tends to have a soporific effect on your penis.

Many men have sex when they are tense because of time pressure, some unfinished business with their partner, something that happened at work or with the kids, or for some other reason. Sex under such conditions frequently is not very satisfying and sometimes it doesn't work at all.

We cannot sufficiently emphasize the importance of being relaxed in sex. Attempting to engage in sex when you are irritated or anxious is one of the best ways we know to have a miserable experience. Good sex is extremely difficult to come by under these circumstances; your arousal, erection, and ejaculation systems simply do not function well when you are feeling tense.

Let's talk a bit about what we mean by tension and relaxation. People differ greatly in this regard. Some are generally easygoing and relaxed, while others are tense and keyed-up most of the time. But even the most relaxed person is more relaxed at some times than at others, and even the most high-strung person is sometimes less tense. As far as sex goes, the important things, regardless of whether you are generally tense or relaxed, are that you be able to recognize when you are more tense than usual for you and that you be able to do something to relax yourself.

Relaxation and tension, as we use the terms, are relative states. You are to consider your own behavior as the standard, being aware that what is tense or relaxed for you may have little to do with what others are like when they employ these terms.

There are two general types of indicators of tension that will help you determine how tense you are in a given situation. The first type consists of physical indicators. People differ as to where in their bodies they experience tension, but some common signs are tensing of the neck and shoulder muscles, a knotty feeling in the stomach, sweaty palms, and clenching of teeth. Whether or not these examples fit for you, tension always has some physical manifestations and you need to determine what yours are.

Your thoughts are the second kind of indicator of tension. The following thoughts all indicate some degree of concern or anxiety: 'Will it stay hard?' 'Am I going to be able to last?' 'Will she like me?' 'Am I going to be able to carry this off?'

Have you ever experienced some of the physical symptoms described above in a sexual situation? Or asked yourself questions similar to the ones we cited? If so, you were probably experiencing tension or anxiety. There is nothing to be concerned about if the experiences were fleeting – if, for example, the question of whether you would last merely floated through your mind. But if it stayed on and nagged at you, the chances are good that you would enjoy sex more if you learned more about relaxing.

It may help you to consider the feelings you experienced in some nonsexual situations to get a better idea of how tension manifests itself in you. How do you feel when you sit in the dentist's chair waiting for him to start drilling? Does your body tense up in some way? Do you hold your breath? Grasp the arms of the chair? Do you wonder if it's going to hurt despite the Novocain? Or consider what you feel when your boss calls you into his office to discuss a mistake you made. And what happens to you when you have to finish a project by a certain time and are aware that you have more work than time left? Consider these questions carefully; they will give you a good understanding of what tension means to you.

Now, to look at the other side of things, give some thought to situations in which you felt free of cares and worries. Perhaps when you wake up late on a Sunday morning knowing there isn't anything for you to do that day. Or when you're lying on the beach during a vacation. Or perhaps after a good sexual experience. How do your body and your mind feel on such occasions?

Although the particular examples we gave may not fit for you, we're sure you can think of similar situations that will help you define what maximum tension and relaxation mean to you.

The following exercise is a useful tool for becoming more aware of your tension/relaxation state.

EXERCISE 9–1: DETERMINING HOW RELAXED YOU ARE
Time Required: 5 to 10 minutes

The first few times you do the exercise, make sure you have privacy and will not be interrupted. Once you are accustomed to it, you can do it any time, any place, even if others are present. The exercise should be done at least ten times, but twenty or thirty times are not too often.

Without changing your posture, breathing or muscle tension, focus your attention on the part of your body that is most tense. Resist the temptation to relax that part: just experience it the way it is for a few seconds. Now check to

see if any other part of your body is as tense or nearly as tense as the part you first focused on. Pay attention to this part, just experiencing it, for a few seconds, again without changing it. Next, spend a few minutes on the rest of your body – feet, calves, thighs, buttocks, back, stomach, chest, hands, arms, shoulders, neck, face, scalp, and insides – asking of each part if it is tense or relaxed. If it feels relaxed, could it feel more relaxed? If tense, more tense? Don't try to make it more relaxed or tense, just determine if it's possible that it could change.

Finally, get in touch with your breathing without changing it. Become aware of how you are breathing. Deeply or shallowly? Slowly or quickly? Is your chest moving? Your stomach? Are you unable to detect movement in either?

POSSIBLE PROBLEMS

1. You find yourself wanting to do something about what you discover. This tendency comes from being judgmental about what you find, e.g., 'I shouldn't be so tense,' 'My breathing should be slower.' These judgments may have little to do with reality and, even when they are correct, trying to do something about them gets in the way of the goal of the exercise, being aware of tension and relaxation. You will have plenty of opportunities to make changes in your level of relaxation later. For now, just try to accept what you find. If the temptation to change something is there, just let it be there and continue with the exercise.

2. You find your mind wandering away from the parts of your body you want to focus on. Everyone's mind wanders during such exercises and it is not a problem. When you are aware that your attention has drifted off, just gently bring it back and continue where you left off. You will have to do this a number of times during the course of the exercise, and that is fine. Of course, should your wandering be due to factors over which you have some control, e.g., the radio

playing or the dog barking, you should take care of these distractions before continuing.

Doing this exercise may be the first time you have paid attention to your body without asking it to *do* something. You will be asked to do more of this type of attending, which we call focusing, in other exercises in the book. It may sometimes be difficult – for men have learned too well how to do and too little about how to be – but it will get easier with practice. Just take it slow and bring your mind back when it wanders.

Now that you have learned to check on your level of tension, let's explore some ways of lessening tension. There are many approaches to relaxation and, as our society grows ever more stressful, increasing numbers of people are turning to them. Among the more popular are meditation, yoga exercises, self-hypnosis, and tai-chi. All of these can be effective if practiced properly and consistently; if you are already involved in one or more of them and found them helpful, we encourage you to continue.

Here are some other effective ways of helping you become more relaxed.

A lot of the anxiety that men experience in sex has to do with trying to please or impress their partners. You want to do it well for her and get concerned about what may happen if you don't. As paradoxical as it sounds, probably the best way of dealing with such tension is to tell your partner about it. Just express what you are feeling: e.g., 'Honey, I know you were disappointed last time and I want it to be good for you tonight. But I'm trying so hard, and I'm so concerned that you'll get mad if I don't stay hard, that I'm worrying like crazy and can't even concentrate on what's happening.' Sometimes the acknowledgment will in itself reduce your anxiety. Or perhaps your statement will lead to a conversation regarding her feelings and expectations, as well as yours, and this may contribute to better feelings on both sides. You might find that she wasn't expecting the kind of performance you imagined.

Most men find it at least a bit difficult to express their

feelings in this way. We learned that we weren't supposed to feel fear or concern, let alone express them. And it's true that there is some risk involved; though not likely, it is possible that your partner won't like what you say or will have the expectations you fear or will feel very disappointed. You have to decide if the potential benefits outweigh the risks. One way or another, you need to reduce your tension if you are to have good sex. Telling your partner about your concern isn't the only way, but it's one of the best. It may be of interest to you to know that of the thousands of instances we know of where men talked to their partners about their tense feelings in sex, there were only a few where the situation was not improved as a result of the talking.

Another type of talking, the kind involved in clearing up unfinished business, is also very helpful in making sex more satisfying. Every relationship is bound to include disappointments, frustrations, and hostilities. The feelings are inevitable but they get handled in different ways. At one extreme, some couples almost immediately deal with any negative feelings that come up. They may talk or scream or do something else, but the bad feelings are dealt with and no backlog results. Each day begins with a more or less clean slate. Other couples do just the opposite. They almost never deal with their negative emotions and, as a result, carry around resentment and hostility from years ago. Each new experience of frustration or anger just gets piled on top of the already existing heap which more and more begins to resemble Mount Everest. The feelings may be expressed in sarcasm or seemingly reasonable complaints, or they may not, but the aura of tension and hostility is often so thick that strangers immediately sense that something is wrong.

Sex usually does not go well in such situations, assuming that there is any sex. The tension and anger may interfere with one or both partner's arousal systems, causing a lack of sexual interest, or with the systems governing erection or orgasm. Simple relaxation exercises are usually not very effective in such cases. Much more beneficial are talks about the sources of one's discontent and negotiations for reaching a resolution of some of the problems.

Rob, age forty-two, came to therapy for help with his sexual relationship with his wife. For the past two years, whenever they had sex he would either not get an erection, get one but lose it quickly, or come very fast. He felt very tense in sex and he also reported feeling tense whenever he was around his wife although he said he cared for her deeply and wanted to make the marriage work. His wife, Margaret, was asked to come in for a few sessions, and the following story emerged.

Rob had been somewhat dissatisfied with their sexual relationship since the beginning of their marriage. Margaret had been inexperienced sexually and reacted negatively to his desires for oral and anal sex. Rob, instead of trying to work it out with her, had an affair with a woman he worked with, feeling that Margaret's primness had driven him to it. Margaret was deeply hurt by the affair and was angry at Rob not only for having sex with another woman but also for not being more patient with her. None of these feelings had been discussed or worked out prior to their coming to therapy, and they had been the basis for ever-increasing tension between Rob and Margaret. Rob felt guilty about the affair and feared Margaret's anger. So he acted very carefully around her, trying not to show too much that he cared for her; he didn't want to give her a chance to reject him. Margaret took his withdrawal as a rejection of her; she wanted, but wasn't getting, his assurance that he loved her rather than the woman with whom he had the affair. All of these feelings, not expressed directly, formed a wall of tension between them all of the time, but especially in sex. The wall began to crumble when they told each other what they had been feeling and what they wanted. Margaret was surprised to hear that Rob cared as much as he did, that the other woman meant very little to him, and that he certainly would not want another affair. Rob was surprised that Margaret still wanted his love and, lo and behold, was quite willing to experiment with new sexual practices if he could respect her inexperience and get into new things slowly. These talks continued for six therapy sessions; the tension between them was reduced to a manageable level and sex became good.

This was a case where less direct methods did not work. Before coming to see us, Rob had been to several therapists, one of whom taught him self-hypnosis and another of whom had given him autogenic training (a form of relaxation training). Such methods were insufficient to deal with the strong and pervasive tension in the relationship. It had to be dealt with directly, by airing grievances and desires and making satisfactory arrangements for future behavior.

If there's a lot of unfinished business between you and your partner, consider how it affects your sexual activities and what you want to do about it. You might benefit from doing what Rob and Margaret did, with or without professional help.

Two more tension-producing situations deserve comment. We have found that many men find it difficult to separate work and leisure. They bring the worries, pressures, and frustrations of their jobs home with them and, in this state of tenseness, interpret anything their families do as more demands and pressure. Needless to say, they are hard to be with, sexually or otherwise.

A very effective way of dealing with this situation is to do something that both literally and symbolically marks the leaving of work and the entering into a more relaxed state. The types of transition activities that men have chosen vary considerably: vigorous physical activity; gardening; a massage; meditation; a relaxing glass of wine either alone or with a partner; a hot bath; a short nap; listening to some favorite music or doing some fun reading. Here is how one man told his wife about wanting to make the transition from work to home:

Honey, I know I'm pretty grouchy in the evenings and difficult to live with. I get all revved up at work and I'm just beat by the time I get home. As soon as I get in the door we get into a conversation and I feel overwhelmed. It just feels like more pressure. I think it would really help if I had some time alone after I got here, just to relax and unwind, without having to talk to you or anyone else. What I'd like to do is still come home at five, but I'd like you to pretend that I'm not here until quarter after six. If the phone rings, either don't answer it or say I'm not home if it's for me. I'm not sure what I'll do in that time, maybe go jogging or take a nap or just sit in our room. I'm pretty sure that if I can get that time to myself, I'll be much better company the rest of the evening.

In looking for transition activities, consider those things that are both pleasurable and relaxing for you. Perhaps one of the activities you chose in Exercise 6–3 will make for a good transition.

You may at first run into some resistance from your lover or children; they may believe that you're just taking more time away from them or that your new activities will upset the household routine. And they may be right. It will help if you carefully explain the reasons for what you're doing. If you choose your transition activities with care and stick with them, it probably won't be long before both you and those you live with agree you're doing the right thing.

You should also be aware of periods of unusually high stress. All of us experience such times: the busy season at work, the days before final exams, working on a project with a deadline, and so on. Many men simply shrug their shoulders during such periods and stoically try to accept their burden, usually not realizing that they are causing others around them much unhappiness. Accepting such high levels of tension without doing anything to relieve them takes its toll, and many men are quite difficult to live with during such periods.

Although you may not be able to do much to change the

pressure-producing situation, you probably can deal with it in a way that creates less tension in you. Taking a few minutes every hour or two to do something relaxing can be helpful; you will probably find that although you have 'lost' a few minutes of work time, the increased productivity brought about by your more relaxed state will more than make up for it. Some men find a few minutes of physical exercise every hour or two helpful, others enjoy a quiet moment alone taking a walk or fantasizing, and some achieve good results from lying down and doing some deep breathing for a few moments. Transition activities are particularly useful during periods of high stress. The most important point is that you recognize that you are under a lot of pressure and make some plans to help you relax.

As surprising as it may sound after all we have said, physical contact with your partner, with or without sex, can be very soothing during times of high stress, providing that the cause of the stress is not the relationship and that you follow a few simple suggestions. Be aware that since you are under a great deal of tension, sex may not be 'as usual'. You may respond differently from when you are more relaxed. As long as you put no pressure on yourself to have an erection or to go on to sex or to have intercourse, there's no reason to avoid touching or sex, should you desire either. Being cuddled or made love to can be wonderful ways of making you feel cared for and relieving your tensions. But this is only true when the touching and sex do not add extra pressure. If they do, they are best avoided.

Following the suggestions in this chapter should help you be more relaxed in sex. However, there may still be times when you are tense. Men tend to try to ignore the tension and push on. We hope you now realize that such a procedure will rarely result in good sex. The best thing to do when you feel tense is to stop what you're doing and see if there are some ways of getting more comfortable. As we said earlier, telling your partner about your feelings is usually quite helpful. You should also check to see if sex is really what you want to be doing. If you get more comfortable, feel free to resume your sexual activities. If the tension remains, it's probably best not to continue with sex but to do something else that feels more comfortable. There will be plenty of opportunities for sex in the future.

TEN

Masturbation: from self-abuse to pleasure and self-help

You may be wondering why a book like this includes a chapter on masturbation. After all, you're an adult and, whether you masturbate or not, probably don't think that any comment or instruction regarding this practice is necessary. Or perhaps you've never masturbated and don't have any interest in the subject.

There are two important reasons for dealing with masturbation. First, it is one of the best ways of enhancing your sexuality and overcoming any sexual difficulties you may be experiencing. This is especially true for men without partners. Second, masturbation as practiced by many men is not as pleasurable as it might be and, moreover, is accompanied by feelings of guilt or shame. Overcoming some of these negative feelings enables you better to enjoy your autoerotic practices.

Following Kinsey, we define masturbation as 'self-stimulation which is deliberate and designed to effect erotic arousal'. Note that neither erection nor orgasm is mentioned. Also note that, by definition, masturbation refers only to self-stimulation. Your partner may play with your penis exactly the way you do yourself but by virtue of the fact that she and not you is doing it, it is not masturbation.

Although the overwhelming majority of men have masturbated at some time in their lives, it is something few feel good about. Even with the recent openness about sexuality and the greater tolerance for sexual expression, masturbation is the most difficult subject for people to discuss. In his study

Sexual Behavior in the 1970s, Morton Hunt sums it up this way:

> Most persons who masturbate remain more or less guilt-
> ridden about it, and nearly all of them are extremely
> secretive about their masturbating and would be horribly
> embarrassed to have anyone know the truth.

For most men it is easier to admit to lying, cheating, or even to
having sex problems than to acknowledge that they sometimes
play with their penises.

The younger generation is only slightly better off. A recent
nationwide study of teenagers by Robert Sorenson reported
that of the boys who masturbated only 17 per cent said they
'never' felt guilty, anxious, or concerned about it, while 45 per
cent 'often' or 'sometimes' did have such feelings about it.
Sorenson concluded:

> There seems to be no sex practice discussed in this study
> about which young people feel more defensive or private
> than masturbation . . . Self-esteem, embarrassment, and
> personal disgust seem to be the major inhibiting factors.

The amazing thing about these results is that all the youngsters
studied were brought up during the 'sexual revolution'; all
were born several years *after* Kinsey had clearly demonstrated the widespread prevalence of masturbation among
men and convincingly argued that it produced no ill effects
whatever.

There are many good reasons for our concern and anxiety
about masturbation. The practice has been condemned,
usually severely, throughout Western history, and not until
Kinsey did anyone of importance have anything good to say
about it. Jewish religious leaders considered it a grave sin since
it was a deliberate waste of sperm that should have been used
to add to the population. Christian authorities were no more
lenient, calling masturbation immoral and unnatural.

In the middle of the eighteenth century, scientists and physicians joined in the attack against what was variously called 'the solitary vice', 'self-abuse', and 'self-pollution'. Masturbation came to be viewed, with absolutely no evidence whatever, as the cause of everything evil. As Kinsey and his colleagues put it:

> Every conceivable ill from pimples to insanity, including stooped shoulders, loss of weight, fatigue, insomnia, general weakness . . . loss of manly vigor, weak eyes, digestive upsets, stomach ulcers, impotence, feeble-mindedness, genital cancer, and the rest, was ascribed to masturbation . . . Patients [in mental institutions] were observed to engage in frequent masturbation, and this seemed sufficient proof that the insanity was a product of the sexual behavior. Since the lives of university scholars were not so easily observed, it was not so generally known that masturbation occurred quite as frequently among them.

If you think that all this happened hundreds of years ago and has nothing to do with you, you may be interested in what follows, taken from a popular book called *What a Boy Should Know*, written by two physicians in 1909 and widely read for many years after.

> Whenever unnatural emissions are produced . . . the body becomes 'slack'. A boy will not feel so vigorous and springy; he will be more easily tired; he will not have so good 'an eye' for games. He will probably look pale and pasty, and he is lucky if he escapes indigestion and getting his bowels confined, both of which will probably give him spots and pimples on his face . . .
>
> The effect of self-abuse on a boy's character always tends to weaken it, and, in fact, to make him untrustworthy, unreliable, and probably even dishonest.

If you're not as 'springy' as you once were, or if you're looking 'pale and pasty', now you know why.

The *Boy Scout Manual*, probably read by millions of children and parents, until 1945 warned about the evils of masturbation, and as late as 1940 a candidate could be rejected at the United States Naval Academy if it were discovered that he masturbated.

Even if you were born after 1945, what do you think your parents had learned about masturbation? Is it any wonder that you got all sorts of messages that there was something terribly wrong about it?

When scientific authority first joined religious authority in attacking masturbation, punishment for offenders was relatively mild. The main objective was simply to stop the evil habit, often with the aid of patent medicines. But since education regarding the grave consequences of self-stimulation and patent medicines proved ineffective, punishment became harsher and harsher until, by the mid-nineteenth century, a persecution of sadistic proportions had been inaugurated.

Some of the more extreme remedies involved tying boys' hands to their bedposts or chaining them to walls when they slept; putting a wire ring through the foreskin of the penis or wearing a spiked ring on the penis, both procedures making erection and stimulation extremely painful; the wearing of straitjacketlike restraints to keep the hands away from forbidden territory; and, in a few cases, even castration and surgical removal of the penis. These bizarre and barbaric practices quickly peaked and declined, but vestiges remained until the Second World War.

The belief that masturbation caused gross mental and physical abnormalities such as epilepsy and insanity declined toward the end of the last century. But it was quickly replaced by a new set of beliefs that did little to ease the anxiety that most people had about masturbation. The conviction grew that masturbation was a common cause of neurotic disorders and marital sexual problems, a view shared by Freud. Thanks to

Freud and others however, a more liberal attitude toward self-stimulation in children arose; it was accepted as a normal, if somewhat repellent, childish habit. Provided, of course, that it was not done 'to excess'. Since 'excess' was never defined – was it once a day? a week? or year? or what? – no one could ever be sure he wasn't doing it too much.

And, the new views maintained, what was legitimate and normal for children was 'infantile' and 'immature' when done by adults. There must be something seriously wrong with someone past adolescence who resorted to self-stimulation rather than engaging in 'normal, healthy heterosexual relations'. Some defect of character was obviously indicated since masturbation was clearly a poor substitute for 'the real thing'. These views were hardly designed to set anyone's mind at ease. An adult who masturbated was compelled to think of himself as somehow neurotic or socially inept, unable to find a partner with whom he could have sex the way it was supposed to be done.

The something-must-be-wrong-with-you-if-you-masturbate school suffered its greatest setback by the work of Kinsey and his co-workers who, in their massive study of male sexuality, reported not only that 92 per cent of men had masturbated at some time in their lives, many of them while they were married, but that no detrimental effects whatsoever were to be found, regardless of masturbatory frequency. Kinsey went even further, claiming that the problem with masturbation lay not in the act itself but in the anxiety and guilt fostered by the traditional teachings.

> The record does include thousands of cases of boys living in continual conflict, oftentimes disturbed over the effect of such behavior [masturbation] on their ultimate sexual capacities, occasionally attempting suicide – as a result of the teachings concerning masturbation. For the boys who have not been too disturbed psychically, masturbation has, however, provided a regular sexual outlet which has alleviated nervous tensions; and the record is clear in

many cases that these boys have on the whole lived more balanced lives than the boys who have been more restrained in their sexual activities.

Kinsey's data and arguments definitely helped undermine the traditional views of masturbation and helped usher in a more tolerant attitude. Many men took some personal comfort from his statistics and some therapists and physicians reconsidered their views. Masturbation started gaining a small measure of respectability. ln 1968, Wardell Pomeroy, a former Kinsey associate and well-known sex expert, published *Boys and Sex*, in which he encouraged his readers to masturbate as much as they wanted. The book was highly regarded by professionals and undoubtedly had some influence. And in the 1970s best-sellers like *The Sensuous Woman* and *The Sensuous Man* sang the praises of self-stimulation.

While masturbation clearly has come out of the closet, it would be a mistake to assume that it is therefore widely accepted. The newer views still represent a minority opinion. Kinsey's work is less than thirty years old, while the myths and misinformation attached to masturbation have been around for almost two thousand years. Things may be better, but how much?

Not a great deal. Masters and Johnson report that the men they studied held fairly traditional views regarding masturbation, all of them believing that 'excessive' self-stimulation might lead to physical or mental abnormality, although none of them could explain how frequently 'excessive' was. We have already noted the findings of a study of teenagers that demonstrated the defensiveness and concern they felt about masturbating. One particularly interesting aspect of that study is that none of the subjects believed the old stories about the emotional and physical damage that was allegedly caused by masturbation, yet they were still concerned about the practice. They felt badly about it even though they knew that it could lead to no harm. How could this be so?

It is well to remember that many authorities have not accepted the newer views of masturbation. Many, if not most, physicians, therapists, religious leaders, educators, and parents still believe, and convey to the people they deal with, that there is something wrong with playing with yourself, although they are no longer able to say just *what* is wrong with it. Then, too, there are still many who believe that masturbation is sinful. A recently issued proclamation on sexual matters by the Vatican repeats the old, familiar line: masturbation is 'an intrinsically and seriously disordered act'.

What is certainly a source of great confusion to many people is that many authorities speak and write with a forked tongue, taking on the one hand a very liberal attitude regarding masturbation (it's normal and healthy) while at the same time conveying the impression that at best it's a necessary evil and there is really something strange about anyone who is doing it.

David Reuben provides a fine example of this procedure. Here are some quotations from his *Everything You Always Wanted to Know about Sex*, a book that sold millions of copies:

> The only thing harmful about masturbation is the guilt that is drummed into children who admit masturbating. [This is the tolerant stance: masturbation is fine. Now watch how he undermines it.]
>
> . . . masturbation is fun. *Certainly not as much fun as full-fledged sexual intercourse*, but the next thing to it. That is exactly what masturbation is, *a substitute form of gratification when sexual intercourse is impossible*.
>
> [In answer to a question regarding when masturbation is desirable, he mentions it is fine for those too young for partner sex and that it may be helpful for nonorgasmic women. He is then asked if there are other situations where self-stimulation is desirable.] *In those who cannot obtain sexual satisfaction in any other way*. Men and women in prison, very old people, and often the blind are restricted in their sexual outlets.

What the good doctor – along with so many others who talk and write about sex – is saying is that masturbation is fine . . . for children, the aged, the infirm, and the incarcerated. Anyone else doing it just doesn't have what it takes to have the real thing – 'heterosexual intercourse' – and is therefore forced to settle for this poor substitute. This is simply a continuation of the view espoused since the beginning of this century that self-stimulation in adults is immature and indicates some deficiency.

Men's attitudes about their own masturbatory activities strongly reflect the unhappy legacy we have been discussing. It is usually experienced as a necessary evil, useful for relieving sexual tension. Very few feel good about masturbating and even fewer talk about it. Even men who brag about all their other sexual activities never seem to say anything, boastful or otherwise, about their autoerotic practices.

When I started masturbating at the age of thirteen, there was a kind of openness about it with my boyfriends. We sometimes masturbated together in what I later learned were called 'circle jerks', with the one who came first or shot the farthest being acclaimed hero of the day. And we often joked about it. But as we turned our attention to girls, the jokes and circle jerks ceased. I continued masturbating fairly regularly even when involved in a sexual relationship but never talked about it to anyone. I was always concerned that one of my partners would find out about it and sometimes had to invent strange excuses for what I was doing in there, the bathroom. One time, a woman I was living with walked in on me unexpectedly and there I was with my hand on my erect penis. I turned twelve different shades of purple and hastily concocted the weirdest story about having a sore spot on my penis which I was trying to examine. I don't know why I was so ashamed of playing with myself but I clearly felt that it was wrong and disgraceful. I was shocked when she said that it was OK with her if I was masturbating and she would like to watch. I immediately lost my erection and sexual desire. But we talked about it and that broke the ice for me. I lost most of my negative feelings about masturbation and have since been open about it with my partners. I'm certainly happy that she walked in on me.

Shame is the feeling that most often accompanies masturbation in adult men, shame that they should have to resort to this 'childish' substitute. If they really had it together, they think, they would be doing something sexual with a partner. The very fact of playing with oneself conveys a sense that, at least on this one occasion, they weren't good enough or clever enough or masculine enough to get a partner with whom they could have 'real sex'.

Because of these feelings, and also because men have had little permission and practice in being sensual, many men do not derive as much pleasure as they could from masturbating. It is usually done very quickly, the whole object being to achieve orgasm and get it over with. Masturbating this way presents some problems. It develops a habit of coming quickly, which may carry over to sex with a partner. And it also reinforces our tendency to ignore bodily sensations more subtle than orgasm and reinforces our inability to linger over and prolong pleasure.

If men have such negative feelings about self-stimulation, and if it's not as enjoyable for them as it might be, why then do they continue to do it? Basically because it feels good. Even when done hurriedly and without much concentration on the sensations prior to orgasm, it still feels good.

There are also other reasons. Masturbation can be a source of comfort. Hunt reported that a number of his respondents said the urge to masturbate was often aroused by feelings of loneliness. The fantasies that so often accompany masturbation in men are another important motivating factor. The fantasies are not only fun but, as Hunt points out, they 'can partially satisfy the psychological need for variety; it enables people to do, in fantasy, sexual things they do not ordinarily have the chance to do, or with partners they have no access to.'

But you don't really need a reason for masturbating other than the fact that you want to do it. Sometimes you may be feeling sexy and also want to be alone (yes, *want* to be alone, not *have* to be alone). You may not want to deal with another person at the time, and there's no reason why you should have to. After all, dealing with a partner requires energy and consideration, and it is ludicrous to assume that you are going to want to expend such energy and give such consideration every time you feel sexy. Sometimes you just don't want to be concerned with someone else's needs and desires. And must you be? You can decide to have a fine time with yourself – not as a substitute or replacement for something better, but just because that's what you want. Sometimes masturbation simply fits your needs and desires better than anything else.

Now that we've said you need no reasons for masturbating we'd like to turn around and give you some reasons. Masturbation, done systematically and in accordance with a few simple rules, has definite therapeutic benefits. You can use it to learn more about your body and its requirements, and to acquire skills useful in sex with a partner. We have found masturbation exercises very helpful in developing ejaculatory control and in dealing with erection problems. And you can learn a lot about yourself with these exercises even if you do not have a specific problem and are primarily interested in enhancing your sex life.

You may be wondering why masturbation exercises are so helpful or why they should be done in preference to partner exercises. While we have nothing against partner exercises and include many later in the book, masturbation exercises have a particular advantage. Namely, that it is easier to experiment with new things when you don't have to concern yourself with how someone else is feeling about what you're doing. In the long run, of course, you are probably going to want to use your new skills and understanding with a partner, but it is much easier to develop the skills without her distracting influence. Focusing, for example, is difficult for many men to learn with their partners present. Once they get the hang of it on their own, it is then much easier to transfer the skills to situations that involve their partners.

Of course, we can't guarantee that you'll feel good about masturbating. The negative ideas about masturbation that we discussed earlier are still very influential for many of us, since they were pounded into us, sometimes literally, as children and adults. You may find yourself feeling somewhat uneasy as you do, or even consider doing, masturbation exercises. You may feel guilty about doing something which you were told was sinful; ashamed that you are playing with yourself rather than getting it on with a partner as a 'real man' should; or worried about what your partner or potential partners would think if they knew what you were doing. Or there may just be a vague kind of discomfort which has no particular content other than that you are doing something which isn't nice.

Unless your negative feelings about self-stimulation are tremendously strong, we suggest you try it. While it is asking a bit too much to expect your negative feelings about masturbation to disappear altogether, many men have found that doing it regularly under therapeutic advice in itself eased their discomfort. Another way of feeling better about self-stimulation is to talk about it to a partner or friend. We realize that not everyone will want to do this, but those who have done it invariably reported that it made them feel much more comfortable.

Before getting on to the concept of focusing and our basic masturbation exercise, we need to talk about how you masturbate. Most men masturbate by stroking up and down the shaft and head of the penis with one hand, although there is much variation with regard to how much of the shaft and head is included in the stroking, how firmly the penis is held, and the rapidity of the movements. We call this method of stroking the penis with one hand the usual way of masturbating.

Some men masturbate in other ways; for example, by

squeezing the penis rather than stroking it, by rubbing it between both hands, or while lying face down and rubbing the penis against the bed or floor. These ways, if practiced exclusively, can lead to problems.

Larry, a man in his late twenties who had problems maintaining erections and ejaculating with a partner, had always masturbated by rubbing his whole body vigorously against his bed. He had never stroked his penis. The types of stimulation he got with partners were so different from what he did by himself that he did not experience them as arousing and often lost his erection or failed to ejaculate.

We certainly don't want to create any problems where none existed previously, so if you masturbate in some of the atypical ways but don't think they are causing you any difficulties, all well and good; stick with what you do. But if you are experiencing some problems with partners, we encourage you to expand your options by masturbating in what we are calling the usual way. How much pressure to use can only be determined by experience. The only thing to be concerned about is if you are squeezing your penis to a pulp; that's probably too much pressure. By asking you to try the stroking method we are not saying you should give up your old ways entirely. We are suggesting you expand possibilities, not limit them. Use the new method in doing the exercise and use your way at other times.

FOCUSING

In the exercise that follows and in others throughout the book, you are going to be asked to focus on your bodily sensations. Since most men have been trained not to pay attention to such things, it may not be easy at first. But it is well worth doing. Focusing has the effect of amplifying sensations, making their impact more powerful. It is also useful in determining the kinds of stimulation you best like. Focusing will assist you in discovering preferences that may not be obvious to you now.

Focusing basically means paying attention. It is a relatively passive attending to what is happening in a particular part of your body. You have already done some focusing in Exercise 9–1 when you attended to the tensest parts and your breathing. That is all that focusing is. It is more passive and gentle than the mode we men are more accustomed to, wherein we grit our teeth and forcefully concentrate on something. No forcing, no gritting of teeth, no pushing and shoving.

Men often get frustrated when their minds wander during focusing. There is no way of preventing your attention from skipping around. If you've ever meditated, you know this. The mind is like a drunken monkey, always jumping from one thing to another. You can't control this activity and, fortunately, you don't have to. When you do an exercise that asks you to focus, start by putting your attention to the part of the body that is prescribed. When you are aware that your mind has drifted off, simply bring your attention back to the part you want to focus on. Try to avoid getting into an argument with yourself and fighting the distracting thoughts.

Focusing is an intuitive process, not an intellectual one. You need to attend to sensations but there is no need to label, analyze, or think about them. You may find yourself engaging in some intellectual activities – 'What should I call this feeling?' 'Why do I feel more here than there?' Simply recognize that these are distractions and return your attention to the sensations.

A common problem with focusing concerns the expectations you have about what you 'should' be feeling. Many men expect bells-ringing-and-bombs-bursting sensations and, when these are not forthcoming, think that there is nothing worth attending to. The sensations you do feel are unlikely to be earthshaking, sensational, or anything of the sort. They are just, well, sensations. They may seem trivial. Sometimes they may even feel uncomfortable or negative.

Whatever is there is there, and that's what you should focus on. As your ability to focus improves, you may be surprised how interesting these little sensations become.

The following suggestions apply to Exercise 10–1 and all subsequent masturbation and partner exercises.

1. Make sure you have at least ten minutes more than the time specified in the exercise. All of it should be private, uninterrupted time. The extra minutes can be used to relax, to get into a sexual mood, and to prevent any rushing or pressure. Since the importance of having plenty of time and not being rushed cannot be overemphasized, do whatever you need to ensure that you will not be interrupted or distracted.

2. Set the scene the way you like it. The time you take to do the exercises is your gift to yourself; make it as enjoyable as possible. Make the room light or dark, as you prefer, and make any other arrangements you want, such as candles or incense. Some men prefer music, which is fine so long as it is not so powerful that it interferes with your focusing. Some men have found that the best gift they can give themselves is to put a lock on the bedroom door.

3. Make sure your conditions are met. This is much easier in masturbation than in partner sex since you don't have to concern yourself about a partner, but check your emotional and physical states to determine if things are the way they should be to maximize the chances of an enjoyable experience.

4. You should be fairly relaxed before starting an exercise. Use what you learned in the last chapter to help you get there. Some days it's difficult to get relaxed no matter what you do. At such times, it's probably best not to do sexual exercises. Wait until you are more comfortable. It will do you no good to do the assignments when you are tense.

5. It can be helpful to get into a sexual frame of mind before beginning an exercise. Erection is not important but feeling sexy is. You might want to recall a good sexual experience, construct a fantasy, or look at some arousing pictures or

literature. Do whatever you want to help yourself become
aroused.

6. In the masturbation exercises, do not immediately go for
your penis. Spend a few minutes touching and stroking other
parts of your body that are enjoyable to touch.

EXERCISE 10–1: MASTURBATION WITH FOCUSING
Time Required: 15 minutes

**The goals of this exercise are to practice focusing on the
sensations in your penis as you play with it and to discover
what types of stroking feel best. Neither erection nor
orgasm is necessary.**

**After you are feeling aroused, start stroking your penis
slowly and gently, putting your attention in your penis so
that you are aware of the sensations produced by the
touching. Unless you have problems lasting as long as you
like, use a lubricant (see the note on lubricants at the end
of this chapter). If you do not have good ejaculatory
control, do not use lubrication at this time.**

**Regardless of how soft or hard your penis is, there are
sensations in it of which you can be aware. Your penis is
richly supplied with nerve endings that produce sensation
whenever they are stimulated. The sensations may differ
depending on how excited you are, how hard or soft your
penis is, and what kinds of touching you are doing. It's up
to you to discover what these sensations are.**

**Take your time. This is not a test of speed. There is
nothing to accomplish and nothing to finish. Just play and
enjoy. Keep focusing and experiment with different
strokes (for example, stroking the length of the entire
shaft and head, just the shaft, just the head, circular
motions), different pressures and different speeds (but not
too fast). See what you like and go with it.**

**Continue playing with your penis in this manner for 15
minutes. If you find yourself close to orgasm before time is
up, stop masturbating and wait a minute or two until the**

urge to ejaculate subsides, then resume stroking. If this does not help, read Chapter 15 now and then return to this exercise. If you want to come after 15 minutes, do so, but keep going slowly and keep focusing. Remember, there's no need to climax; do so only if you want to.

This exercise should be done at least five times. Before going on to the masturbation exercises in Chapter 15 or 18, you should feel comfortable focusing on the physical sensations and able to return your attention to them when you find your mind has wandered.

POSSIBLE PROBLEMS

1. You don't feel any sensations in your penis, or you do but they don't seem very interesting. If you do not experience any sensations, it either means that you are not focusing properly or that there has been severe nerve damage. Since the latter is so rare and so devastating in its implications, we suggest you reread the section on focusing and try again. If the sensations seem dull and uninspiring, that's probably because you were expecting something of a cosmic nature. See if you can just attend to what is there and worry less about whether it feels as oceanic as you thought it would.

2. Your mind keeps wandering. Of course it does. That's what minds do. This is not a problem. Just keep bringing your attention back to the sensation in your penis.

3. You have difficulty with the exercise because you are tense or in a hurry. It is very important that you only do the exercise when you have sufficient uninterrupted time. Don't be like the man who always started to do it 15 minutes before a friend came to pick him up to go to work. Of course he couldn't relax; he kept wondering when his friend was going to knock on the door. Make sure you are comfortably relaxed before starting.

Some men discover new and interesting sensations in their genitals the first few times they do this exercise. For most, however, it takes longer. Whether it happens quickly or not, we hope you'll continue with the exercise. There are sensations in your body when it is being touched, and they are a large part of the raw material from which a state of arousal is built. Focusing helps enhance their power and enables you to feel more pleasure from what is happening to your body.

You may find that this exercise helps you discover some new places and new ways of touching that feel good. There is probably more feeling in your penis than you knew. We hope you will enjoy pleasuring yourself in these new ways and that you'll soon share your discoveries with your partner. We imagine she'd be happy to learn how to give you the most pleasure.

A NOTE ON LUBRICATION

Most men find that using a lubricant on their hand when they masturbate reduces irritating friction and enhances their pleasure. Since lubrication amplifies the sensations in the penis, it also makes focusing easier.

It is difficult to recommend lubricants since preferences vary considerably from person to person. Some men prefer petroleum jelly (Vaseline) since it is not quickly absorbed by the skin and need not be replenished during one masturbation session. But others find it 'greasy and gunky'. It usually needs to be washed off with soap and water. Hand or body lotion (such as Intensive Care or Jergens Lotion) is favored by others. Since lotion is absorbed rather quickly, however, you may need to squirt it on several times in a session. Massage oil, KY jelly, and Albolene also have large numbers of supporters.

Perhaps the best thing to do is start with whatever lubricant is available in your home. If it doesn't please you, try something else. Lubricants, like so much else in sex, are largely a matter of individual taste. There is at least one with the consistency, absorbability, and odor that will satisfy you.

ELEVEN

Virginity and sexual abstinence

Because of the influence of the fantasy model of sex, discussions of virginity and celibacy are rare. It is widely assumed that all men have had sex and want to keep on getting as much as they can. Like almost everything else in the fantasy model, these assumptions are erroneous.

VIRGINITY

It seems that there are many more male virgins than is generally believed, and that they cover a fairly broad age range. A survey of college students commissioned by *Playboy* found that 26 per cent of the men had not had sex with a partner. Covering a much broader age range, a *Psychology Today* survey reported that 22 per cent of the male respondents were virgins. Since it is difficult for a man over the age of eighteen to admit to being a virgin, it is likely that these figures are lower than they should be. We have talked to many men in their thirties and forties, and even to a few in their fifties, who have never had sex. It appears, then, that male virginity is real and widespread.

We all start out as sexual virgins but this status isn't considered a problem until either we start feeling pressure from others to have sex or we want to have it but our attempts are unsuccessful.

There is tremendous pressure on men to be sexual. Virginity is seen as an unnecessary evil, to be eliminated as early as possible. There is little compassion or understanding for those

who haven't had sex or who don't want it. Here is what
Playboy had to say about the subject in an unsigned article
reporting the results of the college survey we cited earlier: 'It is
actually possible to go through four years of higher education
without getting laid, though why you'd want to is beyond us.
Fortunately, the odds are against it.' The pressure comes not
only from sources like *Playboy*, where you would expect it, but
from places closer to home as well. Here is what a nineteen-
year-old college student told us:

> I'm starting to doubt myself because I haven't had sex.
> The thing is that I like girls and I spend time with them.
> But I'm really involved with my studies and playing ball,
> and I don't want to take the time to have a big-time
> relationship. Just picking up some chick to have sex with
> doesn't do it for me. I'm fairly content doing my thing and
> not having sex. But everybody seems to think I'm strange,
> and now I'm starting to wonder. The girls I know don't
> seem to understand where I'm at, and several have asked
> if I like guys more than girls. Of course I like guys, but I
> don't want to screw them. Some of my male friends know
> I'm a virgin. They keep trying to help me get laid, coming
> up with suggestions all the time. They don't understand
> when I say that I'm OK where I am. And even my father
> is on this trip. He never says anything directly, but
> whenever we talk he throws in little jokes or quips about
> it being good for a guy to have fun and sow his oats.
> I think he'd be prouder than hell if I told him I fucked
> some girl.

Other young men we talked to have reported similar stories.
These men are not interested in partner sex or don't feel ready
for it, but the questions and concerns of their friends and
relatives affect them and they begin to doubt their position. It's
hard to feel good about yourself when society at large and
those closest to you view your state as a vile affliction in need
of immediate cure.

If you were surprised by our citing pressure from parents as a factor contributing to the uneasiness of virgins, we should say that we were also surprised. While we have no way of knowing how widespread such pressure is, it is clear in some cases that parents, especially fathers, try very hard to get their sons interested in sex. We have never been able to interview any of these fathers, but from what we have pieced together from the stories their sons told it seems that they view sexual activity as an index of the normality of their boys. Sex with a woman, they seem to think, is a sign that the boy is a real man, or that he isn't homosexual, or an assurance that he won't get overly involved in drugs or alcohol. Such fathers don't understand that sexual activity in itself isn't proof of anything and that pressuring a boy to have sex before he is ready can only result in increased strain in the family and perhaps some serious problems for the boy.

Our views on virginity stem from our beliefs that the importance of sex has been greatly exaggerated in recent times and that people should be allowed to blossom sexually in their own good time. We believe that pressure to have sex is almost always destructive. It pushes people into situations they may not be ready to deal with and, more importantly, deflects them from following their own intuition and good sense.

Having sex is certainly not necessary for a good life, and the idea that one should have had sex by a certain age is ridiculous. We know we are swimming against the societal current, but we want to lend whatever support we can to those boys and men who are reasonably content with their virgin status and want to remain there, either for a while or permanently.

If you fit in this category, you already know it's not easy and we would be doing you a disservice if we told you otherwise. Virginity in males over the age of nineteen is now the exception rather than the norm. Virginity in those over twenty-three or twenty-five is considered by many to be odd and ungentlemanly. Almost any position that is statistically unusual is difficult to maintain because people tend to dislike and ridicule what is different. Others may wonder about you and perhaps make fun of you, and some will do all they can to change your status because, for reasons unclear even to them, your virginity bothers them.

Despite this, we hope you can maintain your integrity and wait until you feel the time is right. If being in love or being married are what you want before having sex, we support your waiting until your conditions are fulfilled. If you think that partner sex just isn't for you, we hope you can feel good about that position. You may want to rely on masturbation for sexual pleasure, or you may not, but your attitude is not an unreasonable or unhealthy one, despite the attempts of *Playboy* and others to convince you of the opposite.

Virginity can also be a problem when it is unwanted by the man himself. Many virgins find themselves in this position. They want to have sex but nothing seems to work.

There are many reasons why a man who wants sex doesn't get it. Several of the longtime virgins we talked with had more of a social than a sexual problem. They were quite shy, fearful of asking a woman out and of making a physical advance. For some of these men, it seemed that if they could somehow get together with a woman and get past the first kiss, they might not have too much trouble. But there's little hope for sex when they can barely talk to a woman.

Many men, virgins and nonvirgins alike, have not developed good social skills. The problem has been largely unrecognized until recently, for it was widely assumed that almost all men knew how to meet women and initiate relationships. A few institutions, such as the Human Sexuality Program, University of California, San Francisco, now offer social skills groups and workshops. Some assertiveness training courses also deal with the development of social skills. Although we know of only two books on the subject, both are good: Eileen Gambrill and Cheryl Richey's *It's Up To You*, and Phillip Zimbardo's *Shyness*.

A large obstacle for many virgins is their fear of what sex might lead to. Although we have no way of knowing if the male virgins we saw in therapy are representative of all males who have trouble losing their virginity, we were very impressed by their fear of involvement with women. It's as if they believed that having sex would lead to entrapment by the woman. They would have to stay with her, marry her, and do her bidding until the end of time. They would lose all rights, autonomy, and personal space. Since they deeply believe that sex would lead to such dire consequences, it's no wonder they have so much trouble getting into it.

While many therapists would undoubtedly argue that the only solution for such fears would be prolonged psycho-therapy, we believe differently. Twenty-one of the twenty-five virgins we worked with got involved in sex after only relatively brief courses of therapy, even though most of them had been trying unsuccessfully for over five years. It wasn't easy for any of them, but those who got what they wanted agreed it was worth the effort.

Another obstacle for many virgins is the heavy performance pressure they put on themselves. Some have tried to have sex a number of times, but the demands to perform have been so great that they caused erection failure every time. Trying again doesn't help because nothing is done to decrease the pressure. Such men should read the chapters on erection problems and scrupulously follow the suggestions in Chapter 12 for sex with a new partner.

Another issue facing those who want to lose their virginity is their feeling of almost hopeless backwardness. They believe their peers are experienced and that women expect a man to know what he's doing. Often these beliefs and expectations are realistic. A man without sexual experience with partners is by virtue of that fact a beginner and has some things to learn.

But there is also another side, one that may give you some cause for optimism. Most women are not as concerned with experience and performance as men think they are. Although it is true that women tend to expect a man in his late twenties or older to be sexually experienced, many are not offended or put off when they find out otherwise. The women we talked to who initiated a man in the ways of sex quite enjoyed the experience. As one of them said:

> To tell the truth, I was shocked when he told me he never had intercourse before. I didn't think a man could reach the age of thirty-three without having sex. But the shock quickly died down and I thought, why not? I had the time of my life. It was fantastic being the teacher and breaking him in. He was so appreciative and I got everything I wanted.

Some men who have had difficulty losing their virginity decide that going to a prostitute would help. While there are no statistics that bear on the success of such attempts, they are not without danger. Prostitutes with hearts of gold are far more common in literature than in reality and we have talked with several men who, after they failed with a prostitute, felt worse than ever about themselves and couldn't bring themselves to attempt sex again for months or years.

A good way of dealing with involuntary virginity is brief treatment with a therapist experienced in working with men on sexual issues (of whom there are very few). Another way is using this book. Much of the material and many of the exercises are the same as those we use in our therapy work with virgins.

If you have not yet had sex with a partner but think you want to, you should ask yourself why you want to change. What would sex add to your life? Then ask yourself what obstacles are in the way of having sex and what prices you would have to pay to overcome them. You can be certain that there are obstacles and prices. You can probably count on being rejected, embarrassed, afraid, and awkward. There may be other costs that only you can determine. When you have listed the prices, try to see or feel yourself paying them. Imagine yourself being rejected, fumbling with the woman because of your lack of experience, facing the fears of involvement or not doing well at sex, or any other costs you came up with. Now that you have faced the worst, ask yourself if you're willing to pay the fare.

If you can answer yes, you are ready to go on, reading the sections and doing the exercises that seem appropriate. If you're not sure, you can proceed anyway and, as you get further into things, perhaps you'll be clearer about your answer. If it's not worth the price, maybe you can stop pushing yourself to have sex and start concentrating on what is important to you. As we said earlier, there is no dishonor in not being sexual.

So, if you want to leave your virginity behind you, there is hope. You may have to confront some of your worst fears, and you may want to get some professional help with this, but there's a good chance that you can get into sex in a way that will be right for you. Make sure that your conditions are met and that you follow the suggestions in Chapter 12 for sex with a new partner. We hope you enjoy the experience. Whatever does or doesn't happen, whether or not it goes the way you think it should, it can be fun. And if it doesn't go precisely the way you hoped, there will be many other opportunities.

ABSTINENCE

We use abstinence and celibacy to mean a voluntary and temporary withdrawal from sexual activity with partners. Since it is generally thought that men always want sex, abstinence is not something one is likely to hear men talk about, at least not favorably. We include this brief discussion because we have talked to a number of men who were considering abstinence but were concerned over what it implied about them as men. We have also talked to a much smaller group of men who have practiced celibacy for varying periods of time with gratifying results.

There are any number of reasons why a man might choose to refrain from sexual activity for relatively long periods of time. Preoccupation with extended projects is one. You might be so involved with an activity – writing a book or musical score, studying for an important exam, spiritual concerns, etc. – that is so demanding and satisfying that there is little time for, and interest in, sex.

Another reason is that, while there may not be an obvious preoccupation with other matters, there is simply little sexual interest or energy. Many men try to ignore their lack of interest or, worse, get concerned about it and try to prove it groundless by engaging in lots of sex. We men simply haven't had much permission to be uninterested and uninvolved in sex. But such times occur for many of us, sometimes lasting for months or longer. While the reasons for the disinterest may not be clear, there is certainly nothing abnormal about it. Probably the best thing to do is honor your feelings and get on with the rest of your life.

Deep depression is one of the more obvious factors that can lead to a loss of sexual interest. The loss of a loved one or a serious setback in one's education or job can result in sexual apathy for some time. Some men get concerned about this and try to have sex anyway, often with negative results. It's best to wait until time heals the wounds and the interest reappears.

Even in the presence of sexual desire, there are times when abstinence can be beneficial. This is true when sex would get in the way of important processes and decisions. A not uncommon example of this occurs when a man decides it's time to rethink his romantic involvements. He has not been satisfied with them, perhaps feeling as one man did that 'It's like I've had the same lousy relationship with eight different women.' He doesn't want to spend the rest of his life in similar involvements. He needs time away from relationships to sort out his feelings, to determine why he continues in the same negative paths and how he can get more of what he wants.

Sexual involvement may not only impede his learning but it may also lure him back into what he is trying to escape. It might be best for him to avoid sexual activity until he is clearer about what he is looking for and how he can get it.

Abstinence can be useful in many situations where a man

wants to get to know himself better and come to some new understanding about where he is going. It can be a time of learning and growing, and it need not be as horrendously difficult as many men might think.

One of us went through a period of eight months of celibacy a few years ago and found the experience relatively painless and also quite gratifying.

It was generally a good time for me. I spent lots of time by myself, part of which was devoted to thinking about past relationships. I also spent time with friends, enjoying their company and sharing many of my feelings with them.

The people who knew I wasn't having sex acted a bit strangely, continuously asking how I could do it. It was as if they thought I were performing some miraculous feat. Men were much more surprised than women. Actually, it wasn't very difficult. At times I was lonely, but it wasn't as difficult as I had anticipated. Sometimes I was aware of missing something, but it usually wasn't sex. What I missed most was sleeping next to someone and the cuddling and playing around in bed. I got lots of hugs from my friends, but nothing could replace the warm sense of snuggling with a lover in bed. And that was really the worst of it.

Often I felt intense relief when alone. I didn't have to concern myself with anyone else's needs or feelings. Many times it felt very good to know that I didn't have to share my bed with someone. It was my bed and I could take it all up and do anything I wanted to there.

To say I learned a lot is a cliché but nonetheless true. I learned about myself and relationships and, surprisingly, about myself and sex. I realized for the first time how often I had not gotten what I wanted in sex because I had been so busy trying to be nice and considerate. And I saw how the resentment I had accumulated during such occasions spilled over into other parts of my relationships. Another important thing I learned was that my need for solitude was much greater than I had ever imagined. I enjoyed my own company and needed some quiet time each day to be with me. This turned out to be quite useful in later relationships: I could get more of my alone time when I wanted it, thus making it easier for me to really be with my partner when I was with her.

Some of the men who've practiced abstinence have reported similar stories, but for others the experience was somewhat different. None of the ones we've talked to regretted their experience; in fact, all thought it quite worthwhile.

We are not trying to sell celibacy any more than we are trying to sell sex. But we do offer our support to those who think that a period of abstinence would be useful. It can be an important experience. Certain problems are encountered by those who undertake such a project, and we want to mention them. A consuming sexual hunger, surprisingly, is not usually one of them, especially since abstinence need not rule out masturbation.

One problem is that of loneliness. Since abstinence rules out what is usually called a romantic or primary relationship, you are not going to get many of the things that occur in such relationships. You may have to manage with much less physical affection, companionship, and the special kinds of communication and closeness that you are accustomed to. Your closest friends may be able to make up for some of it, but not all. You will be deprived of some of your pleasures and you will feel lonely at times.

Another problem is the meaning that you and those close to you put on your behavior. You may find yourself wondering if there is something wrong with you, especially when you realize that staying away from sex isn't terribly difficult. And, as the example given above indicates, your friends may wonder along with you. Sex has been so oversold that many people can't even conceive of not having it regularly. So you'll probably have to put up with some questions and astonishment.

A last issue concerns what happens when you decide to become sexually involved again. Some men, but not all, reported that getting back into sex after a long period of abstinence was a bit awkward. This is hardly an insurmountable obstacle but there can be feelings of strangeness and embarrassment. Following our suggestions in the next chapter for sex with a new partner can alleviate whatever slight difficulties there are in this area.

If you're willing to handle these issues and if a period of celibacy seems like it might be right for you, why not? And don't worry. No matter how long you stay in that state, you won't forget how to 'do it'.

TWELVE

Dealing with a partner

Relationships come in an almost infinite variety and there are countless ways of expressing and dealing with relationship issues. Our focus here is relatively narrow. We restrict ourselves to those issues and problems that play a significant role in the development and maintenance of a satisfactory sexual relationship.

Although the chapter is divided into sections, we see it as a unit and believe you will profit from reading all of it, even those sections in which you have only minimal interest.

The ideas and suggestions presented here are effective but they have limitations. They work best in a caring and supportive atmosphere, or at least one that is not overflowing with hostility. If the relationship is in serious trouble – if bitterness and anger are the norm or if the partners can barely be civil to one another – the relationship, not sex, is what needs attention. While good sex is sometimes possible in bad relationships, the combination is much rarer than most of us believe. This chapter is no substitute for the competent professional help that is usually required to resolve the problems in seriously disturbed relationships.

TALKING ABOUT SEX

Talking to a partner about sex is one of the most difficult things to do. Even though there have been many changes in sexual attitudes and behavior in the last few decades, it probably isn't much easier to talk about sex now than it was twenty years ago. We have heard from people with broad sexual experience, some of whom considered themselves swingers and had had sex in every conceivable way with almost everyone in town, but it was evident that they had problems discussing their sexual thoughts, feelings, and behavior with their partners. We have also talked to many young men and women who were brought up during the sexual revolution. While most of them started their sexual careers at a much earlier age than their parents and are much freer in their thoughts and activities, they aren't much more comfortable discussing sex with their partners. Doing it is obviously much easier than talking about it.

A few years ago we heard the following on a radio program devoted to the new sexuality. The speaker recounted an interview he had done with a young man about a recent sexual experience.

INTERVIEWER: Did you know the woman well?

MAN: No, I met her that night.

I: How was the experience?

M: Fine.

I: Did you have an orgasm?

M: Yeh.

I: Did she have one?

M: Gee, I'm not sure . . . I guess so.

I: But you're not sure. Is there a way you could have found out?

M: Hmmm . . . I don't know.

I: You could have asked her, couldn't you?

M: Asked her? I hardly knew her name!

There is no doubt that the inability to talk about sex is one of the main reasons why sex is not as good as it could be. In earlier chapters, we asked you to talk about sex or at least consider doing so, and much of the rest of the book is also about talking about sex. Since we consider sexual communication so important, we want to say some general things about the subject here and also to deal with some of the objections that men have raised about it.

In saying that talking is important, we do not mean that sex should be primarily a cerebral affair, with long analytical discussions before and after every experience. There are many times when talking is unnecessary or distracting. Talking about sex is a useful option you should cultivate if you want to enhance your sexuality, an option to be used when appropriate.

When is talking appropriate? It's difficult to give general rules but we offer some examples. If you're with a new partner, it's relevant to do something about contraception. How can this be done without words? Another example is when your partner initiates sex and you aren't in the mood. How can you let her know your feelings? Suppose you like a particular type of stimulation or activity and your nonverbal attempts to indicate this to your partner have failed. How can you let her know what you like? Perhaps your partner did or said something that annoyed or angered you. How can you deal with this situation without talking?

Given, then, that there may be some good reasons for talking about sex, let's look at some of the common objections men raise.

One is simply that they would rather communicate nonverbally. In response to this, we say that nonverbal communication is one level of communication and an important one. Not everything has to be spoken; many times it is relevant and effective to indicate your desires or feelings without using words. As a supplement to verbal communication, acts and gestures are fine. As a substitute, they don't quite make it. The man who has sex with his partner every day is shocked when she complains that he never tells her he loves her. Isn't his lovemaking a way of saying that he loves her? It may be, but only on one level, and she also wants to hear it at the verbal level.

Nonverbal communication is important. Use it where it works. And recognize its limitations.

A second objection to talking about sex is that it interferes with spontaneity. A view of spontaneity as something that precludes the use of words strikes us as unnecessarily restrictive and quite unreasonable. Words can be as spontaneous as actions and, besides, where is it written that sex should be spontaneous?

The issue of spontaneity and exclusive preferences for nonverbal communication are in most cases merely screens for the fact that people have great difficulty talking about sex. Rather than admitting the difficulty, they find reasons why talking is unnecessary or a hindrance. This would be fine if they could have the kind of sex they want without using words. The problem is that they usually can't.

We begin with the premise that talking about sex is quite difficult. Rather than trying to sidestep the issue, we prefer to bring it out in the open and then find ways of dealing with it.

One of the reasons why sex talk is so difficult is that there are very few good models. Neither the kinds of sources we examined in Chapters 3 and 4 nor more academic treatments of sex demonstrate much in the way of how human beings can discuss sex. This glaring omission reinforces a myth we all learned – even if you have sex, it's not nice to talk about it. Given this lack of permission to talk and the lack of models for how to do it, it's not surprising that most of us are not very good at it.

Another reason for difficulty in talking is that it can produce a powerful kind of intimacy. Verbally expressing your joy, anxiety, preferences, dislikes, and other feelings is a way of sharing yourself. This holds great promise but also great threat, since we are all at least somewhat ambivalent about the prospect of closeness. How much easier to let two more or less disconnected bodies go through the mechanics of what we call making love.

Man is the only animal that communicates with words. This does not mean that all talk is noble, meaningful, or even interesting. But in certain situations, like sex, talking can open the doors to real sharing between people.

Talk is also threatening in other ways. If you clearly say what you like and want, you are displaying yourself in a very personal way and exposing your vulnerability, since your partner may reject your requests or disagree with your opinions. It's then difficult to say that you didn't really mean what you said; such tactics work much better with nonverbal communications, most of which are subject to many interpretations and therefore are easier to explain away if you run into resistance.

Being clear verbally also seems selfish to many people. It's considered fine to be suggestive, for example, loudly complaining about how much your back hurts in the hope that your partner will offer to give you a massage, or rolling around in a way that your penis innocently ends up close to your partner's mouth. But to come right out and ask her to rub your back or suck your penis, well, that's something else. We can only repeat what we said about selfishness in Chapter 6: it's not such a bad habit. As long as you are willing to give as well as take, you have every right to ask for precisely what you want. It may be difficult at first, but it grows on you.

The last threatening aspect of communication to be discussed involves the fear of criticizing others. People worry about making their partners feel bad. After all, how would she take it if you told her you wish she'd brush her teeth before sex, or that she holds your penis too tightly, or that you'd like her to take a more active part in the lovemaking? Not only might she feel bad, thus perhaps forcing you to deal with your guilt about that, but she might turn around and criticize you.

Many people don't want to rock the boat by saying anything that is or might be construed as negative or critical. Mutual protection societies get formed in relationships, where each partner protects the other, and therefore himself, from disquieting communications. Which may sound very nice, what with all that protection, but which usually means that neither is getting what he or she wants aside from the protection.

This is a nice little game, but the rewards are meager. It's impossible for negative feelings not to exist in relationships. Your partner is going to say and do many things that adversely affect you, and you are going to do the same to her. The two of you can decide not to deal with the negative feelings generated by such occurrences, as discussed above, or you can decide that you are both free to express negative feelings in an attempt to clear the air and get more of what both of you want. Needless to say, we prefer the second alternative because it does result in greater contentment in the long run and also prevents the piling up of resentment. Keeping resentment to a minimal level is important; hostile relationships are often nothing more than the effects of resentment piled so high that it eventually got completely out of control. Putting the pieces back together after that happens is difficult.

There is no doubt that complaining or expressing negative emotions is difficult. But we believe it is something that needs to happen fairly frequently if you want your relationships to stay alive and healthy. The crucial point in expressing complaints is not to blame your partner; just let her know how what she says or does affects you, as in this example:

> 'Martha, it really bothers me that you keep talking about your ex-husband so much. I feel like I'm always being compared to him, especially sexually. It's hard for me to get fully involved in sex with you, because I'm wondering if George had some better way of doing it or if he gave you more pleasure than I do. I'd feel much better if you stopped making these comparisons.'

It is true, of course, that if you make such statements, your partner will probably feel free to do the same. Which means that you'll have to hear some things you'd rather not. That can be excruciatingly painful at times, but the anticipation is often worse than the reality. It can be lived with and, more importantly, can enrich both your relationship and your sexual patterns.

We want to emphasize that there are many levels of

communication and that no one is suggesting that Shakespearian odes are necessary. Understanding this point is important because the concept of communication sounds very serious and frightening to so many people. It can be quite simple and go no further than your level of comfort.

Acts and gestures are one level of communication, and words form another level. But the verbal level itself consists of a number of different levels. These differ in many ways, but the ones we want to discuss have to do with the length, complexity, and difficulty of the messages sent. Our preference is always for the shortest, simplest, and most comfortable messages. Many therapists and educators take the opposite approach, asking their clients or students to talk in ways that are too demanding or threatening. The following example indicates some of the differences between the two approaches.

An intern presented a case that involved a sixty-five-year-old man with erection problems. Because it was obvious that the man made many probably incorrect assumptions about what his wife felt and wanted, he was asked to go home and check out all of his assumptions with his wife. That's a tall order for anyone, but it was worse in this case because the man had never talked to anyone about sex. Although he and his wife had a generally warm and supportive relationship, sex had never been discussed. It seemed highly unlikely to us that the man would even try to carry out the assignment. We predicted also that he would not carry out any further assignments and would become resistant to any suggestions from the therapist, because she had asked for far too much. Unfortunately, we were proved right.

The intern wanted to know whether we thought communication was necessary. We did, but it had to be built around the fact that this man had never talked about sex. It had to be short, simple, and something he felt he could say. Without going into great detail about the case here, we only want to say that two simple messages were worked out that met these criteria. One of them was, when she had stimulated him to erection and was starting to get ready for intercourse (which she thought he wanted): 'This feels good. Don't stop.' The other, to be given after he ejaculated, was: 'What can I do for you?' These brief statements were all that were needed to accomplish what the therapist had tried to obtain through a much more difficult, and in this case impossible, route.

Most of the examples in the book are at a low level of complexity. Short and simple are what work best most of the time. Long speeches are usually not necessary.

You should also choose messages that are most comfortable for you or, if there's no way you can be comfortable saying what you want to say, messages that are the least uncomfortable. You may find that the talk-and-listen format presented below is a useful way of making you more relaxed.

There are of course times when long and somewhat complex messages are required. The problem is that they are often not heard or understood. You might want to check out what you do when someone talks to you at length about a complex issue. If you're like most people, you try to listen but get easily distracted, mainly because you begin formulating your response. So you're busy writing your speech while she's talking, and guess what she's doing when you're talking?

The following exercise is useful for minimizing this type of distraction. It can be used any time you have something important to say, especially if it can't be said in a sentence or two. It's very valuable for saying things that have been or might be misunderstood.

EXERCISE 12–1: TALK AND LISTEN
Time Required: 5 to 10 minutes; 15 minutes maximum

When you have something important to communicate to your lover, tell her so and ask for the amount of time you think you need to get your message across. The time need

not be right now; you can set an appointment for doing it later. It is important that you agree on a time when you are both reasonably relaxed and free from any interruptions.

For your talk-and-listen session, sit facing your partner and tell her what you want to say in as simple and direct a way as possible. You might want to go over your thoughts beforehand to make sure they are clear and concise. Stick to one main point and be as specific as possible.

Your partner should understand before you begin that her job is only to listen and understand. She is not to interrupt you unless she needs clarification. She is not to defend herself, answer you, or comfort you.

Let her know when you are finished. She is then to tell you in a sentence or two what she understood your main point to be (e.g., 'I hear that you're very angry with me because I didn't want to have sex the last four times you initiated; you think that means I don't care about you'). If you think she has correctly understood you, tell her so. If not, correct her and have her give you her new understanding. Continue in this way until you are satisfied that she understands. Try not to be picky, however. Understanding means only that she can correctly summarize your main point, not that she can repeat verbatim all that you said.

If she wants to reply to what you said, use the same format and try to understand what she has to say. It's usually best to take at least a few minutes between your statement and hers.

Some of the people to whom we've suggested this exercise have reported that it also worked quite well in nonsexual areas, with friends, colleagues, and children. It's truly amazing how often we aren't understood and how often we don't understand others. The feeling of being understood is a powerful one and in itself can bring people closer together.

You need to realize, however, that understanding is not the

same as compliance or agreement. Your partner will probably understand you better if you use the talk-and-listen format, but that doesn't necessarily mean that she will agree with you or comply with any requests you make. She may not, for example, apologize for rejecting your last four advances, or feel any different about the next four, but at least she will understand what meaning you are attributing to her actions. If she chooses to tell you what's going on with her, you may better understand what the rejections really mean. And that, though perhaps not exactly what you wished for, may still be something.

Though communication is an important art to cultivate and can make your sex life more enjoyable, it is not a panacea and it has limitations. One of them has already been mentioned – communicating won't always get you what you want. You need to guard against the unrealistic expectation that just because your partner understands your desires, she will agree with them or fulfill them.

Communication is also limited because it may conflict with the equally important right of privacy. Despite what some of the therapy gurus have been preaching, there is no such thing as complete openness or honesty, nor should there be. You have the right to keep private many of your thoughts and feelings, and so does your partner. These rights should never be surrendered. Further, there are times when it is best to keep one's mouth shut. We have seen permanent damage done to relationships when, for example, a man told his partner about an affair he had or when a woman told her partner that the conception of their child was not the 'accident' he thought it was. There is no guarantee that talking is going to produce joy and goodwill. There is simply no substitute for common sense and good judgment in this or any other area. You need to consider the possible consequences of what you say. In most cases, the consideration can be brief because the consequences are not serious. Other issues are potentially more volatile, however, and you should take into account the value of discussing them.

Another limit of communication has to do with its results. If understanding and/or change are not forthcoming the first few times a subject is discussed, further repetition will probably be futile. If your messages are clear and there is no change, then something is getting in the way. The possibilities are many, including that some other issue, like control, is really at stake, or your partner cannot hear the message the way you are sending it, or, even if she can hear and understand, she cannot do what you want. You may want to shift the discussion to these other issues.

Endless repetition is not only purposeless, but it is also destructive since it makes communication sterile and undermines the value of any discussion. Patience is one thing; useless perseverance is something else. It is disappointing, frustrating, and puts a strain on the relationship.

CONTRACEPTION

Contraception is a subject boys and men used to think about but in recent years have learned is none of their business. It wasn't many years ago that the condom or rubber was the primary means of preventing conception. While it would be ridiculous to say that all men took birth control seriously, it was true that they were at least aware that it had something to do with them. Males carried condoms in their wallets or the glove compartments of their cars, practiced putting them on, and traded jokes with friends about their uses and problems (wearing one in sex was like taking a shower in a raincoat, it was said). Boys were often admonished by their fathers, coaches, and friends that while sex was fine, they should take care not to get a girl 'in trouble'.

Times have obviously changed. Since the advent of the birth-control pill and the IUD, the idea has developed that contraception is almost exclusively a female affair. Family-planning agencies have focused their energy almost entirely on women, sometimes treating the rare male who entered their portals as an unwanted intruder. Unfortunately, some women themselves have also contributed to the illusion that birth control has nothing to do with men. Carrying a good idea to ridiculous extremes, they claim that women must be totally responsible for their bodies and have reacted with shock or hostility to the suggestion that a man could be interested or involved in contraceptive decisions and practice. Another factor is the media, which have managed to convey the impression that all women are either taking pills or are equipped with an IUD.

Not surprisingly, men have gotten the message and many indicate no interest in, or concern about, contraception. Why should they, given their impression that women have taken care of the subject? This lack of interest is then taken by some women and by many workers in the family-planning field as proof that men are only interested in sex and care not at all about women and the consequences of sex – an interesting example of a self-fulfilling prophecy in action.

The consequences of excluding men from birth-control planning and participation have been serious. There have been needless arguments and bitterness over who should have taken precautions, numerous broken relationships, and countless unnecessary abortions. Despite the pill and IUD, the rate of unwanted pregnancies has not been reduced; in fact, it has substantially increased in the teenage population.

The involvement of men in contraception will not solve all these problems. But it can make a difference. Perhaps most importantly from your point of view, it can make your sex life a bit more enjoyable.

The fear of pregnancy is one of the factors that make sexual partners uneasy. Even the suspicion that contraception isn't being used, or used effectively, is enough to make them less comfortable than they would otherwise be. While it is true that the woman will bear the brunt of responsibility for a pregnancy or abortion, the man usually finds that, like it or not, he is also involved. Abortions are hassles and unwanted children are disasters.

Birth control is a much more complex subject than most people realize. There are many reasons why people do or do not effectively use contraceptive methods. It is difficult for many women who, though they know they will bear the main responsibility for any unwanted consequences of sex, have also been taught that having children is necessary to their feminine identity. Women experience many such conflicts over the use of contraception, and hence many are not effective contraceptive users.

We believe that women should not have to take sole responsibility for preventing conception, any more than men should have to take sole responsibility for sexual satisfaction. Sex involves man and woman, and so does contraception. Sharing the responsibility for birth control can lead to increased comfort about sex, since both partners know they are doing the best they can to preclude consequences neither wants. It is also a special kind of intimacy which can bring the lovers closer together.

Joint participation in contraception also means more effective contraception. Several studies have clearly indicated that the man's attitude toward contraception is an important factor in how effectively it is used. Should your partner have conflicts about contraception, it will help her and the relationship if she knows she can count on your understanding and support. Should she be using a method inconsistently, you can use one over which you have control and also initiate discussions aimed at finding one both of you are comfortable with.

We hope you won't make the mistake often made by family planning personnel of equating male participation in birth control with the wearing of a condom. Being involved has nothing to do with who ingests, puts in, or puts on a contraceptive. Being involved means only that you share and participate, and there are many ways of doing this.

One good way is simply to ask before the first time you have sex with a partner if she has a contraceptive. If not, you can use a condom if that feels right, or you can suggest engaging in activities other than intercourse until a decision about contraception is made. Another way, if your partner is using the pill or diaphragm, is to offer to pay all or part of the cost. If she needs to see a doctor to get a contraceptive, you can offer to accompany her. Both of you can discuss the various methods and choose the one that seems best. You can listen to any conflicts she has about birth control and do whatever is possible to help her deal with them.

The following story shows how one man participates in contraceptive issues.

One of my first sexual experiences resulted in pregnancy and I resolved that I would do all in my power to prevent that from ever happening again. I've never liked rubbers. I don't care what anyone says – they do dull sensation. So I've always relied on my partner's using something, but I've always been involved. Before having sex with a new partner, I ask if she has anything. Usually they do. But several times they didn't and, surprisingly, I was the one who refused to have intercourse. I just told them that intercourse without birth control is not something I'm willing to do, and I suggested other sexual activities. It always worked out fine.

I like participating in contraception. I talk to my partners about the method they use and, if there's a relationship of any duration, I always pay some of the cost. Most of the women I've been with in the last few years used a diaphragm, and I've bought the cream. Several have showed me how to put it in but, even though I've tried a number of times, I'm not very good at it. But we laugh at my bumbling attempts and that becomes part of our being together. I don't find that inserting the diaphragm interferes with our sex. It's just part of what we're doing and I prefer to have it put in when I'm there. I don't like it when the woman goes off to the bathroom to put it in. It makes me feel excluded. I like to hold her, touch her, or talk to her when she's doing it. It feels nice and close.

A few women have been surprised by my interest in contraception. They later told me that their first reaction was some suspicion at why I was minding their business. But this initial reaction has always given way to appreciation. Because of my interest and participation, my lovers have shared some things with me that they haven't with other men – their feelings and conflicts about conception and contraception, as well as their thoughts and feelings about sex. I think I've also been open about my feelings. My interest in birth control has served me well. I never worry about pregnancy, I feel comfortable with my partners, and I really enjoy them.

While this is not the place for a lengthy discussion of various contraceptive methods, a few words are in order. The pill and IUD have received the most publicity because they are the favorites of most family-planning personnel and appeal to those who like to be up on the latest technological advances. Both, however, have dangerous side effects which need to be considered. And here as elsewhere, there is a great deal to be said for the simple methods. Both the diaphragm and the condom, when used properly with spermicidal jelly or foam, are very nearly as effective, and neither has worrisome side effects.

If you are certain that you never want to have children, or more children, you might want to consider a vasectomy. It is a relatively inexpensive and safe surgical procedure which in no way decreases sexual interest or has any other negative side effects. The only problem with vasectomies is that they must be considered permanent; usually they cannot be reversed. Talk to your doctor if you have any questions about this procedure.

Successful contraception is simply the effective use of whatever method you and your partner choose. Pick a method that makes the most sense and feels most comfortable to use. Then there will be less temptation to take chances with it and, should one partner weaken, the other can be there to give support and implement its use.

SEXUAL CHOICES AND SAYING NO TO SEX

Every sexual feeling and invitation opens the door to a number of alternative actions, some of which will be more satisfying to you and your partner than others. Many men are not aware of all the possibilities and hence end up either not getting their needs met as well as possible or having trouble with their partners. This section is intended to make you more aware of your choices and help you exercise them.

One choice that men have difficulty making is that of refusing to engage in sex at a particular time. This is felt by many to be unmanly since a man should be interested and able all the time especially if he gets a direct sexual invitation from a woman. Aside from being silly (no one is always interested in anything), this piece of mythology is harmful. For many men, being able to say no to sex is a prerequisite for being able to say yes to it. Sex is best when they are confident of their ability to refuse to engage in it. When they have sex, it's because they want to, not because they have to.

The man who can't say no to sex is always at the mercy of his partner's wishes, or what he thinks to be her wishes. This is a very uncomfortable situation for him, one that leads to deception and argument. If he can't refuse her directly, he may pretend to be angry or tired or busy so that she won't approach him. Or he may start a fight, correctly believing that this will dampen her interest. Even without these strategies, the situation is not good because he feels compelled to have sex when he is uninterested or his conditions are not met.

Let's look further at this situation. Suppose your partner indicates a desire for sex and you find that you have no sexual interest at all (remembering that interest refers to how you feel rather than what your penis is doing). You don't have to try to get in the mood or resort to deception. You can simply tell her that you are not interested. The telling should be done with words rather than gestures. Otherwise, she is liable to misunderstand what you are communicating.

What are the best words to use? The best approach to the subject is probably to ask yourself how you would like her to reject your sexual invitations. Word for word, what would you want her to say? Try using the same wording in your rejections. Rejections are almost as hard to give as to get. The first times you give them directly, you will probably be awkward, but you'll feel better about them as you get more practice.

Before you tell your partner that you're uninterested in sex, however, you should consider if you want any contact at all with her. Do you want to be alone, not having anything to do with her? If so, it's probably best to say that clearly ('I'm sorry, honey, but I just want to be alone now'). She may be disappointed and hurt, but at least there won't be any misunderstanding and she will know what you want.

You may find, however, that although your sexual interest is lacking, you do want some contact with her. You may want to cuddle, talk, take a walk, or do something else with her. Even though her desire may have been for sex, she may be willing to settle for something else. Unfortunately, these other alternatives often do not get mentioned or acted on because a hassle develops over the sexual invitation and rejection. Such hassles can be precluded in most cases if you are clear about how you feel and what you are interested in. The following example is but one of many responses when your partner asks for sex and you are not interested.

I really don't feel like sex tonight. I've been feeling down since I found out that I didn't get the promotion at work. I don't want to lead you on but if you're willing, I'd like to lie here with you and talk.

If lying together and talking should lead to some sexual interest on your part, you are free to make another decision. If not, you and your partner may still enjoy each other. What you're doing may not be totally satisfying to her if she was really set on sex, but at least it's something, a way of being together. And it avoids the horrible arguments that can occur when she feels that you have no interest in her at all.

We do not mean to overplay the being together part. Contact is important in relationships, and so is being alone. You have a right to be alone when you want to. Be as clear as you can about what you want at any given time regarding contact and sex, and let her know. We can't emphasize it sufficiently: feeling comfortable rejecting sex and togetherness is crucial to a good relationship and good sex.

While it looks ridiculous on paper, many men act as if they believe it is wrong ever to frustrate or disappoint their partners, and this obviously hampers their ability to say no. There's not much to be said about this idea other than that it's impossible to attain. Every relationship involves rejections, frustrations, and disappointments. All you can do is accept their inevitability. Make them as honest and clear as possible. You can only give what you can give. And that is usually sufficient.

Another area of difficulty arises when you aren't sure what you want. You're not exactly turned-on but not exactly turned-off, either. Suppose, given these feelings, your partner initiates physical contact. Many men hesitate to respond to their partners' touch for fear of leading them on. This issue has been discussed in the chapter on touching. All that needs to be said here is that there is no reason to hesitate (and that's true of your initiating physical contact as well). If you are concerned about misleading her, you might want to say something like: 'I'm not sure what I'm in the mood for. Let's see what happens.' Start doing what you want and see how you feel. You may be content with the touching and, if your partner is also content, there's no problem. If you both get turned-on and want to continue to sex, there's also no problem.

Many men have trouble with the situation where their

partners want to go on to sex and they don't. This is similar to the situation previously discussed, where your partner initiates sex and you aren't in the mood. Let's assume you and your partner have been cuddling and she indicates she'd like sex. Take a minute to consider exactly what you'd like. If you're absolutely not in the mood for any kind of sexual activity, tell her. But perhaps you're interested in something sexual, but not what you think she wants. If your sexual encounters almost always include intercourse, you can still have sex this time without intercourse. If you're not interested in intercourse, but would be willing to do something else, let her know. Don't assume that sex has to include any particular activities or follow any particular pattern. You have choices. Another way of telling your partner what you want is to say 'I'm not interested in anything for myself but I'd like to do something for you.' These kinds of statements let your partner know clearly what she can expect from you and prevent the building up of inappropriate expectations. She will usually appreciate your clarity and your willingness to do what you can.

Several myths stand in the way of applying these alternatives – those that state that a man should always want sex, that sex should always include intercourse, and that sex must always be reciprocal, with both partners simultaneously being involved to the same extent. We have discussed the first two in other places, but the third requires more attention.

The sexual model we learn emphasizes simultaneity. Intercourse is the paragon of the model, since with it both partners are doing the same thing together. If both experience orgasm, everything is perfect. (Fortunately, however, the emphasis on simultaneous orgasm has decreased in recent years.) In other sexual activities, too, many believe that both participants must be busy at the same time. Thus, in oral sex, the 69 position is very popular.

There is nothing wrong with simultaneous sex as long as you realize that it is an option, one that has both advantages and disadvantages. Nonsimultaneous sex is another possibility, one that is appropriate to situations where one partner is more interested in sex than the other. We explore this subject further in the section on working out disagreements. Here we want to add that an advantage of nonsimultaneous sex is that it can result in much stronger physical sensations. Since you are not busy both giving and receiving, you can give directions to her on how best to please you and can devote all your attention to focusing on the pleasurable sensations. We have suggested to many couples that they try oral sex with one partner taking the active and the other the passive role, rather than using their customary 69 format. More than 75 per cent of them reported that the nonsimultaneous way was more enjoyable.

There is one more situation we want to discuss here, and that concerns when you want something sexual for yourself but don't want to give anything at the same time. This is just the opposite of the example we explored earlier, where you are willing to do something for your partner but don't care for anything for yourself. Suppose you'd like a quickie, or would like your partner to use her mouth all over you, or don't have any preferences other than wanting to be on the receiving end of a sexual experience. This is difficult for many men to handle because it sounds so selfish. We are wary because we have heard so much from women and the women's movement about how selfish men are. But when you think about it, why shouldn't you be able to get what you're willing to give to your partner at other times? There's nothing selfish about that at all. A simple request is all that's needed – 'I'd like to just lie here while you make love to me,' or 'I know we've got to leave in ten minutes, but you're turning me on and I want you before we go.'

There are many possible responses to any sexual situation. Consult your feelings about what you want, then work it out with your partner. Most times there will be an option to please both of you.

THE FIRST SEXUAL EXPERIENCES WITH A PARTNER

The first time a couple has sex together is a poignant moment. Two people come together to share an experience and themselves, often in conflict or confusion within themselves, and with differing goals and expectations. Each hopes for at least a tolerable experience and fears a humiliating one, each yearns for acceptance (though this yearning may be ambivalent) and fears something less. Both are concerned that they will not pass the test; that their bodies, behaviors, or personality will be compared to some superior standard and be found wanting.

Men have what they consider to be special concerns about first experiences. Since they believe they are totally or primarily responsible for the management and outcome of the sexual encounter, they wonder if they can get the woman ready, get and maintain their erections, and provide the kind of ecstasy they assume their partners desire. In short, they hope their performances will be, if not fantastic, at least passable.

What men often don't recognize is that their partners go through very similar types of questioning and agonizing. The woman wonders if the man will find her body attractive, if she'll be able to please him, and if the man will find sufficient interest and pleasure to want to return.

It's only logical that people should be uneasy when they have sex with someone new. Even in these days of instant sex and instant intimacy, sex still means something special to most people. It's not something you do with just anyone. In sex you allow a unique access to yourself – to your nudity, to the feel and smell of your body and its fluids. And it can go even further. You may allow access to your emotions, at least to your interest and excitement. In doing so, you run the risk that this may be the start of real contact with the other person, a kind of intimacy, with all the possibilities and dangers that intimacy implies.

Because of the tension that so often accompanies first-time experiences, they are often unsatisfactory. Many men do not get or maintain erections in such situations or ejaculate more quickly than they like, and then feel bad about these 'failures'. Other men function adequately but don't get enjoyment from the sex. Many women do not have orgasms the first time they have sex with a partner, a fact for which many men blame themselves.

It doesn't have to be this way. First-time situations are unique and there is no way of dissipating all the strangeness and tension involved. But the experiences can be more comfortable and enjoyable, with fewer 'failures' and bad feelings.

Saying how to make them better is simple – wait until you are comfortable with her and all your conditions are met – but difficult for many men to practice because this approach flies in the face of the prevailing notion of instant sex. What will the woman think if the man doesn't make sexual advances almost as soon as he has met her? Men think that the woman will feel disappointed, angry, undesirable, or will conclude that the man isn't interested in women or sex. In fact, most women are quite willing to delay sex until they have spent a significant amount of time with their new partners and have gotten to know them. Many women actually experience some turmoil over what to do about sex with new partners. They are torn between their own desires and what they think the man wants, as illustrated by this quote from a woman with whom we talked:

I wish all men were taught the kinds of things you're saying about not getting into sex right away. Often when I'm with someone I'm just getting to know, I'm in a quandary as to what to do. I want to get to know him better. I'd like some physical contact but I'm not really comfortable having sex at the beginning. But I'm supposed to be liberated and I worry that if I don't agree to sex he might feel rejected or get angry. I don't want to hurt him or lose him, but at the same time I wish we didn't have to fuck until we knew each other better and I really wanted to have sex with him.

Many men and women feel this way and go through a lot of difficulty trying to figure out what to do, often making decisions that do not reflect their feelings. How much better it would be if they could just tell their partners how they feel. With only a few word changes, the above quotation could be said to a new partner, probably with little chance of misunderstanding or negative consequences.

There may be times, of course, when a woman you hardly know will want sex immediately. Should you find yourself in such a situation, remember that you don't have to go along with her plans if they don't fit yours. You can tell her how you feel ('I'd like to get to know you better but I'm not ready to go to bed with you now') and see if anything can be worked out.

This suggestion strikes some men as ridiculous, but we know of only a few cases where it didn't work out well. The exceptions all involved men who presented themselves as the greatest lovers since Casanova. One man, thinking about an evening that ended quite badly, remembered that

I really came on like Hot Pants Harry when I met her at the bar. I must have given the impression that I would drive her through the ceiling with ecstasy. I can see why she got mad when I said I wasn't in the mood for sex when we got to her place.

If you don't present yourself as a stud, you won't be in danger of being accused of false advertising.

A second factor that leads to quick sex is spending too much time together at the beginning. We continue to be surprised at how frequently men initiate sex with a new partner, not because they wanted to but because they couldn't think of anything else to do. Here is how Sam, who chronically got sexually involved on the first date with a partner, described his experiences.

Typically I take the woman to dinner or a show, then for a few drinks. Then to my place. We talk a little and then I make my move. You asked if I really wanted sex all those times. The honest answer is no, at least not most of the times. Sometimes I wish I hadn't brought her home. But there she is. How can you deal with that gracefully? I just can't say it's time for her to go. What would she think? Last week there was a weird situation with the woman I met at my cousin's. I definitely knew what I wanted from her when we got home. I wanted a back massage – my back was killing me from helping my cousin move – but how can you ask for a massage on the first date?

Although Sam felt he didn't know the woman well enough to ask for a back-rub, he was willing to have intercourse with her and share her bed for a night. Which is quite interesting, when you think about it: for many people, sex has become less personal and intimate than a massage or conversation.

If you can't tell your partner that you're tired and want to go home, that your back is sore and you'd like a massage, that you don't feel ready to have sex with her, or any similar feelings, sex is probably not going to be very satisfying. If you're not comfortable telling her any of these things, what is sex with her going to do for you?

We use the idea of minimal contact to deal with new partners. Rather than trying to rush a new woman into bed or making a date for Saturday night at your place or hers – a situation that almost begs for a sexual advance – we suggest a few coffee dates first so you can determine just what is your interest and level of comfort. A coffee date need not have anything to do with coffee. It is merely a time-limited get-together during which no physical contact other than a handshake or hug is permitted. The woman should be informed of the time limit when the date is arranged, and the limit should be adhered to no matter what happens. Examples of coffee dates are short walks, giving her a ride someplace, sharing a drink or meal.

Minimal contact allows you to find out how you feel about a woman in small doses, giving you time to make satisfying decisions for yourself and ease any discomfort you may experience. If your interest in her continues and you are comfortable, you can arrange longer get-togethers and do what you want.

We have suggested coffee dates to both men and women and almost everyone who tried them reported that they produced a great sense of relief. They were able to get to know others without feeling pressured to fill up vast amounts of time or have sex with people they didn't care for or feel comfortable with. You might be surprised by the number of times we heard stories like the following.

I was pissed that I had agreed to do the coffee date thing. As soon as I met Jennie at the party I knew we would hit it off just fine. She was so lovely, so warm, and those beautiful eyes . . . I was sure I could take her to bed that night and love it. But I kept our agreement and asked her for lunch the next day. I don't know what happened but she was a different person. She was still lovely, but we really didn't have much to say to each other. I kept looking at her eyes, trying to rekindle what I felt the night before, but it just wasn't there. She didn't even seem very warm anymore. I'm not putting her down. She's an OK person, but I can see that she's not what I need. I wonder how I got so worked up about her at the party. I think I'll vote for coffee dates now. When I think of what might have happened had I gone to bed with her that night, it makes my skin crawl. There's nothing worse than realizing you're not interested in a woman after you've had sex with her. It's so hard to leave gracefully and my feelings are so bad that they wipe out any good feelings that might have happened during sex.

Now for some specific suggestions for sex with a new partner.

1. Get to know her and give her the opportunity to know you. Give yourself time to determine if you really want sex with her.

The only possible problem is that she might misinterpret your lack of sexual attention as meaning that you don't like her or find her desirable. Women are so accustomed to men making sexual overtures as soon as they meet that they may wonder what's going on even though they really prefer to delay sex. A simple explanation is all that's required.

This is lovely but I think I should be going now. I like you and am very turned-on to you but I'd prefer not having sex until I know you a little better. Then I'm sure it'll be good for both of us.

2. Be sensual with her before you even think of doing anything sexual. Hold hands, hug, kiss, snuggle, or do anything else that feels good. The chapter on touching may give you some ideas. Do what feels comfortable and stop when you feel anxious or when you want to stop. If you have concerns that you are being a tease or leading her on, talk to her about them.

3. Do what is necessary to feel comfortable with her and get your conditions met. You might want to talk to her about any concerns you have about being with her, about what she expects in a relationship or sex. You might also want to talk about the types of physical contact you enjoy. This need not be a serious 'There's something I want to talk to you about' event. A simple 'I really like it when you touch me like that' is fine. Establish a habit of discussing your preferences with her; it will serve you well.

If you're feeling adventurous, you might want to discuss the types of sexual activities you enjoy. Here's what one man told us about discussing sex long before he and his partner went to bed:

> It was a new experience for me. Susan and I had gone out four or five times and were strongly attracted to each other. But she said she wasn't ready for sex. It's funny how I can accept that from women but how difficult it was for me to tell them the same thing. Anyway, one day out of the blue she asked what I liked in sex. This took me totally by surprise and it took a few minutes before I could say anything. But I did state some of my preferences and she did the same. That conversation really turned me on and I was looking forward to doing it with her. We didn't get to bed the next two times we were together, however. We continued our sex talk and I got more relaxed about it. The next time we got it on and it was very nice. There was a whole new quality to it. I just felt so cozy with her. Getting to know her was part of the reason and so was the sex talk. I felt that I had already come clean with her, she knew what I wanted and liked. And since I knew what turned her on, I didn't have to try to figure it out.
>
> I learned a lesson from her and I'm grateful. That was several years ago and since then I've usually put off having sex with a new woman until we've spent some time together and we've talked some about sex. I'm happy to say that I'm now the one who initiates this talk.

4. Consider a session or two of massage before having sex. Massage is a good way of getting comfortable with your partner and will also tell you how ready you are for sex. If you're not comfortable in the massage, that's a good warning that some of your conditions are not being met. The massage can be done informally ('I'd like to give you a back-rub') or by using the more formalized instructions given in Exercise 8–3.

You might also want to consider *sleeping* with her, which

can be a nice and cozy way of getting more comfortable with her. We know this sounds a bit old-fashioned, but it has worked very well for the men who've tried it. It's possible, of course, that sleeping together might lead to sex, which is fine if that's what feels right at the time. But make sure your conditions are met and that sex is what you want. If not, just sleep.

5. When your conditions are met, when you are comfortable, and when you are feeling aroused, feel free to engage in whatever sexual activities you like. Try to remember what we said about sexual choices. Intercourse is not required. If you have had erection or ejaculation problems in the past, it is best not to have intercourse the first few times you are with a new partner. Do other things that feel good to both of you.

6. Give feedback about your experiences with her. Feel free to tell her – before, during, and after sexual encounters – what you liked and didn't like, and encourage her to do the same. This eliminates guesswork and misunderstandings, thus helping both of you to know each other better.

7. Express your feelings when appropriate. If you have feelings that get in the way of your sexual responsiveness or, for that matter, your ability to relate to her in any way, you would probably do well to discuss them with her. It will help her to know you and it may also totally or partially resolve some of the difficulties.

8. Don't do anything you don't want to do. If she suggests that you have sex on the front lawn or that her dog join in your sexual activities, and if such things simply aren't your style, let her know immediately. Take care of yourself.

Following these suggestions will allow you to begin sexual activity with a new partner with a maximum of comfort and a minimum of stress. They will not all be easy to follow, but you now have the skills to at least begin. In later chapters, we supplement this list with other ideas for men who have erectile or ejaculation problems.

CHANGING SEXUAL PATTERNS IN
RELATIONSHIPS

Many men suddenly or gradually find that they are not content with the sexual patterns in their relationships. The sources of the dissatisfaction vary: too little (or too much) sex; insufficient variation in practices and positions; not enough initiation or participation by the partner; not enough excitement; and so on. Sometimes the precise nature of the discontent is not clear; the man just knows that sex doesn't feel as good or interesting as it once did.

The best way to begin with this problem is to discuss it with your partner. It is not important whether you know precisely what is bothering you or what changes you want. The feeling of discontent is sufficient basis for a discussion, during which clarity may develop. Some men have been surprised to find that their partners felt exactly the way they did, but whether or not this is true, a talk is beneficial for putting forth your thoughts and feelings, and preparing for change.

The initial conversation about the subject is important and will strongly influence subsequent events. We suggest that you use the talk-and-listen format given earlier in this chapter and that you spend a few minutes beforehand deciding what it is you want to say. Your message needs to be clean and clear, and it should not imply that something is wrong with your partner. Like this:

(A) Mary, I've been thinking that our sex life isn't as exciting as it was when we first met. I'd like to talk with you about it and see if we can make some changes that will make sex better for both of us.

Not like this:

(B) Mary, having sex with you sure hasn't been any fun

lately. I'm going to tell you some things I want you to do to correct the situation.

The man in example A is clearly stating his dissatisfaction and expressing a desire that they both try to work it out. The man in example B is headed for trouble. He's telling his partner that it's all her fault (which very rarely is the case) and putting her on the defensive. Her reaction will probably be such as to make impossible any improvement in their sexual situation.

Be as specific as possible about your complaints. Talk about how you feel dissatisfied and, if you know, what changes you'd like. Ask for your lover's reactions and ideas. Make sure she understands this is a joint venture. Everything need not, and probably cannot, be done in one discussion. Terminate the discussion when one of you gets tired or when progress ceases, and give yourselves some time to think over what has been said. Then you can talk again.

The result of your talks should be specific plans for how change is to be effected. Without specific plans, there is an excellent chance that the changes will not come to fruition. Consideration should also be given to possible sources of resistance to the change and ways of dealing with them.

Charlie wanted his wife to initiate sex more often. He had told her about this in the past and, while she always agreed to initiate more, she rarely followed through. There was good reason for this. If she did initiate when Charlie wasn't in the mood, he became angry. She would feel free to initiate only if she knew that she wouldn't have to deal with his anger. With a little help from a therapist, they worked it out so that Charlie got practice turning down her sexual invitations without getting angry. As he became more comfortable saying no, she felt freer to initiate when she was in the mood.

Of all the sources that one might consult regarding possible changes, the best are your fantasies and past experiences.

What kinds of sexual attitudes, events, and practices have you thought about, fantasized about, or dreamed about? Surely some of these could be carried out in reality. What about your past experiences? What factors made sex better with other partners or with this partner at other times? Can some of these factors be reinstituted now?

While on the subject of fantasies, we want to add that the sharing of sexual fantasies, whether or not they are carried out, is exciting to many couples. You might want to try this if your partner is willing. But take it slowly until you are comfortable with this type of sharing.

Keep in mind that change is rarely easy and don't expect too much too soon. Your partner may well be willing to initiate sex, or have oral sex, or meet some of your other wishes, but she may not always remember to do what you want or do it in quite the way you want. Patience is required, and so is support. Let her know that you know she's willing and is trying. And give feedback so she'll know how she's doing.

You will go a long way to ensuring that your desires are met if you reinforce what you like and correct what you don't like, as long as the corrections are given in a supportive and nonblaming way. If your lover rarely initiates sex, make sure you tell her how much you enjoyed it when she does initiate. If she has a lot to learn about sucking your penis, give her directions and let her know when it feels good.

If you have trouble working out the changes you like, be sure to read the section later in this chapter on working out disagreements.

SEXUAL BOREDOM IN LONG-TERM RELATIONSHIPS

Wanting to relieve boredom in a sexual relationship is a specific example of making changes in a relationship and is therefore closely related to the previous section. But sexual boredom is an interesting phenomenon in its own right.

While many people assume that boredom is inevitable in long-term relationships, we believe that this is just another bit of mythology. Sex is not the same after ten, twenty, or thirty years with the same partner, but it need not be boring or unsatisfactory. The mystery may be gone since the partners know each other well after a number of years, but the increased comfort, trust, cooperation, and knowledge of one another that comes with being together for so long can more than compensate for its absence. For some people, sex gets better as the years go by, while for others it stays at the same high level for many, many years.

Why, then, do so many others complain that sex gets boring after a few years? The people complaining of boredom to whom we have talked can be loosely grouped into three categories, each with a different reason for the boredom.

The first group consists of those who have maintained a rigidly narrow pattern of sexual activity since they began. Sex is programmed down to the last detail and always proceeds according to plan. It's no wonder that they are bored.

Changing the routine can be helpful to people in this group. Having sex at different times, in different places, and in different ways can introduce the kind of variety that will relieve the boredom. You need to talk to your partner about the changes you want or about the idea of making changes. Specific ideas for change can come out of your discussion, from your fantasies, or perhaps from some of the exercises in this book. If you want still more ideas, you might consult some pornographic films or literature and also Alex Comfort's *The Joy of Sex.*

The notion of introducing variety into sexual relationships suffering from boredom is not new and has, in our opinion, been somewhat overdone in recent years. It can be beneficial, but only with the people who are bored because of a lack of variety. Most of the people who complain of boredom, however, do not fit into that group. They fall into two other categories and it is highly unlikely that sexual variety will do anything for them.

The second category of people who complain of sexual boredom consists of those in relationships with little feeling left in them. Some of these people engage in varied sexual techniques and activities but the boredom persists because there is no feeling between the partners (or worse, there is lots of feeling, all negative). Since all the positions and techniques in the world can't substitute for feelings of caring, attraction and passion, this situation is more difficult to work with than the first type of boredom.

Our position is not very optimistic. Unless a way can be found to rekindle the interest, caring, or love that once existed, it may not be possible to relieve the sexual malaise. This is not to say that the relationship must resume its early form or that it must in any sense become ideal. But some feelings must be awakened if sex is to be different. This is sometimes possible and sometimes not. We do not believe that a book is the best way of dealing with this situation. Professional help is required in most cases.

The last category of sexually bored people consists of those whose expectations exceed reality. While they complain of boredom, on questioning it usually turns out that they are not so much bored as dissatisfied because sex no longer is – or never was – what they thought it ought to be. People in this group, like those in the preceding one, have often tried various ways of increasing their sexual enjoyment. They have read all the books, seen all the movies, attended all the workshops. Nothing helps, at least, not for long, because what they are after is unattainable. Rather than exploring the reasonableness of their expectations, however, they continue to look for the methods that will fulfill their fantasies.

This issue is a large one and, because the values of sex have been so exaggerated in recent years, one to which we are all subject to some degree. We discuss it in great detail in Chapter 22. For now it is enough to say that dissatisfaction and boredom are inevitable for those who cling to superhuman expectations. What needs changing are the expectations rather than the behaviors. Our chapter on sex and aging will be useful for those who have unrealistic expectations about sex in the later years.

Sex does not have to get boring in long-term relationships, unless the opposite of boredom is defined in terms of the excitement that characterizes adolescence or fantasy. Sex does not get boring for those who retain some affection for their partners, have realistic expectations about sex, do not do what they don't want to do, and who feel free to have sex in ways, places, times, and positions that feel right to them at the moment. In fact, a number of people have told us that sex became really good for them only after they had been together for more than ten years and that since then it had kept improving. Sex was no longer characterized by youthful passion and awkwardness, but it sure was fun.

WORKING OUT DISAGREEMENTS

Disagreements are an inevitable part of every relationship. Many can be easily and satisfactorily negotiated, but not all. Some people delude themselves into thinking that all differences can be ironed out. Such, alas, is not the case. Some differences cannot be resolved in a given relationship, and for others the amount of effort required, as well as the amount of ill will generated, makes the price too high.

One extremely common type of disagreement revolves around the amount of contact and sharing in the relationship. Usually it is the woman who desires more attention and communication. Without them, she may withdraw sexually. We deal with this situation in greater detail in the next chapter. We mention it here because so many times sexual disagreements are the result of this more basic conflict.

Two other common disagreements have to do with the frequency of sex and types of sexual activity. While many people still believe that it is always the man who wants sex more often and who is eager to try variations, this isn't necessarily so. In fact, in our experience we have found that there are just as many relationships in which the reverse is true.

With either of these types of conflict the first thing to do is to determine precisely what you or your partner want. This can be more difficult than it sounds. A desire for more frequent sex sounds deceptively simple: 'I (or she) just want to do it more often.' But what is 'it' – touching, oral or manual sex, intercourse, orgasm, or something else? The it has to be pinpointed; its precise nature makes a difference as to whether or not it can be fulfilled. The partner less inclined to have more sex may be willing to increase the amount of physical contact or sexual activity other than intercourse, but may not be willing to have intercourse more often.

Another way of looking at the same issue is to ask what would it mean for the requester to get what he is asking. Is he primarily interested in the physical act itself or its symbolic meaning? If it's the meaning rather than the act that's important, the issue can often be resolved without increasing the amount or variety of sex.

For example, a woman may ask for more sex because only during sex does she feel loved; it's the only time her partner pays any attention to her. While an obvious solution is to increase the amount of sex, a better response in some respects would have the partner start paying attention and showing love in other ways. Another example is a man who wants his partner to swallow his semen because he feels this would show her complete acceptance of him. In some cases like this, the women were willing to have the men come in their mouths. But the majority of such situations were worked out in other ways, more acceptable to both partners.

Here again we emphasize the importance of understanding clearly what the disagreement is about. More sex, oral sex, anal sex, more active participation, and similar requests are not specific or clear enough. Exactly what is it that you or your partner want? And what would it mean to you to get it or not get it?

The symbolic meanings of sex are many, and we deal with

some of them in Chapter 22. For now, just be sure you know what you want and what you and your partner are disagreeing about. Of course there are situations where one partner simply has a greater desire for sex than the other.

We recall one man who claimed he wanted sex at least once a day, every day, while his partner was satisfied with once a week. Sex was this man's only way of showing his wife he cared for her. But even after he learned to express his love in words and nonsexual touching, he still wanted sex more often than she did. The discrepancy in desire was resolved in several ways, only one of which will be mentioned here. We suggested masturbation as a sexual supplement for him but that didn't appeal to him because it didn't include his partner. Whereupon she said that she would be happy to hold and stroke him while he masturbated. He wasn't exactly thrilled by the idea but finally tried it. This practice soon became a regular part of their sexual repertoire.

The compromise this couple worked out is something that others who have different preferences regarding frequency might want to try. The main obstacle to its implementation is the myth that in sex each partner does something to the other but no one does anything to himself. It's a powerful myth, but when you think about it there's no good reason for it. While masturbating this way is not as exciting to many people as other forms of sex, it is an alternative that allows for sexual satisfaction with some participation by the partner.

If you and your partner understand each other's position and no agreement seems possible, you both need to consider how important the matter is to you. Is it really vital that you have sex more often or that she suck you or initiate sex? If it's not terribly important, you might want to drop the subject. It may not be worth the hassle. Even if it is important, consider what the chances for resolution are. If your partner is adamant, or if it seems that a change will create considerable ill will in the relationship, ask yourself if it's worth it. Since you're not going to get everything you want, it pays to put your energy into those issues that are most important and that have a reasonable likelihood of being resolved in a way that does not involve serious negative side effects.

If you want to continue with trying to make changes, here are some ideas:

1. Let your partner know how important the issue is to you and how willing you are to try to find a mutually agreeable solution.
2. Ask what her objections are.
3. Taking her objections seriously, see if you can suggest ways of dealing with them, or offer to work with her toward this end.
4. Offer her something in return, something she wants but you have so far been unwilling to grant.

The following story illustrates how these suggestions worked in one case.

George had never had anal intercourse and wanted very much to try it with a woman he was seeing. She refused. Although the relationship was generally sound, fights soon developed over this conflict. We suggested that George ask his partner why she was so opposed to the idea, and that he do nothing but listen while she talked. Her objections were that the whole idea seemed dirty to her and that she feared it would be painful. George asked if she would be willing to keep an open mind on the subject and to see if something could be worked out. She agreed after exacting a promise that he would not push her. A discussion with us and some reading helped free her from the idea that anal lovemaking was shameful. We told her that while this kind of sexual activity might be uncomfortable at first, if she wanted to try it lubrication and the relaxation of the pelvic muscles would help. We suggested that, since she would be doing this for George's enjoyment, she should ask for something for herself. There was something she wanted – a whole evening of George pleasuring her, 'just spending a whole lot of time lavishing physical affection on me' – but George had refused to do it because it involved so much time. The trade was made. She got her evening of loving and enjoyed it. George got what he wanted but the results were not what he had expected. 'It was weird. It just wasn't anything like I thought it would be. I mean, it was OK, but nothing special. God, to think I got so hassled about it.'

There is one situation you need to look out for. If a disagreement assumes major proportions and can neither be resolved nor dropped, and is causing real problems in the relationship, the chances are excellent that sex is not what you are disagreeing about. Something more fundamental is probably at stake. Get some help before it wrecks the relationship.

THIRTEEN

Some things you should know about women

Although men and women spend much of their lives in each other's company, many think and act as if the opposite sex were an alien species. Throughout history – in jokes, folktales, songs and literature – men have bemoaned their inability to understand women. Even the great Freud, after decades of inquiry, finally threw up his hands in despair, crying, 'What do women want?'

Female sexuality has been a particularly vexing area for men, who have believed and vainly tried to reconcile many outlandish and contradictory ideas about how women related to sex. From the wanton slut of the fantasy model, who can never seem to get enough of sex, to the prim Victorian lady for whom any sex, or any thought of it, would have been far more than enough, we have gone from one extreme to the other, never quite knowing which to trust.

Ignorance breeds doubt and fear, and to these emotions must be added others – envy and anger. Men have often thought that women had it too easy in sex. Women didn't have to do anything. They could, if need be, just lie there and spread their legs. Men, on the other hand, had to do all the work; at the very least, they have to achieve erection. The woman got to lie back and evaluate the man's prowess. It just didn't seem fair.

Since the natural order seemed weighted in favor of women, men used their physical and political power to tip the scales their way. Men defined how women should feel and behave sexually, and it wasn't long before women started acting the way men said they should, even to the point in Victorian times of denying that they were sexual at all. But the uncertainties and fears remained.

It would be presumptuous to assume that in one chapter we can clear up issues that have perplexed millions of men over hundreds of years, but we are going to try at least to shed some light on the topic of female sexuality. This chapter is divided into two parts. The first discusses what women say they want in sex and the second deals with some of the anatomical and physiological aspects of female sexuality. The order reflects our priorities: what women say they like is more important than where the parts are and what they do.

We want to emphasize that this chapter is in no way intended as a blueprint for satisfying a woman. There is tremendous variation among women, as there is among men. Nothing is true of all women. This point was underscored powerfully in the preparation of the chapter. A number of women – colleagues, friends, clients – read it and made comments. There is hardly a point in the chapter that was not disputed by at least one of them. The intention of the chapter, then, is to serve as a basis for thought and discussion. Even if your partner disagrees with everything we say, if she lets you know how she differs from what we say and explains what is true for her, then this chapter will have served its purpose.

WHAT WOMEN WANT IN SEX

Female sexuality, as we said above, has traditionally been defined by men. Male authorities – religious, literary, medical, scientific – decided what women were like sexually and what they wanted. Only rarely were women themselves consulted about the matter. When a woman was courageous enough to try to define her own sexuality, no one paid much attention because it didn't seem that a woman would know what she was talking about. It was easy to pass her off as unfeminine, a castrating bitch, or a threat to the established order of things and continue in the delusion that men knew what was best.

This pattern is in the process of change. Women are now studying female sexuality and there is more societal permission for them to explore their own sexual feelings, styles, and preferences. But it is a mistake to think that the tenacious hold of male-dominated ideas has been broken. Many if not most women still find it difficult to assert themselves sexually. Many of them are struggling to do just this, but it isn't easy. One of the most powerful lessons many women learned was that they should defer to men in sex; they certainly shouldn't say or do anything that might be taken as a reproach or criticism. This obviously makes it difficult for them to assert their own sexual desires, especially if the man takes any suggestions as an insult.

In order to find out what women had to say about sex, we decided to ask them. Bernie Zilbergeld and Lynn Stanton did a study in which over four hundred women responded to a questionnaire asking what they liked and didn't like in sex. Most of the material and all of the quotations in this section are from that study.

To get the maximum benefit from the material to be presented, you should do the following exercise before reading further.

EXERCISE 13–1: WHAT YOU THINK WOMEN WANT IN SEX
Time Required: 30 to 40 minutes

Make a list of the kinds of things you think women (your partner, a potential partner, or women in general) want in sex, in terms of attitudes, behaviors, techniques, or anything else. Make another list of the things they don't want. Be as specific as possible in both lists.

You might want to keep your lists handy as you read the rest of the chapter and compare your responses with what is presented. When you find a discrepancy, ask yourself what is the basis for your information. Did a partner say or do something that led to your belief, did you hear it from others, read it in a book, or are you guessing? We do not

mean to imply that you are wrong if you disagree with what we say. As we mentioned earlier, many women disagree with many of our statements. We only want you to make sure that you have good reason for disagreeing. If you believe that a certain point is not true for your partner but aren't sure why you believe this, why not check it out with her?

We were pleased to discover that most of what the women said was congruent with our own thinking and with the approaches we were successfully using to help men enhance their sexuality. This convergence seems to point to the possibility of a more realistic and human expression of sexuality. To be sure, women want more from men, but what they want has nothing to do with bigger penises, harder or more frequent erections, perfect performances, or mind-blowing orgasms. They want more of the kinds of things many men are now realizing that they want to give – equal treatment, understanding, sensitivity, communication, and a greater sharing of themselves. Another way of saying the same thing: women want more of what men have not been allowed to give because of the rigid ordering of human qualities into male and female categories. They want men to be more fully human, more fully themselves, so that women can be who they are.

Before going on, we want to mention that we are not saying that women are right and men are wrong, nor that women are paragons of sexual wisdom. Women's sexual training is at least as unrealistic and cruel as men's, and in many cases much worse. As a result, many women have problems with sex. They are in conflict over what is right for them, or can't get their minds and bodies to operate in harmony. Many of our respondents candidly admitted their problems and confusions. And more than a few said that the reason they hoped for a change in men was that this would make it easier for them to change.

If there is any one point which summarizes what women

want from men it is a greater sharing of themselves. This issue extends far beyond the area of sexual activity but often affects it since a woman who thinks her man is not giving enough in other areas may well be angry or inhibited in bed. There is no doubt that this is the greatest complaint women have about men: that they do not give enough of their time, attention, feelings and understanding.

> He says he loves me but you'd never know it from the way he acts. We never do any touching, talking, or anything else. He doesn't have time for me because he's so busy with all the 'important' things like his job, working on his stupid boat, paying bills and caring for the lawn, and watching a zillion football games on TV. I want more of him. I don't care if the lawn never gets mowed.

A common pattern in contemporary relationships is that the woman makes requests for more contact, which the man often interprets as meaning that she's asking for more than he's able or willing to give. Whereupon he retreats further into his other activities, which makes the woman angry and more demanding. Which makes the man withdraw even further, ad infinitum. In this pattern, it is not the man's aggressiveness that upsets the woman, but his passivity and withdrawal, his lack of responsiveness in expressing his feelings toward her.

Another common pattern, better known than the first because of the widespread publicity given to it by the women's movement, involves a domineering man lording it over his partner. He doesn't respect his partner as an equal and feels free to tell her how to live her life, free to criticize and belittle her, and, in general, not to take her seriously. Curiously, this pattern is more similar to the one discussed above than may seem apparent at first glance. Both involve women not getting what they want (and this is usually also true for the men) because their men refuse to give.

Many of the points that follow are only elaborations of these two patterns. And, unfortunately, we don't have any easy solutions. Women have been trained to focus more on relationships than have men, who learned more about dealing with things like jobs, ideas, and games. Relationship patterns and problems are often merely logical outgrowths of the different socialization patterns. Many times, however, compromises are possible, providing there is some genuine affection between the partners and an ability to listen to what is being requested by the other. Often what is being asked is much less demanding and threatening than what was imagined. In most relationships, there is no reason why the man (or woman, if that be the case) can't have time to work on his boat, while the woman (or man) also gets some of the contact she (or he) desires. We hope that what follows will be of value in helping you hear what some women say they want.

The days are long gone, if they ever existed, when women wanted nothing from sex and submitted to it only to please their men. Women like men who are interested in what they want. They view sex as a cooperative venture between equals and expect to be taken seriously. The man who is concerned only with his own needs and satisfaction is held in contempt.

I like a partner who can be sensitive to my needs while still being true to his own satisfaction. I like to have my requests listened to and to not be forced into doing things I don't like. In short, I like an equal relationship rather than a one-sided one.

What I hate most is when a man is concerned with his own needs to a degree that leaves no room for mine. It feels like a denseness on his part, an unwillingness to listen to me. It makes me feel like I have to struggle to be an equal person in the sexual interaction, and often that I am simply unable to have an impact on him. The behaviors range from near-rape (insisting on intercourse when I don't want it) . . . to berating me for being oversexed when I want sex and he's not in the mood.

In general, women seem much less performance-oriented in sex than men. Sex for them is a process of shared contact and communication rather than a mad scramble to achieve certain goals.

The important things are sharing and mutual pleasure. The sharing of minds, bodies, and souls is where it's at for me.

Men get so busy pursuing performance goals that they forget sensuality, playfulness, the pleasure of taking one's time during a sexual encounter, doing things like exploring fantasies, experimenting with different things, and taking the time to stop in the middle of lovemaking for a sip of wine and some talk.

Women tend to have a fairly differentiated view of sex. Each part is important, to be appreciated for its own sake, whether or not it leads to something else. What is usually called foreplay is not something they see only as a prelude to something better. It is valuable in its own right, and women like men who are sensual enough to enjoy this aspect of lovemaking.

I like sensual men. A man who will spend as much time kissing my neck (if he and I are both enjoying it) as my breasts can turn lovemaking into a slow, delicious exploration and discovery of each other.

I enjoy a man who enjoys all forms of foreplay for their own sake and who doesn't have to have intercourse every time.

Expressions of physical affection are extremely important to most women, and not only sexual touching. They want to touch and be touched at times when sex isn't possible or desirable, as well as times when sex may be a result of the touching. Women who are only touched when their partners want sex are not content.

> Affection is what I crave. Touching is important *all* the time.

> I get so angry when a man thinks that all touching must lead to sex. I want to be able to touch, and want him to touch me, just as a way of saying, 'I like you,' or 'I care for you,' without having to end up in bed.

The hugging, kissing, and stroking called foreplay comprise one example of the physical affection women like. The uniting of genitals is another, but one that is distrusted by women unless it is preceded and followed by other kinds. They resent feeling that they are nothing but receptacles for the man's sperm, useful until he has ejaculated and then discarded like yesterday's newspaper. Afterplay, therefore, is another type of affection that most women like.

> I like a man to hold me after intercourse. There doesn't have to be a lot of conversation, just a few tender words, some physical intimacy, some contact that tells me that the closeness is still there even after the orgasm is over.

> I resent a man who, after orgasm, jumps up and says 'Now on to the important events of the day.'

Another aspect of the affectionate, sensual approach that appeals to so many women is a slow, unhurried attitude.

> I like him to move slowly – to kiss me, fondle my body, to allow me to pleasure his body through kissing and stroking – and to take time to try different things, to be able to stop for a while and start again. I like sex to be a slow, sensuous experience.

> I like a man who is relaxed and unhurried during sex.

When a man rushes, I assume that he is caught up in himself and his feelings and that it is not a sharing experience.

This should not be taken to mean that every sexual act must go on for hours or that women are against quickies. It is true that some women have learned to distrust quickies because they think they are being used without regard for their own needs. Despite this, however, most women do like or can learn to like quick sexual encounters provided that they feel cared for and respected and that this is not the only type of sex they get. A moral we draw from this is that quickies work best in the context of a caring relationship, where both partners trust the other and know without question that they are valued and appreciated. A quickie at the beginning of a relationship, however, is a good way of leaving the woman feeling used and abused, and may end the relationship before it gets off the ground.

Gentleness and sensitivity are greatly admired by women. Women usually do not like feeling that they are in a football game when having sex.

Being gentle is a virtue.

Perhaps what saddens me the most is the way that some men feel they must act in order to fulfill their masculine role. This includes gruffness, a lack of tenderness (such as hugging and soft body stroking), and poor expression of emotion.

Again, this should not be construed to mean that women are not sometimes interested in rough sex. Many are, but usually only in the context of a relationship where they feel respected and cared for. Rough handling outside that context – despite what Harold Robbins and other such experts have to say about it – leaves most women feeling abused and thinking that the man is an insensitive clod.

We realize that we haven't said much about orgasms so far. Surprisingly, the women who responded to the questionnaire didn't have much to say about this topic. Women want orgasms, there is no doubt about that, but they tend to view them somewhat differently than men do. While most men can barely conceive of a sexual experience without an orgasm for them, women are more flexible. They don't see orgasm as necessary every time. Sex can be good even without orgasm.

It follows then that for many women orgasm is not the main reason they engage in sex. They have sex because it's a way of sharing themselves and a pleasurable experience. They want the option of being able to have an orgasm, but don't want to focus on it to the point where everything becomes only a means toward this end.

I don't want to feel that I have to climax every time. I want to be able to get what I need to have an orgasm when I want one, but that isn't every time I have sex. I want to be able to enjoy just doing what feels good, without worrying how it should end.

Women do not like being pressured to have orgasms. Being sensitive to their needs is valued, as is the willingness to give them the kinds of stimulation they want (which may or may not be intercourse). Trying to make them come so that you'll feel like a good lover is not.

If I haven't climaxed but feel warm and happy and sleepy and tell my partner I want to sleep, it makes me *angry* if he insists I must have an orgasm. That says, 'I'm meeting my male ego needs and to hell with you.'

In conformity with the idea that women are more interested in an experience than a performance, the more technical aspects of sex that concern so many men received little attention. Not one woman mentioned penis size as being important and only a very small number said anything about the ability to last a long time. This is not to say that a woman won't feel cheated or frustrated if you ejaculate in twenty seconds every time you are with her – she probably will – but only that this is not the most important consideration for most women. If you are relating in ways that are satisfying to both of you, learning to last longer is a simple matter.

Many women complained about rigid, mechanical patterns on the part of their lovers, where technique was emphasized over personal expression, playfulness, and passion. They don't like to feel that the man is doing something *to* them; they want the man to be *with* them, sharing the experience.

I am not interested in sexual performance. I am interested in sexual expression on a one-to-one basis without a driving manual for instruction and reference.

A mechanical approach is the biggest turn-off for me. I'm treated as a machine or Barbie Doll, to be touched, diddled, rubbed, or sucked in certain parts according to what worked for the last girl or what he read in a book. No emotional communication, no joy, just engineering designed to do the job as effectively as possible so he can get on with what he really wants to do.

Part of the complaints about rigidity dealt with the man's unwillingness to experiment. We were a bit surprised by this because we have so often heard this complaint from men about women. A number of women said their lovers were quite resistant to trying new places, times, positions, and activities. Some said that their partners refused to have intercourse in any but the missionary position, some that their partners would have sex only late at night, while others complained that while their men wanted oral sex from them, they refused to reciprocate.

For all their talk, men seem to be more inhibited than women.

Many women expressed a desire for less seriousness and more playfulness in sex.

I like for men to regard sex as a fun thing, not as something real heavy.

Most of all I love playfulness and rule-breaking in lovemaking. Nothing sacred or orderly or sequential, just experimenting and the shared closeness that it brings.

Reading these comments reinforced an impression we developed in our work with men, in and out of therapy – namely, that many men regard sex as a very serious undertaking, with no levity permitted. The issue here is of course our old friend performance. When you're trying to get the job done, to perform well, humor and playfulness are experienced as distractions. On the other hand, when you are having an experience without much regard for where it ought to go, you can do whatever feels right at the moment, be it laughing, crying, talking, fucking, nibbling, cuddling, or something else.

In line with their desire for a sharing experience, the women requested more communication about sex. They wanted men to be more open about their feelings and preferences and they liked men to ask about their partners' preferences. All in all, women want an atmosphere of openness in talking about sex, where each partner is free to say what he or she likes and dislikes, how he or she is feeling, and to verbalize anything of relevance to the process. Several women were clear that when this atmosphere prevails, orgasms are not a problem. They can say what they want and, when they get it, orgasms usually occur.

Communication plays a huge part in satisfaction and enjoyment. One good thing men can do is give me feedback on what they want and don't want, encourage me to do the same, and do all this not only with body language but also by verbalizing.

When I feel OK about saying what I want, and if he can go along with these things, I don't have to worry about orgasm.

A number of women stated that they need the man to voice his preferences in order for them to feel free to voice their own.

I like for men to tell me what feels good to them and what they like for me to do sexually. It not only helps me know what to do but it also makes it easier for me to tell them what I like.

This is sometimes difficult for men to understand since they know they're relatively uneasy and unskilled in communication and assume that women are much better at it. While this is often true, the problem for women is that they learned that a man should take the lead sexually. For a woman to say what she wanted, to make suggestions – this was taboo unless the man took the lead. Which is precisely what the women in this survey said.

It is vital that men recognize the tremendous influence they wield over how much and what their partners are willing to say. Women want to share their thoughts and feelings, as well as their bodies, with men, but they need support and encouragement.

My least favorite thing is men who make it hard for me to talk to them, in bed or not. I don't think men realize how hard they can make it to share information in bed – simply by being unresponsive, or disinterested, or overtly hostile. And then they wonder why we can't get into a good place together. Even after all these years, I still find it's hard to discuss what I need and want – emotionally, sexually, and in terms of the relationship – unless the man listens actively and is supportive.

This should come as no surprise. All of us need interest and support if we are to say what's important to us, particularly in areas that are difficult to talk about. No one wants to talk to someone who looks as if he'd much rather be somewhere else.

Most of the women were also very clear about wanting to know more about their partners' feelings. Because men characteristically do not say what they feel and think, sexually or otherwise, women often feel left out. One of their most fervent desires is to be included more often, to hear what's happening with their men. And this includes the bad feelings as well as the good ones.

> I really like for a man to tell me how he's feeling (anxious, uncomfortable, distracted, etc.) instead of 'pushing on'.

> I appreciate it when he's able to stop the lovemaking because he's getting tense, and talk or play or get a sandwich and let me in on what's happening with him. It makes whatever he's experiencing as a problem just a part of our sharing, and it gives me permission to do the same.

There is an important message here about what a man can do when he feels uncomfortable in sex or is having a problem. Too often a man will try to hide his feelings or problem, vainly attempting to override the feelings by pushing on. The woman usually senses that something is amiss but can't figure out exactly what it is, a situation hardly conducive to an enjoyable experience. Or she may misinterpret his reticence to mean that the man doesn't like her or that she did something wrong. She wants to know what is happening for him. Sharing feelings with her will be received as a gift.

This is especially important if you are having problems. Time and again we have listened to men tell us that women yelled or berated them for losing an erection or coming too fast. We don't want to say such things never happen because we know they sometimes do. But in those cases where we have been able to hear the woman's side of it, her anger was triggered not by the event itself but by the man's reaction to it – blaming her; refusing to continue the experience; or withdrawing into a sulky isolation, leaving her feeling alone and helpless.

So if you are having trouble, don't withdraw. Let her know what's going on with you, and see what the two of you want to do next. It sounds almost too simple to be true, but listen to what the women said.

> The only time that men's sexual problems become real problems is when the man uses it as a way of distancing himself from me by withdrawing or berating himself, refusing to accept my acceptance of the situation.

> I'm annoyed and uncomfortable when a man is experiencing problems with an erection and works at it so intently that I begin to feel used. It's like the erection is so damn important that nothing else matters. I would rather not have intercourse if he is apprehensive about losing his erection or coming too quickly. I really like for him to stop when this occurs and to tell me how he's feeling, to share the experience with me rather than making the situation uncomfortable for both of us.

We close this section on what women want in sex with three statements that seem to sum up most of the main points.

> We want men, not supermen; lovers, not beasts; and intelligent, warm companions, not Hollywood handsomes stroking their egos at our expense.

> I like a man who feels free to be vulnerable, to give up his masculine stereotype, who can be gentle and sensitive and passive, as well as aggressive. A man who allows me to do the same. A man who can relinquish control of the lovemaking and allow it to be a shared experience. A man who can tolerate imperfections in himself, his penis, and

me... A man who appreciates and enjoys women's bodies – even the not-so-perfect ones.

Actually, the things I respond most to in men are qualities which are traditionally considered feminine: tenderness, gentleness, caring, touching, and sensitivity to emotions.

We have presented what 416 women said they wanted in sex. We wonder how the woman or women you relate to feel about what our sample said. We invite you to find out.

FEMALE SEXUAL ANATOMY AND RESPONSE

While no one denies that there are differences between male and female sexual anatomy and physiology, most modern sex researchers and therapists have been more impressed with the similarities than the differences. Men and women are not as different as was once thought.

The similarities are evident at the very beginning of life. During the first six to eight weeks of life, male and female fetuses are indistinguishable and follow an identical course of development. The fetus is basically female in that it will develop female sex organs unless something external is added. The something external is the hormone androgen, which stimulates the development of male sex organs.

Male and female sex organs develop from the same basic structures. To take but one example, a structure called the genital tubercle becomes the clitoris in girls and the head of the penis in boys. Both of these organs are richly supplied with nerve endings sensitive to touch and both are capable of expansion. In this sense, it is proper to think of the penis and clitoris as counterparts. The similarities between males and females go beyond just these two organs. Almost every part of the male sexual anatomy has a counterpart in an organ or tissue in women which has similar origins and functions.

Despite our common beginning, however, our genitals end up looking quite dissimilar. The external genitals of a woman are illustrated in Figure 7. Of course, all women do not look the same. Just as men's genitals differ in placement, size, color, and other characteristics, so do women's. But the figure will serve well enough for our purposes.

Let's start at the top with the clitoris, a unique organ. Its uniqueness lies in the fact that it has no function other than providing pleasure. Men have nothing quite like it, since their penises are also organs of elimination. The fact that the penis is larger than the clitoris does not mean much. The smaller organ has about as many nerve endings, so it is very sensitive to stimulation.

The importance of the clitoris was not fully appreciated until the work of Kinsey and Masters and Johnson. Before them, it was commonly believed that the vagina was the sexual organ

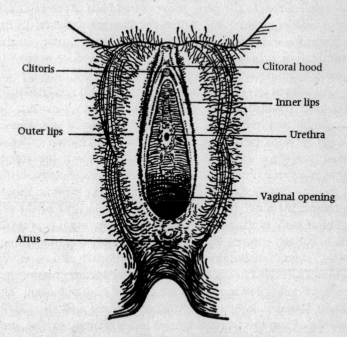

FIGURE 7: EXTERNAL FEMALE GENITALS

in women. Not only should they have orgasms with penile thrusting in the vagina but, should they need some warming up first, that was done by finger thrusting in the vagina. A number of factors helped undermine the idea of vaginal supremacy. One was the finding that when women masturbate, they usually stimulate the area around the clitoris and rarely insert anything into the vagina. Another important factor was that many women who are not orgasmic in intercourse do have orgasms when they or their partners stimulate the clitoral area.

The clitoris rarely gets direct stimulation during intercourse. As you can see in Figure 7, it is quite difficult for a penis to be in the vagina and touching the clitoris at the same time. To accomplish this in most positions you would need an L-shaped penis, and you just don't see many of them anymore. The clitoris does receive indirect stimulation from penile thrusting in intercourse. As the penis moves in and out of the vagina, it tugs on the vaginal lips. Since the lips are attached to the clitoral hood, thrusting does affect the clitoris. However, this stimulation is indirect and insufficient to produce orgasm in many women.

The clitoris can also be stimulated in a more direct fashion by rubbing it against the man's pubic bone. This can be accomplished in the female superior position if the woman leans forward far enough. It can also be achieved in other positions – for example, the male superior – if the couple makes a special effort to do so. In older marriage manuals this practice was called 'riding high', meaning that the man should position his pubic bone so that it pressed against his lover's clitoral area. While pubic-bone clitoral stimulation is possible, such contact is often difficult to maintain during intercourse. And, even if maintained, the stimulation it affords is not always sufficient to allow the woman to have an orgasm.

The outer lips of the vagina are covered with pubic hair. The inner lips are closer to the vaginal opening and are usually closed. When the woman spreads her legs or is aroused, they part, exposing the urethra and vaginal opening. Both the outer and inner lips are sensitive to the touch in many women, although such stimulation in itself is unlikely to produce orgasm.

Since we have made statements about what is and is not likely to lead to orgasm in women, we should add an important qualification. Erogenous zones and orgasms are largely the result of conditioning, and while what we are saying seems true of most women, there are others who do not conform to these ideas. There are women who can have orgasms through breast stimulation alone, and there are others who are orgasmic through stimulation of areas other than the clitoris, vagina, or breasts. It's important to remember that there are many individual differences.

While often thought of as a hole, the vagina is actually a potential rather than a real space. In the unaroused state its walls are relaxed and touch each other. When sexually excited, the walls balloon out, forming an actual space. This space will form itself to fit snugly around whatever object is inside of it, from the smallest penis to a baby's head.

While the erotic sensitivity of the vagina differs from woman to woman, it is true that the outer third of the vagina (the part closest to the entrance) contains the most nerve endings and probably the only nerves in it that are sensitive to touch. The inner two-thirds are, in many women, quite insensitive to touch and, in fact, minor surgery has been performed in this area without the use of anesthetics. However, the inner two-thirds are sensitive to pressure and stretch in many women, and the thrusting and distention that occur during intercourse can be very pleasurable for them.

Fashions change quickly in the sex field, and although it seems not too long ago that women who had little feeling in their vaginas were being called neurotic and in need of psychoanalysis, more recently we seem to be in the grip of what Germaine Greer has called a 'veritable clitoromania'. Some radical feminists and sex authorities talk as if the vagina were of no importance whatever to the woman, being a source of pleasure only for the man. We have more than once observed talks on female sexuality that so overstressed the importance of the clitoris (no doubt in reaction to the previous underestimation of its role) that women with little feeling there, or those who achieved orgasms with penile thrusting in the vagina, asked if something was wrong with them.

Since the vagina will accommodate itself to any size penis, some well-meaning people have argued that women have no preferences regarding penis size and that there is no size difference among erect penises, anyway. Yet the fact is that penises do differ in size, whether hard or soft, and there's no point pretending otherwise. And while most women don't have strong size preferences, it would be folly to think that they have no preferences at all. Of the questionnaire respondents we talked to, some said they liked long, thin penises, others favored short, thick ones, and others had still different choices. But they didn't put these preferences on the questionnaire. Why not? Simply because choices regarding penis size are just not that important to them. We call such preferences druthers. A druther is an ideal, something you'd like if you could have anything you wanted. But it's not necessary or even a high priority.

Perhaps you can think of some of your druthers. If you could have anything you wanted in a woman, you might like a certain kind of smile, nose, hair, behind, breasts, or whatever. But since this world is far from perfect, you easily accept your lover without such qualities. And this is precisely the way the overwhelming majority of women feel about penis size. Even if they have a preference (and not all women do), they can easily live without it. Certainly they are not going to let it dictate their choice of a man.

That's the good news. Now for the bad. Although we have never in our personal lives or work encountered a woman who was so obsessed with penis size that she let it run her sex life, we are sure that a few such women must exist somewhere. Just as there are a few men who absolutely will not have sex with a woman unless her breasts can fill a 38D bra, there are probably a few women who won't be satisfied with anything less than a twelve-inch penis. Should it be your misfortune to run into one of these women, the only reasonable suggestion we can make is that you get away as quickly as possible. Being that concerned about a physical characteristic over which no one can have any control is not a good sign. Besides, if you don't have the requisite number of inches there is nothing you can do about it. Better to spend your time with one of the millions of women who couldn't care less about such things.

We want to discuss briefly some of the physiological changes that occur as a woman goes through a sexual experience. This discussion parallels the one on men in Chapter 7. For the reasons mentioned there, we do not use Masters and Johnson's concept of the sexual response cycle in this discussion. For women as for men, there are many different ways of having a sexual experience.

The main changes that occur for both women and men are the result of vasocongestion, the accumulation of blood in various parts of the body. Muscular tension increases and other changes also occur. Orgasm reverses the blood flow and releases the tension, but these phenomena occur even without orgasm, though more slowly.

A sexual response begins when the woman receives some kind of sexual stimulation, which can be almost anything – touch, smell, fantasy, or sight. An increased volume of blood is pumped into various parts of her body, increasing their size and sensitivity to stimulation. The pelvis is not the only area so affected. While women's reactions differ considerably, usually the breasts, lips, and ear lobes are sensitized.

Vaginal lubrication begins soon after blood starts flowing into the pelvic region. The lubrication is produced by the vaginal walls in a process similar to sweating. Lubrication does not mean, as once thought, that the woman is ready for penetration or close to orgasm. It only signifies that she is beginning to become aroused. The amount of lubrication varies from woman to woman and from time to time in the same woman. Some women lubricate so freely that it seems to flow out of the vagina while others produce only a sparse amount.

The flow of blood to the sexual tissues causes them to enlarge. The breasts, clitoris, and inner and outer vaginal lips puff up. The vagina starts expanding and lengthening at the same time. As stimulation continues, the outer two-thirds of the vagina narrows, creating what Masters and Johnson call the 'orgasmic platform'. Some men and women have taken this narrowing of the vaginal opening as a sign that the woman is not aroused; in fact, it signifies the opposite.

The clitoris, as mentioned, expands as more blood flows into it, in a process quite similar to penile erection. The clitoris always increases in diameter but only in some women does it also get longer. As stimulation continues, the clitoris retracts under its hood. It may no longer be visible and is often difficult to find. Many are the times that men have gone in search of it, wondering where on earth it went. There's no need to look for it because you probably won't find it in any case. Even though not visible, however, the clitoris still responds to stimulation of the area around it.

Increased muscular tension may be evident – in the face, hands, thighs, abdomen, or almost any place. There may also be involuntary contractions or spasms in the pelvis, buttocks, and elsewhere. Other changes include increased blood pressure, heart rate, and respiration rate.

As with men, all these changes are reversible. If the woman is distracted or stops to talk to her partner or starts doing something which is less stimulating for her, her excitement level will drop, accompanied by physical changes reflecting the lesser degree of arousal. This is nothing to get concerned about. A reinstatement of the conditions and activities that led to the higher level of arousal will probably have the same effect again.

But let's stay with the woman in a high state of arousal and discuss what would happen if, for whatever reason, she didn't have an orgasm. Women's orgasms have received so much publicity in recent years that it is easy to think that not having one would be disastrous. In reality, it is no different from what happens to a man who doesn't have an orgasm in a sexual encounter. There may be a feeling of frustration or disappointment or there may not. It depends on many factors, not the least important of which is how the woman feels about her partner and their sexual relationship. If she generally can get what she wants and knows that the man is willing to do what she desires, it's usually no big thing if she doesn't have an orgasm. On the other hand, if she feels that the man cares only about his own satisfaction and isn't willing to do anything for her, the lack of orgasm can be a serious matter.

This discussion refers only to occasional lack of orgasm. If the lack of orgasm is the norm, the woman may lose interest in sex altogether.

If you and your partner are satisfied with your sexual activities, each knowing you usually get what you want, there's no reason why every encounter should end in orgasm. Your sexual experiences can be interrupted or terminated at any point without undue physical or emotional damage to either party. The important thing is that neither of you puts pressure on yourself or the other to have orgasms, for doing so can create a situation that is quite difficult to live with, much more so than an occasional lack of orgasm.

Orgasms in men and women are quite similar, the main difference being that women do not ejaculate. In both men and women, orgasm is a reflex that releases the muscular tension and reverses the flow of blood to the pelvic area.

It is important to know that women require stimulation not only up to the point of orgasm but throughout the orgasm as well. In this, they differ from men. Once men reach the point of inevitability, orgasm will occur even if stimulation ceases. In a woman, however, if stimulation is interrupted a second before the onset of orgasm or in the midst of it, the excitement may decline rapidly, resulting in no orgasm or a truncated one.

In many women orgasm is accompanied by contractions of the pelvic musculature, contractions which you may feel if your finger or penis is in the vagina. While Masters and Johnson and other authorities define female orgasm in terms of these contractions (meaning no orgasm without the contractions), it seems to us that such definition is unreasonably narrow. Irving Singer, in his book *The Goals of Human Sexuality*, argues persuasively that orgasms without contractions are not only possible but the norm for many women. Some women with whom we've discussed this issue agree. Orgasms, like everything else in sex, follow no absolute pattern. There may be evident pelvic contractions or there may not. Only your partner knows if she has had an orgasm.

Traditional thought had it that men's and women's experience of orgasm differed greatly. Men's orgasms were more explosive and short-lived while women's, though less powerful, were more prolonged. It is difficult to know what to make of this information. When men and women talk about their orgasms, the most impressive feature is the tremendous variation among individuals, and among different orgasms in the same individual. The only research study we know of in this area found that neither physicians, psychologists, nor medical students could correctly differentiate between written descriptions of male and female orgasms.

The next logical issue to examine is multiple orgasms. People scoffed when Kinsey reported in 1953 that 14 per cent of the women he interviewed said that they could have two, three, or even more orgasms during one sexual encounter. It was not so easy to scoff when Masters and Johnson demonstrated that women in their laboratory could indeed have more than one orgasm in a relatively short period of time with continued stimulation.

Most men do not seem to have this ability. They experience a period after ejaculation during which no amount of stimulation will produce either erection or ejaculation. Whether or not such a refractory period is necessary is something that cannot be answered at this time. We believe, and there is some research evidence to support the idea, that at least some men can learn to have multiple orgasms similar to women's. Whatever the merits of this viewpoint, the present situation is that very few men have multiple orgasms while a number of women can and do.

But even with women the picture is not clear. While many authorities write and speak as if it had been conclusively proved that all women are capable of multiple orgasms, such proof does not exist. It is simply not known how widespread the ability to have multiple orgasms is.

What is unfortunately clear is that the emphasis on multiple orgasms, by the media and some experts, has created a great deal of confusion and feelings of inadequacy. Many women feel deficient if they have only one orgasm and many men wonder what is wrong with them if their partners are not multiply orgasmic. Imagine what a woman who rarely or never has orgasms might think of herself.

A vast confusion has been created between what may be possible and what should be done. Just because a woman is capable of having several orgasms is no reason that she must have several. But because of all the anxiety surrounding sex, whenever an authority announces that people are capable of something or other, a lot of us take it to mean that there's something wrong with us if we can't or aren't doing it.

If your partner likes to have several orgasms, that's nice, but no nicer and no more proof of anything than if she has only one or none on a particular occasion. The only reason for having more than one orgasm is that it feels good at the time – unless, of course, you or she is training for the orgasm olympics. If your partner desires continued stimulation to have another orgasm, you are free to decide whether or not you want to participate in the process. Try to avoid the compulsion to participate when you don't want to. Also avoid the notion that all her orgasms should come through intercourse.

The last orgasm issue we discuss is the means by which a woman is orgasmic – the old clitoral-vaginal controversy. The old idea, formulated by Freud and his followers, and still very influential, is that women should have orgasms by means of a penis thrusting in their vaginas. This should happen without any simultaneous clitoral stimulation (what Lonnie Barbach calls 'Look ma, no hands' orgasms). This notion plays a large role in the fantasy model of sex where every woman is capable of orgasm via intercourse. Orgasms derived from hand or mouth stimulation, or from intercourse plus hand stimulation, are considered by the adherents of this idea to be immature or infantile.

The truth is that many women do not have 'no hands' orgasms. In a recent work that looks at this issue, *The Hite Report*, it was reported that only about 30 per cent of women consistently achieve vaginal orgasms (meaning through intercourse). The women who are orgasmic through means other than intercourse are no more neurotic, frigid, or hostile toward men than women who have vaginal orgasms. Most of them are perfectly normal and healthy; they just don't have orgasms by means of a thrusting penis.

This wouldn't be a problem were it not for the fact that it differs so widely from the model we learned.

My first sexual experiences fit my model of sex: we did the foreplay thing and, when the woman was ready, we inserted my penis and fucked away until both of us had orgasms. This was the way it was supposed to be. Then I got involved with a woman who liked intercourse but never had orgasms with it. She wanted me to play with her clitoris before or after intercourse in order for her to come. At first I was shocked by what I thought was her problem. Then I thought that I could make her come in intercourse if we had longer sessions of foreplay, used different positions, and a number of other techniques. All of which failed. Then I thought that something was wrong with me. If only I knew the right things to do, I could get her to come 'the right way'. For almost a year I vacillated between thinking that something was wrong with her and something was wrong with me. Finally, with a lot of help from her, I started to realize that nothing was wrong with either of us. The problem lay in my model of sex, which was far too limited. Not too long ago, many years after our sexual relationship had ended, I talked to her about this issue and we had a good laugh about it. She told me that she finally had managed to have a few orgasms in intercourse but that they took too much effort and were not worth the trouble.

The main point here is simply that there is nothing wrong with women who do not have orgasms the 'right way'. There is, in fact, no right way. It is our models that are in need of correction, for they are narrow and limited, far too restrictive to encompass the variety of human sexual experience.

The last part of a sexual experience is basically the same in men and women. It is simply a return to the unaroused state. The swelling in the genitals and other areas decreases as blood flows away from them, the muscles become relaxed, and the organs and tissues return to their normal positions. This process occurs more quickly if there has been an orgasm than if there has not. Sometimes, if there has been a very high level of arousal and no orgasm, the return to the unaroused state can take a considerable amount of time and there may be some discomfort. Masturbating to orgasm can bring relief, if it is desired.

Men and women display divergent tendencies immediately after sex. Many men have a tendency either to go to sleep or to leap into some other activity, whereas many women like to cuddle, talk, and in other ways continue the experience of being together. Our speculation is that these differences are rooted in socialization practices rather than in physiological differences. The time after sex can be difficult for men to handle since there is no longer any agenda or format. There is no task to be done, no goal to be reached, and nothing to be accomplished. We men are not trained to deal comfortably with such situations. There's just you and this other person and nothing in particular to do except relate.

If you are interested in pursuing this, perhaps the best thing to do is tell your partner what you're feeling. Tell her you feel like jumping up and making a sandwich, or turning on the TV, or taking a walk, or whatever – tell her and don't do it. Resist the urge to do something and stay with her. Kiss, hug, talk, listen. It may be uncomfortable if you've never done it before, but try to stick it out for a few times and see if you don't start feeling more comfortable. We've worked with a number of men on this issue and almost all have found that they quickly became more comfortable with this kind of intimacy. They were soon participating for their own satisfaction, not just to please their partners.

Now that you have read about what woman say they like and how they function, you may be wondering, 'How does this apply to my partner? How should I act with her?' Many men ask these questions and we have a simple answer. Namely, that we don't have the foggiest notion.

We can only repeat what we have already said several times – there are tremendous individual variations. What is arousing for one woman may be repugnant to another.

When I was in high school, the word was that blowing in a girl's ear and putting your tongue in there was a good way to get her hot. So, not knowing what else to do, I always did the ear thing. Some girls obviously liked it. But others didn't, and one said that it was a complete turn-off.

What is true about ears and blowing in them is true for every other part of the body and every other technique – some women will like it and some won't.

Take women's breasts, for example. Most men seem to be turned-on by breasts; by seeing them, touching them, kissing them. And they assume that women will be very aroused by such actions. There is no question that this assumption is true for many women. But just how common is women's sensitivity to breast stimulation? Probably not as common as most men think. Kinsey reported that most women were only moderately aroused by having their breasts stimulated. Lonnie

Barbach, who has probably worked with more women on sexual issues than any other therapist, estimates that about 60 per cent of them get a lot of pleasure from having their breasts touched, while the rest either get only a small amount of pleasure from it or are relatively indifferent to such caresses.

This presents an interesting problem, one that is especially evident in new relationships but also present in many older ones as well. The man, we have been taught, should somehow know what his partner likes. But how can he manage this if women are different? Reading all the books in the world won't help since his woman may have different tastes than those discussed in the books. Besides, even the books differ. Lots of experience is often thought to be a panacea, but it isn't. What worked for the last partner, or even the last twenty partners, may not be what the present partner wants. It would be nice to think that the woman will come to the rescue, clearly letting her partner know what she wants. It sometimes happens this way, but rarely. As we saw in our discussion of the questionnaire study, many women are uncomfortable stating their preferences, particularly in a new relationship. What, then, is a man to do?

There are several possibilities. You can just do whatever you want, either not caring about her or figuring that if she wants something different, she'll say so. However, it should be clear from what we presented earlier in the chapter that this option is bound to create problems. Women are less and less willing to put up with it.

Another alternative, used by many men, is to play Sherlock Holmes and attempt, using whatever clues are available, to figure out what would please her. The problem with this method is that it only works well when your partner gives frequent, clear, and relatively consistent clues. Otherwise, you are going to be working very hard trying to decipher all of her nonverbal communications. You will make many errors and put a tremendous amount of pressure on yourself.

Our own bias, one that agrees with what many women want and that has worked very well with the men who have used it under our direction, is for open communication. Since your life will be much easier if you know what pleases her, ask her or somehow give her permission to tell you, perhaps by voicing your own preferences. As we noted earlier, this permission is very important to many women.

The first time I had sex with Carla I asked, 'What would you like?' Not exactly eloquent or brilliant, but it produced some interesting results. She told me what she wanted and we had a very nice time. A few days later she said that since she had orgasms through oral or manual stimulation but not with intercourse, she never indicated her needs the first few times she was with a man. Only after they knew each other better and were more comfortable sexually would she say what she wanted. But my simple question had allowed her to express what she wanted the first time we were together sexually. She appreciated my interest and I must say that I was quite proud of myself.

The power of a few words is well illustrated by this example. Asking, however, should not be confused with demanding. By asking your partner what she likes, you are giving her the opportunity to express herself if she so desires. Be aware that she may not choose to answer, at least not then. For many women, being asked what they want by a man is such a new idea that they need some time to get accustomed to it. It is also possible that she hasn't given much thought to her preferences. If you get no response, feel free to do whatever you want. Do not push her to answer. If you indicate your interest and willingness to listen, you are doing all that can reasonably be expected. The chances are good that she will get around to telling you when she is ready, or the next time you ask in a gentle and nondemanding way.

If initiating this type of discussion is very difficult for you, you might find it easier by making use of an external prop.

This chapter is such a prop. Asking her to read it, followed by a discussion of the points she agrees and disagrees with, can be valuable.

FOURTEEN

On not lasting long enough

Lack of ejaculatory control, usually called premature ejaculation, is one of the most common sexual complaints among American men. Although the phenomenon itself has been known for quite some time, it was not considered a major problem until very recently. As long as the woman's satisfaction and orgasm were not considered to be important, there was relatively little concern with how long a man could last. As long as he enjoyed himself, what was the problem? Just thirty years ago, Kinsey reported that 75 per cent of the men he interviewed ejaculated within two minutes of beginning intercourse. While he recognized that this might be 'inconvenient and unfortunate' from the point of view of their partners, he didn't consider such occurrences to be premature and seemed hard put to figure out what the problem might be.

Much has changed since Kinsey did his work. Although men are as performance-oriented as ever, perhaps even more so, the criteria of a good sexual performance have changed. It is no longer sufficient to 'get a lot', although that is still important. The real test of a good performance these days is the ability to satisfy one's partner, usually defined as giving her at least one, but preferably more, good orgasms in intercourse.

With this change in definition of male sexual prowess has come first an interest, then a concern, and now almost an obsession with lasting longer. As might be expected, the people who write about sex have done their share to promote this obsession. In his *How to Get More Out of Sex*, David Reuben unmercifully lambasts men who ejaculate quickly, implying that they are immature and accusing them of masturbating in the vagina. He warns that it is the man's job to keep his penis in his partner's vagina long enough to provide her with 'satisfactory service'. *The Sensuous Man* tells us that premature ejaculation is a 'major disaster'. It mentions the possibility of satisfying your partner through oral or manual play after you've had your orgasm, but then discounts the utility of this approach because 'the two of you can't really get the most out of your sex life unless you can prolong your intercourse long enough for her to have an orgasm (or lots of orgasms)'. And Gail Sheehy in her book *Passages* several times mentions the importance of the man withholding ejaculation long enough to bring his partner 'through an ascending chain of orgasms'.

Lasting a long time in intercourse seems to be a very important item. After all, who would want to be a major disaster? Or cheat their partners of ascending chains of orgasms?

Many men have been influenced by this type of thinking and have sought treatment to help them last longer. They are convinced that sex will be much better when they can have intercourse for longer periods of time. Their partners will become orgasmic or perhaps multiply orgasmic. And sex will just be better. Everyone will be happy and sated.

We're sorry to disappoint you, but it may not be that way at all. In order to explain this statement, we need to look more closely at what is meant by premature ejaculation. It is not a monolithic entity and, in fact, includes men of quite different ejaculatory behaviors.

There are men who ejaculate at the slightest provocation, sometimes even before touching their partners but more typically shortly after the commencement of any genital contact. Another group of men come as soon as their penises enter the vagina or within a few seconds of vaginal containment. Still other men can thrust for a few minutes before ejaculating, but they do not feel any sense of control over when they come.

The lack of ability consciously to control when ejaculation occurs is what characterizes all the men in the above categories. Ejaculations sort of sneak up on them; many report that 'all of a sudden, it just happens'. Sometimes they have some warning and realize they will soon come, but there's nothing they can do about it. Anything they do to hold off ejaculation only seems to speed it up.

These men are the ones who benefit most from learning ejaculatory control. All those we have worked with enjoyed sex more when they had acquired better voluntary control. Their own orgasms felt better – fuller or more complete, they said – and their partners appreciated the greater duration of intercourse, although many of the partners still did not become orgasmic through intercourse. For the types of men we have been talking about, then, it often is advisable to develop control over their ejaculatory processes.

However, there are many other men who want to last longer. They believe their partners would enjoy sex more or become orgasmic if only they (the men) could last longer. Which sounds reasonable and considerate until you realize that many of these men already have good ejaculatory control. Some of them are able, when they desire, to have intercourse for from ten to thirty minutes.

We'll never forget the man who called himself a premature ejaculator even though fairly regularly he lasted for forty-five minutes of vigorous thrusting. We know he lasted this long because his partner confirmed it. Actually, she had never been orgasmic in intercourse and had no desire to become so. She much preferred shorter intercourse because she sometimes became so sore through almost an hour of thrusting that she could barely sit down the next day. That had little influence on the thinking of our client, who was convinced that she would have orgasms if only he could last an hour.

It is only natural to assume that a few minutes longer might do the trick (more enjoyment, orgasms, multiple orgasms) but this is often an illusion. If you can already last for ten to fifteen minutes, or even longer, the chances that your partner will become orgasmic or find more contentment if you last longer are highly improbable.

If your partner is not orgasmic in the length of time you usually last, it might be a good idea to talk to her about what she wants. Perhaps she is orgasmic in other ways and doesn't care about becoming so in intercourse. Much of the obsession with lasting longer is due to the exaggerated importance most of us have given to intercourse. Maybe she would prefer to get what she wants through some other sexual activity. Whatever her feelings in this regard, we hope you can listen to her. Don't be like the man we cited in the example who thought he knew how things should be for his lover. And remember that there is nothing inherently better about long-lasting sex than the shorter variety. Sex that *has* to last a certain length of time, especially long periods of time, can be very boring. It can also give you a real pain in the crotch.

It is interesting that despite all the interest in premature ejaculation, there is no agreed-upon definition of what it is. Some people, like David Reuben, think a man is premature unless he can thrust for five to ten minutes. Others, following Masters and Johnson, define prematurity as the inability to satisfy the woman 50 per cent of the time in intercourse. Both of these definitions have serious drawbacks.

The definition we use is quite simple and does away with the term premature ejaculation. We are interested in a man's ability to exercise voluntary control over his ejaculatory process. This is not to say that anyone can be in total control of such a bodily function. Rather, a man with good control is one who usually can decide approximately when he will ejaculate. He usually can last a long time when he wants, and he also can come quickly if he so desires. His control of the process allows him to do what feels right at the moment.

Of course, a man without this type of control doesn't necessarily have a problem. If he and his partner are content, there is no reason for change. Only if you are dissatisfied with your lack of control should you follow the procedures in the next two chapters.

Most of the men we've worked with have been consistent in their lack of control. They've experienced it all their lives and with all partners. But there are many exceptions. Some have reasonably good control in some activities, like masturbation or when their partners stimulate them by hand, but not in others, usually intercourse. Some other men report having had good control at some time in their lives but having since lost the ability to delay ejaculation. Still others report good control with certain partners but not others. A great many men come very quickly the first time or times they have sex with a new partner. This is usually a transitory phenomenon, with control returning after the man is more comfortable with his new lover.

If your problem is situational – that is, if it occurs at some times but not others, with some partners but not others – you need to consider if your conditions are being met when you don't have control. The chances are that they are not, and you'll probably reap more benefit from working on them than from doing exercises to develop control. Or perhaps you can do both.

Just as there is no consensus about a definition for premature ejaculation, there is no agreement on what causes it. There has been speculation that men's socialization predisposes them to speedy ejaculations. It is true that men are taught to put a lot of value on speed. And many of our early sexual experiences, whether masturbating in the bathroom or having sex in the back seat of a car, carried the risk of discovery, so the quicker we got them over with the less the chance of being found out. While this type of thinking seems plausible, it doesn't explain why, given similar early experiences, some of us lack ejaculatory control while others have enough to spare.

Some in the psychoanalytic tradition have argued that coming quickly is a neurotic process, a manifestation of conflicts regarding women. They believe that such conflicts must be worked out before the man can learn to delay his ejaculations. However, since treatment based on this idea has not been notably successful, while more direct behavioral approaches have been, serious doubt is cast on the credibility of the whole argument. This, of course, does not rule out the possibility that some cases of premature ejaculation may be caused or maintained by internal or interpersonal conflicts. But even in such cases, the suggestions in the next two chapters, combined with the fulfilling of conditions, are usually all that is needed to resolve the difficulty.

Despite the fact that our understanding of what causes lack of ejaculatory control is inadequate, solutions to the problem do exist. The most widely employed remedies, however, are the ones with the least value. Every man who has come sooner than he wanted has tried to control his ejaculations, usually by gritting his teeth and will in an effort to hold them back. This method rarely works since it only creates tension, which in itself can trigger quick ejaculations.

Another popular method, still advocated by some authorities, attempts to decrease excitement by telling the man to 'think of other things' while he is having sex. While this approach sometimes works, the price is tremendous since the man is asked not to experience his good feelings. What is the point of lasting longer or having sex at all if you are not allowed to enjoy it?

We have the same objection to the use of numbing ointments. These preparations, which can be purchased at most drugstores, partially anesthetize the penis. A numb penis, the theory goes, should last longer than one that feels more. These ointments sometimes work but often they do not. If you are considering using one of them, you might want to consider the costs. Not only do you sacrifice some enjoyment but, since you don't learn anything about controlling ejaculations, you become forever dependent upon the ointment.

Our thinking is that lasting longer should not involve the numbing of feeling. Rather, it should allow you to feel more, to enjoy and luxuriate in high levels of sexual excitement and sensation for as long as you like.

There are several methods that allow you to do just that. Two of them depend on the ability to control the muscles in the pelvis, the muscles developed by the Kegel exercise in Chapter 7. One technique requires that you relax these muscles when you feel close to orgasm, thus delaying ejaculation. The other technique is just the reverse, tightening the same muscles as you near ejaculation. They both work, but experimentation is necessary to determine exactly when to tense or relax the muscles. We will not say any more about these procedures but you might want to explore them on your own. You should first, however, practice the Kegel exercise until you are in good touch with the pelvic muscles.

Both of these methods, as well as the others that have been successful in developing ejaculatory control, have one point in common – training the man to pay attention to his feelings of sexual excitement. Unlike the think-of-something-else notion, the effective methods ask that you pay more attention to the good feelings. By attending to these feelings, you know when you are approaching ejaculation and can take some simple steps to delay it.

While we do not understand why some men have acquired good control with no conscious effort or training, it seems to be true that all, or at least most, men who have control make adjustments in their behavior when they feel close to orgasm. One of us, trying to determine how men controlled their ejaculations, observed that he always changed his manner of thrusting when he felt close to orgasm but didn't want it to happen yet. He then asked a number of other men with good control to observe their behavior to see if they made any adjustments to help them last longer. All of them, including several who before observing themselves adamantly denied making any adjustments, discovered that they did indeed make changes in their behavior. The type of changes made varied considerably: squeezing or relaxing the pelvic muscles, slowing the tempo, changing the depth of thrusting, or changing the type of thrusting (e.g., from in and out to circular motions).

The procedures in the next two chapters are designed to enable you to do what these men do. They somehow acquired their skills without any special training but, at the end of your training program, your skills will be the same as theirs.

Without realizing it, you have already successfully negotiated a very similar training process: when you learned to control your urinary function. When you were very small, you had no control over urination; it just happened when your bladder reached a certain degree of fullness. But then your parents let you know that this was not satisfactory and that you had to take charge of the situation. You gradually learned to recognize the sensations in your body announcing that you were about to urinate, and you could signal that you had to go to the bathroom. At this point your training was incomplete. You could tell if something was about to happen but you couldn't delay its occurrence.

As time went on, you completed your training. You not only knew when urination was imminent but you could also exert some control over when it happened. You might realize that you had to urinate, but if you were in the middle of an interesting game you could squeeze some muscles and wiggle around enough to hold it back, at least for a while.

All this is many years behind you, of course, and you probably have no memory of the experiences. The processes of control have been under automatic pilot for years and you may not be aware that you are doing anything to delay the onset of urination, just as some of the men we questioned didn't realize that they did anything to delay ejaculation. If you have any doubts about what we are saying, focus your attention in your crotch the next time you have to go to the bathroom but are in a situation that requires you to wait.

What you need to learn to control your ejaculations is not much different from what you learned then, and learned very successfully. And this time it will be much easier. Your body is better coordinated and your mind is far more developed, two factors that will help considerably.

Our approach in developing ejaculatory control is based on a simple technique developed in the 1950s by James Semans. The method consisted in the stimulation of the client's penis by his partner until he felt the sensations signaling that ejaculation was near. His partner stopped stimulation, resuming when the man no longer felt close to ejaculation. With practice, the man could enjoy more and more stimulation without ejaculating. Semans's method is the foundation of almost all of the successful procedures used by sex therapists today for developing ejaculatory control.

Masters and Johnson took Semans's stop-start method and added a squeeze; instead of merely stopping the stimulation of the penis, the woman squeezes it where the head and shaft join. We have used both the stop-start and the squeeze and found that they both give the same results. Since the squeeze is a bit more difficult to learn, we no longer use it.

Semans worked only with men who had cooperative partners, and Masters and Johnson argued that ejaculatory control could not be developed without such a partner. Fortunately, they were wrong. We have devised some methods that do not require a partner's participation and that have yielded the same impressive results as the partner exercises.

If you want to gain more control over your ejaculatory process so that you can enjoy intense sexual pleasure without immediately ejaculating, go on to the next two chapters. The training will of course involve conscious attention and effort at first. As time goes on, however, you will be less and less aware that you are monitoring your arousal level and making adjustments in your behavior. You will consciously forget about making adjustments and be free to enjoy fully your partner and yourself.

FIFTEEN

Starting to develop ejaculatory control

Ejaculatory control can be effectively learned either on your own or by doing exercises with a partner. We suggest that even if you want to do the partner exercises, you do at least the first masturbation exercise in this chapter before starting to work with her. The reason for this suggestion is that it is easier to learn the rudiments of control without her distracting presence. Once you have mastered the fundamentals, it will be easier to work with her.

If you absolutely don't want to do the masturbation exercises, you should at least read this chapter before turning to the partner exercises in the next chapter. Should you encounter problems in doing the partner exercises, it may be necessary for you to reconsider your stance regarding the masturbation exercises.

The first step in attaining ejaculatory control is learning to pay attention to your arousal level in a sexual situation so that you will know when you need to change your behavior to delay ejaculation.

Figure 8 (page 282), representing a hypothetical sexual experience, will help facilitate your understanding of arousal levels and the adjustments you need to make. The flat part of the curve, what Masters and Johnson refer to as the plateau phase, is usually experienced as very pleasurable. Men who can last as long as they like do so by spending as much time as they want at this level of excitement. Those who do not have ejaculatory control do not spend much time here. In fact, their arousal level does not seem to flatten out at all, going directly

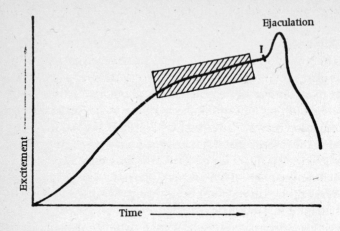

FIGURE 8: MALE SEXUAL RESPONSE WITH EJACULATORY
CONTROL

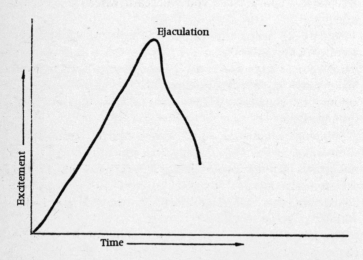

FIGURE 9: MALE SEXUAL RESPONSE WITHOUT EJACULATORY
CONTROL

from zero to orgasm, as illustrated in Figure 9 (page 282). What is needed is a way of staying at the plateau level for longer periods of time, thus prolonging the pleasure and delaying the ejaculation.

Point I in Figure 8 stands for inevitability, shorthand for Masters and Johnson's sense of ejaculatory inevitability. This is the place, a few seconds before the ejaculate appears, where the man senses that ejaculation is about to occur and that there's nothing he can do about it. It will happen even if all stimulation ceases. The reason for this is, as we said in Chapter 7, that the internal sex organs have already begun contracting, starting the ejaculate on its way through the penis.

Before the point of inevitability there is an area (the shaded portion of the curve in Figure 8) where, if stimulation ceases, ejaculation will not occur. This means that you can enjoy high levels of arousal and, providing you stop stimulation somewhere in this area, not ejaculate. There is no precise way of demarcating the point at which you should stop. Any time you are feeling very excited but not yet at inevitability is acceptable. With practice you will learn where you need to stop.

You will be asked to masturbate to a high level of excitement, stopping when you feel close to ejaculation, to learn more about where you should stop. You will undoubtedly make some 'mistakes' – stopping too late to prevent ejaculation – on your way to discovering the boundaries of the stopping area.

Stopping stimulation, meaning complete cessation of stimulating the genitals, is simply a training procedure and will not always be necessary. After establishing good control using the stop-start method, you can learn to make more subtle adjustments that will allow you to control your ejaculations without stopping.

The following guidelines apply to all the exercises in this chapter:

1. Except where noted, each exercise requires fifteen

minutes. We use fifteen minutes because it has produced good results, not because we think this is an ideal or normal time for sex to last. Going longer than fifteen minutes won't do any harm but it probably won't be of much help, either. Some of the men we worked with have proudly announced that they had reached the point where they could masturbate without ejaculating for periods ranging from thirty minutes to over an hour. While this is a great attention-getter, it serves no useful function. On the other hand, you should make sure you are not consistently going for much less than the suggested time. The fifteen minutes refers only to the time you are masturbating and making adjustments. Anything else you do – fantasizing before beginning to masturbate, massaging other parts of your body, and so on – is not included.

2. If you want to ejaculate after you have done an exercise, you may, but it is best if you go slowly, focusing in your penis and being aware of the point of inevitability as you reach it and pass through it. Done this way, ejaculating after an exercise will be an integral part of your learning better ejaculatory control.

3. Since you want to develop new patterns of functioning, it is important to be consistent in your masturbatory practices. Once you start with the exercises, it is best not to alternate with your old ways of masturbating, for this would only impede your progress.

4. The exercises should be done at least three or four times a week. In general, the more frequently you do them, the sooner you will reach your goals.

5 At times you may find that you have difficulty getting an erection, either before starting an exercise or after stopping to allow your arousal level to decrease. This is not a cause for concern. If playing with your penis, accompanied by fantasy if you like, does not result in an erection in a few minutes, do not try to force it. Come back to the exercise later when you are in a sexier mood.

6. Do the exercises in the order in which they are presented. Two criteria should be satisfied before moving from one

can always stop to prevent ejaculation. When you feel you are no longer close to ejaculation, you can resume the more arousing type of stimulation if you want.

POSSIBLE PROBLEM

Progress is more difficult now than with the stopping exercises. This is to be expected. Finding the changes that work best takes some time, as does determining just when to make the changes. Do not be afraid to make them very early; there's no rule that says you have to start sex with wild in-and-out thrusting.

Many men find that their new ways of moving are quite enjoyable and come to prefer them over their old ways. Going slower, making shorter thrusts, moving in circular ways, or squeezing the pelvic muscles just become part of the way they like to have sex. When this happens, lasting as long as they like is no longer an issue.

For many men, what has been presented so far will be sufficient to develop a high degree of ejaculatory control, and they will want to move on to partner sex. They should first, however, do the last exercise in this series, 15–5, which need be done only once. Other men, however, will not yet feel ready to move on and, for them, we suggest two fantasy exercises.

We have found that fantasy is an excellent means of making the transition from masturbation exercises to partner sex. Our use of fantasy might best be called role-rehearsal. Fantasizing a behavior under controlled conditions prepares you to carry out that behavior in your life and also reduces some of the anxiety you may feel about it. You will be asked to fantasize sexual situations while masturbating with the stop-start method, and later, while employing the more subtle means of delaying ejaculation. You will be in a much better position to have ejaculatory control with a partner after doing these exercises.

Some people find it easier to have clear fantasies or images than others. Most of us have some difficulty, at least initially, seeing distinct pictures in our minds. In general, the more you practice, the more vivid and lifelike the images get. Even if this does not occur – and we know that some men never develop clear images – the fantasy exercises can still work. Having fantasies that are less than clear, or having thoughts or feelings rather than pictures, will do as well.

What is most important, whether you have thoughts, feelings, or images, is that you be able really to imagine the scene or idea you are dealing with. You can help yourself get more fully into the fantasy by noticing details. If the scene you are working on is of your partner stimulating your penis with her hand, for example, ask yourself how firmly she is holding the penis. Is she using long or short strokes? What about the texture and temperature of her hand? What's going on in your penis as she touches it? When you fantasize intercourse, be aware of how your bodies fit together, the temperature, texture, and wetness of the vagina, and so forth. Any details that will help you feel more like you are really there will be useful.

EXERCISE 15-3: STOP-START MASTURBATION WITH FANTASY

Step A: Using the stop-start method, masturbate for fifteen minutes while fantasizing having sex with a partner. Start the fantasy with the first touch or kiss and go through all the steps that might occur in this imagined sexual event, or at least as many of them as you can comfortably get through in fifteen minutes. You probably won't get through an entire sexual event in one session. That's fine. Next time you do the exercise, start the fantasy where you left off the last time.

As part of the fantasy, see yourself needing to stop with your partner and doing so. When you stop in the fantasy, stop your masturbating. When the urge to ejaculate has subsided, resume the fantasy and the masturbation. Be sure to include some scenes of needing to stop during intercourse. Needing to stop can be dictated by two

criteria: when you actually feel you need to stop to prevent ejaculation and at places in the fantasy where you feel you might need to stop in reality. Use both; just be sure to stop masturbating at the same time you stop in the fantasy.

Many men have trouble maintaining control with some of the fantasy scenes. The two places where they have the most trouble are when imagining entering the vagina and when thrusting becomes hard and fast. Since what gives you trouble in fantasy will tend to do the same in reality, you want to work with the scenes that are difficult. When you run into a difficult scene that does not get easier after several attempts, go to Step B.

Step B: Instead of masturbating to a fantasy of a whole sexual encounter, fantasize only the scene that gives you trouble. Make sure you are relaxed before beginning. Masturbate slowly, get into the fantasy as fully as possible while at the same time remaining aware of your level of excitement, and stop *before* you need to, both in the fantasy and in your masturbating. Go through the scene again and again until fifteen minutes are up. If at any time during the exercise you feel tense, discontinue it and do something to get more comfortable, then resume the exercise.

As you get more comfortable with this scene, you can shift to stopping when, rather than before, you need to. When you are comfortable and in control while fantasizing the difficult scene, return to Step A and incorporate this scene into the larger fantasy.

If you have trouble with more than one scene, work through all of them, one at a time, in the manner suggested above.

POSSIBLE PROBLEMS

1. You have difficulty staying with the fantasy, perhaps because of drifting into other thoughts and fantasies. When this happens, simply come back to the scene you were imagining. You will need to do this a number of times every session.

2. You don't stop in time to delay ejaculation because you forget about your excitement level. It is, of course, essential that you remain aware of how aroused you are so that you can stop in time. This is difficult for some people, since it means you have to focus on both the fantasy and your arousal. You can try keeping most of your attention on how excited you are, even if this means less distinct images. A better way is to record the fantasy and play it while you masturbate. Since you won't have to put any effort into developing the fantasy you can listen while putting your attention on your level of arousal.

3. You rush through the fantasy in an effort to complete it in one session. This exercise was not intended to be mastered in one session. The important thing is that it be carried out as suggested and without hurry. You need to get through all the possible scenes that might occur in a real sexual event, but there is no need to do so in one masturbation session. Speed is not only unimportant, but it can impede your progress.

When you have mastered that exercise, go on to the next one, which is quite similar.

EXERCISE 15–4: MASTURBATING WITH SUBTLE ADJUSTMENTS AND FANTASY

This exercise is identical to 15–3, with the exception that you now use the more subtle changes you discovered in Exercise 15–2 rather than stopping. Follow all other directions for 15–3. As you make adjustments in your masturbation, imagine yourself making them in the fantasy. Should any scenes cause you discomfort or make you feel that you are losing control, work through them using the suggestions in Step B of 15–3.

You should by now feel even more confident of your ability to exercise control over when you ejaculate. The next exercise sounds silly but is important, and you can have lots of fun with it. Whatever happens, it can be a good learning experience. It requires a minimum of time and need only be done once or twice.

EXERCISE 15-5: QUICKIE MASTURBATION WITH FOCUS

Focusing in your penis, masturbate and ejaculate as quickly as possible. Try to come even faster than you did before starting your training program. Keep focusing until you ejaculate.

If you do come fast, you can learn something about what makes for quick ejaculations. If you find it difficult to do, you will realize how far you've progressed. In either case, you win. And that is the point of the exercise, and of sex.

You might have found the exercise difficult to do because you were afraid that it might undo all that you have learned. Fear not, it will only broaden your horizons. You can control your ejaculations so that you can last a long time. See if you can also control them so that you can last a short time. You now have options; use them.

To use a bad pun, you've come a long way, and are ready to use your newly acquired control with a partner.

SIXTEEN

Lasting longer with a partner

In this chapter we present two basic approaches for developing ejaculatory control with a partner. The first thing you should decide is which best fits your situation and desires. Whichever you choose, it will help if you have read and understood Chapter 12, Dealing with a Partner, and have done at least some of the masturbation exercises in the last chapter.

One approach requires a partner who is willing to work with you on a series of exercises, 16–1 through 16–6. The general outline was developed by Semans, elaborated by Masters and Johnson and others, and has been widely employed. Its main drawback is the necessity of a cooperative partner with whom to do the exercises.

The second approach is not dependent on a cooperative partner and involves no exercises with a partner. It requires complete mastery of the masturbation exercises in the last chapter and the willingness to follow a set of guidelines when having sex with a lover. This approach, though not as well known as the partner exercise method, has yielded approximately the same results. It is presented first in this chapter so that those with partners can get a feel for it before making a decision about whether to do the partner exercises.

EJACULATORY CONTROL WITHOUT PARTNER EXERCISES

It is crucial that you have mastered the exercises in Chapter 15. You should be able to masturbate for fifteen minutes without ejaculating and without stopping. The more subtle adjustments should be sufficient for you to control your ejaculations. You should keep masturbating with subtle adjustments even after you no longer have trouble lasting as long as you want. When you start going out with someone with whom you might want to have sex, incorporate her into your masturbation fantasies.

It is also essential that you have done and feel comfortable with the assertiveness exercises in Chapters 6 and 12. The masturbation exercises and other training procedures will do you no good at all unless you are willing and able to get what you need in a sexual situation. The guidelines below assume that you already have some skill and confidence in asserting yourself. It won't always be easy, but if you have done all the preparatory work, you are ready to use your ejaculatory control with a lover.

Most of the principles you need to follow with a partner have already been given in the section on sex with a new partner in Chapter 12. They should be adhered to without exception. The suggestions below supplement that list.

1. Don't engage in intercourse until all your conditions are met and you are comfortable with her. This means that your first few experiences should not include intercourse. Let her play with your penis and make adjustments to allow you to delay ejaculation a reasonable length of time. This is a good way of checking your control with her. If you have trouble lasting with hand or mouth stimulation, you'll probably have more trouble with intercourse. Have intercourse only after you've established good control in other activities.

2. Stay focused in your penis during all sexual activities with her and make adjustments early. It is important that you be able to indicate that you want to stop, should a stop be advisable.

3. Check your arousal level before vaginal insertion. If it is high, make some adjustments before entering her (e.g., stopping for a minute or so; squeezing your pelvic muscles).

Don't start moving immediately after you have entered. Rest for a minute or so and be aware of your arousal level.

4. Go slowly in all your sexual activities, especially in intercourse. Take your time and experience all the sensations, making adjustments when necessary.

5. Don't expect things to work perfectly in the beginning. They won't. If you run into a problem that doesn't improve after a few experiences, you need not panic. You have the skills to work it out. Figure out as precisely as possible what the difficulty is: for example, 'I have good control except when she starts moving wildly in intercourse.' Then find an appropriate exercise to help you deal with it. In the example given, you could use a masturbation exercise, masturbating to a fantasy of her moving wildly in intercourse, going over the scene again and again while making adjustments to retain control. When you have mastered that, you can have intercourse with her again and now be more confident of your ability to control your ejaculations. If this isn't sufficient, you could ask her to move more slowly, at a pace at which you have good control. Then have her gradually increase the tempo. If you do this a few times, you will extend your control to cover the movements that at first gave you problems.

Remember that you can always ask her to slow down or stop if you feel you are losing control.

6. There will be times when you come fast, either because you lost control or because you wanted to. Don't apologize in either case. Enjoy yourself and do something for your partner if she so desires.

These principles should be carried out to the letter when you are starting to have sex with a new partner or trying to change sexual patterns with a familiar lover. These are the most anxious and trying times, so go slowly and follow the rules. As you become more comfortable with exercising your ejaculatory control with her, you will become less conscious of following the principles and they will become automatic.

That's really all there is to it. The program is simple but quite effective. Should it not work well for you, you should consider whether you have truly mastered the masturbation exercises and are following the guidelines. If you need to return to the exercises to learn the fundamentals better, do so. The same is true for the principles. They have to be followed. Do what is necessary to put them into effect. Should there still be difficulties, you have the option of doing the partner exercises.

PARTNER EXERCISES FOR LASTING LONGER

Before undertaking the program, discuss it with your lover. She should read Chapter 13 and the exercises in this chapter so she will understand what is being asked of her. Discuss your feelings and her feelings about the project and work out any differences before starting.

Everything depends upon clear communication and understanding and, since you don't have a therapist to help you, you need to expend some effort to ensure that the two of you agree on what is going to happen. Your partner should understand that the exercises constitute a training program and will not be needed forever. Since how long they are needed is largely a function of how often they are done, you should reach an agreement about frequency. She should also understand that the exercises need to be executed exactly as described and that you are in total control when the exercises are being done – of the type of stimulation, of when to stop and when to resume. You should be very clear about your willingness to satisfy her manually or orally before or after doing an exercise. Problems often arise because the woman feels she is doing all the work and getting nothing in return. Do everything possible to prevent this from becoming an issue. There will probably be misunderstandings and differences of opinion over this and other matters. They need to be talked out and resolved as quickly as possible.

It is very important that you don't restrict the physical activities with your partner to these exercises. Allow time and space for holding, hugging, kissing, taking baths together, and any other mutually enjoyable expressions of physical affection.

Since the stop-start method is the one used in the exercises, your partner should clearly understand that she must stop immediately when you tell her to. You need to work out how you are going to let her know when to stop. Most men simply say 'stop' or 'now', but any language is fine as long as you both know what is meant. The language must be spoken; nonverbal messages do not work well in these exercises.

The following guidelines apply to all the exercises in this chapter unless otherwise indicated:

1. Both of you should read, discuss, and understand each exercise before you do it.
2. Do whatever is necessary to feel relaxed and comfortable before beginning an exercise.
3. Start a session with some hugging, holding, or a massage. Then go to the exercise.
4. During the exercise, keep focused on your arousal level rather than on your lover.
5. The goal in each exercise is to last for fifteen minutes, including stops, without ejaculating. You can come after fifteen minutes if you wish, but go slowly, be aware of your arousal level and the point of inevitability, and enjoy yourself.
6. You should feel confident that you will be able to delay ejaculation by stopping, and need no more than two or three stops during a fifteen-minute period, before going on to the next exercise. If you have a lot of difficulty with the next exercise, and it doesn't get easier after a few experiences, return to the one before it and practice it until you have further developed your skills.
7. The more frequently you do the exercises, the better. Three times a week is the minimum.

EXERCISE 16–1: PARTNER STIMULATION OF PENIS

Step A: **Lie on your back and have your partner take a position sufficiently comfortable for her to last for fifteen minutes. You might want to try the position recommended by Masters and Johnson, illustrated in Figure 10 (below), but any position is acceptable as long as you both are comfortable. Your partner is to stimulate your penis with her unlubricated hand in ways that are most arousing to you; feel free to give her instructions on how to touch you. Keep focused in your penis and tell her when to stop. Allow sufficient time for the urge to ejaculate to diminish before asking her to resume stimulation. If you find that you need to stop again as soon as stimulation is resumed, try taking longer stops.**

When you can last for fifteen minutes with no more than two or three stops and feel confident of your control, do Step B.

Step B: **This is exactly the same as Step A except that your partner now uses lotion, oil, or some other lubricant on her hand.**

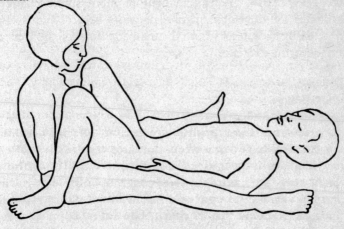

FIGURE 10: POSITION FOR PARTNER STIMULATION OF PENIS
Adapted from Human Sexual Inadequacy, *by William H. Masters and Virginia E. Johnson, 1965.*

POSSIBLE PROBLEM

You aren't stopping in time because you're attending to your partner rather than your level of excitement. You may find yourself wondering if she is enjoying herself, if her hand is getting tired, if she is bored. There is nothing wrong with considering these questions as long as you swing your attention back to your penis as soon as you become aware that your mind has wandered. You might also want to talk to your lover about your concerns. Maybe she is bored some of the time. Can it be OK with you that she is willing to do the exercises even though it's not exciting for her? However you work it out, the important thing is that you have the space to put your attention where it needs to be, on your arousal level.

Now that you feel comfortable delaying ejaculation by stopping with your partner, you're ready to use more subtle changes. The use of changes other than stopping is a departure from the approaches of Semans and Masters and Johnson who use, respectively, only the stop-start and squeeze methods. We have found that the employment of more subtle changes facilitates the development of ejaculatory control and is also more easily accepted by both the man and the woman. Hence, the following exercise.

EXERCISE 16–2: PARTNER STLMULATLON OF PENIS WITH SUBTLE ADJUSTMENTS

Assume the same positions you used for the previous exercise and have your lover stimulate your penis in ways you like. Your goal is to last fifteen minutes without ejaculating and without stopping, by employing any changes you like in your and her behavior. Since types of changes to delay ejaculation other than stopping have been discussed several times, we assume you are familiar with them. Experiment and find out what works best with your partner. You will make some mistakes at first, but

you may still be able to delay ejaculation by stopping. In time, you will learn how and when to use the other kinds of adjustments.

The first few times you do the exercise, your partner should not use lubrication on her hand. When you have good control, she can start using a lubricant.

Should there be difficult problems with this exercise that do not resolve themselves after a few sessions, consider spending some time mastering the subtle adjustments by yourself, following Exercise 15–2.

If you and your partner both like oral sex, you might want to repeat the above two exercises with her using her mouth rather than her hand. If she has any qualms whatever about doing this, don't try it; it will only lead to problems and get in the way of reaching your goals.

EXERCISE 16–3: PENIS IN VAGINA WITH NO MOVEMENT

Lie on your back and have your lover sit on your legs. She is to play with your penis until you have an erection. Then let her rub your penis gently around the outside of her vagina and in her pubic hair. Be aware of your arousal level and make any necessary adjustments. Take as long as you need to get accustomed to the idea of having your penis around her vagina. When you are feeling comfortable with this, and confident that you are in control of your ejaculatory process, then – and only then – should she slowly insert your penis. The two of you will then be in the position illustrated in Figure 11 (page 302). It is crucial, however, that there be no insertion until you are comfortable and in control. If it takes you more than one session to feel that way, that's fine.

Once your penis is safely ensconced in her, she is just to sit and you are just to focus. She should not make any movements as we now explain. Without any stimulation, your erection may tend to go down. If this starts to happen, ask her either to contract her pelvic muscles a few times or to move slightly, just enough to keep your erection firm.

That's all you need to do for fifteen minutes. Focus in your penis and see how it feels to be surrounded by her vagina. You might become aware of the texture, temperature, and lubricity of the vagina. Be aware and get used to being there; it can be a very friendly place.

Should you feel that you are losing control, you can either ask her to get off or you can try relaxing or tensing your pelvic muscles.

If you want to ejaculate after time is up, do so (we assume you have talked to your partner about this), but go slowly and be aware of the point of inevitability.

POSSIBLE PROBLEM

The first time or two you do the exercise, you get very excited and ejaculate. This is not a problem unless it continues to occur. If it does, you have several options. One is to go back to her stimulating you with her lubricated hand and get more comfortable with that. Another is to do

FIGURE 11: FEMALE IN SUPERIOR POSITION
Adapted from Human Sexual Inadequacy, *by William H. Masters and Virginia E. Johnson, 1965*

a masturbation exercise accompanied by a fantasy of being inside her; follow the suggestions for Exercise 15–3, Step B. Still another possibility is to spend several sessions without fully entering her. Rub your penis around the outside of her vagina until that is comfortable, then put it in only a little way. Gradually increase the depth of penetration as you feel more confident and comfortable.

EXERCISE 16–4: PENIS IN VAGINA WITH MOVEMENT

Step A: This is similar to the previous exercise, except that your partner should thrust slowly, at your instructions as to how much and how fast. Use the subtle adjustments or stops to enable you to go for fifteen minutes without ejaculating. It is important that your partner not start thrusting to satisfy herself. That will come later. For now, you are in control of what kind and how much movement there is. Get comfortable with the pace before increasing it.

Step B: Both of you move slowly.

Step C: Gradually increase the pace, employing the subtle adjustments whenever you like, using stops as a last resort to prevent ejaculation. Continue in this fashion until you are both moving as much as you want. Keep in mind that it all doesn't have to happen in one session.

POSSIBLE PROBLEM

You lose control when the movement gets faster. This probably means that you are speeding up too suddenly. It is important that you be comfortable and feel in control with one tempo before increasing it. Take your time.

Since you don't want to spend the rest of your life having sex in only one position, it's time to try different ones. Again, a caveat – go slowly. Having good control in one position does not necessarily ensure good control in others. Most men find the female superior position, the one you have used in the last two exercises, the easiest one in which to maintain ejaculatory control. Side-by-side positions are next best for most men, while the well-known missionary position – man on top – is the most difficult.

EXERCISE 16–5: USING DIFFERENT POSITIONS FOR INTERCOURSE

Step A: **The best new position to start with is probably the side-by-side or lateral position. It is a favorite of Masters and Johnson and many of their clients. Perhaps the best way to assume the position is to start with your lover on top, with your penis in her vagina. She then rolls to one side until she is lying on her side on the bed, while you roll up on one side so that you are facing her. Your penis may or may not remain inside of her. If not, you can have a good laugh while figuring out how to get it back in. Once you get on your sides, you will have to do some shifting of arms and legs and whatnot to get comfortable.**

Remember that the first times you try a new position there may be some awkwardness, minor discomfort, and a loss of control. Take it slow, stay focused on your arousal level, and make changes early.

If this or any other new position presents difficulties, follow the suggestions in Exercise 16–4, gradually building up to abandoned movement.

Step B: **Feel free to try any other positions that you like. Since good control will probably be most difficult to maintain when you are on top, you may want to experiment with other positions first.**

The next exercise is very valuable and can be lots of fun. You are going to be asked to ejaculate as quickly as possible in intercourse. This may sound quite strange to you, given that you've spent so much time and energy learning how to control your ejaculations. The point is that good control means control in any direction. You should be able to come fast or slow. At this stage, coming quickly will increase your knowledge of what makes for quick ejaculations. It will also be good preparation for the time when you come quickly without intending it, and such things happen to almost all men once in a while. You now have many new skills for dealing with a partner and also some new feelings of confidence in yourself. Use them in this exercise. All is not lost if you come quickly. It only means that you decided to ejaculate sooner rather than later. The exercise need be done only once or twice.

EXERCISE 16–6: AN INTENTIONAL QUICKIE

Try to ejaculate as fast as possible in intercourse, even faster than you did before starting your training program. If you succeed in doing this, be aware of a tendency to want to apologize, but don't act on it. Express your appreciation to your partner and see if she would like you to do something for her. You should be pleased that you are now in control of your ejaculatory process.

If you are unable to come fast, you may decide to forget the exercise and rest on your laurels, content that you have achieved your goals. Or you may want to try it again to see if it isn't possible to have a quick ejaculation. After all, you might want to have a quickie some day, and you can view this exercise as preparation for that eventuality.

Whether you have done the partner exercises or followed the principles given at the beginning of the chapter, by now you have attained good ejaculatory control and are enjoying your sexuality in a more confident, relaxed, and carefree way. You will have noticed that results come gradually and that it takes a while for the effects of the training to really sink in and become automatic. This process will continue for months. All you need do to facilitate the process is to stay aware of your arousal level and make adjustments when needed.

You want to remember that there is absolutely no way to avoid losing control some of the time. Whether because you haven't had sex for a long time, are extremely excited, are tense or angry, or perhaps because of some other reason, there will be quick ejaculations once in a while. As time goes on, they will decrease in frequency, but they will probably never completely disappear. This is simply part of normal male functioning. There is nothing you can do about it and there's no need to get concerned about it.

When you realize that you have not made an adjustment in time and are going to ejaculate, don't fight it. Let it happen and enjoy it. No need for apologies; you can do something for her later if she wants. And no need to assume that all your training has been in vain. It hasn't. Just go a bit more slowly the next time, stay focused, and make your adjustments earlier than usual.

We hope you'll keep in mind the discussion in Chapter 9 on the effects of tension. If you get extremely upset about anything, you may start to lose some of your ejaculatory control. So be especially aware and careful in sex during tense times. Anything you can do to relieve or mitigate the tension will of course be extremely helpful.

If for any reason you notice yourself slipping back into your old, quick ways, take some time and figure out what is causing you to lose control. A brief refresher course with some of the exercises in this and the previous chapter may be very useful.

Now that you can last a long time, we hope you won't assume that every sexual encounter must be a long one. Compulsively lasting a long time is not much better than compulsively coming quickly. You have options and we hope you'll use them. Longlasting sex can be a wonderful experience, and so can a quickie.

SEVENTEEN

Erection problems, or why the damn thing won't act like it should

While every sex problem is accompanied by discomfort and concern, nothing equals the devastation wrought by the lack of an erection at the right time. Nothing except perhaps the loss of his job can make a man feel more worthless and hopeless. Impotence, the term traditionally used to signify the inability to get erections, also means a lack of power, strength, and vigor – the negation of all that we consider masculine. Men have securely tied their self-respect to the upward mobility of their penises and, when their penises do not rise to the occasion, they no longer feel like men.

Sam Julty, who interviewed a number of men with erection problems, described their situation like this:

> The man without the erection sees himself as being less than a man, as an unworthy, as a fraud. It is as if the flag of his manhood must remain furled for lack of a mast. Thus the terror, the shame, the withdrawal spurred by the dysfunction far exceed the reaction to almost any other medical condition . . .

Here, in more personal terms, is what a client we saw recently said when asked what he wanted to gain from therapy:

> I want to feel like a whole man again. If I could just function normally at least some of the time when I'm with a woman, that would do it. I know I can use my hand or tongue to satisfy them, and that's fine some of the time, but I'm not going to feel good about myself until I can get

a good hard-on and use it. I feel so useless when that thing
just hangs limp between my legs.

Women are often baffled by the agony a man goes through
when he fails to get or keep an erection, but they have no
parallel experience with which to compare it. The lack of
erection, except in the relatively few cases caused by medical
problems, signifies a lack of readiness for sex – the man is tired,
bored, angry, anxious, or is in some other way preventing his
sexual feelings from influencing his penis. But men have not
had the permission women have to say that something is
getting in their way or that they'd rather not have sex now.

A woman can participate in intercourse (which most of us
learned was *the* sexual act) without being aroused or even
interested. If she fails to lubricate sufficiently, saliva or artificial
lubrication can be brought to the rescue. She might not have
an orgasm, of course, which would be construed by some as a
failure of sorts, but at least she can go through with the act and
give her partner pleasure. A man is in a somewhat different
position. Because of the incorrect but deeply embedded belief
that sex demands a rigid penis, there is nothing that can be
brought to the rescue. And his 'failure' is so obvious. There is
his limp organ, dangling in full view. There is no way to fake
an erection and, though not impossible, it is quite difficult to
have intercourse without at least a partial erection.

So a man without an erection can't have intercourse, which
he usually translates as meaning that he can't have sex, and
feels that he has failed as a man and a human being. Of course
his partner may be sympathetic and offer support and
understanding. But he may be so consumed with self-loathing
that he can't accept what she offers. Many men withdraw from
their partners after such 'failures' and engage in an orgy of
self-flagellation. The result is usually a miserable experience
for them and their partners.

Erection problems are as old as recorded history and so are
the agony and self-torture of men who experience them. Even
today, however, there is no agreed-upon definition of what

constitutes an erectile problem. Almost all men have had at least a few experiences when they wanted an erection and didn't get one or when they lost an erection at some embarrassing point. This is not really a problem. But what about the man who usually does not get or maintain an erection in sexual encounters? Or the man who does fine with one partner but not with others? Or the man who complains that his erections aren't as hard as they used to be?

Our belief is that if it bothers you, it's a problem. But the solution may not lie where you think.

Too many men with erection difficulties think that all they need is some procedure or device to get it up and keep it up. After all, the job of a penis is to get hard, so perhaps the doctor has a pill or shot to get this misguided penis back on the right track. Unfortunately, the situation is usually a bit more complex.

The real problem usually lies not in the man's functioning but in his ideas of how he should function. Far too many men uncritically accept the superhuman standards and myths about men and penises and then get concerned when they discover they are merely human. Erection problems are almost always due to one or more of the following: unrealistic expectations: lack of arousal; absence of the proper conditions; and the undue emphasis placed on the need for an erection.

An example of unrealistic expectations is a man in his forties or fifties who complains that his erections are not as full or firm as they were twenty years ago. If this 'problem' gets the best of him and he becomes obsessed with it, he may end up without any erections at all. Fifty-year-old penises don't feel or act exactly the way twenty-year-old penises do. They can still do their jobs and provide much pleasure to the man and his partner, as long as the fantasy ideal of penises that are hard as steel and always jumping about doesn't get in the way. What need adjusting in such cases are the standards and expectations, not the penis.

The lack of arousal causes much confusion and frustration. Most men think they should have erections even if they aren't really turned-on. While penises can get hard in the absence of arousal, such occurrences are rare and unpredictable. If you aren't interested in sex, your penis will usually remain soft. That's not a problem, but many men succeed in turning it into one by trying to force erections when there is no arousal.

The lack of proper conditions leads to many erection problems, but many men do not understand the importance of meeting their conditions and wonder what is wrong with them for not having erections even under the most adverse circumstances.

Sam came to therapy because he had not had an erection with a woman he had been seeing for three months. He was totally befuddled by his problem. He claimed that Greta was the best thing that ever happened to him. She was European, which he liked, and very experienced sexually. She was lots of fun, a wonderful companion, and he feared losing her unless he could perform. After some probing by the therapist, it turned out that Greta had some other interesting qualities. She had a quick and violent temper, and had several times thrown dishes and other objects at Sam. She continually berated American men in general and Sam in particular for their sexual ineptness. She frequently compared Sam to her last lover, with Sam coming out on the short end. She demanded erections and intercourse, threatening to leave if they were not forthcoming. Although he hardly recognized it when he first came to therapy, Sam was seething with resentment toward her. He trembled as he talked about her callousness toward him. Yet he continued to call himself impotent and wanted to know what was wrong with him.

That Sam could ask such a question demonstrates the power of our sexual mythology. He believed that, no matter what the circumstances, no matter how angry he was, and no matter how fearful he was of his partner's critical outbursts, he should have an erection with her. A more realistic question, but one that didn't occur to him, would have been: how could anyone get an erection in that situation?

If you have a lot of negative feelings toward your partner, if you feel guilty about having sex with her, if you aren't turned-on by her, if you are preoccupied with other matters, if sex with her is a tense experience – if any of these things are true, what makes you think you should have an erection? The answer, of course, is our sexual conditioning, the nonsense we discussed in Chapters 3 and 4.

One aspect of our learning important to consider here is the inordinate emphasis placed on erect penises. We men have so much at stake in getting an erection – not only the success or failure of the particular sexual event, but our entire identity as men. Because so much is at stake, the absence of an erection is greeted with the same degree of calmness as would be the announcement that someone in the neighborhood had the bubonic plague. When a man doesn't get an erection, invariably because the situation isn't right in the first place, he panics. He loses his ability to think clearly and flings himself into an ocean of self-doubt and fear.

A vicious cycle often is set in motion, all because of a penis that refused to get hard on one occasion. The man wonders what is wrong with him, if he is over the hill. He may think that this proves he's not as good as the other guys or perhaps that he's a closet homosexual. In his panic, he distances himself from his partner, thereby ensuring that the event will end badly and that his concerns will grow.

If this panic is not immediately resolved (in ways we will discuss shortly), the stage is set for real trouble. The next sexual encounter is looked forward to with both anticipation and apprehension. If it goes well, the man's worries are over. If it goes badly, his worst fears will be confirmed. The next encounter becomes too important. The stakes are much too high. Too much pressure is being generated. The man's penis is confronted with conditions under which it cannot operate. The more the man peers at his penis, wondering what is wrong with it and whether it will embarrass him again, the more it wilts.

The man is doing everything possible to ensure that this experience will end at least as badly as the first one. He's not doing it purposely, but he doesn't know what else to do. A second bad experience will only make things worse the next time around. And pretty soon the man realizes that he almost never gets erections with a partner. Because he ignored his conditions and put too much pressure on his penis, it now refuses to function at all.

What could he have done differently? What can you do when you don't get an erection when you think you should? Several things.

First, remember that every man sometimes experiences a lack of an erection. It's just one of those things that all men must learn to live with. If you can avoid worrying yourself to death about what it means, things will probably work out fine the next time.

Second, realize that all is not lost. You and your partner can have an enjoyable experience even without an erection. Women are much less concerned with the erectability of penises than are men, and your partner can probably take your soft penis in stride as long as you don't make a catastrophe of it. Resist the temptation to withdraw in shame and anger. You may want to tell her what you are feeling. You may remember that many of the women in the Zilbergeld and Stanton study requested this type of expression. Whether you tell her or not, however, the important thing is to stay with her and do whatever the two of you enjoy.

It's paradoxical but true that if you ignore your lack of erection (that is, don't make a federal case of it), it may not be lacking for long. This won't happen every time, and it rarely happens if you are only pretending to be unconcerned about what your penis is doing, but it happens often if you can leave it alone and not pester it.

A third thing you can do when you don't get an erection is avoid the tendency of launching into an internal dialogue about what the matter is with you. Instead, think whether your conditions are being met, if you are aroused, and if you are getting the kind of stimulation you want. If something is lacking – a certain kind of stimulation, some of your conditions – do what is necessary to get it. If you are not aroused, the best thing is probably to call it a day and wait until you are more in the mood.

Last, if you find yourself thinking that you have to prove yourself the next time, remember that such pressure is self-defeating. You now have many ways of dealing with it, such as having sex only when aroused, meeting your conditions, talking to your partner about your feelings, and clarifying her expectations and desires. You might also want to set a rule for yourself not to use your penis in the next sexual encounter. Any of these methods, used singly or in combination, should reduce your anxiety. The important thing is that you give yourself the opportunity to enjoy yourself and your partner rather than setting yourself a test that can be passed only if your penis behaves in certain ways. Penises respond to pleasure but are only too ready to fail any tests you set for them.

What we have said here, of course, is only a summary of what we discussed in earlier chapters. You are human and operate according to laws governing human sexual behavior. Treat yourself and your penis with respect by having sex only when you are aroused and your conditions are met, and things will usually work out fine. Once in a while they won't, but that's just the nature of the beast.

If you have had erection problems for some time and are wondering specifically what to do, the next two chapters are for you. You have already done most of what is necessary, perhaps without realizing it. The exercises and suggestions in the following chapters will help you put your skills to the best use.

Before going on to them, however, we want to discuss briefly some of the appliances and medications sometimes used to treat erection problems. All sorts of nostrums and remedies have been developed for the improvement of a man's sex life, and particularly for dealing with penises that refuse to do what they're supposed to do. If you have been considering any of these scientific wonders, it will pay you to read on.

Although the search for an aphrodisiac is as old as recorded history, none has ever been found. James Woods, a research pharmacologist and expert on the subject, had this to say:

In reality, there are no known drugs that specifically increase libido or sexual performance, and every chemical taken for this purpose, without medical advice . . . poses the danger of drug interaction or overdose to the user.

That goes for all the common folk potions as well as the sophisticated products of modern chemistry. The well-known Spanish fly is not only not very effective but is also dangerous. It causes acute irritation of the intestinal and urinary tracts, which sometimes leads to a feeling of sexual excitement, but has also led to continued and painful erection (priapism) which sometimes requires surgical treatment. Deaths have also been attributed to its use.

Some massage oils are advertised as having aphrodisiac properties. This is false advertising. Massage oil may be nice; it can lubricate and give you a good, warm feeling, but that's as far as it goes. If that turns you on, that's fine, but the oil itself, no matter what 'secret herbs' it contains, is not going to change your sexual desire or functioning.

As for the bands to be tied around the base of your penis, don't use them. You may keep the erection but there is a possibility of causing damage. The penis is a very sensitive and vulnerable organ, best left untampered with.

Testosterone injections and penile implants are prescribed by some physicians. Testosterone therapy is fashionable in some medical circles and the implants show indications of becoming the next fad.

Testosterone is an androgen, or male sex hormone,

produced in the testicles. It was once thought that production of this hormone decreased abruptly with aging, and that this decline was responsible for decreased sexual interest and performance. Injections of testosterone were therefore recommended as appropriate therapy. Current thinking is that production of the hormone does not suddenly decline at any age, except in rare cases. In cases where there is a hormone deficiency, injections are often very helpful. But such cases are not common.

When no hormone deficiency has been established, results are much less certain. Even when positive, they are often transitory. We have seen many men who had either received no benefit from testosterone shots or who had experienced some change, only to have it fade away soon after the treatment ended. Because of possible side effects (mentioned below), testosterone injections cannot be administered indefinitely.

Some physicians recommend testosterone almost routinely for men over forty who complain of erection problems or decreased sexual desire. Other doctors are more cautious, using it only when a deficiency of the hormone is proved. Before considering this type of treatment, you should know that it is suspected of having a very dangerous side effect. In his book, *Male Sexual Health*, Phillip Roen, a well-known urologist, explains:

> We know that hidden in the depths of the prostate there may be a latent group of cancer cells which ordinarily would not produce any trouble but which can do so when they are stimulated by testosterone injections. This kind of treatment therefore seems to me to carry too high a risk to be justified.

Sometimes testosterone therapy is a desperate last resort on the part of the doctor, who has no idea of what to do if it fails. This can lead to problems for the patient.

Ollie, a man in his early fifties, saw a urologist at a well-known medical center for his erection problems. He was given Afrodex pills (a combination of testosterone and yohimbine, a natural substance thought by some to possess aphrodisiac qualities). When no progress was forthcoming, the urologist began a course of testosterone injections, telling Ollie that if they didn't work, nothing would. The shots didn't work and Ollie was seriously depressed for several months because he believed there was no help for him. After a while, he inquired about other possibilities and someone referred him to us. Six weeks after his first session, he was having enjoyable sex.

We wonder how many men have accepted a sexless life because the testosterone shots failed to help and their doctors said there was nothing else.

The best advice we can give regarding testosterone is don't even consider it unless your doctor says you have a hormone deficiency. If such a deficiency exists and your doctor recommends injections, talk to him about the possible side effects before making a decision. Better yet, try the exercises in the next two chapters first. You'll probably find that you don't need any injections.

Two types of penile implants have been developed in recent years. The first consists of one or two silicone rods surgically implanted in the penis. The result is a permanent state of semierection, firm enough to insert in the vagina for intercourse but usually not so obtrusive as to cause embarrassment in nonsexual situations. The surgery itself is fairly simple and the risk is low. The implant does not impair penile sensation or the capacity for orgasm and ejaculation.

The newer device is much more complex. It is a hydraulic model, involving inflatable cylinders in the penis, a reservoir of fluid placed under the abdominal muscles, and a pumping mechanism in the scrotum. When a man with such an implant desires an erection, he pumps the bulb in his scrotum, causing the fluid in the reservoir to inflate the cylinders in the penis.

He may then engage in whatever sexual activity he desires. Orgasm and ejaculation are not interfered with by the implant. To return his penis to its normal state, the man activates the bulb that deflates the cylinders.

The hydraulic model has both advantages and disadvantages compared to the simple implant. The penis looks and feels more normal than the semi-rigid one produced by the earlier procedure. The erection can be full and firm rather than semi-firm and there is no problem about concealing the erection. On the negative side, it is a much more complex device (meaning that there is more that can go wrong) and much less is known about it. Only a few of the hydraulic models are in use and not enough time has elapsed to have good follow-up information. It is therefore impossible at this time to give a fair appraisal of their usefulness.

Both kinds of implants were originally designed as a last resort. They were to be used for men with severe physical impairment, so severe that the implant was the only way they could ever hope to have an erection again. As so often happens, however, once a procedure exists, it gets used on all sorts of people. Some implants have been done on men who did not have physical impairment.

We have talked to a number of urologists who have either done the surgery or were in some other way involved and the consensus is that the implants often work out well for men for whom it really is the only hope, i.e., those with organic impairment. For those without such impairment, however, and those who have not tried other alternatives, there is often trouble. They complain about the implant, they want adjustments made and none that are made satisfy them, they want them removed, or they just don't ever use them. In other words, the implant only provides new things to complain about.

Implants are tempting to many men. Surgery seems so much simpler than thinking about conditions and how relaxed you are, considering whether or not you want sex, talking to your partner – all these silly human things. Just have an operation and barring equipment failure – you're all set. This logic appeals to many men who are accustomed to technological solutions for all problems.

There is another side, however. Surgery, no matter how simple, always carries a risk. The risk varies according to age, physical condition, type of anesthetic, and other factors. Surgery is also expensive, usually more expensive than short-term therapy and certainly more expensive than this book.

Another consideration is what it means to replace your own functioning with a mechanical device. In some cases, of course, it may be absolutely necessary. If your heart, lungs, or kidneys don't work, having yourself hooked up to a machine may be the only way to preserve your life. If your penis won't work, even after trying the exercises in this book and going to a good sex therapist, an implant may be the only recourse left. But it should be considered only after you have exhausted the other alternatives.

If you are in a hurry to get an implant, we suggest you carefully consider why. What problems do you think it will solve for you? Why are you so unwilling to try the book or see a therapist? It's a terrible mistake to think of the implant as a panacea. It will give you an erection and nothing else. It will not increase your desire or sexual skills, it will not help you find a partner, nor will it necessarily circumvent the need for talking about sex. Your partner, after all, may wonder how come you always have an erection or why you're always pushing buttons. If you are engaging in magical thinking about the wonders that an implant will produce for you, you are probably headed for a huge disappointment.

EIGHTEEN

Resolving erection problems I

Successfully dealing with erection problems requires that the following criteria be met:

1. Having sex only when you feel aroused, and only the kinds of sex that you want;
2. Meeting all your conditions for good sex;
3. Recognizing when you are tense, and getting more relaxed;
4. Getting the kinds of stimulation you like and focusing on this stimulation.

In short, you need to be able to take charge of a sexual situation so that you are enjoying rather than performing.

Each of the four criteria above is composed of a number of separate skills. Having sex only when you want to, for example, requires you to be able to say no to sex when you are not in the mood, to get the type of sexual activity you like, to be able to stop in the middle of a sexual encounter if you realize that you are no longer in the mood, and to initiate sex when you want it. Being able to communicate clearly with your partner is, of course, necessary for the application of these skills.

If you have done the conditions, assertiveness, relaxation, talking, and focusing exercises presented earlier in the book and feel reasonably confident of your ability to apply what you have learned, your erection difficulties are probably all but resolved. The suggestions and exercises in this and the next chapter can help extend your learning and increase your confidence, but you may not need them. Some of the men we've worked with resolved their erection problems without doing any of the exercises in these two chapters. We want to be clear that these exercises are useful only as a supplement to, and not as a substitute for, the conditions, assertiveness, and other exercises given earlier.

Now is a good time to take stock of where you are and what you need to do. Read this and the next chapter without doing the exercises to get an idea of which exercises might be useful and which exercises given earlier in the book require further work. Pay particular attention to the section in the next chapter called Partner Sex without Exercises. If you think you can carry out the suggestions given there without doing any more exercises, feel free to do what you want. If, on the other hand, you feel you need more confidence or better development of certain skills, do what is necessary to achieve these ends.

The guidelines for doing exercises on pages 188-9 apply to all the exercises in this and the next chapter. An additional suggestion for men with erection problems is not to do more than one exercise a day. You want to give your penis the best possible conditions in which to respond, and having sex more than once a day may not be conducive for reaching this goal.

The masturbation exercises require the ability to focus, an ability developed by Exercise 10–1. If you need more time with that exercise, now is the time to get it.

The first masturbation exercise is simple and will help you to understand that a lost erection can often be regained when conditions are right and the stimulation good. Men often forget this and get anxious when their erection goes down. It is useful to remember that it is common for the strength of an erection to fluctuate during a sexual experience. Your penis may be very firm and full one moment, softer the next, and then either regain its firmness or become completely flaccid. If it does get soft, try not to panic. If your conditions are met, if you are reasonably relaxed, and if you are getting the kind of stimulation you like, the chances are good that your erection will return.

EXERCISE 18–1: LOSING AND REGAINING ERECTION
Time Required: 15 to 20 minutes

Masturbate with lubricant and focus inside your penis. When you have an erection, stop. Take your hand away from your penis, stop focusing, and think about something nonsexual. Let your erection go completely down, which may take from a few seconds to a few minutes. When your penis is soft, resume masturbating and focusing. Most of the time your penis will get hard again, in which case you should again stop and let it get soft. Two stops are sufficient in a 15- to 20-minute session.

If your erection does not return in a few minutes after the resumption of stimulation, consider if there is anything you should do to get into a more relaxed, sexier frame of mind (for example, recalling a good sexual experience or looking at some stimulating pictures or literature). If the changes you make result in an erection, just continue the exercise. If not, call it quits for then and return to the exercise some other time. Whatever you do, don't try to force an erection. It won't work.

Do this exercise two to four times, or until you are reasonably confident that an erection can often be regained by the proper atmosphere and stimulation.

POSSIBLE PROBLEM
You *never* regain your erection after letting it go down. (If you usually get it back but not always, that's not a problem.) Be sure you are feeling sexy before you resume stimulation, that you are comfortable, and that all your conditions are met.

You may have found that you did not always regain your erection. If you didn't have this experience in this exercise, you probably will in one of the later ones. This is simply one of those difficult facts of life that all men need to accept. The only reason it's difficult is that our sex education didn't leave room for it.

All you can do about erections is meet your conditions. Sometimes, even when conditions are met and everything seems perfect, you still won't get or maintain an erection. Penises sometimes decide to take brief vacations at the oddest moments. See if you can accept this as a fact that you can do nothing about (assuming, of course, that your conditions are fulfilled). The more you accept this idea, the better you'll feel about yourself and the less pressure you'll put on your penis. The less pressure your penis feels, the more likely it will respond in the future.

The next three exercises involve the use of structured fantasy. Before doing them, read the discussion of the role of fantasy in exercises on pages 289–90.

EXERCISE 18–2: MASTURBATION WITH FANTASY OF SEX WITH A PARTNER
Time Required: 20 to 25 minutes

Step A: **Masturbate with lubricant while fantasizing a sexual experience with a partner. Start the fantasy with the first touch or kiss and slowly go through all the activities that might occur in this imagined sexual event. A typical sequence might go like this: kissing, hugging, removing clothes, caressing while nude, playing with her breasts, playing with her genitals, her touching your penis, oral sex, inserting your penis into her vagina, being in the vagina with no movement, slow movement, and movement that gradually becomes rapid. (We are not implying that a real sexual encounter should include all these activities or that there is a special order in which the activities should occur. The important thing is that you fantasize all the possible sexual activities you might actually encounter.)**

Be aware of your anxiety level and, should it rise, visualize yourself doing something to make yourself more

comfortable. At the same time, actually do something to make yourself more relaxed. When the anxiety decreases, resume sexual activity in the fantasy and resume masturbation. Here is an example of how this might go:

> You are masturbating and enjoying your fantasy until the scene where she touches your penis. At that point your anxiety goes up. Stop masturbating and do something to get comfortable, e.g., taking a few deep breaths. At the same time, visualize yourself doing something to relax with your partner. You might see yourself telling her you want to stop and just hold her for a while; or you might do something for her; or perhaps you could see yourself talking to her about your feelings. When you feel more relaxed, resume masturbating and see yourself continue or resume sexual activity in the fantasy. If your anxiety rises at the same point as before, do Step B.

If you are doing the exercise slowly and carefully, as you should, the allotted time will probably not be sufficient to get through the entire fantasy. That is fine. Next time you can start the fantasy at a later scene, e.g., where you are already undressed and caressing each other. Regardless of how many sessions it takes, make sure you cover all possible aspects of a sexual experience while doing this exercise.

Most men experience some difficulty with one or more of the fantasized scenes. Perhaps your anxiety increases when you imagine her touching your penis or when you imagine starting intercourse. Since what gives you trouble in fantasy will probably do the same in reality, you want to devote special attention to the difficult scenes. When you run into an anxiety-producing scene that does not get easier after a few repetitions, use Step B.

Step B: Instead of masturbating to a fantasy of a whole sexual encounter, fantasize only the scene that causes you trouble. It is essential that you be relaxed before

beginning. Get into a sexual mood, then slowly begin masturbating and gently ease yourself into the difficult scene. Here is an example.

If your difficult scene involved your partner's playing with your penis, first imagine her hand just lightly brushing your penis. When that feels comfortable, see her holding your penis for a second or two. Then holding it a bit longer. Then stroking it for just a moment. Gradually increase the amount of time you can visualize her stroking your penis until you can fantasize it for as long as you like without an increase in anxiety. If you do get tense at any point, stop and get more comfortable, then resume that fantasy at a point preceding the one that caused the increase in anxiety.

Repeat this process as many times as necessary until you can go through the entire scene without any increase in anxiety. When this is accomplished, return to Step A and incorporate this scene into the larger fantasy. You may then find that another scene gives you trouble, necessitating a return to Step B. Continue this procedure until you can go through the entire fantasy in Step A feeling very comfortable.

POSSIBLE PROBLEMS

1. You have difficulty staying with the fantasy, finding yourself drifting to other thoughts and fantasies. When this happens, simply bring your attention back to the scene you were imagining. You will need to do this a number of times each session.

2. You forget about your relaxation level. It is crucial that you be aware of how relaxed you are so you can stop and get more comfortable when you need to. If this is a problem for you, try keeping most of your attention on your relaxation level even though this may result in less distinct fantasy images.

If you have a tape recorder, we encourage you to record the fantasy and play it while you masturbate. Since you won't have to put any effort into developing the fantasy, you can listen to it while keeping your attention on how relaxed or tense you are.

3. You try to do too much in one session. It's important that you really get into your fantasy and slowly go through it, which means that this exercise will take at least a few sessions to complete. You will probably need to stop a number of times to get relaxed, and also need to do Step B at least a few times. Speed is not important. Carrying out the exercise exactly as suggested is.

We generally like to cover in fantasy most or all of the disappointing or anxiety-producing events that may occur in reality, e.g., not getting or maintaining an erection. This helps you think of how you can deal with such a situation, making its actuality less threatening. The next exercise deals with not getting or maintaining an erection, a situation that may have caused you much grief in the past. You need to learn to handle it in a way that makes the sexual experience a good one for both you and your partner.

EXERCISE 18–3: MASTURBATING WITH FANTASY OF LOSING AND
REGAINING ERECTION
Time Required: 15 to 20 minutes

While masturbating, you are to fantasize losing your erection at the point at which this usually occurred in partner activities in the past. If your main problem is not getting an erection when with a partner, fantasize that situation instead. It is important that the fantasy be reasonably vivid and detailed. What is going on the moment that you lose your erection? What are you doing and what is she doing? As you picture yourself losing your erection, stop masturbating. You may experience the awful feelings you usually have in such situations

(hopelessness, anger, and so forth). Imagine yourself doing something to get more comfortable, e.g., asking her to give you a light massage, holding her, talking to her. Get into the fantasy of the relaxing activity and allow yourself to relax. When you are more comfortable, think of what would be needed for you to get aroused again, perhaps a certain kind of stimulation or telling your lover what you are feeling. Then imagine yourself doing it. As you imagine these scenes, resume masturbating. Picture in as much detail as possible getting the things you need to become more aroused. Then visualize yourself regaining your erection and having a good time.

Do this exercise as many times as needed to develop some confidence that you could actually carry out what you fantasized with a partner. For many men, four to six repetitions are sufficient, but others will want to do more.

You probably felt good about regaining your erection in the fantasy in this exercise. But since that won't always happen in reality, we go to a fantasy of a situation that may be quite threatening to you – failing to get or regain an erection regardless of how relaxed and aroused you feel. This situation frightens most men, particularly those who have experienced it and not handled it well. It is important to confront the situation, otherwise your sex life is going to be overcrowded, with the fear of not regaining an erection taking up a lot of space. That fear can be put to rest if you prove to yourself that you can have a marvelous time in bed without an erection. We hope that your reading of Chapter 13 has at least raised the possibility in your mind that your partner can probably be satisfied without an erection. The following exercise is intended to help you realize that you also can have a good time without a hard penis.

EXERCISE 18–4: MASTURBATION WITH FANTASY OF NO ERECTION
Time Required: 15 to 25 minutes

Masturbate to a fantasy where you either do not get an erection, or you have one which goes soft, whichever situation has been most true for you. Stop masturbating and imagine yourself doing something to help yourself relax. When you are relaxed in the fantasy, imagine yourself getting all your conditions met and the types of stimulation you like best. And imagine that none of this brings you an erection. You may at this point experience some negative feelings, similar to those you actually experienced in such situations in the past. You may need to exert some effort to keep control of the fantasy.

Now imagine yourself accepting the fact that your penis is not going to get hard. You may want to visualize yourself telling your partner this ('I guess I'm not going to get an erection tonight', or something of this sort). Then imagine doing whatever seems right to make the experience an enjoyable one for both you and your partner. One possibility is to do something for her with your hands, mouth, or something else (but not your penis). While fantasizing about carrying out these ideas, resume masturbating and have a good time.

As you repeat the exercise, you might want to try different things that can be done after you and your partner accept the fact of your nonerection. Some of the possibilities can be nonsexual, e.g., talking, massage, holding each other, going for a walk together. Keep control of the fantasies and do not let them wander to include such nonproductive alternatives as sulking, fighting, or stomping out of the room. You may have done such things in the past but you're in a different place now, with many more satisfying alternatives to choose from. If you have difficulty keeping control of the fantasy, we suggest you record it and play it back while you are masturbating.

Remember that whatever you do in the fantasy, it does

**not result in an erection. See how many alternatives you
can discover for an enjoyable experience in this situation.**

   **Do this exercise as many times as necessary to give you a
feeling of confidence that you could carry it out in reality.**

You may have had some trouble when you saw yourself
without an erection despite all your fantasy attempts to get
one. Repeating the exercise a number of times will help.
Having good sex is not dependent upon having an erection
and you should be well on your way toward accepting that
fact.

NINETEEN

Resolving erection problems II

This chapter presents two approaches to partner sex for men with erection problems, both of which have been used very successfully. The first approach involves a list of principles to be followed in partner sex and requires no partner exercises. It does require you to meet the four criteria listed at the beginning of Chapter 18. This program has been successfully used by men without steady partners, by men with partners who would not cooperate in treatment, and by men who had cooperative partners but who didn't want to do partner exercises.

The second program requires a partner who is willing to work with you on a series of exercises. It follows an outline developed by Masters and Johnson, but with several of our own variations.

Read both approaches and pick the one that feels right for you. If you do not have a partner, of course, you have to go with the first one. Otherwise, either method can work. The first one is a bit more difficult for most men, so if you have trouble with it, you can always do some exercises with your partner.

PARTNER SEX WITHOUT EXERCISES

If you have done the exercises given earlier in the book, you are ready to carry out our suggestions for sex with a partner. You have already seen most of the suggestions, in the section on sex with a new partner on pages 228–30. You should follow them whether you are in a new or an old relationship. Here we offer some elaboration and a few new ideas.

If you are in a relationship and have broken off physical contact because of your sexual problem, it is important to reestablish that contact as soon as possible. Start holding hands, hugging, snuggling, taking baths or showers together, doing light bodyrubs, or anything else that is mutually agreeable. You need to feel comfortable being physical with your partner, and engaging in these activities is one of the best ways to get there. Of course, you should stop and get more comfortable if at any time you get tense.

Use your list of conditions and systematically go about meeting them. Work out any unfinished business with your partner that is getting in the way, talk to her about how you can satisfy her if you don't have an erection, use transition activities to help you relax – do these or anything else that will fulfill all your conditions. And don't even consider doing anything sexual until they all are met.

While engaged in any type of physical activity with your partner, most of your attention should be on the pleasurable sensations you're feeling. But you should also be aware of how tense or relaxed you are. Whenever you are tense, even if during nonsexual contact with your lover, do something to get more comfortable.

Plan not to have intercourse the first few times you have sex with her and stick to the plan no matter what comes up. It's a bad pun but we're serious. You may get an erection but you shouldn't use it in intercourse. A mistake commonly made by men who've had erection problems is to attempt frantically to 'stick it in' as soon as they have an erection. Such frenzied efforts usually end with the erection disappearing. Let your lover play with your penis and give her plenty of directions so she'll do it just the way you like. If an ejaculation happens, that's nice, and if it doesn't, that's also nice. Enjoy the feelings and don't attempt any 'sticking it in'.

When engaging in sexual activities other than intercourse, see if you can't have a good time. Some men are so busy thinking about intercourse that they don't enjoy anything else that happens. Focusing on the sensations in your penis as it's being stimulated will help keep your mind where it belongs. When you do get around to intercourse, keep focusing in your penis.

It's a good idea deliberately to lose your erection with your partner. You can ask her to stop stimulating you and do something else until your erection has gone away. Then, if you feel like it, ask her to resume stimulation. If your erection doesn't return soon, don't try to push it. Do something else that feels good. You may feel bad because you want to reward her efforts with an erection. She's playing with you because it feels good to you and good to her. That usually is sufficient reward for anyone. You don't owe her an erection, just as she doesn't owe you an orgasm when you stimulate her.

Since you are at some point going to be asking your penis to go into her body, it is helpful if she and it become better acquainted. Have her touch, pat, hold, and caress it when it's soft. Some men find this difficult to do ('I only want her to touch it when it's hard'), but it's well worth practicing. You'll feel much more comfortable if you can let her touch your penis regardless of what shape it's in. Have her do a little at a time, gradually increasing the amount of touching as you feel more comfortable (most women, by the way, like this type of activity).

Another way of developing diplomatic relations between your penis and your lover is to gently rub it on her body. Whether it's hard or soft, you can rub it almost everywhere on her. When you are comfortable doing this, rub it in her pubic hair, between her thighs, on her vaginal lips, and perhaps put it in her vagina just a little way. Of course you should stop and get comfortable if you get tense. Go slowly, keep your attention on your penis, and allow it and you to get to know your partner better.

The business about helping your penis and your partner to get better acquainted strikes some men as silly, but we assure you that the techniques we've suggested are powerful ones.

Besides, they can be lots of fun. You really can play fun games while in bed without feeling that you have to achieve some goal or put on a performance.

Remember to go no further than you are comfortable with. Respect your anxious feelings by not doing anything to increase their strength. If that means that you don't have intercourse the first three, five, or ten times you are sexual with your partner, that's fine. Enjoy what you do with her and, sooner or later, you will be ready for intercourse.

If you don't get an erection after a few times with a partner, she may wonder what is going on. She may even wonder the first time it happens. Many women take a lack of erection as a sign that the man is not attracted to them or that they are not doing the right things to arouse him, just as many men take a lack of orgasm on the part of their partners to indicate some deficiency in the men's attractiveness or lovemaking skills.

Obviously this is a potentially explosive situation and needs to be defused as quickly as possible. You need to let your partner know that she is attractive and desirable to you (assuming that this is true) and that your lack of erection is not her fault. Here are two possible ways:

Mary, I don't exactly understand what's going on but I can tell I'm not going to get an erection. I like you and am really turned-on to you. I've been looking forward to tonight all week and you've been doing everything I could want and I'm turned-on like crazy. I think it's because I like you and want to be a good lover for you. I'm just trying too hard and whenever I do that my penis goes on vacation. I'd like to leave it alone for a while. But I'd also like to touch you some more.

Ginny, I better level with you. I've had problems getting an erection for some time. I've been getting some help with it and I thought things would be different with you because I feel close to you and I really want you. But I can see that I'm still very nervous and that's getting in the way of getting hard. I'm sure I won't get an erection tonight, but I'd love to do whatever you want me to.

What you say may be quite different from either of these examples. Just make sure your partner understands that you are not blaming her. It's also a good idea not to apologize. You haven't done anything wrong or anything to be ashamed of. Apologies in such situations often lead to self-flagellation and other forms of destructive behavior. Just tell her what is happening, in as direct and honest a way as you can. No one has the right to expect more than that.

Regardless of what anyone has a right to expect, however, we want to acknowledge that there are some women who will be put off by your lack of erection, regardless of what you tell them about it. Because of their own insecurities about their attractiveness or sexual competence, or for some other reason, they may not be able to deal with a man who has a problem. Such women are probably few, but should you find yourself with one, you need to realize that you don't have many choices. Since her unwillingness to accept you the way you are is only going to make you feel bad about yourself and put more pressure on your penis, the situation can only get worse. Unless she can become more accepting of your situation, the only reasonable choice you have is to leave. Not a happy prospect, perhaps, but staying with her (assuming she is willing) will probably only add to your sexual woes.

Better to find a woman who is more interested in a man than in a rigid penis. With a more supportive attitude, you'll probably soon have erections.

To avoid unnecessary disappointments, remember that you won't always get erections when you think you should, you will lose erections sometimes and not be able to regain them, and at times your erections may not be as full or hard as you would like. As long as you are following all the suggestions we gave, you are doing all you can to maximize the chances for having good sex.

If you can't seem to get past a certain point, however, or if a problem keeps recurring, you can do something about it. First, figure out as precisely as possible what the problem is. For example, 'I get erections without any trouble but often lose them when she goes to insert it.' If you don't lose your erection when *you* insert it, you could decide to insert it yourself all the time, thus easily solving the difficulty. If you would like the option of her inserting it, one way of dealing with this is to use a scene of her doing that in Step B of Exercise 18–2.

Another option is to create an exercise of your own. An appropriate exercise might go like this. She sits on top of you and stimulates you to erection. She then rubs your penis in her pubic hair, then on the lips of her vagina. All this is done slowly and you move from one step to the next as you are comfortable and feel ready. She can then insert your penis just a little. Gradually, and not necessarily in one session, she can insert your penis deeper and deeper until it is all the way in.

Reading the partner exercises that follow will give you some ideas of the kinds of exercises you can use to deal with any problems that arise. You may not want to tell your partner that what you want to do is an exercise, and there's no reason you should. You can just say that you'd like to try such and such. As long as you proceed slowly enough to keep your anxiety level down, you should be able to handle any difficulties that come up.

That's really all there is to it. This program has worked for hundreds of men and it can work for you. You already have most of the skills and only need practice in applying them. Keep referring back to this section and make sure you are following our suggestions to the letter. When you have developed more confidence, you can be more flexible and do pretty much what you want as long as you are not totally disregarding your conditions. That is a certain invitation to trouble for anyone, no matter how much experience and confidence he has.

PARTNER EXERCISES

Before starting these exercises both you and your partner should read and discuss them. Talk about your feelings about the program and work out any conflicts. You both should understand that these exercises constitute a training program and will not be needed forever. Since how long they are needed is mainly determined by how often they are done, work out an agreement about frequency. Your partner should understand that you are in total control while the exercises are being done; she is not to push you faster or further than you want to go. You need to assure her that you are willing to satisfy her with your hands or mouth when she desires, but that no demands can be made on your penis.

It is common for disagreements to arise in the course of doing the exercises. To get the maximum benefit from the program, work out the disagreements as soon as they occur.

Do not restrict your physical contact with your partner to these exercises. Allow plenty of time for mutually satisfying expressions of physical affection, and be sure to have some physical contact before starting each exercise.

The basic principle to be followed in all the exercises is that you should engage in the suggested activities only up to the point where anxiety arises. When you become anxious, stop what you are doing and do something that will allow you to become comfortable. Then, if you desire, you can resume the previous activity, remembering to stop again if the tenseness returns.

The following suggestions apply to the exercises:

1. If possible, do exercises two to four times a week, no more than one exercise per day.

2. You probably will do best if you don't masturbate while engaged in this program. There are two exceptions to this rule. You may want to masturbate if you and your partner are not

able to get together several times a week. Masturbating is then fine and it will help if you use the focusing technique or one of the exercises in Chapter 18. The other situation in which masturbation is acceptable is if you feel the need to gain more confidence with one or more of the masturbation exercises. If so, take a break from the partner work, returning to it when you have accomplished what you wanted with the masturbation exercises. It's best not to alternate between masturbation and partner exercises on a daily basis. That may be just too much sex.

3. Both you and your partner should read and discuss an exercise before doing it.

4. Make sure you are relaxed and your conditions are met before starting an exercise.

5. Don't try to rush through the program. That will only add pressure. It will take as long as it needs to and there is little you can do to speed up the process. Take it slowly and see if you can enjoy what you are doing.

6. At some point you will get an erection and be tempted to have intercourse. Resist the temptation. Don't attempt insertion until it is suggested in the exercises and never attempt it in a hurried or pressured manner.

Since most of the exercises parallel some of the masturbation exercises in the last chapter and/or the idea in that chapter and the first part of this chapter, we keep our explanations here to a minimum.

EXERCISE 19–1: PARTNER PLAYING WITH YOUR SOFT PENIS
Time Required: 15 minutes

After making sure that you are both in a comfortable position (you may want to try the position recommended by Masters and Johnson, illustrated on page 299), let your partner play with your soft penis. Try not to get an erection since you want the experience of being touched and played with when soft. If you do get an erection, stop for a while until your penis gets soft, then have your partner resume.

Your partner can explore, caress, stroke, and play with your penis in any way she likes. Don't let her do anything that is painful or uncomfortable but, aside from that, keep your hands to yourself and your attention in your penis. Be aware of what it feels like to be touched. You may be aware of some pressure to get an erection. Just let the feeling be there and continue to focus on the sensations in your penis.

Do this exercise three or four times, or until you are quite comfortable with her touching you when you are soft.

POSSIBLE PROBLEM

You find yourself trying to get an erection. That's natural since men were taught that they should be hard when a woman touched them. If they weren't hard to begin with, they certainly should get that way within a few seconds after she started her ministrations. Be aware of the pressure if it is there but don't act on it. Talking to your partner about these feelings can be valuable. Remember that the goal is to keep your penis soft. Having an erection interferes with the purpose of the exercise.

EXERCISE 19–2: PARTNER STIMULATION OF PENIS WITH FOCUSING
Time Required: 15 to 20 minutes

Assume a position that is comfortable for you and your partner and have her stimulate your penis in ways that you like. Pay attention to the sensations in your penis and give her instructions on how to touch it. Suggest different strokes, pressures, and rhythms and see how they feel. If she has any trouble following your instructions, be more specific or show her how to do it. Be sure to tell her when she's doing it the way you like. Give your directions in ways that encourage her to follow them. Do not criticize her under any circumstance. Just tell her what you want as clearly as you can and show your appreciation for what she's doing.

Whether or not you get an erection is not the point. The goals are to give you practice in focusing and giving directions. If you are aroused, your conditions are met, and you are getting the kind of stimulation you want, you probably will get an erection some of the time. It's fine if you ejaculate.

Do the exercise three to five times, or until you feel confident that you usually do respond in a satisfying manner with the proper stimulation.

POSSIBLE PROBLEM

You never get an erection in this exercise, even after doing it a number of times. Check that your conditions are met, that you are aroused and comfortable before starting the exercise, and that you are getting precisely the kind of stimulation you want. If everything checks out and there's still no change, you might want to try the next exercise, particularly if you like oral stimulation.

If you responded in the masturbation exercises but not with your partner, there is obviously something in the relationship that is getting in your way. Ask yourself what it would take for you to be able to have an erection with your partner. What issues, attitudes, or behaviors would have to be resolved or changed? See if you can work them out. If not, you may have no alternative to seeking professional help.

If you responded to neither the masturbation exercises nor the partner exercises, you should definitely see a competent sex therapist.

If you are like most of the men we have worked with, you are now convinced that things are not as bad as you had imagined. In fact, you may be thinking that things are going well and be in a hurry to get to intercourse. We hope you are willing to put that off for a bit.

The next exercise is optional. Many men have enjoyed it and found it valuable. However, not all women are willing to do it, so you and your partner will have to discuss it carefully. If she is not willing to do it, don't push her. It's not a necessary exercise. Perhaps, as your sex life becomes more satisfying, she will be willing to try oral sex.

EXERCISE 19–3: ORAL STIMULATION OF PENIS WITH FOCUSING
Time Required: 15 to 20 minutes

This exercise is identical to the preceding one in all respects except that your partner now stimulates your penis with her mouth rather than her hand. Use whatever position is comfortable for the two of you but resist the temptation to stimulate her orally at the same time. Just focus and give directions.

By now you should be confident of getting erections most of the time when you have the proper conditions and stimulation. You now need to learn that it's really OK to lose your erection with your partner. Most of the time you will be able to regain it. And when you can't you can still have a good time.

EXERCISE 19–4: LOSING AND REGAINING ERECTIONS
Time Required: 20 to 25 minutes

Have your partner stimulate your penis with her hand or mouth. Keep your attention in your penis and give directions as needed. When you have an erection, tell her to stop and allow your erection to go down. You can do anything you want to accomplish this – have a chat, give her a back-rub, or whatever. Take as much time as you need for your penis to become flaccid. Then have her resume stimulation. When your penis gets hard again,

repeat the above procedure. Two repetitions are sufficient for one session.

You will not always regain your erection and, in fact, you will not always get one to begin with. When this happens, let her know that it's not going to get hard ('I guess it's tired today; I'd like you to stop'). Then ask yourself what you'd like to do with your partner. Perhaps you'd like a back-rub, some cuddling or talking, or to do something for her. Whatever it is, let her know and see if you can do it. It is quite important that you master this little procedure. You can be sure your penis will not always respond; you need to let your partner know when this is true and be able to have a good time without an erection.

Do this exercise at least four times or until you are confident that your erection will usually return with proper stimulation and that, when it doesn't, you can still have a pleasurable experience.

POSSIBLE PROBLEMS

1. Your erection doesn't go down in a reasonable length of time. This really isn't much of a problem but it does increase the amount of time it takes to do the exercise. Check to see if what you're doing while waiting for it to get soft is arousing. If so, do something else. You might even have to leave the room and take a walk around the house. That usually does the trick.

2. Your erection, once lost, never returns in a reasonable length of time. Consider whether your conditions are being fully met and whether you are aroused and relaxed when stimulation is resumed. The problem often lies in anxiety about getting the erection back. If that is the case, try to remember that you don't have to do anything to make your penis hard. It gets hard of its own accord. You only need to remove the obstacles that hinder this from happening. Talking to your partner about any concerns you have about regaining the erection can be helpful.

You're probably thinking that it's about time for intercourse. We agree. The next two exercises employ our usual step-by-step approach, moving slowly from insertion to intercourse with full movement. You can, of course, explore insertion and intercourse without following our method, but be sure you do so in a gradual, easy manner, stopping to get more comfortable when you need to. Frantic or pressured activities will only hinder your progress.

EXERCISE 19–5: PENIS IN VAGINA WITH MINIMUM MOVEMENT
Time Required: 20 to 25 minutes

Before beginning this exercise you should make sure your partner's vagina is well lubricated. You may need to use an artificial lubricant such as KY jelly or Albolene. Discuss this with her.

Lie on your back and have your partner sit on your thighs, as in Figure 11 (p. 302). She should stimulate your penis while you give instructions and focus. When you have an erection, rub your penis in her pubic hair. As you feel comfortable doing that, rub it against the lips of her vagina (she will have to shift position for you to do this). When that is comfortable, have her put your penis very slowly into her vagina. You need not insert it all the way in one session. Let your comfort be your guide. Gradually, your penis should be inserted until it is completely inside her. Then be still for a few minutes. Focus in your penis and be aware of how it feels inside of her. Then ask her to move slowly, just enough to provide some stimulation for your penis. Give her directions on how much to move. Feel free to ask her to stop moving or to get off if that is what you want.

Continue intercourse with minimal movement for about ten minutes. You can ejaculate if you want to when time is up.

It is essential that you be in full control over how much movement there is. Your partner should understand that she is not to move for her own enjoyment at this time.

Repeat this exercise as many times as needed for you to feel comfortable with insertion and slight movement. Then, with you still in complete control, increase the pace – which is the goal of the next exercise.

EXERCISE 19–6: PENIS IN VAGINA WITH MOVEMENT
Time Required: 15 to 20 minutes

The position and format are the same as in the preceding exercise. Here you want to increase the amount of movement you can comfortably handle.

With your penis inside her, give her directions to slowly increase the pace. As you become comfortable with a given pace, increase it. You can move too, if you desire.

Take as many sessions as you need to get to the point where you are comfortable with any amount of movement.

POSSIBLE PROBLEM

You lose your erection during intercourse. This happens occasionally to most men, but there are some things you can try if you feel it's a problem. Check to see that you are relaxed; if your penis is still in her vagina you can leave it there and try to get the stimulation that you want – moving in certain ways or having your lover squeeze her pelvic muscles may do the trick. Or you can take your penis out and get the type of stimulation you want, resuming intercourse when you are hard.

If you find that you usually lose your erection at a particular point – for example, when your partner is thrusting very quickly – you can do two additional things. First, using the instructions given in Step B of Exercise 18–2, masturbate to a fantasy of your partner moving quickly in intercourse. When you can handle it comfortably in that exercise, you'll be better prepared to handle it in reality. Then, with your partner, slowly approach the problem activity. Start with a pace that is

very comfortable for you, gradually building up the speed as you are comfortable with the slower movements. Stay focused and, should you become anxious or start to lose your erection, stop and relax, then resume at a slower pace, gradually increasing the speed again. Done consistently, this procedure will allow you to tolerate and enjoy more and more movement.

When you are comfortable with uninhibited movement in the female superior position, you can try other positions. You don't need a formal exercise for this. Try any positions you want, remembering that the first experience with a new position may be a bit awkward and uncomfortable. The first few times you try a new position, go slowly, as in Exercise 19–5, then gradually work up to a pace which you and your partner enjoy.

There is one last exercise to be done. The chances are extremely good that sooner or later you will again lose your erection during a sexual experience. By going through this under instruction, you can learn some useful ways of dealing with the situation and preclude the possibility of its upsetting you when it happens spontaneously. This exercise extends the understanding you developed in Exercise 19–4.

EXERCISE 19–7: LOSING YOUR ERECTION
Time Required: 20 to 30 minutes

You are to reenact your old erection problem and handle it differently than you did in the past. If your problem is that you did not get an erection while hugging and kissing your partner, then hug and kiss her and see to it that you don't get an erection. If your problem was losing erection during insertion, attempt insertion while trying to make your erection go away. Whatever the old problem, see to it that you get your penis soft.

There are many ways of accomplishing this. Worrying whether it will stay hard, if the kids are listening, or how

tired you'll be in the morning are all good methods. If none of these work, try pacing around the room for a while.

Now deal with the situation in a way that is enjoyable for you and your partner. Stick with your partner and find some things to do that satisfy both of you. These activities can be sexual or nonsexual.

Repeat this exercise as many times as required for you to feel comfortable about losing your erection and dealing with the situation after that. For some men, one or two repetitions are sufficient. Others can benefit from more.

Once you can handle this exercise with equanimity, you know you are in good shape. By fulfilling your conditions, you are ensuring that your penis will be hard most of the time you want it that way. And when it doesn't come up to expectations or when you lose your erection in the middle of things, you no longer have to worry about it. You are now prepared to have a good time no matter what your penis does.

As time goes on and your sexual confidence develops even further, you will not need to be as careful about your conditions. Just don't forget about them altogether. If you should ever find yourself getting back into the old rut, if you begin to get tense in sex (which can happen, for example, when you're with a new partner) or find that sex isn't as satisfying as it is now, start being more careful about meeting your conditions and stopping when you get tense, and it probably won't be too long before things are well again.

TWENTY

Male sexuality and the aging process

There is no special age at which one becomes old. We start aging and the inexorable march to the grave the minute we are born. This chapter is not only for men who are over sixty or who think they are old. It is intended for all men because all of us are aging and will someday consider ourselves old, and also because younger men suffer from the same affliction as older men – the inability to live up to the sexual standards that they have accepted.

Sex, we have been led to believe, is for the young and healthy. We glorify youth and health, forgetting that both are gradually lost. We segregate the aged and make jokes about them, such as the one that follows, conveniently forgetting that someday we will be on the short end of these same jokes.

An elderly man was hoping for some solace from the minister speaking on the radio. At one point the minister said that if the members of the radio audience would put one hand on the radio and the other hand on the ailing part of the body, he would pray for healing. The old man put his left hand on the radio and reached for his penis with the right. At which point, his younger wife laughed. 'He said that he was going to heal the sick, not raise the dead.'

Ours is not a good country in which to grow old. Aging is regarded not as a natural and inevitable process, full of possibilities and challenges as well as limitations, but rather as a dread disease to be fought and staved off as long as possible by all the resources of modern technology. The result is those who think they are old or who reach a certain birthday or who notice some wrinkles often feel unattractive, unwanted, and useless. And they are, at least according to the standards that many people in this society subscribe to.

In discussing a subject like aging it is useful to have a reference point, a time of life to which aging or being old can be compared. Although, as we have said, the aging process begins at the moment of birth, this is not the reference point that most people use. Rather, it is the period of life in which most of us reach the peak of our physical abilities – adolescence and early adulthood, which we arbitrarily define as the years between thirteen and twenty-five, give or take a few years – that people use as a standard when they talk about youth and age.

In conformity with this idea, we begin our discussion of aging with a look at adolescence. During the teenage years and for a few years thereafter, males – with few exceptions – are in better physical condition than they will ever be again. It is a time of seemingly boundless energy, enthusiasm, and exuberance. You can play football all day, boogie half the night, masturbate during breaks, sleep for four hours, and still be up in time for class or work in the morning. It is not like this for long and it will never be the same.

Never again will we run as fast, climb as high, move around as strongly and briskly. And few of us will ever again feel so strong and healthy. For in these years most of us hardly know the meaning of ulcers, high blood pressure, arthritis, coronaries, chronic constipation, and the many other discomforts and diseases that the adult body is heir to. Even if we smoke, drink, eat too much, and sleep too little, our young bodies are resilient enough not to be too badly scarred.

Adolescence is a time of great physical and emotional upheaval. Adult size and strength are attained, along with full adult sexual capacity. Hormonal changes cause an increase of sexual feeling. Sex, sex, sex – most teenaged boys are obsessed with it. Masturbation usually begins during this period, as well as the first sexual experiences with partners.

Boys experience and deal with their budding sexuality in different ways. Some find it more of a curse than a blessing. Some stick to masturbation while others quickly turn to partner sex. Some are so concerned with other activities or so repressed that they seem to be almost unaffected by sex. Despite these differences, there seems to be sufficient uniformity of experience to justify talking about an adolescent model of sexuality.

Adolescent sexuality, when not repressed or sublimated, is obsessive. Nothing else matters as much as sex – thinking about it, fantasizing about it, learning about it, doing it, talking about it. We would prefer, at least at times, to concentrate on our schoolwork or other activities, but fantasies and warm tinglings and erections continue to intrude. We are unable to control our sexual feelings. It is not enough that we get turned-on by almost every female we see on the streets and in magazines and movies, but many of us also feel the stirrings of flesh and fantasy when we look at our sisters, cousins and mothers of friends. Where, we wonder, will all this lead? Are there any limits?

In his hilarious and deeply moving account 'Being a Boy', Julius Lester tells of his experience:

> No wonder boys talked about nothing but sex. That thing was always there. Everytime we went to the john, there it was, twitching around like a fat little worm on a fishing hook. When we took baths, it floated in the water like a lazy fish and God forbid we should touch it! It sprang to life like lightning leaping from a cloud. I wished I could cut it off, or at least keep it tucked between my legs . . . But I was helpless. It was there, with a life and mind of its own, having no other function than to embarrass me.

Which brings us to the adolescent penis, a penis that for many of us knew only one position – rigid. As one man said, 'I had a hard-on from the day I was fourteen until I graduated from college.' Whether we were pleased or embarrassed by its erect state, we were always aware of its presence.

Refractory periods were something many adolescent penises had not heard about. A few seconds or minutes after ejaculation there it was again, as hard as if nothing at all had happened. And boy, was it hard! It felt like it was made of steel and would burst apart if something wasn't done to appease it. But there seemed to be no way. No matter how many sexual experiences we had, whether alone or with partners, the insatiable appetites of our penis seemed unaffected.

The ejaculations were marvelously strong, just like explosions. Many of us tried to see how far we could ejaculate, often in competition with our friends. It was something to see, our vigorous bodies sometimes pushing the ejaculate halfway across the room.

The process of sex was quick and explosive. Once we got started – and it took little enough to get us going – there was an awesome rush toward ejaculation. We were out of control; passion (or something we took for passion) pushed us and we exploded in orgasm.

That is adolescent sexuality, something many men look back upon as the good old days. It may not have felt very good at the time, given our anxieties about our pimples, girls, whether anyone would notice our erections, and other teenage concerns, but it did serve as our first experience with adult sexuality. It became a standard against which later experiences would be compared.

It is also a standard that would be reinforced by many sources because, as you may have noticed, adolescent sexuality is very similar to the fantasy model of sex discussed in Chapters 3 and 4. In its obsession with sex, the functioning of the penis, and the uncontrolled nature of sex, adolescent sexuality is the closest most men will ever get to fantasyland sexuality. Our first experience of adult sexuality is therefore similar to the dominant model in our culture that is held up as a standard for the rest of our lives.

And that is quite unfortunate because adolescence is soon

over, with the larger portion of life still to come. Every day and every year takes us further and further away from the only models of sex we know. Which means that we are but poorly equipped to deal with the changes that aging brings.

We go along after our adolescent years, often unaware that time is passing and we are aging, until one day it suddenly hits us. It may be when we develop an illness or condition that we had considered something that only happened to middle-aged or old folks – such as ulcers, back trouble, heart problems – or perhaps when we notice that we have developed a pot belly, or that we can't run as fast or play tennis as well as when we were younger. Or it may be something sexual: when we notice that our erections aren't as full or firm, that our orgasms aren't as powerful, or that we are having sex less often. Whatever the exact stimulus, it is frequently a moving experience.

At one point in my mid-twenties, I realized that my erections were not as firm as when I was in high school. In those days they seemed hard as rock. Now they were hard but not quite rocklike. I couldn't believe that I was over the hill at the tender age of twenty-six. At this rate, I was certain, I wouldn't be able to get an erection at all by the time I was thirty. With some difficulty, I talked about it with my doctor. He assured me that nothing was wrong, that I was simply experiencing the effects of aging, and that I would probably be able to get it up long past thirty, although it might never again be as hard as when I was seventeen. This discussion had repercussions for many months. I often thought about it and tried to make sense of it. I realized that I had always believed that I would be young until one special day, like my seventieth birthday, I would suddenly become old. It was quite a shock to recognize that I was already experiencing the aging process. It was a process that went on continuously, whether one was twenty, forty, or sixty. I had a strong sense of the fact that I, too, was aging and that I, too, would someday die. And I realized that there really were no special days when anything happened. What seemed like special days were those on which I took the time to become aware of how much had changed since the last special day on which I looked.

Men react to aging in many different ways. Some retire from physical activity in their twenties and never again do anything more strenuous than walking to their cars. Others retire for months or years at a time, then suffer attacks of energy and play five sets of tennis or shovel snow for several hours, often causing themselves severe injury in the process. Still others continue regular physical activity – be it walking, jogging, swimming, or something else – for many years, not moving as fast in their sixties as in their thirties, but moving nonetheless. And some of these men continue their activities well into the years where they 'should be too old to do them' and become local celebrities.

Sexual changes are similar. Things slow down for all men as the years go by, but the changes occur at different ages and with different consequences. Some men retire from sexual activity quite early in life, engaging in it only rarely thereafter. Others move along well until some illness intervenes and then they, too, retire. For others, reaching a certain age spells the end of sex. It is as if they had heard that there is no sex after, say, sixty, so they fulfill the prophecy upon reaching their sixtieth birthday. Still others just keep on going. They don't function exactly as they did in their twenties and thirties, but they keep on enjoying sex in their sixties, seventies, and beyond.

We now list and discuss some of the more common sexual changes that occur in men as they get older. Most of them also accompany illness (whether temporary like a cold or flu, or chronic) and some types of injuries. These changes do not necessarily happen at the same time for a given individual; they occur at different times for different men; and not all men experience all of them.

1. *It takes longer to achieve erection.* Since sex is no longer like a new toy, and since the hormones are no longer racing through your body the way they did when you were in high school, your penis is slower to jump up from its naps. Just thinking about sex or kissing your lover may no longer be enough. Direct penile stimulation may be required to achieve erection even in the late twenties or early thirties.

This bothers many men. They remember 'the way it used to be' and feel embarrassed that it isn't that way anymore. Some of them come to therapy wanting to get an erection 'the normal way', meaning without direct stimulation. Sometimes something can be done, especially if the man is bored with his partner or is having sex under less than appropriate conditions. But most often he needs to accept the fact that there isn't any normal way to get an erection, that it is perfectly acceptable to get one through penile stimulation from his partner.

The problem many men have in accepting this is the idea that a man should produce his own turn-on and not need anything from a woman. For some men, needing stimulation (or information or anything else) from a woman means that they are weak and dependent on their partners. Such is the influence of our sexual mythology. Here, as elsewhere, we need to realize that the mythology is just that and not very useful as a guide for human behavior. After all, why should we value a spontaneous erection more highly than one attained through the tender, loving care of a partner?

2. *Erections may not be as full or as hard.* This phenomenon is noticed by some men in their twenties and thirties, and by many who are older. Some men play a numbers game, offering information that their erections are only 60 or 80 or some other per cent as hard as they used to be. This is understandable, given the 'hard as a rock' model we learned, but has unfortunate consequences because it can lead to worrying about what isn't instead of enjoying what is.

3. *It takes longer to achieve an erection after ejaculation* or, in more technical terminology, longer refractory periods are

experienced. Masters and Johnson found that many men in their fifties and sixties could not get an erection, regardless of how much stimulation was applied, for twelve to twenty-four hours after their last ejaculation.

Another related discovery by Masters and Johnson is that some older men who lose their erections without ejaculating may be unable to regain them during the same sexual experience no matter how much stimulation is applied. They may have to wait several hours or longer before again having erections. This phenomenon seems restricted to men over the age of sixty and is by no means universal even within that group.

4. *It takes longer to ejaculate.* Ejaculatory control, a problem for many younger men, often comes automatically with aging. This is not usually experienced as a problem. In fact, many regard it as a gift, particularly those who were quick on the trigger when younger.

Not only does orgasm take longer to reach, but many men past forty find that they have no desire to ejaculate every time they have sex. They can maintain an erection for relatively long periods of time and need not end each experience with an ejaculation. Few men see this as a big problem, but many are surprised and a bit discomforted by it. Sex without orgasm is a new idea for them that takes some getting used to. A few men have great difficulty with this, feeling that somehow they are failing by not having an orgasm. All that is needed is acceptance of the fact that we have stated several times: orgasm is not necessary for a good sexual experience.

Not ejaculating every time he has sex can have positive results for the older man, since the lack of ejaculation means he can have more frequent erections (refractory periods are usually shorter when there is no ejaculation).

5. *Ejaculation is less powerful.* As the male ages, particularly past sixty, the ejaculatory process becomes less efficient. The sense of ejaculatory inevitability may vanish altogether and the orgasm may feel less intense. The ejaculate may seem to seep out rather than being expelled under pressure. This does

not mean that orgasm is not pleasurable, but only that it may feel somewhat different than it did before.

6. *Sex is engaged in less frequently.* On the average, frequency of sexual activity declines with advancing age. There are many reasons for this decline – boredom with sex, decreased desire, the belief that sex is not for the old, physical infirmities – some of which we discuss later in the chapter.

Despite the general decline in activity, however, there are important exceptions. Some men have as much or almost as much sex in their seventies as in their twenties. And one study reported that about 15 per cent of the people over sixty-five in the population studied said they were having more sex than ever before.

7. *Automatic functioning may no longer be possible.* In order to have good sex, an older man may have to consider factors he could safely ignore when younger. He no longer can function automatically; he has to set the stage carefully for a good experience. Arousal, conditions, and proper stimulation become crucial.

Whitney, a man in his late sixties who was having trouble getting erections, had some difficulty understanding why he had to pay attention to things he had never before considered. But, since he wanted to get remarried, he was open to exploration. A surprising discovery was that time of day made a great deal of difference. He almost never got an erection late at night but, after meeting some of his other conditions, he found that a good time for him was immediately following his afternoon nap. He later was able to expand his 'good periods' to include early morning and evening, but the afternoon remained the best time for him.

Four of the age-related changes mentioned have to do with erections. This is quite disturbing to many men who can barely conceive of sexual relations without an erection. God forbid the silly thing shouldn't get hard! For reasons we have discussed throughout the book, men forget that they have fingers and mouths and lots of sensitive skin elsewhere, and also that a penis doesn't have to be hard to be enjoyably stimulated. Older men, as well as many younger ones, would probably have more sex and enjoy it more if only they could let go of the idea that there can be no sex without an erection.

Why do so many older men retire from sexual activity or develop sexual problems? It is easy to jump to the conclusion that the answer is obvious: the aging process destroys both interest and the ability to function. We suggest that this is only rarely the case. Aging may make things different but it doesn't destroy them. A man of ninety is probably not going to run a four-minute mile, no matter how much he trains. But if he wants to and is willing to get himself in condition, there's no reason why he can't enjoy jogging.

Although, as we have seen, aging does have some effect on erections, Masters and Johnson found that the male 'does not lose his facility for erection at any time'. And we have worked successfully with dozens of men in their sixties and seventies who came to therapy complaining that they hadn't had erections or sexual interest in years. It is clear that something other than biological mechanisms is what causes older men to give up on sex. It is to these other mechanisms, psychological and social, that we now turn.

We have already said that our society defines sexuality as something that belongs to the young and healthy. To most people, sex in the aged seems somehow inappropriate and is a source of discomfort. Many of us can't even conceive of a man and a woman in their sixties or seventies in bed. It strikes us, as one young man put it, as 'gross and disgusting'. An elderly man interested in sex is a 'dirty old man', while a younger man with precisely the same interests is admired and praised.

Older men realize that they don't fit the picture of people who are supposed to be interested in sex. They learned the adolescent and fantasy models of sex just like everyone else, and they know how poorly they fit the models. Often they are confused because, contrary to what they have learned, they find that the feelings are still there, they are interested. And many feel guilty for having sexual feelings when they know they 'shouldn't' have them.

For some, the easiest way of reconciling the differences between what they were taught and what they feel is to capitulate to society's view and suppress their own feelings. If this sounds strange to you, perhaps you can think of some examples from your own life where you felt a certain way or wanted to do a certain thing but then, realizing that your feelings or desires were contrary to your image of yourself (as a 'nice boy', 'grown man', 'mature and responsible adult'), you pushed away the feelings or decided not to engage in the activity. In a similar way, older men often decide, consciously or not, that sex is not for them.

And they have plenty of help in making such decisions. That they are asexual is reinforced by the attitudes of those close to them. Adult children, for example, often view their parents' normal sexual urges as embarrassing and put obstacles in the way. A not very subtle example was given by a man in his seventies.

> He was still interested in women and sex but, for financial reasons, lived with his daughter. She was repulsed by his 'carrying on' and frequently criticized him for 'acting like a child' and 'running around with loose women'. She also refused to take messages for him if his women friends called when he was out.

Relatives, friends, and physicians are often shocked and do all they can to remind the man that he is acting with impropriety. As for hospitals and other institutions in which many of the aged spend a fair portion of their time, probably the less said the better. Most such places make no provision for sexual expression of any kind (even for their permanent residents) and anyone caught masturbating or having sex with a partner is subjected to inhuman degrees of embarrassment and humiliation.

The message gets through – sex is not for you.

The elderly are often treated very delicately, as if they were in danger of falling apart, especially if they have had any serious medical problems. Sometimes, the heavy emphasis by the doctor and concerned friends and relatives on taking good care of oneself and not doing anything that might cause harm is taken to mean that the man shouldn't do anything. Since sex is a something, many think it is healthful to stay away from it or at least not to do it too vigorously. Sometimes the man, sometimes his partner, and sometimes both conspire to deny or limit his sexuality, or at least to keep it from being very interesting. All with the purpose of preventing the poor fellow from doing himself harm.

Thus far we have been talking about general ways in which the social definition of the role of older man is inconsistent with active sexuality. There are also other problems. Older men realize that they can't live up to the rules laid down in the fantasy model of sex. Of course, they never could; but now they can't even equal the poor imitation they used to do. The results of this kind of comparison with the fantasy model are often tragic, extending far beyond the area of sex.

After giving a talk about friendships in old age to a group of men and women over sixty-five, I had the opportunity to chat with some members of the audience. One man who had a hearing problem and a hip injury that necessitated using a cane when he walked said that he missed female companionship since the death of his wife, but that nothing could be done about it. When I asked what prevented him from befriending some of the women in his apartment building, he replied: 'Are you kidding? Look at me. I can hardly hear and I don't walk so good. They don't want me. They want a man, someone who is strong and can take care of them. They don't want an old cripple!' What is particularly interesting about this story is that my invitation to speak had come from the women. They outnumbered the men five to one and were desperate for some male attention and company. Not only that, but two of the women had told me that they were interested in this particular man but found him un-approachable. He was so locked into his idea of what a man should be and what he thought women wanted that he couldn't see what was happening right in front of him.

There is no question but that many men feel very bad and apologetic for being old or for not being as healthy as a twenty-year-old. In the country of the young and healthy, being old is in itself something many people feel guilty about, as is being ill. Feeling bad about oneself is, of course, hardly conducive to good sex or good anything.

Still another problem for many older men is a restrictive view of sex. Having learned about sex when the Victorian influence was much stronger than it is today, their ideas about sex are frequently unnecessarily narrow. Many believe that masturbation is totally inappropriate for adults and so deny themselves this form of gratification, or engage in it with a great deal of guilt. Still more are convinced that sex equals intercourse and refuse to have much to do with manual or oral stimulation. Which means, of course, that they view an erect penis as the main actor on the sexual stage. This is a heavy enough burden for men who are young and healthy; it is impossibly difficult for many who are old and in less than perfect health. They get so concerned about the erectility of their penises that they sometimes bring about what they most fear – erection problems. Because they fear failure to get an erection or have already experienced this problem, they stay away from sex.

It is important to recognize that these fears often occur in a context of low self-esteem. The man knows he is growing old, that he cannot do all the things he used to do, and that society does not see much use for old men, and he may feel bad about all these things. His image of himself is deflated; he feels like something less than a man, less impressive than he would like. And perhaps he has heard that old men are usually impotent.

Feeling bad about himself and fearful of being unable to be an adequate lover, an older man may simply give up on sex, claiming to be too old or too sick for such things. Or he may attempt sexual activity but, because of his fears, develop problems. This makes him even more worried, even more concerned if he still 'has it in him'. A cycle of failure and anxiety ensues, leaving him feeling worse about himself each time. After a while he may come to the probably erroneous conclusion, perhaps with the aid of his partner, friends, or doctor, that his age or physical condition is the cause of his problem and that nothing can be done about it.

There is one other reason for retirement from sexual activity. Contrary to popular belief that all men love sex and can't get enough of it, there are men who experience sex as a burden and engage in it only through a sense of duty or in order to avoid hurting their partners' feelings. This is usually not true at the beginning of a relationship. The newness and mystery of the partner and the relationship generate a passion that is often expressed in sex. But as the novelty decreases, the man realizes that sex just isn't what he thought it would be. There are more important things that require his attention (usually his job or career) and sex is just more work without a lot of rewards.

Many women will recognize the pattern – the man who can't get enough sex at the beginning of the relationship but not long after seems to lose all interest in the subject. Some women, as well as some sex experts, put the blame on man's presumed nonmonogamous nature or on the woman for not being seductive enough. We think differently. It is usually the man's unrealistic expectations of what sex can provide and his limited idea of how he should be in sex that cause the trouble.

Once a man starts feeling that sex is something to be endured rather than enjoyed, he's not far from sexual retirement. In his novel *Go to the Widow-Maker*, James Jones gives a realistic picture of sex as obligation.

Grant didn't know if he could. In silence he finished his drink. Finally both pity and a terribly painful sense of how embarrassing it would be for her if he didn't, plus a vague moral obligation which he knew was ridiculous, plus the fact that she was a female, all came to his aid . . . Gracelessly, flat on his back, he groped at her crotch a little to aid him . . . He rolled over onto her, stuck it in her, and pumped away until he came.

With this type of sex, it's no wonder that a man would rather stay late at work or watch TV. Who needs anything as dull and listless? But he needs a respectable reason for leaving the field. The demands of his career, illness, or old age provide it. His partner can't complain because it's not that he doesn't want to, it's just that his job or condition or age won't allow it.

While we can understand why anyone who is disappointed with sex should want to discontinue their participation in it, the fact is that it doesn't have to be this way. Sex can be fun. But, because of a rigid adherence to the fantasy model of sex that they learned while very young, many men see no alternative and decide that sex just isn't worth the trouble.

One of the saddest consequences of giving up on sex is that often this means that all forms of physical affection are dispensed with. Because of the fear that the partner will want more than snuggling or the fear of being unable 'to finish what I start', many men discontinue all forms of affectionate expression – hand-holding, cuddling, kissing, everything. And this at a time when such expressions could convey so much caring, support, and affection. Thus the elderly who have given up on sex often become more isolated and discontented.

While not denying that sexual functioning does change with age, we have said that there is no age at which a man should give up sex or at which sex becomes unseemly or unenjoyable. Sexual expression can be a part of your life for as long as you live. There are no biological or medical reasons for sexual retirement, there are only a lot of cultural myths that cause lots of older people lots of misery.

While we don't mean to say that you should have sex – that decision being yours to make – we do say that there are many enjoyable ways of having sex, some of which may be new to you. If you are interested, the relevant chapters in this book can be valuable. All the suggestions and exercises have been used with men of all ages. Of course you may have to fight some prejudices of your own and those of others, but it may not be as difficult as you think. Societal attitudes about aging have started to change in recent years and while there is still plenty of room for improvement, we think and hope that it won't be too long before being called a dirty old man will be taken as a compliment.

If you have little desire and/or a persistent inability to get an erection, and you are on medication of any sort, it's a good idea to talk to your doctor about this. A number of prescription drugs are known to have, or are suspected of having, negative sexual side effects. If a doctor has told you not to have sex because of a medical condition, find out more about what that means. Sex is not a dangerous activity and there is usually no reason for refraining from it for long, even after major illness or surgery. If you're well enough to take a walk, you're probably well enough to have sex. If your doctor doesn't agree, get a second opinion. If your doctor thinks that men your age shouldn't be interested in sex, find yourself another doctor.

If you decide that sex isn't for you, that's fine, but we would ask you to consider if you're getting as much physical contact as you like. If not, we hope that reading this book has at least raised the possibility that you might be able to get more without having sex or doing anything else you don't want to do.

We close with two stories, one of a woman who is a relative of a close friend and one of a former client. Their stories are close to our hearts and cheer us when we contemplate our own old age.

Auntie Grace, as she is known to all her friends, is now eighty-four and still carrying on. She has always liked men and sex, and survived three husbands and many lovers. Her older sister, with whom she has lived for the past decade, is scandalized by her activities. A few years ago, as Auntie Grace was leaving for a date, her sister started on her usual lecture about how a woman of her age shouldn't act this way and what would the neighbors think. Just before walking out the door, Grace turned and said: 'Don't worry, I won't come home pregnant.' When last heard from, Grace was getting involved with the younger set. She had just returned from a vacation where she had met a 'nice, young doctor' who was only seventy-one.

Norton came for sex therapy when he was seventy-six. He had enjoyed a good sexual relationship with his wife for over forty years but then had had a few erection failures and assumed that he was over the hill. For almost ten years since then, he hadn't tried to have sex. He and his wife still engaged in some physical contact but not as much as before, because he didn't want to lead her on. After reading an article about sex and aging in a popular magazine, he decided to see if anything could be done. He had all the usual, narrow ideas about sex, as did his wife. Intercourse had always been the culmination of their sexual activity and they could barely think of anything that could be done without an erection. But they had a very close and warm relationship and were able to support one another in looking at new models of sex. It took only a few weeks for them to resume satisfying sexual activity. Here is what he said in his last therapy session. 'I guess it's never too late to teach an old dog some new tricks. Hell, I haven't had so much fun in a long time. And to think of all the time we wasted because I was so fired up with concern about that old pecker. He comes around pretty good now, but like you said, not every time. But that's all right, I don't need him every time. I just like to be playing around with Emmy, and she loves it. I haven't seen so much fire in her eyes for twenty years or more. And when she plays with me, it's just like I was back in high school again. Wow, I just want to eat her up. It's really good to be back with her again like this. And I don't intend to stop, ever.'

TWENTY-ONE

Male sexuality and medical conditions

You should be warned that we are entering one of the most confused and least understood areas of sexuality. There is vast disagreement over if, how, and why various diseases and injuries affect sexual functioning and enjoyment, what kinds of sexual expression are possible for those afflicted with the various conditions, and what the patient should be told. Many physicians are no better informed in this area than lay people and, in fact, have themselves been the source of much misinformation and harmful advice. Our intention is to give you sufficient information so that you can start being a better consumer of medical services and find out for yourself what is possible and enjoyable for you.

The diseases and injuries thought to influence sexual functioning are too numerous to be discussed or even listed here. Some of the more common ones are alcoholism, some types of cancer, diabetes, epilepsy, hypertension, multiple sclerosis, and spinal cord injuries or lesions. Sexual functioning can also be seriously affected by what the doctor does for you. Radical prostate surgery, for example, often leads to erection problems. Some types of back operations may also result in sexual problems. Decreased sexual interest and/or impaired sexual functioning is produced in many people by the medications so liberally dispensed in our society. Some of the most widely prescribed drugs, including Valium, have been implicated in sexual problems.

It is not surprising that so many diseases and conditions influence sexuality. Almost anything that affects the way you feel physically or the way you view yourself can have sexual consequences. As a simple example, you might consider what happens to your sexual desire and functioning when you have a bad cold, a severe headache or stomach ache, or the flu. And these, of course, are simple and transient conditions. More severe and chronic conditions involve not only more extensive physical disability and discomfort, but also one's view of oneself as a person (e.g., 'I'm a cripple', or 'I'm a sick man, not as good as other men').

Even given this, however, it is clear that men are affected differently by the same physical problem. There is hardly any physical disability that prevents all men who have it from enjoying sex. Some diabetics, for example, have erection problems. But many do not. And many men who developed a sexual problem after getting a certain disease or sustaining an injury have been able to overcome the problem and have good sex. We will return to this point later.

It is easy to get depressed reading the medical literature about the sexual effects of many physical disabilities. It is full of gloom and doom, citing statistics showing higher frequencies of sexual problems for men with these disabilities than for those without, and spinning many interesting-sounding theories about the supposed mechanisms causing the sex problems.

The depressing conclusions in the literature have been picked up by physicians and the popular culture, and the 'knowledge' has a wide circulation. We 'know' that diabetics have erection problems, that men with spinal cord injuries can't have sex, that sexual problems caused by long-term alcoholism are irreversible, and so forth, just as we 'know' that older men aren't interested in sex and, even if they are, can't function satisfactorily. This 'knowledge', no matter how erroneous it is, has consequences.

It has consequences for the same reasons that the idea that older men don't function well in sex has consequences. The man with a physical disability becomes frightened. Will he be able to have sex or won't he? His fears may be so strong as to discourage him from even trying to have sex. Or he may try but, because of his worries, bring about the failure he is worried about. When statistics are being compiled, this man may well be included among those who are having sexual problems – which is fair because it is a fact. But then things will become confused because it will be said that his physical condition caused the problem. But did it?

Almost everything we said in the last chapter about the sexual situation of older men is true of most disabled men. The sexual model most of us learned has no room for sick or crippled participants. Where is the encouragement for a man with epilepsy or multiple sclerosis or a colostomy or a spinal cord injury to think of himself as sexual? And everyone 'knows' that men who have had coronaries shouldn't have sex or at least should make sure that it's not very exciting.

Like men who feel bad about being old, sick and disabled men may feel bad about their condition. They may not like the way they are – 'only half a man', as a man with a colostomy called himself – and may wonder why anyone would want to make love or do anything else with them. They often have special requirements in sex ('special' meaning anything not part of the fantasy model of sex) and feel guilty about them, just as many healthy men feel guilty about their special requirements. Sometimes they can barely stand to think of their requirements, let alone communicate them to a partner.

Paul, a man in his forties with multiple sclerosis, decided to seek therapy after twelve years of no sexual activity. He claimed that his penis was dead but after a while he found that he could get erections with prolonged penile stimulation. But he was greatly bothered by his condition. Since he was confined to a wheelchair and had only limited strength in his arms, it took some doing to get into a bed. How would a woman feel, he wondered, having to wait the five minutes it took him to make the transition? He felt embarrassed and helpless as he contemplated the possibility. He was also bothered by the vigorous and lengthy stimulation he required to get an erection. He bitterly complained about his rotten luck and wistfully talked about how easy sex would be if he could just hop into bed and get an erection without any help from a partner.

Men who have only recently had surgery or found that they have a serious illness have another issue to contend with. In addition to the discomfort and physical limitations they have to endure, there is the psychological shock of learning that one really is mortal, a realization that is often accompanied by feelings of despair and depression. All these responses add to the man's feelings of inadequacy. He feels bad about himself, he's worried about his condition and his future, and he's not sure what he can or should do. This is quite a bundle of woes to bring to bed, and it can't help but affect what happens there.

There is also an excellent chance that the medical authorities in charge of a sick or disabled man's treatment will add to his sexual worries. We wish this weren't true, but it is a fact that most doctors know very little about sex and don't feel comfortable discussing it with their patients. The situation is beginning to change – most medical schools have instituted required sex courses in the last decade and doctors are now being encouraged to attend workshops and seminars on sex – but it is still very far from ideal or even good. Almost every man with a serious illness or disability whom we have treated – and there have been scores – had been told by at least one doctor that he would not be able to have 'normal sexual relations'. Such words of good cheer served to increase his fears and, sure enough, he developed sexual problems.

We want you to be very clear about what we are saying before going further. We are not implying that illness and injury have no sexual consequences. They certainly do. Nor are we saying that there are no cases where sickness or injury has caused serious and perhaps even irreversible damage to the organs or nerves involved in sexual functioning. There are such cases. But we are saying that the number of such cases has been seriously exaggerated. The fear of being unable to function and all the other worries attendant upon being physically impaired cause the majority of sexual problems for sick and disabled men, not the condition itself. No matter what kind of impairment you have, some kind of enjoyable sex life is possible for you.

To understand why there have been such exaggerations and such confusion in this field, we need to look at how a doctor typically decides that a man is too ill or crippled to be capable of functioning sexually. Doctors view the complaints presented to them – whether a fever, an erratic heartbeat, an erection problem – as symptoms of some underlying disease process. Their job is to determine what that process is and recommend appropriate treatment. Doctors are, of course, trained to think in terms of physical disease or injury such as nerve degeneration or spinal cord lesion rather than in terms of psychological factors such as the ones we discussed above.

Once a physical cause has been found – nerve damage, for example – the options are often limited. The cause should be treated, but this can't always be done. There's not a lot to do about nerve damage, cerebral palsy, or multiple sclerosis, but one can try to get the alcoholic to stop drinking and the diabetic to maintain better control. But if this doesn't help, it is often assumed that nothing can be done. And it sounds so convincing. Not only can the physician supply you with a scientific-sounding explanation of why you have the problem, but he can also cite statistics demonstrating that many men with your condition have the same sexual problem.

The real problem, however, lies elsewhere. Medical deduction works well in many areas but very poorly when dealing with sex problems. The deduction game the doctor plays – we know that disease X damages nervous tissue; this patient has the disease and can't get erections; therefore the disease has damaged the nerves that govern erection – is simply the wrong game. The premises are too loose and inexact. Disease X may damage nerve tissue but not in all patients; we don't know how much damage is necessary to impair or destroy a given function, and it is difficult to determine how much damage has been done; further, even if some nerves have been damaged or destroyed, others may be able to take over some of their work. Such deductions are also wrong because they ignore the many nonphysical factors that can cause sex problems. The following example will help you understand how easy it can be to make a wrong diagnosis when physical illness is involved.

I found that I was diabetic when I was twenty-one. A few years later, the first time I had sex with Allie, I didn't get an erection. I got very worried about this and didn't get an erection on numerous successive occasions. I started wondering what was wrong with me. Since there was no such thing as sex therapy in those days, I didn't consider getting professional help. But apparently I did all the right things. I spent lots of time with Allie in and out of bed and we had plenty of physical contact. My impotence lasted five weeks. Then, all of a sudden, all was well and remained well.

Looking back, it's easy to see what caused my problem. Allie was the first woman I had been with who was sexually assertive. She knew what she wanted and made no bones about it. I was scared. My sexual confidence was precarious and I didn't know if I could satisfy her. My fear was what caused my erection problem. It took several weeks for me to become accustomed to this situation and feel more comfortable with her. When that happened, my erections returned.

But I have sometimes wondered what might have happened had I gone to a doctor for help. Given what I have heard from many doctors, from what other diabetics have told me about what their doctors did, and from what I have read in the medical literature, there is a good chance it would have gone like this. The doctor would have taken a medical history and focused on the diabetes. He would have checked my blood and urine. If I were not well controlled, he would have helped me with that, hoping that resumption of good control would solve the problem. If it didn't, or if I already was under good control, he might have said that the impotence was caused by the diabetes and that nothing could be done. (If this sounds extreme, you should know that it happens all the time.) I would have freaked out – my sexual career over at twenty-four! – and been unable even to think about sex without trembling, which would have ensured that my problem would go on forever. I have many times thought that someone up there must like me, for I didn't know at that time that diabetes was thought to cause erection problems and I didn't consult anyone who might have told me.

It is tragic that standard practice should be such that this man can rightly claim that ignorance is what saved him. We have seen numerous men who sat around for one to twelve years, worrying themselves into total impotence because their doctors had told them that their 'organically caused' impotence was incurable.

The medical deduction game is also called into question by the successful results that some sex therapists have had with men who were told by doctors that they were too impaired to have sex. The results obtained by us and other therapists with almost every condition said to lead to irreversible sex problems indicates that there is more hope for the physically disabled than had previously been believed.

Are we saying, then, that regardless of your physical condition you have the capacity to function sexually as you once did or as a man in very good health can? In truth, we aren't sure. Some men have been able to do so. For others, however, it wasn't the way it used to be. But the way it used to be isn't the only way to be sexual. You may have to learn some new ways of sexual expression, ways that deviate widely from the adolescent and fantasy models of sex but that can still be enjoyable.

Paul, the man with multiple sclerosis mentioned earlier in the chapter, finally got around to having sex with a partner. He was uncomfortable at first because of his problems getting from his wheelchair into the bed and the vigorous stimulation he needed to get an erection. But he learned some things as time went on. He could ask his partner to help him get into bed, a practice which both shortened the amount of time it took and also kept them in close contact. He later realized that it wasn't necessary to have sex in bed; it was much easier for him to roll onto the floor. He also learned some things about his penis. While he continued to need more stimulation than most men, he found some new ways of having his penis stimulated that shortened the amount of time required to get an erection. He also found that he could sometimes have a very good time satisfying his partner and rubbing against her without an erection. Paul is not totally happy. He still wishes he didn't have multiple sclerosis and that he could have sex the way he did before he got the disease. But he's much more content than when we first saw him. He's no longer afraid to go out with women and he no longer backs away from sex. When he has sex, he usually enjoys it. Not too bad for a man who had been told by several doctors, and who himself believed, that nothing could be done for him.

So what does all of this mean for you? Simply that if you haven't been having sex or have been experiencing sexual problems because of what you have been told or think is a physical disability, you have some choices. You can decide that nothing should or can be done. If you are content with this decision, well and good.

Another possibility is to proclaim that you would do something about sex if only things were different, if only you didn't have a disability, if only other people had a different attitude toward your disability, and so on. The 'if only' game is common and often very comforting to those who play it. It places responsibility for the problem on people or factors over which the player has no control, thus relieving him of any responsibility for changing his situation. The man in a wheelchair thinks that he would get his sex life together if only he could walk; the older man, if only he were thirty years younger; the man with a colostomy, if only he could control his elimination functions.

The 'if only' game is also played by many who are not technically disabled. It's easy to see why when you realize that we are all deficient and disabled compared to the unattainable sexual standards we learned. Many young and healthy men say they would have more sex, or better sex, or deal with their sexual problems, if only they had bigger penises, if only they could prolong intercourse for an hour, if only they knew more about turning women on, if only their sexual upbringing hadn't been so restricted and oppressive.

We are reminded of a high school friend.

Billy wouldn't go out with girls and his friends tried to help. If only he knew what to talk about, he said, he would go out. So we suggested some topics and had some practice conversations. He finally felt confident that he had something to say, but strangely he still wouldn't get a date. Now he said that he didn't know how to dance. How, given this deficiency, could he ask a girl out? So one of our girl friends taught him to dance. But he still stayed home. If only he had a car, all would be well. One of us promised him a ride when he got a date, but Billy still wouldn't go out. It turned out that none of the several hundred girls in our school was his type. If only he could meet the right girl. Billy never did have a date in high school.

Many years later Billy told one of us that the problem really had nothing to do with talking, dancing, rides, or any of his other 'if onlys'. The reason he hadn't gone out in high school was simply that he was scared silly of being alone with a girl. She might not like him and make him feel like two cents. Or he might not like her and not know how to deal with that situation. Or worst of all, they might like each other and then what should he do? Billy discovered on his own that all the reasons why he wouldn't go out were only cover-ups for his tremendous fear, a fear, incidentally, that was only a bit more powerful than that felt by most of his friends.

There is no question but that sex, like most human interactions, can be frightening. Possibilities abound for rejection, humiliation, and hurt. This is true for all men, but those with medical problems, because they depart so much from the model of men we all aspire to, are much more vulnerable. 'Who wants a man with a weak heart?' 'What will she think when she finds out how long it takes for me to have an erection?' 'How can I tell her that I sometimes have epileptic fits or insulin reactions?'

Questions like these plague many men. And there are no simple answers. There is always the possibility that you will be rejected and hurt. It is silly to assume that it can be otherwise. You will be rejected not only for the reasons that all men sometimes get rejected but also because of your physical condition. Some women don't want to have sex with a man with heart disease, cerebral palsy, a colostomy, or whatever you have.

So you can sit around for the rest of your life contemplating how wonderful everything would be if only you weren't who you are. A fascinating pastime, perhaps, but always a losing one, for you will never be other than who you are and you will therefore never get any of the benefits that you think would accrue to the person you wish you were. Sex as you are may well carry risks of disappointment and rejection but, since you'll never be anyone else, it might be in your interests to consider if the risks are worth taking.

Which brings us to the third choice you can make. You can decide that, whatever the risks, you are interested in a more enjoyable sex life and that you are willing to find out what is possible for you. This may be a difficult decision. No one can guarantee you'll get precisely what you hope for. Even if you put a lot of time and effort into it, you may not end up performing the way you want. And your ideas about what is acceptable sexual expression will probably have to undergo some revision.

We're not saying it will be easy and we don't want to offer any false hope. But our experience has been that an enjoyable sex life is possible for almost all men, regardless of the type of physical impairment they have, providing that they are willing to work on it and be reasonably flexible about what acceptable sexuality is. You probably won't end up acting like the men in the fantasy model of sex, but then, neither does anyone else.

If you choose to go on, do the exercises in the book that are relevant to you and feel free to make any adjustments required by your physical condition. The suggestions and exercises here are exactly the same as we use in therapy with disabled men. You will have to make some changes in some of them to make them better fit with your situation but that shouldn't be difficult.

It is preferable that you have the cooperation of a doctor who knows you and your condition, and who knows about and is comfortable dealing with sexual issues. If you don't have such a doctor now, we strongly suggested you find one. A local medical school or university with a sex program should be able to give you an appropriate referral. But it is up to you to make sure that you get the kind of medical care that you want. Be a wise consumer. Let the doctor know what your interests and concerns are, ask about his experience and training in the field of sex, and ask all the questions you have. Try not to expect him to perform magic. If you believe that he is not qualified to help you, or that he is uncomfortable discussing what you are concerned about, find someone else. You are as responsible for good medical care as your doctor. Do your part and you'll find a good doctor who can do his.

If a doctor has ever told you that you should not have sex, get some clarification. If the advice remains the same, get another opinion, preferably from a doctor experienced in dealing with sex.

If you are taking medication of any sort, check with your doctor regarding possible sexual side effects. As we mentioned earlier, many prescribed drugs do affect sexual desire and functioning. Switching medications or changing dosages can sometimes help, but this should never be done without a doctor's supervision.

Surgery is another issue that requires your attention. If your doctor recommends surgery, you should talk to him about why and what the potential benefits and side effects are. Ask specifically how it will affect your sexual functioning. If the chances of negative sexual side effects are present, ask if there is another treatment available or another kind of surgery. Some doctors don't give much thought to the sexual lives of their patients and suggest radical procedures when more conservative ones would do as well and not affect sexual functioning. This is sometimes seen in prostate surgery, where the radical approach through the perineum often destroys the nerves that control erection while the other methods of reaching the prostate do not.

Before having any type of surgery, we strongly recommend that you get a second opinion from another reputable doctor. Discuss the options and side effects with both doctors and form your own opinion. Being a wise consumer will help you get the best possible treatment for yourself.

If the suggestions and exercises in the book don't produce the desired results after being given a reasonable chance, that doesn't necessarily mean that you should give up on sex or decide to get a penile implant. Before making any such rash decisions, we suggest you consult a competent sex therapist.

TWENTY-TWO

The uses of sex and sex problems

People have sex for a variety of reasons. Even in one sexual experience, the motivations of the participants are usually numerous and complex. Among the more common motives for, or uses of, sex are physical release; giving or getting comfort, affection, or love; proving one's popularity, masculinity (or femininity), or sexual prowess; and expressing tenderness or hostility.

The point is simple but important – sex has many uses. What feels like a desire for sex can be something quite different, as Erich Fromm pointed out in *Man for Himself* many years ago:

> Intense sexual desire . . . can be caused not by physiological but by psychic needs. A . . . person who has an intense need to prove his worth to himself, to show others how irresistible he is, or to dominate others by 'making' them sexually, will easily feel intense sexual desires, and a painful tension if the desires are not satisfied. He will be prone to think that the intensity of his desires is due to the demands of his body, while actually these demands are determined by his psychic needs.

We are not implying that sex should be engaged in only for certain 'right' or 'correct' reasons. Human sexuality is flexible and can satisfactorily serve many needs. While we have frequently said that sex is for fun, this formulation is obviously too narrow, as the following example indicates.

Peter had sex with a woman he barely knew and wasn't

particularly attracted to, the day after his father's funeral.
When asked what led him to have sex with her, he
replied: 'I really wasn't that turned-on and had some
difficulty getting hard. But I needed to feel close to
someone. Feeling her body and feeling mine respond
helped me feel that I was alive. As a purely sexual
experience it wasn't much but it was important in another
way. It gave me some comfort and a feeling of aliveness
that I really needed.'

Peter certainly didn't have fun with his partner but got
warmth and comfort during a very bad time in his life. He had
no regrets about the experience and remembers it as being
important.

But it would be a different story if Peter always had to have
sex to feel alive. A possible outcome would be that his penis
would refuse to function, which it almost did on that occasion.
Another possible result is that he would have problems with
his partners. He was clearly using the woman. He was too
wrapped up in his own feelings to pay any attention to hers.
Given the circumstances, it is understandable. But as a
consistent pattern, it might not be either understandable or
acceptable to his partners.

While sex can be used to meet a number of needs, it has its
limits. Sex is not appropriate for meeting all human needs and
there are needs which, while they can be satisfied in sex, are
best fulfilled in other ways. When sex is consistently used in
pursuit of goals for which it is not appropriate, disappointment
and problems may develop. In this chapter we discuss a few ill-
advised uses to which sex is put by men and what can be done
about them.

Then we deal with the functions sometimes performed by
sexual problems. If you have had difficulty in changing your
sexual behavior by following the ideas and exercises in this
book, the reason may lie in the function that your present
situation serves.

The purpose of this chapter, then, is to help you better

differentiate among your various needs and desires so that you satisfy them in the most appropriate and enjoyable ways.

SEX AS PROOF OF MASCULINITY

In Chapter 2 we mentioned the tremendous pressure felt by men to continually offer proof that they are indeed worthy of being called men. The types of proof required vary and can be almost anything that we and our peers accept as masculine – making a lot of money, talking tough, having an important job, being good at mechanical tasks, being athletic, and so on.

And, of course, sex. Sex has long been a major way of asserting one's manhood. In earlier times, manhood could be demonstrated by siring children, especially sons. While this notion still retains power for some men, it has been largely replaced by a different kind of sexual demonstration – enthusiastic interest in sex and engaging in it frequently and well. In many circles, men who show little interest in sex – who do not leer at every woman who goes by or talk about their sexual escapades – are regarded suspiciously by other men.

Many of us have known or at least heard of a man who ran around having sex with a different woman every night, and more than a few of us have envied him not only because of all the fun we assumed he was having but also because of the admiration he inspired in us. Anyone having that much sex must be quite a man. Surely he must possess all the manly attributes we feel we are lacking – confidence, aggressiveness, unlimited libido, a way with women, and the techniques of a great lover.

Sexual prowess as validation of one's masculinity is an equation that most of us implicitly accept and, while only a few of us would choose to be Don Juans, it does affect our thinking and behavior. Even if we don't go so far as to have sex every day to prove what real men we are, we are tempted to live up to at least some of the canons of the male mythology, whether or not we are capable of such feats or whether we are really interested in them. But we try anyway, just to reassure ourselves of our manhood.

Otto had been in a bad relationship for several years. As it grew increasingly bitter and disappointing, his partner made a lot of angry comments about his sexual abilities and told him that he wasn't man enough for her. After they separated, Otto was in a bad way. He half believed that his partner was right, that he was no good in bed and couldn't satisfy a woman. He felt like 'not quite a man' and set out to do something about this. Three or four nights a week for over a year he picked up a different woman at one of San Francisco's 'body bars' and attempted to have sex. He was not interested in any of his partners. He just wanted to prove that he was a man. He was rarely turned-on and, to make matters worse, drank a lot to try to still the tremendous anxiety he felt when with these women. A perfect set-up for failure. For over a year, with over one hundred different women, he did not get one erection or have one good experience. And yet he must have looked to all the world as the great stud on the prowl.

Inside, however, he was hurting terribly and finally decided to get professional help. He soon solved his problem, but only after he started paying attention to what he wanted and stopped trying to prove himself. He learned that he valued companionship and intimacy more than casual sex, and stopped going out altogether for several weeks. He then met a woman he liked and formed a friendship with her. As they got close and comfortable, they started having sex. There were a few minor problems at first, but they were soon worked out.

Otto is unusual only in the large number of unsatisfactory experiences he underwent in his great adventure to prove that he was really OK. By using sex inappropriately to try to prove his adequacy as a man and lover, he didn't get what he needed to have good sex.

Many men equate sexual frequency with masculinity. They have read or heard about men who have sex more frequently than themselves and wonder if they are missing something. They think that they should have great sexual interest. This notion is easily reinforced if their partner wants sex more often than they do. These men are often shocked when they discover that they really want something other than sex.

Henry, a man in his early forties, made this announcement after being in therapy for a few weeks. 'You're going to think this is crazy but I'll say it anyway. I don't think I have that much interest in sex. I've thought about it a lot the last few weeks and realized that my sexual needs have never been great. I could probably get by with three or four times a month. What I really like is a lot of touching and hugging and sleeping next to a woman, but I usually don't want to go further. I guess I'm more like a woman in this respect. The problem is that I'm a man and none of this makes sense. I wish I wanted sex more often.'

Henry had tried to live up to what he thought were the masculine norms, pushing himself to have sex when he wasn't interested and when he would have preferred nonsexual physical contact. His penis had tired of the charade and stopped functioning.

Both Henry and Otto tried to force themselves to function in unfavorable situations. They violated their conditions for good sex and expected their penises not to notice. Both of these men had to learn that masculinity is not defined by wanting to fuck rather than wanting a hug or a caring relationship.

Another aspect of this issue is using sex as a means of dominating your partner. Sex is your show, done your way, with you in charge. Your partner can of course participate, but only if she follows your rules.

A woman friend told us this story. A man she was dating insisted on having sex his way, meaning that he always initiated and always got on top of her in intercourse. One day, she initiated and after arousing him, assumed the superior position. He was horrified and yelled: 'Who do you think you are, fucking me? I'm supposed to be on top!' It looks comical on paper but that's not the way he meant it. He couldn't deal with her being in charge and refused to continue the experience. Whereupon she refused to continue the relationship.

The phrase 'making a woman' describes the idea well. You 'make' her – make her submit to your will, do your bidding. Then you feel like a man. The example we gave is extreme in its lack of subtlety and there are many more delicate ways of playing the same game: for example, never being interested when your partner initiates, never following her instructions or her desires, and having lots of reasons why whatever she suggests is wrong.

Aside from the fact that such a game makes for a very one-sided relationship where many things cannot be explored and experienced, it usually also generates a lot of resentment from the partner. Not many women are willing to put up with it anymore.

SEX AS DEMONSTRATION OR PROOF OF LOVE

Sex can be a wonderful way of expressing caring and love. For many men, however, sex is the only way of expressing these feelings. We have given several examples elsewhere in the book of men who were attentive to and communicative with their partners only during sex. This often causes problems.

Most women want affection expressed in both sexual and nonsexual ways. Many of them say things like, 'Just once I'd like him to show me he cares without its leading to sex.'

What do these women want? We can't speak for all of them, but the desires we have heard included shared activities, nonsexual touching, and verbal expressions of appreciation and affection.

You might want to ask yourself if sex is the only way you have of expressing affection. If for some reason you couldn't have sex for a month, would your partner know you cared for her? How?

Exclusive reliance on sex to express certain emotions overburdens sex; and, as we have mentioned several times, the less the burden, the better the sex.

A different twist to using sex as proof of love occurs when the man tries to get a woman to show that she cares by having sex, or engaging in some particular type of sexual activity, with him. It's as if he believed that 'if she'll do even this with me, then she must care'. Some nice male–female friendships have run aground on this rock, well expressed by the following example:

> Janice and I had a great friendship for a year, the only good friendship I've had with a woman. We did lots of neat things together and talked about everything, including our lovers. But after a while, it got to me. I mean, I thought she really cared for me, but here she was fucking other guys and going down on them, and I wondered if she cared enough to do the same for me. So I put pressure on her and she finally gave in, but it was lousy. She wasn't into it and I guess I wasn't either. Our friendship wasn't based on physical attraction or sex and it just wasn't the right thing to do. We still see each other but it's not as good as it was.

Sometimes the man thinks that sex is a good way of determining how far his partner's interest or affection extends. At the beginning of a relationship, her willingness to have sex may be sufficient. Later, the ante may be raised. 'If she'll give me a blowjob (or swallow my come or have anal sex or whatever), then she accepts and loves me.' If she won't do it, this thinking goes on, then obviously something is lacking in her feelings toward the man.

What the man doesn't understand is that what his partner will or will not do may have little or no bearing on her feelings about him. She may not want to have oral sex because she learned that it was dirty or because she had a bad experience with it in the past or because she just doesn't like having a penis in her mouth. On the other side, complying with his demands may also not mean what he thinks or hopes it does. She may comply because she's afraid of losing him or because she was taught always to do a man's bidding in sex or because she thinks he knows what is best for her. None of these motives, of course, has anything to do with caring or love.

Two types of problems derive from this use of sex. First, it can be coercive. Pressuring someone to do something she really doesn't want to do in order to prove she cares is a dangerous game. She may refuse, despite all your entreaties, leaving you feeling that she doesn't love you, and with no recourse but to break up what may have been a nice relationship. Or she may give in because of fear or guilt. Such gifts have a way of being very costly. She will probably harbor a great deal of resentment over the coercion. Relationships built on such foundations rarely do well.

A second problem, common to all proofs and tests, is that there can never be sufficient proof. Even if she complies with your requests, will you feel loved for more than a few minutes? Somehow it doesn't work out this way. The ante must be raised, a new test proposed. And it goes on endlessly.

If you have been using sex as a proving ground and want to change, we offer a few suggestions. Whether you have been trying to prove your masculinity or affection, or getting your partner to demonstrate her feelings for you, the important thing is that you begin gradually to stop acting on your impulses to prove anything. These impulses will not immediately disappear. You need to acknowledge their presence and do what you can to go in another direction.

Let's assume you have been relying solely on sex to express all your good feelings toward your partner and want to expand your repertory. The next time you feel loving toward her or want sex, don't have sex. Express your feelings some other way. Give her a big hug; tell her you love her; share some of your thoughts and feelings with her; offer to give her a back-rub, suggest doing something you know she enjoys; or tell her you'd like to do something for her to express your love and would like to know what she wants.

For a while – at least a few weeks – deliberately express affection in nonsexual ways. You can have sex if you want, but first express affection nonsexually. Make sure that such expressions are not always followed by sex. Do this as an experiment and then determine how you and your partner feel about this new pattern.

You may have some negative feelings when making a change. Many men reported feeling vaguely uneasy, irritated, or frustrated. This is to be expected when you change a habit. In time, however, the uneasy feelings will decrease in intensity and be more than balanced by the positive ones that result from feedback from your body and your partner.

SEX AS SENSATION-SEEKING OR NIRVANA

Most of us, because of the fairy tales we heard as children, believe somewhere in the back of our minds that there is a way of avoiding all the problems and hassles of everyday life, of walking into the sunset and living happily ever after. It's a nice fantasy, but many people are acting as if they took it seriously. In recent years, sex has been advertised as one of the main paths to that walk in the sunset.

The rewards of sexual experience have been exaggerated almost beyond belief. It is the fantasy model all over again, and with a vengeance. *The Joy of Sex* tells us that 'Sex is the one place where we today can learn to treat people as people.' Later it informs us that 'orgasm is the most religious moment of our lives, of which all other mystical experiences are a mere translation.' If all the saints and mystics had only known! Many sex manuals read suspiciously like religious tracts. It is easy to get the impression that eternal happiness or the salvation of one's soul is what is being discussed. Sex, or the right kind of sex, it seems, can unite us with the cosmos, radically changing and fulfilling our lives.

This line of thought, if it can be called that, is supplemented and abetted by the attitude well expressed by Herbert Hendin as the 'unquestioning belief in the unquestioned good of trying everything'. There is pressure from everywhere to 'search for all the gusto you can', as one advertisement put it, to experience every possible activity. Hendin calls it 'a rapacious greed for experience'. It matters little if the experiences are good, bad, or indifferent; the important thing is having them, being able to say that you have done it all. Sex is considered to offer a utopia of unexcelled thrills and vibrations, so it must be experienced with as many people and as many permutations as possible. Nirvana here is not so much a mind-blowing experience as the sheer aggregate of experiences.

Whichever version of heaven is being sought, nothing is too drastic or bizarre for experimentation. Sex with drugs, sex on the floor and ceiling or in the road, sex with children and animals, sex with urine and enemas – everything must be savored. The results are usually disappointing because the ideas that are peddled deal with fantasy while real sex is only human. One is forced either to drop out of the game or to up the ante by trying something even farther out.

But raising the ante never quite does it. As Gregory Curtis says in his fine article on sex manuals, 'The New Facts of Life', 'No matter who one is with or what is happening, real sex seems always to be some place else with someone else.' Many people don't understand that what they experience can never equal what they think they ought to feel. They assume they should have mystical orgasms, and blame themselves for not doing so. They think they haven't yet found the right activity or partner or that they are too uptight to let themselves experience the ultimate joy. And the search continues.

It is tragic that such notions require comment, but the need is a reflection of the degree to which they have been accepted. Literally millions of people peer through countless sex manuals and magazines looking for the secrets that will send them into orbit.

The first thing that needs to be said is that sex simply does not have the power that has been attributed to it. No matter how good it is, sex does not have the power to radically alter your life. You still have to contend with work, taxes, the children's allowances, and all the interesting and annoying nonsexual aspects of your relationship, like who left the top off the toothpaste, how you should spend your weekends, and who should walk the dog. Sex researchers John Gagnon and William Simon put sex in perspective when they say that 'it is by its very nature a dependent variable. It is something that is more caused than causing, and only through its ties with other human experience is it given its meaning.'

A second point is that even if there are no problems, sex is only rarely of the earthshaking variety. Frequently it is merely pleasurable and pleasant in a quiet, lazy way. And sometimes it's just a physical release, enjoyable in a small way but maybe not worth missing Johnny Carson for.

As for sensation-seeking, it is often a very disheartening and disillusioning experience. Nothing lives up to its billing, so newer activities must be found. In the process, people often violate themselves by doing things quite inconsistent with their feelings and values.

We recall a man who for four years tried to force himself to have sex with another man. He had been heterosexual all his life but thought that his inability or unwillingness (he was never sure which it was) to have sex with a man represented a deficiency on his part. Loving a man sexually was an important experience he didn't want to miss. When we asked why he just didn't go and do it, he said: 'I'm not ready yet. I'm too uptight because of my upbringing. I know that everyone is inherently bisexual but my training was so strict that the thought of actually doing it with another man almost nauseates me. But I'm working on it.' We don't know the outcome of this story but we wonder if the agony and self-torture this man went through was worth it.

Another problem with the frenzied scramble to experience all things is that it sometimes leads to an inability to experience anything. You can become so obsessed with the wonders you will someday experience that you don't pay any attention to what's happening now. And even if it doesn't go to this extreme, bizarre experimentation tends to cheapen almost everything and rob you of the joy of experiencing the simple things of life. A hug or even the conventional type of intercourse can seem very dull and not worthwhile if you've been spending the last few months doing it in the road with donkeys and whips.

Real sex is not and never has been a magical solution. It cannot bring intimacy if there is no closeness or affection to begin with. It cannot bring joy if you violate your needs and values.

We are not saying that experimentation is wrong. It can be fun and a nice, sharing experience. But not when it becomes a consuming, labored goal and when expectations run far ahead of what reality can deliver.

If you think your expectations have gotten out of hand, you might want to ask yourself some questions. Whose expectations are you trying to fulfill? Why are they so important to you? See if you can attend to what is happening in your next sexual experiences and then determine what, if anything, was lacking. What would you have to do to make up any deficiencies you noticed? Are you willing to pay the prices involved? Talking about these issues with a friend, partner, or therapist can be valuable.

IMPERSONAL SEX

We define impersonal sex as sex with minimal emotional involvement. The bodies make contact but the people do not. There is little curiosity, warmth, caring, closeness, or feeling of any kind. While the correlation between impersonal sex and casual sex is probably quite high, the two terms are not synonymous. A one-time experience with someone you just met sometimes does include personal sharing and involvement. On the other hand, a long-term relationship is no guarantee against impersonal sex.

Impersonal sex flourishes today. It is the hallmark of prostitution which, contrary to the hopes and expectations of many philosophers of sexual freedom, is doing a thriving business. It is also characteristic of the activities of millions of people – singles and marrieds alike – who would never even dream of paying for sex.

There are a number of reasons for the popularity of impersonal sex. Often it is not a goal in itself but rather a by-product of striving for other goals. When the goal of sex is to prove something – be it one's masculinity, sexual prowess, popularity, or liberation – impersonal contact is the likely result. The proof assumes such importance that the partner, and even one's own feelings and satisfaction, are lost sight of.

Impersonal sex is also a goal in its own right. It is tempting as a release from loneliness and sexual tension. It offers at least a semblance of human contact without the problems that real contact entails. Many people these days seem to have sex rather than shaking hands or talking. In some ways sex is easier, because talking and shaking hands can be risky. They invite contact and sharing. Whether the relationship is long-standing or just beginning, it is difficult to know how much of oneself to reveal and how much involvement and commitment to allow. It often seems safer to hop into bed where, one can hope, the bodies will do their part and it won't be necessary to deal with silly and annoying things like communication and vulnerability.

There is a great deal of talk about intimacy these days, but it is well to remember that intimacy is always difficult and there are powerful forces arrayed against it. In a world where constant happiness is considered a reasonable expectation and where there is much pressure to experience everything, the complexity, responsibility, and pain of intimacy or personal sharing seem somehow out of date and not worth the trouble.

For some, sexual activity itself has become the main defense against involvement. You may be able to recall some examples from your life where you initiated sex not because you wanted sex but because it provided an escape from an otherwise uncomfortable situation. Sex often seems easier and safer than deciding what you really want to do or working out a disagreement, and it therefore can be more of a running away from something else than an activity engaged in because it is attractive in its own right. We agree in large part with Herbert Hendin's claim that the sexual revolution 'has become a revolution against intimacy'.

All of us have impersonal sex at times. Even in the most caring of relationships, there are times when you are so wrapped up in your own thoughts and concerns that you really aren't there when sex is happening. Sex at such times often feels rather blah, but an occasional occurrence isn't something to be concerned about.

But there are people for whom impersonal sex is the norm.

Aldo was forty years old when he came for therapy because of erection problems he had experienced for about a year. He exuded sex, something noticed even by our receptionist to whom he had only said hello. He worked in a bar that catered to young singles and it was a rare night when he was not picked up. He had sex with almost every woman he met and almost never saw them again. It was easy to believe his claim that he was a fantastic lover (at least for those women who didn't want their sex cluttered up by feelings). Satisfying his partners was always his main goal and his only criterion for a good sexual experience.

Involvement of any sort was anathema to Aldo. He rarely thought about whether or not he liked his partners. It was sufficient that he was attracted to their bodies. The worst fate he could imagine was having feelings for a woman and being with her more than a few times. Everything had been going fine for him until his penis stopped performing. Now he was frequently embarrassed in bed. Everything he did, said, or implied with women in one way or another revolved around the moment when he would enter them and give them the greatest sexual experience of their lives. Without an erection, he was lost.

Until he began to have problems with his erections, Aldo was a good example of automatic functioning. He could perform without regard for conditions, arousal, feelings, or anything else. But then, as so often happens, the whole system broke down.

It may sound as if Aldo was exploiting women. We don't see it this way and we don't believe that impersonal sex is always, or even usually, a case of men using women. Women are as implicated as men (Aldo, in fact, rarely initiated contact or gave invitations; the women came after him and he never promised more than sex) and usually both partners are using each other in the same way. They have sex and nothing else, then part, and it is often quite embarrassing if by chance they run into each other again.

The only important question you need to answer is whether impersonal sex works for you. If you are satisfied, fine. We know, however, that many men are not happy with it. They do it but are not content and wish for something better. The human contact it provides is illusory and the sexual release it affords is often less satisfying than what could have been derived from masturbation. Many men who have tried this kind of sex find that they often don't function well. Others can perform but get little from their experiences. Aldo didn't want to feel anything, but other men do.

> One man, very much like Aldo in many ways, loved to talk about all his sexual adventures. When the therapist interrupted his rambling account of his latest exploit by asking if he enjoyed it, the man's tearful reply was, 'No. I feel dead inside.'

If you want to change to a more personal type of sexual expression, you need to consider the prices you will have to pay. You will, at the least, have to deal with some feelings you have kept hidden, you will feel uncomfortable some of the time, you will have to take risks, and you may well be hurt, rejected and disappointed. The costs must be paid.

If you think you are willing to pay the fare, begin by getting to know some women and, for a while at least, stop having so much sex. Do things that are pleasurable and talk about what you want, as long as it's not sex. When difficulties and complications arise, acknowledge at least to yourself the temptation to run. But try to stick it out and work out the problems. The process is not easy and can't be accomplished overnight. It takes a long time and you may want to get some professional help along the way.

It should be obvious by now that we believe that sex is only sex and consequently has a limited area of applicability and utility. This really isn't a problem except when sex gets used for purposes for which it isn't appropriate. There are many better ways of dealing with most issues than having sex. Even when sex is relevant, it still may not be the best course to follow. As an example, we return to our story of Peter, the young man who had sex the day after his father's funeral.

> After recounting the experience presented earlier in the chapter, Peter was asked if there were any ways other than sex that could have been used to make him feel alive

and comforted. He couldn't think of any but agreed to take a fantasy trip back to the day after the funeral. The therapist gave instructions to help Peter reexperience his feelings on that day and then asked Peter what he would want if he could have anything at all (the only thing he could not ask for was that his father be brought back to life). Peter got deeply involved in the fantasy and imagined himself being held by a woman (a cross between his mother and Marti, a woman he knew only slightly but was very attracted to) while he 'cried my guts out'. He actually cried for some time, and then became calm.

Peter said he felt better and was glad he agreed to do the fantasy. In fact, although he felt sad, he said, he felt better about everything than he had since he heard of his father's death. He added that doing what he had done in the fantasy was obviously a better way of dealing with his feelings about his father's death than having sex. He was then asked what he thought he would do if he had that day to live over again. His reply is instructive.

'This sounds contradictory, but I think I'd have sex. Sitting here it would be easy to say that I'd have Mom or Marti hold me, but out there isn't the same as in here. I know how to have sex. It was easy for me to approach Ann [the woman he had slept with], make some moves and notice her response, and just go ahead. I can see now that it didn't meet my needs half as well as the fantasy I went through with you. But I don't know how to ask someone to hold me. How can I ask someone to let me sit in their lap and cry my guts out? My mother is finally starting to treat me like an adult and here I'd go crying like a child. And Marti, I like her and want to get something going with her. Crying on her lap doesn't exactly seem like the best way to start a relationship. It's funny, as I'm talking something is telling me that I'm full of shit, that both Mom and Marti would understand and would even have a special kind of respect for me, for the fact that I could feel the sadness and cry. But, boy, when I think about actually doing it, it still seems hard.'

The fact that Peter, a very intelligent and sensitive man, resorted to sex when other alternatives might have better met his needs is a good indication of how sexualized our lives have become. The chains that bind us are, to use a metaphor from elsewhere, as hard as steel. But they can be slipped out of or broken and, as we get free, we are probably going to feel better about sex and the rest of our lives.

THE USES OF SEX PROBLEMS

If you have done the exercises in this book carefully but have not achieved the results you wanted, or if you thought you wanted to make some changes but couldn't find the time, energy, or privacy, you have three choices. The first is to conclude that nothing can be done for you at this time and call it quits, at least for now. The second is to decide that you can't get the help you need from a book and consider seeing a good sex therapist. Before you do that, however, you might want to consider the third possibility, that your sexual problem may be serving a positive function for you.

Nearly everyone thinks of bad sex or a sexual difficulty as a problem that should be solved. However, and we realize this may sound very strange at first, a sex problem may be a solution to another problem. Of course the sexual difficulty is in itself a problem. It makes you feel bad and creates misery, but it may also protect you against something which might be far worse. Most often the person is not aware of the protective or positive function performed by his problem and is shocked when he discovers it. Here is an example that may help to make this concept clearer.

Harry, a young psychiatrist, came to see us because of persistent erection problems with a woman he had dated for a year. It was immediately clear that Harry was afraid of being overwhelmed by his partner. She had already talked about living together and marriage, neither of which appealed to him at all. But he couldn't tell her about his feelings. He couldn't say no to her or anyone else. When asked what changes would occur in his life if he could get erections, he said: 'There would be no reason for not living together and she would move in.' He was shocked by what he said but after thinking about it for a few minutes realized that it was true. When asked if such an occurrence would be good or bad, he said, 'Disastrous.' It was explained to Harry that there was no sex problem as such. His lack of erection was more of a solution than a problem; it was the only way he could keep his partner from moving in with him (since she wanted to make sure they were sexually compatible before deciding to live together). Since Harry was very intelligent and efficient, once he saw what the problem was it wasn't necessary to tell him much more. He was simply told that when he found another way of dealing with her desire to get closer than he wanted, his penis would behave differently, and that he should call if he wanted another appointment. He never did call but we received a note from him about a month later which said only, 'Now that I'm saying no with my mouth, my penis is saying yes. Thank you.' A few months later we ran into him and a brief conversation revealed that he continued to be more assertive with his lover and that his sex life was fine.

We have worked with many men whose sexual problem was the only thing standing between them and marriage or some other situation that they did not want but could not deal with in a direct way. Sometimes the sex problem is used to hide other problems that would be even more difficult to deal with: for example, the possibility that the relationship is no longer much fun and should either be radically altered or abandoned. The sex problem is a way of denying the larger problem and keeping hope alive. The man acts as if he were thinking, 'If only I could have erections, all our problems would be over and we'd have a good relationship.' So he can hope that a solution to his sex problem will someday be found (while at the same time unconsciously subverting any solution) and all will be well.

Sometimes the sex problem is a way of expressing negative feelings that cannot be communicated more directly. Negative feelings are part of every relationship, but it often happens that these feelings are not dealt with openly and are left to seethe in someone's insides until they are expressed in some inappropriate way. Sex can provide a means of giving vent to the feelings, though the person who is doing the expressing is usually unaware of what he is doing.

Not getting an erection can be a way of saying, 'See, you don't turn me on anymore,' or 'I know you'd like to fuck but I'm not going to do that for you.' Coming before your partner wants you to or never being interested in sex when she is can also express hostility.

The sexual problem allows the man to avoid taking responsibility for his feelings. He can't take responsibility because he isn't aware of his motives. He honestly believes that he wants to resolve the sexual problem so that he can satisfy his partner and himself. But somehow he just can't seem to find the time, space, or whatever to solve his problem. That's a good clue that the problem is serving a protective function.

Marc, a man in his twenties with arousal problems that had not responded to almost two years of treatment with four different therapists, was at the end of his rope when he came to see us. He claimed he had a very loving relationship with his wife and there was no reason not to solve the problem. Things just somehow hadn't worked out with the other therapists. We convinced him to do a variation of Exercise 22–1 with us and he fought us all the way. Nothing, he swore, would be bad about solving his problem. We told him that we didn't think we could help him, given that four therapists whom we respected had already failed, but, since he had already paid for the session, we could chat a bit longer. We asked if he had ever felt angry with his wife. His response told us we were on to something. She had had an affair shortly after they were married and he was furious about it. But he had never let her know how he felt. When asked what prevented him from telling her his feelings, he replied: 'I can't stand it when she gets angry. That's what she'll do. She'll listen a while, then start crying, which bugs the shit out of me, then start yelling and screaming at me, throwing up to me all the bad stuff I did to her then, blaming me for pushing her into the affair. I hate it when she gets like that.'

Marc's lack of sexual interest allowed him to get back at his wife without having to be honest about his feelings or dealing with hers. It protected him from dealing with anger, something quite difficult for him, but at the same time was wrecking their relationship. Marc decided to return for more sessions but we never worked directly on sex. All we did was help him express his own angry feelings and get more comfortable dealing with his wife's expression of hers. They had the worst fight of their marriage about two months after he first came to therapy. They didn't speak to each other for a few days after that, then gradually they started talking about the affair and their feelings for each other. Not surprisingly, the sex problem vanished and the relationship became sounder than it had been since before their marriage.

We want to be clear about what we are saying because we know that these ideas can be easily misunderstood. A sex problem may be protecting you from something that you consider far worse. This is not to say that you enjoy your problem, that you don't want to resolve it, or that you are fully aware of what is going on. Contradictions flourish in human beings and it is possible both to want something so much that it hurts and at the same time to fight tooth and nail against getting it. Discovering why you are resisting resolving the problem is a good first step in coming to grips with this type of contradiction.

The following exercise – adapted from one developed by John Enright, one of the most creative and effective therapists it has ever been our pleasure to learn from – will help you discover the obstacles in your path.

It is not an easy exercise to do. Your mind may recoil from taking it seriously, since it asks you to look at feelings or issues that are not pleasant and that you have so far kept out of your awareness. It may help if you remember that doing the exercise does not commit you to any further action. You may decide, after determining what is in your way, that the price of removing it is too great and you'd rather leave things just as they are. But then you can at least stop worrying about your sex problem and get on with your life.

It's best not to read the exercise until you are ready to do it.

EXERCISE 22–1: WHAT WOULD BE BAD ABOUT RESOLVING MY SEX
PROBLEM
Time Required: 1½ hours

Take your pen or tape recorder in hand and address yourself to whatever version of the question makes the most sense to you.

1. **What would be bad (potentially harmful, negative, destructive) about resolving the problem?**
2. **What does having the problem do *for* me (in a positive sense)?**
3. **How would my life be more difficult or complex if I overcame the problem?**

You may find that you can think only of positive outcomes, like how good you'd feel without the problem. Let yourself go through all the positive results, then for each one ask how it might make your life more difficult or

lead to negative consequences.

Spend no more than 45 minutes on this part. If absolutely nothing comes to you, guess. If that doesn't help, put the exercise aside and come back to it a few hours or days later.

When you have completed this part, put it aside for a day or two. Then reread it and see if you have anything to add. For each item on your list, consider the following:

1. Is the negative outcome you expect a likely probability? If you don't know, can you find out? (e.g., 'Is it probable that Susan will push for a more involved relationship than I want if the problem is resolved?').

2. What price would you have to pay to deal with it? (e.g., 'I'd have to tell her straight out that I don't want to have a closer relationship with her at this point. That would be very hard for me to say.') Picture yourself paying the price in as much detail as possible. Back off if you get very anxious, get yourself comfortable, then start again. You might want to go over some of the relevant sections in this book for assistance. Keep dealing with the fantasy of paying the price until you can actually imagine yourself carrying it out.

3. Now ask yourself if you are willing to pay the price to solve your sex problem. (e.g., 'Am I willing to tell Susan I'm not willing to have a closer relationship in order to solve my sex problem?') Take the first answer that comes to you and put it in the form of a statement. (e.g., 'I am willing to tell Susan that I'm not interested . . .') If the statement rings true to you, you'll know what you have to do. If it doesn't quite sound right, play around with it, changing a word here and there until you arrive at something that feels right.

Just because you know what you need to do is no assurance that you'll feel confident of doing it immediately. Get whatever assistance that you think you need, from this book or elsewhere.

If you concluded that you are not willing to pay the

price, you might want to check your thinking to see if a more acceptable price would do the trick. Or you may decide to accept your situation as it is now.

If you find that you do not implement your decision within a reasonable period of time, it's probably safe to assume that your obstacles have not been fully dealt with and need more attention. Doing the exercise again may help. If not, consider enlisting the aid of a competent therapist.

TWENTY-THREE

Sex and liberation

Saying that we live in an age of transition is a cliché but is true nonetheless. The values that once gave structure and meaning to life have been falling apart for at least the last hundred years, leaving us to play or cry, as the case may be, in the ruins. The decline of religious values has had a great influence, but it can be persuasively argued that traditional sex roles, now in a state of grand disarray, played at least as large a part in supplying order and meaning to life.

The crumbling of the old order has both good and bad aspects. We have argued throughout this book that most of the problems men have with sex are a result of the traditional male role. Forced to bury the expressive, tender side of themselves and to relate in restrictive, stereotyped ways, men have not been well prepared to have real sex with real women. And it goes much further than sex. Our social scripting has not prepared us for meaningful relationships with other men, women, or children, for self-knowledge and expression, or almost anything else. In short, conventional sex roles are both impractical and destructive. They are based on fantasies and illusions, on a world long since past, and probably contribute as much as any other factor to our lives of noisy desperation.

We are accustomed to hearing this kind of talk – from women. For at least the last seventy years many women have been questioning their role and trying to change it. This movement has gathered new momentum and influence in the last fifteen years. Women have taken the initiative in examining the whole institution of sex roles and they have wrought changes that affect men as well as women.

The fact that women have taken the initiative and are bringing about vast changes in the way all of us understand and act is itself a powerful indication of how far the traditional roles have deteriorated. Men have taken a very passive position, mainly confined to watching the women from the sidelines.

The position of men seems similar to that of many women prior to 1965. Although a great deal of dissatisfaction was felt by women in the past, they tended to blame themselves rather than questioning their role. Thus, women who were frustrated and unhappy about being home all day with the children questioned their ability as mothers rather than the idea that all women should be content sitting at home. There is no doubt that many men are today dissatisfied with their lot. We have mentioned that large numbers of men are not content with the sexual part of their lives, but the discontent extends far beyond sex. Men are unhappy about their work and their inability to be successful according to standard definitions. Many of those who have attained success realize how little happiness it brings. But most have been inclined to fault themselves rather than the standards and unrealistic expectations society has imposed.

Change is here to stay and its rate will probably accelerate whether or not men decide to play a more active role. Sex roles and other traditional institutions and values are crumbling precisely because they aren't working. While anything like a men's movement is clearly several years in the future, some men have started to question the established order as it affects them. More and more men are asking if there isn't a better way. They wonder if it's necessary for men to suffer from such a disproportionate number of diseases, to die so much younger than women, to have so many problems expressing themselves and relating to others. They admire the audacity of women in seeking to change their lives, the way women are struggling with issues that men are afraid to face, and they envy the closeness among women. In short, such men think that change may be necessary and positive.

But there is another side to the picture, one that has to be understood lest the opportunity for constructive change be lost in a sea of confusion and chaos. Sex roles and other societal institutions, no matter how harmful they are in some ways, perform useful and necessary functions. They provide the framework in which one can live a meaningful life; they supply the guidelines for thought, feeling, and action, and the standards by which to measure oneself. These guidelines ensure a predictable and orderly world, thereby giving a sense of security. These are not minor matters.

When institutions and values lose their influence, predictability and security are diminished. Nothing can be taken for granted. Issues that before had been ritualized and therefore made trivial now become subjects for thought, debate, and anxiety, with no clear guides for behavior.

A woman told us this story about a man she knows. He had always performed small courtesies for women. One day a woman for whom he had opened a door in a large department store loudly lambasted him ('Don't you think I can open my own door, you pig?'), which was quite different from the smiles and thank-you's he was used to. He was embarrassed and gave serious thought to the matter. He decided that the new order was here and he would have to conform to it – no more courtesies. Things went fine until one day when he was roundly criticized for not offering his seat to a woman on a bus. He thought about this for some time and came to a conclusion: 'There's no way of doing things right. If I act the way I was brought up to act, that's wrong. If I don't act that way, that isn't right either. I'm going back to being the same old asshole I've always been and I don't care if it's right or not.'

Friends who work in restaurants have told us how often they overhear disagreements and arguments between couples, about who should pay the bill. When opening doors and giving up seats and paying for dates become subjects of debate and dissension, where it is no longer clear what is expected or who should do what, you know the old order is in trouble. And so are we all.

The world becomes a strange and frightening place when nothing can be assumed or predicted. A man used to know that sex would happen, if at all, when he wanted it to happen, because God knows women didn't initiate. A man could therefore be secure in the knowledge that nothing would happen until he was good and ready. But now he has no assurance whatever that his date or partner won't make sexual advances when she feels like it.

Despite fashionable talk about how wonderful change is and how nice it is not to know what is going to occur, we believe that uncertainty is difficult. Human beings do like variety and some degree of uncertainty – there is no doubt about that – but they like them best in a context of stability and security, and that is precisely what is lacking today.

Not only is there an absence of external stability and order, but the internal guidelines aren't working so well either. You can't depend on anyone else to follow certain rules and you also aren't sure which ones you should follow. The issue, of course, is freedom, one of the most difficult subjects we humans have to contend with.

To apply freedom to sex means that instead of relying on rules such as 'A man always wants sex' or 'A man should always be in charge of sex,' you need to assess situations as they occur and determine for each what you want to do. If you realize that you don't want sex right now, then you need to ask if you are willing to act on your feelings, even while knowing that there are people, including perhaps your partner, who believe in the rule that says men always want sex. If you decide to act on your feeling of not wanting sex now, you have to let your partner know. If you are serious about being free, you will have to be honest and say that you aren't in the mood rather than relying on some external support (like a new rule that says men don't like sex on Tuesdays).

You will, in short, have to put yourself on the line, and that's rarely easy. You will also have to accept responsibility for your decision. It is conceivable that your partner will not want to be with a man who sometimes isn't in the mood for sex. Accepting responsibility in this case means that you don't blame her or yourself but instead accept the fact that the two of you have a difference of opinion as to what men should be like, a difference that may or may not be capable of resolution.

Of course this is all difficult and that is why, despite all the flag-waving and speech-making about freedom and liberation, few people actually are willing to accept even a small portion of freedom. What is much more common, and we see it all around us today, is freeing oneself from one set of rules and immediately flinging oneself into the arms of another set, different but no less demanding and no more tolerant of individual preference. The current notion demanding that one experience all things, whether one likes them or not, is no better than the Victorian idea demanding that so many things not be experienced. Neither has much to do with being free. The extreme form of the current fad of androgyny, which demands that men express both 'masculine' and 'feminine' qualities, is no more liberating than the system against which it is a reaction – that men express only 'masculine' qualities. The range of acceptable behavior is broadened, but the coercion remains the same.

Freedom is not free. It has many prices but, then, so does everything else. While it is a fact that there is no way of going for free, if you are careful and have a little luck you can have a say about what prices you will pay. And that is no small thing.

Since we live in an age of confusion and turmoil, we all must consider our situations and determine how we want to relate to the changing scene around us.

You can decide to try to live by the old rules, but you should be aware that this is not without problems. For many people, the old system didn't work well and exacted a horrendous toll. Are you willing to keep paying it? It is also true that the old rules are no longer as widely accepted and there will be those people who consider you strange just because you stick to them.

Another choice is to find a new set of rules and values to adhere to. As we have said, there is no shortage of such systems and all of them have advantages and disadvantages. Perhaps the chief advantage of all of them is that they offer the security of having a set of rules. The greatest disadvantage is that they are all narrow and restrictive in their own ways.

The third alternative is to accept to some degree the burden of freedom, adopting external rules to cover situations that are unimportant or where the rules make sense. This still leaves large areas where you will have to exercise your own judgment and be responsible for it. It seems that more and more people are at least willing to try this approach. It is difficult and there are many dropouts, but there are also many who are encouraged by their progress and plan to continue.

If this is your choice – and obviously it is our bias – this is a good time for making it. While there are always sanctions for behaving differently than others expect or want, there is probably more tolerance for individual differences today than at any previous time in history. Not only have restrictive laws and policies been abandoned at an unprecedented rate, but there also seems to be a greater individual desire for understanding and accepting behavior that does not fit the standards.

It is also a good time because everyone is having to deal in one way or another with all the changes that are occurring. We are all in the same boat in this sense, which can be a fine basis for understanding and support. For all the differences between men and women, and despite the angry charges and countercharges of the last few years, it has become increasingly clear that it's difficult to be either a man or a woman and that both share many of the same dilemmas and aspirations.

As we have repeatedly maintained, sex is not the most important part of life. But it is a part and as good a representative as any other of the larger context of our lives.

The hopes and fears and problems that affect us elsewhere usually also show up in sex. In our attempt to assist you in enhancing your sexuality, we have stressed two factors: the need for determining your own feelings and desires and acting on them, and the need for understanding and communicating with others. Both qualities are needed in sex and the rest of life. Insofar as we evaluate our situation and make our own decisions, we are free. Insofar as we understand, consider, and communicate with others, we link ourselves with the rest of humanity. Sex is far from everything, but it can be a beginning.

And for all that, it won't be easy. We will bumble and fall and there will be many misunderstandings, conflicts and frustrations with those for whom we care the most. It can't be otherwise since we are struggling to reach new levels of consciousness and relating while still being mired in the old ways. Old ways die hard and new understanding takes time. An example we have witnessed many times lately is the man who encourages his partner's independence and assertiveness and then feels angry and betrayed when she becomes assertive with him. An example from the other side is the woman who encourages her lover to be more expressive and tender and then gets angry when he isn't more macho in protecting her from other men or doesn't 'take her' sexually. Such occurrences are and will be common, and it's going to take a lot of goodwill and trust and courage to try to deal with them.

We close with a passage from the gentle poet Rainer Maria Rilke, who not only foresaw many of the changes we are experiencing today but also predicted an outcome more realistic and lovelier than any we know. May his words comfort you as they have comforted us.

This advance [of women] will (at first much against the will of the outstripped men) change the love-experience, which is now full of error, will alter it from the ground up, reshape it into a relation that is meant to be of one human being to another, no longer of man to woman. And this more human love (that will fulfill itself, infinitely considerate and gentle, and kind and clear in binding and releasing) will resemble that which we are preparing with struggle and toil, the love that consists in this, that two solitudes protect and border and salute each other.

References

Although it is not possible to list all the sources that have been of value in working with men and writing this book, we use this section to list those works that are of particular interest for further reading, and also to document quotations and other information taken directly from other sources.

CHAPTER 1
While the literature on men is not comparable in quality or quantity to that on women, there are several valuable sources. Two good collections of readings are D. David and R. Brannon, *The Forty-Nine Percent Majority* (Addison-Wesley, 1976), and J. Petras, *Sex: Male/Gender: Masculine* (Alfred, 1975). Several recent surveys of the masculine condition can be recommended: W. Farrell, *The Liberated Man* (Random House, 1974); M. Fasteau, *The Male Machine* (McGraw-Hill, 1974); and H. Goldberg, *The Hazards of Being Male* (Nash, 1976). None of these, however, has improved on the fine work published over a decade ago by Myron Brenton, *The American Male* (Fawcett, 1966).

Page 10:
Some of my early work with men is described in my article, 'Group Treatment of Sexual Dysfunction in Men Without Partners', *Journal of Sex & Marital Therapy* I (1975): 204–14.

Page 11:
Hendin, H., *The Age of Sensation* (Norton, 1975), p. 2.
'Your Pursuit of Happiness', *Psychology Today* (August 1976), p. 31.

CHAPTER 2
The two workers who have done the most to emphasize and explore the role of learning in human sexuality are John Gagnon and William Simon. Their book, *Sexual Conduct* (Aldine, 1973), is excellent though difficult. A simpler presentation of their views is given in Gagnon's *Human Sexualities* (Scott, Foresman, 1977), the best textbook in the field.

Pages 20–1:
The influence of early learning on the sexuality of adult monkeys was explored in a brilliant series of studies by Harry Harlow, *Learning to Love* (Ballantine, 1971). An interesting study reporting on the initial sexual

behavior of monkeys reared in more normal circumstances than Harlow's animals is J. Erwin and G. Mitchell, 'Initial Heterosexual Behavior of Adolescent Rhesus Monkeys', *Archives of Sexual Behavior* 4 (1975): 97–104.
Page 21:
Gagnon, *Human Sexuality*, p. 118.
Pages 24–5:
N. Mailer, *The Armies of the Night* (Signet, 1968), p. 36.
J. Lester, 'Being a Boy', *Ms.* (July 1973), p. 112.
Pages 25–7:
B. Cosby, 'The Regular Way', *Playboy* (December 1968), pp. 288–9.

CHAPTER 3
The fantasy model of sex as described in Chapters 3 and 4 is our own creation. After listening to what hundreds of men said they did and thought about sex, we simply listed the more common beliefs. The original list was changed several times as we checked it against what new clients, students, friends, and other men said. At the same time, we went in search of sources that taught and reinforced these beliefs and were quite astonished to find that they were everywhere.

Some parts of the model have been discussed by writers dealing with one or more of its sources. Among the more valuable works are: J. Atkins, *Sex in Literature* (Grove, 1970); E. and P. Kronhausen, *Pornography and the Law* (Ballantine, 1959), Part 3; G. Legman, *Rationale of the Dirty Joke* (Grove, 1968); S. Marcus, *The Other Victorians* (Basic Books, 1966). A good source of sexual humor is the collection of *Party Jokes* published each year by Playboy Press. The articles entitled 'Sex in the Cinema', appearing yearly in *Playboy*, are valuable guides to what the movies are doing to sex.

Two valuable resources for research on sex in literature are Robert Reisner's *Show Me the Good Parts* (Citadel, 1964) and Norman Kiell's *Varieties of Sexual Experience* (International Universities Press, 1976). Unfortunately, we discovered these two books only after the manuscript was completed.

Page 32:
M. Goldstein and H. Kant, *Pornography and Sexual Deviance* (University of California Press, 1973), p. 148.
Pages 32–3:
H. Robbins, *The Betsy* (Pocket Books, 1971), pp. 101–3.
Pages 34–5:
J. Elbert, *The Crazy Ladies* (Signet, 1969), p. 81.
M. Puzo, *The Godfather* (Fawcett, 1969), p. 28.
Pages 35–6:
H. Miller, *Sexus* (Grove, 1965), p. 287.
S. Marcus, *The Other Victorians* (Basic Books, 1966), p. 212.
'Penile Survey Results', *Penthouse Forum* (March 1976), p. 26.
Pages 36–7:
For an account of some of the manipulations used to make photographed

penises appear larger than what they are, see Ed McCormack's fine article, 'Maximum Tumescence in Repose', *Rolling Stone* (October 9, 1975), pp. 56-71.

Page 39:

N. Mailer, *An American Dream* (Dell, 1965), pp. 49 and 51.

D. H. Lawrence, *Lady Chatterley's Lover* (Bantam, 1968), p. 268.

Page 41:

J. Baldwin, *Another Country* (Dell, 1962), pp. 152-3.

H. Miller, *Sexus*, p. 287.

Page 42:

The original description of orgasm experienced as the earth moving, at least in respectable literature, is found in Ernest Hemingway's *For Whom the Bell Tolls* (Scribner's, 1940), p. 160. The earth moved for Robert, but his lover Maria apparently got even more out of sex since she died each time.

CHAPTER 4

We did not think it necessary to illustrate every myth with literary quotations, although there is no shortage of such quotations. To add them would only have increased the length of an already long chapter.

Page 49:

H. Miller, *Black Spring* (Grove, 1963), p. 85.

Page 50:

From the Broadway musical *Chicago*, book by Fred Ebb and Bob Fosse, music by John Kander, lyrics by Fred Ebb.

Page 63:

H. Robbins, *The Inheritors* (Pocket Books, 1969), p. 363.

Page 64:

J. Elbert, *Crazy Ladies*, p. 256.

D. Danziger, *The Devil in Miss Jones* (Grove, 1973), p. 32.

Page 65:

J. and L. Bird, *Sexual Loving* (Doubleday, 1976), pp. 143–4.

Pages 66–7:

N. Mailer, *American Dream*, p. 49.

M. Spillane, *The Last Cop Out* (Signet , 1973), p. 162.

D. H. Lawrence, *Lady Chatterley's Lover*, p. 187.

Page 68:

P. Benchley, *The Deep* (Bantam, 1976), p. 61.

Page 71:

A. Ellis, *Sex and the Liberated Man* (Lyle Stuart, 1976), p. 35. Emphasis in original.

Pages 72–3:

G. and C. Greene, *S-M: The Last Taboo* (Grove, 1974).

W. Masters and V. Johnson, *Human Sexual Response* (Little, Brown, 1966).

G. Sheehy, *Passages* (Dutton, 1976), pp. 312–13.

Page 73:

H. Goldberg, *The Hazards of Being Male* (Nash, 1976), pp. 42–3.

Page 74:

R. Keyes, *Is There Life After High School?* (Little, Brown, 1976), p. 153.

CHAPTER 6

The concept of conditions has been useful in working with a variety of situations and problems. There are always requirements or conditions which, if met, make it easier for a person to accomplish his goals, whether these involve good sex, meeting others and establishing relationships, doing well in school or at work, or stopping some undesirable behavior such as smoking or drinking.

We were pleasantly surprised to find that even animals other than man have conditions for sex. A fascinating account of this matter is given in H. Hediger's 'Environmental Factors Influencing the Reproduction of Zoo Animals', in F. Beach (ed.), *Sex and Behavior* (Wiley, 1965), pp. 319-54. What he calls environmental factors are conditions.

Page 105:

L. Barbach, *For Yourself* (Doubleday, 1975), pp. 43–4.

Page 116:

R. Alberti, and M. Emmons, *Your Perfect Right* (Impact, 1974).

H. Fensterheim and J. Baer, *Don't Say Yes When You Want to Say No* (McKay, 1975).

A. Lazarus and A. Fay, *I Can If I Want To* (Morrow, 1975).

CHAPTER 7

Everyone who deals with sexual anatomy and physiology owes a great debt to the research of Masters and Johnson. Their work in this area is reported in the difficult *Human Sexual Response* (Little, Brown, 1966).

Page 122:

Our knowledge of penile activity during sleep and upon awakening is largely due to the work of Charles Fisher and Ismet Karacan. The first article on the subject was by Fisher and his associates, 'Cycle of Penile Erection Synchronous with Dreaming (REM) Sleep', *Archives of General Psychiatry* 12 (1965): 29–45. More recent findings are described by Karacan and his colleagues, 'Sleep-Related Penile Tumescence as a Function of Age', *American Journal of Psychiatry* 132 (1975): 932-7.

Page 132:

At least three other workers have questioned the utility of Masters and Johnson's four-stage response cycle, but so far their thinking has had little impact in the sex field. Helen Kaplan briefly discusses a biphasic model in *The New Sex Therapy* (Brunner Mazel, 1974), pp. 13–14. More detailed evaluations are offered by Bernard Apfelbaum, 'A Critique and Reformulation of Some Basic Assumptions in Sex Therapy', a paper presented to the International Congress of Sexology, Montreal (October 1976), and Irving Singer, *The Goals of Human Sexuality* (Norton, 1973).

A. Kinsey, et al., *Sexual Behavior in the Human Female* (Saunders, 1953), p. 594.

Page 140:

Kegel reported on the sexual function of the pelvic muscles in women in 'Sexual Functions of the Pubococcygeus Muscle', *Western Journal of Surgery* 60 (1952): 521–4.

CHAPTER 8

While not much has been written about nonsexual touching, there are a few good sources. Ashley Montagu's *Touching* (Perennial Library, 1971) is the best book on the subject. Other useful works are Chapter 10 of Masters and Johnson's *The Pleasure Bond* (Little, Brown, 1974); Desmond Morris's *Intimate Behavior* (Bantam, 1971); and for those interested in touching exercises, Bernard Gunther's *Sense Relaxation* (Collier, 1968), the source of the epigraph on page 130.

Page 143:

Throughout his book, Montagu documents the unfortunate consequences caused by a lack of touching in both animals and humans.

Pages 146–7:

Montagu's quote appears on page 192 of *Touching.*

Page 149:

Masters and Johnson, *The Pleasure Bond*, pp. 236–7.

Page 162:

Masters and Johnson, *The Pleasure Bond*, p. 238.

CHAPTER 9

Kenneth Pelletier's *Mind as Healer, Mind as Slayer* (Delta, 1977) offers good reviews of the role of stress in modern life, theories of stress, and some methods of dealing with tension. Fensterheim and Baer's book, *Don't Say Yes When You Want to Say No* (McKay, 1975), gives instructions for the behavioral approach to relaxation.

CHAPTER 10

Pages 175–6:

A. Kinsey et al., *Sexual Behavior in the Human Male* (Saunders, 1948), p. 479.

M. Hunt, *Sexual Behavior in the 1970s* (Playboy Press, 1974), p. 66.

R. Sorenson, *Adolescent Sexuality in Contemporary America* (World Publishing, 1973), p. 144.

Pages 176–7:

Kinsey, *Sexual Behavior in the Human Male*, p. 513.

Page 177:

The quotation from *What a Boy Should Know* is given in Hunt, *Sexual Behavior in the 1970s*, pp. 69–70.

Page 178:

A good history of attitudes toward masturbation in the last 200 years is given in Alex Comfort's *The Anxiety Makers* (Delta, 1967), which also includes descriptions and illustrations of some of the devices designed to prevent 'self-abuse'.

Pages 179–80:

Kinsey, *Sexual Behavior in the Human Male*, p. 514.

Masters and Johnson, *Human Sexual Response*, p. 201.

Page 181:

The Vatican proclamation on sex is quoted in the *San Francisco Monitor*, January 15, 1976, p. 2.

D. Reuben, *Everything You Always Wanted to Know About Sex* (Bantam, 1969), pp. 189, 190, and 213. The italics are ours.

Page 183:

Hunt, *Sexual Behavior in the 1970s*, p. 90.

CHAPTER 11

Page 192:

'What's Really Happening on Campus', *Playboy* (October 1976), p. 128.

'Your Pursuit of Happiness', *Psychology Today* (August 1976), p. 31.

Page 193:

Playboy (October 1976), p. 128.

Page 194:

Statistics on age of first intercourse are found in J. Gagnon, *Human Sexualities* (Scott, Foresman, 1977), p. 184; Hunt, *Sexual Behavior in the 1970s*, p. 149; Sorenson, *Adolescent Sexuality in Contemporary America*, p. 190.

Page 195:

E. Gambrill and C. Richey, *It's Up to You* (Les Femmes, 1976). P. Zimbardo, *Shyness* (Addison-Wesley, 1977). Although it does not include material or exercises designed to help readers find partners and combat loneliness, Suzanne Gordon's *Lonely in America* (Simon & Schuster, 1976) presents a marvelous account of being alone and of 'the loneliness business'.

CHAPTER 12

Although there are numerous books and articles dealing with relationships, many are silly and full of romantic mythology. We seem to know far more about sex than we do about intimacy and what makes a relationship work. Some of the works that have been useful to us in thinking about relationships are: G. Bach and R. Deutsch, *Pairing* (Avon, 1971); J. Bernard, *The Future of Marriage* (Bantam, 1972); W. Lederer and D. Jackson, *The Mirages of Marriage* (Norton, 1968); S. Luthman, *Intimacy* (Nash, 1972); W. Masters and V. Johnson, *The Pleasure Bond*; and L. Rubin, *Worlds of Pain* (Basic, 1976). Rainer Maria Rilke writes briefly though beautifully about aspects of love in his *Letters to a Young Poet* (Norton, 1954).

Page 213:

Very little has been written about male involvement in contraception. Three sources can be recommended: Kristin Luker's excellent book *Taking Chances* (University of California Press, 1975), and two articles, one by Tom Clark and one by Bernie Zilbergeld, in *The Male Role in Family Planning* (Office of Family Planning, California Department of Health, 1975).

Pages 214–15:

Two studies reporting that male attitudes toward contraception are influential in the effectiveness of contraception are F. Kane *et al.*, 'Motivating Factors Affecting Contraceptive Use', *American Journal of Obstetrics and Gynecology* 110 (1971): 1050–4, and D. McCalister and V. Thiessen, 'Prediction in Family Planning', *American Journal of Public Health* 60 (1970): 1372–81.

CHAPTER 13

Of the many fine works on female sexuality, the ones that have been most valuable to us are: Lonnie Barbach, *For Yourself;* Boston's Women's Health Book Collective, *Our Bodies, Our Selves* (Simon & Schuster, 1971); Germaine Greer, *The Female Eunuch* (Bantam, 1971); Shere Hite, *The Hite Report* (Macmillan, 1976); and Leah Schaefer, *Women and Sex* (Pantheon, 1973).

Page 243:

The Zilbergeld and Stanton survey, not yet published, consisted of questionnaires returned by 426 women ranging in age from 18 to 63 and in sexual partners from 1 to 250.

Page 256:

Kinsey and Masters and Johnson noted the great sexual similarities between men and women. Kinsey's discussion of these similarities, in Chapter 15 of the *Female* volume, is a classic and still worthy of attention.

Page 259:

Greer, *The Female Eunuch*, p. 36.

Page 261:

E. B. Vance and N. N. Wagner, 'Written Descriptions of Orgasm; A Study of Sex Differences', *Archives of Sexual Behavior* 5 (1976): 87–98.

Page 265:

The clitoral-vaginal controversy is much more complex than is indicated in the text. It has become difficult to discuss rationally because, first, of the Freudian premise that vaginal orgasms are better and more mature than clitoral ones and second, because some radical feminists have made it a political issue. Our own thinking, which owes much to work currently in progress by Carol Rinkleib, is that many, if not most, women can train themselves to have orgasms with intercourse if they want to. A number of women have done this by themselves, while others have had professional help. Whether or not such training is worthwhile is, of course, something only the women involved can say. Hite, *The Hite Report*, p. 135.

Pages 268–9:

Barbach, personal communication.

CHAPTER 14
Page 272:
Kinsey, *Sexual Behavior in the Human Male*, p. 580.
D. Reuben, *How to Get More Out of Sex* (McKay, 1974), pp. 55, 139–140.
Page 273:
'M', *The Sensuous Man* (Dell, 1971), pp. 39–40.
Sheehy, *Passages*, p. 313.
Page 280:
J. Semans, 'Premature Ejaculation', *Southern Medical Journal* 49(1956): 353-8.

CHAPTER 16
The partner exercise format for developing ejaculatory control differs in a number of ways from the work of Semans, cited in Chapter 14, and Masters and Johnson, *Human Sexual Inadequacy* (Little, Brown, 1970), Chapter 3, although we have liberally borrowed many of their ideas and exercises.

The approach that does not use partner exercises gradually evolved as we worked with more and more men who didn't have partners or whose partners refused to participate in treatment. Once developed, this format was frequently chosen by men who had partners but preferred to develop better ejaculatory control on their own.

CHAPTER 17
A recent novel by Romain Gary, *Your Ticket Is No Longer Valid* (Braziller, 1977), portrays well the agony felt by a man who fears that he is becoming impotent. The title itself is of course not without significance.
Page 307:
S. Julty, *Male Sexual Performance* (Grosset & Dunlap, 1975), p. 15.
Page 314:
J. Woods, 'Drug Effects on Human Sexual Behavior', in N. Woods, *Human Sexuality in Health and Illness* (Mosby, 1975), p. 183.
Page 315:
P. Roen, *Male Sexual Health* (Morrow, 1974), p. 148.

CHAPTER 19
The method of resolving erection problems without doing partner exercises evolved as we worked with men who didn't have partners with whom they could do exercises. It was later also used by men who had partners but didn't want to do exercises with them. Several hundred men have learned the principles and the overwhelming majority reported that they were able to follow them when with a partner, with the result that their erection problems were either totally or largely resolved.

Masters and Johnson's partner exercise format is reported in Chapter 7 of *Human Sexual Inadequacy*. Our partner exercise approach differs from theirs in a number of ways.

CHAPTER 20

A number of very good books on aging have appeared in the last few years. Two of the best are R. Butler, *Why Survive?* (Harper & Row, 1975), and A. Comfort, *A Good Age* (Crown, 1976). Masters and Johnson's research on the sexual aspects of aging is reported in Chapter 16 of *Human Sexual Response* and Chapter 12 of *Human Sexual Inadequacy*. We have drawn on many of their findings for the discussion in this chapter. Two other good books on sex and aging are R. Butler and M. Lewis, *Sex after Sixty* (Harper & Row, 1976), and I. Rubin, *Sexual Life After Sixty* (Signet, 1965).

Page 347:

J. Lester, 'Being a Boy', *Ms.* (July 1973), p. 113.

Page 353:

E. Pfeiffer, 'Sex and Aging', in L. Gross (ed.), *Sexual Issues in Marriage* (Spectrum, 1975), pp. 43–9.

Page 354:

Masters and Johnson, *Human Sexual Inadequacy*, p. 326.

Page 359:

J. Jones, *Go to the Widow-Maker* (Dell, 1967), pp. 42–3.

CHAPTER 21

There is not nearly as much good literature as there should be for the man with a medical condition. Although we have only seen a few parts of it, Gay Blackford's *Sex and Disability* (Van Nostrand, in press) looks as if it will do a great deal to remedy this situation. Many health organizations, such as cancer, heart, diabetes, and ostomy associations, distribute pamphlets and articles on sex. A good book for those with spinal cord injuries is T. Mooney *et al.*, *Sexual Options for Paraplegics and Quadriplegics* (Little, Brown, 1975).

Page 372.

We, as well as several colleagues at the Human Sexuality Program, University of California School of Medicine, San Francisco, have worked successfully with men with many different types of disabilities – long-term alcoholism, diabetes, several types of cancer, cerebal palsy, heart disease, multiple sclerosis, ostomy, prostatectomy, and spinal cord injury.

CHAPTER 22

Page 375:

E. Fromm, *Man for Himself* (Rinehart, 1947), p. 184.

Pages 383–4

A. Comfort, *The Joy of Sex* (Crown, 1972) pp. 9 and 51.

Page 384:

H. Hendin, *The Age of Sensation* (Norton, 1975), p. 325.

G. Curtis, 'The New Facts of Life', *Texas Monthly* (March 1976), p. 102.

Page 385:

J. Gagnon and W. Simon, quoted in E. Kennedy, *The New Sexuality* (Image, 1972), p. 43.

Page 388:
H. Hendin, *The Age of Sensation*, p. 336.

CHAPTER 23
Pages 405–6:
R. Rilke, *Letters to a Young Poet* (Norton, 1954), p. 59.

Index

420   INDEX

What Do Women Want?

Luise Eichenbaum and Susie Orbach

Many women today feel that they pour love, commitment and understanding into their relationships, but that it is not returned in kind. He seems secure and independent, she feels insecure and clingy.

The truth is that men and women are *both* dependent. But his needs are catered to so well – first by his mother, then by his girlfriend or wife – that he doesn't know he has them, while her needs – for closeness and tenderness – are constantly rebuffed as he retreats from intimacy.

Susie Orbach and Luise Eichenbaum set out to explore this crisis in the relationships of men and women. They explain how men have learned to 'manage' their dependency needs very differently from women, and *why* women feel dependent and hungry for love. Finally they show why dependency on both sides is the essential core of any successful relationship.

ISBN 0 00 638252 5

☐	UNLAWFUL CARNAL KNOWLEDGE Wendy Holden	0-00-638258-4	£5.99
☐	DEADLIER THAN THE MALE Alix Kirsta	0-00-637849-8	£5.99
☐	LIFE'S DOMINION Ronald Dworkin	0-00-686309-4	£7.99
☐	SEXING THE MILLENNIUM Linda Grant	0-00-637768-8	£7.99

These books are available from your local bookseller or can be ordered direct from the publishers.

To order direct just tick the titles you want and fill in the form below:

Name:

Address:

Postcode:

Send to: HarperCollins Mail Order, Dept 8, HarperCollins*Publishers*, Westerhill Road, Bishopbriggs, Glasgow G64 2QT.

Please enclose a cheque or postal order or your authority to debit your Visa/Access account –

Credit card no:

Expiry date:

Signature:

– to the value of the cover price plus:

UK & BFPO: Add £1.00 for the first and 25p for each additional book ordered.

Overseas orders including Eire, please add £2.95 service charge.

Books will be sent by surface mail but quotes for airmail despatches will be given on request.

24 HOUR TELEPHONE ORDERING SERVICE FOR
ACCESS/VISA CARDHOLDERS –
TEL: GLASGOW 041-772 2281 or LONDON 081-307 4052

Dominique MÉDA

LE TRAVAIL

Une valeur en voie
de disparition

Flammarion

Cet ouvrage est paru en 1995 dans la collection
« Alto », aux éditions Aubier.

© Aubier, Paris, 1995
ISBN : 2-08-081400-1

INTRODUCTION

L'objectif de ce livre n'est ni de présenter une nouvelle
théorie du travail censée régler les problèmes que connaissent aujourd'hui, à des degrés divers, les pays industrialisés, ni d'enrichir la galerie des systèmes philosophiques. Il
est bien plutôt de ramener à la surface — et donc de rendre
disponibles pour le débat public — un certain nombre de
réflexions, anciennes ou récentes, de nature philosophique
sur le travail, et de développer ainsi une approche critique
de cette notion.

Deux idées sont à l'origine de cette tentative. La
première, c'est que les questions légitimes qui devraient
être posées quant à la place, au sens et à l'avenir du travail
sont occultées par le traitement technocratique, économique, politicien et partant réducteur qui en est fait, alors
même qu'elles concernent chaque citoyen et devraient être
au centre d'un vaste débat public et politique. Car il ne
s'agit pas seulement de savoir si le chômage sera mieux
combattu par la suppression du SMIC, l'abaissement des
cotisations sociales patronales ou la mise en œuvre d'une
relance concertée au niveau européen. Le statut du travail
lui-même est en soi une question centrale pour nos sociétés
occidentales, qu'elles soient dites industrielles ou post-
industrielles, parce qu'il constitue l'une de leurs dimensions

essentielles, l'un de leurs fondements et qu'il s'agit aujour-
d'hui, certes, de connaître la nature de la crise que nous
traversons, mais également de choisir le type de société
dans lequel nous voulons vivre.

Nous appartenons depuis peu de temps (moins de deux
siècles) à des sociétés fondées sur le travail. Ce qui signifie
que le travail, reconnu comme tel par la société, c'est-à-
dire rémunéré, est devenu le principal moyen d'acquisition
des revenus permettant aux individus de vivre, mais qu'il
est aussi un rapport social fondamental — Mauss aurait dit
un fait social total [1] — et enfin le moyen jamais remis en
question d'atteindre l'objectif d'abondance. Aujourd'hui
seulement, alors que le fonctionnement normal de nos
sociétés — le plein emploi à temps plein pour tous — est
remis en cause, nous pouvons nous en rendre compte et la
possible diminution ou raréfaction du travail bouleverse
soudain ce que nous tenions pour des évidences.

Des auteurs peu nombreux ont développé depuis quelques années une analyse ambitieuse visant à replacer le
travail dans l'histoire des idées, des représentations et des
civilisations, et ont tenté de s'interroger sur la signification
du travail dans nos sociétés modernes [2]. Mais, la plupart du
temps, la question du chômage reste une question traitée
par des experts, le plus souvent économistes de formation,
qui cherchent à relancer la machine et à faire disparaître
cette anomalie qu'est le sous-emploi. Or, parce qu'il est au
centre d'une constellation très intégrée — Louis Dumont
aurait dit d'une idéologie [3] — et parce que la place qu'il
occupe aujourd'hui dans nos sociétés va de pair avec de
nombreux autres phénomènes qui nous apparaissent
comme des évidences, voire comme des données naturelles
ou de fait (par exemple, la place de l'économie ou la
prédominance de la rationalité instrumentale), la compréhension exacte du rôle que joue le travail dans nos sociétés
nécessite non seulement une approche multidisciplinaire,
capable de saisir la cohérence d'ensemble de ces diverses
manifestations, mais aussi, et surtout, nous semble-t-il,

l'intervention de la plus généraliste et de la plus réflexive de toutes les sciences dites humaines, la philosophie.

Telle est la seconde ambition de ce livre : démontrer que l'analyse critique et réflexive développée par la philosophie est plus que jamais nécessaire à notre temps, en particulier pour nous aider à resituer des notions — que nous croyions bien connues — dans l'histoire des idées et des représentations ainsi qu'à reformuler un certain nombre de questions contemporaines. Cette ambition paraîtra peut-être démesurée, mal à propos, et surtout profondément datée. Certains de nos philosophes eux-mêmes ont en effet glosé sur la fin de la philosophie, c'est-à-dire sur les vaines ambitions d'un certain mode de pensée, volontairement généraliste et aux antipodes du type de savoir qui s'est développé depuis le début du xxe siècle. Dans la grande querelle des sciences de la nature et des sciences de l'esprit qui a émaillé à plusieurs reprises le xixe et le xxe siècle [4], ce sont les sciences « opérationnelles » qui l'ont emporté, celles qui présentaient des garanties à la fois en matière de vérification expérimentale et en termes d'utilité. Le modèle développé par le positivisme logique, qui voulait que l'on n'appelât sciences que les ensembles de raisonnements hypothético-déductifs susceptibles d'être vérifiés et falsifiés [5], semble s'être définitivement imposé contre les sciences plus généralistes incapables d'exhiber leurs fondements, de démontrer l'exactitude de leurs propos ou de montrer en quoi elles se démarquaient des idéologies [6]. La philosophie semble avoir été la principale victime de ce développement, du moins la métaphysique (cible privilégiée du positivisme logique) ou la critique.

La philosophie s'est aujourd'hui enfermée dans la contemplation et l'élaboration toujours recommencée de son histoire. Même Heidegger, le dernier « grand philosophe », s'est bien gardé de traiter des problèmes dits « de société », dans son œuvre du moins, au point de condamner ceux qui, en France, avaient tenté d'utiliser sa philosophie pour prôner l'engagement [7]. La philosophie actuelle, celle qui s'enseigne dans les terminales et dans les universités ou celle qui s'écrit dans les livres, demeure le plus souvent une histoire des idées conçue comme un défilé rationnel de doctrines se succédant logiquement les unes aux autres sans que jamais la relation soit faite avec l'histoire réelle. Quant à la possibilité pour elle de s'exprimer sur les questions dites de société (le chômage, le travail, l'éducation), elle s'en garde bien, de peur de tomber dans les défauts qui lui ont déjà été reprochés. La philosophie chemine ainsi dans un étroit chenal bordé de deux principaux écueils : la tentation normative et l'idéologie — ou sa version neutre, le relativisme. Dès lors, mieux vaut se spécialiser dans le commentaire. Quant à exercer une fonction purement critique, la philosophie s'y est bien essayée depuis Kant, en particulier avec l'école de Francfort[8], mais cette manière de procéder n'a fait d'émules qu'en Allemagne et ceux-ci demeurent peu nombreux. Malgré la demande de sens dont notre époque est avide, nous continuons à exiger des non-spécialistes qui se risquent à un discours général qu'ils indiquent « d'où ils parlent », c'est-à-dire qu'ils dévoilent les intérêts qu'ils représentent, puisque nous sommes tous censés savoir qu'il est aujourd'hui impossible de tenir un discours universel ou même de mener une discussion véritablement raisonnée.

La fonction critique que la philosophie exerçait à une époque aurait pu être prise en charge par les autres sciences humaines, qui après tout se sont bien développées sur ses décombres, en particulier la sociologie. Mais, devant l'offensive du positivisme anglo-saxon et des caractéristiques de la demande politique et sociale retraduite par l'Etat, cette discipline s'est adaptée aux canons de scientificité qu'on lui reprochait de ne pas respecter et se garde bien aujourd'hui, sauf exceptions, de tenir le moindre discours trop généraliste, normatif ou critique. La référence à une norme, à une éthique, à des choix est devenue, pour toutes les sciences humaines, ce qu'il faut à tout prix éviter. Ce qui nous conduit à la situation suivante : d'un côté, des professeurs, chercheurs, écrivains enseignent la philosophie, l'histoire des idées, la théorie politique, censées permettre aux individus d'exercer leur raison et leur faculté critique ; de l'autre, les responsables des institutions politico-sociales au sens large, c'est-à-dire des politiques publiques, gèrent la machine sociale en se gardant bien d'attribuer à son mouvement des fins autres que la pure reproduction de celui-ci. Il ne s'agit pas de dire que les intellectuels ont disparu ou que les responsables publics n'ont aucune idée. Au contraire, chacun a sa « petite idée », mais chacun se garde de la divulguer, car elle relève de la conviction intime. Qui donc exerce aujourd'hui, dans nos pays hautement développés, la fonction critique ? Sur quels principes, sur quelles croyances se fondent les responsables de nos politiques, qu'il s'agisse des hauts fonctionnaires, des hommes politiques ou de tous ceux qui, un jour, participent à la régulation sociale ?

Une manière de le savoir serait de connaître ce qu'ils ont lu, comment ils ont été formés, ou encore sur quel terreau poussent et se développent les idées politiques ou les théories qui périodiquement sont reprises par toute une partie de la classe dirigeante puis diffusées dans l'ensemble du corps social. Un certain nombre de nos responsables possèdent des connaissances en théorie sociale, en histoire des idées, mais n'y font généralement pas appel pour exercer leur tâche quotidienne. En revanche, ils mobilisent des connaissances économiques, souvent érigées en recettes et en dogmes, mêlées de quelques éléments d'histoire économique, de quelques principes de théorie politique et de lectures générales [9], mais qu'ils s'estiment indignes de critiquer. La formation des grandes écoles qui mènent à ces responsabilités l'explique : Polytechnique, l'ENA, les écoles d'ingénieurs ou de commerce en restent à un assez grand niveau de généralités en matière d'histoire des idées, alors qu'elles poussent à l'acquisition de connaissances techniques et spécialisées approfondies.

Où s'exerce la fonction critique dans nos sociétés si le

discours généraliste et intellectuel est condamné comme idéologique ou irréaliste et si ceux qui ont quelque pouvoir n'ont pas eu l'occasion de prendre le temps de la réflexion ou bien considèrent que cela n'entre pas dans leurs prérogatives officielles ? Nulle part, ou dans les lieux dépourvus d'efficacité que sont l'intériorité, les amphithéâtres des universités ou les laboratoires de recherche. Peut-elle d'ailleurs encore véritablement s'exercer alors que la plupart des sciences humaines, se gardant comme de la peste d'être normatives, le sont pourtant sans le savoir ? Le débat public lui-même est-il possible alors même que ceux qui disposent des données nécessaires — les responsables de l'Etat — sont tenus par l'obligation de réserve, que le reste de la population est dépourvu de cette information et que les partis politiques sont devenus incapables d'être des lieux de formation de l'opinion et de mise en évidence des enjeux, tenus qu'ils sont par l'impératif de l'élection ? Cette situation — la séparation des deux fonctions critique et gestionnaire, la méfiance à l'égard de la fonction critique et normative et l'absence d'un véritable espace public — est relativement inquiétante, sauf si l'on pense, comme beaucoup de bons esprits aujourd'hui, que la société n'a besoin de rien d'autre que de son propre mouvement, et surtout pas d'une réflexion critique pour se maintenir en l'état. Mais peut-être cette idée mérite-t-elle elle-même un regard critique, voire une approche généalogique. Car si l'on ne peut certainement pas déterminer dans sa totalité la direction de la machine sociale, peut-être nos sociétés sont-elles néanmoins assez mûres, ou les risques attachés à une option fataliste trop grands, pour tenter de voir s'il ne leur serait pas possible d'infléchir cette direction. « *Sapere aude* », ce défi que Kant lançait à l'individu en inaugurant l'ère des Lumières [10], ne faut-il pas le destiner aujourd'hui à la société tout entière ? Plus simplement, il s'agit de savoir si la marche de nos sociétés est entièrement déterminée de l'extérieur, comme on tente de nous le faire croire, c'est-à-dire par la mondialisation des échanges, l'internationalisation des relations et des communications, l'évolution économique, et si nous devons dès lors adopter sans même les choisir les critères économiques et technocratiques standards, partagés par tous les pays et censés nous permettre de nous « maintenir à niveau », ou bien si nous ne disposons pas plutôt d'une capacité de décider en partie des évolutions de nos sociétés et en particulier de la nôtre. Reste-t-il une place pour le choix des fins — ce que l'on avait coutume d'appeler politique ? Reste-t-il un espace, à inventer ou à redécouvrir, spécifiquement politique, pour discuter et décider collectivement de ces fins ?

La place du travail dans nos sociétés est un élément d'explication de la situation qui est la nôtre aujourd'hui — dont les deux caractéristiques sont la prédominance de l'approche économique et la recherche d'une régulation toujours plus automatique des phénomènes sociaux —, en même temps que le moyen pour nous de recouvrer une nouvelle dignité. Pour cette raison, la question du travail, de son avenir, de son statut et de sa place n'est pas et ne doit pas être l'apanage des seuls économistes. Bien au contraire, elle ne peut être tranchée — comme celle du chômage — que collectivement, consciemment et au terme d'une véritable entreprise généalogique, qui seule nous permettra de comprendre comment l'avènement des sociétés fondées sur le travail, la prédominance de l'économie et le dépérissement de la politique ne sont que les manifestations multiples d'un unique événement.

CHAPITRE I

L'ACTUEL PARADOXE
DES SOCIÉTÉS FONDÉES SUR LE TRAVAIL

La situation dans laquelle se trouvent les sociétés industrialisées apparaît éminemment paradoxale : la productivité du travail a considérablement augmenté depuis un siècle, et particulièrement depuis les années 1950 ; nous sommes capables de produire toujours plus avec toujours moins de travail humain ; un desserrement de la contrainte qu'exerce sur nous le travail apparaît enfin possible, mais un long cortège de lamentations accompagne cette évolution. C'est à qui trouvera la solution miracle pour augmenter le nombre d'emplois « rentables », et c'est l'ensemble de la société qui attend, de ces objurgations diverses, toujours plus de travail. Les politiques économiques et sociales elles-mêmes ont largement visé, depuis vingt ans (depuis le ralentissement du rythme de croissance), à sauver l'emploi : stratégies macroéconomiques visant à relancer la croissance, aides diverses aux entreprises, exonérations de cotisations sociales, renforcement des institutions chargées de « fluidifier » le marché du travail, effort consacré à améliorer la formation des personnes... beaucoup a été fait[11]. Et même si un certain nombre d'experts économiques ou d'hommes politiques s'élèvent aujourd'hui contre les insuffisances de ces politiques, en mettant en évidence qu'elles n'avaient pas pour priorité l'emploi mais les grands équilibres macroéconomiques (les « fondamentaux »), il est cependant clair que la volonté de préserver ces derniers était destinée en dernier ressort à augmenter l'emploi, en accord avec la formule fameuse du chancelier allemand Schmidt : « Les investissements d'aujourd'hui sont les emplois de demain. »

La réaction de tous les pays occidentaux devant l'augmentation massive de la productivité depuis les années 1950 a donc été double : d'abord considérer le travail humain ainsi rendu inutile comme un mal social majeur en continuant de l'appréhender à travers les mêmes catégories qu'auparavant — et particulièrement celle du chômage [12] —, ensuite mobiliser des moyens pour trouver des emplois à tout prix. L'expression « à tout prix » doit être entendue ici dans son sens littéral. « A tout prix » signifie qu'il est légitime, nécessaire, vital de créer des emplois, même temporaires, même sans contenu, même sans intérêt, même s'ils renforcent les inégalités, pourvu qu'ils existent. Ceci s'explique par le fait que nos gouvernements, mais aussi nos sociétés, considèrent le chômage comme un mal social d'une extrême gravité, un cancer qui dévore la société et conduit les individus qu'il touche depuis trop longtemps à la délinquance et les sociétés elles-mêmes à des réactions imprévisibles. Le chômage, c'est l'une des causes de l'arrivée de Hitler au pouvoir, c'est la révolte sociale, c'est l'anomie... Tout cela est bien connu. Mais le bien connu, c'est l'évidence quotidienne dans laquelle nous vivons et que nous ne pouvons donc plus *voir*. Or, si nous prenons quelque recul, nous conviendrons qu'il est tout de même curieux qu'au lieu de prendre acte de cette augmentation de la productivité et d'y adapter les structures sociales, nous nous soyons arc-boutés pour conserver ce que les années 1970 dénonçaient comme le comble de l'aliénation (« perdre sa vie à la gagner ») : le travail. Ce décalage entre les aspirations profondes et la réponse politique et sociale doit susciter notre réflexion.

De l'emploi au travail :
le retour des pensées de légitimation du travail

Nous nous trouvons aujourd'hui au moment adéquat pour engager celle-ci. Le taux de chômage n'ayant en effet jamais été aussi élevé [13], un certain nombre de voix commencent à se faire entendre qui veulent dépasser les traditionnelles litanies politiques et expliquent pourquoi il faut absolument combattre le chômage et créer des emplois. Elles apportent ainsi un certain nombre de justifications théoriques aux politiques spontanément menées depuis vingt ans. Ces voix sont celles d'auteurs issus de courants de pensée très différents et dont les origines sont diverses : représentants de structures socioprofessionnelles, hauts fonctionnaires, universitaires, hommes politiques prennent la plume aujourd'hui [14] pour expliquer qu'il ne suffit pas d'attendre le retour de la croissance ou d'aider les entreprises, mais qu'il faut faire autre chose. Et, ce faisant, ils indiquent les raisons impératives pour lesquelles, à leur avis, de telles mesures sont indispensables. Leurs analyses ont ceci de commun qu'elles utilisent plus volontiers le terme de travail que celui d'emploi, qui avait pourtant eu la préférence jusque-là. On parlait alors du retour du plein emploi, de la création d'emplois, du sous-emploi, et le terme de travail continuait simplement d'être utilisé dans l'expression « conditions de travail ». Le changement de vocabulaire, massif dans cette première moitié des années 1990, n'est pas anodin. Il s'inscrit dans une double perspective pour les auteurs en question : d'une part, expliciter pourquoi l'emploi, considéré comme la manifestation concrète de l'activité humaine qu'est le travail, est essentiel ; d'autre part, relativiser, voire critiquer, les modalités qu'a recouvertes le travail jusqu'ici, pour indiquer que, par-delà celles-ci et même justement peut-être par-delà l'emploi lui-même, ce qui importe, c'est de sauver le travail, cette activité fondamentale de l'homme.

Que disent, en effet, ces auteurs ? Que le travail est une

catégorie anthropologique, c'est-à-dire un invariant de la
nature humaine, dont on trouve la trace toujours et
partout, qu'il permet la réalisation de soi (l'homme s'expri-
mant dans ses œuvres), et surtout qu'il est au centre et au
fondement du lien social. Le travail, c'est cette activité
essentielle de l'homme grâce à laquelle il est mis en contact
avec son extériorité — la Nature, à laquelle il s'oppose
pour créer quelque chose d'humain —, et avec les autres,
avec lesquels et pour lesquels il réalise cette tâche. Le
travail est donc ce qui exprime au plus haut point notre
humanité, notre condition d'êtres finis, créateurs de
valeurs, mais aussi d'êtres sociaux. Le travail est notre
essence en même temps que notre condition. J'appelle ces
pensées « légitimation des sociétés fondées sur le travail » :
leur caractéristique est d'apparaître à un moment particulier de notre histoire, celui où le développement du
chômage menace le fondement même de nos sociétés et
joue comme révélateur de la fragilité de celui-ci — voire de
sa possible disparition —, et où une partie de la société fait
effort pour mettre au jour ce qui était resté jusque-là
largement impensé et inexprimé, c'est-à-dire le rôle décisif
du travail.

Ce faisant, ces pensées se trouvent dans une position
ambiguë vis-à-vis de la conception « banale » que nous
avons de l'emploi. Au premier abord, elles légitiment les
efforts déployés depuis vingt ans pour sauver l'emploi,
puisqu'elles considèrent également celui-ci comme le facteur essentiel d'intégration sociale. Mais elles sont, dans le
même temps, critiques par rapport aux formes concrètes
qu'a prises le travail dans nos sociétés, et donc par rapport
aux politiques qui ont visé à conforter celles-ci. En effet,
même si elles divergent sur les moyens de rendre au travail
son véritable visage, ces analyses ont néanmoins toutes
pour caractéristique commune de considérer le travail
comme une activité, qui a pris avec la Révolution industrielle des formes qu'il est désormais nécessaire de dépasser. Travail salarié, travail marchand, travail abstrait sont

autant de formules que l'on retrouve sous la plume des auteurs considérés, comme si nous devions aujourd'hui surmonter les formes monstrueuses qu'a recouvertes le travail, à son corps défendant, pour en trouver d'autres qui exprimeraient mieux son essence et pour mettre un coup d'arrêt au développement de ce scandale absolu : que des hommes soient privés de la possibilité d'exprimer librement et pleinement leurs capacités et d'exercer l'activité essentielle qui les fait hommes. On en veut pour seule illustration cette prise de position récente du Centre des jeunes dirigeants [15] : « Cette situation nous a fait prendre pour règle ce qui n'a jamais été qu'une exception historique : le plein emploi, nous faisant oublier que l'emploi salarié ne doit pas être le seul vecteur de l'activité sociale, ni l'entreprise le seul lieu de socialisation... Accepter ce questionnement, c'est faire une distinction entre le travail et l'emploi salarié, qui n'en est qu'une forme parmi d'autres. C'est repenser le sens du travail, la place de l'emploi dans la vie des hommes et le rôle de l'entreprise dans la société. C'est s'ouvrir à deux logiques de pensée et d'action. La première, que nous appellerons « logique de l'emploi salarié », confond le travail et l'emploi. [...] La seconde, logique de l'activité, est plus novatrice. [...] Cela nous conduit à nous libérer de la stricte notion d'emploi pour retrouver le vrai sens du travail, conçu comme source d'accomplissement et de lien social et de subsistance pour l'homme. » Cette citation explique, mieux que toute autre, pourquoi l'emploi ne constitue plus, pour les pensées que nous évoquons, le seul objectif. Que cela s'opère par l'emploi, forme somme toute particulière qu'a prise le travail dans nos sociétés, ou par d'autres moyens, l'essentiel est aujourd'hui de permettre au travail de continuer à assurer les fonctions dont il est par essence porteur, et ce, par-delà les confusions ou les errances historiques. Ce faisant, sans qu'elles y fassent toujours référence et sans que les auteurs en soient toujours conscients, ces idées s'inscrivent dans la plus pure tradition de pensée du xxᵉ siècle.

Elles mettent ainsi en évidence ce qui constitue sans doute l'unique mais véritable dénominateur commun des différents courants doctrinaux constitutifs de cette tradition — chrétien, marxiste et humaniste : la croyance en un schème utopique du travail. Selon celui-ci, le travail est l'essence de l'homme, il est actuellement défiguré et il faut donc retrouver, par-delà ces défigurations, les moyens de son expression pleine et entière. Par conséquent, le travail est et doit devenir en réalité le lieu du lien social et de la réalisation de soi.

Le travail, catégorie anthropologique

C'est la première conception commune à l'ensemble des trois grands courants de pensée du XXe siècle. Pour la pensée chrétienne, le travail est l'activité fondamentale de l'homme, qui tout ensemble ajoute de la valeur au monde et à lui-même, c'est-à-dire spiritualise la nature et permet l'approfondissement des rapports avec autrui. Ainsi pour Henri Bartoli : « Le travail est pour l'homme un moyen nécessaire de se réaliser : le monde dans lequel il est jeté est pour lui un monde de tâches dans lequel il a à œuvrer. [...] Par la médiation du travail et de l'œuvre qui en est le produit, l'esprit se distingue des choses, rompt avec l'esclavage de l'environnement et émerge du monde. La nature est alors libérée, le donné cesse d'être donné, l'homme s'expérimente libre et s'achemine vers la cohérence de soi-même [16]. » Le travail humain est donc la continuation sur terre de la création divine, mais aussi un devoir social que chacun doit remplir du mieux qu'il le peut. La pensée chrétienne a développé beaucoup d'arguments en ce sens, avec Jean Lacroix, le père Chenu, le père Martelet [17]... Elle s'appuie sur une certaine lecture des textes bibliques et sur les plus récentes prises de position de l'Eglise sur ce problème. Elle recouvre également une dimension très spiritualiste en assimilant travail, liberté et effort [18].

Un vaste courant de pensée humaniste, qui ne se revendique pas chrétien, défend la même conception qui voit dans le travail l'activité humaine qui exprime au plus haut point la liberté créatrice de l'homme. On pourrait ici accumuler les exemples [19]. Dans un livre consacré au droit du travail, Alain Supiot, que l'on peut inclure dans la catégorie des humanistes, commence son analyse par des considérations historico-philosophiques et écrit : « Dans la langue française, le premier sens attesté du mot travail désigne ce qu'endure la femme dans l'enfantement. Il désigne cet acte où se mêlent par excellence la douleur et la création, acte où se rejoue à chaque fois, comme dans tout travail, le mystère de la création humaine. Car tout travail est le lieu d'un semblable arrachement des forces et des œuvres que l'homme porte en lui-même. Et c'est dans cette mise au monde des enfants et des œuvres que l'homme accomplit sa destinée [20]. »

L'actuelle pensée marxiste, quelle que soit sa diversité, continue de défendre avec vigueur l'idée que le travail est une catégorie centrale et qu'il constitue l'essence de l'homme. Particulièrement bien illustrée par les ouvrages d'Yves Schwarz, de Jacques Bidet et de Jean-Marie Vincent [21], rares philosophes contemporains à s'être intéressés au travail, l'idée est mise en évidence par des recherches très concrètes sur la réalité de l'acte de travail. Jacques Bidet écrit ainsi : « Le travail est, comme le langage, une catégorie anthropologique générale, sans laquelle ne peuvent être pensés ni le processus d'hominisation, ni la spécificité de l'homme [22]. »

Ces différentes idées convergent vers un élément central : il y a une essence, un caractère anthropologique du travail, fait de créativité, d'inventivité et de lutte avec les contraintes, qui lui donne sa double dimension de souffrance et de réalisation de soi.

Le travail, lien social

Ces trois principaux courants de pensée se retrouvent
également en accord sur l'idée selon laquelle le travail
permet l'intégration sociale et constitue l'une des formes
majeures du lien social. Cette conception est assez ambiguë et plurivoque : le travail est facteur d'intégration non
seulement parce qu'il est une norme, mais aussi parce
qu'il est l'une des modalités d'apprentissage de la vie en
société. Il donne donc accès à autrui, à soi-même et à la
règle sociale. Il recouvre en même temps une dimension
de sociabilité, celle que l'on développe au bureau, aux
guichets, dans l'atelier, en équipe, une sociabilité douce
opposée aux rapports hiérarchiques et aux rapports
privés. Enfin, l'idée de lien social se fonde sur celle de
réciprocité, de contrat social et d'utilité sociale : en
apportant ma contribution, je développe mon sentiment
d'appartenance à la société, je suis liée à elle, parce que
j'ai besoin d'elle et que je lui suis utile.

Pour la pensée judéo-chrétienne, le travail s'inscrit
fondamentalement dans une relation à l'autre et dans
l'idée d'utilité sociale. « Une économie du travail ne
saurait être qu'une économie de tous pour tous. C'est à
la construction d'une Cité fraternelle qu'elle nous
convie », écrit Henri Bartoli en citant la majeure partie
des penseurs chrétiens qui s'exprimaient sur ce sujet au
sortir de la guerre. Il ajoute : « Le travail appelle l'usage
commun des biens, la propriété qu'il permet d'acquérir
n'est légitime que dans la mesure où elle est communication, c'est-à-dire jouissance dans et pour la communauté [23]. » Le travail est, pour eux, le mode d'être
ensemble, la manière de construire ensemble un ordre
nouveau, porteur de valeurs communautaires. Le travail
est le moyen de la communication sociale et de la relation avec autrui : les talents doivent être développés dans
une perspective sociale, communautaire. Nous revien-

drons plus longuement sur le caractère d'éthique du devoir qu'a également pris le travail dans la religion protestante.

La pensée humaniste et sociologique, quant à elle, nous semble bien représentée par tout un ensemble d'études qui vont de Friedmann et Naville à Renaud Sainsaulieu et Claude Dubar : le travail — et particulièrement le travail en entreprise — y apparaît comme le véritable lieu de la socialisation réelle et de la formation de l'identité individuelle et collective [24]. Il constitue même le cadre principal où s'opèrent les échanges humains [25]. Certains ergonomes semblent ne pas dire autre chose lorsqu'ils en appellent à la théorie psychanalytique pour expliquer le caractère profondément social du travail. Critiquant une tendance qui viserait à réduire la place du travail dans l'existence, Christophe Dejours écrit : « J'ai indiqué à plusieurs reprises à quel point la question de l'identité, de l'accomplissement de soi, est centrale dans la construction de la santé, mentale et physique. Or, j'affirme que l'identité ne peut pas se construire uniquement sur l'espace privé. La sphère de l'amour elle-même ne peut suffire. Aucun être ne peut jouer entièrement son identité dans le champ de l'économie érotique, car c'est se placer dans une situation extrêmement périlleuse. Chacun cherche donc à former des substitutions, par lesquelles on peut reprendre ce qui ne s'est pas accompli dans la sphère amoureuse, et jouer cela dans un autre champ, au moyen d'un déplacement que la théorie baptise " sublimation " et qui se déroule, selon les termes de Freud, " dans une activité socialement valorisée " [26]. »

La pensée marxiste ne renierait pas ces propos, elle qui voit dans la production des producteurs associés la fin à poursuivre. L'utilité générale est bien le but à atteindre : la réponse collective à des besoins collectifs. Le vrai travail est fondamentalement social puisqu'il unit dans un effort accepté par tous l'ensemble des producteurs, qui réalisent ensemble la production nécessaire non seulement à la satisfaction des besoins humains, mais aussi à la réalisation des désirs, individuels et collectifs. Le travail, c'est l'œuvre réalisée collectivement, et c'est la médiation majeure, le vrai moyen de communication entre des individus qui ne produisent plus de façon aliénée.

La libération du travail

La troisième caractéristique commune à ces courants de pensée est en effet leur espoir dans une transformation qui permettrait au travail de quitter le domaine de l'aliénation pour retrouver son véritable visage. Ils croient en la possibilité de surmonter l'actuelle défiguration du travail et de le libérer pour le rendre enfin conforme à son essence. A part l'intervention de chrétiens, qui, tel Henri Bartoli, se sont profondément engagés pour un changement du travail, allant jusqu'à soutenir un grand nombre des thèses marxiennes, la pensée judéo-chrétienne moderne n'a pas été plus loin que la revendication, à certaines époques, du juste salaire. Au sortir de la guerre, des propositions très concrètes furent néanmoins exposées ou soutenues par les chrétiens, parmi lesquelles la « gestion commune des entreprises et des moyens de production[27] » et le droit à la liberté du travail. Même si ces revendications relèvent plus d'individus isolés que d'une doctrine constituée, on peut dire néanmoins qu'une partie de la pensée judéo-chrétienne sur le travail vise à rendre plus humaines les conditions de travail et reprend à son compte la notion d'aliénation.

« Toute économie qui emploie le travail comme un pur outil et le détourne de ses fins pour le mettre au service d'un fétiche, l'argent ou le capital, toute économie " avare " est une économie esclavagiste. [...] Dès que le travail perd sa fonction d'hominisation et de spiritualisation et devient pure fabrication, l'aliénation de l'homme s'instaure, l'organisation se vide de son contenu " explosif " : elle devient une technique au service d'un ordre des choses[28]. » Il y a bien dans la pensée judéo-chrétienne de notre siècle une pensée de l'aliénation du travail, de sa perversion et de sa défiguration lorsqu'il est exercé pour autre chose que l'amélioration du monde et des hommes qui l'habitent. Le travail acheté et vendu comme une marchandise, le travail émietté et mutilé, le travail dans lequel le travailleur ne peut s'exprimer et qui ne sert à rien sinon à valoriser un capital, tout cela est fermement condamné[29]. Il s'agit de retrouver le véritable sens du travail, d'organiser les conditions qui permettront de le rendre conforme à son concept. La pensée humaniste reprend globalement le même schéma, ainsi évidemment que la pensée marxiste, construite sur le modèle même de l'aliénation. Mais les différents courants ont en commun de croire que la désaliénation du travail est possible, c'est-à-dire que le travail peut devenir le lieu de l'épanouissement de soi en même temps que de l'utilité sociale.

Ainsi, au moment où le chômage se développe et où il apparaît que le travail humain pourrait se raréfier, les réflexions contemporaines sur le travail renouent-elles avec les grandes pensées ou les grandes eschatologies qui ont structuré le XXᵉ siècle et organisent-elles une défense et illustration du travail pour mettre en évidence sa valeur.

La fin des sociétés fondées sur le travail ?

C'est donc une véritable mobilisation du fond théorique auquel s'alimente le XXᵉ siècle qu'opèrent aujourd'hui les auteurs dont nous avons cité les propos. Il ne s'agit de rien de moins, nous semble-t-il, que de défendre l'ordre exis- tant, celui-là même sur lequel nos sociétés modernes se sont construites. Cette situation rappelle étrangement le siècle qui inaugura l'entrée dans la modernité, c'est-à-dire le moment où, sous la menace d'un nouvel ordre — celui auquel ouvrait le système héliocentrique —, toutes

les forces traditionnelles se rassemblèrent pour faire obstacle à son émergence. Le système héliocentrique remet-
tait en cause les ordres sur lesquels était édifiée la société
d'alors : non seulement le rapport de l'homme au monde,
non seulement les Ecritures, mais aussi, plus profondément, les hiérarchies et les ordres sociaux et politiques
établis sur les anciens fondements. Lorsque le système
héliocentrique ne fut plus seulement une fable, une simple
hypothèse permettant aux savants d'élucubrer, lorsqu'il
fut clair que sa réalité allait être démontrée, alors une
partie des hommes de science et de pouvoir de l'époque
mobilisèrent leurs forces pour « sauver les phénomènes »,
c'est-à-dire pour trouver des explications aux anomalies
dont ne parvenait pas à rendre compte le système ptolé-
maïque.

Il en va de même aujourd'hui. Devant les fractures qui
s'ouvrent dans nos sociétés, des pensées s'élèvent pour
expliquer les anomalies et pour « sauver le travail ».
Pourquoi ? Par peur d'avoir à revenir sur cette notion elle-
même, par peur de devoir y renoncer. Parce que le travail
est évidemment bien plus que le moyen dont dispose
chaque individu pour gagner sa vie et la société pour
satisfaire ses besoins. Le travail n'est pas ce moyen,
existant de toute éternité, dont l'humanité souffrante a
hérité à la sortie du Paradis, ce moyen naturel qui nous
sert simplement à satisfaire nos besoins tout aussi naturels. Le travail est notre fait social total. Il structure de
part en part non seulement notre rapport au monde, mais
aussi nos rapports sociaux. Il est le rapport social fondamental. Il est de surcroît au centre de la vision du monde
qui est la nôtre depuis le XVIIe siècle. Il s'agit d'une
catégorie construite dont l'émergence a correspondu à une
situation politico-sociale particulière. Sa disparition, à
l'évidence non souhaitée, remettrait en cause les ordres
qui structurent nos sociétés : ainsi s'explique la véritable
panique qui saisit gouvernants et gouvernés devant la
montée inexorable du chômage. Car, là où il faut inventer

de nouveaux rapports sociaux, il y a toujours de la place pour l'arbitraire, et donc aussi pour la contestation, la violence et la guerre. Notre tendance immédiate va à la conservation, jusqu'au moment où cela devient vraiment insupportable...

Un certain nombre de voix, pour l'instant peu écoutées ou peu relayées, ont tenté de se faire entendre, attirant l'attention sur le fait que nous étions en train de sortir du modèle sur lequel nous vivons depuis deux siècles, celui des sociétés fondées sur le travail. Habermas annonçait ainsi, en 1985, au détour d'un paragraphe de son livre *Le Discours philosophique de la modernité*, « la fin, historiquement prévisible, de la société fondée sur le travail [30] », reprenant, en une formule lapidaire, les idées qu'il développe depuis trente ans sur l'irréductibilité du travail et de l'interaction. Claus Offe, sociologue allemand, écrivait à la même époque un long article consacré à « l'implosion de la catégorie travail [31] » dans lequel il mettait très fortement en cause la capacité du travail à structurer dans l'avenir la société : « Il n'est guère vraisemblable, écrivait-il, que le travail, la production et les revenus puissent jouer un rôle central comme éléments normatifs d'une manière de conduire sa vie et d'une intégration sociale de la personnalité. Il n'est pas non plus très vraisemblable que l'on puisse les revendiquer et les réactiver politiquement comme normes de référence. Pour ces raisons, de tels essais de revalorisation " morale et spirituelle " renouvelée de la sphère du travail ne sont apparemment plus entrepris que dans les situations de crise aiguë ». Ralf Dahrendorf, autre sociologue allemand, avait publié peu auparavant un article intitulé « La disparition de la société fondée sur le travail [32] » et quelques années plus tard, un autre, lecteur de Heidegger, publiait un livre au titre suggestif : *Quand le travail vient à manquer [33]*. Si ces réflexions se sont développées en Allemagne, elles n'ont guère été portées, en France, que par André Gorz. On dira peut-être que l'apparition de ces pensées correspondait à un moment de crise, dû au ralentissement du rythme de la croissance économique, et donc à une « panne » du modèle. Ceci n'est certainement pas faux, mais il n'est néanmoins pas anodin, comme nous le verrons plus précisément, que ces pensées se soient développées en Allemagne, pays qui a une longue tradition de réflexion sur le travail, le lien social et la politique. De surcroît, au lieu de se renvoyer à l'infini l'argument qui consiste à ne voir dans les pensées que des prurits apparaissant à chaque raté de la régulation économique, peut-être vaudrait-il mieux prendre celles-ci pour ce qu'elles sont et nous interroger sur la naissance, l'évolution et, d'une manière plus générale, la généalogie des sociétés fondées sur le travail.

Quand sont-elles apparues ? Pourquoi ? En réponse à quel contexte, à quelles questions, à quel problème et au nom de quoi ? C'est à une analyse des discours et des représentations que nous invitons le lecteur, à une analyse des discours philosophiques essentiellement, tout en sachant que le discours philosophique et la réalité sociale entretiennent des rapports complexes, les premiers précédant, accompagnant et explicitant tout à la fois la seconde, sans qu'il soit question — telle est notre position — d'une totale détermination « en dernière instance » du discours philosophique par la réalité sociale ou de celle-ci par le poids des idées. Les discours et les théories économiques et politiques seront également analysés non pas en tant que discours scientifiques mais en tant que représentations, à travers lesquelles la société a exprimé ce qu'il en était pour elle du travail.

L'énigme que nous cherchons à résoudre — et dont la résolution structurera l'essentiel de notre propos — est donc la suivante : comment en sommes-nous venus à considérer le travail et la production comme le centre de notre vie individuelle et sociale ? Au terme de quel cheminement le travail a-t-il pu être interprété comme le moyen privilégié de réalisation — pour les individus — et comme le cœur du lien social — pour la société ? Si le travail n'a pas toujours existé, quelles ont été les raisons et les étapes de son « invention » ? Dans quelle mesure l'utopie propre aux sociétés fondées sur le travail permet-elle de comprendre les contradictions que recèlent aujourd'hui les pensées de légitimation du travail ?

CHAPITRE II

DES SOCIÉTÉS SANS TRAVAIL ?

Nous ne parvenons pas, aujourd'hui, à distinguer le travail lui-même des fonctions dont il est le support. Lorsque les réflexions contemporaines portent aux nues le travail parce qu'il serait le lieu par excellence de l'intégration sociale et de la réalisation de soi, elles ne font pas la différence entre des fonctions (assurer le lien social, permettre l'épanouissement ou l'expression de l'individu) et le système qui permet à ces fonctions, à un moment donné, de s'exercer. Or, cette distinction est essentielle. La faire permet d'affirmer, premièrement, que le travail n'est pas *en soi* porteur de ces fonctions ; deuxièmement, que celles-ci sont donc susceptibles d'être portées ou assurées par un autre système ; enfin (ce qui revient au même), que le travail n'a pas toujours été utilisé pour porter ces fonctions, autrement dit que sa signification à travers les époques a varié. Le travail n'est pas une catégorie anthropologique, c'est-à-dire un invariant de la nature humaine ou des civilisations qu'accompagneraient toujours les mêmes représentations. Il s'agit au contraire d'une catégorie profondément historique dont l'invention n'est devenue nécessaire qu'à une époque donnée, et qui s'est de surcroît construite par strates. Ceci signifie que les fonctions aujourd'hui remplies par le travail dans nos sociétés l'étaient, dans d'autres, par un ou des moyens différents, par un ou des systèmes différents. Trois exemples nous serviront ici à illustrer ce propos. Ils ont en commun de se situer dans la préhistoire des sociétés économiques et d'être régis, pour parler schématiquement, par des logiques à la fois sacrées et sociales, où l'organisation des sociétés est structurée autour de principes transcendants, non explicités et dont la vocation est de ne pas l'être. Dans ces exemples, on trouve bien parfois du travail au sens d'effort ou au sens d'approvisionnement, mais le travail n'assure en tout cas pas les fonctions de lien social et de réalisation de soi.

Les sociétés non industrialisées

Les sociétés primitives offrent un premier exemple de sociétés non structurées par le travail. Nous devons à la recherche ethnologique et anthropologique des lumières précieuses sur cette question. Qui n'est d'ailleurs pas très aisée à poser, ni à résoudre. Car, l'ethnologue est, comme chacun d'entre nous, enfermé dans la signification actuelle des mots, mais aussi des représentations et du découpage de la réalité qui accompagnent ceux-ci. Pour nous, le travail est une catégorie homogène, même si nous ne disposons — et n'avons besoin — d'aucune analyse approfondie et explicite de ses différentes significations. Nous le savons intuitivement et nous mettons derrière l'expression plusieurs notions : celle d'effort, celle de satisfaction des besoins, celle de production-transformation, celle d'artifice, celle d'échange, celle de rémunération. Comment s'articulent-elles, nous ne cherchons pas vraiment à le savoir. Par quels présupposés historiques et idéologiques est structurée cette constellation, nous ne le savons pas non plus.

Les travaux ethnologiques visent à nous faire pénétrer dans l'organisation même des sociétés primitives. Pour les comprendre, nous devons donc absolument nous départir

de nos propres catégories. Par exemple, la catégorie
économique n'est pas une des modalités de compréhension
et d'action du monde primitif, au moins si l'on entend par
économie la « science » des comportements rationnels
développés par l'homme cherchant à acquérir des biens
rares. Les recherches des anthropologues nous apprennent
qu'il est impossible de trouver une signification identique
au terme de travail employé par les différentes sociétés
étudiées. Certaines d'entre elles n'ont pas même de mot
distinct pour distinguer les activités productives des autres
comportements humains et ne disposent d'aucun terme ou
notion qui synthétiserait l'idée de travail en général,
« c'est-à-dire l'idée d'un ensemble cohérent d'opérations
techniques visant à produire tous les moyens matériels de
leur existence. La langue ne comporte pas non plus de
termes désignant les procès de travail au sens large, comme
la pêche, l'horticulture ou l'artisanat, et nous nous trouvons d'emblée confrontés au phénomène de l'intelligibilité
de catégories indigènes qui découpent tout autrement que
nous les procès de travail [...] Le lexème indigène dont le
champ sémantique est le plus proche d'un des usages
contemporains du mot travail est le mot *takat* [...] qui
désigne une activité physique pénible, mobilisant un savoir-
faire technique et la médiation d'un outil [34] ». Dans d'autres sociétés, où le terme est présent, il ne recouvre pas ce
que signifie notre terme moderne, mais soit le déborde, soit
rassemble d'une autre manière que nous certains éléments
appartenant à notre conception. Ainsi, dans une tribu
d'Amazonie, le terme est-il employé pour l'activité de
pensée du chaman. Des sociétés ont ainsi une conception
très extensive du travail, d'autres au contraire ne désignent
par ce terme que les activités non productives. En
revanche, on trouve des mots pour évoquer la peine et la
souffrance. Mais celles-ci ne sont pas liées à un certain type
d'activité, par exemple celles visant à satisfaire les besoins.
Ces dernières présentent d'ailleurs des différences incommensurables avec notre « travail ».

En premier lieu, le temps consacré à l'approvisionnement ou aux activités de reproduction de la force physique est faible, parce que les besoins dits naturels sont limités. L'un des constats majeurs des recherches anthropologiques est que la recherche des moyens permettant la subsistance et la satisfaction des besoins ne s'inscrit pas dans un processus indéfini tendant à une abondance jamais atteinte, mais n'occupe au contraire qu'une petite partie du temps et des intérêts des peuples considérés. Marshall Sahlins[35], l'un des premiers, a montré qu'il fallait en finir avec l'image d'une humanité primitive écrasée par la tâche de satisfaction des besoins physiques et naturels. Au contraire, la place qu'occupe cette recherche est strictement circonscrite, et les besoins y sont satisfaits en peu de temps et avec un minimum d'efforts[36]. L'idée de besoins illimités est inexistante. C'est pour cette raison que Sahlins parle de sociétés d'abondance, au sens où ces peuples maîtrisent leur rapport avec la nature parce que leur conception des besoins, et sans doute de la vie, les y pousse. Que ces sociétés parviennent à satisfaire un nombre de besoins donnés dans un temps donné et sans y employer la totalité de leur énergie signifie que rien ne les contraint à produire plus qu'elles n'en ont besoin. Les activités de subsistance sont traversées par d'autres logiques que la satisfaction des besoins, et cette recherche n'occupe pas le tout de la vie. Les chasseurs-cueilleurs ne consacrent ainsi que deux à quatre heures par jour à cette activité.

En second lieu, l'activité de production en vue de la subsistance n'est presque jamais exercée à titre individuel et pour des motivations purement individuelles : « Un seul cas bien choisi suffirait pour démontrer à quel point est absurde l'idée d'un homme, et spécialement d'un homme de culture peu développée, qui serait mû par des motifs purement économiques d'intérêt personnel bien compris[37]. » Le mobile du profit personnel n'est pas naturel à l'homme primitif et le gain ne joue jamais le rôle de stimulant du travail. L'homme n'assume pas non plus seul les activités de subsistance et le résultat ne lui est jamais personnellement destiné : « Ce qui importe, c'est que tous ou presque tous les fruits de son travail, et à coup sûr le surplus qu'il peut obtenir par un effort supplémentaire ne va pas à l'individu qui s'est donné de la peine, mais à ses parents par alliance... Les trois quarts de la récolte d'un homme vont pour une part au chef, à titre de tribut, et pour l'autre part au mari et à la famille de sa sœur (ou de sa mère) par obligation [38]. » La distribution des biens matériels est régie par des mobiles non économiques et le travail est bien plutôt traité comme une obligation qui n'exige pas d'être indemnisée, mais fait partie des contraintes sociales. Mais, en même temps, le travail n'est pas organisé socialement, par l'ensemble de la société pour l'ensemble de la société.

Par ailleurs, si des efforts sont bien déployés, ils ne concernent pas les activités liées à la subsistance, mais bien plutôt des activités sociales situées à mi-chemin entre l'effort et le jeu : « Le Trobriandais travaille guidé par des mobiles fort complexes, où interviennent la société et la tradition ; ses objectifs réels n'ont absolument rien à voir avec la satisfaction des besoins présents ou la réalisation immédiate de projets utilitaires. C'est ainsi que le travail ne se base pas sur la loi du moindre effort. Bien au contraire, beaucoup de temps et d'énergie est consacré à des tâches tout à fait superflues. En outre, le labeur, au lieu de représenter un moyen en vue d'une fin, est en un sens une fin en soi [39]. »

Le travail, s'il n'est pas accompli en vue du gain individuel, ne l'est pas non plus en vue de l'échange. Car l'échange n'est pas de nature économique ; il ne vise pas à obtenir un exact équivalent, il recouvre d'autres logiques, plus directement sociales : « Comme le travail, l'échange, dans les sociétés tribales, obéit aux " rapports sociaux directs d'ordre général ". Il est souvent suscité comme expression de ces rapports et toujours contraint par les liens de parenté et de communauté qui existent entre les parties concernées. La majeure partie des échanges, dans les sociétés tribales, ressemble à ce qui est chez nous leur aspect mineur, appartenant à la même classe que l'échange de cadeaux entre des gens socialement intimes ou que l'hospitalité que nous leur manifestons. Contaminés qu'ils sont par des considérations sociales, ces gestes de réciprocité sont conçus par nous comme non économiques, qualitativement différents du mouvement de l'échange véritable et confinés à un monde où celui qui estime habile de faire de bonnes affaires en envoyant au diable ces considérations est cordialement invité à aller au diable lui-même. Mais dans les tribus, de la même façon que le travail n'existe pas en tant qu'activité spécifique et indépendante des autres fonctions sociales du travailleur, l'échange n'existe pas en dehors des rapports non économiques [40]. »

Trois caractéristiques de cette activité apparaissent donc : d'abord elle est exercée pour le regard des autres, elle est une forme de compétition ludique, de jeu social [41]. Le travail vise d'abord à la parade. Il sert à être vu et à entrer en compétition avec les autres. Ensuite, la satisfaction des besoins pas plus que le souci d'accumulation ne sont primordiaux : le Trobriandais de Malinowski accorde le plus grand soin à l'esthétique et à la bonne disposition générale du lopin de terre ; l'effort n'est pas synonyme de pénibilité. De plus, il produit souvent beaucoup plus que le nécessaire, apportant un immense soin à ce travail, mais sans perspective de thésaurisation : le fruit de cet effort peut être gaspillé en quelques minutes. Enfin, le travail est traversé par des logiques sacrées et sociales : selon les Trobriandais, le magicien des jardins contrôle le labeur des hommes et les forces de la nature. La magie exerce un rôle coordonnateur, régulateur et directeur sur les travaux des champs, un peu à l'image des rites agricoles chez Hésiode, dont la logique est avant tout religieuse et sacrée. « Le Trobriandais n'est pas essentiellement mû par le désir de pourvoir à ses besoins, mais il obéit à un système très

complexe de forces traditionnelles, d'obligations et de
devoirs, de croyances magiques, d'ambitions et de vanités
sociales [42]. »

Tout ceci est parfaitement explicable puisque, nous dira-
t-on, il s'agit d'économies domestiques qui n'ont pas besoin
de l'échange économique et ont adapté leurs besoins à cette
situation. Certes, mais ce qui nous intéresse ici, c'est que,
dans un contexte radicalement différent du nôtre, c'est-à-
dire où les besoins naturels sont limités, où l'individu n'a
pas encore fait irruption en tant que tel, où les échanges
économiques ne sont pas développés, la notion de travail
n'existe pas. C'est dire que l'on ne peut trouver, ni entre
ces sociétés elles-mêmes, ni entre ces sociétés et les nôtres,
le moindre dénominateur commun quant au sens du
travail. « Le travail n'est pas une catégorie réelle de
l'économie tribale », écrivait Marshall Sahlins. Autant dire
que ce n'est pas par le travail que se définit le statut social
ou que se noue et se conserve le lien social. Ces sociétés
sont structurées par d'autres logiques : elles ont un rapport
particulier à l'extériorité (la tradition, la nature, les
dieux...) qui détermine les règles sociales et rend celles-ci
suffisamment « fortes » pour tenir ensemble la société.
Elles n'ont pas besoin d'autres types de régulation.

Dans ce contexte, de ce mode d'activité parmi d'autres
qu'est l'action pour la subsistance ne découlent ni directive
particulière ni hiérarchie sociale. Comme l'ont montré les
études de Mauss ou de Malinowski, les faits sociaux qui
structurent ces sociétés sont d'une nature autre qu'économique. Ils sont prioritairement " sociaux " : ils font intervenir des liens de sang et de parenté, des symboles,
certaines relations avec la nature, avec la tradition, etc.
L'échange lui-même n'est pas l'échange économique que
nous connaissons et qui ne sera défini et représenté comme
tel qu'au XVIIIe siècle. Cela peut d'ailleurs paraître paradoxal, puisque l'on aurait pu penser que ces sociétés
seraient obsédées par la peur de manquer et donneraient
donc une place privilégiée à ceux qui s'occupent des

activités de subsistance. Mais il n'en est rien, justement sans doute parce que ces activités sont tellement importantes qu'elles sont réglées de l'extérieur, exercées collectivement, de façon que personne ne puisse se les approprier.

Le paradigme grec

Dans la question du rapport au travail, la Grèce constitue une référence. En effet, la société grecque, celle que nous connaissons à travers les textes philosophiques, historiques et littéraires, non seulement présente un certain nombre de caractéristiques propres aux « économies domestiques » précapitalistes, mais se distingue aussi par un ensemble de réflexions et d'institutions dont nous savons qu'elles constituent une part fondamentale de notre héritage philosophique, scientifique, culturel et politique. La question du travail a été pensée en tant que telle par les philosophes grecs, même si le terme de travail ne présente pas les mêmes significations que dans nos sociétés modernes. Par rapport aux sociétés étudiées précédemment, la société grecque possède donc l'avantage d'avoir articulé rationnellement sa position par rapport au travail ou par rapport à un certain nombre de tâches qui relèvent aujourd'hui de notre idée du travail. L'interprétation en est d'autant facilitée.

Les philosophes grecs, au-delà de leurs différences, partagent globalement la même conception du travail : il est assimilé à des tâches dégradantes et n'est nullement valorisé. L'époque grecque représente à ce titre une sorte d'idéal type des sociétés dans lesquelles le travail n'est pas glorifié, au nom du développement d'autres activités. Il ne s'agit certes pas de revenir à ce modèle, mais nous sommes persuadés qu'il faut en saisir toutes les implications pour mieux comprendre notre époque. Autrement dit, il ne suffit pas de se débarrasser du modèle grec en arguant du fait qu'il appartient à une civilisation définitivement dépas-

sée et en ajoutant au postulat d'incompréhensibilité (cette
époque serait trop différente de la nôtre pour que nous la
comprenions, nous ne pouvons que projeter nos propres
catégories sur elle) un postulat d'intransférabilité (ces
sociétés sont trop différentes des nôtres, particulièrement
du point de vue du développement économique, pour que
nous puissions le moins du monde nous en inspirer). Afin
de mesurer la pauvreté de ce dernier argument, il nous
suffira de nous rappeler que c'est en Grèce classique qu'ont
été en partie inventées la démocratie, la science, la
philosophie ou encore les mathématiques et que toute
notre histoire n'est, d'une certaine manière, qu'un long
dialogue, parfois interrompu, avec l'héritage grec, dialogue
scandé par la redécouverte d'Aristote au Moyen Age, via
les philosophes arabes, ou le « retour » à la Grèce du
XVIIIe siècle français et du XIXe siècle allemand.

Avant d'analyser la représentation que les Grecs se sont
faite du travail, il nous faut rappeler très rapidement
comment s'ordonnent le monde et les sociétés grecs, tels
qu'ils sont présentés dans les principaux textes qui vont de
l'*Iliade* d'Homère à *La Politique* d'Aristote. Le monde grec
est clos et discontinu : il est constitué d'un ensemble fixe
(les astres) et du monde sublunaire, soumis à la génération
et à la corruption, c'est-à-dire à la mobilité, à la transformation et à la mort. L'ensemble du monde soumis à la
« mortalité » tend à ressembler à ce qui est immortel, ce
qu'Aristote exprime de la façon suivante : Dieu, premier
moteur, meut par amour. Les activités humaines sont
valorisées en fonction de la plus ou moins grande ressem-
blance qu'elles peuvent avoir avec l'immobilité et l'éternité. D'où la valorisation de la pensée, de la *theoria*, de la
contemplation ou plus généralement de la science, qu'elle
soit mathématique ou philosophique, dans la mesure où
elle a pour objet des essences ou des figures immuables, qui
échappent au perpétuel mouvement. Cette activité, comme
par contagion, est la seule susceptible de nous rendre
semblables à ce qui est contemplé, et donc, d'une certaine

façon, de nous soustraire à l'action du temps. Elle est exercée par l'âme ou la raison et non par le corps. Deux autres activités sont également valorisées, particulièrement chez Aristote : l'activité éthique et l'activité politique. La première, encore appelée *praxis,* désigne les activités qui ont leur fin en elles-mêmes, d'autant plus valorisées qu'elles sont soustraites à la nécessité : elles ne visent pas à autre chose qu'elles-mêmes, ne sont pas des instruments au service d'une autre fin. La seconde permet à l'homme d'exercer son humanité, c'est-à-dire la raison et la parole et elle s'emploie à rendre toujours meilleure ce sans quoi l'homme seul n'est rien : la cité.

A ces activités fortement valorisées, parce qu'elles relèvent de la sphère de la liberté, s'opposent les activités qui nous attachent à la nécessité et qui constituent, à des degrés divers, le pôle non valorisé des activités humaines. Le travail y appartient. Trois caractéristiques majeures le définissent, à quelques variations près : le travail, compris comme notion univoque englobant les différents métiers ou les différents « producteurs », n'existe pas. Les activités qu'il recouvre sont méprisées. Enfin, le travail n'est en aucune manière au fondement du lien social.

Les travaux et les jours

On trouve en Grèce des métiers, des activités, des tâches ; on chercherait en vain *le* travail. Les activités sont au contraire classées dans des catégories irréductiblement diverses et traversées par des distinctions qui interdisent de considérer le travail comme une fonction unique. La plus importante concerne la différence entre les tâches rassemblées sous le terme de *ponos,* activités pénibles, exigeant un effort et un contact avec les éléments matériels, un contact dégradant, donc (c'est la logistique ou l'intendance), et celles qui sont identifiées comme *ergon* (« œuvre »), dont la caractéristique est de pouvoir être imputées à quelqu'un et qui consistent dans l'application d'une forme à une matière (le potier façonne par exemple une coupe en mettant en forme une matière donnée). Traversant cette première distinction, on trouve également une série d'activités bien séparées : les activités agricoles, dont la logique est encore proche des pratiques religieuses et qui constitue un mode de vie à part entière, une série de métiers manuels exercés par le cordonnier, le charpentier, etc., et les activités serviles. Chacune a son domaine et sa logique propre, et le plus souvent aussi, sa « classe-support » : les agriculteurs, les artisans et les esclaves. Dans la Grèce archaïque, connue à travers les textes d'Homère ou d'Hésiode, la hiérarchie des activités s'ordonne selon le plus ou moins grand degré de dépendance par rapport aux autres qu'elles impliquent : en bas de l'échelle, on trouve l'activité de l'esclave et du thète (le mercenaire qui loue ses bras à un propriétaire pour un temps déterminé et qui peut être utilisé pour toutes les tâches, à la différence de l'artisan qui maîtrise un savoir spécialisé). Dans l'*Odyssée*, l'ombre d'Achille déclare à Ulysse que la vie d'un simple thète chez le plus indigent laboureur lui paraîtrait préférable à la royauté chez les morts, pour signifier qu'il préférerait à la mort même l'état le plus bas de la vie sociale. Viennent ensuite les démiurges, ou encore artisans. Certes, ceux-ci maîtrisent une « technique » mais ils sont également frappés de dégradation sociale, car ils travaillent pour le *demos*, le peuple, et sont donc redevables à autrui de leurs moyens d'existence. Artisans et mendiants appartiennent à la même catégorie : celle où l'on ne vit que de la commande et de la rétribution d'autrui. Les activités commerciales sont également condamnées : elles révèlent une avidité indigne de l'homme. Seules les activités agricoles échappent à la condamnation, car seules elles permettent d'échapper à la dépendance d'autrui. Ainsi les activités laborieuses ne sont-elles pas méprisées en elles-mêmes, mais surtout en raison de la servitude par rapport à autrui qu'elles entraînent. Hésiode ne méprise pas le travail, il le considère comme nécessaire depuis que les hommes ont perdu l'âge d'or, mais si le travail est obligatoire pour pourvoir aux besoins de la vie, il doit s'opérer dans des conditions qui permettront de sauvegarder l'indépendance, c'est-à-dire la liberté et la dignité.

Le travail méprisé

La Grèce classique ne s'arrête pas là dans le mépris porté aux activités de travail. A travers les textes de Platon et d'Aristote, on voit se mettre en place un idéal de vie individuelle et collective d'où le travail est exclu ou presque. La structure sociale grecque elle-même en est la preuve : l'ensemble des tâches directement liées à la reproduction matérielle est en effet entièrement pris en charge par des esclaves, et sa théorisation repose sur l'opposition loisir/travail. Toute la philosophie grecque est en effet fondée sur l'idée que la vraie liberté, c'est-à-dire ce qui permet à l'homme d'agir selon ce qu'il y a de plus humain en lui, le logos, commence au-delà de la nécessité, une fois que les besoins matériels ont été satisfaits. Sans nourriture, sans vêtements, sans confort, pas de philosophie, certes ; mais dans la simple activité de satisfaction des besoins, de philosophie — donc de sagesse, de vie conforme à la raison — point. C'est ce qu'indique Aristote dès l'ouverture de la *Métaphysique* : « Presque toutes les nécessités de la vie et les choses qui intéressent son bien-être et son agrément avaient reçu satisfaction quand on commença à rechercher une discipline de ce genre[43]. » Cette discipline, qui n'est autre que la philosophie, est la seule des sciences qui soit une discipline libérale, puisque nous ne la recherchons pas pour autre chose qu'elle même, « aussi est-ce encore à bon droit qu'on peut estimer plus qu'humaine sa possession ».

A l'opposé de la sphère de la liberté, qui nous rapproche du divin, se déploie la sphère de la nécessité, qui est celle du travail, et en premier lieu du *ponos*, du travail pénible, des tâches dégradantes, par essence serviles. Chez Platon[44], l'ensemble des activités manuelles est regroupé sous ce terme et est exercé par la « troisième classe », laboureurs et autres artisans, à laquelle correspond, dans la tripartition de l'âme platonicienne, l'appétit sensuel, celui qui pourvoit aux besoins élémentaires de nutrition, de conservation et de reproduction. Chez Aristote, ces activités sont exercées par les esclaves. Plusieurs textes fameux et intensément commentés par la suite louent l'esclavage[45], dont l'existence est la seule condition permettant aux citoyens grecs d'exercer leur humanité. L'esclave est destiné à la satisfaction des besoins indispensables, il est semblable aux animaux domestiques car il partage la même fonction : l'aide physique en vue des tâches indispensables. L'esclave est un instrument animé, il appartient à un autre. Il n'est pas homme. Au-delà du scandale qu'ils ont provoqué plus tard dans la bonne conscience européenne, il faut bien comprendre le sens de ces textes : les tâches de pure reproduction matérielle de la vie sont par essence serviles parce qu'elles nous enchaînent à la nécessité ; si nous voulons développer ce qu'il y a de plus humain en nous, nous rapprocher du divin, nous devons nous écarter de ces tâches et les abandonner à l'esclave, qui n'est justement pas un homme. Etre vraiment humain sera tout autre chose : faire de la philosophie, contempler le beau, pratiquer l'activité politique, dans tous les cas utiliser sa raison, car l'homme est un être raisonnable. Il y a dans la philosophie grecque un intense effort pour rejeter au loin l'animalité de l'homme et cultiver ce que la Grèce vient de découvrir : la raison.

Travail et citoyenneté

Si le *ponos* est condamné, qu'en est-il des activités des artisans pour lesquels Platon, par exemple, semble éprouver une certaine sollicitude ? Leur activité, parfois désignée par le terme d'*ergon*, n'est pourtant guère plus valorisée.

Certes, ils possèdent une certaine *technê* et on peut trouver chez eux une certaine vertu ou perfection, celle qui consiste à très bien faire ce qu'on leur demande de faire (un objet parfaitement adapté à l'usage pour lequel il est attendu), mais ils n'échappent pas à la condamnation : « On doit considérer comme propre à l'artisan, écrit Aristote, toute tâche, tout art, toute connaissance qui aboutissent à rendre impropres à l'usage et à la pratique de la vertu le corps, l'âme ou l'intelligence des hommes libres. C'est pourquoi les arts de ce genre, qui affligent le corps d'une disposition plus mauvaise, nous les disons dignes des artisans et nous le disons de même des activités salariées. Car ils rendent la pensée besogneuse et abjecte [46]. » Là encore, et contrairement à ce que pourrait laisser penser ce texte dans un premier temps, le problème n'est pas tant le caractère manuel des activités exercées, mais le fait qu'elles sont réalisées en vue d'autre chose (gagner de l'argent, par exemple) et non pour elles-mêmes. Car l'artisan réalise des chaussures ou des meubles pour vivre, et non pour son plaisir.

Ajoutons encore que l'artisan n'est jamais considéré, chez les Grecs, comme un producteur qui arracherait à la nature un nouvel objet, exerçant par là même un pouvoir transformateur. Rien de tel chez les Grecs, d'abord parce que leur conception de la nature ne le permet pas (la nature n'est pas un vaste champ à transformer en valeurs et en objets susceptibles de satisfaire les besoins humains), ensuite parce que l'artisan n'est pas perçu comme un créateur, mais comme un imitateur. Il imite la forme qu'il a dans l'esprit pour l'imposer à la matière. Il est d'autant moins considéré comme un producteur d'objets ou de valeurs que son rôle se limite strictement à fabriquer un objet bien adapté à l'usage qui en est attendu et que les besoins sont limités. Son excellence particulière consiste donc à satisfaire du mieux possible un certain nombre de besoins limités, le tout dans une relation qui est essentiellement de service.

Cette faible considération accordée aux artisans va de pair avec une exclusion politique totale. Plusieurs chapitres de *La Politique*[47] sont consacrés à la question de savoir si l'artisan peut ou non être citoyen. La réponse d'Aristote, même si on la sent gênée — l'artisan est tout de même un homme —, n'en est pas moins ferme. L'artisan ne peut pas, ne doit pas être citoyen et si, par malheur, il arrivait qu'une cité mette au nombre des citoyens les artisans, il faudrait, écrit Aristote, ne pas considérer tous les citoyens de la même manière. Il s'en explique : le citoyen est d'abord un homme libre ; or, est véritablement libre l'homme qui s'affranchit des tâches indispensables, qui n'est pas soumis à la nécessité. On ne peut pas participer à la gestion de la cité, à la définition de son bien-vivre si l'on demeure soumis à la nécessité. Dans cette mesure, l'esclave et l'artisan ne sont pas très différents, ajoute Aristote : ce que l'esclave fait pour un seul individu, l'artisan le fait pour l'ensemble de la communauté. Mais l'un et l'autre s'occupent de la reproduction de la vie matérielle, et le font poussés par le besoin ou la nécessité. Ce texte, beaucoup moins commenté que ne l'ont été ceux qui sont consacrés à l'esclavage, est pourtant sans doute plus important pour notre propos parce qu'il permet une meilleure compréhension du lien qui peut exister, en Grèce, entre ce que l'on appellera un jour les activités économiques et la politique, autrement dit de la nature du lien social. Le lien social ou politique n'a aucun rapport, ou plutôt est en rapport inverse avec la dépendance économique et sociale qui peut exister entre les individus d'une même société : telle est la signification principale de ce texte.

Certes, Platon reconnaît que la société est née parce que les hommes avaient besoin les uns des autres, et donc que le besoin, l'échange et une certaine division du travail y ont eu leur part. Mais cela ne suffit pas à faire une société, comme l'exprime le mythe de Prométhée dans le *Protagoras*[48] : les hommes ayant été oubliés dans la distribution des capacités, Prométhée court voler chez les dieux les arts et les techniques et distribue à chacun une capacité différente. Ce geste aurait dû fonder l'échange, et donc être à l'origine du rassemblement des hommes en société. Or, justement, il ne suffit pas. Pour atteindre la cité politique, il faudra qu'Hermès parte en quête des capacités proprement politiques, puis les distribue à chacun. Mais comment doivent-elles être réparties entre les hommes ? demande Hermès à Zeus ; d'une manière inégale, comme les techniques, ou bien de sorte que chacun ait exactement les mêmes ? Il faut les partager également entre tous, répond Zeus, car « les villes ne sauraient exister si ces vertus étaient, comme les arts, le partage exclusif de quelques-uns[49] ». C'est alors seulement que la société politique sera possible. Aristote ne dit pas autre chose dans le texte consacré aux artisans : le lien politique est d'une nature radicalement différente du lien « matériel », qui oblige les hommes à s'utiliser les uns les autres pour subsister. Dans ce dernier cas, chaque homme est doté de capacités différentes et le métier définit en chacun de nous ce qui le distingue des autres. Au contraire, le lien politique est fondé sur l'égalité et l'identité, ou encore sur la *philia*, que l'on traduit souvent par amitié. Le lien politique unit des égaux et presque des amis. Le lien matériel oblige des individus dotés de capacités différentes à s'insérer dans des relations de service et de dépendance qui sont aux antipodes du lien politique.

Travail, loisir, politique

Comme on le voit, la place du travail dans la société grecque s'appuie en dernier ressort sur une idée — on dirait aujourd'hui une conception — de l'homme qui lui donne tout son sens : l'homme est un animal rationnel et sa tâche est de développer cette raison qui le fait homme et qui le rend semblable aux dieux. Exercer sa raison, c'est dans l'ordre théorique, faire de la philosophie ou des sciences, dans l'ordre pratique, agir selon la vertu, et dans l'ordre politique, être un excellent citoyen. C'est dans tous les cas utiliser de manière excellente nos facultés, et cela ne peut se faire qu'en étant libre, c'est-à-dire en développant des activités qui ont leur fin en elles-mêmes et non en dehors d'elles-mêmes. La vraie vie est la vie de loisir, et devenir apte à mener une telle vie est le but de l'éducation. Il n'y a dans une telle philosophie ni ascétisme [50] ni paresse, car le loisir grec n'a évidemment rien à voir avec ce que nous entendons par ce terme aujourd'hui. (« Ce n'est certainement pas jouer, car alors le jeu serait nécessairement pour nous la fin de la vie. ») L'une des plus hautes activité pratiques consiste à faire de la politique, c'est-à-dire à définir ensemble les objectifs de la vie en société et à utiliser à cette fin nos plus éminentes facultés, la raison et la parole. Il y a chez Aristote un plaisir à être ensemble, à jouir d'être en société qui conditionne aussi le bonheur individuel, et donc une articulation entre l'homme et la cité qui constituera pour un certain nombre de philosophes des siècles suivants une source très féconde de méditation. La sagesse grecque s'appuie sur un sens de la mesure et de la limitation qui permet de comprendre, en un sens, la différence avec nos sociétés. La sphère de la consommation et des besoins matériels a une place limitée parce que, pour les Grecs, les besoins sont limités : non pas qu'ils méprisent les besoins et leur légitime satisfaction, bien au contraire ; mais on trouve chez eux, profondément ancrée, l'idée que le bonheur ne vient pas de la satisfaction d'une série illimitée de besoins. Le bonheur individuel et collectif passe par la mesure et le fait que chaque chose soit à sa place.

C'est sans doute ce qui permet de répondre à un certain nombre d'objections qui sont souvent faites aux auteurs qui continuent de présenter la Grèce comme un modèle. Celles-ci consistent essentiellement à affirmer que le mode de vie grec n'est possible qu'au prix de l'esclavage et seulement dans le cadre de petites cités, mais aussi que les textes qui nous ont été transmis ont été écrits par une élite réactionnaire qui se serait attachée à dévaloriser les activités qui commençaient justement à émerger et à menacer la suprématie et le pouvoir des « intellectuels » et hommes de lettres, en l'occurrence les activités commerciales. Mais nous savons que les Grecs ont eu à leur portée un certain nombre d'inventions, qu'ils auraient pu développer mais auxquelles ils n'ont pas consacré d'efforts[51]. Pourquoi ne pas l'avoir fait? Certes, parce que la main-d'œuvre servile, gratuite, était abondante, mais surtout parce que les philosophes et les savants, reflétant l'esprit de l'époque, ne voyaient pas la nécessité de produire plus : produire en plus grande quantité aurait signifié produire en vue de la vente, conception étrangère à l'idéal de vie de l'époque. Il semble bien que c'est la valorisation diversifiée des activités, et en l'occurrence la dévalorisation du travail, qui a constitué la cause principale du blocage technologique dont on parle parfois à propos de la Grèce. Comme si les Grecs avaient réussi à comprendre le lien qui existe entre illimitation des besoins et écrasement de l'humanité sous le travail, et qu'ils avaient réussi à imprimer de la mesure aux premiers pour éviter le second[52].

Dieu travaille-t-il ?

Tout au long de la domination de l'Empire romain, et même jusqu'à la fin du Moyen Age, la représentation du travail ne connaît pas de bouleversement majeur. L'Empire romain n'accorde en effet aucune place particulière au travail, et persiste au contraire, sur le modèle grec, à le mépriser. Ce sont toujours les esclaves qui prennent en charge la majeure partie des travaux dégradants et pénibles et la classification des activités, telle qu'on la trouve exposée par exemple chez Cicéron, se fait autour de l'opposition libéral/servile, les activités serviles étant celles qui sont effectuées sous la dépendance d'un autre, et les activités libérales, exercées pour elles-mêmes, étant au

contraire le fait des hommes libres. La classification
médiévale des arts reprendra ces distinctions, en isolant les
sciences, qui relèvent à la fois du domaine du contemplatif
et du libéral, les arts libéraux, à la fois opératoires et
libéraux, et les arts et métiers, dans le double domaine de
l'opératoire et du servile. Comme chez les Grecs, l'opposition essentielle passe chez les Romains entre *labor* et
otium, le loisir. L'*otium* est le contraire du travail mais il ne
consiste pas en repos ou en jeu ; il est l'activité première.
Le *negotium*, le non-loisir, s'y oppose. D'où la condamnation de ceux qui sont payés pour travailler : « On regarde
comme ignobles et méprisables les gains des mercenaires et
de tous ceux dont ce sont les travaux et non les talents qui
sont payés. Car, pour ceux-là, leur salaire est le prix d'une
servitude[53]. » Et aussi celle des commerçants, qui se
« spécialisent » dans les affaires et le *negotium*. De surcroît, comme on l'a vu pour la Grèce, la nécessité sociale
d'inventions qui permettraient de rendre plus faciles les
travaux humains ne se fait pas sentir. Marc Bloch a ainsi
montré que le moulin à eau était à disposition du monde
gréco-romain dès le début de l'ère chrétienne, mais qu'il
n'a pas été utilisé massivement. Certes, ceci s'explique, au
même titre que pour la Grèce, par l'existence d'une main-
d'œuvre servile nombreuse, ainsi que par la volonté de
conserver l'organisation sociale en l'état : Vespasien aurait
répondu à un inventeur qui lui présentait une machine
permettant de monter des pierres au Capitole : « Laissez-
moi nourrir le petit peuple[54]. » Mais surtout, la nécessité
sociale des inventions ne se fait pas sentir. Ainsi, tout au
long de l'Empire romain, et en réalité jusqu'à la fin du
Moyen Age, dans les sociétés occidentales, le travail n'est
pas au cœur des rapports sociaux. On dira que la division
de la société en deux parties, l'une soumise à la nécessité de
travailler et l'autre vivant du travail des premiers, prouve le
contraire. Cela est exact. Mais le travail ne structure pas la
société au sens où il ne détermine pas l'ordre social[55]. Au
contraire, celui-ci est déterminé par d'autres logiques (le

sang, le rang...), qui permettent ensuite à certains de vivre du travail des autres. De ce fait, le travail n'est pas au centre des représentations que la société se fait d'elle-même ; il n'est pas valorisé, précisément parce qu'il n'est pas encore considéré comme le moyen de renverser les barrières sociales et d'inverser les positions acquises par la naissance.

Le travail entre malédiction et œuvre

Cependant, c'est au cœur de l'Empire romain que se développe et se diffuse le christianisme avec sa nouvelle image de l'homme. On a coutume de dire que le Nouveau Testament a entraîné une valorisation de l'idée de travail, en particulier sous l'influence paulinienne. Il serait plus exact de dire que le christianisme contenait en germe les éléments nécessaires à cette valorisation, qui ne pourront néanmoins pas s'épanouir avant la fin du Moyen Age. La pensée chrétienne issue tout ensemble de l'Ancien et du Nouveau Testament s'inscrit en effet, d'une certaine manière, dans le cadre hérité de la pensée grecque : supériorité de l'esprit sur le corps, vocation en dernier lieu céleste des hommes, sous la forme de l'immortalité, forte opposition du temps de l'ici-bas et de l'éternité qui est celle de Dieu. Voilà pourquoi le travail ne sera pas plus valorisé dans les débuts de l'ère chrétienne que dans l'Antiquité : l'homme doit avant tout se consacrer à Dieu et son passage sur cette terre doit en priorité lui servir à assurer son salut, essentiellement par la foi et la prière. C'est pourquoi le texte de la Genèse doit être compris strictement : le travail est bien une malédiction, une punition. A la suite du péché d'Adam, la condamnation divine est ainsi formulée : « Le sol sera maudit à cause de toi. C'est à force de peine que tu en tireras ta nourriture tous les jours de ta vie, il te produira des épines et des ronces et tu mangeras de l'herbe des champs. C'est à la sueur de ton visage que tu mangeras du pain, jusqu'à ce que tu retournes dans la terre, d'où tu as été pris ; car tu es poussière et tu retourneras à la poussière[56]. » Et l'on ne peut tirer argument du « repos » divin du septième jour pour en conclure que Dieu a travaillé et donc pour soutenir que la doctrine chrétienne, dès la Genèse, a véhiculé une très forte valorisation de l'idée de travail. Certes, la plupart des traductions mettent en évidence la dimension d'œuvre de l'acte divin et laissent à penser que la création est un travail divin, Dieu travaillant six jours durant, s'arrachant de soi-même de quoi produire le monde, dans un effort créatif qui doit dès lors constituer le modèle de référence pour l'homme : « Dieu acheva au septième jour son œuvre, qu'il avait faite : et il se reposa au septième jour de toute son œuvre, qu'il avait faite[57]. » Mais la Genèse n'a pas été interprétée ainsi pendant les premiers siècles de l'ère chrétienne. Les termes mêmes de la Bible montrent d'ailleurs bien que Dieu n'agit pas lui-même, mais ordonne aux choses de se mettre en place, selon la structure : « Dieu dit... et cela fut ainsi. » L'acte divin passe tout entier par la parole. La compréhension de cet acte en termes de travail est le résultat de plusieurs siècles de réinterprétations. De plus, on ne peut pas plus tirer argument de la fameuse phrase paulinienne — « si quelqu'un ne veut pas travailler, qu'il ne mange pas non plus[58] » — pour soutenir l'idée d'une reconnaissance, voire d'une valorisation du travail par le Nouveau Testament. L'exhortation de Paul s'inscrivait en effet dans la lutte contre les éventuels désordres issus de la paresse et dans une optique de définition des bonnes normes de vie en société, comme l'indique la suite du texte : « Nous apprenons, cependant, qu'il y en a parmi vous quelques-uns qui vivent dans le désordre, qui ne travaillent pas, mais s'occupent de futilités. Nous invitons ces gens-là, et nous les exhortons, par le Seigneur Jésus-Christ, à manger leur propre pain, en travaillant paisiblement[59]. »

En revanche, le Moyen Age va être le théâtre d'une lente conversion des esprits et des pratiques. Peu à peu, sous la pression des redécouvertes des textes grecs, des interprétations arabes, mais aussi de la nécessité de définir des normes de vie — en particulier monacales — les Pères de l'Eglise et les théoriciens vont promouvoir une nouvelle idée du travail. C'est seulement à la fin du Moyen Age que théorie et pratiques auront changé au point de permettre l'éclosion d'une modernité centrée sur le travail.

La démarche augustinienne est un bon exemple de cette interaction entre les nécessités de la vie pratique et le remaniement en profondeur de la théorie. C'est dans le même temps que saint Augustin expose, durant les premiers siècles de la chrétienté, sa conception du travail monastique et son interprétation de la création divine. On voit ainsi s'entremêler, dans les textes eux-mêmes, les deux actes, divin et humain, le pauvre travail monastique et l'œuvre divine. S'adressant aux moines du monastère de Carthage qui s'adonnent exclusivement à un apostolat spirituel et vivent de la charité publique, saint Augustin expose sa propre conception du travail pour y exhorter les moines. Il oppose radicalement d'un côté l'*otium,* qui est devenu synonyme de paresse, et de l'autre le travail, pour lequel il utilise indifféremment les termes de *labor* et d'*opus,* alors même que les Romains conservaient entre ces deux mots une différence essentielle. Les deux notions d'œuvre et de travail commencent donc à se confondre, alors que le loisir se voit soudainement condamné. Par ailleurs, saint Augustin emploie le même terme pour désigner le travail humain et l'activité de Dieu — *opus Dei* —, l'œuvre par excellence, dont les hommes devront s'inspirer. L'emploi du même mot pour désigner les deux actes humain et divin, s'il n'invite qu'à penser l'analogie — car ce n'est que de façon métaphorique que l'on peut dire de Dieu et de l'homme qu'ils font la même chose —, marque néanmoins une phase capitale : la Création de la Genèse commence à être réinterprétée dans le sens d'une œuvre divine.

Que l'acte divin puisse être interprété comme une œuvre, certes nullement semblable à l'œuvre humaine, mais néanmoins comme son modèle lointain, comporte d'innombrables conséquences. Deux nous importent particulièrement. La première est que cette interprétation constitue le premier pas vers la compréhension du monde non seulement comme œuvre-résultat de l'acte divin, mais surtout comme processus en train de s'accomplir, comme travail-histoire de l'Esprit, qui s'épanouira au XIXe siècle avec l'idéalisme allemand et qui sera la mise en philosophie de cette unique idée : Dieu travaille. La seconde est que, dans l'autre sens, la Création divine est réinterprétée par saint Augustin à l'aide d'un schéma techniciste. Comme si la relecture des textes grecs à cette époque avait eu pour conséquence d'enfermer l'idée chrétienne absolument nouvelle de création dans le vieux schéma démiurgique grec, c'est-à-dire dans le plus « humain », le plus proche de l'activité humaine et, qui plus est, de l'activité de l'artisan... Les Grecs ne disposaient pas de l'idée de création *ex nihilo* : la figure qu'ils utilisent souvent — chez Platon, en particulier — est celle du Démiurge, figure mi-mythique mi-divine à laquelle la philosophie recourt souvent pour expliquer pourquoi une réalité peut présenter telle ou telle caractéristique : le Démiurge, chez Platon, crée par exemple le monde en ayant les yeux fixés sur un Modèle. La création n'est chez les Grecs qu'une imitation. C'est pourtant à cette activité d'imitation — désormais sans modèle — que la pensée chrétienne va se référer pour décrire la Création divine. Dieu est alors compris comme le grand artisan qui impose une forme à une matière [60]. Est-ce l'acte divin qui est pensé sur le modèle du travail humain, parce que celui-ci est en train de devenir une catégorie particulière de la réalité ? Est-ce au contraire la réinterprétation des textes qui entraîne un intérêt nouveau pour les tâches quotidiennes des hommes ? Quoi qu'il en soit, le vocabulaire fait désormais le pont entre les deux sujets, si différents, d'un acte qui doit bien, au-delà des différences, avoir une même nature. Mais nous n'en sommes pas encore là. A l'époque d'Augustin, que les moines s'adonnent au travail ne va pas de soi.

Quels sont donc les arguments de l'évêque d'Hippone en
faveur du travail ? D'abord, l'argument d'autorité : Paul l'a
dit et a lui-même donné l'exemple en s'adonnant au travail
manuel [61]. Ensuite, c'est une loi de la nature que l'on se
procure par le travail personnel et collectif ce dont on a
besoin pour vivre. Enfin, le travail est une forme de la
charité, puisqu'il permet de venir en aide aux pauvres.
Néanmoins, tous les types de travaux ne sont pas bons.
Saint Augustin distingue [62] les métiers infâmes (voleur,
cocher, gladiateur, comédien), les métiers peu honorables,
qui sont essentiellement les métiers de négociants, et enfin
les métiers que ne réprouve pas l'*honestas*, qui recouvrent
deux catégories principales de travailleurs : les paysans et
les artisans. Ces métiers laissent l'âme libre, car ils ne
visent pas à l'obtention d'un gain et permettent donc à ceux
qui l'exercent de continuer à se consacrer à la tâche
essentielle, la contemplation. Le travail des mains permet
d'avoir l'esprit tout occupé de Dieu. Malgré tout, à côté du
travail manuel, le travail intellectuel, lire et écrire,
demeure le plus important. Les règles suivantes, celles de
saint Benoît par exemple, accorderont une place moindre
au travail intellectuel ; en revanche, le travail manuel sera
l'objet d'une attention toute particulière, parce qu'il apparaît comme le meilleur remède contre l'oisiveté : « La
paresse est l'ennemie de l'âme, et c'est pourquoi il faut qu'à
certaines heures les frères soient occupés au travail manuel,
il faut qu'à d'autres ils soient occupés à la méditation des
choses de Dieu [63]. »

Le travail, contribution à la vie de la communauté en
tant qu'elle doit subvenir à ses besoins, apparaît donc
comme une loi naturelle à laquelle personne ne peut
déroger ; il est considéré pour les moines, et a fortiori pour
les autres, comme l'instrument privilégié de lutte contre
l'oisiveté et la paresse, voire les mauvaises tentations,
toutes choses qui détournent de la tâche principale que sont
la contemplation et la prière. Le travail aide l'âme à se
concentrer sur l'essentiel, il occupe le corps en libérant

l'esprit. Mais il ne s'agit là en aucune façon d'une valorisation du travail : celui-ci sera souvent loué précisément pour
son caractère pénible, il prendra alors le visage de la
pénitence. De plus, les tâches principales du moine demeurent la méditation, la contemplation et la prière, le travail
n'étant qu'un adjuvant. Et, surtout, tout type de travail
n'est pas bon : si le travail manuel et intellectuel, effectué
en communauté, est recommandé, tout ce qui touche à des
activités exercées pour le gain, le commerce, etc., est
farouchement critiqué. Cependant, le terme utilisé pour
désigner le travail intellectuel des moines, *opus*, est désormais le même que celui qui désigne l'œuvre de Dieu. Une
correspondance, certes non univoque, se met en place, qui
peut laisser à penser qu'un certain type de travail ressemble
au travail divin. Si le travail agricole où le travail artisanal
ne sont pas comparables à l'œuvre divine, le vocabulaire ne
parvient néanmoins désormais plus à distinguer parfaitement les activités. Dans les faits, et en dehors des monas-
tères, le verbe *laborare* se spécialise dans le sens du travail
agricole et signifie labourer. Le travail réel prend la forme
du *labor*, qu'il s'agisse des paysans ou des artisans qui sont
des ruraux, des esclaves puis des serfs domaniaux. Ceux qui
travaillent apparaissent toujours dans le bas de l'échelle
sociale, qu'ils soient opposés aux prêtres, aux guerriers ou
aux autres classes. Néanmoins, une part du prestige social
des moines, qui désormais travaillent, commence à rejaillir
sur le travail. D'une certaine manière, le cadre est prêt
pour une valorisation du travail, et sans doute aussi pour la
fusion des deux significations d'œuvre et de peine. En
revanche, rien n'est plus éloigné des conceptions de cette
époque que l'idée d'un travail marchand, et exercé en vue
de la vente profitable.

On pourrait dire qu'à l'époque les deux principaux
obstacles au développement d'un véritable intérêt pour le
travail — la condamnation de toute activité exercée en vue
d'un gain individuel et la surdétermination de l'au-delà par
rapport à l'ici-bas — tiennent tous les deux à la conception

commune et éminemment religieuse du temps. Si les activités lucratives sont condamnées, en particulier celles du marchand, c'est non seulement parce qu'elles détournent le chrétien du seul intérêt qu'il doit avoir, celui de Dieu, mais aussi parce qu'elles font mauvais usage de ce qui n'appartient pas aux hommes mais bien à Dieu : le temps. Spéculer sur celui-ci, comme le font les marchands ou les usuriers, revient à faire des hypothèses sur un bien qu'il est interdit de s'approprier. De plus, et sans entrer dans les détails, il est évident que la conception du temps introduite par le christianisme — ce temps orienté qui se déroule de la Création à la Parousie — est et sera déterminante pour l'intérêt porté au travail et à l'ici-bas. Plus précisément, celui-ci est et sera fonction du rôle plus ou moins décisif assigné ou reconnu à l'homme dans le processus qui mène à la Fin des temps. D'où l'extrême importance des querelles doctrinales qui parcourent le Moyen Age, mais aussi les siècles suivants, sur la prédestination, le libre arbitre de l'homme, etc., et, au cœur du débat, la notion d'œuvres [64] : en attendant le Royaume de Dieu sur terre ou pour le faire arriver plus vite, l'homme doit-il ou non s'investir dans l'ici-bas ? C'est certainement dans ces débats théologiques que s'est joué en partie l'avenir du travail. Nous y reviendrons.

Mépris du gain et métiers interdits

La classification augustinienne des métiers licites et illicites va perdurer tout au long du haut Moyen Age [65] : dresser la liste exhaustive des métiers interdits dans la société de l'Occident médiéval, « ce serait risquer de dénombrer presque tous les métiers médiévaux [66] ». Car aux tabous issus des sociétés antérieures, tabous du sang, de l'impureté, de l'argent, le christianisme a ajouté ses propres condamnations et allongé la liste des professions interdites ou méprisées. Tous les métiers que l'on ne peut exercer sans risquer de tomber dans l'un des sept péchés

capitaux sont ainsi proscrits, et particulièrement les professions lucratives. Les seuls travaux autorisés sont ceux
qui ressemblent à l'œuvre divine, c'est-à-dire qui transforment l'objet sur lequel ils agissent, donc ceux des
artisans ou des paysans : « L'idéologie médiévale est
matérialiste au sens strict. Seule a valeur la production
de matière [67]. » Deux grandes ruptures s'introduisent
ensuite : aux VIIIe et IXe siècles, une forte revalorisation
du travail, appuyée sur une idéologie de l'effort producteur, mais qui se manifeste d'abord en matière agricole,
puis dans la promotion scientifique et intellectuelle des
techniques. Une classe homogène commence à se distinguer, celle des *laboratores*, constituée de ruraux puis
englobant les artisans, face aux deux autres classes, celles
des prêtres et des guerriers [68]. La seconde s'opère autour
des XIIe et XIIIe siècles, et contribue à réduire considérablement le nombre des métiers illicites et à assouplir la
condamnation auparavant totale de l'usure. Ainsi est-ce
seulement lorsqu'ils agissent par cupidité et par amour du
gain que les marchands sont condamnés.

Saint Thomas codifie ce nouveau contexte en développant l'idée d'utilité commune. Ainsi, les métiers mécaniques, comme ceux du textile, de l'habillement ou autres
semblables, qui sont nécessaires aux besoins des
hommes, reçoivent une certaine considération. Cette idée
d'utilité commune va de pair avec l'idée de valeur : « La
valeur de la chose ne résulte pas du besoin de l'acheteur
ou du vendeur, mais de l'utilité et du besoin de toute la
communauté [...] Le prix des choses est estimé non pas
d'après le sentiment ou l'utilité des individus, mais de
manière commune [69]. » Le juste prix est celui qui reflète
la valeur de la chose. Si le prix excède cette valeur ou le
contraire, l'égalité de la justice est supprimée. Ainsi saint
Thomas peut-il revaloriser un certain nombre de métiers
(ceux qui sont exercés par les marchands, par exemple)
ou de notions (la vente ou l'usure), à condition qu'elles
soient réalisées pour le bien de la communauté, et non

dans un autre but : « Si on se livre au commerce en vue
de l'utilité publique, si on veut que les choses nécessaires
à l'existence ne manquent pas dans le pays, le lucre, au
lieu d'être visé comme une fin, est seulement réclamé
comme rémunération du travail. » L'utilité commune
justifie donc le travail, et aussi la rémunération de celui-
ci. On passe des mercenaires, honnis auparavant, aux
professeurs justement rémunérés pour leur travail
d'enseignement. Il en résulte une nouvelle considération
pour le travail [70] qui ne s'explique pas seulement par un
subit intérêt de l'Eglise et de ses théoriciens pour la vie
quotidienne des hommes sur terre, mais aussi par l'ascen-
sion sociale d'un certain nombre de classes qui se développent et veulent obtenir leur reconnaissance : artisans,
marchands, techniciens. A la fin du Moyen Age et avec
l'accord de l'Eglise, une nouvelle ligne de partage sépare
les travailleurs manuels des autres, dont l'utilité est
désormais reconnue [71]. C'est à ce moment seulement,
ainsi que le souligne Marc Bloch à plusieurs reprises, que
les inventions qui jusque-là étaient restées des curiosités,
comme le moulin à vent, vont être développées, parce
que la représentation du travail s'est modifiée. Se dessine
donc un contexte intellectuel qui se refuse encore à faire
du travail une activité essentielle et valorisante, mais
porte en même temps en germe un certain nombre d'évolutions. Le refus de faire du travail une activité essentielle se lit à la fois dans la structure sociale, où dominent
prêtres, nobles et guerriers — dans la place réservée
à ceux qui ne travaillent pas — et dans les termes. Au
XVIᵉ siècle, le nouveau mot de travail, *tripalium*, se
substitue aux deux précédemment en usage, labourer et
ouvrer. On utilise donc pour désigner cette activité un
mot qui permettait jusque-là de nommer une machine à
trois pieux, souvent utilisée comme instrument de tor-
ture. Au XVIIᵉ siècle, le mot continuera à signifier gêne,
accablement et souffrance, humiliation [72]. Les solitaires
de Port-Royal, à la recherche d'un moyen de pénitence

efficace, choisissent le travail manuel. Le travail reste donc tenu pour une activité dégradante au sens fort. Au gré des « hasards » de l'étymologie, le terme d'*opus* a été absorbé dans le terme global de travail pour prendre la seule signification d'effort, de peine. La connotation créatrice a subitement disparu. Parallèlement, les activités de commerce restent considérées avec méfiance et l'idée de pouvoir travailler pour réaliser un gain individuel et non pour le bien de la communauté demeure intolérable. La perspective d'un individu travaillant pour son profit propre grâce au commerce tout comme l'idée d'échange inégal restent fortement condamnées par l'Eglise.

Mais, en même temps, une série de clarifications et d'inflexions majeures sont en cours : les philosophes s'attachent à mieux décrire le contenu de l'acte divin et à résoudre la contradiction d'un Dieu travaillant alors même qu'Il est immobile, tout-puissant, non affecté, inaccessible à la souffrance... Les textes pauliniens, en particulier la fameuse IIe épître aux Thessaloniciens, mais aussi ceux de Calvin rencontrent une très grande audience chez les Français de la Renaissance : « Ainsi s'explique qu'au xvie siècle une sorte de vague de fond ait ramené au jour le culte, la glorification du travail manuel [73]. »

La prise en charge des besoins humains par une organisation plus rationnelle des tâches se fait jour peu à peu. Mais sa réalisation nécessitera encore quelques bouleversements intellectuels. A la fin du Moyen Age, pas plus qu'en Grèce le travail n'est conçu comme une activité unique englobant tous les métiers, créatrice d'artifice et de valeur sociale : « Le travail ou les travaux dont on parle encore, c'est celui du paysan ou de l'artisan, le travail qui procure le pain quotidien et le vêtement mais ne vise pas à procurer la richesse, le travail qui sauve le travailleur du plus grand des vices, qui engendre tous les autres, l'oisiveté. La grande révolution n'est pas accomplie, celle dont nous parle Michelet dans la préface de son *Histoire du XIXᵉ siècle,* lorsqu'il nous décrit la vieille Angleterre, celle des campagnards, s'évanouissant en un quart de siècle pour faire place à un peuple d'ouvriers enfermés aux manufactures [74]. »

CHAPITRE III

ACTE I : L'INVENTION DU TRAVAIL

Transportons-nous en 1776, date de la publication des *Recherches sur les causes de la richesse des nations*[75] d'Adam Smith. Le titre à lui seul constitue une fantastique rupture par rapport au contexte intellectuel qui prévalait encore quelques dizaines d'années auparavant, par exemple au moment de la parution de *La Fable des abeilles*[76] de Mandeville, qui avait fait grand scandale en raison de l'éloge de la passion de l'enrichissement qui y était développé. On recherche désormais les lois — semblables à celles qui expliquent les phénomènes physiques — qui déterminent l'accroissement des richesses. L'ordre des valeurs s'est brutalement inversé, de part et d'autre de la Manche, et presque au même moment. A la condamnation de la volonté d'enrichissement a succédé une frénésie d'expériences, de recherches, d'essais, de théories visant à augmenter la richesse. Weber cite cette exhortation de Benjamin Franklin, qui date de 1748 : « Souviens-toi que le temps, c'est de l'argent [...] Souviens-toi que l'argent est, par nature, générateur et prolifique [...] Celui qui assassine (*sic*) une pièce de cinq shillings détruit tout ce qu'elle aurait pu produire : des monceaux de livres sterling[77]. » A la simple tolérance accordée au commerce à la fin du Moyen Age a succédé l'idée que le commerce est doux[78] et le travail, quasi absent des œuvres du début du XVIIIᵉ siècle, est omniprésent. Il est soudainement clair, chez Smith et encore plus chez ses successeurs, que la richesse est ce qui est absolument désirable. Et si Smith donne encore, bien que discrètement, les raisons de ce choix, ses successeurs ne s'en donneront même pas la peine. Voyez les introductions des *Principes d'économie politique*[79] de Malthus ou le *Traité d'économie politique*[80] de Jean-Baptiste Say. Elles considèrent cette recherche et son objet comme un postulat dont la démonstration n'est pas à faire. Cette obsession de la richesse, encore appelée opulence, abondance, bien-être général, prospérité n'explique pas à elle seule l'apparition du travail sur la scène de l'économie politique. Encore fallait-il pouvoir concevoir le travail humain comme une puissance susceptible de créer et d'ajouter de la valeur, ce que les physiocrates[81], par exemple, pourtant également à la recherche de la nature de la richesse, n'avaient pas fait, réservant à la seule nature la force capable de créer, *ex nihilo*, du nouveau.

Smith franchit ce pas et soudainement le travail humain envahit la scène de l'économie politique : tout le début de son ouvrage y est consacré. Les premiers mots de l'introduction présentent « le travail annuel d'une nation » ; le second paragraphe explique que la richesse d'une nation dépend exclusivement de deux facteurs, l'habileté du travail et la proportion entre le nombre de travailleurs utiles et inutiles ; le premier livre est consacré aux « causes qui ont perfectionné les facultés productives du travail » et le premier chapitre s'intitule « De la division du travail ». Il n'est d'ailleurs pas anodin que le chapitre consacré à la division du travail soit le premier. C'est précisément la faculté du travail humain, correctement organisé, de créer de la valeur de façon exponentielle qui fascine Smith. Ce premier chapitre est un hymne à la productivité du travail qui permet, comme le montre le fameux exemple de la manufacture d'épingles[82], de fabriquer toujours plus dans un temps donné, comme s'il y avait dans le travail une

puissance magique. Mais qu'est-ce que le travail pour
Smith, et à quoi tient donc ce qu'il dénomme « puissance
productive » ? Il ne s'en explique pas directement. Son
ouvrage n'est pas consacré à une recherche sur la nature du
travail lui-même. Le fait que le travail soit le moyen
principal d'augmentation des richesses est le seul élément
qui intéresse Smith, et si l'on voulait donner une définition
smithienne de celui-ci, elle serait purement instrumentale :
le travail, c'est cette puissance humaine et/ou « machini-
que » qui permet de créer de la valeur.

L'invention du travail abstrait : le travail, c'est le temps

Smith construit sa notion de travail avec les outils dont
dispose la pensée scientifique de l'époque. D'un côté, le
travail de l'individu apparaît comme une dépense physique,
qui a pour corollaire l'effort, la fatigue et la peine et qui
admet pour traduction concrète une transformation matérielle de l'objet. Mais à cette dimension concrète et
accessible au sens commun Smith en ajoute une autre, plus
abstraite : le travail est décrit comme une substance
homogène identique en tous temps et tous lieux et infiniment divisible en quantums (en « atomes »). Le problème
qu'il cherche à résoudre, comme toute une tradition
philosophique avant lui d'ailleurs, est celui du fondement
de l'échange. Qu'est-ce qui fait que des objets peuvent
s'échanger ? Qu'est-ce qui fonde la commensurabilité de
choses différentes ? A cette question Smith répond : le
travail. Tous les objets que nous échangeons contiennent
du travail, toutes les choses sont transformables et décom-
posables en travail, en quantités de fatigue ou de dépense
physique. « Le travail a été le premier prix, la monnaie
payée pour l'achat primitif de toutes choses [...]. C'est avec
du travail que toutes les richesses du monde ont été
achetées originairement[83]. Ce ne sont pas les travaux des
champs, les métiers divers, le caractère concret du travail

exercé qui intéressent Smith, mais cette substance en quoi toute chose peut se résoudre et qui permet l'échange universel.

On peut désormais parler *du* travail. Celui-ci vient bien soudainement de trouver son unité, mais c'est pour y perdre en contenu. Pouvoir dire *le* travail se paye. Le prix, c'est l'abstraction du concept. Qu'est-ce que le travail? Smith ne le dira pas. On saura seulement que « des quantités égales de travail doivent être, dans tous les temps et dans tous les lieux, d'une valeur égale pour le travailleur. [...] Ainsi le travail, ne variant jamais de sa valeur propre, est la seule mesure réelle et définitive qui puisse servir, dans tous les temps et dans tous les lieux, à apprécier et à comparer la valeur de toutes les marchandises[84] ». Le travail est conçu exactement dans les termes dans lesquels on décrivait le temps ou l'espace dans les œuvres scientifiques de l'époque. Le temps en particulier apparaît souvent comme une sorte d'étendue dont les éléments constitutifs sont les instants. Or, lorsqu'il s'interroge sur le moyen de mesurer et de comparer les quantités de travail elles-mêmes (comment mesurer ce qui sert de mesure universelle à toute chose?), Smith donne deux critères : le temps de travail, d'une part, et l'habileté ou la dextérité, d'autre part. Puisque, dans les faits, l'habileté et la dextérité sont souvent difficiles à évaluer, c'est le temps qui sera utilisé. L'égalisation et la comparaison des différentes quantités de travail se font par le temps, donc par ce qu'il y a de plus abstrait et de plus homogène. Le travail n'est donc pas seulement *comme* le temps, il *est* le temps ; celui-ci est sa matière première, son ultime constituant. Le travail est lui-même, en dernier ressort, un cadre vide, une forme homogène, dont le seul intérêt est de rendre les différentes marchandises comparables.

Cette perspective permet de comprendre les options fondamentales sur lesquelles reposent les *Recherches*. Elle fonde en effet la logique de la valeur et de la productivité. Si le travail est divisible en quantités identiques, il est alors possible de décomposer tout travail complexe en multiples quantités de travail simple, mais aussi de combiner le plus intelligemment possible ces différentes quantités en autant d'opérations. L'identité de toutes les quantités simples permet leur utilisation *ad libitum* et est au fondement de la productivité du travail, issue d'un effet de répétition (« la division du travail, en réduisant la tâche de chaque homme à quelque opération très simple et en faisant de cette opération la seule occupation de sa vie, lui fait acquérir nécessairement une très grande dextérité[85] ») et de combinaison (« dans chaque art, la division du travail, aussi loin qu'elle peut y être portée, amène un accroissement proportionnel de la puissance productrice du travail[86] »). Le taylorisme est là en germe : l'idée que le travail est sécable en unités simples susceptibles d'être combinées mécaniquement et réparties entre différentes personnes est promise à un bel avenir... Dans le même mouvement, l'échange est compris comme l'effet d'une double transmutation : d'une quantité d'effort en une création de valeur et de celle-ci en une quantité d'argent. Le travail est alors considéré dans sa dimension physique, comme une quantité d'énergie dont la valeur est constante et dont les possibles compositions et décompositions mécaniques fondent les équivalences entre effort, valeur ajoutée dans les choses et prix de vente. Cette conception physique et mécanique du travail va de pair avec les idées scientifiques de l'époque, tant sur le temps que sur la « force ». Les marchandises « contiennent » vraiment la valeur d'une certaine quantité de travail. C'est ce qui permet de considérer la « puissance productive de la Nation », donc la quantité totale de travail susceptible d'être fournie, comme le résultat, d'une part, de la proportion entre ceux qui exercent un travail productif et les autres, et, d'autre part, de la combinaison des différentes « industries » particulières.

Ainsi Smith introduit-il, probablement sans s'en rendre compte, une nouvelle définition du travail. Celle-ci n'est pas le résultat d'une analyse qui aurait recensé toutes les

formes concrètes et empiriques de travail pour en dégager
la caractéristique commune (qu'y a-t-il de commun entre
cultiver un champ, faire un meuble, tailler un tissu, peindre
une fresque dans une église... ?), mais l'aboutissement
d'une recherche dont l'objet n'était pas le travail. Au terme
de celle-ci, il apparaît comme un instrument de calcul et de
mesure, qui a pour qualité essentielle de fonder l'échange.
Ce sont donc bien les économistes qui « inventent » le
concept de travail : pour la première fois, ils lui donnent
une signification homogène. Mais le travail est construit,
instrumental et abstrait. Son essence est le temps.

**L'invention du travail abstrait (suite) : le travail, facteur
d'accroissement de la richesse**

Le concept de travail continue d'être construit tout au
long du XVIIIᵉ siècle. Au terme de cette construction, qui va
faire l'objet de nombreux débats — en particulier de part et
d'autre de la Manche — et qui se stabilise vers le milieu du
XIXᵉ siècle, la fonction de mesure du travail n'est plus
première. Désormais, le travail est ce qui crée de la
richesse ou, dans des termes plus modernes, le travail est
un facteur de production. Malgré ce changement, sa
définition n'en reste pas moins, comme on le voit, entièrement instrumentale. Cette nouvelle construction s'opère
par le biais de la notion de travail productif. Smith opérait
déjà une distinction entre travail productif et travail
improductif, regroupant néanmoins les deux notions sous
la catégorie générale de travail. Le travail productif étant
celui qui produit de la valeur, et celle-ci devant, pour
exister, être durablement inscrite dans les choses, toute une
série d'activités s'étaient trouvées exclues du travail productif, alors même que le concept de travail venait d'être
unifié : le travail du domestique[87], mais aussi celui du
souverain, des magistrats civils et militaires, de l'armée, de
la flotte, des ecclésiastiques, des gens de loi, des médecins,

des gens de lettres de toute espèce, des comédiens, des
farceurs, des musiciens, etc., étaient tenus pour non
productifs. Cette analyse sera reprise par tous les successeurs de Smith et en particulier par Say et Malthus, ce
dernier illustrant le mieux comment se construit le nouveau
concept de travail. Il propose en effet que l'on cesse
d'appeler travail l'activité des personnes qui n'exercent pas
un travail productif, mais plutôt de les appeler « services ».
Ainsi conservera-t-on le terme de travail pour les seules
personnes qui correspondent en quelque sorte au concept
qui a été créé. Le « vrai » travail, c'est le travail productif,
autrement dit le travail matériel, vecteur d'échange.

Pourquoi ? Parce que le concept de travail n'est pas le
résultat d'une analyse des situations vécues mais qu'il est
construit pour les besoins de la cause, et plus particulièrement déduit des définitions de la richesse données par les
auteurs. Tous les ouvrages de l'époque montrent comment
la définition du travail n'est qu'une conséquence de la
définition que les auteurs donnent de la richesse : le travail
n'est que « ce qui produit la richesse ». Mieux, les caractéristiques du travail sont déduites de ce que les différents
auteurs entendent par richesse. D'où l'extrême importance
de la définition qu'en donnent ceux-ci, en particulier Say et
Malthus. Car les deux auteurs parviennent au même
résultat, c'est-à-dire à une conception extrêmement restrictive de la richesse. Certes, écrit Malthus, la richesse peut
bien correspondre à tout ce que l'homme désire comme
pouvant lui être utile et agréable : « Cette définition
embrasse évidemment toutes les choses, matérielles ou
intellectuelles, tangibles ou non, qui procurent de l'utilité
ou des jouissances à l'espèce humaine, elle comprend par
conséquent les avantages et les consolations que nous
retirons de la religion, de la morale, de la liberté politique
et civile, de l'éloquence, des conversations instructives et
amusantes, de la musique, de la danse, du théâtre et
d'autres services et qualités personnels[88]. » Mais cette
définition est beaucoup trop large et n'est pas du tout

opérationnelle : elle ne peut en particulier servir à calculer l'accroissement exact de la richesse d'un pays d'une année sur l'autre[89].

La volonté d'obtenir des résultats concrets et de faire de l'économie politique une science est tellement forte que c'est cette préoccupation qui va dominer toutes les autres. Nos auteurs ne s'en cachent d'ailleurs pas, dont les introductions sont toujours consacrées à mesurer et à louer les progrès de la science économique. Et, au terme d'un épique débat, après de longues pages, où il dispute des mérites relatifs d'une conception extensive — et plus exacte — de la richesse, et d'une conception restrictive, certes un peu fausse, mais sans laquelle le calcul est impossible, Malthus conclut par cet extraordinaire aveu : « Si donc, avec M. Say, nous voulons faire de l'économie politique *une science positive* fondée sur l'expérience et susceptible de donner des résultats précis, il faut prendre le plus grand soin d'embrasser seulement, dans la définition du terme principal dont elle se sert, les objets dont l'accroissement ou la diminution peuvent être susceptibles d'évaluation ; et la ligne qu'il est le plus naturel et le plus utile de tracer nettement est celle qui sépare les objets matériels des objets immatériels[90]. » Parce qu'il est nécessaire que l'économie politique devienne une science, et surtout une science opérationnelle, capable de donner des conseils, Malthus tranche donc en faveur d'une conception éminemment réductrice de la richesse, limitée aux objets matériels : « J'appellerai richesse les objets matériels nécessaires, agréables ou utiles à l'homme, et qui sont volontairement appropriés par les individus ou les nations aux besoins qu'ils éprouvent. La définition ainsi limitée contient presque tous les objets que nous avons ordinairement en vue en parlant de la richesse. [...] Un pays sera donc riche ou pauvre, selon l'abondance ou la rareté des objets matériels dont il est pourvu, relativement à l'étendue de son territoire[91]. » Ce choix est décisif non seulement parce qu'il fixe à l'ensemble de la société la poursuite d'un objectif singulièrement réduit, mais surtout parce qu'il entraîne des conséquences immenses pour la définition du travail. A conception réduite de la richesse, conception réduite du travail. Travail signifie désormais travail productif, c'est-à-dire travail exercé sur des objets matériels et échangeables, à partir desquels la valeur ajoutée est toujours visible et mesurable.

Il est clair désormais que les économistes ont inventé et unifié le terme de travail, c'est-à-dire englobé dans une même catégorie des activités qui jusqu'alors étaient vécues comme « fatigantes », mais qui étaient néanmoins perçues et classées dans des registres très différents : les travaux des champs, l'artisanat... Mais la raison de leur réunion dans un même concept n'est ni le degré de fatigue engendrée par l'effort, ni l'objet sur lequel s'exerce cette activité, ni même la manière dont elle s'effectue. La raison est purement externe : relève de la catégorie de travail toute activité qui est à l'origine d'un accroissement de richesse — ou de ce qui est défini comme tel —, c'est-à-dire toute activité capable d'ajouter de la valeur à un objet matériel. Après Smith, les auteurs ne feront plus référence à la notion d'effort ou de fatigue : le travail sera une catégorie économique, coupée de ses référents concrets.

Gardons-nous cependant de croire, comme cela est encore trop souvent le cas aujourd'hui, que l'économie aurait opéré une réduction par rapport à un concept ou une réalité plus riche et plus large du travail, dans lequel elle aurait en quelque sorte procédé à une découpe. Ce serait commettre un contresens, car ce fameux concept ou cette fameuse réalité n'existait pas auparavant, ni en soi ni comme représentation. C'est tout ensemble que le XVIIIᵉ siècle a inventé le travail comme catégorie homogène et comme facteur d'accroissement des richesses. Ce n'est donc que par une opération de l'esprit, effet d'une illusion rétrospective, que l'on peut imaginer que la catégorie de travail était déjà présente et que l'économie n'en a retenu qu'une partie, oubliant par là même l'activité concrète de l'homme.

L'invention du travail abstrait (suite et fin) : le travail-marchandise

Les formes qu'a recouvertes le travail lors de son émergence ne sont pas anodines : il est apparu à la fois comme la plus haute manifestation de la liberté de l'individu et en même temps comme la partie de l'activité humaine susceptible de faire l'objet d'un échange marchand. Le travail a constitué le symbole de l'autonomie individuelle dans la mesure où, grâce à lui, l'individu devenait capable, par le seul exercice de ses facultés propres, de subvenir à ses besoins en négociant librement la place que ses facultés lui permettaient d'obtenir dans la société. L'idée du travail comme manifestation de la liberté individuelle remonte à Locke, qui avait fondé le droit de propriété non plus sur des ordres établis, mais précisément sur l'exercice de ses facultés par chaque individu. Pour Locke, l'homme a un droit de propriété sur son corps et un devoir de conserver celui-ci dans son intégrité qui lui donne droit à la propriété, pour autant que celle-ci constitue une condition essentielle de la protection et de la conservation de cette intégrité physique : « Chacun a un droit particulier sur sa propre personne, sur laquelle nul autre ne peut avoir aucune prétention. Le travail de son corps et l'ouvrage de ses mains, nous le pouvons dire, sont son bien propre[92]. » C'est par le travail, la fatigue qu'il dépense à acquérir les biens, que l'homme obtient le droit de les posséder[93], ce droit lui-même s'appuyant sur un droit encore plus fondamental à la conservation de soi, donc de son corps. Dès lors, l'individu acquiert, grâce au seul exercice de ses fonctions, de son corps, un certain nombre de droits, qui ne sont plus fondés sur d'autres lois. Cet exercice, c'est le travail. Le travail est donc le nom de l'activité humaine dont l'exercice autonome permet à tout individu de vivre.

Smith se réfère à cette théorie[94], mais y ajoute un élément essentiel. Le travail auquel il fait référence n'est pas le travail par lequel toutes les choses ont été originellement acquises, ce n'est pas l'effort premier et toujours recommencé par lequel l'individu définit son territoire et acquiert les ressources nécessaires à son existence. C'est le travail en société et donc, certes, celui qui permet à l'individu de négocier ses talents, de vivre avec sa force de travail dans la poche, comme le dira Marx plus tard, mais c'est aussi le travail lui-même objet d'échange. Car, comme l'explique Smith, nous sommes sortis de cet état primitif où les hommes soit n'échangeaient pas, soit échangeaient directement des produits où étaient cristallisés leurs efforts, précisément sur la base de la quantité d'effort ou de travail qui avait été nécessaire[95]. Depuis l'appropriation des terres et l'accumulation des capitaux, que Smith accepte comme une donnée de fait, l'échange n'est plus direct : les hommes, pour une partie d'entre eux du moins, doivent vendre à d'autres non pas leurs produits, mais leur travail. Et cela complique singulièrement la situation. Auparavant, les individus échangeant directement des produits dans lesquels n'entrait que leur travail, il était assez facile de comparer les quantités de travail contenues dans chacun, même si l'opération n'était pas totalement exacte et s'il était parfois délicat de s'assurer que deux quantités de travail étaient strictement équivalentes (mais Smith s'en tirait par une pirouette en renvoyant à l'arbitrage du marché : « C'est en marchandant et en débattant le prix de marché qu'il s'établit, d'après cette grosse équité qui, sans être fort exacte, l'est bien assez pour le train des affaires de la vie »). Il n'était surtout pas nécessaire de donner un prix au travail, puisque celui-ci était déterminé lors de la vente du produit. Désormais, il devient nécessaire de trouver le prix de ce qui fonde justement la comparabilité de toutes les marchandises, le prix du travail lui-même... Nécessaire de trouver des critères justes pour récompenser le travailleur, mais aussi celui qui avance les capitaux et encore le propriétaire des terres. Nécessaire de trouver les critères du bon partage, et donc de savoir ce que vaut exactement le travail.

Les débats qui occupent Smith, et qui occuperont ses successeurs, y compris Marx — la valeur ajoutée au produit vient-elle de la quantité de travail incorporée par le travailleur ou bien de l'utilité que les acheteurs potentiels lui trouvent, ou des deux... ? — sont moins importants que ce qu'il officialise sans s'y attarder : le fait que le travail humain lui-même peut avoir un prix, qu'il est un type d'activité susceptible de faire lui-même l'objet d'un achat et d'une vente. Ce qui nous apparaît aujourd'hui comme une révolution [96] — avoir pu considérer le travail humain comme une marchandise comme les autres — n'était sans doute pas interprété comme tel à l'époque par Smith. Au contraire, on voit bien que, pour l'auteur des *Recherches*, la possibilité pour chacun de vendre son travail était une manière de promouvoir une conception révolutionnaire de l'individu, désormais autonome, capable de vivre du simple exercice de ses facultés sans être sous la dépendance de quiconque, à l'opposé de toutes les formes d'utilisation de la main-d'œuvre qui existaient à l'époque, esclavage, servage, etc. [97] Il n'en reste pas moins que, si cette étape constituait certainement un progrès par rapport aux formes de non-droit qui prédominaient auparavant, elle contribuait également à asseoir une conception très particulière du travail humain. Car c'est bien parce que le travail est conçu par Smith comme une quantité de dépense physique mesurable, s'inscrivant durablement sur un objet matériel et dès lors susceptible d'augmenter d'autant la valeur de celui-ci, que sa « marchandisation » est possible. Autrement dit, là encore, le fait de pouvoir traiter le travail comme une marchandise se paye très cher : par une conception totalement matérialiste du travail. D'où la double révolution dont Smith prend acte : d'une part, le travail est désormais le moyen de l'autonomie de l'individu, d'autre part, il existe une partie de l'activité humaine qui peut être détachée de son sujet et qui ne fait pas obligatoirement corps avec celui-ci, puisqu'elle peut être louée ou vendue. Smith n'invente pas cette nouvelle conception du travail : il ne fait que donner forme aux différents éléments qui se mettent en place sous ses yeux pour constituer le travail salarié.

A l'époque, le droit — français et anglais en particulier — se réfère à une conception semblable, encore que non explicite. Est-ce le droit qui s'est saisi d'une interprétation d'abord développée par les économistes ? Sont-ce au contraire les économistes qui se sont pliés aux conceptions juridiques existantes[98] ? La question dépasse notre propos. Quoi qu'il en soit, à la fin du xviiie siècle, c'est une même conception du travail abstrait que promeuvent l'économie et le droit, ce dernier confirmant le caractère « détachable » du travail. Pothier, juriste qui écrit à la même époque que Smith[99], distingue le louage de choses et le louage d'ouvrages et range le travail dans la première catégorie : parmi les choses qui peuvent être louées, Pothier énumère ainsi les maisons, les fonds de terre, les meubles, les droits incorporels et « les services » d'un homme libre[100]. Le travail apparaît bien comme une chose dont dispose le travailleur et dont il peut user moyennant un paiement, une chose qui, bien qu'étant ce travailleur, lui est néanmoins étrangère, puisqu'on peut en parler et en user sans, semble-t-il, toucher à la nature du sujet qui la porte. C'est également cette conception que confirment avec éclat les textes de la Révolution française, qui tous reconnaissent le travail comme chose détachable, susceptible d'être achetée et vendue, et considèrent acheteurs et vendeurs comme des individus qui, au moment où ils contractent, sont parfaitement libres et égaux. Les organisations qui réglaient l'accès aux métiers et les rémunérations liées à leur exercice, ainsi que les corporations diverses qui protégeaient de fait l'individu seront supprimées au nom de cette conception :

la loi du 17 mars 1791 consacre l'idée que le travail est un négoce en le soumettant au principe de la liberté du commerce et de l'industrie, stipulant qu'« il sera libre à toute personne de faire tel négoce, d'exercer telle profession, art ou métier que bon lui semble [101] ». Le Code civil confirmera cette conception [102]. Le travail apparaît ainsi comme une « capacité » dont l'individu dispose librement et dont il négocie les conditions de vente avec un employeur, stipulées dans une convention, résultat d'un acte libre. Les révolutionnaires français ne disent pas autre chose que Smith, qui a peut-être simplement sur eux l'avantage de ne pas être dupe : il sait fort bien que ce ne sont pas des individus libres et égaux qui se rencontrent et contractent, mais que les employeurs peuvent se coaliser alors que les travailleurs ne le peuvent pas ; que, de plus, les employeurs, disposant des capitaux, ne sont pas soumis à la même urgence que les travailleurs, qui, eux, ont absolument besoin d'exercer cette faculté s'ils veulent éviter la mort [103].

Dès l'origine, donc, au travers du droit et de l'économie s'invente un concept de travail immédiatement matériel, quantifié et marchand. Le travail est l'activité qui porte exclusivement sur des marchandises, donc sur des objets susceptibles d'être échangés et il est lui-même une marchandise, au centre d'un échange. L'échange apparaît comme le centre de la société smithienne et le travail comme la condition de celui-ci. Tout se passe comme si le travail était devenu la raison de la nouvelle société. Il est à la fois terriblement concret (son essence, c'est la fatigue, l'effort, la peine, et c'est à ce prix que s'achète la participation à la vie sociale), et éminemment abstrait (le travail est l'instrument de comparabilité de toute chose). Tout se passe comme si le lien social se construisait grâce à la vente de cette substance individuelle qu'est l'effort. Le travail est bien le nouveau rapport social qui structure la société. En cela, et en tant que travail marchand permettant l'échange de marchandises, il répond à un besoin, et constitue une solution.

Pourquoi le travail ?

Pour comprendre dans quelle mesure le travail est une « solution », il nous faut remonter quelque peu en arrière et nous attarder sur la brutale inversion de l'ordre des valeurs au milieu du XVIIIe siècle. Pourquoi la richesse est-elle soudainement apparue comme la véritable fin que doivent poursuivre les sociétés ? Pourquoi cette énergie consacrée à mettre en évidence les lois de son accroissement ? Pourquoi cette soudaine attention portée à l'intérêt individuel, devenu une véritable catégorie de l'économie politique naissante ? Beaucoup d'explications ont été données de ce moment, qui n'est autre que celui de la fondation de nos sociétés modernes. Les unes, plutôt déterministes, voient dans la Révolution industrielle, et particulièrement dans la révolution technique qui en constitue le cœur, le phénomène déclenchant, qui a permis le développement de la productivité, et, de là, l'intérêt porté à la richesse. Dans la même catégorie, on peut faire entrer les explications qui en appellent à la démographie, à la surpopulation rurale, à la constitution de grands centres urbains, à la découverte de nouveaux gisements de métaux précieux, à un degré plus intense d'accumulation du capital... Mais ces explications qui font appel à un *deus ex machina* sont incapables d'expliquer pourquoi des industriels ont soudainement été intéressés par des machines et des techniques dont certaines avaient été jusque-là considérées comme des curiosités, pourquoi certains y ont investi des capitaux, pourquoi d'autres ont jugé important, à un moment donné, d'augmenter la productivité du travail.

D'autres explications font au contraire appel à un autre type de causalité : les croyances, les représentations, ou ce que Weber appelle encore l'*ethos* [104]. On connaît « l'explication » de Weber : ce phénomène n'aurait pu exister, dit-il, sans la conversion des mentalités qui s'est opérée à cette époque, et qui consiste essentiellement en une valorisation des activités terrestres, issue d'une réinterprétation des grands textes bibliques. Les interprétations successives de Luther et de Calvin, même si elles ne visaient pas à exalter les activités terrestres et qu'elles récusaient la notion controversée d'œuvres, conduisirent néanmoins, selon Weber, à ce résultat[105]. Comme s'il avait fallu l'intervention d'un principe de même nature et de même force (c'est-à-dire religieux) pour vaincre la condamnation qui pesait depuis des siècles sur la volonté d'enrichissement, la chrématistique et l'investissement dans l'ici-bas[106]. Cette explication, qui en appelle aux mentalités, a certes fait l'objet de débats. Elle est, comme toutes les explications historiques qui s'élèvent un tant soit peu au-delà de l'exposition tautologique de la succession des événements, discutable, car, par définition, à jamais invérifiable. Elle a néanmoins le mérite de faire la place à ce qui détermine profondément la conduite des hommes, et en particulier à l'époque, aux préceptes religieux diffusés par les Eglises.

D'autres théories encore accordent une plus grande place aux phénomènes sociaux qui ont accompagné la naissance du travail, et mettent l'accent en particulier sur la double émergence de l'économique comme domaine de réalité spécifique et de l'individu. Ainsi Albert Hirschman reconnaît-il qu'un « bouleversement stupéfiant de l'ordre moral et idéologique » s'est produit, pour ainsi dire du jour au lendemain, et a entraîné « une large approbation de la volonté d'enrichissement ainsi que des activités qui en témoignent, en très peu de temps[107] ». Ces mutations doivent, dit-il, être comprises à la lumière du principe de la passion compensatrice. Si le XVIIe siècle est celui de la découverte des passions et de leur force destructrice, la fin du XVIIe siècle et le XVIIIe siècle vont s'employer à les utiliser les unes contre les autres au lieu de les réprimer, visant ainsi à l'obtention d'un équilibre destiné à détourner la violence. Au cœur de cette révolution, on trouve, selon Hirschman, la notion d'intérêt : d'abord employé en référence à l'ensemble des aspirations humaines, ce terme en viendra peu à peu à ne plus désigner que l'avantage économique ; et c'est ainsi que l'égoïsme, sous la forme de l'intérêt individuel, sera progressivement considéré comme le plus grand rempart contre la violence. L'intérêt offre de surcroît l'avantage de fonder un ordre social prévisible et calculable : il n'est qu'à combiner l'ensemble des intérêts individuels pour prévoir les conséquences attendues. Surtout, de la confrontation des intérêts individuels sur le seul terrain économique peut naître un équilibre des forces permettant d'éviter la guerre. D'où aussi le retournement dans l'appréciation du commerce, qui, honni quelques décennies auparavant, est devenu subitement « doux » dans la bouche de Montesquieu : « C'est presque une règle générale, que partout où il y a des mœurs douces, il y a du commerce ; et que partout où il y a du commerce, il y a des mœurs douces [108]. » On comprend mieux ce que veut dire Montesquieu lorsqu'il ajoute que l'esprit de commerce « entraîne avec soi celui de frugalité, d'économie, de modération, de travail, de sagesse, de tranquillité, d'ordre et de règle » avant d'expliquer que le commerce (ou l'intérêt pour l'économique) constitue un contrepoids à la tentation de l'Etat de s'emparer de tout le pouvoir. Dans la mesure où elle vise à accroître la prospérité générale, l'activité économique est donc une manière de dérober au pouvoir politique une partie de l'espace qu'il aurait pu sans cela occuper.

Mais cette interprétation n'explique pas suffisamment, selon nous, pourquoi un tel bouleversement est intervenu. Pas plus d'ailleurs que l'interprétation de Louis Dumont [109]. Celui-ci fait appel, globalement, au même ressort. Dans sa genèse de l'idéologie économique, il met au premier plan l'autonomisation d'un type de réalité particulier, l'économique, brutalement isolé par rapport au politique : la relation primordiale devient dès lors celle qui confronte les hommes aux choses et non plus les hommes à d'autres hommes. On passerait donc ainsi, sous la poussée de l'individualisme du xviie siècle, d'une société globalement holiste, dont la caractéristique est de reposer sur la subordination des hommes vis-à-vis d'autres hommes (et dont la régulation est la politique), à une société individualiste, où priment les relations hommes/choses, et dont la régulation est d'abord économique. Dumont tire ainsi un long fil rouge qui va de Mandeville à Marx et qui voit l'épanouissement conjoint de l'individualisme et de la pensée économique. Nous aurons à revenir plus tard sur l'assimilation ou sur la continuité que tisse Dumont entre la pensée de Smith et la pensée de Marx. Contentons-nous pour l'instant de souligner que l'inversion des valeurs, qui éclôt chez Mandeville et dont les conséquences sont théorisées chez Smith, n'est pas plus expliquée.

La fin de l'ordre géocentrique

Il faut donc sans doute revenir au bouleversement des représentations classiques du monde qui s'est opéré au XVIIe siècle. On peut présenter ce bouleversement, pour la clarté de l'exposé, sous trois rubriques : l'effondrement de la conception géocentrique du monde, et par là même des rapports traditionnels homme/nature ; la remise en cause des représentations classiques de l'ordre social ; l'apparition de l'individu.

Le terme « effondrement de l'ordre naturel » ne doit pas laisser croire à la substitution rapide d'un modèle à un autre : il a fallu plus d'un siècle aux idées nouvelles pour s'imposer. Alors que Copernic avait livré dès 1543 les premiers éléments d'une démonstration de l'héliocentrisme, en 1633, apprenant la condamnation de Galilée au moment même où il achève son traité de physique (*Le Monde*), Descartes renonce à publier celui-ci. Le Saint-Office défend d'affirmer le mouvement de la Terre « même si on le propose à titre d'hypothèse ». Ce n'est qu'avec Newton, qui publie son ouvrage majeur en 1687, que la vérité éclate avec assez de force pour que nul ne puisse plus s'y opposer et pour qu'il devienne clair que la Terre tourne autour du Soleil — et donc que l'homme n'est plus au centre du monde. On a suffisamment glosé sur l'importance capitale de ces découvertes pour qu'il soit inutile de s'y attarder. Il n'en reste pas moins qu'outre la blessure narcissique infligée à l'homme d'autres conséquences extrêmement concrètes doivent être soulignées. Une nouvelle image de la nature, de l'homme et du rapport qui les unit est en effet en jeu.

Descartes propose la synthèse la plus claire de tous ces bouleversements [110]. En reprenant et en démontrant les propos de Galilée selon lesquels la nature est écrite en langage mathématique, Descartes montre que la nature n'est plus cet ensemble peuplé de forces, de formes, de qualités sensibles, voire d'esprits, qu'une certaine lecture des textes grecs au cours du Moyen Age avait légué à l'Europe. La nature apparaît désormais comme homogène, totalement vide et transparente. Elle consiste en une matière parfaitement perméable à l'esprit, connaissable par lui. Le monde est construit selon les lois de la mathématique universelle. Tout se passe comme si Dieu s'était retiré de ce monde, de même que toute l'efficace humaine a reflué dans l'âme et dans la volonté. Le monde est désormais strictement divisé entre l'étendue, dès lors livrée à la connaissance et à l'action de l'homme, et l'esprit (attribut de Dieu au plus haut point, de l'âme humaine de moindre façon). Le fait que Dieu lui-même ait créé le monde, l'ait posé en dehors de lui et le soutienne à chaque instant nous rend ce monde totalement perméable. D'où deux types de réactions, qui sont d'abord celles des hommes de sciences ou de lettres, mais qui vont influencer l'esprit du temps : une réaction de peur, voire de terreur, et une réaction d'allégresse, nourrie de l'idée que la nature n'est désormais plus perçue comme un ensemble de forces inconnues et non maîtrisables et qu'il sera possible de l'apprivoiser.

La réaction de peur est bien exprimée par Pascal [111] ; c'est la peur d'un monde sans Dieu, d'un monde où l'homme est sans repères fixes, entre deux infinis, d'un monde froid, vide, désenchanté, où rien n'a de sens, où il n'y a plus de signes. Tout se passe comme si Pascal voyait déjà se profiler un monde sans Dieu à travers l'univers décrit par Descartes. Ce dernier cède au contraire à l'allégresse : « Sitôt que j'ai eu acquis quelques notions générales touchant la physique et que [...] j'ai remarqué jusques où elles peuvent conduire et combien elles diffèrent des principes dont on s'est servi jusqu'à présent, j'ai cru que je ne pouvais les tenir cachées sans pécher grandement contre la loi qui nous oblige à procurer autant qu'il est en nous le bien général de tous les hommes : car elles m'ont fait voir qu'il est possible de parvenir à des connaissances qui soient fort utiles à la vie et qu'au lieu de cette philosophie spéculative qu'on enseigne dans les écoles on en peut trouver une pratique, par laquelle, connaissant la force et les actions du feu, de l'eau, de l'air, des astres, des cieux et de tous les autres corps qui nous environnent aussi distinctement que nous connaissons les divers métiers de nos artisans, nous les pourrions employer en même façon à tous les usages auxquels ils sont propres, et ainsi nous rendre comme maîtres et possesseurs de la nature, ce qui n'est pas seulement à désirer pour l'invention d'une infinité d'artifices qui feraient qu'on jouirait sans aucune peine des fruits de la terre et de toutes les commodités qui s'y trouvent, mais principalement aussi pour la conservation de la santé, laquelle est sans doute le premier bien et le fondement de tous les autres biens de cette vie [112]. »

On a vu dans ce passage, l'un des plus commentés de l'histoire de la philosophie, le début de l'esprit technicien et conquérant qui caractérise les sociétés occidentales à partir du XVIIIe siècle. Or, Bacon rédige ses principaux écrits, et en particulier *Du progrès et de la promotion des savoirs*, le *Novum organum* et *La Nouvelle Atlantide* [113], au même moment. Pour Bacon, la raison doit nous permettre, non seulement de trouver les causes, mais aussi de ne nous en remettre qu'à nous-mêmes. L'ordre naturel des choses n'est pas donné de l'extérieur, il est simplement, et il ne tient qu'à nous de le dévoiler et de l'utiliser à notre profit. La raison et donc la science doivent nous servir à transformer le monde : « La mission de la science ne réside ni dans les discours plausibles, divertissants, empreints de dignité et faisant beaucoup d'effet, ni dans quelque argumentation évidente, mais dans l'action et le travail, ainsi que dans la découverte de détails inconnus auparavant et permettant un meilleur aménagement de l'existence. » Une triple révolution est à l'œuvre dans ces deux textes : le modèle de la science n'est plus la métaphysique ou la rhétorique, mais la physique, qui permet à la fois de découvrir les causes et qui rend possible l'action transformatrice. Descartes appelle ces moyens d'action les artifices. La science n'a plus pour vocation de découvrir la vérité, mais de mettre au jour des causes qui permettent à l'homme de transformer le monde : connaître, c'est désormais agir. Enfin, cette transformation est orientée : non seulement vers l'artifice, mais surtout vers l'artifice utile. A la relation de crainte et de respect vis-à-vis de la nature se substitue une relation utilitaire. D'où l'enthousiasme des hommes qui prennent soudainement conscience du champ des possibles qui s'ouvre devant eux [114]. C'est à dessein que nous employons le terme d'enthousiasme, dans sa première signification de « transport divin », car tout se passe comme si le manque de Dieu et l'éclatement du monde nourrissaient, chez les hommes, une sorte de folie ; comme si les forces qui avaient été tournées jusque-là vers la nature pour tenter de l'adoucir se déchaînaient pour construire un nouvel ordre, dont l'homme est désormais le maître ; enfin, comme si ce vide devait maintenant être domestiqué. Le moyen de tout ceci, le moyen de ce connaître qui est en même temps un agir, c'est le travail. Le travail, moyen d'aménager l'existence, de la rendre plus douce. Dans ce bouleversement où la nature apparaît soudainement tel un champ à labourer, où la raison se fait efficace, le travail est le véritable moyen d'accéder à une nouvelle existence, à l'abondance universelle, et en même temps l'instrument de l'artifice. Dans les creux de la nature désenchantée, place est faite pour l'artifice humain.

La fin des communautés naturelles

Au moment même où les principes et les connaissances issus de la tradition et légitimés par la seule autorité sont remis en cause dans le domaine de la nature, les justifications traditionnelles qui servaient de fondement à l'ordre social établi commencent à s'effondrer. De même que l'ordre naturel « géocentrique » était appuyé sur une conception du monde issue des Grecs et réinterprétée par les Ecritures, selon lesquelles la Terre, centre du monde, a été créée par Dieu, la théorie politique s'appuie jusqu'au Moyen Age sur l'argument d'autorité, issu de la formule paulinienne : *non est potestas nisi a Deo* [115], confortée plus tard par saint Augustin. Il n'y a point de puissance qui ne vienne de Dieu, et toutes celles qui existent ont été instituées par lui. Dans l'esprit de Paul, cela implique une soumission absolue au gouvernement établi et interdit en particulier toute résistance au pouvoir institué. Cette théorie, dite du droit divin, place l'autorité divine au fondement de l'autorité politique : l'obéissance au pouvoir civil trouve son origine et sa raison dans l'obéissance que l'on doit à Dieu. Les magistrats civils ou les princes sont les ministres de Dieu. Droit divin et droit naturel sont dès lors assimilés par les juristes, qui identifient par là même aussi le naturel et le juste : le droit est naturel parce qu'il fait partie de l'ordre des choses universellement voulu par Dieu. Dès lors, l'ordre social est bien lui aussi un ordre naturel, et la place de chacun dans la société est à chaque instant justifiée, l'ordre social à chaque instant légitime. Mieux, l'unité sociale elle-même trouve son fondement, en dernier ressort, dans l'Eglise. La communauté sociale, l'*universitas*, est une communauté naturelle, hiérarchisée, dont l'unité est organique et où chacun trouve sa place naturellement.

Au moment même où écrivent Descartes et Bacon, Hobbes [116] porte un coup décisif à cette théorie de l'autorité politique, également au nom de la raison. Il soumet la représentation commune des fondements politiques de la société civile au même type de critique que les deux premiers formulaient à l'égard de la représentation classique de la nature. Il dissocie état naturel et état social en établissant une généalogie des sociétés civiles, c'est-à-dire en proposant d'examiner ce qui se passait avant que les hommes ne se mettent en société. Grâce à la fiction de l'état de nature, il distingue un avant de la société — naturel — et un après, qui trouve son fondement et sa légitimité non plus dans l'autorité divine, mais au contraire dans la volonté humaine. L'autorité politique, c'est-à-dire ce qui fait que chacun doit obéir aux lois de son pays, réside en l'homme lui-même, dans sa dépossession volontaire d'un certain nombre de droits qui étaient les siens et qui sont transférés à une autorité supérieure. La sortie de l'état de nature, que Hobbes présente comme un état de guerre, nécessite un effort, un artifice, une invention humaine. La société humaine n'est donc pas le simple prolongement de l'état qui préexistait à son établissement. Elle est l'œuvre de l'homme. L'ordre social n'est donc pas un ordre naturel, donné de toute éternité. Hobbes met par là en évidence un élément fondamental : le caractère arbitraire de l'ordre social. On mesure bien la tonalité éminemment révolutionnaire d'une telle découverte, dont on conçoit qu'elle puisse susciter tout à la fois, comme les découvertes scientifiques de l'époque, terreur et enthousiasme. Terreur devant la totale instabilité — l'anarchie ou la guerre —, qui peut découler de l'absence de lois naturelles, de repères, voire de critères. Enthousiasme devant l'absolue liberté donnée à l'homme d'inventer la société qui sera la plus propice à la poursuite de ses fins. Mais, dans un premier moment, la terreur domine, ce qui explique le caractère affreusement pesant de la machine mise en place par Hobbes pour établir l'autorité politique sur des fondements fermes et stables.

Hobbes construit une véritable machine-Etat capable de cimenter l'ordre social, c'est-à-dire d'établir et de maintenir celui-ci sur des bases aussi solides et aussi incontestables que si elles étaient naturelles. Mais qu'est-il donc nécessaire de cimenter aussi fortement ? Qu'a donc découvert Hobbes qui l'oblige à définir des règles aussi contraignantes ?

Des individus qui sont autant de forces primaires guidées par le seul souci de la conservation de soi, autant de forces qui, non canalisées, non réglées, ne pourront que se heurter et se détruire. L'ordre politique consiste dès lors à déterminer l'autorité supérieure qui donnera la règle de cette coexistence et disposera du pouvoir de la faire respecter. L'ordre politique a essentiellement pour fin de mettre chaque individu à sa place dans le tout social, de l'intégrer dans un ordre, d'où découleront ses droits et ses devoirs. Avec l'effondrement des communautés naturelles, le problème majeur est de trouver la règle de coexistence de ceux qui se reconnaissent et se revendiquent désormais comme des individus, en évitant une remise en cause perpétuelle de celle-ci.

L'individu, l'ordre social et le travail

C'est bien l'apparition de l'individu sur la scène publique qui pose en effet problème. Les ordres naturels, cosmologiques ou sociaux se sont décomposés en leurs constituants premiers, les individus, d'ailleurs en partie sous la pression de ceux-ci. Le cosmos organisé s'est résolu, au sens chimique du terme, en deux produits : d'une part, une nature désenchantée, sans qualités et réductible aux lois mathématiques, et, d'autre part, un sujet, pensant, libre, certain de son existence, conscient d'être différent et séparé de cette nature qui lui fait désormais face. Quant à la décomposition de l'*universitas*, de l'ordre naturel décrit par le droit naturel classique, elle a libéré une multiplicité d'individus réduits à leur plus simple expression et à leur

désir premier : se conserver. L'individu n'est certes pas une
« invention » du xviie siècle. Il s'agit bien plutôt de l'une
des inventions majeures du christianisme, pour lequel
chaque homme est créé par Dieu et en lien direct avec
Lui [117]. Découverte qui s'approfondira avec la Réforme et
ne se manifestera concrètement qu'au xviie siècle. Toute la
philosophie de cette époque, en revanche, s'organise
autour de cette nouvelle image de l'homme, compris tantôt
comme individu porteur de droits et de devoirs particuliers
(à travers les analyses politiques et la notion de liberté
individuelle, par exemple chez Locke), tantôt comme sujet
pensant, pleinement conscient de soi-même (chez Descartes), tantôt encore comme une combinaison spécifique
d'atomes et de sensations (chez Hume), voire comme une
monade sans portes ni fenêtres, à la fois radicalement
différente de toutes les autres mais n'en différant qu'imper-
ceptiblement cependant (chez Leibniz). L'individu qui est
désormais reconnu l'est à la fois comme élément d'une
multiplicité, doté d'une réelle spécificité, mais surtout
comme porteur de sa propre loi, principe d'après lequel il
agit [118].

La critique à laquelle ont été soumis les ordres naturels a
en même temps brisé à jamais les cadres qui permettaient
d'ordonner les composants premiers. C'est ce que signifie
l'utilisation de la métaphore de l'état de guerre chez
Hobbes : avant l'intervention d'un principe unifiant, la
multiplicité n'est pas ordonnée, les individus sont livrés à
eux-mêmes, au désordre de leurs pulsions et de leurs
rencontres. L'état de guerre n'est autre que la coexistence
naturelle et non réglée des individus. En même temps que
l'enthousiasme suscité par l'idée d'un possible aménagement de la nature selon les vœux de l'homme et par la
perspective d'une nouvelle Atlantide, le xviie siècle lègue
donc au siècle suivant l'inquiétude que provoque une
question nouvelle, celle du fondement de l'ordre social. Le
problème majeur est de trouver un nouveau principe
d'ordre, susceptible de fonder l'unité de la société et

d'organiser les liens entre des éléments qui n'avaient jamais été considérés dans leur isolement auparavant, mais toujours déjà comme les parties intégrées d'un ensemble hiérarchisé et articulé. Il faut donc repartir de l'éparpillement des individus eux-mêmes pour trouver ce *nouveau* principe. Ainsi s'explique la forme que prennent les représentations imagées auxquelles les théoriciens politiques[119] font appel pour expliciter le moment fondateur de la société : c'est d'un contrat, d'une convention, que naît le corps social. La souveraineté réside en la volonté des hommes et la société est le résultat d'un accord passé entre tous les individus présents. Mais comment faire en sorte, si la société naît de la volonté humaine, que ses fondements ne soient pas considérés comme arbitraires et ne soient pas perpétuellement remis en cause ? Quel est le fondement de l'ordre social, des positions sociales, de la hiérarchie sociale, si la société est une construction humaine ? Qui empêchera les individus de remettre chaque jour en cause cet ordre, quelle est la règle de sa conservation ? Comment garantir la nécessaire intangibilité de l'ordre social, la nécessité pour lui d'être respecté et presque considéré comme sacré ? Qui déterminera les règles qui régiront les rapports — de contribution et de rétribution en particulier — des individus entre eux et qui pourra garantir que ces règles sont justes, s'il n'y a plus d'ordre naturel ?

Le XVIIIᵉ siècle est celui où s'élaborent les théories susceptibles de répondre à ces questions. Deux solutions radicalement différentes se mettent en place : l'économie et la politique. Elles se donnent toutes deux pour tâche de trouver le principe qui donnera une unité à la multiplicité non ordonnée des individus de l'état de nature. Les deux recourent, dans un premier temps, à la forme du contrat, pour représenter la manière dont les individus se mettent en relation. Mais dans un cas, celui de la politique, le contrat est l'acte par lequel se constitue une autorité politique et grâce auquel se réalise l'unité du corps politique[120] ; dans l'autre, le contrat détermine les conditions de l'échange, et donc énonce les lois de l'équivalence de deux grandeurs (objets, efforts, prestations...). Dans le premier cas, le contrat permet à tous les individus de se reconnaître comme corps politique et de se doter des règles selon lesquelles il sera organisé ; dans l'autre, il n'y a pas un contrat originel, mais une infinité de contrats, d'ailleurs la plupart du temps implicites, selon lesquels se règlent les échanges. C'est grâce à l'échange que naît et se maintient la société chez Smith. C'est la multiplicité des échanges qui constitue, à chaque instant, le lien social. L'économie est donc une philosophie de la société fondée sur la méfiance : l'intervention humaine n'est pas suffisante pour garantir l'ordre social. Au libre choix par les individus de leurs règles de vie et de leurs fins l'économie préfère la rigueur des lois. Comme une certaine philosophie politique, par exemple celle d'un Rousseau, l'économie ne se donne au départ ni instinct de sociabilité ni inclination naturelle pour les autres. Mais, à la différence de la politique, elle considère comme inutile l'idée d'un moment fondateur où les hommes se rassemblent pour décider des règles de leur vie commune : elle ne s'en remet qu'au besoin, c'est-à-dire au désir d'abondance. Elle décentre de ce fait l'objet du désir humain : ce n'est pas directement la société, mais l'abondance. La société ne naît pas de la volonté de faire du bien à autrui, mais de l'intérêt individuel : « Ce n'est pas de la bienveillance du boucher, du marchand de bière et du boulanger que nous attendons notre dîner, mais bien du soin qu'ils apportent à leurs intérêts[121]. » Mais ce désir d'abondance est tellement fort, tellement partagé par toute la société qu'il va déterminer une mécanique sociale bien plus solide — telle est la croyance de l'économie — que l'ordre auquel aurait conduit le désir de société ou la définition collective par les individus des règles de leur vie commune.

L'économie se présente donc, au xviiie siècle, et très clairement chez Smith, comme une réponse philosophique au problème de la naissance et du maintien de la société, mais c'est une philosophie sombre et inquiète, qui ne croit pas en la possibilité pour les hommes de déterminer les conditions de leur vie commune et qui préfère énoncer les lois « naturelles » de celle-ci. Le désir d'abondance est le principe qui donne son unité, de l'extérieur, à la société : tous les individus sont habités par ce désir. Il est désormais le premier moteur social, qui meut l'ensemble des individus par « amour », comme le Dieu d'Aristote [122]. Il donne de cette manière une première sorte d'unité au corps social. Mais ce désir structure de surcroît toute la société. A partir de lui, l'économie définit en effet les lois naturelles de l'enrichissement et en déduit l'ordre social et la structure des rapports sociaux, entièrement déterminés, au sens fort du terme, par la capacité des hommes à produire et à échanger. Les relations sociales, les liens entre les individus, les places, la hiérarchie sociale ne sont pas le résultat du choix des individus, mais celui d'un déterminisme strict, dont l'économie dit les lois. Cette déduction de l'ordre social et des rapports sociaux s'opère de deux manières. D'abord, le désir d'abondance est tel qu'il oblige à l'efficacité et conduit à une division accrue du travail, donc à un approfondissement de la dépendance aux autres... Le premier chapitre des *Recherches* met cet ordre en scène : ce n'est pas en réalité la démultiplication de la puissance productive du travail qui fascine Smith dans la division du travail, mais l'ordre social qu'elle induit. Dans ce texte extraordinaire, dont la forme entrelacée est elle-même symbolique de l'absolue dépendance réciproque dans laquelle se trouvent les individus, la manufacture d'épingles représente en petit la grande société dépeinte à la fin du chapitre : c'est une société où chacun est absolument enchaîné aux autres. Chaque objet consommé a nécessité des milliers d'opérations, qui ont été réalisées par des centaines d'individus différents. Aussi l'individu est-il lié aux autres non seulement dans l'exercice de son travail, mais aussi pour acquérir les produits dont il a besoin. Ces besoins réciproques forment la base d'un ordre social qui

fonctionne « automatiquement ». Ensuite, les lois de l'économie déterminent ce que valent les efforts des individus,
comment leur contribution à la réussite de l'objectif du
corps social tout entier (la Nation) détermine leur propre
enrichissement. L'effort des individus, la mesure dans
laquelle ils augmentent l'ensemble de la richesse et la
manière dont se diffuse l'opulence entretiennent des liens
logiques. Rien de cela n'est laissé au hasard, l'économie est
la science de ces lois. La mécanique sociale est donc tout
entière construite autour de cet impératif d'abondance et
découle strictement de la manière dont chaque individu
participe au grand devoir social.

Le travail est évidemment au centre de cette mécanique
sociale, il est son instrument de prédilection : il est à la fois
l'effort humain qui transforme et l'instrument de mesure
qui indique, scientifiquement, combien vaut cet effort,
c'est-à-dire contre quelle somme d'argent ou quel autre
produit il peut être échangé. Il est le rapport social central
parce qu'il est le moyen concret par lequel on poursuit
l'abondance, parce qu'il est un effort toujours destiné à
l'autre et surtout parce qu'il est la mesure générale des
échanges et des rapports sociaux. Il détermine le prix de
toute chose et garantit l'intangibilité de l'ordre social. Ce
dernier est donc déterminé des deux côtés par le travail :
par la dynamique des besoins et de l'interdépendance, par
la mesure et la comparaison des efforts. Par lui, les
individus non seulement sont tenus ensemble, obligés à la
sociabilité, mais de surcroît leurs échanges sont réglés. Le
cœur de la réponse économique à la question de l'ordre
social, c'est le travail matériel et marchand et l'échange.
Celui-ci est le seul moyen de substituer à l'ancienne
universitas un ordre tout aussi solide, dont l'inflexibilité a la
dureté du naturel, mais qui n'oblige pourtant les individus
ni à s'aimer ni à poursuivre autre chose que leurs propres
souhaits. L'échange est le producteur de lien social, le cœur
de la logique économique. C'est pour cette raison que
Smith fait de lui la chiquenaude qui met les individus de

l'état de nature en branle : notre penchant à troquer est bien le signe que telle est la loi de la société. Le vocabulaire (" troc ") attire enfin notre attention sur un point fondamental : nul besoin de passage traumatique de l'état de nature à l'état civil chez Smith. Le troc est l'étincelle de civilité qui nous épargne ce détour. L'échange est ce qui rend la société toujours plus riche, toujours plus civilisée, car l'échange économique est toujours un échange humain, il rapproche les hommes, aussi éloignés soient-ils. Mieux, il est la condition d'une plus grande égalité des conditions, ainsi que de la liberté individuelle et politique : « Sans l'aide et le concours de plusieurs milliers de personnes, le plus petit particulier, dans un pays civilisé, ne pourrait être vêtu et meublé même selon ce que nous regardons assez mal à propos comme la manière la plus simple et la plus commune. Il est bien vrai que son mobilier paraîtra extrêmement simple et commun, si on le compare avec le luxe extravagant d'un grand seigneur ; cependant, entre le mobilier d'un prince d'Europe et celui d'un paysan laborieux et rangé, il n'y a peut-être pas autant de différences qu'entre les meubles de ce dernier et ceux de tel roi d'Afrique qui règne sur mille sauvages nus et qui dispose en maître absolu de leur liberté et de leur vie [123]. » L'échange est le creuset du lien social : alors que nous croyons échanger pour nous enrichir, nous sont donnés par surcroît le lien social et le rapprochement des conditions. L'économie concilie l'arbitraire et le naturel : nous échangeons dans l'illusion d'une abondance promise et derechef nous construisons l'ordre social, sans l'avoir voulu.

Mais l'économie n'est pas l'au-delà du politique : elle est son autre. Elle résout le problème de l'ordre social en cherchant des lois, en incitant les individus à se servir les uns des autres et aussi à se servir d'eux-mêmes, à se donner à la fois en vente et en spectacle. La politique, si elle utilise aussi le moyen du contrat, est de nature radicalement différente, car, ne serait-ce qu'une fois, elle met les hommes volontairement en contact les uns avec les autres et elle leur fait accomplir ensemble quelque chose, qui n'est pas un échange. Elle ne détourne pas leur intérêt. Elle n'a donc pas besoin du travail ni de l'échange marchand. L'économie n'est pas une solution qui prend la place du politique, comme semblent parfois le laisser penser Louis Dumont ou Pierre Rosanvallon [124]. Pour le premier, le moment qui va de Smith à Marx voit l'épanouissement et l'approfondissement d'une unique idéologie, celle de l'économie, qui s'autonomise et se construit contre le politique. Pour le second, qui lui emboîte le pas, les théories économiques viennent après l'échec des théories du contrat parce que celles-ci sont incapables de régler le problème de l'institution de la société [125]. Mais les théories économiques sont elles aussi des théories du contrat et le développement de l'économie, comme mode de régulation du social, ne met pas fin aux solutions proprement politiques. Au xviiie siècle, les deux types de solution se sont développées conjointement : les solutions de Rousseau ne sont pas économiques. Elles sont politiques, au sens que l'on dirait « ancien » du terme : elles reposent sur la volonté du lien social et croient possible de le construire et de le vouloir pour lui-même. La lecture de l'article « Economie » de l'Encyclopédie, dont Rousseau est le rédacteur, suffirait à nous en convaincre. Certes, dans les faits, l'économie va prendre une place grandissante, au détriment d'une régulation politique. Mais la possibilité de celle-ci existe. Toute une tradition a d'ailleurs tenté de la penser avec d'autres instruments que le contrat. Ainsi Rosanvallon et Dumont confondent-ils peut-être le droit et le fait, ou acceptent-ils peut-être trop rapidement l'effacement d'un type de régulation, jugé caduc, ainsi que l'assimilation entre société régie par la politique et société hiérarchique et holiste. Notre ambition est justement d'attirer à nouveau l'attention sur cette autre tradition, qui n'aboutit pas, comme l'économie, à mettre le travail au centre de la vie sociale. Car c'est bien là, en définitive, la conséquence majeure de la régulation économique : elle installe le travail au fondement de la vie sociale, elle oblige la société, si elle veut exister, à ne pas cesser de produire, d'échanger, de travailler. Elle fait du travail le signe majeur d'appartenance à la société et le devoir de chacun. La Révolution française ne dira pas autre chose, par exemple lorsque la commission dirigée par La Rochefoulcauld-Liancourt, chargée de trouver une solution au problème de l'indigence, écrira : « Si celui qui existe a le droit de dire à la société : " Faites-moi vivre ", la société a également le droit de lui répondre : " Donne-moi ton travail [126]. " » La typologie des pauvres à laquelle aboutit le Comité de mendicité sera dès lors organisée autour du travail [127]. D'un côté, les vrais pauvres, ou du moins ceux qui ont vraiment droit à l'assistance de la société : les enfants, les vieillards et les invalides. De l'autre, les faux, ceux qui mendient par paresse mais qui pourraient très bien vivre autrement. Les premiers doivent être assistés, les seconds punis ou mis au travail. La capacité de travailler constitue désormais le critère qui sépare les « bons » des « mauvais ».

Gardons-nous cependant d'anticiper. A l'époque de Smith comme au moment de la Révolution française, le travail n'est pas encore glorifié. Il est déjà conçu comme artifice, dans les discours les plus en avance sur leur époque, en particulier celui de Bacon, mais il n'est pas encore véritablement théorisé comme tel. Il est né abstrait et matériel, il l'est encore. Tel est le premier acte.

CHAPITRE IV

ACTE II : LE TRAVAIL, ESSENCE DE L'HOMME

A la fin du XVIIIe siècle, le travail apparaît donc sous la double figure du facteur de production et du rapport contributif qui permet la mise en relation de l'individu et de la société. Il reste conçu de façon mécanique et abstraite et sa nature n'est jamais analysée en tant que telle. Il ne fait surtout l'objet d'aucune valorisation particulière et n'est pas encore interprété comme puissance créatrice d'artifices. L'*Encyclopédie* de Diderot et d'Alembert le définit ainsi : « C'est l'occupation journalière à laquelle l'homme est condamné par son besoin, et à laquelle il doit en même temps sa santé, sa subsistance, sa sérénité, son bon sens et sa vertu peut-être [128]. » Le XIXe siècle va profondément transformer cette représentation en faisant du travail le modèle de l'activité créatrice par excellence. Cette révolution conceptuelle s'opère cependant sans changement de vocabulaire, laissant croire à une invariance de la notion, alors que la signification est transformée de fond en comble : le travail apparaît désormais comme l'essence de l'homme. Cette transformation va évidemment de pair avec un profond remaniement des conceptions du monde et du savoir, ainsi que des conditions d'exercice du travail concret lui-même. Au même moment se met en place le grand schème utopique du travail — porté par les socialistes —, qui indique de quelle manière les conditions concrètes et juridiques du travail doivent être bouleversées pour que le travail devienne en réalité ce qu'il est véritablement. Une pensée de l'aliénation se met donc en place, qui dénonce le travail tel qu'il se développe dans les manufactures et y voit une défiguration du travail tel qu'il devrait être. Il faut donc distinguer, dans l'exposition au moins, trois moments : la glorification du travail ; la critique du travail réel ; la mise en place du schème utopique.

Ce bouleversement conceptuel dont nous sommes les héritiers s'opère au même moment, quoique sous des formes différentes, en France et en Allemagne [129]. En France, c'est la dimension technique qui focalise l'attention. Le travail apparaît d'abord comme le moyen dont dispose désormais l'humanité pour progresser vers le bienêtre. Les formidables possibilités ouvertes à l'humanité par le développement technique imprègnent cette pensée et les caractéristiques du travail, résultat de la puissance créatrice des hommes, sont immédiatement et sans problèmes transposées à chaque individu, comme si chacun était désormais le dépositaire de cette puissance. Pendant ce temps, en Allemagne, et sous une forme moins directement accessible, se développe une philosophie idéaliste dont Hegel est le principal représentant, et qui fonde philosophiquement l'idée selon laquelle le travail est l'essence de l'homme.

La philosophie hégélienne est en effet celle qui permet le mieux de comprendre, nous semble-t-il, l'ensemble de ces transformations. Il ne s'agit certes pas de dire que l'idéalisme allemand [130] a déterminé à lui seul un nouveau concept de travail, mais bien plutôt que les profondes transformations intervenues dans les conditions réelles de travail (le développement de l'industrie et de la productivité du travail) se sont accompagnées d'un discours philosophique qui permet de mieux comprendre comment ces transformations ont été vécues et représentées. Ne croyons pas non plus que l'idéalisme allemand a été simplement le produit de la révolution industrielle allemande. Hegel écrit en effet ses premières œuvres au tout début du XIXᵉ siècle, alors que la Révolution industrielle ne s'est pas encore véritablement développée en Allemagne. Comme le dit Marx, l'Allemagne opère ses révolutions et absorbe les bouleversements d'abord en esprit, en les théorisant. C'est pourquoi la lecture des textes philosophiques s'avère instructive. La philosophie de Hegel n'a pas à proprement parler pour objet l'élucidation du concept de travail. Mais elle permet de comprendre pourquoi celui-ci a rapidement acquis une place centrale, et surtout pourquoi il a pu être interprété de façon « dynamique » comme essence de l'homme.

Le travail de l'Esprit

La philosophie de Hegel est spiritualiste, elle s'intéresse à l'esprit, et même à l'Esprit, comme si le monde et son histoire se confondaient avec le développement de cet Esprit, que Hegel appelle justement parfois Esprit du monde. Dans les philosophies antérieures, nous l'avons vu, Dieu était décrit comme immobile, éternel, réalisant l'acte de création hors du temps, n'étant pas « affecté » par ce qui se passait « après » cet acte de création. Hegel introduit, lui, l'histoire en Dieu : Dieu ou l'Esprit n'est pas extérieur au monde, il n'est pas une Personne que nous pourrions nous représenter, il n'est pas identique au début et à la fin de l'histoire. Dieu ou l'Esprit est d'abord *en soi* ; il a besoin de s'exprimer pour se connaître, pour développer en quelque sorte ses potentialités, pour mettre au grand jour ce qu'il contient au plus profond de lui-même et dont il n'est pas conscient. Dieu doit devenir *pour soi* — c'est-à-dire en en étant conscient — ce qu'il est en soi, comme un enfant doit exprimer, à travers toute sa vie, ce qu'il était en puissance pour devenir adulte. Mais ce qui arrive à Dieu ne nous est pas étranger : notre histoire et celle des représentations que nous nous faisons de Dieu est l'histoire même de Dieu. Nous nous le sommes d'abord représenté comme élément physique (le feu, l'eau...), puis comme multiple (l'animisme, le polythéisme...), puis comme une personne en colère (l'Ancien Testament), et enfin comme Esprit (le Nouveau Testament). L'essence de l'Esprit consiste à se connaître, à nier ce qui n'est pas lui, et ceci est une seule et même chose. Pour Dieu ou l'Esprit, se connaître, c'est agir. Dieu se crée et l'histoire de cette autocréation, au terme de laquelle Dieu est pleinement lui-même, est aussi l'histoire de l'humanité, de ses institutions, de ses représentations, de sa connaissance d'elle-même, exprimée à travers ses productions matérielles et spirituelles. Entendons : l'histoire de l'humanité, c'est-à-dire des hommes, des créatures les plus spirituelles, est en même temps celle de Dieu ; Dieu accède à lui-même, à ce qu'il est réellement, à travers l'homme. Comme si Dieu ne parvenait à se connaître qu'a travers les « productions » humaines, parmi lesquelles on compte aussi des représentations — que celles-ci se développent à travers les sciences, l'art, la philosophie ou la politique. L'histoire humaine est en même temps celle de l'assomption de l'Esprit, à travers laquelle celui-ci se connaît. D'où les multiples formules hégéliennes qui identifient substance et sujet [131].

Les conséquences d'une telle représentation de l'Absolu sont immenses. D'abord parce que l'Histoire humaine est ainsi dotée d'un sens, c'est-à-dire d'une finalité et d'une signification, d'une manière encore plus stricte que chez saint Augustin, par exemple. La fin, le terme de l'Histoire, c'est la parfaite coïncidence de l'Esprit avec lui-même. En quoi consiste-t-elle ? Pour le comprendre, il faut bien saisir ce que signifie pour Hegel « se connaître » : il s'agit de s'assimiler l'extériorité. La démarche du connaître consiste, pour l'Esprit, celui de l'homme ou celui du monde, à s'opposer à un élément extérieur, à le transformer et, en le transformant, à mettre au jour ce qui était caché en soi et à comprendre l'objet extérieur comme faisant désormais partie de soi. Pour se connaître, l'Esprit prend des formes diverses, à travers lesquelles et grâce auxquelles il se connaît, et qu'il lui faut alors dépasser pour aller toujours plus loin dans la connaissance de lui-même. Tous les progrès de l'esprit humain et des institutions humaines sont ainsi autant de formes qu'a prises l'Esprit pour approfondir la connaissance qu'il a de lui-même. Au terme de l'Histoire, l'Esprit est « chez lui », il sait que tout ce qui lui semblait extérieur est lui-même, l'Esprit est devenu pour soi, c'est-à-dire consciemment, ce qu'il était en soi. Hegel appelle ce moment le « Savoir absolu ». C'est aussi la fin de l'Histoire.

Une telle représentation peut paraître abstraite. Qu'est-ce que cet Esprit qui se promène à travers les siècles et revêt des formes successives pour mieux se connaître ? Il faut s'installer dans le système hégélien pour voir combien la représentation qu'il donne de son siècle est extraordinairement significative. Ce siècle est en train de découvrir l'histoire, l'évolution, la puissance technicienne de l'homme... Hegel en révèle le squelette logique. Dans le même temps il met en évidence ce en quoi a cru ce siècle, en particulier la profonde transformation de la science qui, de purement contemplative qu'elle était, devient fabricatrice (l'acte technique et la connaissance ne sont plus séparés). L'histoire de l'Esprit est à la fois celle de l'humanité et celle de chaque homme : l'acte de connaissance du donné extérieur est un acte qui transforme le sujet connaissant, lui révèle les capacités dont il était plein. Le connaître est un pouvoir. L'acte de connaissance est conçu sur le modèle de la fabrication et de la consommation : l'objet connu n'est qu'un prétexte à se découvrir, donc à s'enrichir soi-même. Ce processus où la connaissance est un agir, où se connaître signifie pour l'Esprit se plonger dans l'Histoire, être l'Histoire, Hegel l'appelle travail. Voilà qui est absolument sidérant. L'acte par lequel l'Esprit se connaît est un travail qu'il accomplit sur lui-même : « L'Esprit est dans le travail de sa propre transformation [132] », écrit Hegel dans les toutes premières pages de la

Préface à la Phénoménologie de l'esprit. Le travail est pour Hegel l'activité spirituelle par laquelle l'Esprit s'oppose un donné extérieur pour se connaître lui-même, s'invente en quelque sorte des obstacles extérieurs pour s'obliger à dévoiler ses potentialités. L'Esprit travaille donc sans cesse, jusqu'à la fin de l'Histoire. Et le moteur de l'activité de l'Esprit réside dans sa volonté de se connaître entièrement, c'est-à-dire d'amener à l'extérieur tout ce qui était à l'intérieur, non révélé ; ce qui revient à reconnaître que tout ce qui semblait être extérieur, le naturel, ce qui est donné, imposé, était déjà en fait de l'Esprit.

Autrement dit, le but ultime est la spiritualisation totale de la nature ; à terme, il ne doit plus y avoir de nature capable de résister à l'Esprit, puisque l'Esprit est pure activité. Hegel légitime ainsi philosophiquement ce que nous avons vu naître avec Descartes et Bacon : la volonté d'aménager totalement la nature pour en faire un monde humain. Hegel ne dit pas que nous devons rendre habitable et confortable le monde naturel qui nous est donné, que nous devons accroître notre bien-être. Il n'est en rien hédoniste ou utilitariste. Il affirme simplement que la vocation de l'Esprit est de nier tout donné naturel [133]. La recherche de l'abondance et de la richesse, Hegel la traduit en termes de loi du monde, l'objectif ultime de l'Histoire du monde étant l'humanisation complète de la nature. Il n'est donc pas anodin que Hegel parle du travail de l'Esprit. Il voit d'ailleurs dans le travail humain le même schème à l'œuvre : dès ses premiers écrits [134], il a insisté sur la dimension spirituelle de l'outil. En s'opposant à la nature physique, en la transformant, en inventant des prolongements de son corps pour l'utiliser, en rusant avec elle, l'homme non seulement s'est révélé à lui-même ses capacités, mais il les a créées, il s'est créé [135]. Par le travail, l'humanité s'est autocréée, et l'Esprit du monde à travers elle. Le travail est donc le médiateur entre la nature et l'Esprit. Par le travail, l'homme détruit le naturel (« Travailler signifie anéantir le monde ou le maudire » [136]) et se fait toujours plus humain.

Le travail abstrait, moment à dépasser

Néanmoins, ce n'est pas le travail-effort par lequel l'homme satisfait ses besoins qui intéresse Hegel, pas plus que celui qui se développe sous ses yeux dans les manufactures. Ce type de travail est abstrait et sa principale caractéristique est de dissoudre les communautés naturelles et d'enserrer les individus dans une dépendance universelle : « Par cette division, non seulement le travail de l'individu devient plus simple, mais l'habileté de l'individu dans son travail abstrait et la quantité de ses produits deviennent plus grandes. Du même coup, cette abstraction de l'habileté et du moyen rend plus complets la dépendance et les rapports mutuels entre les hommes pour la satisfaction des autres besoins, au point d'en faire une nécessité absolue [137]. » Ce travail-là est condamné à terme, car il recèle trop de contradictions : « Une multitude d'ouvriers est condamnée dans les fabriques, les manufactures et les mines à des travaux entièrement abrutissants, insalubres, dangereux et qui restreignent l'habileté. Des branches de l'industrie qui entretenaient une nombreuse classe d'hommes sont épuisées d'un coup à cause de la mode ou de l'effondrement des prix dû aux découvertes dans d'autres pays [...], et toute cette multitude qui ne peut se tirer d'affaire est livrée à la pauvreté. Alors intervient l'opposition de la grande richesse et de la grande pauvreté. [...] Cette inégalité de la richesse et de la pauvreté devient le plus grand déchirement de la volonté sociale, la révolte intérieure et la haine. [...] Il apparaît ici que, malgré son excès de richesse, la société civile n'est pas assez riche, c'est-à-dire que dans sa richesse elle ne possède pas assez de biens pour payer tribut à l'excès de misère et à la plèbe qu'elle engendre [138]. » Mais ce moment demeure essentiel parce qu'il rapproche les hommes, les enserre dans une dépendance réciproque et ouvre la voie à la véritable communauté. De plus, il conduit à l'invention de la machine, produit de l'esprit humain qui fascine Hegel, parce qu'elle est un automatisme capable de mener sans répit la tâche de négation et de transformation : la machine, c'est l'inquiétude du subjectif, du Concept, posé en dehors du sujet, ou encore le pouvoir de négation de l'homme acquérant une existence objective autonome [139]. Comme s'il n'y avait plus besoin de l'homme pour accomplir la tâche d'anéantissement de la nature. Le travail abstrait de Smith est donc un moment nécessaire, qui porte l'esprit à un degré de conscience et d'approfondissement supérieur, mais il est destiné à être dépassé.

Cela est vrai pour les sociétés humaines et également pour l'Esprit. Autrement dit, si l'Esprit est « en travail », c'est-à-dire en activité jusqu'à la fin de l'Histoire, ce travail, qui consiste à s'incarner dans des formes finies et à les dépasser, ne prend qu'un temps la forme du travail conçu comme opposition à la nature ou du travail industriel, salarié et abstrait. Sans être appelé à disparaître totalement, celui-ci n'aura néanmoins été qu'un temps le moyen majeur d'expression de l'Esprit. Ce qui sera prolongé, c'est le travail de l'humanité sur soi, mais ce « travail » prendra d'autres formes que celles qu'il a prises au XIXᵉ siècle. Ce que décrit Hegel sous ce terme de travail de l'Esprit, cette tâche de négation infinie, est bien plutôt ce que nous-mêmes appellerions culture ou formation. Hegel emploie le même terme pour l'ensemble du processus, pour la vie de l'Esprit, qui est perpétuel approfondissement de soi et qui prendra des formes de plus en plus spirituelles (institutions politiques, œuvres artistiques, religions, systèmes philosophiques...) [140] et pour le travail industriel, qui n'est que l'une des formes que prend l'histoire de l'humanité. La polysémie du terme atteint son acmé.

Le concept de travail est donc, avec Hegel, considérablement enrichi et transformé, puisqu'il désigne désormais l'activité spirituelle elle-même, l'essence de l'histoire de l'humanité, qui est activité créatrice et expression de soi. A ce titre, on peut dire que Hegel a mis en évidence l'apport spécifique du XIXᵉ siècle : la construction d'une essence du travail, c'est-à-dire d'un idéal de création et réalisation de soi. Marx et une partie des socialistes identifieront cet idéal avec l'essence vraie du travail, à quoi ils compareront le travail tel qu'il se développe sous leurs yeux : c'est l'acte de naissance du schème utopique du travail.

Le travail, essence de l'homme

Rappelons rapidement que Marx connaît parfaitement Hegel et qu'il en récupère l'héritage théorique. Certes, il remet, dit-il, la dialectique de Hegel de la tête sur les pieds : ce ne sont ni l'Esprit ni les Idées qui dirigent le cours du monde ; ce sont les hommes qui font leur propre histoire. Marx reprend donc à son compte l'idée de vaste développement historique que présentait Hegel ; cependant, le sujet de celui-ci n'est plus l'Esprit mais l'humanité elle-même. Le travail n'est pas celui de l'Esprit, mais le travail quotidien des hommes, le travail réel, réalisé avec des outils, de la sueur, de la douleur et de l'invention. Sur ces bases, Marx construit une vaste opposition entre le vrai travail, qui est l'essence de l'homme, et la réalité du travail, celle qu'il observe tous les jours à Manchester, et qui n'en est qu'une forme aliénée. Le travail est l'essence de l'homme, parce que l'histoire nous montre que l'homme est devenu ce qu'il est par le travail : « L'histoire dite universelle n'est rien d'autre que la génération de l'homme par le travail humain, rien d'autre que le devenir de la nature pour l'homme [141]. » Mais ceci ne suffit pas. Il faut comprendre l'affirmation de Marx comme celle d'une véritable identité : l'essence de l'homme *est* le travail. L'homme ne peut pas exister autrement qu'en travaillant, c'est-à-dire — et ici Marx reprend le schème hégélien — qu'en créant de l'artifice, qu'en mettant ses propres œuvres à la place du donné naturel. Et il faut même aller plus loin : l'homme n'est pleinement homme, selon Marx, que s'il imprime sur toute chose la marque de son humanité. L'acte qui semble le plus naturel, la procréation, est déjà, chez Marx, humain, donc travail. Dès lors, la fin de l'histoire n'est plus un Esprit qui se connaît lui-même mais un homme ayant humanisé tout le naturel, ce que Marx appelle humanisation de la nature ou naturalisation de l'homme [142]. Marx marque dès lors une sorte d'acmé de l'humanisme technologique dont nous avons vu la naissance chez Bacon. L'homme ne doit avoir de cesse (ou plutôt n'a de cesse, car il n'y a pas d'impératif moral chez Marx, pas plus que chez Hegel), d'humaniser le monde, de le modeler à son image, de réduire le naturel, y compris en lui-même. Il y a chez Marx une haine du donné naturel identique à celle que l'on trouve chez Hegel. Elle va de pair avec un refus de l'animalité en l'homme et avec la croyance profonde que l'homme est fragile et toujours menacé par l'animalité en lui [143]. Celle-ci sert constamment de repoussoir chez Marx, comme dans les philosophies précédentes qui ont vu dans la raison de l'homme le moyen d'éviter la rareté et la guerre. Il se situe dans le droit-fil de cette pensée faite de peur et d'allégresse qui voit dans la technique le moyen d'aménager la nature, de la domestiquer, de l'apprivoiser et d'en faire un havre pour l'homme. L'objectif, c'est bien de se prémunir contre la rareté. « L'homme appppartient à une espèce d'êtres qui, pratiquement et théoriquement, font d'eux-mêmes et de toute chose leur propre objet. [...] Concrètement, l'universalité de l'homme apparaît précisément dans le fait que la nature entière constitue son prolongement non organique, dans la mesure où elle est son moyen de subsistance immédiat et la matière, l'objet et l'outil de son activité vitale. La nature, pour autant qu'elle n'est pas le corps humain, est le corps non organique de l'homme [144]. » Dès lors, homme et travail sont des termes quasi interchangeables.

Mais si tout acte humain est du travail, comment définir celui-ci, quelle est sa différence spécifique ? Certes, comme autocréation : « C'est précisément en façonnant le monde des objets que l'homme commence à s'affirmer comme un être générique. Cette production est sa vie générique créatrice. Grâce à cette production, la nature apparaît comme son œuvre et sa réalité. L'objet du travail est donc la réalisation de la vie générique de l'homme. L'homme ne se recrée pas seulement d'une façon intellectuelle, dans sa conscience, mais activement, réellement, il se contemple lui-même dans le monde de sa création. [...] L'histoire universelle n'est rien d'autre que la génération de l'homme par le travail humain, rien d'autre que le devenir de la nature pour l'homme. [...] L'immense mérite de la phéno-ménologie de Hegel et de son résultat final — la dialectique de la négativité comme principe moteur et créateur — consiste d'abord en ceci : Hegel conçoit l'autocréation de l'homme, l'autocréation comme un processus, l'objectifica-tion comme négation de l'objectification, comme aliéna-tion et suppression de cette aliénation ; de la sorte, il saisit la nature du travail, et conçoit l'homme objectif, véritable, parce que réel, comme résultat de son propre travail [145]. » Mais ceci est encore une tautologie. Ou toute création serait-elle du travail ? Marx, reprenant le concept le plus large de Hegel (« travail de l'Esprit ») et l'appliquant à l'homme [146], englobe en effet sous ce concept la quasi-totalité de l'activité humaine : tout est travail, toute activité humaine, de la procréation à l'activité de connaissance. Il va même plus loin : le vrai travail n'est pas le travail physique, celui qui s'accomplit dans l'effort et sous la contrainte du besoin. Car l'homme ne produit vraiment que libéré du besoin, à la différence de l'animal. Le travail, le vrai travail, pourrait-on dire, n'est pas lié au besoin, il est une activité consciente, visant consciemment à faire du monde naturel un monde humain.

Marx a hérité de Hegel un concept du travail dont le modèle est profondément artisanal et technicien. L'homme travailleur, c'est l'*Homo faber* qui, en créant, se découvre lui-même. Mais l'objet transformé est en même temps l'occasion pour l'homme d'exprimer sa personnalité. Paradoxalement, au moment où se développent les produits industriels déjà standardisés, c'est un modèle plus ancien qui paraît inspirer Hegel et Marx, celui de l'artisan et de son œuvre. En réalité, le maître mot est « expression » : le travail, c'est toute activité humaine qui permet d'exprimer l'individualité de celui qui l'exerce. Mais de s'exprimer aussi *pour* l'autre, donc de montrer à l'autre à la fois sa singularité et son appartenance au genre humain. Telle est la signification de cet extraordinaire texte de Marx : « Supposons, dit-il, que nous produisions comme des êtres humains : chacun de nous s'affirmerait doublement dans sa production, soi-même et l'autre. 1. Dans ma production, je réaliserais mon individualité, ma particularité ; j'éprouverais, en travaillant, la jouissance d'une manifestation individuelle de ma vie, et dans la contemplation de l'objet, j'aurais la joie individuelle de reconnaître ma personnalité comme une puissance réelle, concrètement saisissable et échappant à tout doute. 2. Dans ta jouissance ou ton emploi de mon produit, j'aurais la joie spirituelle de satisfaire par mon travail un besoin humain de réaliser la nature humaine et de fournir au besoin d'un autre l'objet de sa nécessité. 3. J'aurais conscience de servir de médiateur entre toi et le genre humain, d'être reconnu et ressenti par toi comme un complément à ton propre être et comme une partie nécessaire de toi-même, d'être accepté dans ton esprit comme dans ton amour. 4. J'aurais, dans mes manifestations individuelles, la joie de créer la manifestation de ta vie, c'est-à-dire de réaliser et d'affirmer dans mon activité individuelle ma vraie nature, ma sociabilité humaine. Nos productions seraient autant de miroirs où nos êtres rayonneraient l'un vers l'autre [147]. »

Non seulement le travail est la plus haute manifestation de mon individualité, mais il constitue également ce milieu au sein duquel se réalise la véritable sociabilité. Là où Smith pensait la sociabilité et le lien social sous la forme de la dépendance réciproque non voulue, Marx le voit dans le travail réalisé pour l'autre. Ce sont les liens d'échanges réciproques, mais aussi des liens volontaires, qui sont au fondement du lien social, c'est la société civile de Smith et de Hegel rendue humaine. Voilà pourquoi Marx peut se passer de l'Etat comme structure supérieure qui subordonne la lutte des intérêts individuels de la société civile : celle-ci est immédiatement pacifiée parce qu'elle est fondée sur l'échange égal et sur le désir du produit de l'autre comme image de l'autre. Le travail possède dès lors cette triple qualité de me révéler à moi-même, de révéler ma sociabilité et de transformer le monde. En lui se réalise l'échange réciproque de ce que chacun est véritablement... La production consiste à mettre quelque chose de soi-même dans un produit, ce quelque chose pouvant être lu soit dans un sens économique (la valeur travail), soit dans un sens symbolique (une image de moi-même)[148]. Le travail véritable est donc au plus haut point un rapport social, il est la vérité du rapport social, du moins de celui qui est rêvé par Marx. Mais, il faut insister sur ce point, et Marx est le premier à le savoir, cette essence n'a jamais existé *in concreto,* et c'est seulement parce que les circonstances historiques l'ont voulu que le travail peut être pensé de cette manière. Il a fallu, pour en venir là, sortir des conceptions féodales, inventer le travail comme capacité susceptible d'être exercée librement par l'individu. L'essence du travail est pensée à l'horizon de l'avenir et non comme un trésor perdu : un jour, lorsque les forces productives seront suffisamment développées et que les contradictions deviendront trop fortes, les conditions seront réunies pour que le travail devienne adéquat à son essence.

Le concept de travail rêvé est donc au centre d'une triple relation : de l'individu au donné naturel ; de l'individu aux autres ; de l'individu à lui-même. Le travail est à la fois un rapport de l'homme à la nature et un rapport social, mais si l'on pousse l'utopie à son terme et si l'on se place au moment où tout donné naturel a disparu, où tout est humain, donc, le travail apparaît dans son essence, sous la forme de ce qu'il est réellement. L'homme étant libéré du besoin, le travail n'est plus un rapport à la nature, il n'est plus qu'un rapport social, le rapport social dans sa pureté. Si l'activité essentielle de l'homme est de s'exprimer, lorsque le donné naturel n'existe plus comme prétexte à l'expression de l'homme, le travail perd son caractère laborieux. Dès lors, il est ce qui fonde et maintient le lien social, qui apparaît comme un pur rapport d'expression : je te comprends à travers ton œuvre, tu me contemples à travers la mienne. Alors, en effet, l'échange marchand devient superflu. La marchandise qui faisait écran entre les hommes peut être supprimée. Elle déformait le pur rapport d'expression qui peut désormais se développer, elle tordait les images. La représentation que la philosophie marxienne se fait du travail dévoile le fantasme social qui la sous-tend : le rêve d'une société d'individus libérés et auto-nomes qui s'exprimeraient à l'infini les uns les autres, d'une société à l'ordre social pacifié et dont le rapport fondamen-tal serait d'expression.

Le travail aliéné

Le travail ainsi compris explique le type de critique que Marx développe à l'égard du travail « réel », qui se met en place sous ses yeux. L'essence du travail voit sa réalisation entravée ; le travail réel est un travail aliéné. Toute pensée de l'aliénation est en même temps une pensée de l'essence, une pensée qui condamne la réalité, qu'elle tient pour déformée par rapport à ce qu'elle devrait être, ou ce qu'elle sera. La critique majeure de Marx consiste à dire que, dans la société qu'il voit et dans l'économie politique, le but n'est justement pas le développement de l'homme grâce au travail, médiateur par essence, mais au contraire l'enrichis-sement. Le travail réel est une abstraction sans contenu, dont le but est extérieur à lui-même. Le travail dans la

société industrielle capitaliste est toujours déjà aliéné.
« Plus la production et les besoins sont variés, plus les
travaux du producteur sont uniformes et plus son travail
tombe sous la catégorie du travail lucratif. A la fin, le
travail n'a plus que cette signification-là, et il est tout à fait
accidentel ou inessentiel que le producteur se trouve vis-à-
vis de son produit dans un rapport de jouissance immédiate
et de besoin personnel. Peu importe également que l'activité, l'action de travail soit pour lui une jouissance de sa
personnalité, la réalisation de ses dons naturels et de ses
fins spirituelles [149]. » Il est aliéné justement parce qu'il
empêche l'homme d'atteindre le but que nous avons vu
Marx lui assigner : développer, spiritualiser et humaniser
l'humanité. Dans l'économie politique, le travail n'exerce
plus cette fonction, il est détourné de son véritable but.
Parce qu'il détourne l'humanité de la réalisation de ses plus
hautes fins, le travail ramène dès lors l'humanité à l'animalité ; au lieu d'être une activité vitale consciente et volontaire, le travail est rabaissé au rang de moyen : « En
dégradant au rang de moyen la libre activité créatrice de
l'homme, le travail aliéné fait de sa vie générique un
instrument de son existence physique. [...] l'homme fait de
son activité vitale, de son essence, un simple moyen de son
existence [150]. » L'essence de l'homme, c'est le développement de son activité vitale volontaire et le simple souci de
l'existence doit lui être subordonné.

   Quelle forme concrète prend l'aliénation de cette
essence ? Marx en cite deux dans les *Manuscrits de 1844* ; la
première concerne le rapport de l'ouvrier à son produit :
l'ouvrier se trouve devant le produit de son travail dans le
même rapport qu'avec un objet étranger. Il travaille pour
recevoir un salaire — de surcroît, le plus souvent, un salaire
qui ne lui permet pas de vivre —, il produit pour un autre,
qui le paiera. La seconde concerne le rapport de l'ouvrier à
la production : dans son travail, l'ouvrier ne s'affirme pas,
mais se nie, son travail n'étant pas volontaire, mais
contraint [151]. Marx voit l'origine de cette défiguration du

travail dans l'existence de la propriété privée, et il accuse l'économie politique de traiter celle-ci comme un fait naturel [152]. La propriété privée explique en particulier que ceux qui possèdent les moyens de production engagent avec ceux qui ne possèdent que leur travail une relation telle qu'ils chercheront toujours à spolier le travailleur et à valoriser leur capital. Avec la propriété privée et l'assimilation du travail à une marchandise, les rapports humains sont faussés et toute la suite en découle logiquement : la division du travail, destinée à rendre celui-ci plus efficace, la tendance à la baisse des salaires ou à l'augmentation du temps de travail pour améliorer le profit et, d'une manière générale, la subordination de toute chose au processus d'autoconservation et d'autovalorisation du capital, qui finit par faire des travailleurs, mais aussi des capitalistes, de pures marionnettes agies par un processus qui les dépasse.

Marx pousse même le raisonnement plus loin : ce n'est pas la propriété privée qui est à l'origine de l'aliénation du travail, c'est bien plutôt le travail aliéné qui est lui-même la cause de toutes les aliénations. A l'origine même de la double aliénation du travail, on trouve une défiguration primitive. Dès le départ, l'homme est conçu sous le rapport de la propriété privée : son travail vise à obtenir de la propriété, et est donc en contradiction avec sa véritable essence. Selon Marx, l'économie politique opère un double mouvement : certes, elle reconnaît le travail comme son principe, mais en même temps elle pose l'homme dans un rapport de tension extrinsèque à la nature extérieure de la propriété privée : « Il est devenu lui-même cette nature et cette tension de la propriété privée [153]. » Ainsi peut-on dire que Locke (que Marx cite peu), qui voit dans le travail le moyen d'acquérir les choses, et Smith, qui fait du travail un simple facteur de production, ramènent le travail à son abstraction au moment même où ils le reconnaissent. En son cœur même, car il est immédiatement posé comme moyen d'acquérir des richesses, le travail naît aliéné. Marx voit dans ce moment originel la cause de tous les maux à

venir : dès lors que le travail est considéré comme facteur
de production et comme essence de la richesse, il est aliéné.

Comment rendre le travail conforme à son essence ?

En opposant la réalité du travail et son essence, Marx
fonde leur continuité et trace le chemin qui mène de l'une à
l'autre. En désignant par le même terme ce que les
économistes ont inventé, le travail abstrait et le travail-
essence, Marx imprime de façon définitive sa marque sur la
pensée du travail, en mettant en place les principaux
éléments de ce que nous avons appelé le schème utopique.
L'utopie ne consiste pas à vouloir changer les conditions de
travail. Elle consiste à donner le même nom à deux réalités
dont on nous dit que l'une est la caricature de l'autre, mais
qui n'ont rien à voir. Il fusionne de cette manière deux
traditions, la tradition anglaise (de l'économie politique) et
la tradition allemande (de l'expression de soi). Dès lors,
l'économie politique est la science du travail aliéné : Smith
a méconnu la nature profonde du travail en le présentant
comme peine ou sacrifice. Certes, historiquement le travail
est apparu comme contrainte extérieure, mais « [Smith] ne
voit aucunement la réalisation de soi, l'objectivation du
sujet, donc sa liberté concrète qui s'actualise précisément
dans le travail [154] ». L'économie politique commet deux
erreurs qui consistent, d'une part, à considérer le travail
comme un simple facteur de production et, d'autre part, à
continuer de traiter le travail comme peine et sacrifice,
donc comme quelque chose de négatif, alors que le travail
est une force positive et créatrice [155]. Néanmoins, par cette
critique, Marx assure la continuité entre les deux traditions : l'économie politique ne pouvait pas concevoir la
vraie nature du travail. D'une certaine manière, Ricardo a
un peu mieux compris celle-ci que Smith, sa théorie de la
valeur-travail signifiant que l'homme met quelque chose de
lui-même dans son travail. Mais, avec la critique mar-

xienne, le moment approche où nécessairement le travail, enfin conçu dans sa réalité, deviendra ce qu'il est dans son essence.

Marx distingue ainsi entre un avant et un après. L'avant — avant de l'abondance — fonde un productivisme déchaîné où l'impératif d'humanisation joue à plein et contraint l'homme à exercer sa tâche d'anéantissement du donné naturel à travers le travail. L'après — lorsque l'abondance est atteinte — ouvre à un brutal changement de signification du travail. Alors seulement, le travail n'est plus opposition, il est le lieu de la pure expression de soi. Alors, il coïncide avec son essence. Mais cela n'est possible qu'une fois l'abondance atteinte, qu'une fois la rareté conjurée. Ainsi s'expliquent les apparentes contradictions de Marx quant à l'avenir du travail. Car tantôt il indique que le but est la réduction du temps de travail, l'objectif étant donc de se libérer du travail, et tantôt que le travail deviendra le premier besoin vital, appelant de ce fait à libérer le travail, c'est-à-dire à le rendre différent et à le conserver. Il n'y a contradiction que si l'on oublie que les deux propositions correspondent à des stades différents de l'évolution historique et sociale.

En effet, dans un premier moment, celui du développement accru des forces productives, la machine remplace progressivement l'homme et le temps de travail humain n'est plus une bonne mesure de la production de richesse : « A mesure que la grande industrie se développe, la création de la richesse vraie dépend moins du temps et de la quantité de travail employés que de l'action des facteurs mis en mouvement au cours du travail. Elle dépend plutôt de l'état général de la science et du progrès technologique, application de cette science à cette production[156]. » Le développement des forces productives permet de se passer, de plus en plus, du travail humain comme facteur de production et du temps de travail comme mesure de la richesse. Cette première évolution, qui s'opère au sein de la société capitaliste, constitue la base de l'émancipation :

« Ceci n'est pas sans importance, car le capital réduit dès à présent le travail et l'effort humain à leur minimum. Cela sera d'un grand profit pour le travail émancipé, et c'est là la condition de son émancipation[157]. » Dans ce premier moment, l'action politique qui accompagne ce développement doit donc soutenir les revendications de réduction du temps de travail. Car elle doit permettre d'augmenter encore plus le développement de forces productives et d'amener ainsi le capitalisme vers son point de rupture. Cela permet également aux ouvriers de se constituer en force de résistance collective contre les employeurs, d'apprendre un autre type de rapport aux autres et de s'épanouir dans le loisir. Dans cette configuration, travail et loisir continuent de s'opposer : « L'économie vraie, l'épargne, consiste à économiser du temps de travail. [...] Economie de temps de travail signifie augmentation de loisirs pour le plein épanouissement de l'individu[158]. » Le temps de travail demeurant la mesure de la production et de la distribution des richesses, l'objectif à poursuivre ne peut être que la réduction de sa place.

C'est ce qu'explique Marx dans la *Critique du programme de Gotha*[159], rédigée en 1875, mais qui ne sera publiée qu'en 1891 : dans la dernière phase de la société capitaliste comme dans la première phase de la société communiste, le temps de travail continue d'être la mesure sociale du travail et la base de la contribution de chacun. C'est pour cette raison que le programme d'Erfurt, très inspiré par les marxistes à la différence du précédent, réclame, « pour la protection de la classe ouvrière », la fixation d'une journée de travail normale de huit heures au maximum et fait donc figurer en première place de ses revendications celle de la réduction du temps de travail[160]. Si cette idée n'est pas contradictoire avec celle du travail considéré comme premier besoin vital, c'est bien parce que cette conception ne peut se développer que dans « une phase supérieure de la société communiste [...] quand, avec le développement multiple des individus, les forces productives se seront accrues elles aussi et que toutes les sources de la richesse collective jailliront avec abondance [161]. » Dans cette seconde phase, la signification du travail a changé : il n'est plus aliénation mais expression de soi. C'est alors que l'opposition classique entre travail et loisir perd son sens : le travail lui-même est épanouissant. Dans la nouvelle phase de la société communiste, le travail et le loisir ne s'opposent plus : ils sont, dans leur essence, identiques [162]. En même temps, le travail a également changé de nature : il est devenu immatériel et consiste alors en tâches de surveillance générale, de gestion, de contrôle de processus de production, qui seront eux directement assurés par les machines [163]. Le travail est épanouissant, moins d'ailleurs en raison de son nouveau contenu que parce qu'il n'est plus détourné de son but : faire de la production l'acte le plus social.

Néanmoins, une certaine ambiguïté persiste chez Marx. En quoi consiste exactement ce travail de la seconde phase et pourquoi est-il épanouissant ? L'est-il par nature ou parce qu'il est réalisé directement pour les autres ? Comment les tâches nécessaires à la reproduction de nos conditions de vie pourraient-elles être épanouissantes ? Le travail devient-il premier besoin vital parce que toutes les tâches difficiles et sans intérêt sont prises en charge par les machines et qu'il se réduit donc à la pure communication avec les autres ? Autrement dit encore, comment concilier la position que Marx défend dans la *Critique du programme de Gotha,* en 1875, et celle qu'il a exposée dans le livre III du *Capital*, en forme de conclusion de celui-ci : « Le règne de la liberté commence seulement à partir du moment où cesse le travail dicté par la nécessité et les fins extérieures ; il se situe donc, par sa nature même, au-delà de la sphère de la production matérielle proprement dite. Tout comme l'homme primitif, l'homme civilisé est forcé de se mesurer avec la nature pour satisfaire ses besoins, conserver et reproduire sa vie ; cette contrainte existe pour l'homme dans toutes les formes de la société et sous tous les types de production. [...] Dans ce domaine, la liberté ne peut consister qu'en ceci : les producteurs associés — l'homme socialisé — règlent de manière rationnelle leurs échanges organiques avec la nature et les soumettent à leur contrôle commun au lieu d'être dominés par la puissance aveugle de ces échanges ; et ils les accomplissent en dépensant le moins d'énergie possible, dans les conditions les plus dignes, les plus conformes à leur nature humaine. Mais l'empire de la nécessité n'en subsiste pas moins. C'est au-delà que commence l'épanouissement de la puissance humaine qui est sa propre fin, le véritable règne de la liberté qui, cependant, ne peut fleurir qu'en se fondant sur ce règne de la nécessité. La réduction de la journée de travail est la condition fondamentale de cette libération [164]. » Dans cette formulation très aristotélicienne (la liberté ne commence que lorsque les besoins essentiels sont satisfaits, qu'après qu'il a été fait justice à la nécessité), Marx semble donc confiner le travail au règne de la nécessité : on peut certes améliorer les conditions de notre soumission à la nécessité, les rendre en particulier plus dignes et moins inégales, mais nous y restons enchaînés.

Il nous semble qu'il ne faut pas chercher à résoudre à tout prix cette contradiction, car Marx continue d'utiliser le terme de travail dans un double registre : le travail matériel, qui vise essentiellement à satisfaire nos besoins, appartient bien au règne de la nécessité. Et, quels que soient les développements techniques, un certain nombre de tâches devront toujours être prises en charge. Ce problème doit être résolu par une réorganisation de la production. Et c'est bien ce type de travail dont parle Marx dans le passage que nous venons de citer, puisqu'il a indiqué quelques lignes auparavant qu'il s'agissait d'obtenir « une réduction accrue du temps consacré au travail matériel en général ». En revanche, il nous semble également qu'il continue souvent d'employer le terme de travail dans un sens plus large et plus « spirituel », dans un sens hégélien, comprenant par là la plus haute forme d'activité

humaine, dont la nature est d'être en même temps individuelle et sociale, épanouissante et expressive. Bien plus, il
nous semble que cette ambiguïté ne sera pas tranchée par la
suite, entraînant des conséquences multiples. Autrement
dit, Marx renforce l'équivocité du terme tel qu'il apparaît
dans la philosophie de Hegel. Hegel ayant utilisé le terme
de travail pour désigner l'ensemble du processus de développement de l'Esprit et ayant érigé en modèle de toute
action celle qui consiste à s'opposer un donné naturel, la
tentation était grande de voir dans le travail quotidien des
hommes un pâle reflet, une défiguration de cette activité
supérieure. C'est ce que Marx a fait. D'où l'enchaînement
qui caractérise les pensées du XIXe siècle sur le travail :
après avoir défini une essence du travail, elles critiquent
l'état de choses existant et assignent à l'action politique
l'objectif de rendre l'existant conforme à l'essence. La
pensée marxienne est la plus cohérente car elle parvient à
conserver l'énorme distance qui sépare le travail existant de
l'idéal : seule une révolution profonde, concernant à la fois
la propriété des moyens de production, les modalités de
détermination de la production sociale, l'avancement des
progrès « technologiques », pourra permettre de « désalié-
ner » le travail. En attendant, c'est bien la réduction du
temps de travail qui doit être poursuivie. Mais l'idéal d'un
travail épanouissant imprègne toute son œuvre.

La glorification française du travail

La France connaît la même évolution, exprimée néanmoins d'une manière moins « philosophique ». Les trois
moments (essence, critique du travail réel, schème utopique) sont exactement identiques : les années pendant
lesquelles Hegel écrit la *Phénoménologie de l'esprit* (1806-
1807), la *Science de la logique* (1812-1816) et la *Philosophie
du droit* (1820-1821) sont celles pendant lesquelles s'opère,
en France, le retournement conceptuel qui conduit à la

glorification du travail. On peut en effet faire remonter aux années 1815-1820 le moment où se développe soudainement en France un discours de valorisation du travail, qui s'effectue à travers la notion d'industrie. Celle-ci bascule à ce moment précis de son sens ancien à son sens moderne. L'un des auteurs qui cristallise le mieux cette mutation est Alexandre de Laborde : alors qu'en 1814 il considérait comme centrales les questions relatives à la propriété, il écrit, quatre ans plus tard : « Quel est le but des actions des hommes qu'ils méconnaissent ou dépassent, qu'ils cherchent encore, après tant de fatigues et de mécomptes, qui n'est pas la gloire, qui n'est pas la puissance ? Ce but est le bien-être, c'est la participation à toutes les jouissances que peut procurer le travail, à toute la considération que doit inspirer la vertu ou le talent. [...] Que faut-il aux hommes pour y parvenir, pour s'en montrer dignes ? Il leur faut l'amour, la passion du travail, ou autrement l'industrie, mais l'industrie libre, puissante, honorée. [...] Le travail est l'art pratique du bonheur, comme la philosophie en est la science spéculative. Il est le remède des passions, ou plutôt une passion lui-même qui tient lieu de toutes les autres ; il se compose des intérêts les plus chers de la vie, ceux de la famille, de la cité, de la patrie [165]. » Le mot industrie est encore employé dans son sens proche du sens latin [166]. On voit que le terme met essentiellement en valeur la capacité technique de l'homme, son inventivité. Il en résulte une sorte de romantisme naïf : « Honneur à toi, sentiment généreux, passion des hommes éclairés, utile laboriosité, honneur à toi [167] ! » Dans le discours des essayistes et des hommes proches du pouvoir, l'objet de fascination réside dans les découvertes techniques de l'homme, qui sont en passe de bouleverser les conditions de la vie quotidienne et de décupler les pouvoirs humains. Saint-Simon est l'un des penseurs les plus représentatifs de cette période et il subit la même fascination que Laborde. Il ajoute à l'enthousiasme pour la technique l'idée de progrès de l'humanité, qui prend désormais le sens d'un progrès technique, vers

toujours plus de bien-être, mais également l'idée d'utilité.
Le bonheur apparaît à portée de main. Le travail est décrit
comme une substance ou une énergie précieuse, dont la
nation a besoin. Saint-Simon inscrit donc son éloge du
travail dans le contexte plus général de l'utilité sociale et de
la lutte contre les oisifs[168]. D'où un discours de valorisation
tout à fait neuf : « Je propose de substituer le principe
suivant à celui de l'Evangile : l'homme doit travailler.
L'homme le plus heureux est celui qui travaille. La famille
la plus heureuse est celle dont tous les membres emploient
utilement leur temps. La nation la plus heureuse est celle
dans laquelle il y a le moins de désœuvrés. L'humanité
jouirait de tout le bonheur auquel elle peut prétendre s'il
n'y avait pas d'oisifs[169]. » Dès cette époque, le travail
apparaît tout à la fois comme contribution au progrès de
l'humanité, fondement du lien social, car c'est la forme du
travail que doit prendre la contribution de chacun au
progrès de la société, et source d'épanouissement et
d'équilibre personnels.

Il n'est pas inutile de remarquer que, chez Saint-Simon,
l'idée de bien-être et d'abondance universelle qu'il est
possible d'obtenir grâce à l'industrie de tous et au développement des techniques aboutit à la même conception des
rapports entre individus et société et à la même conception
globale de la société que chez Smith : l'essentiel étant
l'obtention de ce bien-être, la pure et simple administration
de ces progrès et du travail destiné à y parvenir suffira à
tenir la société ensemble. La politique devient science de la
production, qui doit permettre de produire le plus et le
mieux possible. Le travail est un lien social suffisant
puisque, par lui, tout individu contribue à cet objectif
commun. L'administration des choses remplacera donc le
gouvernement des hommes, dont on n'aura plus que faire,
car que pourrait-on bien désirer de plus ? Le pouvoir
politique devient superflu. A cela s'ajoute la possibilité
d'en finir avec les conflits de classe. Contrairement à la
propriété, le travail est distribué également à chacun, et

chacun peut l'utiliser à sa guise. Il fonde la liberté de *chacun* de contribuer à la richesse sociale et il donne à *chacun* l'impression d'être lié aux autres pour un combat essentiel [170]. Dans ces exemples, le terme de travail n'est pas défini, ce qui signifie que les auteurs qui l'emploient supposent bien connue sa signification, qu'ils contribuent pourtant à profondément transformer. Ils désignent en fait par ce terme non pas le travail concret, mais cette activité humaine qui prend le visage de la puissance transformatrice et dont les résultats s'inscrivent de façon visible sur le territoire, le paysage, avec les progrès techniques. Le travail est décrit comme une force vitale qui transforme l'aspect physique des choses. D'une conception mécanique, on passe à une conception dynamique. La plupart des théoriciens socialistes de la première moitié du XIXᵉ siècle reprennent cette conception, en particulier Proudhon, pour qui le travail est l'essence métaphysique de l'homme, une liberté qui ne doit pas voir son exercice empêché [171].

La France et l'Allemagne construisent donc au même moment, le premier quart du XIXᵉ siècle, le même concept. L'Allemagne a traduit cette nouvelle vision du monde dans sa philosophie, mais celle-ci, dans ses schèmes les plus abstraits, met bien en évidence le noyau humaniste, historique et technique de l'évolution réelle. La France semble s'être exprimée d'abord par la voix de ses hommes d'Etat et technocrates, fascinés par le fabuleux pouvoir technique dont dispose désormais l'homme. En dépit du formidable paradoxe que constitue, en première lecture, la glorification du travail au moment où ses conditions réelles d'exercice sont les pires, cette réaction est néanmoins tout à fait explicable. On conçoit en effet que, saisis par les prodigieuses capacités de développement ouvertes par l'industrie, et emportés par le mouvement de l'histoire qui semblait s'accélérer (c'est le moment des conquêtes napoléoniennes), philosophes et théoriciens aient fait l'éloge d'une activité humaine qui semblait exprimer à la fois la liberté de chaque individu et la puissance d'une humanité triomphante en marche vers le bien-être. Si l'humanité peut à ce point transformer le monde, créer des objets nouveaux, transformer les paysages, chaque individu doit disposer de la même « force créatrice », le travail. C'était là évidemment confondre technique et travail et ne pas tenir compte des conditions d'exercice, pour chaque individu, de ce travail. Il faut bien se représenter combien l'idée que le travail était une activité que chacun « possédait » et qui permettait à chacun de se construire sa place dans la société était importante. Avec le travail, également accessible à chacun, un ordre social entièrement fondé sur les capacités se mettait en place [172]. Et il n'est pas anodin que la théorie de Ricardo, selon laquelle la valeur ajoutée à un objet correspond très exactement à la quantité de travail fournie, ait particulièrement inspiré les socialistes du XIXe siècle : chacun doit pouvoir enfin être récompensé selon ses efforts sans qu'aucune autre considération, de naissance, d'idéologie, de rang, soit prise en compte. Une compétition sociale enfin acceptable se profile.

A de très rares exceptions près, la situation extrêmement préoccupante des ouvriers, officiellement reconnue dans les milieux politiques et objet de nombreux ouvrages, n'a pas remis en question la représentation désormais dominante que la société se fait du travail. Sismondi est l'une de ces exceptions : il dénonce l'évolution qui, selon lui, mène la société à la catastrophe et dont il voit l'origine chez Smith. Les économistes ont promu la chrématistique, cette science de l'enrichissement dont Aristote avait, dès l'Antiquité, dénoncé les dangers, puisqu'il s'agit d'une science de la démesure, de l'accumulation sans fin des richesses. A partir de là, Sismondi dénonce le mouvement général d'industrialisation et d'intérêt pour la richesse, qui vont de pair. Mais la majeure partie des autres critiques, et en particulier les théoriciens socialistes, présentent la caractéristique commune de critiquer l'organisation du travail, c'est-à-dire les conditions de travail au sens large, sans jamais remettre en cause l'idée majeure que le travail est la plus haute activité de l'homme. Il ne s'agit donc bien que de rendre les conditions concrètes de travail conformes à cette essence.

Même Fourier, que l'on présente souvent comme un critique radical de toute la société de son époque (il est contre le développement du commerce, contre l'organisation du travail, pour le développement des plaisirs et l'épanouissement de l'homme), est paradoxalement celui qui met le mieux en évidence le rêve secret qui habite son époque. Car son organisation en phalanstères, dans lesquels les individus regroupés par affinités échappent à la tyrannie du travail ennuyeux et monotone et développent les trois passions majeures, la cabaliste, la papillonne et la composite [173], vise finalement à rendre le travail agréable et l'industrie attrayante. Le titre lui-même de l'ouvrage de Fourier est instructif. *Le Nouveau Monde industriel et sociétaire* [174] est entièrement construit sur l'industrie et le travail, les deux étant simplement rendus conformes à leur essence. Dès lors, « on y verra nos oisifs, même les petites maîtresses, être sur pied dès quatre heures du matin, en hiver comme en été, pour se livrer avec ardeur aux travaux utiles [175] ». Le plus utopiste des utopistes du XIXᵉ siècle est en réalité celui qui trahit le plus clairement l'esprit de celui-ci : le travail est, dans son essence, épanouissant. Il ne reste plus qu'à le rendre conforme à sa nature.

Liberté du travail ou droit au travail ?

Les revendications concrètes développées par les ouvriers au cours du XIXᵉ siècle manifestent cette révolution au grand jour. Les journées de 1848 marquent en quelque sorte solennellement le moment où la conception du travail comme moyen de la réalisation de soi prend le pas sur la conception du travail comme simple moyen de subsistance. Quelles sont en effet les revendications de Proudhon, de Louis Blanc ou des ouvriers ? Elles sont au nombre de trois : la création étant issue du travail, c'est le travail qui doit être récompensé, et non le capital ; le travail étant collectif, c'est ce collectif en tant que tel qui doit recevoir rémunération ; l'exercice du travail étant devenu la condition de maintien en vie des travailleurs, la production doit être organisée de manière à répondre aux besoins sociaux en évitant le gaspillage, d'une part, et de manière à ce que chacun puisse obtenir un revenu, d'autre part. Sous cette forme, le travail apparaît d'abord, dans les discours socialistes, comme une liberté dont dispose chacun, et dont l'exercice doit pouvoir être assuré et récompensé. Dans la mesure où le travail est devenu le moyen majeur d'acquisition des revenus, reconnaître un droit à la vie, c'est assurer le libre exercice du travail.

Le caractère soudain de cette question s'explique. Le milieu du XIXᵉ siècle en France est à la fois le moment de l'industrialisation et celui de crises périodiques qui jettent des milliers d'ouvriers au chômage. C'est aussi le moment où toute une partie des paysans, qui disposaient encore d'une parcelle de propriété ou d'autres moyens de subsistance que le travail, se retrouvent avec la seule force de leurs bras. C'est également l'époque où l'on se rend compte que ce que l'on n'appelle pas encore le marché du travail présente des déséquilibres délicats à combattre. C'est enfin celle où l'on comprend que le retour à la propriété ne peut pas constituer une solution. A la différence de la Révolution de 1789, où l'idéal des sans-culottes, par exemple, était celui du partage de la propriété et d'une garantie accordée à chacun de disposer d'une petite propriété, celle de 1848 contribue à faire passer l'idée que les revenus s'acquièrent désormais par le travail, et que c'est donc autour de celui-ci que se posent les questions essentielles [176]. La question de la pauvreté et de l'éventuel emploi de main-d'œuvre par l'Etat était d'ailleurs posée depuis longtemps et Turgot lui-même avait défendu en son temps l'idée d'ateliers de charité qui permettraient d'employer les personnes sans travail et ainsi de les occuper et de leur donner de quoi se nourrir. Mais les conceptions de cette époque voyaient aussi dans l'existence des diverses limitations à la pleine liberté du travail la cause essentielle des périodes d'inemploi. Turgot pensait ainsi que la suppression des privilèges ou des organisations corporatistes rationnant l'entrée dans certains métiers permettrait de fait à tous de trouver un travail. Or, en 1848, les corporations ont été abolies par la loi Le Chapelier et les diverses entraves et privilèges assouplis. On s'aperçoit qu'il peut néanmoins y avoir des individus sans travail.

Le droit à la vie se confond avec le droit au moyen de pouvoir gagner sa vie, et donc le droit au libre exercice d'un travail. Par rapport à l'époque où Turgot déclarait : « Nous devons à tous nos sujets de leur assurer la jouissance pleine et entière de leurs droits ; nous devons surtout cette protection à cette classe d'hommes qui, n'ayant de propriété que leur travail et leur industrie, ont d'autant plus le besoin et le droit d'employer, dans toute leur étendue, les seules ressources qu'ils aient pour subsister [177] », ce qui a changé en 1848, c'est que le nombre d'individus se trouvant dans cette situation a considérablement augmenté. En 1848, on demande à l'Etat de prendre sous sa protection l'ensemble des personnes ne disposant que de leur corps pour vivre, c'est-à-dire de permettre à ce corps de travailler pour assurer au moins sa propre reproduction : « L'Etat doit assurer à tous droit et protection [...] et la propriété du riche, et l'existence du pauvre, qui est sa propriété, doivent être également placées sous la sauvegarde de la loi publique [178]. » On assiste ainsi, dans la première moitié du XIXᵉ siècle français, à un glissement qui s'opère du devoir de protection du corps, conçu comme chose fragile à mettre en sûreté, en sécurité, au devoir de protection du corps conçu comme moyen de reproduction de l'existence. Les deux types de protection que l'on demande à l'Etat sont d'ailleurs de même nature : il s'agit de protéger l'individu contre les autres. Mais, dans le cas du droit au travail, les implications sont bien sûr plus sérieuses, car elles remettent en cause l'organisation sociale tout entière.

En effet, que signifie la reconnaissance du droit au travail ? Que l'individu dispose d'une créance sur la société et qu'il va pouvoir obliger celle-ci — donc l'Etat — à lui fournir du travail. De plus, cette reconnaissance ébranlerait l'organisation sociale fondée sur la coexistence d'une classe d'employeurs qui donne, quand elle le peut, du travail aux ouvriers : « Est-il vrai, oui ou non, que tous les hommes apportent en naissant un droit à la vie ? Est-il vrai, oui ou non, que le pouvoir de travailler est le moyen de réalisation du droit de vivre ? Est-il vrai, oui ou non, que si quelques-uns parviennent à s'emparer de tous les instruments de travail, à accaparer le pouvoir de travailler, les autres seront condamnés, par cela même, à se faire esclaves des premiers, ou à mourir ? Est-il juste que, tous ayant apporté, en naissant, le droit à la vie, le pouvoir de réaliser ce droit soit concentré aux mains de quelques-uns, de telle sorte que l'espèce humaine se trouve divisée en deux classes d'hommes dont les uns vendent la vie, que les autres sont réduits à acheter [179] ? » Louis Blanc s'attaque par là même à ce rapport social fondamental. Les socialistes de l'époque se livrent donc également à une véritable critique en règle du contrat, masque d'une pure relation de domination : la pseudo-liberté qui est celle de l'ouvrier contractant avec le patron est un mythe, car l'ouvrier est obligé de vendre son corps-travail, alors que le patron peut toujours attendre ou faire jouer la concurrence. Les deux parties ne sont pas à armes égales, situation d'autant plus grave, disent-ils, qu'il en va de la vie. Et c'est justement parce qu'il s'agit de la vie que l'ouvrier est prêt à accepter n'importe quelles conditions. C'est pourquoi le contrat, sous sa forme de mise en relation de deux individus libres et égaux, est une duperie, à l'instar de la liberté du travail.

La vraie liberté du travail ne peut donc prendre son sens que si elle est appuyée sur le droit au travail, sinon les conditions sont toujours déjà inégales. Seul le droit au travail, véritable droit réel, droit-créance, est capable de venir à bout de cette inégalité et de mener à son terme la

Révolution de 1789 qui n'a su mettre en place, reconnaître et protéger que des droits formels[180]. Si elle n'est pas appuyée sur le droit au travail, la liberté du travail n'est qu'un mot creux et un privilège.

Que répondent les libéraux à ces arguments? Que le droit au travail attente à la liberté et à la réciprocité contractuelle[181]. Qu'est-ce à dire? Qu'en lieu et place des individus libres et responsables on va définir une entité, qui sera le support d'obligations, et qu'il ne pourra s'agir que de l'Etat. On entend donc donner à celui-ci le pouvoir de contraindre des individus[182]. La méconnaissance de la liberté et de la réciprocité contractuelle, la substitution aux rapports entre individus de rapports obligeant la société tout entière ouvrent de surcroît la porte à la guerre civile, à l'opposition de classes entre elles : l'Etat risque tout simplement d'être pris en otage par la classe ouvrière pour réclamer à la classe possédante, celle qui donne du travail, l'ensemble des richesses. L'Etat deviendrait ainsi l'instrument de la lutte des classes. Mais, surtout, la reconnaissance du droit au travail, outre qu'elle donnerait un droit sans obligation réciproque à une classe, ferait de l'Etat le grand planificateur de la production : car comment assurer du travail à tous, si l'Etat ne prend pas lui-même en charge, de proche en proche, l'acte d'embauche, puis celui de production, et enfin celui de rémunération? Le droit au travail porte en lui la remise en cause complète de la liberté du commerce et de l'industrie, des prérogatives du chef d'entreprise ou de l'employeur et l'étatisation de toute la production : « Décréter le droit au travail, c'est constituer l'Etat en pourvoyeur de toutes les existences, en assureur de toutes les fortunes et en entrepreneur de toutes les industries[183]. » Enfin, c'est aller contre le libre choix des individus, qui ne pourront plus choisir leur métier, mais devront travailler là où on les réclame.

Le droit au travail épanouissant

Mais l'opposition essentielle n'est déjà plus entre socialistes et libéraux. Elle se situe désormais entre ceux qui s'arrêtent à la conception du travail comme simple moyen de vivre et ceux qui en font une liberté créatrice. Ce débat majeur accélère donc l'isolement de quelques individus, dont Lamartine, vis-à-vis d'une majorité pour laquelle il est désormais clair que le travail est synonyme de réalisation de soi. L'examen des propositions concrètes qui furent faites, en particulier par Lamartine, pour tenter de donner satisfaction aux ouvriers, le montre clairement. Lamartine entendait proposer la mise en place d'ateliers nationaux, sur le modèle des ateliers de charité de Turgot ; ils n'auraient fonctionné qu'en cas de crise, et dans l'hypothèse où certains ouvriers n'auraient pas trouvé à s'employer pour un salaire leur permettant de subsister : « Nous entendions par droit au travail le droit pour tout individu vivant sur le territoire de la République de ne pas mourir de faim ; non pas le droit à tout travail, mais le droit à l'existence, la garantie des moyens d'existence alimentaire par le travail fourni au travailleur [184]. » Or, cette manière de considérer le travail ne rencontre à l'évidence l'approbation ni des socialistes ni des libéraux, et, semble-t-il, pour des raisons identiques. Non seulement parce que le travail est considéré comme simple moyen de subsistance, mais aussi parce qu'il s'agit d'un travail non qualifié dont les ouvriers doivent se contenter, quelle que soit leur qualification. On ne saurait mieux montrer qu'à l'époque, pour une partie de la classe politique, le travail est déjà un véritable moyen d'autoréalisation pour l'individu : faire remuer de la boue à des ouvriers qualifiés apparaît comme une sorte de péché contre la nature même du travail. Socialistes et libéraux emploient d'ailleurs les mêmes arguments : Louis Blanc reproche à Lamartine de vouloir donner aux ouvriers un travail factice, humiliant et stérile,

équivalant à une aumône. Les libéraux opposés au droit au
travail posent également la question : « Quel genre de
travail donnera l'Etat ? [...] Le droit au travail n'a pas de
sens ni de valeur, s'il ne veut pas dire que tout individu,
s'adressant à l'Etat pour obtenir de l'emploi, aura droit au
genre d'emploi auquel il est propre [185]. » On voit mieux par
là que la véritable ligne de partage passe en réalité entre
ceux pour qui le droit au travail est encore l'équivalent d'un
droit à la survie ou à la vie, et ceux pour qui ce droit est un
droit au travail épanouissant [186].

Le travail-épanouissement, mythe du XIXᵉ siècle

En 1848, le retournement s'est donc définitivement
opéré des deux côtés du Rhin. Le travail est désormais
conçu dans son essence et rêvé comme épanouissement de
soi et moyen du développement de toutes les facultés
humaines. Cette évolution va de pair avec l'idée que le
progrès technique ouvre à l'humanité des chemins infinis
vers les lendemains qui chantent et une conception de
l'homme comme ensemble de facultés qui doivent se
développer, comme homme en devenir. En France, socialistes et libéraux sont en accord sur la nature du travail,
dans son double caractère d'expression de soi et de rapport
social et sur l'objectif général d'augmentation de la production, qui doit désormais être celui de la société. Ils ne
s'opposent plus dès lors que sur les moyens de parvenir le
plus vite possible à ce bien-être général. Les libéraux
croient à la vertu de l'incitation individuelle. Ils reprochent
aux socialistes de préparer une société de misère, où
l'incitation au travail aura disparu, où la fainéantise se
développera et où la production risque de baisser : « La
proclamation du droit au travail dispenserait l'homme
d'une partie de cette activité pénétrante qu'il met à la
recherche des travaux productifs [187]. » La proclamation du
droit au travail et les chimères socialistes ignorent que le

meilleur moyen de faire travailler les hommes est l'aiguillon de la faim, le besoin. Le système individualiste, où
l'employeur prend des risques et où le travailleur tente de
gagner davantage par ses efforts et son mérite, est, de fait,
la meilleure méthode pour tirer de l'homme ce qu'il a de
meilleur, et donc pour l'obliger à produire plus.

A quoi les socialistes répondent que la concurrence
entraîne un vaste gaspillage qui nuit à l'augmentation
globale de la production et qu'il est nécessaire d'organiser
le travail autrement si l'on veut produire plus. Car le travail
est devenu collectif et cette nouvelle situation n'est prise en
compte ni dans le système de rémunération ni dans
l'organisation du travail. C'est ce que Proudhon appelle
l'erreur de compte : « Le capitaliste, dit-on, a payé les
journées des ouvriers ; pour être exact, il faut dire que le
capitaliste a payé autant de fois une journée qu'il a
employé d'ouvriers chaque jour, ce qui n'est point du tout
la même chose. Car cette force immense qui résulte de
l'union et de l'harmonie des travailleurs, de la convergence
et de la simultanéité de leurs efforts, il ne l'a point payée.
[...] Lorsque vous avez payé toutes les forces individuelles,
vous n'avez pas payé la force collective, par conséquent il
reste toujours un droit de propriété collective que vous
n'avez point payé et dont vous jouissez injustement. [...]
Voici ma proposition : le travailleur conserve, même après
avoir reçu son salaire, un droit naturel de propriété sur la
chose qu'il a produite [188]. » La contradiction interne du
capitalisme vient donc, pour Proudhon comme pour Blanc,
du fait que la production est sociale, qu'elle fait appel à des
forces collectives, que tout capital est le fruit d'une
conspiration d'efforts et que « de même que la création de
tout instrument de production est le résultat d'une force
collective, de même aussi le talent et la science dans un
homme sont le produit de l'intelligence universelle et d'une
science générale lentement accumulée [189] », mais que l'appropriation du produit y reste individuelle. La réponse
socialiste est l'association : l'association fait naître une

force collective homogène, dont la production est bien supérieure à ce qui pourrait être obtenu par la coexistence difficile au sein d'une entreprise d'ouvriers en concurrence et qui n'ont aucun intérêt au développement de la production et, à un niveau plus macroéconomique, par la coexistence d'entreprises se faisant la guerre. Les individus comprennent qu'il est de leur intérêt propre de contribuer à une production plus grande, chacun stimule et surveille en même temps les autres. Les différentes associations se viennent en aide grâce à la constitution de fonds qui permettent d'assurer une régulation globale.

Dans les deux cas, les individus travaillent donc ensemble arc-boutés vers un objectif unique : l'augmentation de la production, donc des rémunérations, de la consommation et de la satisfaction des besoins. En cela aussi socialistes et libéraux sont d'accord : si Thiers explique que la concurrence permet l'augmentation des salaires parce que les prix baissent, Blanc reconnaît à son tour que c'est également l'augmentation des salaires qu'il poursuit. Non seulement l'association permet une augmentation de la production, mais elle présente l'avantage de concilier les deux dimensions du travail : son caractère épanouissant pour chaque individu et son caractère social. Avec le système de l'association, l'individu comprend que son intérêt individuel et l'intérêt collectif coïncident : « Le régime de l'association lie l'intérêt personnel à l'intérêt général, de manière à sanctifier le premier en centuplant la puissance du second [190]. » L'œuvre réalisée est une œuvre commune, où chacun a intérêt à l'augmentation de la productivité de chaque autre. Mais surtout, comme chez Marx, la vraie solution est dans la formule « De chacun selon ses facultés à chacun selon ses besoins ». De chacun selon ses facultés, c'est le libre épanouissement par chacun de son talent créateur, dans le travail. A chacun selon ses besoins, c'est la récompense de la production collective. L'individu qui se réalise dans son travail est un individu qui travaille pour les besoins de toute la société, donc les siens propres, qui s'épanouit dans son travail parce qu'il travaille pour les autres et finalement pour la réalisation et la satisfaction de ses besoins propres. On peut considérer soit que l'individu est déjà social et que la contribution à la satisfaction des besoins sociaux le satisfait comme tel, soit que sa satisfaction vient du fait que, par la contribution à la production sociale, il accroît sa propre capacité à consommer.

Dans le second cas, il s'agirait encore d'un cas d'aliénation à la Marx, car la jouissance n'est pas trouvée directement dans le travail, mais dans le salaire et la future consommation permise par le travail. Dans le premier cas, on retombe dans le schéma marxien, et c'est d'ailleurs la solution que semble indiquer Blanc : « Tout se réduit donc à transformer le travail en plaisir, et c'est ce à quoi répond la grande formule socialiste : de chacun suivant ses facultés [191]. » Comme chez Marx, le produit, déterminé par le collectif et voulu comme tel par chaque individu, permet la réalisation de chaque individu au cours de sa fabrication, car l'individu produit en fin de compte pour lui, puisqu'il a participé aux choix et que les besoins à satisfaire sont sociaux et parce que le plaisir vient de cette production même où chacun fabrique pour les autres une image de soi-même. La question reste néanmoins ouverte. On ne comprend en effet pas très bien, pas plus chez Blanc que chez Marx, comment le développement de chaque individu dans le travail est compatible avec le caractère collectif de la production, d'autant que cette conciliation est censée s'opérer non pas dans une société politique qui dépasserait les oppositions de la société productive, mais au sein même de celle-ci. On le voit d'autant moins que les deux auteurs militent pour un développement maximal des forces productives et de la grande industrie, lieu par excellence du travail abstrait. Pour parvenir à cette conciliation, il semble que plusieurs conditions doivent être remplies : que les choix productifs soient faits par tous les individus et que ces choix répondent aux véritables besoins sociaux ; que l'on soit déjà dans une société d'abondance et que l'individu soit déjà « social ». Car développer ses facultés créatrices ne signifie pas, pour l'individu, développer sa particularité, mais bien plutôt créer, en lui imprimant sa marque, un objet voulu par la société.

En fin de compte, on peut se demander si, dans ce type de société qui assure la conciliation entre individu et collectivité, et qui le fait exclusivement par le travail, la sociabilité ne devient pas elle-même quelque chose d'extrêmement abstrait, qui s'opère par des signes, et même si, l'abondance étant acquise, le but ultime de la production n'est pas de permettre aux individus de s'échanger des signes, des miroirs de ce qu'ils sont. Il s'agit dès lors peut-être moins de fabriquer des objets visant à satisfaire les besoins matériels que de produire des signes dans lesquels la société éprouve sa propre sociabilité. Comme si le travail et la production n'étaient plus qu'un prétexte ou une scène où se mettre, collectivement, en représentation, chacun montrant aux autres ce qu'il est et faisant signe à la fois vers ce qu'il est intimement et vers ce qu'il est socialement, un lieu où le produit n'est plus qu'un support d'autre chose.

Quoi qu'il en soit, en 1848, le pas est franchi : le travail est devenu le moyen de la réalisation de soi et du lien social. Il a été investi, en l'espace d'une trentaine d'années, d'une charge utopique extrêmement forte : « Les classiques de la théorie sociale, de Marx à Max Weber, étaient en cela d'accord : la structure de la société civile-bourgeoise porte en elle la marque du travail abstrait à travers le type de travail qu'est le travail salarié, régulé par le marché, mis à profit par le capitalisme et organisé par la forme de l'entreprise. Dans la mesure où la forme de ce travail abstrait a déployé une force qui a pu tout imprégner, et qui a pénétré tous les domaines, les attentes étaient conduites à se porter elles aussi vers la sphère de production, ou pour le dire d'une formule, à vouloir que le travail s'émancipe de ce qui l'aliénait. C'est dans l'image du phalanstère que les utopies des premiers socialistes se sont cristallisées, c'est-à-dire dans l'image d'une organisation sociale fondée sur le travail et réunissant des producteurs libres et égaux. Dans la mesure où elle était correctement organisée, c'est de la production elle-même que devait procéder la vie en commun des producteurs librement associés. [...] Et, en dépit de toutes ses critiques à l'encontre des premières formes de socialisme, c'est encore néanmoins à la même utopie spécifique à la société du travail qu'obéit Marx dans la première partie de l'*Idéologie allemande*[192]... »

Tel est le second acte.

CHAPITRE V

ACTE III : DE LA LIBÉRATION DU TRAVAIL AU PLEIN EMPLOI

Le troisième acte est tout aussi nécessaire que les deux précédents pour comprendre la manière dont la représentation du travail moderne s'est construite. Il se distingue néanmoins des deux autres en ceci qu'il n'a pas véritablement été théorisé à travers des disciplines particulières, philosophie ou économie. Sa compréhension vient donc plutôt d'une analyse des actes et des institutions que d'un examen des textes. Concrètement, ce moment est celui de la social-démocratie ou encore de ce que l'on a appelé l'Etat social ou l'Etat-providence. Il se différencie très précisément de la période antérieure par son pragmatisme. A la fin du XIXᵉ siècle, il n'est plus question de rêver l'essence du travail mais de rendre supportable sa réalité. Il ne s'agit plus de penser la nature du travail mais de mettre en place les institutions permettant de concilier les aspirations contradictoires dont le travail est l'objet. Mais le programme politique des sociaux-démocrates va se développer dans un contexte théorique non retravaillé, c'est-à-dire dans lequel les contradictions que recelait la pensée socialiste n'ont pas été résolues : contradiction entre les conditions épouvantables de travail [193] et le discours de valorisation qui accompagne celui-ci ; contradiction entre la haine du travail et la croyance que lui seul est capable de fonder une hiérarchie sociale juste[194] ; contradiction entre un objectif de libération du travail et donc de réduction radicale de la place occupée par le travail dans la vie des individus et des sociétés et une volonté de libération du travail qui s'opérerait à l'intérieur de celui-ci, par une opération de transsubstantiation[195]. La social-démocratie va donc s'installer sur des fondements plus que fragiles : non seulement elle n'engage aucune réflexion théorique sur ces contradictions, mais elle n'a plus les moyens d'éviter leur mise en évidence. Le « grand soir », la proximité du moment où le temps est suspendu et où les signes s'inversent, artifices grâce auxquels la pensée socialiste parvenait à tergiverser, n'est plus de mise. Car la social-démocratie se caractérise justement par son réalisme, le fait qu'elle est « dans le temps ».

Travail et social-démocratie

On a coutume de considérer la création de la IIe Internationale, en 1889, comme l'acte de naissance de la social-démocratie[196]. Mais il convient de distinguer les deux significations du terme « social-démocrate » : la plupart des programmes ou des partis influencés par le marxisme dans la deuxième moitié du XIXe siècle se disent en effet sociaux-démocrates[197] ; cependant, à la suite de la rupture entre réformistes et révolutionnaires au début du XXe siècle dans tous les partis socialistes européens, on a coutume de réserver la qualification de sociaux-démocrates à une idéologie non marxiste, dont Edouard Bernstein[198] fut, en Allemagne, le meilleur représentant et dont la méthode d'action n'est plus le renversement des institutions politiques et sociales du capitalisme, mais au contraire une « longue marche à travers les institutions ». La pensée sociale-démocrate se développe au moment où il semble à beaucoup qu'il sera plus avantageux de recueillir les fruits de l'adhésion populaire et de répondre légalement aux revendications ouvrières que de continuer à rêver d'une prise du pouvoir par la violence. Dans cette mesure, elle substitue à l'idée de grand soir — cet arrêt brutal du temps à partir duquel le temps lui-même se recompose — un temps plus long, plus épais, au sein duquel les revendications trouveront, plus lentement mais plus sûrement, leur satisfaction. Elle s'appuie de surcroît sur une critique des lois formulées par Marx et Engels, en particulier celle du paupérisme croissant du prolétariat. Au contraire, écrit Bernstein « le nombre des possédants s'accroît au lieu de diminuer. Il ne s'agit pas là d'une invention d'économistes bourgeois partisans de l'harmonie sociale, mais d'un fait incontestable, souvent désagréable pour les contribuables mais reconnu et enregistré par le fisc. [...] Admettre qu'un nombre croissant de possédants — et non l'inverse — s'approprie le surproduit social, cela revient à enlever une des pièces maîtresses de l'échafaudage [199]. » De plus, les lois dont parlent Marx et Engels peuvent être mises en défaut par une action volontariste : « Il est évident que là où la législation, c'est-à-dire l'action systématique et consciente de la société, intervient efficacement, elle peut contrecarrer, voire supprimer certaines tendances de l'évolution économique. » Enfin, Bernstein dénonce l'action révolutionnaire brutale et violente et lui préfère la voie légale au nom d'une double exigence : la maturité économique et la maturité politique de la classe ouvrière.

La pensée sociale-démocrate présente ainsi deux caractéristiques majeures : elle se refuse à penser l'évolution de la société en termes de saut qualitatif; elle fait une place majeure à la stratégie et à l'action politique. Les sociaux-démocrates réformistes sont donc pragmatiques : ils n'approfondissent pas l'analyse théorique mais souhaitent obtenir une amélioration de la situation concrète des ouvriers. Ce faisant, ils ne précisent pas si les objectifs poursuivis demeurent les mêmes que ceux que visaient les socialistes et ils ne retraitent pas leur héritage théorique à la lumière de cette nouvelle option politique : le credo de l'abondance comme but ultime de la société n'est pas remis en cause, pas plus que l'idée du travail créateur[200]. La stratégie sociale-démocrate privilégie, dans son action, le court terme, les résultats électoraux et l'amélioration de la condition ouvrière. Ce faisant, elle va conforter, volontairement ou involontairement selon les cas, les principales institutions sur lesquelles reposait le travail abstrait et dont la suppression était nécessaire — dans la pensée socialiste du moins — pour obtenir une libération du travail.

Concrètement, en revendiquant un partage différent des gains issus de la production de celui qui est en vigueur à l'époque, en réclamant une augmentation de la part revenant au travail et une diminution de celle réservée au capital, ou encore en faisant en sorte qu'une véritable protection soit accordée aux travailleurs en échange de leur travail (les grandes lois sur la protection sociale datent de la fin du xixe siècle en Allemagne[201]), l'action sociale-démocrate aboutit à consolider le rapport salarial, qui était pourtant au centre des critiques socialistes. Celui-ci est désormais considéré, d'une manière assez smithienne, comme le canal par où se répand l'augmentation générale des richesses. Plutôt que de le supprimer, sans doute vaut-il mieux le tourner au profit des salariés, telle est la pensée sociale-démocrate. Elle tombe ainsi dans l'erreur, dénoncée par Marx, qui consiste à croire que l'on peut traiter des problèmes de répartition des richesses sans s'interroger sur les positions respectives dans le processus de production[202]. Dès lors, la confusion est totale : car l'idéologie sociale-démocrate réussit le tour de force de continuer à croire à une libération future du travail, en fondant néanmoins l'amélioration de la situation de la classe ouvrière sur la reconnaissance du rapport salarial. Elle persiste aussi à penser positivement l'essence du travail en contribuant néanmoins à instrumentaliser celui-ci, puisque l'intérêt du travail réside désormais dans sa capacité à garantir des revenus décents et donc un pouvoir de consommation toujours plus grand[203]. Cette contradiction n'est pas analysée par les sociaux-démocrates, mais elle contribue à circonscrire très strictement toutes les politiques futures. Et cela est d'autant plus vrai que le travail est en passe de devenir la forme principale d'acquisition des revenus. Dans le même temps, le salariat en effet s'étend au point de devenir une modalité essentielle d'organisation du travail et de distribution des revenus. La pensée sociale démocrate, profondément liée à cette situation, est en réalité son idéologie.

L'Etat social et le plein emploi

La pensée sociale-démocrate repose sur un fondement fragile, puisqu'elle continue à focaliser les énergies utopiques sur la sphère du travail sans remettre en cause le rapport salarial. Elle s'oblige de ce fait à rendre le plus supportable possible ce rapport en améliorant ses conditions concrètes d'exercice (amélioration des conditions de travail, réduction du temps de travail, hygiène et sécurité, institutions représentatives...) et en garantissant à ceux qui le subissent un accès à des compensations toujours plus grandes, sous forme de revenus toujours croissants, de biens de consommation ou des services plus nombreux, d'une protection toujours améliorée. Ce faisant, elle rend nécessaire une régulation globale du système social, de sorte que celui-ci permette la production de quantités de richesses toujours plus grandes (garantie de taux de croissance positifs) et la répartition homogène de celles-ci (plein emploi et règles de répartition). Elle rend donc obligatoire l'intervention d'un Etat capable de garantir la marche régulière de la grande machine sociale. C'est à ce prix seulement que l'on pourra compenser le rapport salarial et faire oublier aux travailleurs que l'on n'est pas — et que l'on ne sera jamais — dans le travail libéré. Ainsi s'explique le développement, dès le début du xxᵉ siècle[204], mais surtout après la Seconde Guerre mondiale, d'un Etat-providence ou Etat social.

L'Etat-providence n'est pas, comme on l'entend dire souvent, un Etat qui colmate les brèches du système capitaliste ou qui cicatrise à coup de prestations sociales les blessures que celui-ci inflige. L'Etat-providence se donne pour impératif de maintenir absolument un taux de croissance, quel qu'il soit, pourvu qu'il soit positif, et de distribuer des compensations, de manière à toujours assurer un contrepoids au rapport salarial. Comme l'écrit Habermas, « le citoyen est dédommagé pour la pénibilité qui reste, quoi qu'il en soit, attachée au statut de salarié, même s'il est plus confortable ; il est dédommagé par des droits dans son rôle d'usager des bureaucraties mises en place par l'Etat-providence, et par du pouvoir d'achat, dans son rôle de consommateur de marchandises. Le levier permettant de pacifier l'antagonisme de classes reste donc la neutralisation de la matière à conflit que continue de receler le travail salarié [205]. » Ce qui entraîne plusieurs conséquences : d'abord, une intervention économique de l'Etat telle que les principaux mécanismes permettant la régulation de la croissance soient de fait contrôlés [206]. La politique keynésienne sera la juste illustration de cet état de choses. Ensuite, une intervention, dans certaines limites, de l'Etat pour que le plein emploi soit garanti, c'est-à-dire pour que chacun puisse bénéficier des avantages désormais attachés au statut de travailleur même si sa capacité de travailler vient à diminuer ou disparaître : les grands rapports de Beveridge ou les politiques qui s'en inspirent, mises en place au sortir de la Seconde Guerre mondiale, ont elles aussi été l'illustration du nouveau rôle désormais dévolu à l'Etat.

Dans cette configuration, les fins poursuivies n'ont plus réellement d'importance ; seul le caractère régulier de la régulation est pris en compte. Certes, on prône la réduction du temps de travail ; on affirme que la recherche de l'abondance doit permettre de se libérer un jour de la contrainte du travail. Mais, en même temps, l'essentiel est, dit-on, d'humaniser le travail. En fait, le travail n'a plus véritablement besoin d'être libéré, puisqu'il est à l'origine d'avantages certains, en particulier de la participation aux fruits de la croissance : l'Etat social a réussi à substituer à l'utopie socialiste d'un travail libéré une visée plus simple, qui consiste à fournir au travailleur, en échange de son effort, une somme croissante de bien-être et à lui garantir le plein emploi. Le xxe siècle n'est plus celui du travail mais de l'emploi : il revient à l'Etat de garantir à chacun un poste à partir duquel il aura accès aux richesses et une place dans la vie sociale. L'emploi, c'est le travail considéré comme structure sociale, c'est-à-dire comme ensemble articulé de places auxquelles sont attachés des avantages et comme grille de distribution des revenus. L'emploi, c'est le travail salarié dans lequel le salaire n'est plus seulement la stricte contrepartie de la prestation de travail, mais aussi le canal par lequel les salariés accèdent à la formation, à la protection, aux biens sociaux. L'essentiel est donc que chacun ait un emploi.

Mais la garantie du plein emploi et de l'accroissement indéfini de la richesse ne va pas de soi : en développant la productivité, on finit en effet par avoir de moins en moins besoin de travail humain, on s'oblige à inventer toujours plus de travail. Actuellement, les Etats soumis au processus de mondialisation des échanges ne sont plus toujours capables d'assurer cette fonction. Les sociétés fondées sur le travail sont traversées par une double logique, explosive à terme : d'une part, elles persistent à vivre sur l'impératif de développement qui repose sur des progrès de productivité toujours plus grands ; d'autre part, elles doivent garantir le plein emploi pour tous car le travail les structure. Cette contradiction n'a pas encore éclaté parce que les pays développés ont connu une croissance de leur production qui a permis de faire jouer le mécanisme de redistribution, d'intégration et de distribution de compensations. Mais, dès lors que les taux de croissance sont moins élevés ou que des personnes n'ont plus accès au système de distribution des richesses, la machine s'enraye. C'est alors que se posent à nouveau les questions refoulées par la social-démocratie et jamais résolues sur la nature profonde et l'avenir du travail. C'est alors qu'il devient nécessaire de s'interroger sur les fins que poursuivent nos sociétés. Est-ce une toujours plus grande satisfaction des besoins, au prix de toujours plus de travail ? Est-ce un travail plus épanouissant ? Deux siècles d'héritages non retravaillés ont abouti à des représentations équivoques : quelle est la représentation qui domine parmi toutes celles qui nous ont été transmises ? Est-ce le travail-facteur de production ? Est-ce le travail-liberté créatrice ? Est-ce le travail-emploi, système de distribution des richesses et des places ? Mettre de l'ordre dans ces représentations permettrait sans doute de mieux savoir ce que nous pouvons souhaiter pour nos sociétés. Si le travail est d'abord un facteur de production et si son caractère de liberté créatrice est un mythe, alors nous pourrions collectivement décider de réduire sa place, à moins que nous ne préférions prendre cette représentation au mot et faire du marché du travail un marché identique aux autres, de manière à fabriquer encore plus de richesses. Si nous continuons, au contraire, de croire que le travail peut être épanouissant, ne nous faut-il pas énumérer les conditions d'une telle transformation ? S'il est d'abord un système de distribution des richesses, peut-être le chômage n'est-il lui-même que le signe d'une inadaptation de celui-ci. Aujourd'hui, nous sommes écrasés par un héritage trop lourd et confus, dont nous ne parvenons pas à distinguer les différentes strates historiques. Nous confondons essence et phénomènes historiques, nous feignons de croire que l'exercice par chacun d'une activité rémunérée est une constante des sociétés humaines ; que l'absence de travail est, en soi, une punition. Nous continuons de parler de travail épanouissant sans mener une réflexion sur ce que cela recouvre. Le travail est devenu une nécessité telle dans notre société que nous sommes prêts à tout pour lui

conserver sa place sans nous interroger sur les conséquences d'un tel attachement pour notre vie sociale.

Les chapitres suivants ont pour ambition de mettre
précisément en lumière les contradictions sur lesquelles
repose l'actuel discours de légitimation du travail, et de
tenter de comprendre la nature et les fondements de cette
régulation générale dont le travail est un élément central.

CHAPITRE VI

L'UTOPIE DU TRAVAIL LIBÉRÉ

Une partie des pensées et des pratiques actuelles (qu'il s'agisse de celles des entreprises, des hommes politiques, des technocrates, des syndicalistes) défend l'idée que le travail est déjà et sera de plus en plus le moyen de l'accomplissement personnel et de l'expression de soi, le lieu de l'autonomie retrouvée. On parle de valeurs post-matérialistes et de travail épanouissant [207]. La frontière entre loisir et travail serait, dans cette perspective, remise en cause. Appartenant à des courants de pensée très divers, ces idées et ces pratiques ont pour caractéristique commune de s'appuyer sur l'idée désormais bien connue qu'il existe une essence du travail — liberté ou puissance créatrice — qui, ou bien n'est pas encore concrétisée mais le sera au prix de quelques bouleversements, ou bien est en voie de réalisation : le travail serait en train de changer de nature. Il faudrait donc l'exalter, voire augmenter son temps invisible [208] — et non pas le mutiler : toute idée de réduction de la place du travail dans la vie individuelle et sociale, tout « désinvestissement » du champ du travail est par conséquent tenu pour un renoncement de l'homme à son essence.

Pour ces pensées, un desserrement de la contrainte du travail est inutile : « Il n'y a plus aujourd'hui, sauf pour certaines catégories, de nécessité vitale à une réduction du temps de travail[209]. » Et pour cause, puisque celui-ci n'est pas, en dernier ressort, une contrainte, mais le plus haut pouvoir d'expression de l'homme : « Le travail qui s'inscrit dans cet océan d'informations en progression constante est souvent un travail qui n'est plus hypothéqué par le sentiment permanent de la contrainte et de la frustration, mais au contraire provoque un sentiment passionnel de recherche de connaissance et d'action. [...] Le postulat sur lequel repose le partage du travail est que les individus ont la passion du temps libre et rejettent le travail comme une contrainte. Or, rien ne valide cette hypothèse. Pour beaucoup de salariés, le travail est une passion positive[210]. » Mais on peut aisément voir que le travail est ici conçu sur le modèle des professions intellectuelles, chercheurs, professeurs, journalistes, qui organisent leur activité eux-mêmes[211]. A partir de ce genre d'exemples — qui sont le plus souvent développés par les chercheurs qui écrivent sur le travail, en référence à leur propre expérience —, le travail est assimilé au travail intellectuel. De ce fait, il n'est plus distingué de la vie elle-même : travailler et s'exprimer sont une seule et même chose. Où l'on retrouve ce que la pensée du XIXe siècle avait de plus utopique, avec la dimension critique en moins...

Que deviennent dans cette perspective les 4,6 millions de personnes qui ont un emploi non qualifié en France et les millions de personnes dont le métier n'est ni intellectuel, ni organisé par l'individu à sa guise ? Peut-on vraiment soutenir que la majeure partie des métiers sont épanouissants ? N'est-ce pas le cas, au contraire, d'une très petite minorité ? Peut-on continuer à affirmer que le travail (c'est-à-dire potentiellement tout travail, toute tâche réalisée dans le cadre économique et juridique actuel, et rémunérée par la société) est épanouissant ? Qui exerce aujourd'hui un travail qui lui permet d'exprimer sa personnalité ? Sans doute les professions intellectuelles ou vraiment manuelles, c'est-à-dire celles où l'ensemble du processus de travail, son rythme, son développement sont organisés par la personne elle-même. Mais les autres ? Il serait évidemment extrêmement précieux de disposer d'études fines et détaillées sur les représentations actuelles du travail pour progresser sur cette question [212].

Le travail n'est pas épanouissant : les trois logiques de développement du travail

Ces pensées sont fondamentalement contradictoires. Elles oublient en effet la forme sous laquelle le travail est né et sous laquelle il continue d'exister, elles oublient sa dimension économique. Elles font donc l'impasse sur les logiques qui ont présidé à l'apparition du travail et qui continuent de présider à son développement. Elles soutiennent que le travail est une œuvre alors même que sa détermination économique l'en empêche à jamais ; elles sont également incohérentes parce qu'elles ne se donnent pas les moyens de le faire devenir tel et parce qu'elles sont incapables de remettre en cause les présupposés économiques qui sous-tendent leurs raisonnements.

Le travail, moyen au service de la logique capitaliste

Le travail n'est pas apparu comme une fin, poursuivie pour elle-même par des individus cherchant à se réaliser. Dans les discours comme dans la réalité, il a été dès l'origine un *moyen*, pour la nation d'augmenter les richesses produites, pour l'individu d'acquérir un revenu, pour la classe capitaliste de faire du profit. Il est né facteur de production, moyen physique permettant de transformer la matière en produits utilisables par l'homme. Il est également apparu comme *moyen* permettant d'aménager la nature et plus tard comme *moyen* d'humaniser le monde. Il a donc dès l'origine été soumis à une logique d'efficacité, qui a pris la figure du capitalisme, forme de l'économie

dont le principe est la rentabilité en matière d'accroissement du capital investi. Weber, l'un des premiers, a
thématisé l'analyse marxiste du travail dans ces termes de
rationalité et d'efficacité, démontrant comment l'entrepreneur et le capitaliste avaient dès leur apparition rationalisé
le travail. S'interrogeant sur les présupposés du capitalisme
dans son *Histoire économique*[213], Weber explique que la
condition préalable essentielle à l'instauration d'un régime
capitaliste est l'usage d'un compte de capital rationnel par
les entreprises[214]. Cela présuppose, dit-il : 1. Une appropriation de tous les moyens matériels de production par des
entreprises lucratives autonomes privées qui en ont la libre
jouissance ; 2. La liberté du marché ; 3. Une technique
rationnelle ; 4. Un droit rationnel, c'est-à-dire là aussi
calculable ; 5. Le travail libre, « c'est-à-dire la présence de
personnes qui sont non seulement dans la position juridique, mais encore dans la nécessité économique de vendre
librement leur force de travail sur le marché. [...] Le calcul
rationnel du capital n'est réalisable que sur la base du
travail libre, c'est-à-dire lorsqu'il devient possible, du fait
de la présence de travailleurs qui s'offrent de leur plein gré
— du moins formellement, car ils le font, de fait, contraints
par l'aiguillon de la faim —, de calculer préalablement le
coût des produits au moyen de tarifs forfaitaires[215] ».

Le travail apparaît donc comme un pur moyen pour le
capitaliste d'atteindre ses fins, la production d'un surplus,
et il n'est d'ailleurs exercé par les individus que sous
l'aiguillon de la faim. Ceux-ci sont obligés de vendre leur
force de travail et les ouvrages sont légion qui expliquent
comment il a fallu en quelque sorte « domestiquer » les
paysans pour les faire travailler selon des horaires précis et
les rendre sensibles à l'appât du gain. Le capitalisme est
porté et accompagné par le développement d'une rationalité instrumentale qui, la fin étant fixée, utilise le travail
comme un simple moyen pour atteindre ce but. L'émergence du capitalisme et de l'industrialisation a eu pour
condition essentielle la libération du travail des anciennes

structures dans lesquelles il était auparavant englué et diversifié et la transformation du travail en une simple force détachable du travailleur. Alors, écrit Polanyi, que « le travail n'est que l'autre nom de l'activité économique qui accompagne la vie elle-même, laquelle, de son côté, n'est pas produite pour la vente mais pour des raisons entièrement différentes, et [que] cette activité ne peut pas non plus être détachée du reste de la vie, être entreposée ou mobilisée[216] », le travailleur est devenu une marchandise comme les autres, sur un marché comme les autres. Le travail-marchandise a représenté à la fois la condition du développement du capitalisme en même temps que le premier concept et la première réalité unificatrice du travail. De ce point de vue, on ne peut pas dire que Marx se soit beaucoup trompé : la production s'étant développée à partir de critères de rentabilité, elle est devenue toujours plus abstraite et le travail toujours plus instrumentalisé.

Aujourd'hui, la mondialisation de la production le confirme. Le processus de travail est régi, de l'extérieur, par des processus qui n'ont rien à voir avec la libre expression du travailleur. Il en va ainsi pour l'industrie mais aussi pour les services, et plus particulièrement pour les services aux entreprises qui fonctionnent en sous-traitance et sont donc totalement soumis à une logique extérieure. La logique capitaliste attire le travail pour sa propre reproduction : elle a étendu le marché aux dimensions du monde, divisé le travail d'une manière qui n'avait jamais été atteinte et fait de l'homme un simple appendice, d'ailleurs parfois superflu, du capital. De même que le paradoxe du paupérisme était resté un mystère pour la pensée politique du XIXᵉ siècle, de même il nous est difficile de justifier aujourd'hui les conditions de vie qu'ont connues des millions d'êtres humains au XIXᵉ et au XXᵉ siècle au nom du développement des besoins et de l'avancée de l'humanité.

Il faut aussi relire Simone Weil[217], Georges Friedmann[218] ou Di Ciaula[219] pour se souvenir de la manière dont la logique qui vise au développement du capital ignore le travail et en fait un simple facteur. Plus encore que l'économie (neutre vis-à-vis de ce facteur, car elle vise simplement à abaisser son coût ou à le faire disparaître), le taylorisme a poussé à son point extrême le mépris du travail humain, en le chronométrant, en le divisant, en lui enlevant tout sens : « Pour moi, personnellement, voici ce que ça a voulu dire, travailler en usine. Ça a voulu dire que toutes les raisons extérieures sur lesquelles s'appuyaient pour moi le sentiment de ma dignité, le respect de moi-même ont été en deux ou trois semaines radicalement brisées sous le coup d'une contrainte brutale et quotidienne. Et je ne crois pas qu'il en soit résulté en moi des mouvements de révolte. Non, mais au contraire la chose au monde que j'attendais le moins de moi-même — la docilité. Une docilité de bête de somme résignée. [...] Il y a deux facteurs dans cet esclavage : la vitesse et les ordres. La vitesse : pour " y arriver ", il faut répéter mouvement après mouvement à une cadence qui, étant plus rapide que la pensée, interdit de laisser cours non seulement à la réflexion, mais même à la rêverie. Il faut, en se mettant devant sa machine, tuer son âme pour huit heures par jour, sa pensée, ses sentiments, tout. [...] Cette situation fait que la pensée se recroqueville, se rétracte, comme la chair se rétracte devant un bistouri. On ne peut pas être conscient [220]. »

Diviser le travail en temps élémentaires, décrire chaque mouvement et enregistrer son temps, reconstituer les combinaisons de mouvements élémentaires les plus fréquentes dans l'atelier, enregistrer les temps de ces groupes de mouvement et les classer, repérer les mouvements inutiles et les examiner : la logique du taylorisme est la fille spirituelle de celle de Smith et l'aboutissement inéluctable du capitalisme. Comme l'explique Simone Weil, « Marx rend admirablement compte du mécanisme de l'oppression capitaliste. [...] Il a bien montré que la véritable raison de l'exploitation des travailleurs, ce n'est pas le désir qu'au

raient les capitalistes de jouir et de consommer, mais la
nécessité d'agrandir l'entreprise le plus rapidement possible afin de la rendre plus puissante que ses concurrents[221]. » Ce qui, à l'échelle de l'entreprise, s'appelle
taylorisme devient, à l'échelle du pays, la poursuite de la
seule efficacité productive et de la compétitivité. Certes,
nous sommes en train, nous dit-on, de sortir du taylorisme,
mais il n'en demeure pas moins que le travail reste
considéré, par la pensée économique par exemple, comme
un pur facteur de production.

La subordination, cœur du travail salarié

D'où la seconde logique sous la pression de laquelle
continue de se développer le travail, ou au moins le travail
salarié. Celui-ci consiste en l'échange d'une prestation
contre un salaire, cet échange faisant l'objet d'un contrat.
La caractéristique majeure du travail salarié, qui le distingue radicalement du travail indépendant, est le lien de
subordination qui existe entre le salarié et son employeur,
celui-ci se déduisant quasi logiquement de la nature du
contrat de travail. Autrement dit, à partir du moment où
l'on considère que le travail humain peut faire l'objet d'un
négoce, cet achat a pour conséquence la libre disposition de
ce qui a été acheté, c'est-à-dire sa direction, dans le double
sens de « donner des objectifs » et de « conduire ». La
dénomination de « louage de services » pour désigner
l'utilisation du travail d'autrui a, il est vrai, été abandonnée
(en 1973 seulement), et le travail ne peut plus être, au
moins juridiquement, considéré comme une simple marchandise. Pourtant, aucune définition du contrat de travail
n'est venue interdire une telle interprétation. En France,
c'est la jurisprudence qui a fini par faire de la subordination
le critère du travail salarié, le contrat de travail étant dès
lors analysé par la doctrine comme « la convention par
laquelle une personne s'engage à mettre son activité à la
disposition d'une autre, sous la subordination de laquelle

elle se place, moyennant une rémunération[222]. » La notion
de subordination signifie donc que le travailleur salarié se
place sous la direction, sous l'autorité de l'employeur, qui
lui donne des ordres concernant l'exécution du travail, en
contrôle l'accomplissement, en vérifie les résultats. Autrement dit, même si la subordination n'est pas personnelle
mais juridique, elle est néanmoins totale : elle implique
que le salarié fasse ce qui lui est demandé, de la manière
qui lui est demandée, le plus souvent suivant une organisation qui lui est imposée. Il le fait de surcroît aujourd'hui
sans connaître les finalités de ce travail, puisqu'il ne
participe pas aux décisions de l'entreprise. Cette subordination va de pair avec une très forte indétermination de ce
qui est demandé au travailleur au moment de la signature
du contrat : l'engagement ne porte pas sur une ou plusieurs
prestations définies à l'avance, auquel cas il ne resterait
plus de place pour l'exercice du pouvoir de direction de
l'employeur. La notion de subordination s'accompagne
donc de l'absence d'engagement précis, sauf celui de
renoncer à sa volonté autonome et de la soumettre à celle
de l'employeur. Cette subordination, nous dit-on, constitue
la contrepartie logique de l'absence de tout risque économique assumé par le salarié dans son activité. Quoi que l'on
pense de cette justification, difficile à défendre à une
époque où 90 % des embauches se font sous contrat à
durée déterminée ou en intérim, et où le risque majeur est
celui du chômage, il faut prêter attention à cette définition
du travail salarié par la subordination, pour pouvoir mieux
comprendre comment l'on peut défendre l'idée qu'une
activité entièrement dirigée de l'extérieur puisse être
source d'expression de soi et d'autonomie.

Certes, le droit du travail a peu à peu indiqué les limites
que ce pouvoir de direction ne pouvait pas dépasser, en
réduisant progressivement la très grande latitude qui était
donnée au départ à l'employeur : il n'est pas possible
d'engager n'importe qui pour lui faire faire n'importe quel
travail. Il existe des grilles de classification, des grilles

d'emplois à quoi correspondent des niveaux de formation et des niveaux de salaire. Mais la subordination n'en a pas pour autant été supprimée. D'autres objections tentent également de restreindre la portée de la dépendance dans laquelle se trouve le salarié. Trois arguments sont invoqués. Selon le premier, l'intervention du droit du travail aurait permis de passer d'une conception marchande du travail à une autre, où le travailleur est considéré comme sujet : « Au lieu d'être appréhendé comme une chose, une marchandise, le travail se trouve alors saisi comme l'expression de la personne du salarié, c'est-à-dire comme une œuvre [223] », et ceci parce que des dispositions ont fini par assurer un minimum de sécurité physique, puis économique au travailleur. Comme preuves de la reconnaissance de la dimension personnelle du travail, on cite le droit d'expression des salariés et le droit à la qualification professionnelle. Il n'est pas certain que ces exemples suffisent à nous persuader que la personne du travailleur est aujourd'hui prise en compte dans l'entreprise et qu'elle s'exprime dans une œuvre.

Selon le second argument, l'aporie de la soumission volontaire (une même personne étant considérée à la fois comme une volonté pleinement autonome au moment de la signature du contrat de travail et comme une « personne » subordonnée une fois le contrat signé) se résoudrait grâce à l'intervention du droit collectif du travail [224]. Le droit collectif et, d'une manière plus générale, l'ordre public social permettraient ainsi de surmonter la subordination individuelle. Il s'agit là d'une vision tout à fait optimiste, car l'ordre public social, s'il fonde un sujet collectif aux droits collectifs, ne supprime néanmoins pas la relation individuelle de subordination. Assurément, les dispositions légales et professionnelles qui ont pour objet d'améliorer la condition du salarié sont impératives et le contrat individuel ne peut y déroger. Il n'en reste pas moins que, jusqu'à preuve du contraire, l'employeur reste celui qui embauche, licencie et organise le travail. La subordination dans l'exercice quotidien du travail n'a pas été remise en cause par les dispositions collectives. Croire le contraire reviendrait, semble-t-il, à considérer que nous nous trouvons dans une tout autre tradition que celle du contrat, et plus particulièrement dans la tradition allemande, où la communauté de travail a une existence antérieure au contrat de travail et où celui-ci ne crée donc pas la relation de travail, mais s'efface devant elle. Certains juristes français ont tenté d'introduire cette conception en France, mais n'y sont pas parvenus : le contrat reste donc bien en France la source majeure d'obligations [225].

Enfin, le troisième argument consiste à soutenir que la subordination est de moins en moins réelle aujourd'hui [226]. Mais, là encore, il semble que l'exception soit hâtivement généralisée : peut-on vraiment arguer de l'intégration, par pure commodité, de travailleurs indépendants dans les rangs du salariat, pour démontrer que la subordination est en voie de dilution [227] ? Avons-nous vraiment des signes tangibles et des indicateurs démontrant que le travail est, d'une manière générale, moins subordonné ? Et d'ailleurs, quelle est la justification dernière de la subordination ? Il nous faudra revenir sur les raisons d'une telle organisation du travail et nous interroger sur la validité du raisonnement qui invoque l'efficacité productive pour justifier la relation de subordination. Pour obtenir la plus grande efficacité, il faudrait, nous dit-on, qu'un seul dirige et conduise l'entreprise, ce navire dont le capitaine doit être maître à bord. C'est également une autre manière de présenter la thèse de l'aiguillon de la faim : la subordination, la mise à disposition du travail humain serait ce qui permet à une organisation d'extraire le maximum de la force de travail achetée. Quoi qu'il en soit, le travail salarié, mais également le travail sous statut [228] restent aujourd'hui caractérisés, juridiquement et en raison de la manière dont la propriété et la gestion des entreprises sont conçues, par la subordination. Dès lors, comment concilier la subordination avec l'autonomie et l'épanouissement ? Que signifie responsabiliser les personnes dans ce contexte ?

Il faut évoquer ici la thèse de Louis Dumont, qui oppose la société prééconomique, où les relations sont des relations hiérarchiques, d'homme à homme, et, dit-il, de *subordination,* aux sociétés économiques, caractérisées par les rapports des hommes aux choses. L'économie, libérant l'individu, permettrait de substituer aux relations de pouvoir personnelles des relations purement marchandes, vidées de leur puissance et réduites à leur pouvoir monétaire. La crainte de Louis Dumont est de voir se développer la remise en cause de la société économique et de voir réapparaître la subordination et son cortège de hiérarchies et de violences. La première partie de l'allégation est classique, c'est même un des leitmotive de Marx : le travail salarié nous a délivrés des rapports de dépendance personnels, fondés sur la parenté, le sang, la naissance... La seconde l'est moins : Louis Dumont raisonne comme si le simple fait de sortir d'une situation insupportable rendait la situation suivante absolument désirable. Il omet de dire que la violence se trouve également au sein des sociétés économiques, de même que la hiérarchie et que la *subordination*, puisque c'est précisément sur cette même subordination qu'est fondé le rapport de travail, rapport foncièrement inégalitaire, même si certains juristes ont tenté de démontrer qu'il s'agissait d'égalité concrète plus que d'inégalité [229]. Le rapport salarial est un rapport fondamentalement inégal, qui n'est pas si éloigné de la relation d'esclavage et de servitude comme le signalaient déjà Marx [230], Weber [231], Polanyi [232] ou Simone Weil [233] : la différence majeure est certes que le maître devait entretenir son esclave alors que, dans le rapport salarial, l'employeur verse un salaire, qui peut être supérieur aux sommes nécessaires à l'entretien du travailleur. Mais, comme l'écrivait Simone Weil en 1934 : « Ainsi, en dépit du progrès, l'homme n'est pas sorti de la condition servile dans laquelle il se trouvait quand il était livré faible et nu à toutes les forces aveugles qui composent l'univers ; simplement la puissance qui le maintient sur les genoux a été comme transférée de la matière inerte à la société qu'il forme avec ses semblables[234]. » Nos sociétés n'ont pas totalement rompu avec les modèles des sociétés antérieures : il s'agit toujours de faire travailler les autres à sa place, ou de leur faire faire les tâches les plus pénibles en jouant du rapport salarial et de l'échange de temps valorisés de manière inégale. La violence constitutive du rapport salarial est domestiquée par les multiples avantages et garanties qui sont attachés au statut de salarié. Le statut du salarié se normalisant à travers des droits civiques d'intéressement et de participation sociale, la masse de la population obtient la possibilité de vivre dans la liberté, la justice sociale et le bien-être croissant, comme le souligne Habermas[235]. Mais la violence ne disparaît pas pour autant et le rapport de travail se caractérise soit par la subordination, soit par l'asservissement à des directives extérieures. Et il importe peu, pour la vérité de cette affirmation, que la figure du patron ait fait place à une cascade de pouvoirs anonymes propriétaires de parts de capitaux et à une technostructure elle-même salariée. Ainsi que l'avait prévu Marx, même si les puissances sociales ne sont plus incarnées, elles n'en deviennent que plus étrangères, plus aliénantes, la totalité du corps social étant désormais prise dans un ensemble de relations que personne ne maîtrise plus. Mais la relation d'aliénation constitutive du travail marchand perdure. Les flux internationaux de production et de consommation se sont substitués au patron ou au contremaître.

Le travail, moyen d'aménager le monde

Enfin, le travail est régi par une troisième logique : celle du développement technique. Il s'agit ici de bien autre chose que ce que l'on entend habituellement par déterminisme technologique. On ne peut nier, au demeurant, que le travail humain ait à s'adapter aux évolutions technologiques. Pourtant, l'essentiel est ailleurs. Il réside dans le rapport « technique » que nous entretenons avec le monde et dans l'idée de son nécessaire aménagement que les siècles précédents nous ont léguée. Les deux premières logiques qui régissent actuellement le développement du travail (celle du capitalisme et de la subordination) s'expliquent finalement elles aussi par ce rapport au monde. Car quelle est la justification dernière du capitalisme et de la subordination, si ce n'est de rendre le travail plus efficace, et donc de permettre d'augmenter les richesses, l'abondance, le bien-être, et — plus abstraitement — de nous donner l'occasion de nous civiliser toujours davantage, en humanisant le monde ? Depuis le XVIIIᵉ siècle, le travail est un moyen en vue d'aménager le monde. Au départ, il s'agissait seulement d'augmenter notre bien-être. Mais quand considérerons-nous que celui-ci est atteint ? Quand aurons-nous le sentiment d'avoir atteint l'abondance, le véritable bien-être ou la totale coïncidence à nous-mêmes, si ce n'est dans un terme mythique de l'histoire, toujours repoussé en fait. Nous avons conservé le mouvement, la tension et tout ce qu'ils déterminent en sachant secrètement que nous n'atteindrons jamais l'objectif que nous sommes censés poursuivre. Nous ne parlons plus aujourd'hui d'abondance ou de richesses, mais de compétitivité, de besoins toujours plus nombreux à satisfaire, de menace extérieure. Nous avons réussi à externaliser en partie le moteur : désormais, nous devons nous développer pour résister aux autres car l'immobilisme équivaudrait à la disparition de notre pays de la scène mondiale. On parle plus grossièrement de la nécessité d'avoir un gâteau toujours plus large pour pouvoir redistribuer sans heurter les corporatismes, pour satisfaire les besoins des plus pauvres, pour inventer de nouveaux produits. Cela trahit une unique ambition : nourrir le feu du développement, préserver à tout prix celui-ci. Nous avons conservé le mouvement qui devait nous mener vers plus de liberté, plus de conscience, plus de dignité, mais nous avons fini par oublier sa raison et par nous faire dominer, en retour, par les moyens que nous avions mis en œuvre pour y parvenir, en particulier par le travail, la technique et les immenses moyens et appareils rationnels que nous avons mis en branle.

Nous sommes devenus, comme le dit Hannah Arendt [236], une société de travailleurs ; nous ne savons plus pourquoi nous travaillons, pourquoi nous développons cette activité avec un tel sentiment de l'urgence. Au point que nous sommes maintenant les habitants d'une société rivée à la nécessité et que l'éventuelle libération de cet esclavage nous apparaît terrible : « [...] Une société de travailleurs que l'on va délivrer des chaînes du travail, et cette société ne sait plus rien des activités plus hautes et plus enrichissantes pour lesquelles il vaudrait la peine de gagner cette liberté [237]. » Cette liberté nous fait clairement peur aujourd'hui. Les politiques craignent la délinquance, l'ennui. L'idée d'une diminution de la place du travail dans nos vies amène sur la scène le spectre de la surconsommation et de l'individualisme.

Nous sommes soumis à la nécessité parce que notre vie entière est consacrée, dans sa plus grande partie, à gagner les moyens de reproduire cette vie. Certes, c'est une reproduction élargie. Mais nous avons fini par y consacrer toutes nos forces, sans garder de temps pour en jouir et même en oubliant comment en jouir, c'est-à-dire en oubliant que l'homme peut avoir d'autres occupations que la seule transformation de ses conditions de vie matérielles. C'est bien là ce que montre Hannah Arendt lorsqu'elle dessine le chemin parcouru depuis les Grecs jusqu'aux modernes. Chez les Grecs, coexistaient plusieurs modes de vie, ceux que l'on pouvait choisir et exercer librement et ceux dont le but ne visait qu'à la pure reproduction de la vie. Parmi les premiers, Aristote distinguait la vie consacrée au culte du beau, celle consacrée aux affaires de la cité et celle vouée à la contemplation. La thèse de Hannah

Arendt est que le mode de vie voué à la pure reproduction des conditions matérielles s'est développé jusqu'à rendre inimaginables les trois autres. D'où son expression : nous ne savons plus quoi faire du temps libéré car nous ne savons plus ce que signifie la contemplation ou l'action, qui portent le principe de leur plaisir en elles-mêmes. Si nous poussons la thèse de Hannah Arendt un peu plus loin qu'elle ne le fait, il faut dire que nous n'imaginons plus d'autre rapport au monde et à l'action que celui de la production et de la consommation : nous ne pouvons plus nous exprimer que par la médiation d'objets ou de prestations et de productions, nous ne pouvons plus agir qu'en consommant. Ce faisant, Hannah Arendt renoue avec le fond de la philosophie heideggerienne, dont on peut dire qu'elle est l'une des rares philosophies modernes à avoir développé une pensée cohérente du travail moderne, même si elle n'en fait apparemment pas son objet de réflexion.

Le travailleur, figure du xxᵉ siècle

La pensée de Heidegger ne traite en effet pas directement du travail, ni d'ailleurs de ce que l'on appelle parfois les « questions de société ». Elle consiste en une vaste réinterprétation de la métaphysique occidentale qui, selon Heidegger, commence avec Platon et s'achève avec Nietzsche. Pourtant, à plusieurs reprises, Heidegger évoque brièvement le concept de travail, laissant à penser qu'il s'agit là en réalité d'un aspect majeur de son œuvre. Dans la « Contribution à la question de l'Etre [238] », il évoque en particulier le livre de Jünger, *Le Travailleur* [239], et indique que « la question de la technique est redevable aux descriptions du *Travailleur* d'un soutien qui s'exerça tout au long de [son] travail [240] ». Le travail apparaît en fait chez Heidegger comme la manifestation la plus visible de ce qu'est devenu l'homme, au terme de la métaphysique, et surtout de ce qu'est devenu le rapport de l'homme à l'Etre.

Commentant la phrase de Jünger « La technique est la façon dont la forme du travailleur mobilise le monde », Heidegger ajoute, fidèle à son style, que « la volonté de puissance se présente partout et pleinement comme travail [241] ». Il faut, pour bien comprendre ce propos, rappeler que, pour Heidegger, l'apparition de la métaphysique avec Platon constitue l'avènement d'un nouveau rapport de l'homme à l'Etre (ce qui est), dans lequel la vérité est définie comme « ce qui apparaît » (à l'homme). Platon inaugure une époque où la vérité, peu à peu, ne sera plus déterminée que par rapport à l'homme. Nietzsche achève cette époque : le fondement de la réalité est déterminé comme volonté de puissance, l'homme devient la mesure de toutes choses et le nihilisme est avéré, puisque toute vérité n'est qu'interprétation issue du subjectivisme. Dans cette généalogie, Heidegger met en évidence un double mouvement : pendant que l'homme s'érige en sujet pleinement conscient de lui-même se constitue face à lui, posé en face de lui, un monde-objet, privé de vie et d'être, susceptible d'être aménagé. Ce nouveau rapport entre un homme-sujet et un monde « sous la main », Heidegger l'appelle technique ; on pourrait aussi l'appeler humanisme. Cette généalogie met en effet en évidence l'identique racine de ce double mouvement, d'aménagement du monde — qui est théorisé dès le XVIIe siècle et qui se fera concrètement à l'aide de la technique et de la science — et d'humanisation, que l'on a retrouvé justifié chez Hegel et chez Marx. Humanisation du monde et technique ne sont qu'une seule et même chose, puisque humaniser signifie anéantir le naturel et que cette opération se fait à l'aide de la technique.

Nous sommes donc aujourd'hui dans l'ère de la technique et par ce dernier terme, il faut entendre bien plus qu'un ensemble de procédés mécaniques visant à rendre le monde plus confortable. Il s'agit d'un type de rapport au monde où celui-ci est considéré à la fois comme un champ à transformer, comme un réservoir d'où l'homme tire ce qui lui est utile et comme l'extériorité qui lui permet de se construire en tant qu'homme. L'histoire de la métaphysique est en quelque sorte, pour Heidegger, l'histoire du fondement philosophique de cette évolution. On est ainsi passé du *logos* présocratique, qui signifiait écoute et recueillement de l'homme, à un rapport inversé, où le logos s'est fait raison formelle, principe de raison[242]. La technique n'est donc pas un simple moyen que l'homme pourrait maîtriser ou dont il pourrait contrôler à son gré l'utilisation : la technique moderne n'est pas un outil. « L'homme subit le contrôle, la demande et l'adjonction d'une puissance qui se manifeste dans l'essence de la technique et qu'il ne domine pas lui-même[243]. » On comprend alors mieux où la pensée de Hannah Arendt prend son origine : comme Heidegger, elle voit dans l'avènement des Temps modernes la réduction des multiples rapports que l'homme entretenait avec le monde (rapports d'écoute, de contemplation, d'action), à un seul, la production-consommation. Nous sommes passés dans l'ère du produire, où c'est l'homme qui oblige les éléments à se plier à sa volonté, alors même qu'en Grèce l'activité n'était pas réservée à l'homme seul, mais était aussi le fait du monde : en Grèce, produire signifiait d'abord se dévoiler, et la *physis*, que nous traduisons par « nature », était aussi le sujet de ce produire, comportait une dimension dynamique. La *physis* désignait la vie de la nature, la croissance des choses qui s'ouvraient d'elles-mêmes. Aujourd'hui, c'est l'homme qui enjoint à la nature de s'ouvrir : « Le dévoilement qui régit la technique moderne est une provocation par laquelle la nature est mise en demeure de livrer une énergie qui puisse être extraite et accumulée[244]. » Technique et humanisme ont donc profondément la même origine. D'où le refus de Heidegger, exprimé officiellement en 1946, de voir sa pensée assimilée à un humanisme[245]. L'humanisme a en effet pour principe de mettre l'homme au centre du monde, des significations, de la vérité, de l'Etre. Ce qui revient, pour Heidegger, à oublier ce dernier.

On comprend mieux dès lors comment le travail, qui est en quelque sorte la forme concrète que prend le rapport de l'homme au monde à l'ère de la technique, peut représenter pour Heidegger l'essence du monde moderne, en même temps que le comble de l'oubli de l'Etre, certes, mais aussi d'autres manières d'être homme. Ce n'est d'ailleurs pas une condamnation totale que porte Heidegger sur ce destin de l'Etre, puisque, comme on le sait, il y voit une sorte de fatalité contre laquelle l'homme lui-même ne peut s'insurger. Il appelle simplement de ses vœux un retour aux sources de la pensée qui permette de comprendre l'essence de l'époque dans laquelle nous nous trouvons : « Je ne vois pas la situation de l'homme dans le monde de la technique planétaire comme s'il était en proie à un malheur dont il ne pourrait plus se dépêtrer, je vois bien plutôt la tâche de la pensée consister justement à aider, dans ses limites, à ce que l'homme parvienne d'abord à entrer suffisamment en relation avec l'être de la technique[246]. » Notre pensée actuelle est provisoire et inadaptée à cette situation.

La pensée de Heidegger ne peut laisser indifférent, sans qu'il soit même question de son rapport avec le national-socialisme. Elle met en évidence un certain nombre de nœuds dans l'histoire de l'humanité, qui forcent l'interrogation. Que l'on soit d'accord ou non avec cette vaste démonstration, que l'on puisse lui opposer nombre d'arguments (Que propose-t-il ? Rester à l'écoute de l'Etre, cela fait-il vivre une société ? Les progrès techniques n'ont-ils pas rendu nos conditions de vie infiniment plus supportables ? Heidegger n'est-il pas qu'un réactionnaire qui appelle à un retour à la nature ? N'y a-t-il pas une contradiction à dire que cette « histoire » est un destin, et à pouvoir l'écrire et en appeler, d'une certaine manière, à une conversion de la pensée ?), il nous faut en tout état de cause prendre en compte les effets en retour d'un tel rapport de l'homme au monde. Car qu'est-ce qui fait obstacle à ce que nous continuions de développer cette idéologie du travail et de l'artificialisation des rapports naturels et sociaux ? Ce qui fait obstacle, c'est la manière dont les instruments intellectuels et pratiques que nous avons forgés se retournent contre nous, sociétés et individus, au point de bouleverser de façon radicale — mais aussi de rendre insupportables — nos rapports sociaux. La condamnation de Hannah Arendt, au moins dans la *Condition de l'homme moderne*, reste encore faite du point de vue de la dignité de l'homme, c'est-à-dire d'une certaine conception de ce que doit être l'homme, qui serait bafouée aujourd'hui. Dans cette société de travailleurs, où la vie se passe à reproduire les conditions de la vie, nous sommes privés de ce qui fait l'essence de l'homme, la pensée, l'action, l'œuvre, l'art. L'homme s'est mutilé dans cette histoire au point de se perdre. Le résultat, c'est une humanité dégradée, où la dignité de l'homme n'est pas sauvegardée, où la volonté de se différencier à jamais de l'animalité nous a fait sombrer dans une certaine forme d'animalité, peut-être supérieure, mais en tout cas infiniment éloignée de la véritable *humanitas*.

D'autres élèves de Heidegger, regroupés plus tard sous le nom d'école de Francfort — Marcuse, par exemple —, sont allés plus loin. Certes, il y a sans doute chez Hannah Arendt un lien de causalité entre cette condition de l'homme moderne et ce phénomène qu'elle a passé une partie de sa vie à décrire : le totalitarisme, et en particulier l'événement qu'elle dit inexplicable et qui a partie liée avec lui, l'Holocauste. Mais Adorno et Horkheimer ont mis plus clairement qu'elle en évidence la causalité existant entre ce nouvel état de l'humanité, qu'ils appellent également technique, et le sommet de barbarie qui a été atteint. Dans *La Dialectique de la raison*[247], publiée en 1947, Adorno et Horkheimer écrivaient : « Ce que nous nous étions proposé de faire n'était en effet rien de moins que la tentative de comprendre pourquoi l'humanité, au lieu de s'engager dans des conditions vraiment humaines, sombrait dans une nouvelle forme de barbarie[248]. » L'effet en retour des instruments dont l'homme s'est doté pour domestiquer le

monde est leur objet de réflexion. Comme Heidegger, ils
désignent le moment où s'est selon eux opéré le retournement fatal : l'Aufklärung[249]. Après avoir fait remonter
l'origine de l'Aufklärung à Bacon, Horkheimer et Adorno
reprennent l'héritage heideggerien, en retraçant l'histoire
de la raison : celle-ci, qui était d'abord pensée, réflexivité,
critique, a surdéveloppé en quelque sorte son côté formel,
en mesurant son pouvoir sur les choses. La raison est
devenue calculatrice, le monde est devenu un livre de
mathématiques ou un champ d'expérience pour l'homme,
la science a perdu sa dimension de connaissance et de
critique pour devenir un appareil de maîtrise : « Sur la voie
qui les conduit vers la science moderne, les hommes
renoncent au sens. Ils remplacent le concept par la
formule, la cause par la règle et la probabilité. [...] La
logique formelle fut la grande école de l'unification. Elle
offrait aux partisans de la Raison le schéma suivant lequel
le monde pouvait être l'objet d'un calcul[250]. » La science se
transforme en appareil d'action ; il ne s'agit plus de
connaître mais de faire : « La Raison se comporte à l'égard
des choses comme un dictateur à l'égard des hommes : il les
connaît dans la mesure où il peut les manipuler[251]. » D'où
le double effet en retour : parce que la science s'est
transformée en auxiliaire de la technique, le réel, le monde
et l'homme sont devenus inconnaissables à eux-mêmes. Les
instruments sont devenus des obstacles à la connaissance de
soi, à la réflexion critique sur l'essence des choses : « Les
hommes paient l'accroissement de leur pouvoir en devenant étrangers à ce sur quoi ils l'exercent[252]. » En produisant toujours de nouveaux artifices, les hommes construisent des éléments qui les écrasent en retour. Cette instru-
mentalisation se retourne contre l'homme et contre la
société : les rapports entre les hommes eux-mêmes se
chosifient ; c'est lorsque l'homme est une chose que la
barbarie peut se développer. En instaurant une relation de
domination sur la nature, l'homme a en même temps
instauré une relation de domination sur ses semblables et

sur lui-même et s'est privé de la possiblité de les comprendre. Et là encore, le travail est au cœur du processus :
moyen d'aménagement de la nature, il est le nouvel
organisateur des rapports sociaux. Le rapport de domination sur l'extérieur entraîne l'existence d'un rapport identique entre ceux qui sont censés s'orienter ensemble vers
l'objectif donné ; « La domination confère à l'ensemble
social où elle se fixe une cohésion et une force accrues. La
division du travail à laquelle tend la domination sert à
l'autoconservation du groupe dominé [253] », et c'est le retour
au naturel que l'on voulait chasser : « Dans le monde
rationalisé, la mythologie a envahi le domaine du profane.
Débarrassée des démons et de leur postérité conceptuelle,
l'existence retrouve son état naturel et prend le caractère
inquiétant que le monde ancien attribuait aux démons.
Classée dans la catégorie des faits bruts, l'injustice sociale
est aujourd'hui aussi sacrée et intangible que l'était le
sacro-saint guérisseur sous la protection des dieux [254]. » On
comprend dès lors pourquoi le travail a pu occuper la
totalité de l'activité humaine : né comme moyen d'atteindre une fin, la richesse, il a fini par devenir lui-même la fin,
de la même facon que la raison instrumentalisée a oublié en
vue de quelle fin elle s'était instrumentalisée. D'où la
nécessité d'une théorie critique qui redonnerait à la raison
sa pleine dimension et cette fonction réflexive dont elle
s'est privée [255]. D'où la critique, commune à Heidegger et à
l'école de Francfort, du positivisme et du pragmatisme qui
mutilent la raison pour ne faire de celle-ci que l'appendice
d'une pratique, et la volonté de sauvegarder les deux faces
de la raison, instrumentale et objective.

L'impossible travail autonome

Le travail, parce qu'il est d'abord apparu comme facteur
de production, moyen d'augmenter les richesses, puis
d'humaniser le monde, est donc emporté par une logique

qui le dépasse infiniment et fait de lui un moyen au service d'une autre fin que lui-même. Il ne peut pas dès lors être le lieu de l'autonomie et de l'épanouissement. Etre le moyen d'une fin, c'est la définition de l'hétéronomie ou de l'aliénation. Comment le travail pourrait-il donc être le lieu de l'autonomie ? Comment pourrait-il être une œuvre ?

Autogestion et autonomie

Certains affirment que le travail reste certes aujourd'hui le lieu de l'aliénation, mais qu'un bouleversement des conditions de son exercice pourrait lui rendre enfin sa nature. Où l'on retrouve le schéma utopiste en lequel a cru le XIXe siècle, en imaginant des bouleversements plus ou moins radicaux. L'appropriation des moyens de production par les travailleurs et la fin du salariat, rendues possibles par un très fort développement des forces productives et l'inutilité de fait du travail humain, permettraient, selon le marxisme, de rendre le travail conforme à son essence et d'en faire le véritable lieu de l'autonomie. En dépit de ses critiques à l'encontre des premières formes du socialisme, c'est encore néanmoins à la même utopie spécifique à la société du travail qu'obéit Marx dans la première partie de *L'Idéologie allemande* : « Nous en sommes donc arrivés aujourd'hui au point que les individus sont obligés de s'approprier la totalité des forces productives pour parvenir à une activité autonome. [...] C'est à ce stade que l'activité autonome se confond avec la vie matérielle, ce qui correspond à l'épanouissement en individus complets et à l'affranchissement vis-à-vis de toute nature première[256]. » Tout se passe comme si Marx n'avait pas saisi la raison exacte pour laquelle le travail est aliéné, ou plutôt comme s'il avait bien vu les deux premières (la logique capitaliste et la subordination) sans comprendre qu'elles-mêmes s'expliquent, en dernier ressort, par la troisième : la volonté d'abondance ou d'humanisation, fondement du productivisme.

Redisons d'abord ce que nous savons tous aujourd'hui : le caractère aliénant du travail ne disparaîtrait pas du fait de l'appropriation collective des moyens de production. Que les capitaux soient détenus par les travailleurs plutôt que par les capitalistes changerait finalement peu de chose aux conditions concrètes de travail ; l'organisation sera toujours le fait de quelques-uns et non de tous. Comme l'a bien montré Gorz en son temps [257], il n'y a aucune raison pour que ce sujet magnifié, le Prolétariat, ou même l'ensemble des travailleurs, s'approprient le Plan au point de le considérer comme leur. Là encore, l'erreur marxienne est de croire que le grand sujet autonome est conscient et que l'ensemble de ses membres, les travailleurs, possèdent aussi cette conscience tout entière. Qu'elle soit organisée par le marché ou par le plan, l'extériorité de la production à réaliser est identiquement étrangère aux travailleurs, et l'on ne voit pas pourquoi le vote du Plan, ou encore la réalisation d'un Plan correspondant totalement et exclusivement aux besoins des travailleurs, changerait le caractère du travail en quoi que ce soit, sauf à s'autopersuader. Pourquoi ? Parce que le problème n'est pas la propriété des moyens de production, mais le caractère même du travail aujourd'hui, le fait que l'efficacité productive reste son but. Dès lors, le travail demeure un facteur, subordonné au développement technique de l'industrie ou des services. C'est ce qui explique pourquoi une bonne partie des réflexions socialistes, celle de Louis Blanc comme celle de Marx, ont un jour opéré un saut inexplicable entre l'appropriation des moyens de production ou l'organisation du travail par les « producteurs associés » et la libération du travail. Autrement dit, l'abolition du rapport salarial ne suffit pas à rendre le travail autonome [258] : « Aujourd'hui, l'utopie qui se rattache à la société du travail a épuisé sa force de conviction — et ce pas seulement parce que les forces productives ont perdu leur innocence ou parce que l'abolition de la propriété privée des moyens de production ne débouche manifestement pas *per se* sur l'autogestion des travailleurs [259]. » La propriété aura beau être transférée à l'Etat ou à l'ensemble des individus, tant que le travail sera subordonné à la logique de développement des besoins, et donc à celle de la division et de la rentabilité, l'essentiel du travail ne changera pas, et l'on ne voit pas comment l'on pourrait soutenir que le travail moderne, totalement éclaté et de plus en plus abstrait, pourrait être, aujourd'hui ou dans le futur, le lieu ou le moyen de l'autonomie. Pourquoi ? Parce que la force des rapports sociaux de travail tire son origine de la puissance de l'impératif qui lui donne sens : l'organisation du travail est dirigée par le principe d'efficacité, qui vient lui-même de l'impératif absolu d'accroître toujours les richesses. C'est ainsi qu'elle se justifie.

Marx lui-même n'a pas remis ce premier principe en cause, bien au contraire. Dans la mesure où le royaume de la liberté ne pourra éclore que lorsque le capitalisme aura été poussé à son terme, la fin de l'Etat capitaliste et le début de l'Etat communiste doivent eux aussi pousser à sa limite la logique du travail, développer les forces productives jusqu'à ce que, l'abondance ayant été atteinte, le travail change de sens. Quoi que l'on pense de la réalité soviétique dans son rapport à Marx — c'est-à-dire qu'elle s'en réclame sans pourtant que l'on puisse la déduire des œuvres marxiennes — il est clair qu'elle a développé à un point sans doute inégalé la sacralisation du travail et de la production. Ainsi s'explique la critique radicale que des femmes comme Simone Weil ou Hannah Arendt adressent à Marx, qu'elles prennent (paradoxalement, car elles partagent sa révolte) comme cible de leurs attaques contre le « productivisme [260] ». En raison de cette croyance fondamentale dans le nécessaire développement des forces productives, Marx ne nous donne pas les moyens de comprendre comment l'appropriation des moyens de production par les travailleurs — même si elle est désirable — permettrait au travail de devenir brutalement autonome. La pensée marxiste actuelle ne nous donne pas plus les moyens de penser une transformation du travail [261]. C'est également cette croyance en une possible autonomie du travail (dont on ne nous donne pas la clef) qui explique aujourd'hui l'opposition de la pensée marxiste à une réduction du temps de travail[262].

La fin de la division du travail?

Un deuxième argument est souvent avancé pour soutenir la possibilité de l'autonomie dans le travail : le travail industriel serait en train de voir sa place se réduire et il prendrait un autre visage, dû à la sortie du taylorisme et au développement du travail intellectuel. La société post-industrielle, après avoir développé un travail immatériel et des processus très complexes demandant des interventions humaines hautement qualifiées, serait capable aujourd'hui, à condition d'adapter la formation de ses membres, de rendre au travail son autonomie. Nous entrerions dans une société de services, dans laquelle la productivité serait moindre, la division du travail moins poussée, la possibilité de dominer l'ensemble d'un processus, d'une opération ou d'une relation, plus grande. C'est ce que soutiennent un certain nombre de recherches en économie industrielle en France et en Allemagne, où par exemple la publication d'un livre de deux chercheurs allemands, Horst Kern et Michael Schumann, intitulé *La Fin de la division du travail*[263], a relancé ce débat. La thèse défendue par ces deux auteurs et par tout un courant de pensée est que nous sommes sortis de la société industrielle classique caractérisée par le travail à la chaîne exercé sur une matière et entrés dans une société de l'immatériel, où le travail change de sens et est susceptible de devenir autonome. L'autonomie viendrait de ce que le travail consisterait désormais à concevoir, à gérer ou à surveiller la bonne marche d'un processus, donc à avoir un point de vue global sur une série articulée d'opérations, point de vue recomposant par rapport à l'ancienne division du travail (il permettrait l'utilisation des capacités intellectuelles et redonnerait initiative et responsabilité aux agents). Les travailleurs du futur seraient plus responsables, plus autonomes, car amenés à faire appel à leurs capacités cognitives, à faire circuler l'information, à maîtriser des processus complexes, à prendre des décisions susceptibles d'influencer l'ensemble du processus de production. Que l'on nous pardonne, mais on voit mal en quoi la faculté de surveiller un processus complexe serait plus source d'autonomie que celle de tourner 8 000 fois par jour un boulon dans le même sens. Qu'un tel travail soit moins abrutissant ou qu'il fasse appel à d'autres capacités, on le concédera volontiers ; mais aller jusqu'à dire qu'il permet à l'individu de s'exprimer et d'être autonome est sans doute abusif. Nous serions également, nous dit-on, à l'aube d'une société de services où le travail de 90 % de la population ne consistera plus à transformer une matière, mais à organiser des flux d'informations, avec d'autres et pour d'autres. Dès lors que ces mutations s'accompagnent d'une implication accrue des personnes, le travail deviendrait un possible lieu de réalisation de soi, permettant à chacun d'entrer en communication avec les autres et de développer ses compétences (par le biais des organisations qualifiantes par exemple, conçues pour permettre aux individus d'exploiter leurs qualités professionnelles et les compétences acquises). Bref, les relations de travail pourraient aujourd'hui devenir le lieu d'expression de toutes les personnalités.

Trois objections doivent être formulées à l'encontre de ces analyses. En premier lieu, ces pensées ne se donnent pas les moyens de leur ambition : si nous voulons en effet que le travail soit notre œuvre et devienne notre grand médium social, nous devons rompre avec sa dimension essentielle, c'est-à-dire économique. Nous devons renoncer à la recherche infinie de l'abondance et de l'efficacité et du même coup à la subordination. Mais ces pensées, en voulant concilier l'abondance et le sens du travail, n'osent pas mener leur raisonnement à son terme. Ensuite, ces pensées confondent les fonctions et le support qui leur permet de s'exercer. Certes, nous pouvons tenter de donner un sens aux activités que nous exerçons toute la journée pour satisfaire les besoins de la société, et il serait étonnant que nous n'y mettions pas un peu du nôtre. Mais ce n'est pas parce que l'organisation du travail aujourd'hui laisse quelque peu la place à la personnalité et qu'elle permet un minimum d'expression de soi qu'elle le permet par nature. Elle ne le fait que par accident. La vraie autonomie et la vraie expression de soi sont quelque chose de différent. Elles consistent à se donner sa loi à soi-même, à se fixer des objectifs et les moyens de l'atteindre. Le plus étonnant, enfin, dans toutes ces analyses — et celle de Marx relève de la même critique —, ce n'est pas tant que « toute œuvre devienne travail [264] », mais surtout que tout travail puisse être considéré comme une œuvre. Car ce sont bien les catégories de l'œuvre qui sont employées pour décrire le travail aujourd'hui ; il permettrait à chacun d'exprimer sa singularité à travers des objets, des services, des relations et, en même temps, serait profondément socialisant. C'est bien là ce qui est étonnant : non pas que l'on ait pu ramener toute l'activité humaine au seul travail, mais que tout travail soit conçu, depuis Hegel, comme une œuvre. Comme si toute production consistait à mettre sur la place publique une image de soi, que cette production soit un objet, un service, un écrit. Par où l'on peut juger de la prégnance de l'héritage humaniste qui, au terme d'une considérable réduction, fait de la production l'acte le plus humain qui soit.

Tout se passe donc comme si le travail avait pris une place telle dans nos sociétés que nous avions décidé qu'il vaut mieux tenter de le rendre épanouissant — en dépit de la gageure que cela représente — plutôt que de charger un ou d'autres systèmes de cette fonction. L'argument le plus répandu aujourd'hui est que le travail doit rester central parce qu'il permet la satisfaction de tous les besoins, et pas seulement des besoins matériels : le travail est le moyen de réaliser tous nos désirs. L'homme est un être de désir dont l'essence est de consommer et tout désir a besoin d'un travail pour se réaliser. Mais quel travail ? C'est ici que les pensées humanistes sont extrêmement gênantes : elles emploient le terme de travail dans un sens général en omettant de préciser les conditions de sa réalisation. Elles confondent sans cesse le travail au sens large, qui peut recouvrir des réalités très différentes (écrire un poème, se cultiver, peindre, lire, apprendre...), avec ce que nous appelons travail depuis le XVIIIe siècle, et qui est d'abord un facteur de production régi par des règles économiques et juridiques précises, et visant à une fin déterminée. Et elles ne disent jamais comment on passe de l'un à l'autre. Les plus cohérentes, comme celle de Marx, permettent de comprendre ce que signifie cette confusion : considérer toute œuvre comme du travail et tout travail comme une œuvre, c'est considérer que toute vie est production et que tout acte de production est expression. Le seul mode d'expression individuelle possible est la production et le seul mode de communication sociale, la production d'objets ou de services. Nous sommes donc aujourd'hui dans une époque entièrement soumise à cette contradiction qui consiste à penser le travail comme notre œuvre alors qu'il reste régi, plus que jamais, par la logique de l'efficacité. La seule raison pour laquelle cette contradiction ne nous saute pas aux yeux, c'est que nous avons désormais intégré le raisonnement humaniste et productiviste dont Marx est le représentant le plus exceptionnel et le plus rigoureux.

LE TRAVAIL, LIEN SOCIAL ?

Cette aporie nous invite à nous intéresser à l'autre catégorie d'arguments utilisée par les défenseurs du travail : elle regroupe un ensemble de raisonnements selon lesquels le travail est au fondement du lien social, c'est-à-dire non seulement le moyen majeur de socialisation et d'intégration sociale, mais aussi ce qui tient quotidiennement le lien social. Dans l'esprit des auteurs qui la défendent, cette thèse recouvre plusieurs éléments, qui sont le plus souvent confondus et que l'on peut classer sous quatre chefs principaux : le travail permet l'apprentissage de la vie sociale et la constitution des identités (il nous apprend les contraintes de la vie avec les autres) ; il est la mesure des échanges sociaux (il est la norme sociale et la clef de contribution-rétribution sur quoi repose le lien social) ; il permet à chacun d'avoir une utilité sociale (chacun contribue à la vie sociale en adaptant ses capacités aux besoins sociaux) ; enfin, il est un lieu de rencontres et de coopérations, opposé aux lieux non publics que sont le couple ou la famille. Les discours de valorisation du travail qui s'appuient sur cette argumentation pèchent cependant en deux endroits : d'une part, en prenant le travail comme modèle du lien social, ils promeuvent une conception éminemment réductrice de ce lien ; d'autre part, en soutenant que le travail exerce des fonctions macrosociales, ils oublient la réalité du travail et des instruments économiques et juridiques par lesquels celui-ci est régi dans notre société.

Qu'est-ce que le lien social si le travail est sa raison ?

Tentons de comprendre si c'est le travail en soi qui est générateur de lien social ou s'il n'exerce aujourd'hui ces fonctions particulières que « par accident ». Réglons d'un mot la question de la norme : dans une société régie par le travail, où celui-ci est non seulement le moyen d'acquérir un revenu, mais constitue également l'occupation de la majeure partie du temps socialisé, il est évident que les individus qui en sont tenus à l'écart en souffrent. Les enquêtes réalisées chez les chômeurs ou les RMistes et qui montrent que ceux-ci ne veulent pas seulement un revenu, mais aussi du travail, ne doivent pas être mal interprétées. Elles mettent certainement moins en évidence la volonté de ces personnes d'exercer un travail que le désir de vouloir être comme les autres, d'être utiles à la société, de ne pas être assistés. On ne peut pas en déduire un appétit naturel pour le travail et faire comme si nous disposions là d'une population-test qui nous permettrait de savoir ce qu'il en est, en vérité, du besoin de travail. Mais, nonobstant la question de la norme, le travail est-il le seul moyen d'établir et de maintenir le lien social, et le permet-il réellement lui-même ? Cette question mérite d'être posée, car c'est au nom d'un tel raisonnement que toutes les mesures conservatoires du travail sont prises : lui seul permettrait le lien social, il n'y aurait pas de solution de rechange. Or, que constatons-nous ? Que l'on attend du médium qu'est le travail la constitution d'un espace social permettant l'apprentissage de la vie avec les autres, la coopération et la collaboration des individus, la possibilité pour chacun d'entre eux de prouver son utilité sociale et de s'attirer ainsi la reconnaissance. Le travail permet-il cela aujourd'hui ? Ce n'est pas certain, car là n'est pas son but : il n'a pas été inventé dans le but de voir des individus rassemblés réaliser une œuvre commune. Dès lors, le travail est, certes, un moyen d'apprendre la vie en société, de se rencontrer, de se sociabiliser, voire d'être socialement utile, mais il l'est de manière dérivée. Les collaborations et les rencontres occasionnelles qui s'instaurent dans les usines ou dans les bureaux constituent une manière d'être avec les autres, mais il s'agit somme toute d'une forme de sociabilité assez faible. L'utilité sociale peut sans doute parfois se confondre avec l'exercice d'un travail, mais cela n'est pas nécessaire. Autrement dit, le travail permet aujourd'hui l'exercice d'une certaine forme de sociabilité, mais c'est essentiellement parce qu'il est la forme majeure d'organisation du temps social et qu'il est le rapport social dominant, celui sur lequel sont fondés nos échanges et nos hiérarchies sociales, et non parce qu'il aurait été conçu comme le moyen mis au service d'une fin précise : l'établissement du lien social. Les arguments en sa faveur sont d'ailleurs le plus souvent des raisonnements par l'absurde : bien sûr, le travail n'exerce peut-être pas ces fonctions au mieux ; bien sûr, il n'est fondamentalement pas fait pour cela, mais nous ne disposons d'aucun autre système d'organisation sociale équivalent qui pourrait assurer autant de fonctions à la fois. Les associations ou toute autre forme permettant le regroupement d'individus susceptibles d'œuvrer ensemble ne sont pas une alternative crédible, entend-on dire.

Cette question est évidemment majeure : si le travail ne fonde pas par nature le lien social, alors peut-être devrions nous réfléchir au système qui pourrait s'en charger, et de manière plus efficace que le travail. Mais auparavant, sans doute est-il nécessaire de s'entendre sur la notion de lien social. Quelle est notre conception du lien social pour que nous puissions aujourd'hui considérer que le travail est sa condition majeure ? Quel type de représentation en avons-nous pour que le lien établi par le travail — qui relève plus de la contiguïté que du vouloir-vivre ensemble — soit confondu avec lui? Nous sommes les héritiers de la représentation léguée par l'économie et que nous voyons à l'œuvre chez Smith d'abord, chez Marx ensuite. Le nerf du raisonnement de Smith, même s'il n'est pas développé de façon explicite, est que le travail *est* le lien social, car il met les individus obligatoirement en rapport, les oblige à coopérer et les enserre dans un filet de dépendance mutuelle. Mais ce lien social est d'une nature très particulière : il consiste essentiellement en une coexistence pacifique imposée, coexistence entre des individus dont le lien est l'échange marchand et matériel, c'est-à-dire visible, mesurable, exhibé. C'est pourquoi la richesse et le travail sont nés matériels et marchands : ils n'ont d'intérêt social que s'ils sont fondateurs de sociabilité. La richesse ne peut apparaître qu'à partir des objets : objets fabriqués, dans lesquels certains individus ont mis de leur travail, objets achetés par de l'équivalent-travail. Le travail est devenu non seulement la mesure des choses, mais de surcroît la condition de possibilité du lien social. Ce lien social n'est ni voulu ni aimé ; il est sans parole et sans débat ; les actes sociaux s'y font automatiquement. C'est aussi un lien social où l'Etat n'a pour seule fonction que de permettre une fluidité toujours plus grande des échanges économiques, afin de prévenir les tensions sociales. Ce qui est tout à fait curieux et paradoxal, c'est que le système « idéal » imaginé par Marx n'est pas très éloigné de ces conceptions. Car, dans la seconde étape de la société communiste, lorsque le travail est devenu premier besoin vital en se dépouillant de ses caractéristiques originelles d'effort et de contrainte, le travail est un pur rapport social, immédiatement perceptible [265]. Le travail de chacun est à la fois immédiatement œuvre (il exprime la personnalité de son auteur) et social (il est destiné à être lu, vu par les autres). La médiation de l'argent ou même de l'échange n'est plus nécessaire : les rapports sont de purs rapports d'expression, chaque objet exprime à l'infini son auteur, qui se contemple dans les produits des autres. La société est une vaste scène où chacun vient présenter ce qu'il est, son travail. Elle est transparente à elle-même, unie entièrement, comme les monades de Leibniz[266]. L'échange est superfétatoire (il est en quelque sorte déjà inscrit dans l'objet, qui est un « de moi-pour l'autre »), de même que la parole et la régulation extérieure. L'autorégulation passe toujours par des objets ou des services (elle doit pouvoir se manifester), mais elle n'a pas besoin du reste. Voilà pourquoi le travail est un premier besoin vital : il est tout simplement notre rapport aux autres.

Les tentatives d'autorégulation fondées sur le travail au XVIIIe siècle apparaissent alors dans leur vérité : elles n'étaient rien d'autre que des tentatives de fonder le lien social et sa totale autosubsistance. L'activité humaine fondatrice du rapport social est la production, qui n'est désormais plus parasitée par l'intervention d'autres motifs et n'est plus une production aliénée. Produire, c'est faire le lien social. C'est là qu'est la grande similitude, inattendue, entre Smith et Marx. C'est là aussi qu'apparaît la congruence entre les pensées actuelles qui voient dans le travail à la fois le lieu de l'œuvre et du lien social.

Mais à cette première conception s'oppose une autre définition du lien social, radicalement différente, qui voit en lui quelque chose de plus substantiel dont l'origine ne peut se trouver dans la production. Cette tradition parcourt les siècles, d'Aristote à Habermas, et considère que le lien social n'est pas réductible au lien économique ou à la simple production, parce que la vie, et en particulier la vie en communauté, « est action et non production ». Dans *Les Economiques*[267], Aristote a montré la spécificité de l'ordre économique : celui-ci concerne le seul domaine « privé », la famille élargie, elle-même lieu de l'inégalité[268]. L'économique est l'art qui concerne les relations naturelles d'une communauté elle-même naturelle. Le lien sur lequel repose cette communauté, constituée du chef de famille, de la femme, des enfants et des esclaves, est un lien inégal qui se fonde sur d'autres logiques que le véritable lien social qui est, lui, d'essence politique, et qui rassemble des égaux[269]. La famille se distingue donc de la véritable communauté, celle qui est vraiment première (non pas au sens chronologique mais au sens logique, comme Aristote aime le dire), la communauté politique, qui donne son sens, rétrospectivement, à toutes les autres communautés et les précède selon la finalité. Il existe une différence fondamentale, de nature, entre les préoccupations qui ont pour objet la gestion du domaine et la propriété[270] et celles qui concernent la cité tout entière. La seconde ne peut pas dériver de la première : le lien social ou encore le lien qui unit les individus d'une société ne dérive pas du lien économique, c'est-à-dire de la simple préoccupation individuelle de l'accroissement des richesses ou de la bonne gestion. Les deux sont irréductiblement différents. Et c'est bien la confusion de l'un et de l'autre, la progressive réduction du lien social au lien économique, que Hannah Arendt passe une partie de son œuvre à récuser : dès lors que le souci privé est érigé en préoccupation publique, dès que « nous imaginons les peuples, les collectivités publiques comme des familles dont les affaires quotidiennes relèvent de la sollicitude d'une gigantesque administration ménagère[271] », c'en est fini. Alors, non seulement le lien social est issu des relations naturelles entre les individus, mais il s'y réduit : le lien social devient un lien naturel, l'objet de la politique se confond avec celui de chaque petite communauté naturelle.

L'analyse de Hegel met clairement ce processus en lumière : Hegel montre que, dès lors que la communauté politique ne se distingue pas de la société civile, le lien social se réduit au lien économique. Dans le vocabulaire hégélien, la société civile est le lieu des besoins, du travail et des échanges, c'est-à-dire le lieu où les hommes sont dépendants les uns des autres. Dans cette société individualiste, les hommes, conçus comme des atomes, ne sont régis que par le principe de la concurrence et de l'intérêt individuel et ne visent qu'à la prospérité matérielle. L'intérêt individuel est le moteur de cette société civile, moyen terme entre le groupe naturel qu'est la famille et le monde spirituel de l'Etat. Composée des hommes privés agissant les uns à côté des autres, elle correspond à l'Etat du libéralisme économique. Hegel connaît très bien l'économie politique anglaise, Smith, Ricardo et aussi Steuart. Il a lu Smith dès 1805 et le *Système de la vie éthique*[272] en porte la trace ; il a commenté les écrits de Steuart[273]. Il reconnaît l'importance de ce moment dans la préparation du moment suivant, car c'est dans la société civile que l'individu fait son apprentissage de l'universel : dans ce monde économique, l'homme se croit libre, mais se heurte en fait partout à des contraintes ; au lieu de vouloir l'universel, il le trouve partout face à lui comme une puissance étrangère contre laquelle il est impuissant. La société civile est une réalisation médiate de l'universel : son harmonie résulte d'une sorte de ruse ; ce qui est réalisé en fait (l'universel), et ce qui est voulu (l'intérêt individuel) sont distincts.

Ce domaine est celui de l'atomisme et de la séparation, un atomisme poussé à son comble qui fait de la société civile le résultat d'un assemblage d'atomes en concurrence que ne lie aucun lien substantiel. La société civile, libérale ou marchande, image de liens sociaux où les individus sont en totale extériorité les uns avec les autres est, pour Hegel, le contraire du véritable lien politique. Dans l'Etat seulement la société civile, domestiquée, trouvera sa place. Hegel prend donc en compte les dernières découvertes de l'économie politique, il admire que l'on ait pu découvrir des lois dans un tel domaine, il reconnaît l'émergence du marché, des échanges et de la société moderne, mais il n'en fait pas pour autant le but ultime. Il suffit, pour le bien comprendre, de relire la section des *Principes de la philosophie du droit*[274] consacrée à la société civile : « La personne concrète qui, en tant que particulière, est à elle-même son propre but, est, comme ensemble de besoins et comme mélange de nécessité naturelle et de volonté arbitraire, l'un des deux principes de la société civile. [...] Ce but égoïste, ainsi conditionné dans sa réalisation par l'universalité, fonde un système de dépendance réciproque tel que la subsistance, le bien-être de l'individu et son existence juridique sont si étroitement liés à la subsistance, au bien-être et au droit de tous qu'ils ne deviennent effectifs que dans cette liaison. [...] C'est l'Etat du besoin et de l'entendement. » Dans *L'Encyclopédie*, Hegel disait : « C'est le système atomistique. » Par conséquent, ce système qui fonde le rapprochement des individus sur le besoin et sur la dépendance réciproque est le contraire d'un lien substantiel : il met côte à côte des individus qui poursuivent leur objectif propre. L'Etat n'a pour fonction que de protéger la propriété privée des individus. « Si l'on confond l'Etat avec la société civile et si on lui donne pour destination la tâche de veiller à la sûreté, d'assurer la protection de la propriété privée et de la liberté personnelle, c'est l'intérêt des individus comme tels qui est le but final en vue duquel ils se sont unis et il s'ensuit qu'il est laissé au bon vouloir de chacun de devenir membre de l'Etat. Mais l'Etat a un tout autre rapport avec l'individu ; étant donné que l'Etat est Esprit objectif, l'individu ne peut avoir lui-même de vérité, une existence objective et une vie éthique que s'il est membre de l'Etat. L'union en tant que telle est elle-même le véritable contenu et le véritable but, car les individus ont pour destination de mener une vie universelle [275]. »

Il faut mesurer combien cette idée est en rupture avec la conception du droit issue du XVIIIe siècle. En défendant cette conception d'un Etat capable de réconcilier l'individu et le tout social, Hegel ne satisfait pas seulement son admiration pour la Grèce. Il contribue aussi à définir une théorie du droit en rupture profonde avec une certaine tradition juridique issue du droit romain, c'est-à-dire justement de ce droit que Hegel considère comme largement responsable du développement de l'individualisme.

Relayée au xviiie siècle par les conceptions anglaise, française (atomisme, libéralisme, contrat social) ou allemande (individualisme kantien), l'émergence de l'individu dans la sphère juridique a conduit à un droit construit à partir de la personne. Il en est résulté une conception de l'Etat comme visant exclusivement à protéger et surveiller les libertés et les intérêts individuels. A cela Hegel oppose, dans son opuscule *Le Droit naturel*[276], et surtout dans *Les Principes de la philosophie du droit*, l'idée d'un droit organique, dont l'intuition fondamentale est que le tout précède les « parties » qui le composent et leur est supérieur. Dans le droit individualiste issu du droit romain et approfondi avec les penseurs de la Révolution française, Hegel voit un droit abstrait, au service d'un égalitarisme abstrait et issu d'une conception purement mécanique du tout social. Il lui oppose une vision plus organique, où le tout social est semblable à la vie, qui par définition ne se maintient que par l'existence de toutes ses parties, dont elle est à la fois le résultat et la cause. L'Etat apparaît ainsi bien plutôt comme une organisation vivante qui règle harmonieusement les rapports entre les individus qui le composent et les rapports des individus au tout à travers un ensemble d'institutions. C'est à partir de cette analyse de Hegel que se développera, en Allemagne, au xixe siècle, une critique approfondie des relations individualistes et contractuelles héritées du droit romain.

Dès lors, le travail dont Hegel voit l'émergence sous ses yeux, le travail abstrait, est destiné à être à la fois dépassé et domestiqué, de même que la sphère dans laquelle il a pris naissance. La société marchande, la dépendance réciproque induite par le travail et l'échange ne sont en aucune façon le but ultime de l'Esprit et des hommes. Le type de lien qu'une telle société permet d'instaurer reste abstrait et ne parvient pas à replacer l'individu en harmonie avec le tout social. Celle-ci ne peut advenir que grâce au lien politique, qui est d'une autre nature. La construction d'un monde pleinement humain est d'abord celle d'une

société politique aux institutions pleinement développées ;
c'est en cela aussi que consiste le travail de l'Esprit. Celui-ci
ne sera « chez lui » que dans un Etat totalement harmo-
nieux, où art, religion et philosophie constitueront les
activités suprêmes. Hegel est parvenu à réintroduire les
concepts grecs au sein même du monde moderne. La
production matérielle, ou même la production tout court,
n'est pas la seule manière d'être ensemble, de faire une
société : il faut aussi compter avec la parole, le débat, les
institutions. L'être ensemble se parle et le lien politique
n'est pas réductible au lien économique. C'est cette dimension proprement politique que Marx a éludée.

C'est exactement le point de vue développé par Habermas dans son article fondateur « Travail et interaction »[277],
souvent mal interprété. Dans cet article, Habermas mène
une longue argumentation sur les rapports entre Hegel et
Marx et montre comment ce dernier a occulté, comme le
Hegel de la maturité d'ailleurs, une des idées de jeunesse
de Hegel selon laquelle il y a plusieurs domaines de réalité
fondamentaux de l'Esprit objectif et comment, chez Marx,
ces différents domaines sont ramenés à un seul. On
pourrait s'étonner parfois de l'insistance de Habermas à
dire, comme Hannah Arendt, que le travail n'est que le
rapport de l'homme à la nature. La tentation est grande de
penser qu'il a oublié une dimension essentielle du travail,
que celui-ci n'est pas seulement un rapport de l'homme à la
nature mais aussi un rapport éminemment social. Or, c'est
précisément ce que dénonce Habermas : que l'on ait pu
penser que le travail, rapport à la nature, système destiné à
satisfaire nos besoins naturels, déterminait en même temps
nos rapports sociaux (ce que dit Marx lorsqu'il affirme que
les forces productives déterminent les rapports de production) ou que le travail était avant tout un rapport social. Il
critique principalement l'idée que l'on pourrait rabattre la
totalité de la vie sociale sur le travail, donc que le travail
expliquerait et serait le tout des rapports sociaux (les places
dans le système de production déterminent tout le reste),

devenant ainsi leur unique modalité. Fidèle en cela à la tradition hégélienne, Habermas démontre au contraire l'irréductibilité du travail et de l'interaction, autrement dit des rapports de production et des rapports sociaux, de l'économie et de la politique, de la production et de la discussion.

C'est évidemment la même idée que poursuit Hannah Arendt dans sa critique du travail : mettre le travail au centre de la société, justifier le travail comme lien social, c'est défendre une idée éminemment pauvre de celui-ci, c'est refuser que l'ordre politique soit autre que l'ordre économique ou que la simple régulation sociale, c'est oublier que la société a d'autres fins que la production et la richesse et que l'homme a d'autres moyens de s'exprimer que la production ou la consommation. Nous sommes donc clairement ici devant une double tradition, qui interprète de façon très différente le lien social, l'une comme lien économique, l'autre comme lien politique. On voit bien que dans l'un et l'autre cas, le travail comme espace des échanges marchands n'occupe pas la même place. Dans le second cas, le travail sert simplement à la satisfaction des besoins naturels; dans le premier, le travail est en même temps le lien social et tout le lien social dérive du travail. On voit également comment les deux notions modernes qui voient dans le travail une œuvre, d'une part, et le lien social, d'autre part, vont de pair. Elles correspondent au même mouvement de pensée qui, reprenant la dynamique utopique du XIXe siècle, a élu la sphère de la production comme celle d'où viendrait la libération, mais n'a pas procédé, dans le même temps, à la généalogie qui était nécessaire. Récupérer l'héritage du XIXe siècle sans prendre en compte celui qui a été légué par le XVIIIe siècle, c'est ne comprendre qu'une partie du concept de travail et de ses diverses fonctions : c'est oublier la dimension « économique » du travail, c'est-à-dire sa destination première, qui est de produire des richesses et d'asseoir le rapport entre individus de façon autorégulée. C'est donc sombrer de manière évidente dans les contradictions.

Le travail peut-il exercer une fonction macrosociale ?

La même ignorance de la dimension originellement « économique » du travail est à l'origine de la troisième contradiction dont font preuve les pensées de légitimation du travail lorsqu'elles soutiennent que le travail, outre qu'il est le lieu de la réalisation de soi et du lien social, exerce des fonctions macrosociales. Le travail selon elles jouerait aujourd'hui un rôle éminent dans le renforcement des solidarités collectives, il serait la manière moderne d'être ensemble et de coopérer, il permettrait aux individus d'être partie prenante à une relation sociale majeure (la relation de travail) et de s'intégrer par elle dans la communauté, la société en miniature qu'est l'entreprise. Telle est bien l'idée sur laquelle s'appuient une partie des théories sociologiques[278] actuelles, mais aussi les politiques menées depuis une vingtaine d'années en matière d'insertion, de lutte contre l'exclusion ou d'apprentissage : le travail est conçu comme le moyen principal de trouver une reconnaissance, une utilité sociale, une intégration, et l'entreprise comme creuset de cette alchimie, qu'il s'agisse du premier contact du jeune avec la société ou du retour à celle-ci après une longue période d'exclusion. D'où l'impact des « nouvelles » notions d'entreprise citoyenne, de responsabilité sociale de l'entreprise...

Fonction macrosociale et incitation individuelle

Ces pensées conçoivent donc le travail comme une activité collective. Elles sont de ce fait profondément contradictoires parce que, dans le même temps, elles reconnaissent que les techniques qui continuent de régir le travail sont profondément individualistes. Modelé, au XVIIIᵉ siècle, par des sciences ou des techniques adaptées au traitement des relations individuelles, le travail a, certes, été rêvé comme œuvre collective de l'humanité triomphante ou des producteurs associés ; il a, il est vrai, été considéré par nos plus éminents sociologues comme la structure de base de la société et le moyen d'une solidarité organique entre les membres de celle-ci[279], mais il reste aujourd'hui conçu, à travers le contrat de travail et les équations de la microéconomie, comme une prestation individuelle, sanctionnée par une rémunération individuelle, et objet d'un contrat individuel même s'il s'inscrit dans un ordre juridique collectif. Assurément, le droit du travail a considérablement contribué à gommer ce que la conception originale avait d'hypocrite, quand elle laissait croire que l'ouvrier et l'employeur négociaient à égalité. Il a contribué à ériger l'ensemble des travailleurs en un collectif ayant des droits reconnus et une véritable existence. En outre, la reconnaissance des institutions représentatives de salariés et la possibilité d'action des travailleurs groupés se sont développées ; peu à peu un droit spécifiquement collectif s'est élaboré, source de règles collectives applicables à tous les salariés, qui a contribué à profondément transformer la relation de travail et particulièrement celle de contribution-rétribution que nous analysons. Un droit collectif du licenciement, du salaire et de la protection sociale s'est constitué qui a rendu plus lâche le lien de personne à personne qui existait auparavant. En particulier, dans les secteurs couverts par les accords, les augmentations de salaire, l'accès à la formation, le reclassement en cas de licenciement, la durée du travail sont régis par des conventions collectives. Surtout, deux grands types de protections se sont consolidés au long du XXᵉ siècle, la protection contre le risque que constitue le chômage et celle contre les risques sociaux, qui permettent de compenser l'état de subordination du salarié. Ceci a eu, en particulier, pour conséquence de brouiller les caractéristiques idéaltypiques du contrat de travail, une partie des revenus des salariés ne dépendant plus directement de leur contribution à la production mais s'étant socialisée.

Pourtant, cette évolution n'a pas porté atteinte à l'existence du droit individuel, ou du moins à l'architecture fondamentalement individualiste du droit du travail qui s'exprime à travers le contrat de travail. La culture issue du droit romain reste au cœur de notre droit du travail, qui saisit le travail comme l'objet d'une opération d'échange entre individus. Le travail, et c'est un point fondamental, fait l'objet d'un contrat ; il est ainsi placé dans l'orbite du droit des obligations, qui « renvoie à une idéologie individualiste et libérale, qui postule la liberté et l'égalité des individus et affirme la primauté de l'individu sur le groupe et de l'économique sur le social [280] ». Le droit collectif s'est surajouté au droit individuel : le contrat de travail est toujours passé entre un employeur et un employé ; l'acte d'embauche, l'acte de licenciement et l'organisation du travail restent des prérogatives du chef d'entreprise ; le salaire demeure le paiement du travail d'une personne donnée, son niveau étant déterminé grâce à un système de classifications et de qualifications dans lequel chaque individu employé trouve sa place. Le droit collectif, qui a permis de défendre l'individu contre les employeurs capables, quant à eux, de se coaliser et disposant des capitaux nécessaires à la production, a donc agi par correction, addition et modulation des règles individuelles, mais n'a pas supprimé celles-ci. Le fondement du droit du travail, son noyau dur, reste bien l'individu. Le droit du travail continue donc de se référer aux conceptions économiques nées au XVIIIe siècle à partir du travail abstrait et marchand, et précisées plus tard par la pensée marginaliste. Les lois de l'échange que règle le droit du travail sont les « lois naturelles » de l'échange, déterminées par l'économie classique ou néoclassique. Nous vivons encore sur l'idée qu'il existe des lois économiques, donc naturelles, qui déterminent scientifiquement l'apport de chacun à la production (sa contribution), la manière dont il doit être rétribué (selon sa productivité marginale) et la hiérarchie salariale. La loi naturelle énonce que tout facteur de production tend à recevoir une rémunération égale à sa contribution à la production. Le salaire représente dès lors le prix de cette marchandise comme les autres qu'est le travail et qui peut être scientifiquement calculé. Malgré les correctifs apportés à ces idées dans les discours et dans la réalité (par exemple la prise en compte du rôle des syndicats dans la fixation des salaires [281]...), le travail reste considéré, dans ces conceptions, comme une marchandise vendue par un individu à un autre et comme l'objet d'un échange.

Cette vision, fondée sur des instruments qui représentent et organisent le travail d'abord comme un acte individuel, entre donc en contradiction non seulement avec l'idée que le travail serait un acte collectif, mais aussi avec le fait bien réel que la richesse est de plus en plus le produit d'un ensemble d'interactions complexes entre des capitaux, des systèmes d'information, du travail « machinal » et du travail humain, donc que le travail humain n'est pas le seul producteur de richesse. Le travail humain est aujourd'hui si imbriqué dans un ensemble de machines et de systèmes que son efficace ne peut être distinguée de la leur. Par ailleurs, le travail humain lui-même a une efficacité productive qui varie non seulement grâce aux efforts et à la bonne volonté de ses « porteurs », mais aussi en fonction des progrès généraux de toute la société en matière d'éducation, de formation, de santé, etc. Enfin, la manière dont un individu contribue lui-même à l'augmentation de la production ne peut pas être scientifiquement déterminée, pas plus que la contribution relative de deux individus. C'est d'ailleurs ce que mettent en évidence les macroéconomistes lorsque, analysant les causes de la forte augmentation de la production entre les années 1950 et 1970, ils imputent près du tiers de celle-ci à un facteur « résiduel », fait tout ensemble de progrès technique, d'efforts de rationalisation de la production et d'élévation générale du niveau de formation. Il semble devenu de plus en plus difficile de mesurer scientifiquement la contribution du travail humain à la production, sinon par un raisonnement tautologique consistant à dire que cette contribution est mesurée par l'ensemble des salaires ! Qu'est-ce que la productivité ? Qui a décidé que la contribution d'un cadre à l'augmentation de la production était plus forte que celle d'un ouvrier spécialisé ? Sur quoi est fondée la hiérarchie salariale ? On nous dit que c'est sur une grille de qualifications et de classifications, donc en dernier ressort sur un diplôme ou une qualification au sens scolaire. Mais comment sait-on qu'un travailleur diplômé contribuera plus à la production que les autres ? On est très éloigné en tout cas des critères que Smith déterminait [282].

Pourquoi continuons-nous à vivre avec des techniques (l'économie et le droit) si décalées non seulement par rapport à ce qu'est devenue la réalité du travail mais également par rapport à nos rêves et à nos discours politiques ? La principale raison nous semble être la volonté de sauvegarder le pivot essentiel de la construction capitaliste et de la société autorégulée : l'incitation à travailler. Conserver l'idée d'une contribution et d'une rétribution proportionnelles au travail accompli, au diplôme, au mérite, c'est garder l'idée de l'incitation au travail, de l'aiguillon individuel, de l'intérêt individuel ou, ce qui revient au même, de la peur de la faim. S'il n'y avait pas l'appât du gain, les gens ne travailleraient pas ; il est donc impossible d'envisager la dissociation des revenus et du travail accompli. Là est le nerf du raisonnement économique parfaitement congruent, à cet égard, avec l'approche du droit du travail (et en totale contradiction avec l'idée que le travail serait épanouissant). L'économie conçoit le travail comme facteur de production individualisé et comme « désutilité » pour l'individu : elle vit sur le mythe de l'effort individuel payé de retour par une récompense. Les théories microéconomiques actuelles et les politiques publiques sont assises sur la peur de la désincitation ou la croyance que l'individualisation renforce la productivité.

L'histoire de la protection sociale [283] est un bon indice de la prégnance de cette croyance quasi religieuse sur nos comportements sociaux : considérées de ce point de vue, les cent années qui séparent les enquêtes de Villermé (1840) du Plan français de sécurité sociale (1945) content l'histoire de la résistance acharnée d'une partie de la France à l'idée de dissociation du travail et de la protection, c'est-à-dire à l'idée de socialisation des risques. Pendant ce siècle, l'idée qu'on pourrait encourager ou aider l'individu à se couvrir contre les risques issus de son travail, ou de l'interruption de celui-ci, fut considérée comme la plus à même de désinciter au travail, d'amollir l'individu et d'ouvrir la porte à la décadence générale [284]. Au contraire, la prévoyance individuelle paraissait la plus susceptible de contribuer au développement de l'individu et de la productivité du travail. Mais lorsque l'on parvint à mettre en place un plan de sécurité sociale obligeant les individus à se protéger et que des institutions prirent cette protection en charge, lorsque c'est en quelque sorte toute la population qui décida de se couvrir collectivement contre les risques sociaux, la peur de la désincitation ne disparut pas pour autant. Il s'agissait moins d'elle, d'ailleurs, que de la volonté de voir le travail dignement récompensé et la hiérarchie sociale, fondée sur le travail, respectée. Il ne fallait donc pas que tout le monde puisse avoir droit à la même protection : tel était le raisonnement quelques mois après la sortie de la guerre. Aujourd'hui la protection sociale n'est toujours pas universalisée, c'est-à-dire détachée de l'acte de travail. Pour bénéficier des prestations de l'assurance-maladie, il est nécessaire d'avoir travaillé ou cotisé un certain nombre de mois, sauf à accéder à des formules spéciales (RMI, aide sociale) dont le bénéfice est soumis à des conditions. Celui qui travaille peut s'ouvrir des droits à la protection, pas les autres ; et la protection est d'autant plus grande que l'emploi est meilleur. Alors que plus du tiers des revenus des Français sont aujourd'hui socialisés (ils ne sont pas la contrepartie directe du travail), l'idée d'une protection pour tous fait encore frémir, et les remises en cause de l'Etat-providence ont toutes ce petit goût de moralisme qui voit dans la sensation de l'effort le meilleur des aiguillons au travail. C'est ce qui nous empêche, certainement plus encore que les problèmes financiers ou institutionnels, de généraliser la couverture maladie, c'est-à-dire de la dissocier totalement du travail. Car, s'ils sont couverts, pourquoi les individus feraient-ils encore un effort pour travailler ? Les constructions microéconomiques actuelles reposent sur la même logique : l'arbitrage des individus entre travail et loisir fait que si des revenus sociaux s'approchent du salaire minimum, alors chacun s'arrêtera de travailler. Mais on oublie que tous les chômeurs ne sont pas, loin s'en faut, des chômeurs volontaires et qu'un tel arbitrage entre travail et loisir n'est possible que si les circonstances s'y prêtent.

S'il n'est pas question de soutenir ici que l'incitation individuelle n'a aucune efficace ou qu'il n'y aurait aucun danger à dissocier travail et revenu, protection sociale et travail, nous souhaitons mettre en évidence le décalage qui existe entre des discours selon lesquels le travail serait le lieu d'une coopération et d'une solidarité effective et les instruments et/ou les représentations qui régissent nos rapports au travail aujourd'hui. Car tout se passe donc comme si, en dépit des rêves et des discours, un certain nombre de croyances étaient encore trop fortes pour laisser s'épanouir une conception du travail comme acte collectif, appelant des instruments conceptuels et des techniques réellement collectifs.

Le mythe de l'entreprise citoyenne

Le décalage paraît encore plus flagrant lorsqu'il s'agit de l'entreprise. Celle-ci est présentée aussi bien dans les discours politico-administratifs que dans une grande partie des théories sociologiques qui analysent le travail et la construction des identités, comme un haut lieu de socialisation, celui où s'épanouirait le collectif de travail, où s'acquerraient les identités, où se développerait une solidarité objective. L'entrée en entreprise est toujours présentée comme l'initiation à la vie sociale : en être tenu écarté équivaut à l'exclusion sociale. Dans les années 1980, l'entreprise est également devenue une « organisation », objet d'une sociologie particulière, dont le but était de maximiser son efficacité, de trouver les organisations les plus performantes... Ce courant d'analyse, globalement antitaylorien, a conduit à la stratégie des ressources humaines, à la notion d'attachement des salariés à l'entreprise, à l'idée que la productivité serait plus élevée si la motivation au travail était plus grande et donc si les conditions de travail, la communication, les rapports entre salariés et direction étaient meilleurs. Peu à peu l'idée s'est fait jour d'une entreprise qui assurerait, en plus de la fonction de production, d'autres fonctions de nature sociale, permettant l'expression, la cohésion, la sociabilité des salariés : l'entreprise, société en miniature, serait devenue un haut lieu de vie sociale [285]. Mais la définition de l'entreprise permet-elle la prise en charge de ces nouvelles tâches ?

L'entreprise est généralement définie par sa fonction : elle a vocation à combiner différents facteurs de production pour aboutir à un produit [286]. D'où deux conséquences immédiates : d'abord, la réalisation d'une communauté de travail ne fait pas partie des objectifs de l'entreprise et n'appartient pas à son concept. Ensuite, le travail auquel il est fait allusion dans la définition précédente (et qui n'en constitue en aucune manière un élément nécessaire) est le travail-facteur de production, ou encore le travail abstrait. L'entreprise n'est pas d'abord conçue comme une communauté de travail ; il peut y avoir entreprise sans travail humain. On peut concevoir une production de biens sans intervention aucune de main-d'œuvre, et tel est d'ailleurs certainement ce à quoi tend l'entreprise, *volens nolens*, non pas parce que le travail serait trop cher par rapport au capital, mais parce que le travail n'est considéré, dans la définition de l'entreprise, que comme un facteur et un coût. Et il n'est pas certain que les théories qui se développent depuis quelques années en France, et qui tentent de remettre à l'honneur le capital humain détournent l'entreprise de cette tendance radicale [287]. Non seulement le travail n'appartient pas à la définition de l'entreprise, dont la vocation est de produire, mais de surcroît l'organisation de l'entreprise est tout simplement l'antithèse d'une organisation « démocratique » — pour reprendre la substance de l'expression « entreprise citoyenne ». Ceci ne signifie pas que l'entreprise soit un lieu antidémocratique, mais simplement que cette catégorie ne peut lui être appliquée. Le lien de citoyenneté concerne en effet des égaux qui, par le suffrage, selon le principe « un individu = une voix », décident collectivement des fins à rechercher. L'entreprise est exactement le contraire : elle admet une totale distinction entre les propriétaires et les employés, les seconds exerçant sous la direction des premiers ou de leurs mandants, mais n'ayant pas à intervenir sur les fins poursuivies ou la manière dont celles-ci le sont. Le contrat de travail salarié est en petit ce que l'entreprise est en plus grand : un lien de subordination qui est l'inverse du lien de citoyenneté [288]. Le développement du syndicalisme — qu'il s'agisse de la participation des syndicats à la préparation des textes concernant les salariés ou de la négociation des accords collectifs, mais aussi de la vie syndicale à travers les institutions représentatives au cœur des entreprises — n'a changé que peu de chose, sur le fond, à cet état de fait [289]. L'entreprise ne peut pas être considérée comme une communauté d'égaux qui coopéreraient ; elle est bien plutôt éclatée entre des logiques et des légitimités diverses : sont-ce plutôt les salariés qui constituent son essence, ou le patron, ou les actionnaires ? Qu'est-ce que l'entreprise, qui fait son unité, d'où tire-t-elle sa cohérence ?

Ces questions sont d'autant plus légitimes aujourd'hui que les entreprises se transforment, de manières diverses, et que les licenciements qui accompagnent souvent ces bouleversements mettent en évidence le caractère purement conjoncturel du lien qui les attache aux salariés : ceux-ci n'appartiennent pas « substantiellement » à l'entreprise, puisque son identité n'est pas affectée par leur départ. Les entreprises se recentrent sur leurs fonctions essentielles, en externalisant les autres tâches, c'est-à-dire en les confiant à des réseaux de sous-traitants (PME ou indépendants) [290] : parallèlement, elles réduisent leur personnel stable à un noyau dur, les autres étant soumis à des contrats différents ou allant grossir les rangs des sous-traitants. Jusqu'où peut aller ce processus ? L'entreprise peut également décider de délocaliser tout ou partie de sa production et ne plus garder qu'un siège. Ce serait encore une entreprise, qui ne se caractériserait que par le fait qu'elle paye l'impôt sur les sociétés. Quand bien même elle n'employerait quasiment plus personne ou ne produirait plus de biens, elle conserverait son statut d'entreprise. Dès lors, ni l'emploi de personnes ni l'établissement d'une communauté de travail n'appartiennent au concept de l'entreprise : lorsqu'elle se dissout sous les chocs externes, elle montre que sa nature réelle est d'être un ensemble d'individus dont ni la présence ni la coopération ne sont nécessaires. Ses fins ne sont ni celles d'un lieu démocratique, ni celles d'une communauté réalisée en vue du bien de ses membres.

Cette description ne porte en elle aucune condamnation de fait. La vocation de l'entreprise est de produire, et de la manière la plus efficace. En revanche, on se méprend quand on raisonne comme si elle était une sorte de communauté politique, destinée à favoriser l'épanouissement des individus qui s'y trouvent et à leur permettre d'exercer les principales capacités qu'exige la vie en société ; pis, comme si elle était le lieu principal où peuvent s'exercer celles-ci. Non seulement l'entreprise n'est pas chargée de cette fonction, mais, de plus, ceux qui tiennent ce discours ne sont absolument pas prêts à se donner les moyens de l'en rendre capable. Car, pour que l'entreprise soit citoyenne, il faudrait que le pouvoir, les responsabilités, les choix soient réalisés par l'ensemble de ses acteurs ; en d'autres termes, que le lien existant entre l'entreprise et chaque individu et entre les individus eux-mêmes soit un lien substantiel. Cela supposerait une profonde réforme de l'entreprise, de ses fonctions, de son organisation, que nous sommes certainement moins prêts que jamais à accepter. Il suffit pour s'en convaincre de relire les propos que pouvait tenir sans choquer Bartoli dans les années 1950 : « La finalité du travail exige aussi que la gestion des entreprises soit une gestion commune. La liberté du travail n'existe pas si le travail est abandonné aux seules volontés individuelles et aux seuls contrats interindividuels de travail. [...] Elle implique une organisation sociale [291]. » Sans doute devons-nous renoncer à notre hypocrisie et reconnaître que l'entreprise n'est en rien citoyenne et ne vise qu'à la production — ce qui n'empêche pas de tout faire pour rendre ces conditions de production le plus humaines possible. Elle n'est donc ni un lieu d'expression de soi, ni un lieu d'apprentissage de la vie sociale. A moins que, si nous souhaitons qu'elle soit telle, nous ne la réformions de fond en comble. La résolution de cette question suppose tranché le problème de savoir si l'entreprise *doit* devenir ou pas l'un des principaux lieux de sociabilité, donc si nous le *voulons*.

Aujourd'hui, l'entreprise ne constitue donc pas une communauté de travail et de vie, pas plus que la relation de travail n'est la relation sociale majeure ou le lien substantiel qui attacherait chaque individu à cette communauté et lui permettrait d'exercer ses droits et d'avoir une vie sociale. Mieux vaut dire aujourd'hui que l'évolution va plutôt dans le sens contraire. Car en lieu et place des grandes entreprises où s'étaient, en effet, bon gré mal gré, forgées des identités collectives à travers les conflits, et où s'était développé un droit collectif efficace, se multiplient aujourd'hui des types de contrat très particuliers (en général accompagnés d'un très faible contenu de protection, ou passés pour un temps très court), qui, de plus en plus fréquemment, ne sont pas des contrats de travail mais des contrats commerciaux (entre une grande entreprise et un travailleur indépendant, qui supporte ainsi tout le risque sans avoir aucun des avantages du contrat de travail), et qui constituent peut-être les premiers signes d'une disparition du droit du travail au profit du simple droit civil. Une telle transformation ne ferait que mettre en évidence, plus qu'aujourd'hui, la vérité du lien qui est au fondement de l'entreprise et son manque constitutif d'« âme ».

Le travail, contrat ou relation ?

A vrai dire, il a existé, à côté de cette tradition contractuelle qui s'appuie sur une représentation du travail comme prestation individuelle et de l'entreprise comme simple somme des contrats individuels, une tradition qui a justement théorisé le travail comme relation sociale et l'entreprise comme société politique en miniature. Ecoutons Paul Durand, juriste français adepte de cette théorie : « L'employeur dispose comme chef d'entreprise de trois prérogatives : d'un pouvoir législatif, d'un pouvoir de direction et d'un pouvoir disciplinaire. Ainsi pourvue d'un législateur et d'un juge, l'entreprise rappelle la société politique[292]. » Alors que la première tradition est issue du droit romain — droit de la personne — et s'est épanouie en France, en particulier au moment de la Révolution française et dans le Code napoléonien, la seconde plonge ses racines dans la philosophie et la théologie allemande, médiévale d'abord, hégélienne ensuite. Elle considère la partie comme toujours déjà déterminée par le tout : autrement dit, ce n'est pas l'individu passant contrat qui est premier, mais la relation qui s'instaure entre une personne et une institution. Dans cette optique, l'entreprise apparaît

en effet d'abord comme une communauté, dont le fondement est organique, et qui a donc une véritable unité. Le
travail, quant à lui, se définit toujours comme une relation,
par laquelle l'individu est intégré dans la communauté.
« L'ancien droit germanique [...] connaissait, à côté de la
relation de travail servile, un contrat de vassalité par lequel
un homme libre se mettait au service d'un autre, qui lui
accordait en retour protection, aide et représentation. Ce
contrat faisait naître un lien personnel de fidélité réciproque, qui s'apparentait aux liens familiaux et faisait participer ceux qu'il unissait à une même communauté de droits
et de devoirs. Cette idée de lien personnel et d'obligation
de fidélité se retrouvera naturellement dans l'organisation
corporative, telle qu'elle se structure au Moyen Age et
survit jusqu'à la Révolution industrielle [293]. » Il s'agit là
d'une conception radicalement différente de la tradition
issue de la culture de droit romain et qui s'attaquera
d'ailleurs, au XIXe siècle, à la vision individualiste du travail
sur laquelle s'appuie celle-ci. Très fortement inspiré de
Hegel [294], le juriste Gierke soutient qu'on ne peut penser
juridiquement l'individu indépendamment de la communauté à laquelle il appartient. Pour lui, l'essence du droit ne
peut être recherchée dans la volonté, qu'il s'agisse de la
volonté individuelle ou de celle de l'Etat, car « la source
dernière de tout droit est toujours la conscience commune [295]. » Autrement dit, « l'esprit du peuple », le
Volksgeist incarné dans une langue, une histoire et des
institutions politiques et sociales, est premier par rapport à
l'individu. Il en est le terreau. La relation de travail est
donc interprétée comme une relation d'appartenance à une
communauté, qui prend naissance au moment de l'intégration du travailleur dans celle-ci, et non comme un rapport
contractuel entre deux individus : « C'est cette appartenance de fait à l'entreprise qui est la véritable source de la
relation juridique de travail, c'est elle qui lui confère le
statut de membre de cette communauté [296]. » La relation
qui unit l'employeur et le travailleur n'est pas une pure

relation d'échange portant sur la force de travail, mais d'abord une relation entre deux personnes : elle inclut des droits et des devoirs comme la fidélité, la loyauté, la protection... L'ensemble communautaire, qui a une véritable unité, ne résulte donc pas d'une association de hasard ou d'une simple contiguïté accidentelle, mais du lien personnel qui unit le « chef » à chacun des membres et de la préexistence d'une « âme » de la communauté, antérieure aux parties. Pour cette tradition, l'entreprise, fondée sur une évidente communauté d'intérêts, constitue une communauté organisée et hiérarchisée sous l'autorité naturelle de son chef[297].

Cette théorie montre que l'on ne peut se payer de mots : dire que le travail est une relation sociale et qu'il fonde l'intégration et l'appartenance d'un individu à une communauté a un sens dans cette tradition, pas dans la nôtre. Cela s'explique en particulier parce que la conception allemande de l'entreprise ou du travail se comprennent elles-mêmes par rapport à une philosophie politique dans lesquelles la société est pareillement conçue comme communauté. L'entreprise est à la fois une société politique en petit et l'un des moments de la grande société politique. Autrement dit encore, il ne suffit pas d'affirmer que le travail a telle ou telle qualité, encore faut-il disposer d'une théorie de l'entreprise et d'une théorie politique qui rendent ceci possible. C'est d'ailleurs ce que des juristes français tentèrent de réaliser au début du xxe siècle. Durand, Duguit et Hauriou, baptisés « institutionnalistes » parce qu'ils démontrent le caractère premier des institutions sociales par rapport aux actes sociaux, menèrent une critique en règle du contrat et de la théorie qui voit dans celui-ci la source des rapports de travail[298]. Peine perdue, semble-t-il, puisque, selon un rapport de 1964 établi pour le compte de la CECA, la théorie allemande était « une conception très largement dépassée par le mouvement de l'histoire et liée à une philosophie politique condamnée[299] ». Elle devait également être abandonnée en raison de « l'inconsistance de la construction de l'entreprise comme communauté de travail[300] ». Le fondement du droit du travail applicable dans l'Union européenne serait donc de nature contractuelle, c'est-à-dire assis sur une tradition plutôt romaine, la relation de travail restant dès lors considérée comme un cas particulier de la théorie des échanges. Il n'en reste pas moins qu'aujourd'hui encore le droit allemand « se refuse à identifier le rapport de travail à un rapport d'échange. [...] Il reste fidèle à cette idée d'un rapport régi par le droit des personnes ou de type communautaire[301] ». Comme on le voit, cette théorie est à la fois séduisante et inquiétante par certains aspects. Séduisante parce qu'elle semble offrir les moyens de penser un type de coopération moins abstrait que celui auquel nous ouvre la tradition romaniste contractuelle, et parce qu'elle explicite les conditions d'un vrai lien d'appartenance et d'un lien social substantiel. Inquiétante, dans la mesure où elle continue de reposer sur une forme de subordination — qui cette fois n'est pas juridique, donc impersonnelle, mais bien personnelle —, et parce que l'unité qu'elle décrit est de type hiérarchique, construite autour d'un chef, reposant sur des liens personnels de fidélité, de loyauté, de soumission.

Ce passage par la conception germaniste de la relation de travail et de l'entreprise est essentiel. Il nous permet, en effet, de mettre en évidence l'opposition majeure qui a été celle du XIXe siècle et dont nous ne parvenons pas à sortir : d'un côté, une théorie du contrat, individualiste ; de l'autre, une théorie de la communauté hiérarchisée et antérieure aux individus. Cette opposition ne s'est pas seulement nourrie de la question du travail ; elle a structuré les débats et les options idéologiques du XIXe et du XXe siècle[302]. Mais tout se passe comme si l'histoire s'était enrayée et comme si nous ne parvenions plus aujourd'hui à trouver une troisième voie.

Avant d'envisager comment cette voie pourrait s'ouvrir, revenons sur l'image constrastée du travail que nous ont livrée nos analyses. Le travail a constitué une solution à la question de l'apparition sur la scène publique de l'individu et aux risques de bouleversement de l'ordre social que celle-ci comportait. Il a été le moyen privilégié d'intégration de l'individu au tout social, et donc le moyen d'assurer une certaine automaticité de la régulation sociale. Dans cette mesure, en tant qu'attribut de chaque individu, il s'est substitué aux anciens ordres fondées sur des hiérarchies naturelles ou héritées, et a fondé un principe d'ordre nouveau, reposant sur les capacités et engendrant une nouvelle hiérarchie sociale. Il a donc bien été le moyen de l'émancipation de l'individu, ce que prouvent les techniques fondamentalement individualistes qui le régissent, en particulier l'économie, qui représente la traduction concrète d'une vision contractualiste de la société. Travail, économie et vision contractualiste sont allés de pair. Mais le formidable développement de « la puissance productive du travail » et l'explosion des énergies utopiques, qui se sont fixées sur la sphère de la production, ont ajouté des dimensions radicalement différentes à cette première idée, sans que pourtant la vision économique développée au XVIIIe siècle soit remise en cause. D'où les contradictions que recèlent les pensées actuelles de légitimation du travail, pour lesquelles la sphère du travail et de la production est celle où se réalise l'essentiel de notre vie individuelle et sociale : elles sont issues, telle est notre thèse, d'une reprise non critique des différentes strates historiques qui constituent la notion contemporaine de travail. Car ces pensées n'ont pas tranché entre les différentes représentations du travail qui leur étaient léguées ; elles ont fait i'économie du choix. Ce faisant, elles commettent une triple faute : elles ne présentent le travail que sous la forme rêvée qu'il a prise au XIXe siècle — comme liberté individuelle et collective créatrice —, en omettant de rappeler sa dimension économique, donc le fait qu'il a d'abord été et reste conçu comme simple facteur de production et comme travail abstrait. Elles considèrent de surcroît ce que le XIXe ne considérait que sous la forme du rêve ou de l'utopie (le travail désaliéné), comme quelque chose de déjà advenu : elles croient à la magie. Enfin, n'ayant pas accompli de réflexion critique — continuant donc malgré tout à accepter la dimension économique du travail, qu'elles occultent — elles ne s'aperçoivent pas qu'elles ont elles-mêmes été envahies par l'idéologie économique originelle qui constitua le contexte de l'invention du travail. Les contradictions auxquelles mènent ces pensées naissent en général de l'impensé économique qui les hante et dont elles sont sans le savoir le produit. Elles oublient sous quelle forme est apparu le travail et pourquoi il est apparu : pour donner sa cohérence à une société qui avait perdu ses cadres d'organisation traditionnels.

Mais le plus intéressant, ce qui nous en dit le plus long sur ces pensées et sur notre époque, c'est que ces contradictions ne sont même plus ressenties comme telles : considérer comme le plus haut moyen de nous réaliser, individuellement et socialement, ce qui était originellement un moyen de tenir ensemble les individus, et dont la nature était l'effort, la souffrance, ne nous semble plus inquiétant. Cela signifie que nous nous sommes totalement abandonnés à l'économie : nous n'imaginons plus la vie sociale que sous la forme de l'échange et l'expression de soi que sous la forme de la production. En ce sens, nous sommes certainement devenus marxistes dans la mesure où nous considérons que la société peut en effet s'autoréguler par l'interexpression, l'échange de signes et de services et que, de ce fait, le travail doit devenir ou rester notre médium social central. C'est donc bien à l'économie qu'il nous faut revenir désormais, car c'est elle qui est à l'origine de notre attachement — aujourd'hui voulu, jadis forcé —, au travail. Il nous faut montrer pourquoi les trois phénomènes majeurs qui caractérisent la modernité des sociétés industrialisées — la domination de la pensée économique, l'élection de la sphère du travail et de la production comme cœur de la vie individuelle et sociale et le dépérissement de la politique — ont partie liée, et sur quels postulats cette constellation parvient à se maintenir. Il s'agit également de savoir, d'une part, si l'économie n'a pas hérité de son passé un certain nombre de présupposés qui l'empêchent de s'adapter aux problèmes que nous connaissons aujourd'hui ; d'autre part, si le choix que représentait l'économie au XVIIIe siècle — individualisme contre holisme — se pose encore dans les mêmes termes aujourd'hui ; enfin, si nous n'avons pas, avant tout, besoin désormais d'une conception de la société radicalement différente de celle à laquelle continue malgré tout de se référer l'économie.

CHAPITRE VIII

CRITIQUE DE L'ÉCONOMIE

L'économie est devenue notre science sociale, celle qui, sous sa forme vulgarisée, inspire décideurs, hauts fonctionnaires et hommes politiques ; celle qui prétend être la science générale du comportement humain et la plus exacte — donc la plus objective — des sciences sociales ; enfin, celle qui a même réussi à imposer ses méthodes à la réflexion dont l'objet est pourtant le plus « social » : la philosophie politique. Inventée comme la méthode qui devait permettre de garantir l'autorégulation d'une société conçue comme une simple association des individus, l'économie est aujourd'hui incapable de promouvoir une autre conception de la société. La tenir pour la science qui convient à notre temps, c'est donc se résigner à vivre avec une conception réduite de l'homme et de la richesse, n'imaginer pour seul mode de régulation que le travail et refuser de faire appel à la politique comme méthode alternative susceptible de servir de guide à la vie en commun.

L'économie, une méthode au service d'une vision contractualiste de la société

L'économie s'est présentée, au xviiie siècle, comme la solution la plus « forte » pour résoudre la question du lien social. Sa spécificité a consisté à partir des individus et à les pousser à tisser des liens non volontaires : le désir d'abondance constitue le principe extérieur qui meut les individus et les oblige à l'échange, et qui, de surcroît, met en marche une mécanique sociale où les relations interindividuelles sont réglées automatiquement. L'ordre social se déduit logiquement des échanges entre individus. Dès lors, l'économie va nécessairement de pair, à l'origine, avec une conception contractualiste de la société.

Postulats et réquisits de l'économie

L'économie doit, pour remplir sa fonction, exhiber des lois naturelles, partir de l'individu, valoriser l'échange.

L'économie, science des lois naturelles de la vie en société

Dès le départ, l'économie s'est voulue une science capable de rivaliser en exactitude avec les sciences de la nature dont le modèle avait été donné par Newton. Celui-ci est la référence constante de tous les auteurs d'économie politique du xviiie siècle. Trouver les lois des phénomènes sociaux comme on a trouvé celles des phénomènes naturels, telle est l'ambition de la pensée économique. Montesquieu et Condorcet développent au même moment l'idée d'un déterminisme social analogue au déterminisme physique. Quesnay et les physiocrates en général défendent également cette conception. Pour eux, les lois naturelles sont inscrites dans l'ordre physique du monde : « Les lois naturelles de l'ordre des sociétés sont les lois physiques mêmes de la reproduction perpétuelle des biens nécessaires à la subsistance, à la conservation et à la commodité des hommes. » Say revendique le premier l'idée d'une science qui a pour objet un domaine particulier de réalité : l'économie[303]. Le premier siècle de recherches économiques (1750-1850), s'il tente bien de dégager des lois et se représente l'économie comme une science, n'utilise pourtant aucun appareil formalisé. Avec Cournot, la situation change. La revendication des économistes de construire une science s'accompagne d'un discours et d'un appareil beaucoup plus détaillés qu'auparavant : l'économie politique doit être abordée comme une véritable science qui « a pour objet essentiel les lois sous l'empire desquelles se forment et circulent les produits de l'industrie humaine, dans des sociétés assez nombreuses pour que les individualités s'effacent et qu'il n'y ait plus à considérer que des masses soumises à une sorte de mécanisme, fort analogue à celui qui gouverne les grands phénomènes du monde physique[304] ». Cournot publie en 1838 un mémoire intitulé *Recherches sur les principes mathématiques de la théorie des richesses*, dans lequel il démontre l'intérêt que présente l'utilisation du langage mathématique pour exprimer des relations économiques qui se prêtent à une formulation algébrique. Léon Walras saluera plusieurs années plus tard cette tentative, restée sans écho au moment de sa publication : « Voilà plusieurs années que je travaille, de mon côté, à élaborer l'économie politique pure comme une science naturelle et mathématique[305]. »

Le même Walras continuera dans cette direction, en orientant délibérément ses travaux vers l'économie pure. S'insurgeant contre une vision trop fonctionnelle de l'économie, il conçoit celle-ci comme un domaine scientifique à part entière et qui tient sa place dans la classification des sciences : « Les faits qui se produisent dans le monde peuvent être considérés de deux sortes : les uns ont leur origine dans le jeu des forces de la nature, qui sont des forces aveugles et fatales ; les autres prennent leur source dans l'exercice de la volonté de l'homme, qui est une force clairvoyante et libre[306]. » Walras distingue ainsi trois types de sciences : la science pure, qui s'occupe des faits naturels, la science appliquée, qui s'occupe des relations homme/nature, et la science sociale, qui s'occupe des relations homme/homme. L'économie peut être pure, appliquée et sociale (Walras écrira trois livres consacrés à chacune de ces questions). Mais, lorsqu'elle est pure, l'économie s'occupe de faits naturels : « Le blé vaut 24 francs l'hectolitre. Voilà le fait de la valeur d'échange. [...] Ce fait a le caractère d'un fait naturel. Cette valeur du blé en argent, ou ce prix du blé, ne résulte ni de la volonté du vendeur, ni de la volonté de l'acheteur, ni d'un accord entre les deux. Le fait de la valeur d'échange prend donc, une fois établi, le caractère d'un fait naturel, naturel dans son origine, naturel dans sa manifestation et sa manière d'être[307]. » Il justifie l'utilisation d'outils mathématiques et la recherche en économie pure de la manière suivante : « Je pense que l'économie politique ne sera une science que le jour où elle s'astreindra à démontrer ce qu'elle s'est à peu près bornée jusqu'ici à affirmer gratuitement. [...] Chacun sait parfaitement, pour peu qu'il ait fait de la géométrie, que les rayons d'une circonférence ne sont égaux entre eux, et que la somme des trois angles d'un triangle n'est égale à celle de deux droits, que dans une circonférence et dans un triangle abstraits et idéaux. La réalité ne confirme qu'approximativement ces définitions et démonstrations; mais elle en permet une très riche application. Pour observer cette méthode, l'économie politique pure doit emprunter à l'expérience des types d'échange, d'offre, de demande, de capitaux, de revenus, de services producteurs, de produits. De ces types réels, elle doit abstraire, par définition, des types idéaux et raisonner sur ces derniers, pour ne revenir à la réalité que la science une fois faite et en vue des applications. Nous aurons ainsi, sur un marché idéal, des prix idéaux qui seront dans un rapport rigoureux avec une demande et une offre idéales. Et ainsi de suite. Ces vérités pures seront-elles d'une application fréquente ? A la rigueur, ce serait le droit du savant de faire de la science pour la science, comme c'est le droit du géomètre d'étudier les propriétés les plus singulières de la figure la plus bizarre, si elles sont curieuses. Mais on verra que ces vérités d'économie pure fourniront la solution des problèmes les plus importants, les plus débattus et les moins éclaircis d'économie politique appliquée et d'économie sociale [308]. »

Derrière cette conception, on trouve l'idée que les lois de l'économie sont bien semblables aux lois de la nature et que, de même que les mathématiques ont, par abstraction et idéalisation, révélé les lois de la physique, l'économie pure va se dévoiler comme toile de fond de l'économie réelle. Soulignons l'extraordinaire pari que représente cette conception : non seulement la vie en société, mais cette partie particulière de la vie en société qu'étudie l'économie, présente des régularités qui peuvent être comprises comme des lois. En cela, les économistes de la fin du XIXe siècle ne sont pas extrêmement originaux, car les sociologues croient également être en mesure de révéler des lois de la société aussi solides que les lois de la nature. De ce point de vue, l'économie semble néanmoins l'une des sciences humaines les plus avancées à l'époque, ou du moins l'une des plus ambitieuses, puisqu'elle se permet cet éclatement entre un versant pur, sorte de recherche sur les catégories ou la logique formelle, et un versant appliqué, censé permettre la vérification empirique, à l'instar de la physique, par exemple. Partie de la recherche des causes de l'accroissement des richesses, l'économie se retrouve à la fin du XIXe siècle à la tête d'un appareil mathématique formalisé déjà impressionnant. La démarche économique est plus que jamais soutenue par l'idée qu'elle met en évidence des lois inflexibles.

L'individualisme de l'économie

L'économie s'est construite à partir des individus qu'il lui revenait précisément d'inscrire dans un ordre. Elle s'est présentée comme une philosophie du contrat dans lequel l'objet de l'échange n'est pas constitué de libertés individuelles, mais de capacités et de produits ; où les individus ne se débarrassent pas de ce dont ils disposent au profit d'un autre (acte politique de délégation du pouvoir), sans cesser pourtant d'échanger ; où le lien social, enfin, ne naît pas d'une dépossession au terme de laquelle éclôt la société, mais de la permanence de l'échange : le lien social est, dans un sens quasi physique, ce flux incessant d'échanges. Son défi, c'est donc de faire coexister des individus qui n'ont précisément pas d'intérêt pour les autres : des individus qui ne sont pas déjà sociables, ne sont intéressés qu'à leur propre conservation et sont réduits à leur plus simple expression. Ainsi s'explique que l'économie soit, dès l'origine, individualiste, hédoniste et utilitariste. Non seulement elle emprunte ses représentations et ses concepts de base à la psychologie et à la philosophie anglaises de l'époque, mais elle radicalise les présupposés de celles-ci en refusant de déduire la société de la seule présence des individus. L'équilibre social ne naît pas de la sociabilité, mais d'une combinatoire autorégulée des échanges. D'où le concept de base, l'intérêt, qui est le seul que s'autorise l'économie en réaction contre toutes les philosophies ou les morales qui, quant à elles, se donnent toujours d'autres points de départ : la sympathie, l'inclination, quand ce n'est pas l'instinct de sociabilité [309]. D'où également les deux caractéristiques de l'économie, dont elle ne se départira pas : elle part toujours de l'individu ou d'agrégations d'individus ; elle fait abstraction de toute préoccupation autre que purement individuelle chez l'individu considéré. Celui-ci est simplement rationnel, ce qui signifie qu'il préfère toujours le plaisir à la peine. Au XVIIIᵉ siècle, l'utilitarisme de l'économie est d'abord hédoniste, non par conviction philosophique, mais parce que l'hédonisme est la forme la plus simple, la moins élaborée de la rationalité brute. L'hédonisme est ce qui reste de l'individu quand on a enlevé la sociabilité et les impératifs moraux.

L'intérêt et l'utilité se traduisent donc, dans un premier moment, en termes de plaisir et de souffrance, notions physiologiques de base. Comme l'explicite Jeremy Bentham, « inventeur » de l'utilitarisme : « On désigne par principe d'utilité le principe qui approuve ou désapprouve toute action conformément à la tendance que celle-ci semble avoir d'augmenter ou de diminuer le bonheur du parti dont l'intérêt est en question, ou, pour le dire en d'autres termes, de promouvoir le bonheur ou de s'y opposer [310]. » John Stuart Mill ajoutera : « Par bonheur, on entend le plaisir et l'absence de peine. Par absence de bonheur, on entend la peine et la privation du plaisir [311]. » L'essentiel demeure qu'aucune autre considération n'intervienne chez l'individu et que ces expressions primaires que sont le plaisir et la peine soient mesurables. Ainsi le calcul des plaisirs et des peines auquel se livre Bentham est-il censé permettre de réformer la société tout entière. La notion de plaisir ainsi conçue est homogène et continue : on peut en calculer facilement l'augmentation et les degrés. Même si, au début, la notion de plaisir, à l'instar de celle de richesse, provoque débat et discussion au sein du camp utilitariste (Stuart Mill, grand lecteur de Bentham et auteur de *L'Utilitarisme* [312], remet ainsi en cause la conception purement quantitative du plaisir qui est celle de son maître et lui oppose une définition plus large, incluant aussi les plaisirs de l'esprit, exactement comme Malthus s'interrogeait sur l'opportunité de ranger les œuvres de Shakespeare parmi les richesses), il n'en ira pas longtemps ainsi. Dans sa recherche de ce qu'est « le plus grand bonheur du plus grand nombre », l'économie doit pouvoir additionner et comparer des éléments homogènes. Et, de fait, elle va rapidement abandonner la référence à des situations ou des sensations concrètes : en lieu et place des notions de plaisir et de peine, c'est la stricte notion d'utilité qui sera définitivement retenue, plus simple de maniement et plus consensuelle.

Au XIXe siècle, l'hédonisme, figure encore primaire et

trop incarnée de la rationalité, laisse place à une rationalité plus formelle. L'*Homo economicus,* déjà notion fondamentale de l'économie naissante, machine de guerre contre la « sociabilité », trouve son épanouissement sous la figure de l'individu rationnel qui poursuit son intérêt et cherche à maximiser son utilité. Jevons[313] écrit que « l'économique est la mécanique de l'utilité et de l'intérêt individuel ». Les néoclassiques s'appuient sur une conception radicalement individuelle, mais d'un individu désormais abstrait dont la caractéristique est de pouvoir exprimer des préférences entre des paniers de biens ou de situations qui lui sont présentés. Son activité se résume à ordonner ses préférences et à effectuer des choix alternatifs en vue de maximiser sa satisfaction globale : cette opération est nommée rationalité. L'utilité est le critère de choix qui permet de classer les préférences des individus. D'où l'importance du prix, qui doit précisément permettre de trancher entre les différents désirs et de les combiner. Cette conception s'affinera par la suite, prenant non seulement en compte les désirs des différents individus, mais introduisant de plus la considération du temps et des quantités disponibles d'un bien donné au cours du temps pour un même individu. C'est ce que l'on a appelé le marginalisme. Il focalise son attention sur la dernière unité de bien détenue, appelée utilité marginale, qui tend à décroître au fur et à mesure que la quantité de ce bien déjà détenue augmente[314].

A partir de cette approche, qui se prête particulièrement bien à la formalisation, puisqu'elle raisonne sur des quantités et du temps, un certain nombre de principes vont pouvoir être dégagés, tel celui de la maximisation. En vertu de celui-ci, une personne ressentant un besoin fait un effort ou accepte une dépense pour obtenir un bien aussi longtemps que son besoin ne sera pas satisfait. Lorsque l'ampleur de la dépense ou de l'effort contrebalancent le désir du bien, l'équilibre est atteint : la satisfaction est parvenue à son maximum. Ainsi tous les comportements

peuvent-ils faire également l'objet d'une telle formalisation, qui permet de mettre face à face la dépense que l'on
est prêt à faire et ce que l'on veut obtenir. Il ne s'agit pas
d'autre chose que d'une formalisation du principe utilitariste qui veut que l'on poursuive le plaisir et que l'on fuie la
peine. Celui-ci est désormais affiné : tout besoin ou désir
humain peut être représenté par une « courbe d'utilité »
qui montre à partir de quel moment la personne ne
souhaite pas faire plus d'effort ou de dépense, c'est-à-dire
comment, pour chaque bien, il est possible de maximiser la
satisfaction, point d'équilibre entre désir et satiété ou entre
peine et plaisir. On peut ainsi exprimer les différentes
utilités marginales ou désutilités marginales des biens en
fonction des quantités détenues.

L'utilité est devenue le concept central de l'économie.
Dans le même mouvement, l'individualisme originel et
atomistique de l'économie s'est approfondi. C'est l'individu, et plus particulièrement l'intensité de son désir, qui
détermine la valeur : la conception substantialiste de la
valeur, en germe chez Smith et pleinement épanouie chez
Ricardo, a fait place à une conception de part en part
subjective. La valeur d'un bien se fonde sur le jugement de
chaque individu quant à l'utilité de la détention d'un bien et
quant à la rareté de ce même bien, ce qu'exprime parfaitement Walras en parlant de « valeur-utilité » ou « valeur-
utilité-rareté » : « Il y a dans la science trois solutions
principales au problème de l'origine de la valeur. La
première est celle de Smith, de Ricardo, de Mac Culloch,
c'est la solution anglaise ; elle met l'origine de la valeur
dans le travail. Cette solution est trop étroite et elle refuse
de la valeur à des choses qui en ont réellement. La seconde
est celle de Condillac et de Say : elle met l'origine de la
valeur dans l'utilité. Celle-ci est trop large et elle attribue
de la valeur à des choses qui, en réalité, n'en ont pas.
Enfin, la troisième, qui est la bonne, est celle de Burlamaqui et de mon père, A.A. Walras : elle met l'origine de la
valeur dans la rareté [315]. » Dès lors, l'individualisme restera

la méthode de l'économie. De l'individualisme « atomistique » et psychologique des débuts, on est passé à l'individualisme méthodologique de l'école de Lausanne, qui s'est ralliée à l'idée qu'il n'y a de valorisation que subjective, rejoignant ainsi les représentations philosophiques de l'époque : au même moment, Kierkegaard ou Nietzsche développent l'idée qu'il n'y a que des « points de vue » sur le monde, et donc pas de vérité [316]. L'école de Vienne [317] ira encore plus loin, son individualisme méthodologique s'accompagnant d'un discours idéologique qui dénie toute existence à des réalités autres qu'individuelles, telles les classes sociales ou la société. Il ne s'agit donc plus d'une démarche d'abstraction, comme celle d'un Walras, qui simplifiait le réel pour mieux comprendre sa logique interne, mais d'une démarche philosophique qui postule que seul l'individu existe, ou encore d'un nominalisme radical : « Qu'il s'abstienne logiquement de traiter ces pseudo-entités comme des faits et qu'il parte systématiquement des concepts qui guident les individus dans leurs actions et non des résultats de leur réflexion théorique sur leurs actions, c'est là le trait caractéristique de cet individualisme méthodologique étroitement lié au subjectivisme des sciences sociales [318]. » Pour Hayek, il faut donc laisser les individus se comporter de la façon qu'ils jugent la meilleure et il en résultera la meilleure situation pour la société tout entière [319]. L'économie apparaît donc de plus en plus comme la gageure qui consiste à trouver un équilibre à partir d'individus n'ayant aucune vocation sociale mais exclusivement des préférences, qui portent de surcroît sur les mêmes biens. Sa tâche est dès lors de déterminer les conditions de cet équilibre — équilibre social ou équilibre des échanges — ou encore de voir comment les diverses préférences individuelles qui portent sur des biens en nombre réduit vont néanmoins s'ordonner. L'économie trouve des principes d'ordre : pour chaque individu, le principe de maximisation de son utilité, qui lui permet de choisir des quantités de biens en fonction de leur prix ; pour l'ensemble des individus, le principe de la maximisation du bien-être collectif. Tout ceci s'opérant sur la scène désormais nécessaire à l'économie, le marché.

Le silence du marché

Le marché est le lieu central de l'économie, celui où s'opèrent les véritables rencontres entre des offres et des demandes, celui où se tranchent les différends, mais dans le calme et l'intangibilité des déterminations naturelles et des lois. L'utilisation de l'appareil mathématique et du vocable d'« économie pure » met mieux encore en évidence la signification hautement symbolique de ce lieu et de sa fonction : là se dénouent et se décident, souverainement et sans qu'il y ait à rendre d'arbitrage, l'allocation des ressources, la distribution des richesses, l'échange. Là se noue le lien social. Le marché permet d'économiser les interventions humaines, de réduire au minimum les risques de désaccord et de conflit : car, les règles étant données au départ, les prix doivent être le seul moyen de régler les prétentions diversifiées des individus et de déterminer la rétribution que mérite chacun en fonction de sa contribution. Les physiocrates, Smith, Mandeville, Ricardo et Malthus, cherchaient déjà l'ordre naturel et ces fameuses lois de l'équilibre vers lesquelles tendaient, selon eux, à long terme, les grandeurs économiques. C'est pourquoi l'Etat, symbole de l'intervention humaine dans un domaine qui doit s'autoréguler, ne pouvait être, dans cette mesure, qu'un empêcheur de tourner en rond. Avec Walras, il n'en va plus de même : l'équilibre qui est recherché est instantané, et il prend son origine dans le marché lui-même[320].

La théorie de l'équilibre général, outre qu'elle constitue une performance intellectuelle, représente surtout l'aboutissement de la recherche entreprise par l'économie au XVIIIe siècle : prouver qu'il existe un équilibre des offres et des demandes sur tous les marchés en même temps (en système de concurrence pure et parfaite), et donc que la

société peut être totalement autorégulée ; démontrer que,
si les règles énoncées à l'avance sont justes, elles doivent
permettre, grâce aux prix, de déterminer strictement toutes
les lois de la vie sociale, sans qu'aucune intervention
humaine, nécessairement arbitraire, soit nécessaire. Après
la main invisible, le marché et l'équilibre sont des schèmes
profondément autorégulateurs, des lieux où s'harmonisent
par eux-mêmes tous les désirs, où ils s'ordonnent et où une
puissance anonyme extérieure et inébranlable permet de
rendre commensurables et en même temps de satisfaire ces
désirs. Le marché est le haut lieu d'un règlement a priori,
automatique et silencieux des conflits sociaux (ceux-ci ne
doivent théoriquement même pas pouvoir naître : on ne se
révolte pas et on ne discute pas de lois qui ont la puissance
du naturel). Point focal d'une pensée économique apoliti-
que, il exclut tout principe originel qui pourrait toujours
être remis en cause (comme, par exemple, un premier
choix des règles de base par les individus eux-mêmes).
L'équilibre naît à partir d'éléments simples et éternels : des
individus rationnels et des règles de formation des prix, les
uns et les autres étant donnés, dans l'évidence du naturel [321].

Tels sont les réquisits de l'économie. Ils ont été déterminés au XVIIIe siècle en fonction du problème majeur
auquel toutes les réflexions étaient confrontées : faire tenir
ensemble des individus que rien ne disposait à coopérer et à
entrer en société et garantir l'autorégulation de l'ordre
social. L'économie a défini à cette époque un appareil
théorique et un type de valorisation adaptés à cette tâche ;
elle a donc déterminé la ligne de partage entre ce qui devait
être tenu ou non pour une richesse (rien n'est en soi source
de richesses ou de valeur, ainsi que l'ont mis en évidence
les débats du XVIIIe siècle sur la nature de la richesse) [322]. Il
y a donc un lien de causalité évident entre le type de société
que l'économie avait pour tâche de rendre possible et de
promouvoir (une société associant contractuellement des
individus sans désir de coopération, sans instinct de sociabi-

lité et sans autre patrimoine que leur force de travail), et ce qu'elle a désigné comme étant producteur de richesse : l'échange marchand et matériel. Autrement dit, parce que l'économie avait pour fonction de fonder l'unité d'une société dont le lien ne pouvait consister qu'en l'échange, c'est l'échange marchand et matériel qui a été considéré comme facteur de richesse ; l'augmentation des échanges et de la production a ainsi été assignée comme but à la société [323].

Comment l'économie conçoit la richesse des nations

Dès l'origine, l'économie s'est voulue science des causes de l'accroissement des richesses de la société tout entière (c'est bien pour cette raison que Smith emploie le terme de « nation » : la société est par là conçue comme un tout) [324]. Mais elle a immédiatement assimilé la richesse sociale à la somme des enrichissements individuels issus de l'échange marchand [325]. Parce qu'elle a conservé l'armature théorique qu'elle requérait au moment de son invention, elle demeure aujourd'hui incapable de concevoir la richesse d'une autre manière.

Du point de vue théorique, ceci se traduit par le fait que l'économie se réfère toujours à l'utilité individuelle pour définir l'utilité globale : celle-ci est toujours conçue comme la maximisation ou l'agrégation d'utilités individuelles ou en relation avec celles-ci. Pour certaines théories, la maximisation de l'utilité de chaque individu s'accompagne de la maximisation de l'utilité sociale globale [326]. D'autres cherchent à maximiser le bien-être collectif — somme du bien-être ou de l'utilité des individus — en choisissant, parmi toutes les options possibles, celles dont les conséquences sont telles que la somme des utilités individuelles qui lui est associée est au moins aussi grande que celle associée à toute autre option possible. Autrement dit, dans tous les cas, le bien-être collectif, ou encore la richesse sociale, ne se conçoit qu'à partir d'une prise en considération des points de vue individuels, quelle que soit la manière dont ceux-ci sont agrégés. Sans rentrer dans les subtilités par lesquelles l'économie parvient à construire cette maximisation de la somme des utilités[327], il est clair que l'optimum social ne peut jamais être conçu, dans la théorie économique, en dehors de la prise en considération des points de vue individuels entre lesquels il détermine un compromis.

Ainsi, après beaucoup de débats (sur la possibilité d'agréger les utilités individuelles, de mesurer leur intensité et de les comparer), la théorie économique est parvenue à faire émerger le critère de Pareto : un état social est défini comme optimal au sens de Pareto si, et seulement si, il est impossible d'augmenter l'utilité d'une personne sans réduire celle d'une autre personne, ou encore si aucun individu de la collectivité considérée ne préfère une autre option, et si au moins un individu préfère cette option à toute autre[328]. Dès lors, chaque état social est jugé à partir du point de vue de chaque individu sur lui. Tout se passe comme si la société n'était jamais considérée que comme le produit de tous les points de vue individuels sur le tout social et comme si l'économie tentait le tour de force de se mettre simultanément du point de vue de chaque individu pour trouver l'état optimal, celui qui convient à la fois le mieux et le moins mal à chacun ; comme si, enfin, l'économie tentait de compenser son individualisme foncier en se plaçant en même temps de chaque point de vue particulier pour en réaliser une sorte d'intégration supérieure. Quoi qu'elle en dise, elle ne peut jamais saisir une utilité qui ne trouverait pas son origine dans le point de vue individuel, isolé ou agrégé,˙ et elle s'interdit donc de concevoir un bien auquel la maximisation de l'utilité individuelle ou l'agrégation de toutes les préférences individuelles n'auraient jamais conduit.

Du point de vue pratique, la représentation concrète que nous nous faisons de la richesse sociale est mise en évidence par la manière dont est conçu notre indicateur de richesse, le produit intérieur brut (PIB). Les options originelles de l'économie l'inspirent considérablement. Tout d'abord, la richesse sociale est définie comme la somme des valeurs ajoutées par chaque unité productive [329] (que celle-ci soit une entreprise, un individu ou une administration). La richesse sociale est donc déterminée, par construction, comme l'agrégation de l'enrichissement de chaque centre productif, de chaque unité qui échange. De plus, la conception de la richesse sociale que révèle la comptabilité nationale, et en particulier le Système élargi de comptabilité nationale [330], est certes plus vaste que celle de Smith ou de ses successeurs : elle fait place aux biens immatériels et aux services, et particulièrement aux services non marchands (depuis 1976 seulement). Mais la même logique l'inspire. Car notre comptabilité ne considère comme richesse sociale que la production socialement organisée [331], donc la production organisée en vue de la vente ou de l'échange (même si la prestation ne donne pas lieu à une vente couvrant le prix de revient de celle-ci). N'est donc valorisé que ce qui est l'occasion d'une rencontre sociale, que celle-ci se traduise par un échange marchand ou non : ne sont comptabilisés dans la richesse sociale ni ce qui échappe à la logique de l'échange (l'éducation personnelle, la santé...) ni ce qui échappe à la socialisation (le travail domestique) [332]. D'ailleurs, seul l'échange marchand est véritablement valorisé dans notre comptabilité : les services non marchands — par exemple, toutes les fonctions collectives exercées par l'Etat, telles la santé, l'éducation... — ne sont pris en compte que sous la forme du coût qu'ils ont représenté, et non de la valeur ajoutée qu'ils sont censés avoir dégagée : on estime que l'exercice d'une fonction collective ne permet donc pas un enrichissement, un surcroît de richesse. Nous savons donc aujourd'hui valoriser les biens immatériels et les services, à la différence de Malthus, mais nous ne sommes jamais revenus sur l'idée qu'un bien ou un service ne sont une source d'augmentation de la richesse sociale que s'ils peuvent être vendus ou faire l'objet d'un échange.

En agrégeant des valeurs ajoutées, c'est-à-dire en considérant la richesse sociale comme l'addition des enrichissements particuliers générés par chacune des unités de production particulière, les comptables nationaux omettent de prendre en compte les désutilités, c'est-à-dire ce qui est produit comme nuisance à l'occasion de l'acte de production, ou encore le fait que lorsqu'elle produit chaque unité productive ne considère que sa propre utilité et désutilité — son propre intérêt —, sans prendre en considération ce qu'elle peut occasionner comme désutilité pour les autres. Les agents économiques privés ne tiennent compte dans leur raisonnement que des utilités et des désutilités « privées ». Ils fabriquent un produit « privé », qui seul intervient dans la construction de la production totale. Si, en produisant de l'acier, une entreprise pollue une rivière, détruit le paysage ou provoque des nuisances pour autrui, seule la valeur ajoutée par cette production sera comptabilisée : n'est pris en compte, pour la construction de la richesse globale, que ce qui a constitué une utilité ou une désutilité du point de vue privé. Dès lors, il n'y a pas d'utilité « générale », ni même de tentative pour corriger, par la soustraction des désutilités générales, l'agrégat obtenu par la somme de toutes les valeurs ajoutées individuelles. On essaye aujourd'hui, il est vrai, de prendre en compte quelques effets nuisibles provoqués par la production, sous le nom d'« externalités ». Mais cette désignation montre bien qu'il ne s'agit là que d'une anomalie extérieure au processus de production, qui appelle certaines corrections, sans que l'ensemble du raisonnement soit remis en cause. Il est clair que l'incapacité à concevoir l'utilité ou la nuisance du point de vue de l'ensemble social demeure un problème. Considérer la production nationale comme la somme des productions individuelles, c'est considérer que le bien général résulte de l'agrégation de tous les biens particuliers — de tous les biens considérés comme biens du seul point de vue particulier —, sans considérer les maux qui sont générés à cette occasion.

Une partie des économistes néoclassiques, tenants de

l'économie du bien-être, l'ont souligné. Ainsi Pigou (pourtant futur souffre-douleur de Keynes), qui distinguait entre produit net privé et produit net social : « Nous devons distinguer avec précision deux sortes de produits marginaux nets que j'ai respectivement appelés " social " et " privé ". [...] En général, les industriels ne s'intéressent qu'au produit net privé, et non social, de leur opération[333]. » Chez Pigou, mais aussi chez Marshall et d'autres, cette approche qui consiste à dire que le marché ne tend pas nécessairement à l'optimum, et donc que la somme des productions « privées » ne correspond pas nécessairement à la production maximale, a conduit à légitimer quelques interventions de l'Etat ; le principe est alors d'obliger le producteur privé à prendre en compte la désutilité produite grâce à une taxe ou une subvention, c'est-à-dire par un mécanisme de correction. Mais l'approche générale n'en est pas pour autant modifiée : elle persiste à additionner des productions individuelles et donc à agréger des points de vue individuels sans jamais s'interroger sur ce que pourraient être le bien social ou la richesse sociale, considérés du point de vue de l'ensemble. Certes, on pourrait rétorquer que Keynes est justement celui qui a rompu avec cette approche individualiste, puisqu'il considère au contraire des agrégats, dont il observe les évolutions, au point que, dans sa théorie, les individus ont quasiment disparu. Mais les agrégats de Keynes regroupent des classes d'individus ou des fonctions ayant le même rôle économique. Quant aux agrégats principaux, la production et la consommation, ce sont des grandeurs déjà agrégées d'aspirations ou de comportements individuels, sur lesquelles Keynes travaille de manière « macroéconomique ». Autrement dit, Keynes part en quelque sorte des résultats acquis par ses prédécesseurs, accepte leurs conclusions, pour ne plus manier par la suite que des grandeurs agrégées. Mais, ce faisant, il ne trouve pas plus que ses prédécesseurs une méthode permettant la détermination d'un bien social qui ne serait pas l'agrégation de préférences individuelles. Pour Keynes, le bien social, c'est encore la production, et celle-ci n'est rien d'autre que l'agrégation des productions « privées ».

Comment parviendrons-nous à définir ce qui, conçu comme un enrichissement du point de vue « privé », constitue en réalité un appauvrissement pour l'ensemble de la société, si nous ne disposons pas d'un inventaire de la richesse sociale ? Autrement dit, si nous n'avons inscrit nulle part que l'air pur, la beauté, un haut niveau d'éducation, une harmonieuse répartition des individus sur le territoire, la paix, la cohésion sociale, la qualité des relations sociales sont des richesses, nous ne pourrons jamais mettre en évidence que notre richesse sociale peut diminuer alors que nos indicateurs mettent en évidence son augmentation. En effet, il s'agit d'une richesse qui n'est pas réductible au(x) point(s) de vue individuel(s), qui ne peut pas être produite par un acte ou des actes individuels, puisqu'elle concerne justement tous les individus ou résulte de leur acte commun. Ce n'est donc qu'à condition de disposer d'un inventaire de la richesse sociale que nous pourrions savoir si celle-ci augmente vraiment d'une année sur l'autre. A cette condition, nous pourrions éviter de faire passer ce qui n'est qu'une usure ou une diminution de la richesse sociale pour une augmentation de celle-ci [334]. A cette condition seulement, nous pourrions considérer comme faisant partie intégrante de la richesse sociale ce qui renforce la cohésion ou le lien social, ce qui est un bien pour tous, comme l'absence de pollution ou de violence, l'existence de lieux où se rencontrer, se promener, réfléchir, mais également toutes les qualités individuelles : l'augmentation du niveau d'éducation de chacun, l'amélioration de sa santé, le bon exercice de toutes ses facultés, l'amélioration de ses qualités morales et civiques. Ainsi seulement, ce qui est considéré aujourd'hui par les centres individuels de production, les entreprises, comme des désutilités privées — c'est-à-dire comme des coûts (la formation, par exemple, qui, financée par l'Etat ou les

entreprises, apparaît toujours comme une dépense) —
pourrait être tenu pour un bien social et encouragé à ce
titre.

La différence entre l'indicateur dont nous disposons
aujourd'hui et ce que nous proposons est claire : dans un
cas, c'est l'échange ou la production socialisée qui est
valorisée, conformément à la fonction originellement assignée à l'économie, à savoir favoriser l'échange entre les
individus parce que le lien social ne peut se tisser qu'à
partir de l'échange de biens. La richesse vient de l'échange
et de la valeur ajoutée par l'acte « privé » de production et
d'échange ; elle se mesure à partir de flux socialisés. Dans
l'autre, la richesse est patrimoniale, elle se réfère à une
conception totalement différente de la société : celle-ci
n'est pas appréhendée comme un ensemble d'individus
isolés qui se trouvent dans l'obligation d'échanger pour se
rencontrer, mais comme un tout uni où les individus sont
toujours déjà en relation et où ce qui importe est la qualité
de ces individus et la densité des liens qui les unissent. Dans
cette dernière conception, tout ce qui est bénéfique à
chacune des parties et à leur lien est considéré comme
richesse.

La première conception donne de la richesse sociale une
idée beaucoup plus réduite que la seconde. Elle se trouve
également à l'origine de la distinction entre l'économique
et le social sur laquelle nous vivons aujourd'hui. Dans cette
optique, l'économique est le domaine de la production des
richesses, et le social se limite à un « reste » : désutilités
générales non prises en compte dans la comptabilisation
des utilités privées, et utilités générales que l'Etat doit
prendre en charge parce qu'elles sont définies comme des
désutilités privées. La production doit viser à l'efficacité
(l'état social optimal de Pareto correspond aussi à « l'efficacité économique »), de manière à produire des richesses
(le PIB marchand) qui permettront de « faire du social »,
c'est-à-dire de panser les éventuelles plaies ouvertes à
l'occasion de l'acte productif dans le tissu social, réparées

grâce aux dépenses engagées. La vie sociale est ainsi coupée en deux : d'un côté, des acteurs économiques produisent la richesse la plus grande possible, issue des échanges interindividuels. De l'autre, l'Etat dépense une partie de ces richesses pour exercer des fonctions collectives, dont une partie est employée à refaire le tissu social... De fait, tout ce qui relève de la société (le lien social, l'aménagement du territoire, la beauté, le niveau général de connaissance) n'est pas économique, mais « social ». Le social ne procure pas d'enrichissement individuel, n'augmente pas la production. Le social apparaît uniquement comme un facteur de dépense. Le social est un résidu. Telle est la conception à laquelle se réfère le PIB, qui ne reflète donc qu'une image tronquée du bien social.

A cette critique, déjà engagée depuis plusieurs années par de nombreux auteurs, les économistes répondent qu'il ne faut pas confondre l'instrument qui nous permet de mesurer la production nationale avec ce que nous tenons pour le bien-être collectif ; ils se défendent en relativisant la signification du PIB : « L'ensemble des phénomènes sociaux n'est pas réductible aux seules dimensions économiques : la comptabilité nationale, qui mesure en termes monétaires la création et les échanges de droits économiques, n'a pas pour objet de mesurer le bien-être, le bonheur ou la satisfaction sociale », écrivent les comptables nationaux dans leur présentation des méthodes du Système élargi de comptabilité nationale [335]. C'est croire que l'on peut dissocier l'image de la réalité que donnent les instruments de mesure de cette réalité elle-même. On opère aujourd'hui un amalgame entre richesse sociale et PIB, quand ce n'est pas PIB marchand, alors qu'il ne s'agit en effet que d'une représentation particulière de la réalité, qui s'appuie sur de nombreux présupposés, non explicités de surcroît. Malthus disait, souvenons-nous-en, exactement la même chose. Il fallait, disait-il en substance, faire la distinction entre prix et valeur : les objets matériels auraient un prix, et à ce titre pourraient entrer dans la catégorie « officielle » de la richesse, mais les œuvres de Shakespeare auraient une valeur tellement supérieure qu'elles ne devraient pas avoir de prix, qu'elles ne devraient même pas être prises en compte, puisqu'elles participent d'un autre ordre... : « Estimer la valeur des découvertes de Newton ou les jouissances causées par les productions de Shakespeare et de Milton par le prix que leurs ouvrages ont rapporté, ce serait en effet une bien chétive mesure du degré de gloire et de plaisir qui en est résulté pour leur patrie [336]. » Certes, mais à force de penser que les richesses intellectuelles, la beauté, la force du lien social sont des valeurs bien trop hautes pour rentrer dans la classification officielle, nous avons fini par les oublier.

Un certain nombre d'expériences ont été tentées aux Etats-Unis pour corriger le PNB et en faire un indicateur de bien-être élargi. Ainsi James Tobin et William Norhaus lui ont-ils fait subir un certain nombre de corrections, au terme desquelles le PNB était transformé en MBE (Mesure du bien-être économique). Mais, comme l'indique Serge Christophe Kolm [337], le bien-être collectif était toujours obtenu au terme d'une démarche d'addition des revenus individuels. C'est donc bien la conception même de l'indicateur qui devrait être revue. Certes, une telle opération n'irait pas sans difficultés : comment faire l'inventaire de tout ce qu'une société considère comme facteur de richesse ? Comment valoriser les qualités individuelles ? Comment comparer les bienfaits relatifs d'un beau paysage et d'une ville nouvelle ? Comment prendre en compte des nuisances ressenties de manière différente par les individus ? Ce sont ces mêmes problèmes que s'étaient posés les classiques, en particulier Say et Malthus, ce dernier l'exposant de façon saisissante au début de ses *Principes d'économie politique* [338] en mettant très exactement en évidence cette difficulté : il faudrait, écrivait-il, disposer d'un inventaire. La raison pour laquelle ces auteurs ont fini par trancher pour une conception réduite de la richesse n'est pas seulement technique. La définition de ce qu'est la

richesse sociale, la description de ce dont elle est composée, de ce qui constitue un bienfait et un mal pour une
société est un acte éminemment politique : elle nécessite
des débats et peut-être des conflits... Nous avons préféré
laisser cette responsabilité aux comptables nationaux.

Nous avons aujourd'hui besoin d'une autre conception
de la richesse, qui ne se contente plus de comptabiliser les
flux mais soit également patrimoniale[339]. Elle seule permettrait de valoriser les situations qui favorisent et amélio-
rent la cohésion sociale et de prendre également mieux en
compte les véritables intérêts individuels. Car notre
conception actuelle de la richesse sociale, agrégation
d'échanges de produits entre individus, oblige chacun à s'y
plier (alors qu'il n'a pas participé à sa définition), et le
contraint à passer le plus clair de sa vie à effectuer un
travail qui ne l'enrichit peut-être pas toujours, pas plus
qu'il n'enrichit peut-être, au fond, toujours la société.

La religion de la production, pour quoi faire ?

Si l'économie est incapable de concevoir un bien social
autre que celui qui résulte de l'échange entre les individus,
peut-elle fonder le postulat fondamental selon lequel
l'augmentation de la production est destinée à augmenter
le bien de chacun ? L'idée est née en même temps que la
religion de la production, au moment où la poursuite de
l'abondance était désignée comme profitable à l'ensemble
du corps social — la Nation — et à chaque individu en
particulier, pour améliorer son sort. Dans sa structure
même, le mythe de l'abondance était voué à souder les
sociétés et à constituer leur principe régulateur : chacun,
en poursuivant l'abondance, permettait également au corps
social de progresser et devait être récompensé en retour de
sa contribution, les deux opérations (contribution et rétribution) s'opérant par le canal du travail ; une abondance
universelle se répand jusqu'aux dernières classes de la
société, dit Smith en employant à dessein cette métaphore

liquide. L'économie est la science qui énonce les lois de cette contribution-rétribution, les lois du travail.

Production et répartition

Pour Smith, l'augmentation de la richesse générale est destinée à augmenter le bien-être de tout le peuple, et en particulier de la classe la plus nombreuse qui vit le plus difficilement. Il s'agit de faire en sorte que les prix baissent pour que de plus en plus de marchandises deviennent accessibles à celle-ci. De plus, même s'il croit aux lois de l'économie et estime que la classe capitaliste est celle qui permet d'accroître la production, de faire baisser les prix et d'amener l'opulence[340], Smith sait aussi que les lois naturelles de répartition du revenu issu de la production sont ancrées dans des rapports de force : la diffusion de l'abondance à toutes les classes du peuple, grâce à la hausse des salaires ou à la baisse des prix, n'est pas automatique ; elle peut être entravée.

En effet, la société dépeinte dans les *Recherches* n'est pas homogène et les intérêts des différentes classes ne sont pas les mêmes. Les trois classes que distingue Smith, celle qui vit de rentes, celle qui vit de salaires et celle qui vit de profit, n'ont pas tout à fait le même rapport à l'intérêt général : si « les intérêts de la première et de la seconde sont étroitement et inséparablement liés à l'intérêt général de la société », celui de la troisième classe, constituée de ceux qui emploient des ouvriers et vivent de profit, « n'a pas la même liaison que celui des deux autres avec l'intérêt de la société ». Comme ils sont occupés de projets et de spéculations, les membres de cette troisième classe, poursuit-il, ont en général plus de subtilité dans l'entendement que la majeure partie des propriétaires de la campagne. Mais, dans la mesure où leur subtilité s'exerce plutôt sur leurs propres affaires que sur l'intérêt général, il faudra se méfier de leurs avis et de leurs recommandations : il s'agit de gens, conclut-il, « dont l'intérêt ne saurait jamais être exactement le même que l'intérêt de la société, qui ont, en général, intérêt à tromper le public et même à le surcharger et qui, en conséquence, ont déjà fait l'un et l'autre en beaucoup d'occasions [341] ». Smith se méfie : certes, l'augmentation de la production est l'objectif à atteindre parce qu'elle permet normalement la diffusion de l'abondance à toutes les classes du peuple, mais le respect de cette loi nécessite un certain nombre de précautions.

Les successeurs de Smith et la science économique, y compris dans les siècles suivants, ne prendront plus la peine de s'expliquer sur les finalités et le pourquoi de l'objectif d'augmentation de la production, pas plus d'ailleurs que sur les mesures à prendre pour que cette augmentation serve à tous : la recherche des moyens permettant l'augmentation des richesses constituera au contraire l'impératif qui définit la science économique, « science dont le but principal est la recherche des causes qui influent sur les progrès de la richesse [342] ». Celui-ci devient l'objectif évident, mais jamais explicité et jamais remis en cause, de l'économie. Dès lors, ayant à se doter des instruments de mesure les plus efficaces pour repérer tout accroissement de la richesse, l'économie va devenir une simple science formelle, une science instrumentale, dont la tâche sera de trouver les moyens les plus performants pour atteindre une fin qui ne sera plus jamais discutée. Plus tard, les néoclassiques ne parlent plus de richesse, mais d'équilibre et d'efficacité productive, de maximisation de l'utilité et de la production. Quant aux keynésiens, leur obsession de l'augmentation de la production est élevée à la hauteur d'un dogme [343]. Chez les uns et les autres, l'augmentation de la production et de l'efficacité productive est considérée en soi, tel un bien absolu, indépendamment des éventuels effets recherchés, et donc indépendamment du fait que ceux-ci soient ou non atteints. On omet de dire que la production doit être augmentée pour que le bien-être de tous, donc de chacun, s'accroisse. On oublie qu'un jour on a souhaité augmenter les richesses pour augmenter celles du peuple. La répartition a été totalement oubliée ; pis, elle semble, en réalité, n'avoir jamais intéressé l'économie.

Si l'on examine à nouveau les grands textes néoclassiques, on voit bien que l'optimum économique peut parfaitement être atteint alors même que la répartition est totalement inégalitaire. C'est la critique que l'on a très souvent adressée à Pareto : un état peut être optimal, au sens de Pareto, même si certains individus sont extrêmement pauvres et d'autres excessivement riches, dès lors qu'on ne peut pas améliorer le sort des indigents sans toucher au style de vie des riches. L'optimum de Pareto peut sortir tout droit de l'enfer[344]. Il ne se préoccupe que de l'efficacité et n'accorde aucune attention aux questions de répartition. L'ensemble du raisonnement néoclassique est biaisé à l'origine, car l'augmentation de la production ou la maximisation de l'utilité générale considérée comme somme des utilités individuelles demeure un postulat absolu. Aussi aboutit-on fatalement à une dichotomie qui nous est familière : l'économie se consacre à l'augmentation de la production, à l'accroissement du gâteau, et le social se charge de la répartition. Ou à cette autre, tellement à la mode, mais tout aussi peu intéressante : l'économie se préoccupe de l'efficacité, les autres sciences s'occupent de la justice... Les keynésiens ne raisonnent pas autrement : sans doute la répartition est-elle analysée, mais elle n'est jamais considérée qu'en tant que moyen d'augmenter la production. Ainsi vaut-il mieux distribuer des revenus aux plus déshérités parce que leur propension à consommer est plus forte que celle des autres classes ; il vaut mieux diriger les capitaux vers l'investissement, parce que tel effet va permettre d'accroître encore davantage la production. Mais la question de la répartition en tant que telle, de la diffusion des avantages issus de cette augmentation, ne les intéresse pas.

Les politiques économiques actuelles des pays industrialisés le confirment : la manière dont les richesses sont réparties n'est pas une question qui relève de l'économie, sauf si elle peut influer sur la production. C'est exclusivement en référence à ce principe que certains types de répartition seront considérés comme préférables à d'autres. Plus généralement, l'économie, dans la mesure où elle est utilitariste, mérite la critique que Rawls inflige à l'utilitarisme dans la *Théorie de la justice*[345] en remettant en cause la manière dont celui-ci cherche à augmenter le bien-être collectif sans prendre en compte le bien de chacun. L'économie se donne aujourd'hui comme la science objective et mathématisée qui vise à trouver les meilleurs moyens d'augmenter la production. Obtenir le taux de croissance le plus fort sur une longue période, telle est sa tâche. Si l'on interroge des économistes sur les raisons d'un tel impératif, ils répondront que la croissance est bonne en soi, mais aussi qu'elle permet d'augmenter le niveau de vie de chacun. Mais ils ne le démontrent pas. L'économie ne s'occupe ni des fins ni de la répartition, mais de la seule production. Dès lors, puisqu'elle considère cet objectif comme un impératif, tout est bon pour le réaliser, y compris, par exemple, le développement des inégalités. Pourtant, s'il s'avérait que l'obtention d'un taux de croissance plus élevé nécessitait une augmentation des inégalités, et que de surcroît cette croissance ne bénéficiait qu'à quelques-uns, nous nous trouverions alors dans un véritable cercle vicieux. Mais peut-être ce cercle vicieux n'intéresse-t-il pas non plus l'économie.

Les lois naturelles de l'échange

La véritable raison du désintérêt de l'économie pour la structure de la répartition est évidente : l'économie elle-même se veut la science des lois naturelles de l'échange. Elle n'a pas à se préoccuper de la répartition et du caractère plus ou moins juste de celle-ci, parce qu'elle édicte elle-même les lois de la répartition naturelle, c'est-à-dire de la répartition juste. Elle ne fait que dévoiler la répartition naturelle (qui est celle qui maximise l'utilité collective et récompense chaque individu selon sa contribution à la production) et les conditions de celle-ci : chacun doit être rémunéré selon sa productivité marginale, ou, pour parler plus généralement, chaque facteur doit être rémunéré selon sa productivité marginale. La bonne société est par conséquent celle où les efforts que chacun a consentis sont rétribués naturellement. S'écarter de ces lois « naturelles », c'est risquer le déséquilibre, donc risquer de ne pas obtenir le maximum de production possible. La hiérarchie salariale est « naturelle » en ce sens. L'économie, au moins l'économie néoclassique, mais aussi celle du sens commun qui revient au galop aujourd'hui, croit que l'on peut isoler la contribution d'un individu à la production, qu'on peut lui imputer une partie de l'augmentation, que l'on peut dire quelle rémunération appelle cette contribution. L'économie croit qu'il existe une rétribution naturelle, de même qu'il existe un taux de chômage naturel, un salaire naturel... Elle croit à la naturalité des lois qu'elle met en évidence, et celle-ci est toujours finalement la justification de l'ordre établi.

L'économie détache les individus et les phénomènes de leur histoire et de leur contexte social et feint ensuite de croire que leurs relations sont naturelles. Elle se plaît à ignorer que les états sociaux et les relations sociales résultent d'une histoire, de conflits, de rapports de force, de compromis. Elle ne reconnaît que des individus dont les désirs, les relations, les comportements seraient identiques. On sait pourtant qu'il n'y a pas de loi naturelle : l'économie confond naturel avec existant, le droit avec le fait. Il n'y a pas plus de contribution naturelle et calculable d'un individu à la production que de valeur naturelle du diplôme. Pourquoi un diplôme de polytechnicien, d'énarque ou d'élève d'une école de commerce devrait-il être plus payé qu'un autre, pourquoi posséder un tel diplôme signifierait-il une plus grande contribution à la production ? Pourquoi le marché trouverait-il de lui-même l'optimum social ? Ce que l'économie appelle « naturel », n'est-ce pas, au contraire, le résultat d'un rapport de force et l'état qu'a déterminé la victoire du plus fort ? Ici apparaissent au grand jour les lacunes de l'économie : elle ne regarde pas les positions dans la production ou les positions sociales, les héritages divers, les rapports de force qui ont décidé des équivalences qu'elle considère comme naturelles. Elle fait comme si les « décisions » du marché n'avaient pas d'explication sociale. Elle omet de considérer, derrière le caractère apparemment objectif du marché et des compétences, la façon dont celles-ci ont été plus ou moins valorisées, rendues plus ou moins accessibles aux différentes catégories sociales, puis plus ou moins rémunérées. La hiérarchie des salaires n'est pas naturelle même si le marché sanctionne des différences réelles de compétence qui, à court terme, fondent des différences de rémunération : elle résulte de multiples négociations et rapports de forces. Il s'agit d'un pur produit historique.

L'économie confond le fait et le droit : Elie Halévy illustre cette réflexion profondément institutionnaliste (la relation sociale et l'institution précèdent et expliquent la relation économique) en critiquant en profondeur l'idée selon laquelle la rémunération de chaque individu selon sa productivité serait naturelle et conforme aux lois éternelles de l'économie : « Les marchandises s'échangent, et elles s'échangent à leur valeur, mais quelle est cette valeur ? Les premiers théoriciens voulaient mesurer cette valeur par la quantité de travail. [...] Il s'agissait pour eux, plus ou moins inconsciemment, de justifier l'ordre social qui se fonde sur l'échange, en démontrant que c'est un ordre des choses où chacun, comme paraît l'exiger la justice, reçoit en proportion de son travail. La preuve, c'est que depuis l'abandon de la théorie selon laquelle le travail mesure la valeur, les économistes ont constamment essayé, sous l'empire des mêmes préoccupations, de démontrer que le mécanisme de l'échange a pour effet d'assigner spontanément aux individus le produit de leur travail, la juste rémunération de leurs peines. [...] Le droit du plus fort est-il aboli par l'organisa-

tion de l'échange ? Il est seulement régularisé, et utilisé de
la même manière qu'on régularise le cours d'un torrent,
pour en faire une rivière navigable. [...] Comment donc et
en vertu de quels principes se fixe la hiérarchie des
salaires ? C'est un principe de distribution des richesses qui
ne résulte pas de l'opération spontanée des lois de la
nature : il suppose un système compliqué d'institutions
juridiques. Il consiste dans une sorte de transaction entre le
droit du plus fort et la loi du nombre. Il repose donc sur
deux vérités de fait, la première que les forts ont, dans la
lutte pour l'existence, l'avantage sur les faibles, la seconde
que les forts sont plus faibles que la coalition des faibles, et
doivent accepter le contrôle de la majorité sur leurs actes,
dès qu'il a plu aux faibles de se concerter pour agir [...].
Nous ne voyons en conséquence rien d'absurde à ce que ce
principe rende compte de l'inégalité des salaires. Nous
demandons seulement si, en fait, il suffit à rendre compte
des énormes inégalités qui se font actuellement observer
dans la distribution des richesses entre travailleurs. [...]
Nous croyons que l'inégalité actuelle des salaires tient,
pour une grande part, non pas à l'inégalité des capacités de
travail exigées, mais à l'inégalité des besoins, due à la
constitution aristocratique de la société [346]. »

Raymond Aron ne dira pas autre chose quelques décennies plus tard : s'interrogeant sur les différents types de
société industrielle et comparant, comme c'était la mode à
l'époque, les sociétés capitalistes et socialistes, puis s'attar-
dant sur l'une des critiques adressées aux sociétés capitalistes, qui comporteraient un large degré d'inégalité dans la
répartition des revenus, Aron conclut en disant : « La
conclusion minimum que l'on doit tirer de ces considérations, c'est que le problème de l'inégalité ne peut pas se
trancher par oui ou par non, par bon ou par mauvais. Il y a
une inégalité proprement indispensable dans toutes les
sociétés connues comme incitation à la production. Il y a
une inégalité qui est probablement nécessaire comme
condition de la culture afin d'assurer à une minorité la

possibilité de se livrer aux activités de l'esprit, ce qui ne laisse pas d'être cruel pour ceux qui n'en ont pas le loisir. Enfin, l'inégalité, fût-ce l'inégalité de propriété, peut être considérée comme la condition d'un minimum d'indépendance de l'individu par rapport à la collectivité[347]. »

La critique de Marx doit donc être prise au sérieux : l'économie ne fait que justifier a posteriori des situations issues d'une histoire. Parce qu'elle croit que l'individu est ce qu'il y a de plus naturel et qu'elle imagine celui-ci sans relation avec les autres, sans histoire, sans héritage, elle ne parvient pas à distinguer ce qui est légué à tous les membres d'une société en raison même de leur appartenance à celle-ci et ce que chaque individu obtient par son seul effort. Elle feint de croire que chacun a fait seul tout le chemin menant à la qualification sociale, comme si l'ensemble de l'héritage transmis par la famille, par l'éducation et, d'une manière plus générale, par toute la société, était le fruit du seul mérite individuel et devait donc être récompensé comme tel. Elle transforme la chance qu'ont certains d'avoir accès à cet héritage en efforts individuels méritant rémunération ; de ce fait, elle finit par trouver naturelles les inégalités qui sont l'effet d'une rente, comme Marshall lui-même, pourtant néoclassique, le reconnaissait[348]. Autrement dit, l'héritage de progrès, de savoirs, de sciences, de techniques, de capital qui est légué par toute une génération à une autre échoit en réalité de façon disproportionnée aux individus qui disposent des moyens de s'emparer de cet héritage, au premier titre desquels figure l'emploi. Il existe une grille des emplois, plus ou moins rémunérés, auxquels les individus accèdent à partir de leurs diplômes ou de leur qualification. Cet accès est rationné et socialement déterminé. Ceux qui accèdent aux emplois les mieux rémunérés recueillent seuls le bénéfice du travail des générations antérieures. Car aujourd'hui, parce que la rémunération du travail reste d'essence individuelle, seuls ceux qui sont dans le système y ont accès : ils accaparent le résultat du travail combiné des

hommes et des machines de toutes les générations antérieures. Et, ce faisant, l'économie légitime et considère
comme naturels des effets de rente cumulés : la hiérarchie
salariale est fondée sur une valorisation implicite réalisée
par ceux qui obtiennent les postes de pouvoir et transforment leurs propres qualités en éléments objectifs de
productivité pour l'entreprise ; l'accès à ces salaires et à ces
postes est quasiment destiné à ceux qui ont bénéficié de la
formation nécessaire, et l'accès à cette formation elle-
même, c'est-à-dire à l'enseignement supérieur, est infiniment plus aisé pour ceux qui appartiennent à une certaine
catégorie sociale. Dès lors, dire qu'un individu qui se
trouve dans le système productif a droit à voir son effort
rémunéré selon sa qualification, c'est faire comme si
l'ensemble de l'héritage qui lui a été transmis n'était issu
que de son seul effort.

L'effort individuel existe, certes, et il doit être récompensé ; mais il ne peut pas être pensé indépendamment de
la dimension sociale de l'héritage qui échoit à chaque
individu ni de la dimension collective de la production.
Conservant un système de rémunération adapté à son
idéologie — la rémunération individuelle censée récompenser le mérite et inciter à la productivité —, l'économie
légitime, sous une façade scientifique, la plupart des
inégalités qui préexistent à la répartition des richesses, et
qui sont ensuite renforcées par celle-ci. En se cachant
derrière l'idée de lois naturelles et en soutenant que chacun
bénéficie des fruits de la production, l'économie a en
réalité totalement oublié l'objectif qu'elle disait poursuivre. L'augmentation de la production, même si celle-ci doit
se faire au prix des plus grandes inégalités, est le véritable
objectif de l'économie. Car ce à quoi elle tend, c'est à la
multiplication des échanges, et donc à l'augmentation de la
production en tant que celle-ci est déterminée à partir des
échanges. Les inégalités ne la gênent pas ; elle les considère
même comme intéressantes dans la mesure où elles sont
génératrices d'effort productif. Mais jusqu'où doivent-elles

aller ? Schumpeter justifie le profit de l'entrepreneur par l'innovation : c'est pour son rôle central dans la croissance économique que celui-ci doit être récompensé (puisqu'il met ainsi à disposition de la société un nouveau produit, dont le prix ne va cesser de baisser) ; mais il ne dit pas jusqu'où peut aller cette récompense. Certainement jusqu'à l'endroit où le marché le supportera. Cela aussi est naturel.

Incitation individuelle et cohésion sociale

Partie de l'individu, c'est à l'individu que revient l'économie : elle ne peut donc pas être la technique d'une société qui voudrait mettre en avant sa cohésion sociale ou imaginer des mesures susceptibles de renforcer celle-ci. On l'a bien vu depuis vingt ans et depuis que, nous dit-on, les Etats-providence sont entrés en crise : l'Etat-providence est l'Etat qui, à la fois, utilise l'économie (donc l'incitation et la rétribution individuelle) et tente de préserver la cohésion sociale (donc panse les plaies et colmate les inégalités provoquées par la conception individualiste et inégalitaire de l'économie). L'économie ne peut pas promouvoir une idée de la société autre que celle dont elle est partie : partie de l'atomisme, elle y revient. Partie d'un ensemble d'individus tous autosuffisants, qui ne considèrent la société que comme un décor, elle aboutit normalement à la dissolution du lien social : la société n'a jamais été pour l'économie qu'un cadre extérieur aux individus. Il est, dès lors, normal que les individus eux-mêmes vivent sur cette idée. Aujourd'hui, la lente dissolution du lien social à laquelle nous assistons prend sans doute des formes plus sourdes et plus subtiles que le retour au pur atomisme : les individus restent groupés par ensembles homogènes. Il ne s'agit plus de classes, mais d'ensembles plus réduits, réunis par une même réaction vis-à-vis des autres ensembles, qui leur semblent menaçants, et unis par les mêmes intérêts. C'est une stratification sociale qui s'épanouit en corps et même en castes et se dessine avec force aux deux bouts de l'échelle. Les comportements qui commencent à poindre de nos jours en matière de protection sociale en sont une bonne illustration.

Rappelons qu'en 1945, alors que le Plan français de sécurité sociale avait pour ambition de couvrir et de protéger toute la population française — salariée ou non salariée, travailleuse ou non travailleuse — dans les situations de maladie, de vieillesse, de maternité, de handicap[349], l'idée échoua sous la poussée des corporatismes, tous mus par l'idée qu'il était impossible de traiter chacun également. Les cadres souhaitaient que leurs revenus différés soient en rapport avec leurs revenus d'activité, les agriculteurs trouvaient le prélèvement trop élevé, les professions indépendantes ne souhaitaient pas être mises dans le « même sac » que les salariés, les médecins ne voulaient pas non plus être salariés. Il en résulta une double conséquence : une invraisemblable mosaïque de régimes offrant des protections différentes aux différents groupes sociaux et une généralisation très tardive à l'ensemble de la population, celle-ci n'étant même pas acquise aujourd'hui, puisque la Sécurité sociale continue d'exiger des durées de travail minimales pour couvrir ses ressortissants. Contrairement à ce qu'on pourrait penser, ce corporatisme est encore bien plus fort aujourd'hui. Alors que les données concrètes et chiffrées dont on dispose ne sont pas suffisantes (les dernières comparaisons entre efforts contributifs des différents régimes remontant à 1982), chaque groupe social se considère moins bien payé de retour que les autres, payant trop pour ce qu'il consomme, souhaitant une modulation conforme à ses principes et à ses habitudes de vie. Aujourd'hui que le système de Sécurité sociale est en crise — les dépenses sont de plus en plus élevées et elles sont surtout difficilement régulables —, certains proposent pour principal remède de diminuer la couverture obligatoire et de rendre à chacun sa liberté : que chacun ou que chaque groupe choisisse ses propres modalités de couverture ; dépenses et protection élevées pour les uns, plus faibles pour les autres. La tentation est de régler la protection soit sur une logique individuelle (plus on travaille, plus on gagne, plus on a droit à de la protection), soit sur une logique de groupes sociaux, aux conceptions, aux revenus et aux habitus proches. Autrement dit, que chacun paye pour ce qu'il veut vraiment, et surtout que personne ne risque de payer pour quelqu'un d'autre. Mieux, que chaque groupe social ayant les mêmes habitudes, les mêmes revenus, le même profil de risques et de consommation soit couvert par le même organisme, mais que les différents risques et comportements sociaux cessent d'être mutualisés, comme c'est encore le cas aujourd'hui pour la protection obligatoire de base [350]. Car à quoi sert-il de travailler, si c'est pour payer des cotisations sociales qui vont ensuite servir à la protection de ceux qui n'ont pas fait d'effort pour prévenir la maladie, qui présentent beaucoup plus de « risques », ou qui ont une tendance à gaspiller… ? La tentation, c'est donc celle de petits groupes identitaires, dans lesquels on se retrouve et qui partagent, disons-le, les mêmes valeurs. On parle également de développer plus fortement la protection d'entreprise, ce qui constituerait un nouvel outil de gestion de la main-d'œuvre, renforcerait l'attachement du salarié à son groupe et mettrait mieux en évidence le lien entre effort consenti et avantages accordés en retour. C'est ainsi que se présentent aujourd'hui un certain nombre de projets dont l'ambition en matière de protection sociale est d'instituer un socle de base assurant une protection minimale aux individus, un second « étage » dépendant de l'entreprise et lié au travail, et enfin un dernier « étage », facultatif et surcomplémentaire. Lorsque ce système sera en place, chacun sera donc strictement couvert selon les moyens dont il dispose et selon son intégration dans le monde du travail.

Ce raisonnement ressemble d'ailleurs étrangement à la philosophie individualiste en vogue à la fin du XIXe siècle et au début du XXe siècle, qui inspirait les premiers débats relatifs à la protection sociale : il ne faut pas obliger les

gens à se protéger, non pas tant parce que cela coûtera cher
aux entreprises que parce que cela diminuera l'envie de
travailler. L'obligation, concept majeur de la Sécurité
sociale, a toujours été dénoncée par les individualistes
comme un danger pour la liberté de l'individu : danger de
ne pas avoir la liberté de se protéger quand il le veut,
danger de lui ôter sa capacité à prévoir, danger de faire de
lui un être mou qui perd son pouvoir d'innovation. Comme
il y a un siècle, l'obligation, clef de voûte du système de
protection sociale [351], est aujourd'hui remise en cause, au
nom d'un raisonnement purement économique. Il n'est pas
indifférent que ces thèses très individualistes retrouvent un
certain écho aujourd'hui, au moment où nous doutons de
l'efficacité de l'Etat-providence. Nous nous trouvons en
effet au cœur de la contradiction que recèle celui-ci.

D'un côté, l'Etat-Providence accepte la vérité de l'économie classique. Or, le terme du raisonnement économique classique, c'est une société qui n'est rien de plus que la
somme de ses parties, et donc qui ne modifie en rien la
hiérarchie originelle. L'économie est censée permettre que
de la multiplicité désorganisée naisse un ordre, à partir des
seuls échanges entre individus, mais de telle sorte que,
grâce aux lois naturelles dont elle est la science, l'association ne touche en rien à la distribution naturelle des
capacités qui prévalait avant la mise en place de la société.
Le rôle de l'économie se limite à donner les règles de
transformation des capacités en relations. Chaque individu
dispose à l'origine d'un capital donné de facultés dont la
mise en valeur a un prix, que dit l'économie. La société qui
résulte des échanges entre individus, c'est-à-dire de la
vente de leurs facultés, doit se déduire logiquement de la
situation originelle, de l'état naturel. Autrement dit, l'économie est la science qui révèle l'ordre naturel, parce qu'elle
se borne à effectuer une translation entre l'état naturel et
l'état de société. Il n'y a dans le second rien de plus que ce
qui était déjà contenu dans le premier. L'Etat-providence,
mais aussi la politique keynésienne qui en est le cœur,

accepte ce raisonnement économique. Dans cette mesure, il entérine une organisation de la production individualiste dirigée par l'impératif d'efficacité, mais aussi l'incitation individuelle, l'augmentation de la production — fût-ce au prix du développement des inégalités et de l'exclusion du système productif d'un nombre toujours plus grand d'individus —, et enfin la réduction de la protection sociale et la nécessaire proportionnalité de celle-ci au travail accompli.

D'un autre côté, l'Etat-providence vit sur l'idée que la société est plus que la somme de ses parties. Au nom de cette conception ont été mis en place les instruments censés renforcer la solidarité originelle qui tient les individus liés ensemble. D'où la contradiction, car c'est simultanément que l'Etat reconnaît deux conceptions de la société qui fondent des interventions radicalement différentes. Le résultat, c'est que les instruments de l'Etat-providence « social » ont été ajoutés à la conception de l'Etat-providence " économique " : la redistribution qu'est censé permettre l'Etat n'est qu'une correction des inégalités générées lors de la distribution primaire des revenus. A un premier stade, l'Etat laisse faire (même si certaines règles générales doivent malgré tout être respectées, comme le SMIC...); ensuite, il corrige. D'un côté, l'efficacité productive et le respect de ce à quoi donne lieu l'incitation individuelle, de l'autre une redistribution au nom de la solidarité. Mais, dans la mesure où l'Etat-providence n'a jamais osé tenir le discours qui justifiait son intervention sociale, où il a toujours craint d'effrayer les individus en affirmant sa croyance dans la société et dans la force du lien qui unit les individus, et où il croit lui-même à la naturalité et à la vérité des lois de l'économie, peu de gens comprennent aujourd'hui au nom de quoi ils payent des impôts et des cotisations toujours plus élevés ou ce qui justifie que l'on vienne leur prendre, sur le fruit de leur travail, des sommes destinées à d'autres, qui n'ont peut-être pas autant travaillé. D'où la tentation d'un vrai retour au naturel. Laissons donc le marché décider totalement de la juste répartition des revenus, supprimons tous les obstacles aux échanges naturels et ne faisons intervenir l'Etat que pour assister ceux qui s'en tireraient trop mal au terme de l'évolution. Les propositions qui fleurissent depuis quelques années et visent à revenir sur le SMIC, réduire la protection sociale, baisser le taux d'imposition, c'est-à-dire supprimer les instruments de prédilection de l'Etat social, s'inscrivent dans cette même logique. Ces revendications sont parfaitement compréhensibles dans la mesure où l'Etat n'a jamais osé dire au nom de quelle conception de la société il intervenait, et où il a continué à accepter la prétendue neutralité du raisonnement économique. Car c'est évidemment là que le bât blesse : il n'y a pas plus de loi naturelle que d'individus autonomes vivant à l'état naturel. L'économie croit pourtant à sa propre naturalité et à sa neutralité totale vis-à-vis de quelque conception philosophique ou éthique que ce soit. Là est le problème.

L'économie, science du comportement humain ?

Tout ceci n'aurait en effet que peu de conséquences si l'économie, d'une part, s'était reconnue comme une idéologie au service d'une conception particulière de la société et, d'autre part, avait bien voulu rester une simple technique au service des gouvernants et du débat social, chargée de tester des hypothèses et de faire des calculs, tout en se limitant très précisément à son objectif originel : trouver les moyens d'augmenter la prospérité et la richesse matérielle. Or, à la recherche des lois naturelles de la vie en société, l'économie a fini par étendre considérablement son objet et s'est proclamée science naturelle et générale du comportement humain, sans pourtant s'être aucunement débarrassée de ses postulats réducteurs. Alors même qu'elle se réfère à une conception de la société historiquement datée dont elle est l'idéologie, l'économie affirme, en effet, sa neutralité axiologique.

Où l'on reparle de l'« Homo economicus »...

Cette prétention de l'économie à accéder au rang de science est déjà en elle-même sujette à caution : car de quoi l'économie pourrait-elle être la science ? Des faits économiques, nous répondra-t-on, et de leur rationalité. Preuve en est que l'on peut faire des prévisions et que des lois peuvent d'ores et déjà être considérées comme acquises. Mais l'économie, comme l'histoire — dont elle est une partie lorsqu'elle s'intéresse au passé — constate des régularités pour tenter de dégager des causalités partielles. Elle ne peut guère plus. Il faut relire Paul Veyne [352] pour se pénétrer de l'idée que les faits économiques passés n'ont pas d'autre rationalité que celle qu'on veut bien leur prêter. Il faut surtout rappeler que l'économie, alors qu'elle revendique le titre de science et même de la plus exacte des sciences sociales, ne s'est jamais occupée de faire son épistémologie, à la différence des sciences exactes, ou même de l'histoire. Elle ne s'est jamais interrogée sur la construction de ses notions de base, sur leur rapport avec la réalité ou avec le contexte historique, sur ce qu'elle empruntait à la philosophie, à la psychologie ou au sens commun de chaque époque. Contrairement à la physique, à la mathématique et à l'histoire, elle n'a encore jamais connu ces crises qui permettent d'interroger les fondements d'une discipline. Peu à peu, ses adeptes ont affirmé sa neutralité et son indépendance vis-à-vis de toute considération éthique ou politique. Le vrai problème, ce n'est pas tellement que, ce faisant, l'économie en soit venue à « passer sous silence toutes sortes de considérations éthiques complexes qui influent sur le comportement humain réel [353] », mais surtout qu'elle ait cru qu'il suffisait de se proclamer neutre pour le devenir.

Or, en dépit de ce handicap, l'économie a renforcé ses prétentions depuis une cinquantaine d'années : elle se considère, au moins dans sa partie théorique, comme la science du comportement humain en société, ainsi que le met en évidence la querelle qui a opposé économistes et ethno-anthropologues dans les années 1950 et 1960. Certains économistes défendaient des conceptions radicalement naturalistes : l'*Homo economicus* existe et a toujours existé ; les catégories dont use l'économie sont universelles ; l'économie est « la science qui étudie le comportement humain comme une relation entre des fins et des moyens rares qui ont des usages alternatifs [354] ». Au même moment, l'économie déclarait clairement que son objet n'était pas un domaine particulier de la réalité — les activités visant à la production matérielle —, mais plus généralement le comportement humain face à des biens rares. L'économie s'est donc autoproclamée science du comportement de l'homme en société, tout en conservant ses présupposés individualistes et utilitaristes et en postulant leur universalité. Un certain nombre d'économistes [355] ont ainsi décidé que les catégories économiques étaient applicables aux sociétés primitives, parce que les « concepts de l'économie politique élaborés pour rendre compte d'un système économique de production marchande industrielle sont considérés porteurs d'une vérité universelle dans la mesure où ils expliciteraient les lois naturelles du comportement rationnel de l'*Homo economicus* qui sommeille en tout individu et à toute époque, et n'auraient pu s'appliquer et s'épanouir qu'avec l'apparition de l'économie de marché capitaliste moderne, devenue ainsi la norme et l'incarnation de la rationalité économique [356] ».

Robbins Burling revient ainsi sur la théorie de la maximisation et la généralise en écrivant : « L'idée que le comportement humain est en quelque sorte orienté vers la maximisation d'une fin souhaitée est apparue dans un grand nombre de théories des sciences sociales. La maximisation est, naturellement, un concept fondamental en économie car un des principaux axes de cette discipline pose que les besoins sont illimités mais que nous nous

efforçons constamment de maximiser nos satisfactions. [...]
L'économie n'est cependant en aucun cas la seule branche
des sciences sociales qui a considéré l'homme comme s'il
maximisait quelque chose. Le principe plaisir-douleur est
profondément enraciné dans la conception freudienne de la
personnalité. [...] Cette personnalité freudienne est remar-
quablement semblable à celle de l'homme économique.
Toutes deux ont un objectif en vue, toutes deux font des
projets, toutes deux veulent parvenir à une fin déterminée
et toutes deux s'efforcent par tous les moyens dont elles
disposent d'atteindre ce but et d'en tirer autant que
possible. [...] Déclarer qu'un individu s'efforce de maximiser ses satisfactions est un truisme. [...] Tout ceci signifie
simplement que notre comportement est finalisé et que les
divers objectifs immédiats sont eux-mêmes mesurables les
uns par rapport aux autres et qu'ils peuvent être classés par
ordre de préférence [357]. »

Edward LeClair ira encore plus loin. Critiquant ceux qui
assimilent économique à matériel, il écrit : « Les économistes ne croient plus, si ce fût jamais le cas, que, dans les
sociétés marchandes, les besoins humains sont limités aux
biens matériels et ils ne supposent pas non plus que ceci
puisse être vrai d'une autre société quelconque. Et l'hypothèse de la nature matérialiste des besoins humains n'est
pas non plus un élément nécessaire de la théorie économique contemporaine. [...] C'est pourquoi il peut être question d'économie de moyens, par exemple dans le cas de
l'autorité, du prestige ou des mérites religieux ; les biens et
services peuvent inclure les services d'un spécialiste en
matière rituelle ou en politique ou en esthétique, bref, le
champ de l'économie peut englober tous les besoins
humains et non pas les seuls besoins matériels. [...]
*L'économie semble être une science sociale générale traitant
de la totalité de la vie sociale* [358]. »

Il s'agit là, à l'évidence, d'une prise de position décisive :
après avoir déclaré que l'*Homo economicus* est universel et
éternel, l'économie se définit désormais non plus par son

objet, mais par sa méthode ; elle est la science qui étudie le comportement humain dès lors que l'homme est confronté à la rareté [359]. Cette définition formelle sera adoptée par une grande partie des économistes : von Mises, Samuelson, Burling... La totalité de la vie sociale est désormais justiciable d'une approche économique, de même que l'ensemble de l'activité humaine [360]. L'économie devient la science sociale de tous les temps... Plus rien ne retient alors l'économie de se présenter comme la science du principe de rationalité : « L'activité économique est le domaine le plus vaste du principe de rationalité, et également celui où ce principe est apparu tout d'abord, mais il n'est pas le seul [361]. » En outre, le principe économique s'est conquis et continue à se conquérir de nouveaux domaines. L'économie se veut donc la science qui découvre et promeut le principe de rationalité conçu comme le principe universel de toute action rationnelle.

A cette prétention se sont opposés les anthropologues de l'époque, critiquant tout à la fois la définition de l'économie dans sa dimension formelle et la prétention de l'économie à révéler des catégories économiques et un homme universels alors qu'elle ne faisait qu'extrapoler les conceptions du xixe et du xxe siècle. Polanyi oppose ainsi à la définition formelle de l'économie la définition substantive : « Le terme d'économique a deux significations aux racines indépendantes que nous nommerons sens substantiel et sens formel. Le sens substantif dérive du fait que l'homme dépend, pour sa survie, de ses semblables et de la nature. Ce sens renvoie à l'interaction entre l'homme et son environnement, naturel et social, interaction qui lui fournit les moyens de satisfaire ses besoins matériels. Le sens formel dérive du caractère logique du rapport fins-moyens, comme le montrent les expressions « processus économique » ou processus qui économise les moyens. Il se réfère à une situation de choix, à savoir le choix entre les usages alternatifs de différents moyens par suite de la rareté de ces moyens. Si les lois gouvernant le choix des moyens sont appelées logique de l'action rationnelle, nous pouvons désigner cette variante de la logique d'un terme improvisé : l'économie formelle. Les deux significations qui sont à la racine du terme économique n'ont rien en commun. La première découle du fait et la seconde de la logique. [...] Selon nous, seul le sens substantif de l'économique est capable de produire les concepts qu'exigent les sciences sociales pour analyser toutes les économies empiriques du passé et du présent [362]. »

Les fameuses catégories universelles de l'économie ne sont donc que celles de l'économie moderne marchande et le choix rationnel en situation de rareté ne vaut que dans cette économie-là. Malinowski, Dalton, Polanyi et d'autres anthropologues ont ainsi montré que, d'une manière générale, la dimension économique existait bien dans les sociétés primitives, en tant que fonction d'approvisionnement et de satisfaction des besoins, mais que cette fonction était enchâssée dans les rapports sociaux, voire régie par ceux-ci, et que nos catégories actuelles ne pouvaient leur être appliquées [363]. L'homme aux besoins naturellement illimités [364], dirigé par l'appât du gain et désirant naturellement les biens rares, se réduit à une invention de l'économie [365].

De même que la notion d'*Homo economicus* revendiquée par l'économie ne résiste pas à un examen sérieux, de même on peut s'interroger sur le caractère premier de la notion d'échange. Là encore, ce que l'économie tient pour la catégorie la plus simple et la plus universelle est une catégorie dérivée : « Un échange de biens n'est qu'un épisode momentané au sein d'un rapport social continu. Les termes de l'échange sont réglementés par les rapports existant entre les parties. Si les rapports changent, les termes changent [366]. » Ce que l'anthropologie et l'ethnologie démontreront, le courant institutionnaliste [367] l'avait déjà mis en évidence : « Si l'on vise à démontrer que toutes les relations économiques sont des relations d'échange, c'est donc que l'on trouve à la notion d'échange un caractère privilégié. Elle seule, entre toutes, serait primitive et irréductible à l'analyse : et voilà pourquoi analyser une notion économique serait toujours, en fin de compte, la réduire à cette notion première. Mais, précisément, il est faux de croire que l'échange soit une notion inanalysable et que les lois de l'échange soient, en quelque sorte, antérieures à toutes les institutions juridiques, analogues, pour l'homme vivant en société, à ce que les lois de l'attraction moléculaire sont pour la nature inanimée. L'échange suppose tout un système d'institutions juridiques, élaborées par la société humaine en vue de fins déterminées. Loin que la distribution des richesses doive être considérée comme expliquée lorsque les formes en sont ramenées aux lois de l'échange, c'est au contraire l'échange qui est susceptible d'une explication et d'une réduction inverses : il constitue un mode artificiel de distribution des richesses. [...] L'échange a pour condition première le consentement, exprès ou tacite, de la société à la possession, par les individus entre lesquels a lieu l'échange, d'un certain fond. C'est ce consentement social qui consacre la possession. [...] La seconde condition de l'échange, c'est l'existence d'un régime de libre concurrence. [...] Encore faut-il qu'il y ait un marché. [...] Mais ce marché, sur lequel vendeurs et acheteurs se retrouvent, c'est une institution politique : pour qu'il existe et qu'il soit effectivement le lieu de rencontre de ceux qui veulent échanger leurs produits, il faut des règlements, une police, bref, une intervention de l'Etat. *La véritable concurrence économique suppose non pas, comme cela paraît à première vue presque évident, la dispersion absolue des individus, mais au contraire leur concentration par un acte de l'autorité sociale*[368]. »

En réponse à la question du fondement et du maintien de l'ordre social, l'économie a trouvé l'échange marchand, acte social majeur, fondateur de sociabilité. Mais, ce faisant, elle se référait à un contexte historique et intellectuel précis en fonction duquel sa méthode, ses hypothèses et son objet furent construits. Mais, au lieu de reconnaître qu'elle s'enracinait dans l'histoire, elle a transformé le contexte de sa naissance et les données historiques du problème qu'elle avait à résoudre en données universelles. Sourde aux critiques qui lui ont été adressées à tant de reprises, elle continue à régir nos sociétés sur des bases dépassées.

L'économie hantée par la politique

L'économie continue aujourd'hui à véhiculer les mêmes postulats alors même que le contexte et les questions à régler ont totalement changé. On objectera que l'économie n'est pas une, mais diverse, qu'il n'y a plus grand rapport aujourd'hui entre microéconomie (issue de l'économie classique et néoclassique) et macroéconomie (essentiellement issue de Keynes), dont « l'unité » constitue l'un des problèmes majeurs posés à la discipline, et que l'on ne peut donc affirmer que l'économie reste l'idéologie d'une société conçue comme association d'individus régis par des rapports contractuels et continue de se référer à un hypothétique *Homo economicus,* ou encore à des lois naturelles... L'économie qui inspire aujourd'hui les hommes politiques et les administrations consiste, en effet, en un mixte aux sources d'inspirations diversifiées, que l'on appelle communément « politique économique ». Les fondements théoriques de la politique économique demeurent flous et divers : on y trouve pêle-mêle des raisonnements de type keynésiens mâtinés de constructions microéconomiques, le tout intégré dans des modèles économétriques qui permettent de calculer les effets de certaines décisions de la puissance publique. Ce flou est reconnu par certains économistes eux-mêmes : « L'économie politique présente tous les signes extérieurs d'une bonne santé. Des assises institutionnelles solides, une scientificité largement reconnue (certains pensent même qu'elle est la plus scientifique des sciences sociales), une insertion étroite dans le débat politique. Mais, en y regardant de plus près, on s'aperçoit qu'il est impossible de porter un jugement global car l'économie n'est plus du tout un ensemble homogène. Elle est à la fois florissante et entrée dans une crise profonde [369]. »

En dépit de cette diversité, l'économie présente pourtant toujours des caractéristiques homogènes. Elle continue de se vouloir neutre, science positive et formelle indépendante de tout jugement de type politique ou éthique et se refuse à juger des fins. Elle se revendique science des moyens et non des fins, tout en persistant également à désigner l'augmentation de la production comme un bien en soi. Au lieu de se mettre au service de la science ou de l'art spécialisé dans les fins, elle se substitue à celui-ci, l'éclipsant et le renvoyant aux oubliettes de l'histoire. Elle maintient qu'il n'existe qu'une forme de rationalité, le « reste » relevant du domaine de l'idéologie : « Il apparaît donc que le principe de rationalité économique est le principe de toute activité rationnelle de l'homme tendant à réaliser au maximum une fin donnée [370]. » L'économie se prétend l'incarnation de la rationalité, elle-même réduite à la rationalité de l'économie, devenue pure logique formelle, adaptation des moyens à des fins données : « On ne saurait trop le souligner, en dehors de la condition de cohérence, il n'y a pas de critère de la rationalité des fins considérées en elles-mêmes. Ces fins sont absolument arbitraires. [...] Il en est ici comme en matière des goûts. Ils sont ce qu'ils sont. Ce sont des données qui diffèrent d'un individu à l'autre [371]. » L'idée majeure qui guide l'économie n'est pas qu'il ne lui appartient pas de déterminer les fins, mais bien plutôt qu'il n'y a pas de fins. Il n'y a pas de bien social, seulement des fins individuelles, tel est le présupposé de l'économie. Le keynésianisme n'a remis en cause aucun des éléments de la vision sociale sur lesquels était fondée l'économie classique, il a simplement globalisé ce qu'elle isolait : « La différence est plutôt de méthode. La microéconomie est d'abord une théorie pure analysant un monde idéal, celui où règne une concurrence parfaite organisée. La macroéconomie entend partir du monde réel et de ses imperfections. [...] Elle se satisfait d'hypothèses de comportements assez frustes, mais qui lui paraissent admissibles comme représentation moyenne de comportements individuels ou comme résumé d'interactions nombreuses dont l'analyse rigoureuse serait d'une effrayante complexité [372]. » La macroéconomie non plus n'a pas renoncé au postulat d'une société constituée d'individus qui échangent.

L'économie pratique actuelle ne cherche même plus à faire référence à des hypothèses théoriques : elle n'a plus recours qu'à la seule notion de besoin. Celle-ci n'est d'ailleurs jamais explicitée par l'économie, qui la considère comme une catégorie naturelle et derechef infiniment extensible : les besoins humains sont tout ensemble individuels et sociaux, matériels et spirituels... En réalité, ces besoins sont tout autant des désirs : de nourriture, d'habillement, de temps libre, de sociabilité, de beauté, d'amour. Cette vision est tout à fait congruente avec la conception de l'homme comme être de désir, jamais rassasié : l'économie se présente comme la science et la technique au service de la satisfaction des besoins et des désirs humains [373]. Elle gère la rareté et donne les règles d'ordre qui président à la distribution de tous les biens dont l'homme a besoin.

Le paradoxe de cette situation ne doit cependant pas nous échapper. La logique des besoins est une logique naturelle à l'origine — et c'est bien ainsi qu'était conçue l'économie au départ, les besoins matériels devant être satisfaits par une production matérielle —, mais elle a été peu à peu étendue à la totalité des désirs humains. En d'autres termes, l'économie prend désormais en charge tout désir ; elle le socialise, l'officialise. L'économie nous fait donc croire que tout désir 1. peut être comblé, 2. par une production ou un service, 3. d'autrui, 4. et d'une manière socialisée. Comme si la tâche de la société était aujourd'hui de se saisir de l'ensemble des désirs humains pour les transformer en besoins et d'organiser la production collective susceptible de les satisfaire. L'homme n'est dès lors plus appréhendé que comme un producteur/consommateur[374]. D'où les invraisemblables exhortations à consommer : consommer est devenu un acte civique. Consommez n'importe quoi, pourvu que cela apparaisse dans les statistiques officielles. Qu'importe qui consomme, pourvu que cela soit visible. Situation paradoxale, donc : on croyait l'économie soucieuse de protéger l'individu, méfiante vis-à-vis de toute réalité extérieure aux individus ; en socialisant tous ses désirs, elle le soumet doublement à la société : ses désirs sont transformés et pris en charge par l'organisation sociale, et lui-même consacre l'essentiel de ses forces, chaque jour, à réaliser une production qui a pour but de satisfaire les désirs retraduits des autres.

Ce faisant, on conçoit que le désir de chacun ait perdu sa particularité, et qu'il soit devenu totalement standardisé. Que tout désir soit interprété en termes de besoin signifie que l'homme doit passer toujours davantage par la médiation du système productif public pour être satisfait ; que tout besoin humain soit susceptible d'être satisfait par le système économique suppose donc que se développe un système de publicisation des besoins, puis de retraduction, et enfin de prise en charge par la société. Comme Habermas[375] l'a bien mis en évidence, une telle traduction n'est pas anodine, car elle transforme le système social de médiation en un appareil condamné à se reproduire, à peser de plus en plus sur les décisions et à supprimer tout ce qui ne contribue pas à nourrir ce mouvement, en particulier les formes de vie autonomes. Ce système médium n'est pas seulement constitué de l'Etat, mais bien de l'ensemble des institutions qui ont pour but d'organiser la « publicisation » des besoins, de les repérer, de les mettre en forme, d'y répondre... Les entreprises en font donc également partie, au même titre que l'Etat.

Dès lors on voit combien économie classique et keynésianisme sont au fond peu différents. Keynes a simplement donné une autre dimension à l'économie en l'élevant au rang de politique : l'Etat assure désormais lui-même la fonction de régulation dont l'économie classique et néoclassique avaient cru bon de le tenir écarté. L'Etat prend le relais des individus et des unités de production pour opérer cette régulation globale : la hantise du déséquilibre[376], de l'absence de régulation est si forte que l'Etat a désormais le droit d'intervenir. Ainsi, il n'est plus le symbole de la fragile intervention humaine, il représente au contraire la puissance de calcul et de régulation : si l'on a fait appel à lui, c'est qu'il peut mieux que tout autre garantir la régularité des évolutions économiques et sociales. Certes, on débat encore aujourd'hui pour savoir jusqu'où l'Etat doit aller et si l'ordre ne serait pas plus sûrement garanti par le marché pur ; mais nos sociétés modernes ont répondu d'une manière assez générale que cette tâche revenait en grande partie à l'Etat et cela, au fond, n'importe guère. Il lui incombe donc de soutenir le processus, de le nourrir, de le stabiliser, de le calculer... L'économie n'est plus seulement l'instrument privilégié de la régulation, elle fixe les fins : ce que poursuit l'Etat, c'est non pas telle ou telle fin particulière, mais l'augmentation du taux de croissance et/ou de la consommation. Les indicateurs économiques ont été érigés en indicateurs politiques : « Les objectifs une fois définis, on tend vers une sorte de pilotage automatique assuré par des experts et des modèles. Les objectifs eux-mêmes finissent par être largement déterminés par la technicité des instruments (la représentation qu'ils impliquent constitue une construction/réduction du réel) ainsi que par toutes les contraintes internationales et les rigidités internes. Au total, la fonction politique n'est plus séparable des choix techniques en matière économique : l'intendance ne suit plus mais précède, le politique s'incorpore dans la technocratie[377]. »

L'Etat social ou l'Etat-providence n'est donc lui-même que la forme moderne qu'a prise l'impératif d'abondance et de production. Désormais, l'Etat est le médiateur, c'est par son intermédiaire que les individus sont liés. En distribuant

toujours plus de revenus aux consommateurs, l'Etat-
providence a gagné tout le monde au système et chacun est
obligé de faire sien l'objectif d'augmentation de la production, qui permettra la satisfaction de toujours plus de
besoins, qui donnera toujours plus d'emploi... jusqu'à la
fin des Temps. On obtient par là une forme d'ordre social
très efficace, à condition que puissent être inventés des
besoins en nombre suffisant. Du coup, l'ensemble de la
société ne travaille plus que pour un seul but : nourrir ce
feu de la consommation. En face d'un Etat qui régule et
prend en charge les besoins par une politique économique,
une politique de l'emploi et une politique d'assistance, les
individus persistent dans l'état d'isolement où les avait
trouvés l'économie[378]. Purs individus autonomes qui ne
peuvent communiquer que par l'échange, leur vie se passe
à produire, c'est-à-dire à transformer leurs capacités en
services susceptibles d'être vendus ou à recycler leurs désirs
en besoins : ils sont dès lors entièrement socialisés, c'est-à-
dire entièrement voués et attachés aux autres. Par conséquent, l'économie contemporaine continue de produire
l'ordre social par les mêmes moyens qu'à l'origine : elle fait
dépendre l'éventuel enrichissement des individus (voire
leur survie) de leur participation au métabolisme social,
grâce à une définition de la richesse purement « échan-
giste ». Tel est le fondement du processus social d'autore-
production dans lequel sont entraînés, bon gré mal gré,
tous les individus.

On comprend mieux alors la critique fondamentale
d'Hannah Arendt à l'égard de l'économie : considérer la
tâche d'un pays comme exclusivement économique, et
l'homme comme un producteur et un consommateur,
revient à rendre l'homme entièrement « public ». En le
livrant pieds et poings liés à la régulation sociale, on pose
que l'individu ne peut plus vivre autrement qu'en tant
qu'être social. D'où, poursuit-elle, deux conséquences en
forme d'échec : la disparition de la sphère privée, où
l'individu disposait de son espace propre, et celle de

l'espace politique, où les citoyens étaient égaux. Echec qui, pour l'économie, a le goût de la victoire, puisqu'elle se fait passer pour la politique même.

L'économie et le dépérissement de la politique

L'économie n'est pas une simple technique neutre : elle va de pair avec une vision du monde, celle qui a déterminé le contexte de sa naissance, mais aussi avec le refus absolu de la politique et de l'éthique, c'est-à-dire des arts humains portant sur les fins. L'économie portait en soi le dépérissement de la politique, elle se présentait au XVIIIᵉ siècle comme l'autre choix, et elle s'est bien substituée, au moins dans nos sociétés, à la politique. En s'affirmant comme la science qui édictait les lois naturelles de la recherche de l'abondance, l'économie prétendait également dévoiler celles des rapports sociaux et entrait de fait en concurrence avec les autres systèmes susceptibles de constituer un principe d'ordre (religion, morale, philosophie, politique...). Il y a une relation évidente entre d'une part, le dépérissement des systèmes traditionnels de « légitimation » (pour reprendre l'expression de Habermas), qui expliquaient le sens du monde, la place des hommes et de la société et fondaient l'obligation, et, d'autre part, la nécessité de construire de toutes pièces de nouveaux modes de régulation et de laisser une plus large place à l'intervention de la volonté humaine. Alors que deux solutions radicalement antithétiques se présentaient, au XVIIIᵉ siècle, pour asseoir l'ordre social à partir du nouveau contexte, l'économie et la politique, l'économie s'est imposée.

Au fur et à mesure que s'affirmait l'impératif d'efficacité productive, l'économie augmentait son emprise sur l'ensemble de la vie sociale, réduisant celle-ci à l'organisation des moyens d'atteindre cet unique objectif. Alors que disparaissaient les systèmes de légitimation ou les traditions, et que se développait la rationalisation de la vie

sociale au service d'un seul but, la politique comme art de
trouver les fins de la vie sociale ou, plus simplement,
comme art de choisir devenait de plus en plus inutile. Ce
constat concerne toutes les sociétés qui ont adopté la
régulation économique, quelque important que soit le rôle
dévolu à l'Etat. Comme l'écrit Habermas : « Dans la
mesure où l'activité de l'Etat vise à la stabilité et à la
croissance du système économique, la politique prend un
caractère négatif : elle oriente son action de façon à
éliminer les dysfonctionnements, à éviter les risques susceptibles de mettre le système en danger, et non pas de
façon à réaliser des finalités pratiques mais à trouver des
solutions d'ordre technique. [...] La politique de type
ancien était tenue de se déterminer par rapport à des buts
pratiques, ne fût-ce qu'en raison de la forme de légitimation qui était celle de la domination : l'idée d'une vie bonne
faisait l'objet d'interprétations qui étaient tournées vers des
relations d'interaction. La programmation de remplace-
ment qui prévaut aujourd'hui ne concerne plus que le
fonctionnement d'un système faisant l'objet d'un guidage.
[...] C'est pourquoi la nouvelle politique de l'interventionnisme étatique exige la dépolitisation de la grande masse de
la population[379]. » Dans la mesure où elle édicte des lois
naturelles et sociales, qui doivent être respectées pour
atteindre un objectif qui ne souffre pas la discussion,
l'économie porte en soi le dépérissement de la politique ;
elle rend inutiles non seulement la réflexion prudente de
l'homme politique, mais également les débats, voire la
consultation et la discussion nationales.

Economie et technocratie

La grande masse doit être dépolitisée, la classe politique
également. Elle est appelée soit à se transformer en une
technocratie spécialisée dans le choix des moyens les plus
adaptés pour parvenir aux objectifs prédéterminés, soit à se
perdre dans un bavardage sans efficace. Dès lors, la

politique se réduit à quelques discours sur les marges de manœuvre laissées par l'économie, mais jamais sur les finalités mêmes de la vie en société. Elle est devenue aujourd'hui un sous-produit de l'économie qui a pour fonction de faire croire qu'il existe plusieurs manières d'atteindre le même objectif et entretient une apparence de liberté et de débat. Mais la division du travail « politique » lui-même montre qu'il ne s'agit bien que d'une illusion.

La régulation sociale actuelle prend, en effet, appui sur une double division du travail : d'une part, entre une classe politico-administrative censée déterminer les fins et les moyens de la vie en société et le reste de la population, qui, en dehors de l'acte de vote, exercé en moyenne une fois par an, ne se préoccupe plus de ceux-ci et délègue à la première le soin de s'en occuper ; et, d'autre part, au sein de la classe politico-administrative elle-même, entre une technocratie de plus en plus nombreuse, de mieux en mieux formée et responsable de la régulation d'une partie de plus en plus importante de la vie sociale et les hommes politiques qui ne sont « que » les représentants du peuple. Cette division s'est considérablement accentuée depuis la fin de la Seconde Guerre mondiale ; elle a conduit à la constitution d'une classe spécialisée dans le traitement des problèmes publics et, plus généralement, dans le traitement de la régulation de l'ordre social ; elle se veut une classe neutre, ne se référant qu'à un savoir neutre — l'économie — et tentant d'obtenir l'ordre social le meilleur. La constitution d'une telle classe était justifiée par le caractère éminemment complexe et technique des problèmes à traiter et par l'incapacité de l'ensemble de la population ou des hommes politiques classiques à pénétrer tous les arcanes de la décision. La division a atteint son apogée depuis que cette classe, formée pour la gestion des problèmes mécaniques et techniques de régulation, est devenue en même temps celle qui exerce le pouvoir politique. Résultat atteint par plusieurs voies : soit parce que les hommes politiques, et en particulier ceux qui exercent les fonctions les plus éminentes, sont eux-mêmes issus de cette classe, soit parce que les rapports entre pouvoir exécutif et Parlement sont tels que les députés ne disposent pas des moyens de maîtriser et de vérifier la pertinence des calculs ou des décisions de l'administration. Autrement dit, la dépolitisation des citoyens, mais aussi des hommes politiques, est inévitable depuis qu'il est préférable d'avoir fait une grande école technique spécialisée dans le traitement des problèmes de régulation (Polytechnique, l'ENA ou d'autres) pour devenir un homme politique. L'Ecole nationale d'administration est devenue l'école où s'enseignent les mécanismes de régulation de la société, où l'on apprend, comme le voulait Saint-Simon, à administrer les hommes comme les choses, où l'on se pénètre de l'idée qu'il n'existe que des problèmes techniques et jamais des problèmes portant sur les fins. A l'ENA, on apprend le secret de la régulation. Aujourd'hui, être un homme politique, c'est soit être passé maître dans l'art de la régulation, soit être capable d'être à l'écoute d'une technocratie spécialisée dans les questions économiques.

Ce faisant, ce n'est évidemment plus le caractère économique ou non des questions qui est primordial (car aucun sujet n'est véritablement économique et l'économie prétend édicter, en tout état de cause, les lois de tous les domaines), mais le fait qu'il existe des lois et que seuls ceux qui connaissent ces lois sont aptes à diriger la société. La direction de la société apparaît de plus en plus semblable à la direction d'une entreprise, avec une dérive technocratique similaire dans les deux cas, celle dont Galbraith parlait en visant les seules entreprises[380]. C'est ce qu'invite à penser Max Weber lorsqu'il parle de « l'entreprise politique » (qui nécessite un état-major administratif et des moyens matériels) et lorsqu'il s'interroge sur la signification de la figure moderne de l'homme politique professionnel. Dans la conférence qu'il prononce en 1919 et que l'on a coutume de traduire en français par « Le métier et la vocation d'homme politique » (« *Politik als Beruf* »)[381],

Weber désigne la fonction de l'homme politique par le terme même de *Beruf*, qu'il a longuement analysé dans *L'Ethique protestante et l'esprit du capitalisme*. Ce terme, qui signifie à la fois vocation et métier, a acquis son sens moderne à travers la traduction de la Bible par Luther. Il concentre l'essentiel des transformations par lesquelles le travail est devenu la tâche des hommes dans le monde et le fondement de nos sociétés[382]. *Beruf*, la tâche assignée aux hommes sur terre, et qui a contribué à donner au capitalisme son visage, est également la tâche assignée à l'homme politique ; celui-ci conçoit lui aussi sa fonction comme une activité qui doit être exercée le plus efficacement possible, en rendant des comptes, et qui doit être menée de la même façon que toute autre entreprise. Derrière la similitude des termes, on trouve bien l'idée que la société est une entreprise et qu'il s'agit de la diriger comme telle. Weber précise : « L'évolution qui transformait la politique en une " entreprise " exigeait une formation spéciale de ceux qui participent à la lutte pour le pouvoir et qui en appliquent les méthodes, suivant le principe du parti moderne [...] Les choses ne se passent pas autrement dans une entreprise privée[383]. » Il faut prendre la comparaison de Weber au mot : aujourd'hui, la fonction de l'homme politique spécialisé est de diriger la société comme on dirige une entreprise. Parce que la société *est* une entreprise qui, comme les « petites » entreprises, fixe son budget, doit être efficace et vise à maximiser sinon son profit, au moins sa production ; elle possède ses travailleurs, son équipe de direction, sa division des tâches. Dans le monde moderne, l'organisation économique a pris le pas sur toute autre : de même que l'entreprise moderne est celle qui possède un compte de capital, la société moderne est celle dont la comptabilité nationale est celle d'une grande entreprise[384]. Nous croyons aujourd'hui faire de la politique alors que nous faisons de l'économie et nous appelons politique ce qui n'en est pas. Nous croyons parler des fins alors qu'un seul objectif nous importe : chercher à rendre toujours plus rentable l'entreprise France.

Ne poussons pas l'angélisme jusqu'à croire que l'on peut se passer d'être compétitif, de produire et de consommer. La survie d'un pays est à ce prix aujourd'hui et cela ne peut être contesté. Ce qui peut l'être néanmoins, nous y reviendrons, c'est la plus ou moins grande place donnée à cet objectif de survie, c'est le nom qu'on lui donne et c'est l'espace qu'il laisse libre pour d'autres préoccupations. Pendant ce temps, ce qui pourrait ressembler à de la politique — à savoir déterminer les fins de la vie sociale, parler, débattre, participer — apparaît bien évidemment comme une vieille lune : le débat est inutile, puisqu'il existe des lois et une classe spécialisée dans leur lecture et leur interprétation. Laissons-la donc faire pendant que le reste de la population s'attache aux fonctions de base de la société, produire et consommer. C'est bien parce que la société est comprise comme une entreprise que l'ensemble des fonctions collectives — et pas seulement le travail — peut faire l'objet d'une division toujours plus poussée : l'économie est également l'instrument de la division du travail social.

Quand la philosophie politique adopte les postulats de l'économie

Il nous semble que le terme de l'évolution est atteint lorsque la théorie politique elle-même emploie la méthode — et de ce fait accepte en même temps l'ensemble de la vision du monde, des présupposés et des réquisits — de l'économie. C'est le cas aux Etats-Unis depuis une vingtaine d'années (mais en réalité depuis que s'est développé le positivisme, dans les années 1920) et désormais également en France. Un très grand nombre d'ouvrages américains de philosophie politique s'inspirent, en effet, sans jamais l'expliciter ni le justifier, des méthodes issues de la « science » économique et utilisées dans la discipline qu'on appelle, aux Etats-Unis, théorie du choix social ou du choix rationnel. Dans la *Théorie de la justice,* Rawls explique ainsi que dans la situation initiale — celle dans laquelle se trouvent les individus qui vont choisir les principes selon lesquels ils vivront ensemble —, les partenaires sont des êtres rationnels, et il ajoute : « Le concept de rationalité doit être interprété au sens étroit, courant dans la théorie économique, c'est-à-dire comme la capacité d'employer les moyens les plus efficaces pour atteindre des fins données. [...] La théorie de la justice est une partie, peut-être la plus importante, de la théorie du choix rationnel [385]. » L'ensemble de l'ouvrage s'inspire effectivement très fortement non seulement de la méthode, mais également des situations, des hypothèses et des raisonnements utilisés en économie. Dès lors, l'ensemble de la démarche s'appuie sur les postulats d'une autre discipline, simplement empruntés à celle-ci et qu'il ne s'agira plus que de développer. A titre de fiction lui permettant de réfléchir sur la nature de la société et la notion de justice sociale, Rawls choisit exactement la situation-type dont partaient l'économie et la politique au XVIIIe siècle, c'est-à-dire la fiction d'un état de nature dans lequel les individus sont isolés, dispersés ; l'enjeu était alors de mettre en évidence les raisons pour lesquelles les individus pourraient décider de vivre ensemble. Le choix de cette fiction, matrice de la pensée économique, n'est évidemment pas innocent chez Rawls.

Les économistes contemporains de Rawls se réfèrent à une situation originelle identique. Comparons. Rawls écrit, en 1971 : « Posons, pour fixer les idées, qu'une société est une association, plus ou moins autosuffisante, de personnes qui, dans leurs relations réciproques, reconnaissent certaines règles de conduite comme obligatoires, et qui, pour la plupart, agissent en conformité avec elles. [...] Supposons, de plus, que ces règles déterminent un système de coopération visant à favoriser le bien de ses membres. Bien qu'une société soit une tentative de coopération en vue de l'avantage mutuel, elle se caractérise donc à la fois par un conflit d'intérêts et par une identité d'intérêts[386]. » En 1962, Robbins Burling, l'un des chefs de file des économistes américains, écrivait : « On peut considérer une société comme une collection d'individus faisant des choix et dont chaque action implique des options conscientes ou inconscientes entre des moyens et des fins alternatives. Les fins sont les buts de l'individu, colorées par les valeurs de la société dans laquelle il vit et vers lesquelles il essaye de se diriger[387]. » Dans les deux cas, les individus sont dispersés mais rationnels et autosuffisants. Chez Rawls comme dans toute la démarche économique, les individus ont des préférences qu'ils souhaitent maximiser. Comme dans un vaste pan de la tradition économique, même si Rawls s'attaque à l'utilitarisme, l'optimum social résulte également de la prise en compte des points de vue individuels, qu'il faut concilier pour obtenir un équilibre. Dans les deux cas, la société est considérée comme une agrégation, une collection, une association d'individus rationnels, ou encore un décor qui « colore » simplement des fins qui demeurent individuelles. L'entrée en société n'a rien changé.

Mais, nous dira-t-on, pourquoi le fait de partir de cette multiplicité d'individus dispersés serait-il plus économique que politique ? Car cette hypothèse, nous l'avons vu précédemment[388], est commune aux théories économiques et politiques du XVIIIe siècle, dont la plupart ont également pour caractéristique commune de considérer le contrat comme l'instrument par lequel les individus sortent de l'état de nature pour rentrer dans l'état civil. Mais trois différences majeures nous semblent différencier les deux types de solution. En premier lieu, les théories politiques considèrent comme une question ce que l'économie fait passer pour une réponse : l'articulation entre l'individu, ses désirs, sa volonté d'un côté et la société de l'autre. Il n'est que de voir les difficultés dans lesquelles se débat Rousseau lorsqu'il lui faut montrer comment l'on passe de la multiplicité des volontés particulières à la volonté générale[389]. De la même façon, et c'est la deuxième différence, la théorie politique approfondira la conception de l'individu à laquelle elle se réfère. Rares sont les théories politiques du XIXᵉ siècle qui osent faire leurs les hypothèses de l'état de nature, florissantes au siècle précédent. Elles prennent acte de l'impossibilité de déduire la société à partir d'individus dispersés qui ne seraient pas socialement et historiquement situés. Enfin, et surtout, l'économie, comme le met en évidence l'étymologie, dévoile des lois. Sa différence spécifique réside dans l'automaticité de l'ordre qu'elle découvre, alors que la politique est l'art qui cherche les fins de la vie en société et qui reconnaît par là que nous sommes toujours déjà en société. La politique, même lorsqu'elle part des individus dispersés et qu'elle les fait contracter, même lorsqu'elle imagine que le contrat transforme magiquement en un instant la multiplicité désordonnée en un corps social organique[390], exige que les individus se parlent. Chez Rousseau, les individus s'adressent la parole et échangent autre chose que leurs facultés. Chez Smith, mais également chez tous les économistes qui suivront, et jusqu'à Marx, la parole est inutile. Le lien social est produit, il n'est pas parlé. Le lien social se déduit des échanges entre individus, il se tisse automatiquement, il n'est pas soumis à la fragilité du discours, au bavardage, à la possible inefficacité ou vacuité de la parole, à ses éventuelles carences[391]. Il en va exactement ainsi chez Rawls.

Dans la *Théorie de la justice*, tout se passe comme si les individus dispersés mais parfaitement autosuffisants se réunissaient un moment pour décider des règles qui leur permettront chacun de vivre encore mieux — grâce aux avantages tirés de la coopération — puis repartaient vivre chacun de leur côté, comme si le moment de face-à-face devait être le plus bref possible. Que les individus réalisent ce choix sous un voile d'ignorance n'est d'ailleurs pas indifférent : craignent-ils de voir des signes extérieurs qui entameraient l'innocence nécessaire au choix « équitable » des règles ? Ou se prémunissent-ils de cette manière contre les risques de la rencontre et de la parole ? On désigne un principe et tout est fini. D'ailleurs, tout est déjà fini parce qu'une fois les règles choisies les hommes n'auront plus jamais besoin de se parler, de se rencontrer, de s'assembler : ce moment fictionnel est le seul où les hommes courent le risque d'être en société et d'avoir un intérêt qui pourrait être commun. Après, les règles édicteront, chaque fois, et pour chaque cas, ce qui doit être fait et l'équilibre sera, dans tous les cas, préservé[392]. Paradoxalement, ce moment fondamental est en quelque sorte volé aux individus, qui en définitive ne choisissent rien : leur seul moment de sociabilité leur est retiré, leur est masqué au sens propre du terme. Tout se passe comme si les économistes, Rawls et les théoriciens politiques proches de sa pensée, étaient hantés par une double terreur dont la racine est la même : terreur qu'on puisse reconnaître une réalité à la société, la considérer comme plus que la somme des individus qui la composent, qu'on puisse la désirer ou l'aimer ; terreur que les relations sociales puissent ne pas être totalement déterminées, déduites à partir de règles sur lesquelles les hommes se sont accordés de toute éternité, dans un moment de fiction qui n'a jamais vraiment existé. « Nous devons imaginer que ceux qui s'engagent dans la coopération sociale choisissent ensemble, par *un seul* acte collectif, les principes qui doivent fixer les droits et les devoirs de base et déterminer la répartition des avantages sociaux. [...] Un groupe de personnes doit décider, *une fois pour toutes*, ce qui, en son sein, doit être tenu pour juste ou injuste », écrit Rawls[393]. Tout se passe enfin comme si l'idéal de la vie en société, selon Rawls, consistait en ce qu'une fois les règles « choisies » l'ordre social tout entier (la hiérarchie, les chances, la répartition des biens) soit calculé automatiquement, comme par une machine.

La démarche de Rawls a le mérite de la systématicité : dispersion originelle des individus, conformément à toute la tradition économique ; contrat tenu pour seule manière de faire coexister des individus[394] ; société considérée comme agrégat[395] ; refus de reconnaître la société comme une réalité différente des individus, susceptible d'avoir des fins différentes des fins individuelles. Elle manque pourtant de cohérence.

Car Rawls accepte une certaine correction des inégalités sociales. Non point d'ailleurs qu'il ait pour idéal une réduction des inégalités : celles-ci ne sont critiquables que lorsque leur augmentation s'opère sans procurer le moindre gain aux défavorisés. Cependant, en indiquant que certaines inégalités sont injustes, Rawls accepte non seulement la vie en société, l'idée que celle-ci comporte des avantages, mais aussi l'idée que l'Etat peut aider à remédier à certaines de ces inégalités. Cette position nuancée lui permettra d'être enfin traduit en France, et surtout d'être abondamment commenté[396]. Néanmoins il n'a pas poussé la démarche à son terme, comme l'ont fait avant lui Hayek ou Friedmann, ou après lui Nozick ou d'autres représentants du courant que l'on a appelé libertarien ou néolibéral[397]. Ces auteurs ont en commun de reprendre les hypothèses et les réquisits de l'économie et de faire du type d'ordre que permet l'économie l'ordre le plus naturel ; c'est à dessein que Hayek utilise le terme de *nomos*, radical essentiel dans le vocable d'économie, pour en faire le modèle de l'ordre social : *nomos*, c'est la règle de droit, d'un droit naturel qui est également celui qui correspond à un ordre spontané[398]. Si la régulation sociale que décrit l'économie est la meilleure, c'est parce que l'ordre qui se déploie spontanément à partir du marché est un ordre naturel, presque biologique, résultat des actions des hommes et non de leurs desseins. D'où une remise en cause totale de l'Etat. Mais ce que les libertariens montrent, mieux que tout autre, c'est que l'ennemi intime de l'économie n'est pas, comme on pourrait le croire, l'Etat et ce qui l'accompagne, impôts, biens collectifs..., mais la politique en tant qu'elle nous oblige à vivre en société et à choisir ensemble la manière dont nous voulons le faire. Ainsi chez

Robert Nozick, où l'idée que seuls les individus existent,
que les droits individuels sont absolus et que la liberté
individuelle est totale, conduit à une marchandisation
généralisée, y compris de soi-même : comme si l'ordre
économique, qui ne conçoit de rapports sociaux que sous la
forme de l'échange réglé, de préférence marchand, trouvait
son terme absolu dans la transformation de toute chose en
marchandise ; c'est le prix de la liberté de l'individu et le
seul mode de reconnaissance d'autrui. Les libertariens
démontrent ainsi la justesse de l'analyse de Polanyi, qui
considère la transformation de toute la substance naturelle
et humaine de la société en marchandises[399] comme le
corollaire absolu du développement de l'économie.

Le devenir économique des sciences sociales

Elaborée comme moyen d'éviter à tout prix l'arbitraire
et la discussion sur les fins, l'économie porte en elle la
tendance à se présenter comme politique. Et, comme on l'a
vu, elle y parvient. Elle le fait également d'une manière
plus subtile, en absorbant peu à peu les principaux résultats
issus des « disciplines » originellement assises sur une
représentation différente de la société et en les intégrant
dans sa propre matrice, donc en imprégnant progressivement l'ensemble des sciences sociales, y compris les
sciences et les courants de pensée qui s'étaient construits en
s'opposant à elle. Ainsi l'institutionnalisme, qui s'était
clairement présenté, à ses débuts, comme un courant de
pensée farouchement opposé aux modes de raisonnement
de l'économie, et en particulier à l'idée que le contrat ou la
convention peuvent être premiers par rapport à l'organisation sociale, a-t-il vu toutes ses critiques peu à peu
réintégrées dans la théorie économique dite standard.
Depuis une vingtaine d'années, en France, plusieurs
« écoles » (dites respectivement de la régulation, de l'économie des conventions, de l'économie des institutions) se
sont appliquées à corriger les simplifications les plus

criantes de la théorie économique standard grâce aux résultats des recherches engagées en sociologie, en droit ou en anthropologie. On dispose aujourd'hui de nombreux modèles et de nombreuses théories économiques qui font une large place aux institutions, à l'histoire, aux conventions, aux accords implicites... Mais il est tout à fait extraordinaire que l'économie ait pris en compte ces éléments sans changer le moins du monde ses présupposés majeurs : les hypothèses sur la rationalité restent dans tous les modèles extrêmement restrictives ; il s'agit toujours d'individus cherchant à maximiser leur profit, d'égoïstes rationnels dont les seules modalités d'existence demeurent la production et la consommation. L'ensemble de la vie individuelle et sociale reste régi par ces deux modes d'être et il s'agit toujours pour l'économie de trouver la régulation générale de l'ensemble social qui permet de maximiser la production. Certes, les hypothèses sont beaucoup plus riches : ainsi les théories sur les salaires prennent-elles en compte les négociations, l'existence de syndicats, de collectifs... L'échange non marchand est également pris en compte : l'économie s'ouvre à la prise en considération du don et du contre-don [400]. Mais elle le fait sans révision de ses postulats de départ, ce qui aboutit à des résultats pour le moins surprenants : les travaux des anthropologues sur le don, issus de la tradition maussienne, sont ainsi retraités à partir des hypothèses de la microéconomie, en complète contradiction avec les ambitions et le type d'approche développés par l'ethnologie et l'anthropologie [401]. Il en va de même dans ce que l'on a appelé le « marxisme analytique », où les analyses marxistes sont réinterprétées dans le cadre de l'individualisme méthodologique [402]. L'institutionnalisme et le marxisme semblent donc avoir subi des transformations radicales au cours de leur exportation outre-Manche. L'institutionnalisme s'est coulé, aux Etats-Unis, dans le moule de l'individualisme et du pragmatisme, en particulier chez J. R. Commons [403]. D'une manière plus générale encore, l'institutionnalisme et le marxisme n'étant alors peut-être qu'un cas particulier d'un phénomène plus large, la sociologie elle-même, destinée à l'origine à analyser la société comme un tout, a largement intégré la méthode et les hypothèses de base de l'économie, sans toujours s'en rendre compte, mais par le simple fait qu'elle recourait massivement à la théorie des jeux ou aux méthodes dites du choix rationnel [404]. Il y a là une évolution majeure, la spécificité de l'économie se dissolvant à mesure que toutes les autres sciences sociales adoptent sa méthode. Sur cette évolution il nous faudra également réfléchir.

Car le plus grave n'est pas que les autres sciences adoptent la méthode ou la conception de la société de l'économie, mais que, ce faisant, elles prennent à leur compte la fin implicitement poursuivie par celle-ci. Comme le fait remarquer A. Sen, ce qui est gênant n'est pas tant que l'économie se dise indépendante de l'éthique, mais qu'elle fixe comme objectif aux sociétés, sous le vocable d'utilité, le seul bien-être, qu'elle ne définit d'ailleurs jamais [405]. Il est en effet extrêmement troublant que l'économie opère une série de valorisations implicites, un partage entre le bon et le mauvais que les économistes présentent ensuite comme des vérités : « S'il n'y avait pas de conseil à donner à la nation, il n'y aurait pas d'économistes. La seule attitude positive et scientifique consisterait pour l'économiste à considérer que le partage entre l'utile et l'inutile n'est pas de son ressort, mais de celui de la société entière », écrit un économiste [406]. Il nous faut réfléchir sur ce que l'économie nous oblige à valoriser aujourd'hui, sur son périmètre d'investigation lorsqu'elle effectue ses calculs et réalise des bilans coûts/avantages, sur ce qu'elle considère comme efficace, et nous nous rendrons compte que la rationalité qu'elle promeut est pour le moins limitée, sa conception de la richesse très réduite et son périmètre de calcul trop étroit : il fut une époque où il n'y avait de richesse que d'hommes [407]. Aujourd'hui, nous sommes prêts à consacrer trois cents milliards de francs à la politique familiale, c'est-à-dire à une opération dont la rentabilité ne se mesure que dans le long terme : cette dépense trouve en définitive sa justification dans la volonté de voir notre pays survivre. Pourquoi ne recourons-nous pas plus fréquemment à cette notion moins limitée de rentabilité ? Pourquoi ne parvenons-nous pas à élargir le périmètre de rentabilité ? Une population en bonne santé, capable de civisme et de coopération et soucieuse de paix est également désirable. L'économie mesure la rentabilité des investissements publics à l'aune d'une année. Elle oublie toujours de prendre en considération les moments de crise ou de guerre, qui ont pourtant été fréquents, où des milliers de vies humaines ont été sacrifiées : sa comptabilité est étriquée.

CHAPITRE IX

RÉINVENTER LA POLITIQUE :
SORTIR DU CONTRACTUALISME

Les sociétés occidentales industrialisées, qu'elles soient capitalistes ou ex-socialistes, traversent aujourd'hui une crise où leur capacité à constituer un lieu d'ancrage des identités individuelles est en jeu. Le bouleversement des ordres géopolitiques issus de la Seconde Guerre mondiale, la constitution d'ordres dits supranationaux tels que l'Europe ou encore l'existence d'un quasi-ordre mondial de l'économie, des échanges et des communications, à la fois sont très perturbateurs pour les individus et ouvrent la porte à des regroupements sur des bases différentes, religieuses, ethniques, nationalistes... La dissolution de l'ordre soviétique a ainsi ouvert le champ à des revendications visant à constituer des communautés sur des fondements de toute nature : la nation, d'abord, puis l'ethnie, puis la famille élargie. Où s'arrêtera la régression ? Comment empêcher qu'elle aille à l'infini et ne bute en dernier ressort sur l'individu ? Sur quel fondement, quelles ressemblances, quelle identité fonder une communauté de vie et de droits ? Au nom de quoi cette communauté est-elle acceptée ? Nos sociétés occidentales « capitalistes » sont également confrontées à ces questions. Elles sont secouées par la même crise identitaire, la même peur des ordres supranationaux, la même difficulté pour chaque individu à se reconnaître lié à plusieurs dizaines de millions d'autres personnes, la même interrogation sur la nature du lien social, sur ce qui fonde notre coappartenance et sur ce à quoi celle-ci nous oblige. Notre société est menacée de devenir une société duale ou une société balkanisée, segmentée en de multiples groupes coexistant soit pacifiquement, soit dans une forme de guerre civile larvée, chacun ayant ses habitus, sa religion, ses écoles, sa protection sociale, ses ghettos. Nous nous trouvons à un moment décisif parce que tout est possible : que nos sociétés parviennent à être des ensembles structurés, où les individus trouvent leur place — c'est-à-dire où puissent s'épanouir leur liberté, leurs projets, leurs convictions —, mais où en même temps cette coappartenance constitue pour eux quelque chose d'essentiel, une part de leur réalité — des instruments et des institutions matérialisant l'existence et l'épaisseur de ce lien social ; ou qu'elles n'y parviennent pas et laissent se développer en leur sein des comportements qui les mineraient et les condamneraient à terme.

De la nécessité de disposer d'une philosophie politique

Les questions les plus urgentes que doit résoudre notre société touchent au lien social ; elles ont toutes à voir avec la conception la plus intime que nous nous faisons chacun de la nature du lien qui nous unit à nos concitoyens. Car, parmi les questions essentielles auxquelles nous devons répondre, figurent celle de la cohésion sociale (comment allons-nous l'assurer, la garantir ?), celle de l'exclusion (quelles mesures devons-nous prendre pour qu'une partie de plus en plus grande de la population ne soit pas privée de travail, de logement, de soins et ne soit pas exclue de la vie sociale, faute de pouvoir exercer ses droits fondamentaux ?), celle des inégalités (quelle est la dose d'inégalités supportable pour une société ?), même s'il n'est pas encore de bon ton de la poser aujourd'hui. Personne n'ose dire que c'est du lien social et de notre conception de la société qu'il s'agit. Sans doute les discours politiques parviennent-ils à mettre en évidence un certain nombre de problèmes ou de dysfonctionnements (rôle de l'école, du chômage, des banlieues, de la protection sociale, de l'exclusion), chacun faisant l'objet d'analyses spécifiques. Mais il n'apparaît pas encore clairement qu'il ne s'agit là que des différents aspects d'une seule et même question : notre représentation de la société, notre conception du lien social nous permettent-elles de répondre aux risques de dissolution de la société, à l'aggravation des inégalités et à la marginalisation d'un nombre de plus en plus grand de personnes ? La conception de la société et du lien social qui est la nôtre permet-elle d'asseoir une société solide, capable de résister à l'instauration d'un ordre européen et d'intégrer les corporatismes, les poussées individualistes, les tentations des petits groupes identitaires, sans pourtant avoir besoin de recourir à des concepts ambigus — celui de nation, par exemple — qui, bien souvent, ne parviennent à fonder l'attachement des individus que sur la passion et le sentiment ou sur des éléments prétendument « naturels », comme la langue, le folklore, les habitus, la religion... ? Plus concrètement encore, il s'agit de savoir si notre conception de la société est telle qu'elle fonde des droits et des devoirs spécifiquement sociaux, de se demander quel type d'obligations implique notre coappartenance, comment s'articulent précisément les rapports de l'individu et de la société et qui peut en décider. Mais nous n'osons pas encore formuler la question dans les termes qui permettraient de la résoudre.

C'est là sans doute que nous fait défaut une véritable philosophie politique capable d'expliciter les représentations que la société se fait d'elle-même. Nous manquons d'une théorie politique, et donc de l'occasion de disposer d'un miroir qui nous permettrait de comprendre comment nous envisageons la nature de notre lien et notre avenir ; miroir qui nous permettrait également de débattre, peut-être de combattre, de faire de la politique enfin. Nous n'en disposons pas, non pas parce que, dans notre pays, aucun penseur ne serait capable de théoriser l'air du temps, mais parce que aucun n'ose aujourd'hui poser cette question, trop chargée d'interprétations, de luttes, de contresens, de rendez-vous historiques manqués. Nous ne possédons pas, en particulier, une théorie politique qui nous donnerait les moyens de penser la société comme une réalité à part entière, un ensemble ayant une valeur et un bien propres. Dès lors, nous ne pouvons pas non plus rendre légitime l'utilisation d'instruments qui nous permettraient de remédier aux inégalités, de renforcer la cohésion sociale ou de rendre plus effective la recherche de ce que nous considérons comme le bien de la société. La Révolution française avait une théorie politique légitimant des interventions de la société sur elle-même [408]. Malgré (ou à cause de) sa croyance foncière en l'individu, elle avait reconnu la responsabilité de la société à l'égard d'un certain nombre de maux sociaux et en avait déduit un mode d'intervention sociale et une véritable politique. On peut dire également que le XIXᵉ siècle a eu sa théorie de la société, individualiste, qui l'a conduit à refuser l'intervention sociale au nom de la prévoyance [409]. Mais le XXᵉ siècle ne dispose pas d'une théorie politique capable de fonder en raison des interventions de la société sur elle-même. Cette absence nous interdit de justifier conceptuellement une intervention de l'Etat qui aurait pour objectif de renforcer la cohésion sociale. La fraternité ou la solidarité n'ont jamais été véritablement fondées en raison, sauf dans des théories sociologiques qui — comble du paradoxe — attendaient de la division et de la spécialisation des fonctions sociales un surcroît quasi automatique de solidarité [410]. Notre Etat-providence ne possède pas de fondement conceptuel : ses interventions sont bien plutôt issues d'une pratique qui s'est greffée sur une représentation figée de la société. C'est d'ailleurs ce qui explique le caractère profondément ambigu d'un certain nombre de nos systèmes sociaux [411]

Il faut relire les discours de Pierre Laroque [412] au moment de la création d'un grand système de sécurité sociale ou les ouvrages d'Henri Bartoli pour voir combien les esprits étaient prêts, à l'époque, à passer à une société plus solidaire, plus attentive à sa cohésion, à la répartition de ses biens et à la discussion publique. Mais, pour de multiples raisons, dont la moindre n'était pas ce qui s'était passé et continuait de se passer en URSS (au nom d'une conception marxiste-léniniste de l'Etat et au nom du bien supérieur de la société), une véritable théorie politique, reconnaissant à la société une valeur et une existence propres, n'a pas pu être élaborée. Notre Etat-providence, c'est-à-dire les interventions menées par l'Etat pour corriger la répartition primaire des revenus et des biens, est donc toujours en attente d'un fondement théorique. Notre conception de l'Etat-providence est accidentelle et arbitraire ; elle résulte de la seule pratique qui a pu se développer à ce point uniquement parce qu'elle rencontrait une doctrine économique complémentaire : on pouvait consacrer des sommes importantes à combattre les inégalités et à renforcer la cohésion sociale, car cela favorisait la croissance. Mais, dès lors que les évolutions économiques et la théorie économique ont ébranlé la théorie keynésienne, c'en était fait de l'Etat-providence. Les critiques qui se développent depuis maintenant une quinzaine d'années ne viennent donc pas uniquement d'un refroidissement des passions de l'après-guerre ou d'une interrogation sur la nécessité de réduire les inégalités [413]. Elles viennent plus profondément de ce que les interventions de l'Etat-providence n'ont jamais été légitimées par une théorie politique adéquate, au point que la moindre critique, par exemple économique, suffit à les remettre en cause.

Communauté ou société ?

Pourquoi ne disposons-nous pas d'une telle théorie ? Parce que nous ne sommes pas parvenus à sortir de l'opposition stérile entre deux traditions, deux visions de la société également anachroniques, l'une considérant la société comme une simple agrégation d'individus (*societas, Gesellschaft*), l'autre comme une communauté dans laquelle le tout prime sur les parties (*universitas, Gemeinschaft* [414]). La première, issue du XVIIIe siècle et qui s'exprime dans l'économie, est restée en quelque sorte tétanisée par l'émergence de l'individu. La découverte de celui-ci a été si radicale que cette tradition ne peut pas imaginer la société autrement qu'issue d'un contrat volontaire entre les individus. Non seulement la société est l'œuvre des individus, mais elle n'existe que pour permettre à ceux-ci de poursuivre en paix leurs fins : elle n'est qu'un cadre assurant que l'ordre naturel sera en mesure de se déployer. La théorie politique, qui voit dans la société le résultat d'un contrat, et l'économie vont de pair au XVIIIe siècle : l'économie est en quelque sorte la théorie politique la plus radicale, celle qui prend le plus en compte le risque d'insociable sociabilité [415] qui oblige les individus à vivre ensemble en les incitant à poursuivre leurs fins propres et n'imagine comme solution, pour faire coexister des individus non désireux de l'état social, que l'appât de l'échange mutuellement avantageux. Il y a là une constellation historique très précise dont nous avons déjà énuméré les éléments constitutifs.

Cette tradition est très exactement opposée à l'idée antique selon laquelle la communauté politique est première, précède tout autre groupement humain, et, parce qu'elle forme un tout, possède un bien qui lui est propre. Aristote, dans *La Politique*, définissait cette conception en ces termes : « Nous voyons que toute cité est une sorte de communauté et que toute communauté est constituée en vue d'un certain bien. [...] Cette communauté est celle qui est appelée cité, c'est la communauté politique[416]. » Pour Aristote, l'homme ne peut vivre en dehors de la cité ; tous les autres groupements humains ne se conçoivent que par rapport à elle. En elle seulement l'homme trouve son plein épanouissement et déploie ses véritables facultés humaines, la raison et la parole. La cité est le fait premier, celui qui donne son existence à l'homme, dont la définition est d'être un animal politique, c'est-à-dire un animal qui ne développe son humanité qu'en étant avec les autres dans un relation de coappartenance, et qui n'est rien en dehors de celle-ci.

Les Temps modernes, dont tout le monde s'accorde à situer le début avec l'émergence de l'individu, se sont voulus radicalement opposés à la conception antique : il n'y a ni communauté, donc ni bien social, ni fins qui pourraient être communes à l'ensemble des individus. Cette idée, très fortement exprimée par Benjamin Constant en France par exemple, deviendra par la suite un lieu commun[417] : la conception antique de la politique est définitivement impossible. L'apparition de l'individu et de sa liberté infinie a rendu impensable une société qui serait autre chose qu'une association bien réglée d'individus. La communauté n'est qu'un mythe. Il n'y a ni bien social, ni politique au sens d'une recherche ensemble de la bonne vie en société ou de la bonne société. Nous ne pouvons pas vouloir de bien commun parce que nos sociétés sont construites sur la pluralité irréductible des individus, des conceptions et des biens poursuivis. L'accord de tous les individus sur une unique fin n'est pas envisageable. Rawls exprime parfaitement ce point de vue lorsqu'il indique que, dans sa démarche, le juste précède le bien. Sa définition « procédurale » de la justice exprime la même idée : nous ne pouvons avoir qu'une conception formelle de la justice, sinon il faudrait comprendre que le bien précède le juste et qu'il existe donc un bien susceptible d'être considéré comme tel par tous les individus. Or cela est impossible. Il ne peut y avoir de bien en dehors des biens multiples considérés comme tels par chaque individu [418]. Reconnaître la possibilité d'un Bien commun, ce serait risquer de négliger les aspirations d'une partie de la société, et donc risquer de l'opprimer. Reconnaître que la société peut être une communauté et qu'il existe un bien commun, c'est toujours risquer l'oppression de l'individu. Alors que les Temps modernes s'appuient précisément sur la découverte que la liberté de l'individu est infinie. Pour cette tradition, toute entreprise visant à chercher un bien commun à l'ensemble des individus est interprétée comme une volonté de supprimer la liberté individuelle. C'est pourquoi la politique se réduit alors au minimum : elle se borne à garantir le bon fonctionnement de l'ordre naturel, dont les lois sont déterminées par l'économie.

Cette tradition, fondamentalement anglo-saxonne, n'a cessé de soumettre à la critique et de soupçonner toutes les théories qui tentaient d'ériger la société en une réalité indépendante des individus et supérieure à ceux-ci. Elle s'est en particulier dressée contre les tentatives allemandes qui visaient à renouer avec la conception antique de la politique et avec la notion de communauté. La tradition allemande a, en effet, profondément entretenu l'idéal d'une conception communautaire de la vie en société. Ancrée dans la philosophie, la théologie et la vision juridique du haut Moyen Age, cette conception a connu un regain de faveur au début du XIXᵉ siècle, lorsque Schelling, Hegel et Hölderlin firent du retour à la belle totalité antique leur cri de ralliement. Ces philosophes souhaitaient rompre avec l'individualisme qui avait caractérisé la période précédente et réconcilier l'individu avec la communauté politique, en le réintégrant dans celle-ci, dès lors fondée sur d'autres bases. Le XIXᵉ siècle allemand a été, en philosophie, celui de l'espoir en une communauté politique retrouvée. En cela, les philosophes allemands rejoignaient la nostalgie de Rousseau pour la cité grecque ou la vertu civique romaine. Mais, plus que Rousseau, les Allemands souhaitaient opérer une véritable conciliation de l'individu et de la communauté, surmonter le déchirement qui s'était, selon eux, opéré, depuis l'Empire romain et le christianisme, au sein même de l'individu entre l'intérêt personnel et les devoirs du citoyen.

Ces tentatives ont toujours été considérées avec beaucoup de méfiance par les Anglo-Saxons et toujours condamnées, en particulier lorsque la révolution russe se recommanda de Marx et de Hegel pour asseoir sa conception de l'Etat et de la société [419]. La tradition anglo-saxonne n'a eu de cesse de démontrer que les théories de la communauté quelles qu'elles soient portent toujours en elles le risque de l'étouffement de l'individu et du totalitarisme. Elle a pris prétexte des errances historiques pour condamner en bloc les diverses représentations politiques de la société comme une totalité, qu'il s'agisse des efforts visant à concilier individu et principe d'unité ou qu'il s'agisse des conceptions les plus nationalistes, holistes ou totalitaires [420]. Il est vrai qu'une partie de la tradition allemande à laquelle nous avons déjà fait allusion est plus proche de l'*universitas* thomiste que de la *societas* moderne. Elle pense l'ordre comme d'abord issu d'un principe supérieur : de la même façon que, chez Aristote, l'idée de communauté ou de cité préexiste, d'une certaine façon, à l'individu, au couple, à la famille, il existe dans la philosophie allemande de la communauté, y compris chez Hegel, un certain nombre d'expressions qui prêtent à confusion et dont l'ambiguïté demeure extrêmement gênante : elles peuvent en effet laisser à penser que le bien de la société peut être atteint au mépris des désirs des individus. Chez un certain nombre d'auteurs allemands, en effet, la notion de communauté s'appuie sur une vision parfois hiérarchique, ou organique, voire également nationaliste de la société. La notion d'esprit du peuple, de *Volksgeist*, est ainsi employée de manière parfois ambiguë.

Mais une grande partie de la philosophie allemande du xixᵉ siècle a également consisté en un gigantesque effort pour intégrer l'individu dans le tout social selon un ordre qui ne soit ni celui de la simple contiguïté ni celui de l'attraction d'un principe extérieur. La philosophie allemande possède une longue tradition de pensée de l'ordre à partir d'un centre, d'une unité qui préexiste et qui donne sens aux parties. Elle fait souvent place à un principe interne, l'âme, l'esprit, la conscience commune ou la morale incarnée, qui imprègne et détermine tellement les individus qu'il leur semble antérieur : l'individu ne peut ainsi jamais se concevoir indépendamment de l'histoire, de la langue, des institutions politiques, de la morale incarnée, du lieu où il se trouve. C'est dans cette mesure que l'on peut dire que le tout préexiste aux parties. Il n'y a rien de plus éloigné de cette tradition que l'idée d'un ordre qui se construirait par collage ou agrégation et permettrait néanmoins d'obtenir une unité. Leibniz, l'un des premiers, avait donné cet objectif à la philosophie allemande en réfléchissant sur la notion d'ordre et en proposant son système des « monades » : il s'agissait déjà de faire naître un ordre interne et substantiel à partir d'éléments radicalement différents et isolés. Leibniz y était parvenu par une théorie de l'expression, imaginant que chaque monade (ou individu) exprime, de son propre point de vue, toutes les autres. S'il est vrai que les efforts de la philosophie allemande de l'époque ne vont pas sans écarts vers des théories qui ne parviennent pas à se détacher du nationalisme ou du holisme, il n'en reste pas moins que cette tentative, traduite en termes politiques par Hegel, est sans précédent.

En frappant d'un même anathème les tentations nationalistes d'un Fichte, les conceptions juridiques qui confondent responsable et chef, les représentations de la société comme un tout hiérarchisé où les relations sont de dépendance, et des tentatives comme celles de Hegel pour parvenir à une conciliation supérieure, la tradition anglosaxonne, confortée par les deux expériences totalitaires qui se réclamaient de penseurs allemands, a réussi à faire croire

que toute représentation de la société dérogeant à l'hypothèse de l'association portait en elle la mort de l'individu.
Elle a également laissé penser que la seule alternative était
la suivante : d'un côté, une société d'individus libres et
égaux, liés par l'échange marchand, régie par l'économie et
laissant se développer les inégalités ; de l'autre, une société
holiste, unie mais hiérarchisée, régie par la politique et
pour laquelle l'individu n'est rien. Louis Dumont est
l'auteur français qui a le plus approfondi cette opposition
en la résumant ainsi : l'économie est le type de régulation
sociale qui succède à la politique. La politique est le
principe d'ordre qui régit les sociétés avant l'économie, un
principe d'ordre holiste, où les relations de personne à
personne sont structurantes, où les rapports sont nécessairement hiérarchiques. L'économie est le type d'ordre, au
contraire, des sociétés individualistes et égalitaires, quoi
qu'il en soit en réalité de cette égalité. Sortir de l'économie,
c'est retomber dans la subordination, la dépendance personnelle, un type d'ordre où les individus ne sont pas
considérés comme libres et égaux. Par là, Louis Dumont a
également considérablement contribué à conforter l'assimilation entre société pensée comme un tout et risques
encourus par l'individu, omettant de souligner combien les
efforts théoriques pour penser l'unité sociale se distin-
guaient les uns des autres en profondeur[421]. Il a conforté
l'opposition grossière entre égalitarisme et hiérarchie.
L'idée la plus répandue aujourd'hui est donc que nous
avons le choix entre d'un côté, les inégalités et de l'autre,
l'oppression de l'individu, et qu'entre les deux il vaut
évidemment mieux choisir les inégalités. En témoigne cette
phrase de Louis Dumont : « Les faits que nous avons
devant nous sont suffisamment lourds pour justifier une
réflexion. Ils montrent que jusqu'ici l'alternative entre la
richesse comme fin et des formes forcées, pathologiques de
subordination est notre lot. C'est ici, selon toute vraisem-
blance, que se noue le drame du totalitarisme. C'est ici en
particulier que les doctrinaires généreux qui ont prétendu

nous tirer de " l'individualisme possessif " font figure
d'apprentis-sorciers [422]. » Telle est la représentation commune sur laquelle nous continuons à vivre aujourd'hui.
Tout se passe de surcroît comme si l'effondrement de
l'empire soviétique et la confirmation de ce qu'était vraiment cet ordre n'avaient fait que renforcer nos convictions
sur l'impossibilité d'un ordre autre que l'ordre naturel qui
s'appuie sur la liberté individuelle. Comme si la liberté
individuelle était le défi de notre société.

Notre horizon indépassable est-il la défense de la liberté individuelle ?

C'est ainsi que se présentent, quoi qu'elles en aient, les
théories de Rawls ou de ses successeurs : le défi actuel des
sociétés démocratiques occidentales serait avant tout de se
protéger contre une possible remise en cause de la liberté
individuelle. Il suffit pour s'en persuader de relire le
chapitre V de la *Théorie de la justice* consacré à la critique
de l'utilitarisme. Celui-ci est critiqué non pas parce qu'il
pourrait conduire à une répartition inégalitaire de biens,
mais avant tout parce qu'il ne fait pas suffisamment de
place à la liberté individuelle : « La pluralité des personnes
n'est donc pas prise au sérieux par l'utilitarisme », écrit
Rawls en conclusion, remettant ainsi en cause, au nom d'un
individualisme supérieur, l'individualisme primaire de l'utilitarisme [423]. Celui-ci porte toujours en lui, selon Rawls, le
risque de sacrifier la personne, la liberté infinie de l'individu au bien social. L'utilitarisme est tellement obnubilé
par l'augmentation du bien collectif qu'il est prêt à sacrifier
quelques individus à cette augmentation. Ce que Rawls
remet donc profondément en question, c'est la possibilité
pour une société d'augmenter un prétendu bien social en
faisant fi de la liberté individuelle. D'où son extrême
précaution à bien distinguer deux moments ou deux aspects
du système social : « Ainsi, nous distinguerons entre les

aspects du système social qui définissent et garantissent
l'égalité des libertés de base pour chacun et les aspects qui
spécifient et établissent les inégalités sociales et économiques[424]. » Cette distinction est essentielle. Ce qui est
absolument premier, c'est donc ce que Rawls appelle les
libertés de base : les libertés politiques (droit de vote et
droit d'occuper un poste public), la liberté d'expression, de
réunion, liberté de pensée et de conscience, la liberté de la
personne (protection à l'égard de l'oppression psychologique et de l'agression physique), droit de propriété personnelle... qui doivent être égales pour tous. Quant à la
répartition des richesses et des revenus, elle n'a pas besoin
d'être égale, elle doit simplement être à l'avantage de
chacun. Et, comme l'explique Rawls, l'ordre existant entre
les deux principes de base est lexical, c'est-à-dire que le
premier est antérieur au second. Les atteintes aux libertés
de base égales pour tous, protégées par le premier principe,
ne peuvent donc pas être justifiées ou compensées par des
avantages économiques ou sociaux plus grands[425]. Toutes
choses que les analyses politiques du XVIIIe siècle avaient
déjà démontrées. Avec ce raisonnement, nous sommes
ramenés un siècle en arrière.

Rawls s'attache à démontrer l'intangibilité des libertés
individuelles. Aucune inégalité économique ou sociale ne
peut être diminuée, dit-il, si, en la diminuant, on attente
aux libertés individuelles. Rawls fait comme si Marx n'avait
pas existé, comme si les analyses développées depuis le
milieu du XIXe siècle sur la différence entre libertés réelles
et libertés formelles n'avaient eu aucun écho, comme si
Beveridge n'avait jamais dit qu'il ne peut y avoir de
véritable liberté si les besoins fondamentaux des individus
ne sont pas assurés, c'est-à-dire si les politiques des
revenus, de l'emploi et de la santé ne viennent pas rendre
réelles ces libertés. Rawls théorise donc sans doute l'Etat-
providence, c'est-à-dire l'idée qu'il est du devoir de l'Etat
de corriger les inégalités les plus criantes provoquées par le
processus économique et qu'il lui revient d'assurer une

redistribution des richesses issues de ce processus ; mais il persiste à se référer à une société conçue comme une agrégation d'individus, poursuivant chacun leurs fins et produisant à cette occasion des inégalités, que l'Etat viendra corriger sans cependant attenter à la structure des incitations individuelles ou à la liberté des individus. Rawls théorise la différence entre l'économique et le social, mais il ne nous donne pas les moyens de penser la société autrement que comme *societas* ; il ne permet pas d'éviter qu'un jour les interventions de l'Etat soient remises en cause précisément au nom de cet ordre naturel qui est premier. La théorie de la justice ne parvient pas à fonder en raison l'unité de la société. Tout se passe comme si la théorie de la justice était une énorme machine destinée à protéger définitivement l'individu contre les interventions intempestives de la société ou de l'Etat, et, en particulier, contre cette méthode rusée qui, au nom du bien collectif, risque de sacrifier l'individu. Comme l'explique de façon très convaincante J.-P. Dupuy[426], Rawls — ainsi que la tradition de pensée à laquelle il appartient — fait comme si la reconnaissance d'un bien social impliquait le « sacrifice » (c'est bien le mot employé) nécessaire de l'individu. Il n'y a pas de place, dans cette tradition, pour une véritable pensée de la société.

Pour en finir avec le contractualisme

La critique de la démarche contractualiste a été réalisée depuis longtemps, magistralement par Hegel[427] dès le début du XIXe siècle, et par les sociologues, ethnologues, anthropologues ensuite. La critique essentielle consiste à dire que l'état de nature est en effet une fiction, dangereuse de surcroît : les individus ne sont jamais seuls et auto-nomes, ils ne peuvent pas être rationnels avant d'être entrés en société, il est absurde de considérer des individus « tout faits » et ne vivant pas en société. Plus encore, les

individus sont toujours déjà en société, toujours déjà
pénétrés de leurs relations avec les autres, toujours déjà en
train de parler avec eux. Quant à l'idée d'une société
naissant du contrat, elle est également indéfendable, puisqu'elle fait croire que des individus dont la raison et le
langage sont parfaitement développés (mais cela dans la
plus totale solitude) pourraient un jour décider de s'associer pour bénéficier des avantages de la coopération
sociale. Qu'elle ait été largement utilisée au XVIIIe siècle
pour mettre en évidence que la société était œuvre humaine
et non divine, cela se comprend aisément ; mais il est
inquiétant que cette fiction demeure en usage aujourd'hui,
surtout lorsqu'elle concerne la rencontre originelle et la
décision de s'associer. On n'a pas suffisamment insisté, en
France, sur le formidable anachronisme qui entache la
pensée rawlsienne quand elle recourt à un concept dont on
comprend certes l'intérêt (mettre en évidence le fait que les
individus doivent d'une certaine manière acquiescer à leur
existence en société), mais qui n'a plus aucune valeur,
même méthodologique, aujourd'hui. L'idée même d'un
contrat social entre des individus qui ne sont pas encore en
société et décident des modalités de celle-ci est profondément fausse et à l'origine de toutes les autres erreurs : c'est
d'elle que vient l'illusion que les individus continuent de
poursuivre leurs fins et que la société n'est là que pour les y
aider. C'est d'elle que naît l'idée d'individus pleinement
libres qui sacrifient une partie de cette liberté lors de
l'entrée en société, ou encore celle qu'ils pourraient peut-
être arbitrer entre ce qu'ils donnent et ce qu'ils gagnent...

Cette représentation n'est pas seulement fausse, elle se
révèle de surcroît incapable de fonder quelque obligation
que ce soit. Telle est la seconde grande critique que Hegel
lui adresse ; le contrat ne peut régir la société politique car
cela signifierait que le lien substantiel de cette dernière
dépend d'un accord arbitraire entre individus : « Le
contrat, accord dépendant du libre arbitre et portant sur
une chose contingente, renferme aussi la position d'une

volonté accidentelle[428]. » Le contrat n'est que l'entente entre deux ou plusieurs individus qui décident arbitrairement de s'accorder sur l'acquisition d'une chose ou la réalisation d'une opération. Dans libre arbitre, il y a arbitraire. Le contrat repose donc sur un choix arbitraire alors que la société doit, elle, pouvoir reposer sur quelque chose de plus solide : elle précède toujours tout contrat. La société ne peut pas être le résultat d'une construction et d'un accord entre les individus. La théorie contractualiste, parce qu'elle conçoit la société comme le résultat de l'accord arbitraire entre les individus, est incapable de fonder l'obligation, car ce que l'individu a décidé arbitrairement, il peut le renier, ce que l'individu a fait, il peut le défaire. La troisième grande critique à l'encontre de cette conception a été développée, dans des termes proches, par Hegel et Tocqueville. La vérité d'une telle société, disent-ils, c'est l'individualisme et le caractère arbitraire, non fondé, donc éminemment fragile du lien social. Avec des individus, on n'obtient jamais davantage que des individus. Avec une multiplicité sans principe d'ordre interne, on n'obtient jamais de l'unité. La vérité de ce genre de société, c'est le droit du plus fort ; si la société n'est que le lieu où s'épanouissent les intérêts particuliers des individus, l'Etat lui-même n'est qu'un instrument au service de ces intérêts : il apparaît peu à peu comme l'instrument des désirs des individus, il est confisqué par des groupes de pression, il n'existe plus que pour défendre la propriété individuelle[429]. L'Etat n'est qu'une association d'individus qui finiront par se trouver prisonniers du groupe de pression le plus fort. La fin d'une telle société, c'est donc le retour au droit naturel, au droit du plus fort, et en l'occurrence du plus riche. Mais une société qui ne se reconnaît d'autre fin que les fins des individus qui la composent n'a pas besoin d'Etat. Sa fin, c'est la dissolution totale du lien social, dont sont victimes les perdants de la course à la richesse. Telle est la société civile décrite par Hegel.

Reconnaître l'individu, préserver le lien social

Hegel et Tocqueville, aussi éloignées que soient leurs pensées, développent pourtant la même analyse : pour les deux auteurs, la société civile (ou bourgeoise) représente la destruction de l'ancien ordre politique, féodal et aristocratique, et l'avènement d'un nouvel ordre, plein de promesses, car fondé sur l'idée de liberté individuelle et d'égalité. L'un et l'autre s'accordent sur le contenu émancipatoire [430] de la société civile qui a permis l'universalisation des droits de l'homme. L'un et l'autre reconnaissent que les Temps modernes se caractérisent par la reconnaissance de l'individu [431] et que la société doit faire une place majeure à celui-ci, et les deux portent cependant le même diagnostic : en rester à l'individu, c'est accepter la dissolution de toute solidarité sociale et ne pas parvenir à reconstruire un ordre qui instaurerait une nouvelle solidarité. Le défi des Temps modernes consiste donc à reconnaître l'individu tout en l'intégrant dans une communauté de droits et de devoirs qui ne se résume pas au simple échange marchand.

Ces deux auteurs s'y efforceront, de manière différente. Hegel tente de dépasser le point de vue abstrait qui voit dans l'individu et le contrat l'essence de la société : un tel individu est abstrait ; le véritable individu est celui qui s'incarne dans une communauté et dans un Etat. C'est seulement dans la communauté politique que l'individu peut trouver son accomplissement [432]. Quant à Tocqueville, il imagine une société démocratique allant de pair avec une conception communautaire de la liberté. L'étape de la liberté négative doit être dépassée et l'individu intégré dans un ordre supérieur, une communauté où sa liberté prendra tout son sens [433]. Chez les deux auteurs, la liberté individuelle doit donc être, certes, pleinement reconnue, mais également harmonieusement intégrée dans une communauté. La société peut avoir ses propres fins.

Le prétexte de la liberté individuelle

Car la thèse selon laquelle une société ne pourrait plus aujourd'hui avoir de bien commun sans opprimer l'individu repose sur un abus de langage : la reconnaissance de la société comme un ensemble ayant une réalité différente de celle de tous les individus qui la composent ne mène pas forcément au « sacrifice » de ceux-ci, comme le reconnaît bien Isaiah Berlin, l'un des philosophes contemporains qui ont poussé le plus loin la réflexion sur la liberté individuelle et la vie en société : « A mon avis, il serait souhaitable d'instaurer dans tous les pays un système unique d'enseignement primaire et secondaire, ne serait-ce que pour en finir avec les inégalités de statut social que crée ou que favorise l'existence d'une hiérarchie des écoles dans certains pays occidentaux, notamment le mien. Si l'on me demandait pourquoi, je répondrais [...] : le droit à l'égalité sociale en tant que telle ; les maux engendrés par les inégalités de statut social dues à un système où les ressources financières et la position sociale des parents sont plus déterminantes que les capacités et les besoins des enfants ; l'idéal de solidarité ; favoriser le développement physique et intellectuel du plus grand nombre, et pas seulement des privilégiés ; et plus particulièrement permettre à un maximum d'enfants d'exercer leur liberté de choix, que l'égalité à l'école ne pourra qu'accroître. Si l'on me disait que ceci constituerait une atteinte sérieuse à la liberté des parents de choisir le type d'enseignement qu'ils désirent pour leurs enfants, le type d'environnement intellectuel, religieux, social ou économique dans lequel ils souhaitent les voir grandir, je n'écarterais pas cette objection d'un revers de main. Je répondrais que, lorsque d'authentiques valeurs entrent dans un conflit, il faut faire des choix. En l'occurrence, le conflit se situe ici entre plusieurs exigences : préserver la liberté des parents de déterminer le type d'éducation qu'ils souhaitent pour leurs enfants, satisfaire d'autres besoins sociaux et, enfin, créer les conditions qui permettront à ceux qui en sont privés d'exercer les droits (la liberté de choisir) qu'ils possèdent juridiquement mais dont ils ne peuvent faire usage[434]. »

Quant à l'idée selon laquelle il serait imposible à nos sociétés de concevoir un bien commun parce que les sociétés modernes se caractérisent par la multiplicité des points de vue et des convictions des individus qui la composent, elle est également abusive. Lorsque Rawls soutient cette idée, il pense essentiellement aux convictions religieuses, aux croyances philosophiques, aux modes de vie, etc. Mais lorsque l'on parle du bien social, il s'agit de tout autre chose. En effet, il n'est pas question d'obliger toute une société à adopter telle religion, tel point de vue philosophique ou tel mode de vie. Il n'est nul besoin d'avoir les mêmes convictions religieuses pour décider ensemble de la manière dont la richesse doit être répartie, ce que l'on considère comme richesse, comment doit s'organiser le système de santé, qui doit payer les impôts et selon quels principes, comment l'éducation doit être organisée, comment le territoire doit être aménagé, jusqu'où on doit combattre la pollution, selon quel principe les entreprises doivent être gérées... La pluralité des convictions intimes n'est donc en aucune façon un obstacle à la recherche en commun et au débat sur les fins sociales. Il va de soi que la reconnaissance d'un bien social peut entraîner des obligations pour les individus. Mais nous devons peut-être oser reconnaître aujourd'hui que la bonne vie en société a un prix et une valeur pour l'individu et que certains de ses désirs (et non de ses libertés individuelles) peuvent être limités du fait de la vie sociale. Car il ne nous est rien donné d'autre. Nous sommes toujours déjà des êtres sociaux et mieux vaut tenter de construire un type de société capable de concilier au plus haut point la double aspiration au développement de la liberté individuelle et à la densité du lien social. Il nous faut donc aujourd'hui repartir des acquis des théories qui défendent la liberté individuelle. Certes, celle-ci doit être inscrite dans les textes et constituer la première de toutes les valeurs. Mais ensuite, il reste à la théorie politique à garantir l'unité sociale. C'est ce qu'avait tenté Hegel et qu'il n'a pas réussi.

L'échec de Hegel

Pourquoi revenir à Hegel ? Tout d'abord parce qu'il est l'un des seuls théoriciens politiques à avoir mis en évidence que le problème des sociétés modernes était de concilier la liberté individuelle et la communauté, et à avoir construit les instruments de cette conciliation. Il est le penseur politique qui a le mieux reconnu que le principe des Temps modernes était l'individu et qui a le mieux mis en évidence que si ce principe ne parvenait pas à s'incarner dans une communauté, nos sociétés couraient à leur perte. Il a également tenté de trouver une troisième voie, au-delà de l'atomisme et du holisme, sans tomber dans le nationalisme. Il est ainsi parvenu à reconnaître l'économie comme science des échanges marchands de la société civile bourgeoise, tout en la circonscrivant et en la subordonnant à la politique, art d'un type d'ordre supérieur. De plus, il se situe à un moment historique majeur, parce qu'il connaît et intègre la réflexion de l'économie politique anglaise et les tentations nationalistes ou communautaristes réactionnaires de son pays. Ce faisant, il a compris qu'il fallait à la fois prendre en compte la sphère des intérêts individuels et de l'échange marchand pour fonder la société politique, mais également que cette dernière devait s'appuyer non seulement sur une histoire, une langue, un esprit, mais surtout sur des institutions politiques, des droits, des devoirs, des ordres. Enfin, il a surtout montré qu'il existait une relation dialectique et de causalité réciproque entre la représentation d'une société comme communauté et l'Etat. C'est dire que si l'unité de la société ne s'incarne pas dans un Etat, alors elle risque toujours de se confondre soit avec

l'ordre économique « naturel », soit avec l'ordre holiste
« naturel », soit avec l'ordre national (géographique, historique et linguistique) « naturel ». Seul l'Etat met la société
à distance d'elle-même, lui représente son unité à travers
un ensemble d'institutions et d'instruments divers et lui
donne véritablement son unité. Seul un Etat peut représenter l'unité symbolique d'une nation et fonder celle-ci en
raison, soutient Hegel ; lui seul peut l'asseoir non pas sur le
sentiment mais sur des institutions. L'individu appartient
toujours déjà à une communauté politique qui lui donne
son sens et l'imprègne toujours déjà ainsi que les diverses
communautés naturelles ou artificielles qui se déploient en
son sein. L'individu participe de ce fait à plusieurs ordres
dans lesquels il trouve son ou ses identités : la sphère du
couple, celle de la famille, la sphère économique, celle de
la représentation des intérêts professionnels, la sphère
politique. Le lien social ne prend pas son origine dans
l'échange économique, dans la production ou le travail ;
ceux-ci n'en sont au contraire que des moments. L'homme
s'exprime ainsi dans diverses sphères, sous divers modes.
Et l'Etat n'est d'ailleurs pas le dernier mot de l'évolution et
de l'expression sociale : l'homme trouve également son
identité dans l'art, la religion, la philosophie ; les modes
d'être sont multiples mais tous s'épanouissent à l'intérieur
de cette communauté politique, qui est première et leur
donne sens.

Hegel a construit une théorie politique extrêmement
ambitieuse et cohérente dans laquelle la représentation de
la société, communauté respectueuse de l'individu, s'accompagne d'une théorie de l'Etat très développée, qui non
seulement donne toute leur légitimité aux interventions de
celui-ci au nom de la cohésion sociale, valeur première,
mais fonde en quelque sorte la multicitoyenneté des
individus, c'est-à-dire leur manière diversifiée d'être
citoyen et d'avoir une identité dans cette communauté.
Mais la théorie hégélienne n'a pas pu être poussée jusqu'à
son terme. Certaines expressions de Hegel prêtaient à

confusion[435] et les critiques du siècle suivant n'hésiteront pas à les utiliser pour faire de Hegel l'apologue de l'étatisme, et particulièrement de l'étatisme prussien, donc l'ancêtre tout à la fois de Bismarck, puis de Hitler. D'autre part, la théorie politique de Hegel aurait nécessité des approfondissements : la souveraineté populaire pas plus que la représentation n'ont été théorisées par Hegel, qui considère la monarchie constitutionnelle comme la meilleure forme de gouvernement. Enfin, sa conception du lien entre Etat et individu n'est pas toujours très dynamique. La participation des citoyens à la vie politique s'opère à travers les responsabilités diverses qu'ils occupent dans les multiples institutions ou corporations qui servent à médiatiser les rapports entre individu et Etat. Mais Hegel ne parvient pas à élaborer, au cœur des Temps modernes, un mécanisme identique à celui qui permettait de faire véritablement participer les individus à la vie de la démocratie dans l'Antiquité. Il n'en a pas moins fait considérablement progresser la science politique de son temps : c'est certainement de cette tentative que nous devons nous-mêmes repartir, car tout s'est passé comme si les terribles expériences du xxᵉ siècle nous avaient ramenés, du point de vue de la théorie politique, plus d'un siècle en arrière. La philosophie politique doit reprendre cette tâche délaissée, car depuis Hegel nous ne sommes pas davantage parvenus à fonder en réalité ce lien social.

Les successeurs de Hegel, en effet, qu'il s'agisse des jeunes-hégéliens de gauche — dont Marx fait partie — ou de droite, ou encore la tradition anglo-saxonne ne parviendront pas à séparer à nouveau économie et politique, sauf à passer par le nationalisme. La majeure partie d'entre eux, Marx au premier chef, rêveront d'une société autorégulée d'où la nécessité d'un Etat a disparu, d'une société immédiatement transparente à elle-même, sans besoin d'un organe symbolique où pourrait se dire et se faire l'unité du lien social. Marx n'aura de cesse de se gausser du concept d'Etat créé par Hegel[436] : selon lui, l'Etat est l'instrument dont s'emparent les classes dominantes pour faire croire qu'elles défendent l'intérêt général alors qu'elles défendent le leur. Pour Marx, il ne peut y avoir d'ordre qu'issu des rapports de production, les deux sphères de l'économie et de la politique ne peuvent pas être séparées ; l'économie dit la vérité des rapports sociaux, elle *est* la politique. Quant au nationalisme, il prendra également la figure de la transparence de la société à elle-même, coïncidant avec son histoire, son lieu et ses traditions. L'Etat, lorsqu'il est accepté, n'est alors que l'instrument de ce peuple à nouveau en accord avec lui-même. Dans les deux cas, la coïncidence est telle que l'ordre social ne nécessite plus de médiations ou d'incarnations, il est autoproduit, naturel, non conflictuel : politique et Etat sont identiquement inutiles, la société étant capable, en pleine coïncidence avec elle-même, de s'auto-organiser.

L'Etat et la communauté

Aujourd'hui, notre pensée politique ne nous permet pas de fonder en raison une intervention de l'Etat qui aurait pour objectif de renforcer la cohésion sociale. Car nous ne disposons ni d'une représentation de la société comme une communauté ayant un ou plusieurs biens propres (parmi lesquels sa propre cohésion), ni d'une conception de l'Etat comme symbole de l'unité sociale et comme instance utilisant de façon légitime les instruments propres à rendre celle-ci concrète. Peut-être ces deux incapacités sont-elles liées, peut-être notre méfiance vis-à-vis de l'Etat et notre représentation classique de l'Etat expliquent-elles en partie notre difficulté à penser la société comme une communauté.

Nous avons vu que chez Hegel la société ne prend elle-même le caractère d'une communauté qu'à partir du moment où elle s'incarne dans un ensemble d'institutions dont le foyer est l'Etat. Or, nous continuons, dans nos sociétés, à ne pas vouloir pleinement reconnaître la légitimité de celui-ci et à ne pas vouloir le considérer comme l'instance capable de donner corps à cette communauté. Ce n'est d'ailleurs pas un hasard si c'est à la Nation et non à l'Etat que notre Constitution confie un certain nombre de responsabilités éminemment sociales [437]. Nous nous représentons l'Etat, d'une manière générale, comme un instrument utilisé par ceux qui occupent le pouvoir pour leur propre usage. Nous en avons donc une conception à la fois économique (l'Etat est un parasite qui empêche les ajustements), marxiste (l'Etat est l'instrument du pouvoir des classes dominantes), webérienne (l'Etat a le monopole de la violence légitime) et « moderne » (l'Etat est la pire des bureaucraties). Nous continuons à penser l'Etat comme une excroissance dont la fonction première (œuvrer pour l'intérêt général) finit toujours par être oubliée, au profit d'une logique de prise en charge de tous les domaines de la vie.

Alors même que les interventions de l'Etat occupent, en effet, une très grande partie de l'espace social, nous raisonnons sur l'Etat tel qu'il est et non sur ce qu'il devrait être. Nous condamnons, autrement dit, l'idée même de l'Etat tandis qu'il nous faudrait réfléchir sur sa fonction et sur le type de réforme qui permettrait de mieux promouvoir celle-ci. C'est dans ce piège qu'est tombé le courant de pensée qui s'est développé dans les années 1970 et 1980, dont la devise était de rendre son épaisseur à la société civile, grâce à la capacité d'auto-organisation de celle-ci, au développement des associations et à la prise en charge de leurs problèmes par les individus eux-mêmes ou par les groupements d'individus [438]. L'Etat, accusé de s'être développé sur les décombres des corps intermédiaires, à la suppression desquels il avait largement participé pour mieux pouvoir apparaître comme l'instance suprême de recours vis-à-vis d'un individu sans défense, devait laisser la place, libérer l'espace social, réduire considérablement ses interventions.

Si elle prenait bien en compte et l'expérience historique
et les risques potentiels toujours attachés au développement de l'Etat, cette analyse ne s'en privait pas moins d'un
élément essentiel dans la constitution d'une véritable
société communautaire. Car celle-ci ne peut advenir qu'au
terme d'un mouvement de médiation sans cesse recommencé, dont le principe régulateur ne peut être qu'un
ensemble de droits, de devoirs et d'institutions. Sinon, le
risque est de retomber dans des théories, soit de la parfaite
coïncidence à soi-même de la société, soit de l'autoconstitu-
tion d'un intérêt commun à partir de regroupements
d'individus dont les intérêts sont toujours particuliers. Une
société moderne ne peut être une véritable communauté si
un Etat ne lui sert pas de catalyseur et de médiateur. Cela
ne signifie pas que tout Etat remplit cette fonction, bien au
contraire. Mais bien plutôt que la tâche d'une philosophie
politique qui viserait à fonder une communauté serait au
premier chef d'établir une théorie de l'Etat comme moyen
conscient que la société se donne à elle-même pour réaliser
les fins qu'elle a librement choisies et comme instance dont
la fonction première est de permettre la médiation de la
société avec elle-même, en aidant à la formation et à
l'expression de la volonté générale.

Avant même d'être un régulateur de la croissance ou un
correcteur des inégalités [439], un tel Etat aurait pour tâche
première d'organiser continûment l'espace public, c'est-à-
dire de libérer un espace pour l'information et la diffusion
des données nécessaires au débat public, de permettre aux
citoyens d'y accéder, de s'y exprimer et donc de participer à
la décision publique au sens large, au choix de la bonne
société ou encore à la fonction politique [440]. Seule une telle
transformation et « une telle combinaison, au plus haut
point novatrice, de pouvoir et d'autolimitation intelligente [441] » pourraient permettre à la fois de rendre possible
l'idée d'une communauté [442] sur un fondement autre que
naturel et de faire reculer la sphère autorégulée par les
impératifs économiques ou administratifs. Seule l'assigna-

tion à l'Etat d'une telle tâche permettrait de renouer, au cœur des Temps modernes, avec la conception antique de la politique et de la citoyenneté. Mais il s'agit là d'une tâche infinie car, à la différence du type de rapport qui se nouait jusque-là entre l'individu et la volonté générale — dans un même espace en Grèce, par la participation à des ordres chez Hegel, par la représentation simple et la pure délégation dans nos démocraties parlementaires —, c'est à un véritable travail de construction, d'explication, de publication que devrait se livrer un tel Etat. Cette tâche infinie [443], qui est celle de l'Etat appuyé sur la société et celle des citoyens, n'est rien d'autre que le tissage, lui-même toujours remis sur le métier, du lien social.

Il y a là une très grande différence avec la fonction avouée et la réalité de nos Etats, y compris de nos Etats-providence. Et donc un véritable défi pour la pensée et la pratique politique, qui consiste, en lieu et place d'une condamnation de l'idée que nous en avons, à transformer profondément leur réalité, à les rendre conformes à ce que nous souhaitons qu'ils soient, à mettre en place des règles et des pratiques qui préviennent, autant que faire se peut, les « dérapages ». Une telle question n'est d'ailleurs pas très éloignée de celle qui occupait les Grecs lorsqu'ils disaient se consacrer à la recherche du bon gouvernement. Mais c'est une question dont la dimension pratique est essentielle : réformer l'Etat est sans doute l'une des choses les plus difficiles à faire, et il paraît tout à fait certain que les deux démarches qui consisteraient, l'une à promouvoir une société plus communautaire, l'autre à réformer l'Etat, ne peuvent s'opérer l'une sans l'autre, ne peuvent que se féconder l'une l'autre.

Le choix de la communauté

Il faut sans doute oser faire le pari aujourd'hui que nos sociétés sont suffisamment riches, suffisamment mûres ou suffisamment menacées dans leur cohésion pour se donner de nouvelles ambitions. Comme l'histoire passée et présente le montre, les sociétés ne survivent pas uniquement grâce à la production de richesses matérielles. Elles parviennent aussi à résister aux assauts intérieurs et extérieurs de toute nature en étant capables de sécréter du sens, de la sagesse, de la solidarité, de la beauté. Ces ressources-là ne produisent aucun enrichissement immédiat mais elles permettent certainement à long terme d'éviter la violence, le nationalisme, l'avilissement, la guerre et finalement la dissolution sociale. Pourtant, personne ne tire jamais ce bilan et personne n'ose réaliser ce calcul qui ne peut s'envisager du point de vue de la rationalité limitée. Sommes-nous assez mûrs ou assez menacés pour choisir désormais de reconnaître que notre société est une sorte de communauté qui a une valeur, qu'elle a un ou des biens — parmi lesquels sa propre cohésion — qu'il nous incombe de rechercher en commun ? Sommes-nous assez mûrs ou assez menacés pour abandonner les images qui nous présentent la vie en société comme un sacrifice, la diminution des impôts comme un idéal et tout acte collectif comme profondément ennuyeux ? En un mot, sommes-nous assez mûrs ou assez menacés pour accepter les bouleversements qu'imposerait l'adoption d'un tel point de vue ?

Une telle conception supposerait en effet trois grands types de remise en cause : une remise en cause de la place de l'économie ; une remise en cause de l'Etat ; une remise en cause des instruments, des institutions et des dispositifs fiscaux et sociaux. Une réforme de la place de l'économie, d'abord. On le conçoit aisément : dès lors que l'on reconnaît que la société a plusieurs biens, que l'on s'interroge sur ses fins, que l'on réintroduit les considérations éthiques et politiques, il devient malaisé de faire croire que nos sociétés poursuivent un objectif unique, l'augmentation de la croissance, à quoi tout devrait être subordonné, que le lien social est issu de la seule sphère productive et enfin que l'ordre économique est l'ordre naturel sur lequel viendraient se greffer l'ordre politique et l'ordre social. Au contraire, l'idée que c'est désormais la société tout entière qui a une valeur, et que celle-ci est déterminée par les individus la composant, réintroduit une dimension politique, donc de débat et de choix, qui est antithétique avec celle d'une autorégulation et constitue une source concurrente de « production » de lien social. Aussi reconnaître la dimension communautaire de la société suppose-t-il de subordonner l'économie à la politique — c'est-à-dire de considérer l'économie comme un simple instrument technique qui nous indique comment produire certaines richesses [444] —, de créer de nouveaux indicateurs de richesse sociale capables de valoriser toutes les formes de richesses — le patrimoine naturel, les individus, le lien social [445] —, à la place ou à côté des indicateurs dont nous disposons aujourd'hui, et de libérer de l'espace, individuel et collectif, pour permettre à ce nouveau mode de socialisation, politique, de s'exprimer.

Aujourd'hui, la fonction politique du citoyen s'exerce au moment des élections et la politique est une tâche spécialisée. Vouloir augmenter la participation des individus au choix de la bonne société suppose à la fois de mettre fin à cette spécialisation (autrement dit de cesser de soumettre la fonction politique à la division du travail social), d'inventer les modalités d'exercice de cette participation, et donc de revoir les modes d'action de l'Etat. Il ne suffit pas de modifier les responsabilités respectives du Parlement et du pouvoir exécutif et d'améliorer la manière dont les élus représentent la volonté générale (par exemple en supprimant les possibilités de cumul des mandats, en renforçant l'assiduité des parlementaires ou même, pourquoi pas, en dissociant les deux fonctions de représentant des intérêts locaux et de législateur national). Il s'agit également de trouver de nouveaux modes d'expression de la volonté générale, concurrents de ce type de représentation ou même de l'actuelle médiation réalisée par les partenaires sociaux. En effet, la représentation parlementaire ne suffit plus à l'expression des individus, les partis ne parviennent plus à être des lieux de formation de la volonté générale et les syndicats, originellement créés pour représenter des intérêts professionnels, ne sont pas faits pour représenter tous les types d'intérêts sociaux. L'enjeu est donc de trouver de nouvelles modalités d'expression de la volonté générale qui ne consistent ni en une simple représentation non préparée et non retravaillée, ni en une simple procédure d'enregistrement des vœux des individus, par exemple par le biais de sondages [446]. Trois fonctions pourraient dès lors être assignées à l'Etat : informer, diffuser, éclairer [447] la prise de décision et aider à la formation et à la prise en compte de la volonté générale, d'une part. Fixer, à partir de ces consultations, des objectifs et des cadres nationaux (en matière de politique de santé, d'éducation, de logement, de revenus, de répartition de la population sur le territoire...) et se doter des moyens disponibles pour contrôler et évaluer la réalisation de ceux-ci, d'autre part. Enfin, déléguer la majeure partie de la mise en œuvre concrète de ces politiques à d'autres que lui, collectivités locales, regroupements spécialement conçus pour la prise en charge de tel intérêt commun, associations, entreprises, qui tous auraient à se soumettre à des obligations de publication, de comptes et de transparence extrêmement précises, à des autoévaluations et à des évaluations. Par le biais de ces contrats d'un type assez particulier, on verrait ainsi un vaste champ couvert par l'intérêt public, sous la responsabilité de l'Etat sans être pris en charge directement par lui [448].

Quant à cet Etat, on voit bien qu'il serait très différent de celui que nous avons connu et connaissons encore aujourd'hui : exerçant des fonctions beaucoup moins nombreuses, mais de nature plus stratégique, médium actif entre la société et elle-même, il aurait pour tâche essentielle, outre l'alimentation du débat social, de traduire l'intérêt général en objectifs et de renvoyer les tâches particulières ainsi définies vers la société elle-même. Un tel

Etat, qu'il s'agisse du pouvoir exécutif ou du pouvoir législatif, devrait également — il s'agit sans doute là de l'élément le plus utopique et le plus stratégique de notre propos — ne plus pouvoir être *pris en otage* par une classe, qu'elle soit politique ou administrative. Cela suppose à la fois une réforme de l'accès à la fonction parlementaire (congés spéciaux, non-renouvellement des mandats, voire tirage au sort) de sorte qu'il n'y ait plus de carrière politique, car rien n'est plus opposé à l'idée même de la politique ; mais aussi une réforme de l'accès aux écoles menant aux carrières publiques[449], des fonctions auxquelles elles conduisent, des passerelles actuelles entre les deux fonctions ; et, enfin, que l'Etat lui-même soit soumis à un certain nombre d'obligations, en particulier en matière d'information sur ses propres activités.

En dernier lieu, si cette conception de la société comme communauté nécessite une nouvelle relation à l'économie et la définition d'un nouveau rôle de l'Etat, elle suppose également la réforme des instruments de prélèvement et de redistribution existants. Il ne s'agit d'ailleurs pas tant de rendre légitimes les interventions correctrices et redistributrices de l'Etat-providence que de repenser l'ensemble des interventions de la société sur elle-même, sachant que son objectif primordial est la réalisation concrète d'une certaine cohésion à laquelle sont subordonnés les autres objectifs[450]. Ceci suppose réalisées au moins trois conditions : que soient abandonnées en partie les notions d'incitation individuelle ou de rémunération individuelle selon la contribution à la production, comme le proposait déjà Bartoli il y a quarante ans[451] ; qu'une partie du revenu national soit consacrée au renouvellement et à l'amélioration du patrimoine commun inventorié comme tel (individus, lien social, fonctions collectives) et valorisé comme un véritable investissement ; que la réduction des inégalités constitue un objectif affiché par l'ensemble de la société et inscrit dans l'ensemble des dispositifs de prélèvement, et qu'elle s'effectue non seulement par le prélèvement, mais également par un accès facilité à certains biens premiers (qui ne sont pas seulement les biens premiers de Rawls, car il faut y ajouter la Sécurité sociale, un minimum de travail, l'exercice des droits sociaux...). Ces trois idées trouvent leur origine dans une même conviction : il n'y a pas d'ordre naturel ; et, par conséquent, la notion d'équité[452], cette nouvelle vertu à la mode dont chacun parle sans jamais la définir, ne peut appartenir au vocabulaire de la philosophie politique. L'équité, selon le dictionnaire, c'est la notion de la justice naturelle dans l'appréciation de ce qui est dû à chacun. C'est donc l'idée de rendre à chacun ce qui lui appartient, de se régler sur la répartition dictée par l'ordre naturel. Nous sommes toujours ramenés, dans cette question, à l'état de nature. L'idée d'augmenter les impôts pour financer des mesures qui seraient bonnes pour tous — par exemple une véritable politique de santé publique ou encore une universalisation de la branche maladie de la Sécurité sociale, ou un véritable service performant d'accueil des enfants préscolarisés et scolarisés rendant l'activité des parents plus facile — continue d'être taboue dans notre pays. Pour la simple raison, si l'on pousse l'analyse jusqu'à son terme, qu'il est préférable, quoi qu'il en soit et de toute éternité, de faire jouer l'arbitrage individuel. Eviter des dépenses plus élevées n'est donc pas le motif des « politiques » actuelles : on préfère aujourd'hui laisser la société dépenser davantage tandis que, ce faisant, les inégalités augmentent, plutôt que d'augmenter les impôts pour financer une activité utile à tous (des crèches, par exemple, qu'il faut comparer au mécanisme d'exonérations de cotisations familiales mis en place[453]). Accroître les possibilités d'arbitrage individuel (donc ne pas décider à la place des individus), respecter l'ordre naturel ou s'interdire de dépasser des seuils dits « insupportables », par exemple pour les prélèvements obligatoires[454], tels sont aujourd'hui les grands principes de notre fiscalité et de notre système de redistribution.

Il semble prioritaire pour une société qui donne à sa

cohésion une valeur, non seulement d'éviter de trop gros écarts de revenus et de patrimoines, mais également d'organiser une véritable distribution, le plus tôt possible, des chances, des accès et des biens. L'entreprise est à l'évidence extrêmement délicate et ce n'est pas un hasard si l'économie prétend ne découvrir que des lois existant de toute éternité ou si Rawls [455] est obligé de recourir à une procédure de décision sans décideurs... En effet, le choix des principes selon lesquels seront réparties les richesses est l'acte le plus politique, donc à la fois le plus antinaturel, le plus humain et le plus risqué qui soit. Ce n'est pas non plus un hasard si tous les grands théoriciens politiques qui ont cru à la nécessité de la participation du citoyen à la fabrication des lois, qu'il s'agisse des Grecs ou de Rousseau, en ont pourtant appelé à un premier législateur mythique, un nomothète, capable de choisir au moins quelques principes inébranlables qui revêtiraient un caractère sacré. Car la politique se définit par la possible remise en cause de tout ordre.

CHAPITRE X

DÉSENCHANTER LE TRAVAIL

Le paradoxe actuel de nos sociétés modernes — qu'il soit aujourd'hui possible de desserrer la contrainte qu'exerce sur nous le travail, mais que nous ne parvenions pas à nous y résoudre, ou encore que nous ayons inventé de toutes pièces et conservé une catégorie spécifique, celle de chômage, qui ne signifie rien d'autre sinon que le travail est la norme et l'ordre de nos sociétés — a constitué la première source d'étonnement et le point de départ de ce livre. Il montre que le travail représente pour nos sociétés bien plus qu'un rapport social, bien plus qu'un moyen de distribuer les richesses et d'atteindre une hypothétique abondance. Il est en effet chargé de toutes les énergies utopiques qui se sont fixées sur lui au long des deux siècles passés. Il est « enchanté », au sens où il exerce sur nous un « charme » dont nous sommes aujourd'hui prisonniers. Il nous faut maintenant briser ce sortilège, désenchanter le travail [456].

Lorsque Weber utilisait l'expression « désenchantement du monde », il désignait par là le résultat d'un processus historique mais aussi d'une action volontaire : l'élimination de la magie en tant que technique de salut [457] était à la fois une procédure consciente, entamée par les prophètes juifs et poursuivie par Calvin, et la conséquence des découvertes scientifiques qui, peu à peu, révélaient un monde vide, inhabité, sans âme, un monde à travers lequel Dieu ne faisait plus signe à l'homme, un monde dépourvu de sens. Désenchanter le travail supposerait de notre part une décision, mais qui prendrait acte d'une évolution historique selon laquelle « l'utopie qui se rattache à la société du travail a épuisé sa force de conviction[458] ». Désenchanter le travail impliquerait de la part de nos sociétés une décision douloureuse et risquée, dont le refus serait néanmoins encore plus grave.

Que nous manque-t-il pour prendre une telle décision ? On entend aujourd'hui dire que font défaut, soit les forces sociales sur lesquelles pourrait prendre appui une réforme, soit une nouvelle attitude des élites incapables de rompre avec un conservatisme frileux. Il nous semble que, plus profondément, il nous manque d'abord une généalogie convaincante qui mette en évidence pourquoi le travail s'est ainsi vu chargé de toutes les espérances, ensuite un lieu de substitution où projeter nos énergies utopiques, et enfin seulement une ébauche de procédure concrète nous permettant d'opérer sans risque ce « transfert ». Cette réponse doit beaucoup à la philosophie allemande, et en particulier aux instruments d'analyse que celle-ci est parvenue à forger au cours du dernier siècle[459], mais dont nous ne nous sommes, semble-t-il, pas encore véritablement inspirés. Cette philosophie repose sur une anthropologie de la peur, du désir et de l'utopie qui ouvre à une pratique du changement. Sans rentrer dans les détails, le fait qu'elle conçoive l'homme comme un être habité par une peur primordiale — qui est à la fois celle d'être au monde, de mourir, d'être parmi les autres et différent d'eux —, donc par le manque et le désir, lui permet de comprendre l'homme et les sociétés comme détenteurs d'une énergie « fabricatrice » de stabilité, de catégories, d'ordre, de valeurs et de sens. Ainsi Nietzsche voit-il dans les arrière-mondes platonicien ou chrétien, mais aussi dans les catégories logiques, la rationalité, l'ordre social, la morale, l'art, ou la culture, le résultat de l'investissement d'une énergie primitive, à la fois peur et volonté de puissance, crainte et énergie créatrice [460]. Dans la philosophie de Nietzsche, tout ordre est toujours en même temps d'une certaine manière un « enchantement », une manière de mettre en forme, de donner un sens à ce qui n'en a pas et d'y croire [461]. Weber ne dit pas autre chose lorsqu'il impute les transformations essentielles qui adviennent aux hommes et aux sociétés aux motivations (*Antriebe*) psychologiques, qui ont leur source, dit-il, dans les croyances et les pratiques religieuses. Un vaste pan de la pensée allemande, y compris Marx, fait de l'homme un être dont la peur originelle et constitutive se transforme en énergie créatrice, capable de créer de toutes pièces des mondes, des interprétations, des idéologies. L'utopie est la tension qui précède, soutient et dépasse ainsi les objets ou les mondes investis par ces énergies. Cette pensée nous apprend que tout ordre ou tout système de valorisation a une « raison », dont il convient de faire la généalogie, que la croyance quasi utopique dans le système créé ne peut être supprimée qu'au terme d'une démarche « curative » et que cette guérison ne peut consister qu'en un transfert de ces énergies sur d'autres systèmes de valorisation.

On peut de cette manière interpréter la naissance, le développement et l'adaptation du capitalisme, de même que le prodigieux accroissement de richesse, de technique et de productivité qui l'a accompagné, comme le résultat du désinvestissement des énergies utopiques (d'aucuns diraient des espérances eschatologiques) de l'au-delà vers l'ici-bas. Ce relâchement des tensions jusqu'alors dirigées vers l'au-delà, à la fois sous la forme d'attentes, de raffinements de la doctrine et d'appareils d'interprétation et de pouvoir, et son investissement massif dans le monde sont seuls susceptibles d'expliquer la frénésie du développement dans laquelle nous vivons encore aujourd'hui et dont personne n'a encore véritablement réussi à trouver la cause. La grande peur qui commence à la fin du Moyen

Age et se poursuit jusqu'au début du XVIIe siècle — à l'origine de laquelle on peut repérer des « événements » aussi divers que la peste, l'éloignement divin ou l'effondrement des ordres naturels — pourrait ainsi expliquer un regain de l'utopie, tournée cette fois vers le monde et mise au service d'un ordre rationnel mondain : « Même aujourd'hui, la peur peut être considérée comme la principale force motrice de la croissance économique et technologique [462] », écrit un commentateur moderne de Hans Jonas, qui voit dans l'engouement des deux derniers siècles pour le progrès, la croissance et la technique la conséquence de la peur et de la recherche de la sécurité. Le moment baconien apparaît ainsi essentiel, Bacon étant celui qui soudainement a permis la transmutation de la peur en énergie.

Au XVIIIe siècle, en réponse à cette « grande peur », le travail devient donc le vecteur privilégié du réinvestissement des énergies vers l'ici-bas, le moyen de l'abondance, de l'aménagement, du progrès. Au milieu du XIXe siècle, il se voit soudainement chargé d'une nouvelle moisson d'attentes : la production devient le centre de la vie économique et sociale et le travail, le médium privilégié par lequel la société s'exprime. La production n'est plus seulement le moyen de satisfaire les besoins matériels, mais aussi celui de mettre en valeur et d'amener au jour toutes les potentialités. Aujourd'hui, la société continue de se vivre comme productrice d'elle-même et l'ensemble de nos dispositifs sociaux s'organise autour de cette opération de maïeutique perpétuelle de la société sur elle-même. C'est à partir de ce foyer que tout prend sens : est valorisée chez l'individu la manière dont ses capacités naturelles sont ou non adaptées à la mise en valeur du monde. L'homme est pensé en termes de capacité à apporter de la valeur.

La volonté de mise en valeur du monde et de l'homme est la forme commune de l'humanisme. La culture consiste, de fait, à dé-naturaliser l'homme et le monde, à affiner l'humanité de l'homme, à modeler ce qui demeure toujours encore naturel en lui[463]. Le capitalisme semble être la forme la plus efficace et la plus rapide de cette mise en valeur : il s'appuie, en effet, sur l'intérêt qu'a chacun à valoriser ses capacités pour en retirer un bénéfice. Dans cette mesure, il a accéléré dans des proportions jamais connues la mise en valeur du monde. Néanmoins, il demeure la forme la plus perverse et la plus réductrice de l'humanisme. Car jamais avant le XIXe siècle on n'aurait osé tenir la production de biens et services pour la manière la plus haute de « civiliser » le monde. La mise en valeur de celui-ci se présentait jusqu'alors, au contraire, sous une pluralité de dimensions : l'art, la religion, la morale, les institutions, la politique, le raisonnement, le savoir constituaient autant de possibles « approfondissements » de l'homme et du monde. Autrement dit, la culture et son double objet, l'homme et le monde, présentaient encore une irréductible diversité. Le capitalisme a rendu sans intérêt un certain nombre de ces mises en valeur : en ne reconnaissant comme facteur de richesses qu'une partie d'entre elles, il a rendu inutile toute forme de « culture » qui ne serait pas une prestation susceptible d'être extériorisée, montrée, ajoutée, bref, qui ne serait pas « utile ». Les logiques de la production et de l'expression vont de pair : la réduction de la culture qui s'est opérée au milieu du XIXe siècle a consisté à ne plus tenir compte que des potentialités humaines ou naturelles propres à s'inscrire dans un objet ou à prendre la forme du service et donc à être utilisées dans une relation à l'autre. Les activités dites « pratiques » — qui possèdent leur raison en elles-mêmes, et non en dehors d'elles-mêmes, et qui ne sont donc pas destinées à être produites à l'extérieur —, qu'il s'agisse de la science au sens large, de la morale ou de la politique, ont donc dès lors été considérées comme sans intérêt.

On a assisté, au XIXe siècle, à la réduction de la culture au travail. Le terme de ce développement est double : c'est d'abord un homme qui n'est plus qu'un « fond » déterminé de l'extérieur ; une matière qui ne prend forme qu'en fonction du stimulus externe ; un ensemble de capacités naturelles qui ne sont mises en avant qu'au gré de la demande sociale. L'individu n'est plus qu'une simple matière dans la mise en forme de laquelle il investit pendant sa jeunesse pour en tirer ensuite un revenu. Le système d'éducation se transforme en dispositif chargé de moduler les capacités naturelles des individus pour atteindre à la qualification [464] ; la formation est conçue en fonction de la qualification sociale ou professionnelle qu'elle permettra. Cette « qualification » prend acte de ce que les capacités naturelles de l'individu ont pris la forme requise pour une mise en valeur maximale du monde. La meilleure formation est, selon les modes, ou bien celle qui sculpte les capacités de la manière la mieux adaptée au futur métier, ou bien celle qui rend les capacités les plus plastiques. L'Antiquité et le Moyen Age avaient interdit la vente des capacités humaines, considérant qu'il était indigne de l'homme de développer ses capacités exclusivement pour en retirer un gain, et qu'au contraire la formation et l'éducation devaient être l'acte le plus libre de toute considération extérieure. Aujourd'hui, les capacités humaines ne sont plus développées qu'en fonction de l'utilisation et du revenu futurs qu'elles permettront. Les individus s'utilisent eux-mêmes comme moyen de vivre, mobilisent leurs capacités dans cette perspective. La société décide ainsi entièrement des capacités que l'individu devra développer et de celles qu'il devra mettre en jachère.

L'autre terme de ce développement, c'est une société de services, où chacun se présente comme une capacité modelée exclusivement pour l'utilité de l'autre. Un certain nombre de réflexions actuelles prédisent l'avènement ou appellent de leurs vœux une telle société [465], indiquant que, d'ici une décennie, l'industrie sera réduite à la portion congrue — l'activité de transformation et de production des biens matériels étant prise en charge par des machines et des systèmes automatisés, ou bien délocalisée, ou encore abandonnée aux pays moins riches — et que 80 % ou plus des effectifs seront employés dans les services. Dans ces réflexions, les services constituent la forme la plus accomplie que peut prendre une société (la pure relation d'échange sans détour par l'objet), en même temps que la solution au problème de l'emploi. Les services à la personne apparaissent en effet comme une réserve inépuisable de besoins, et donc d'emplois. Il ne resterait plus, indiquent certains, qu'à transformer chaque employeur en entreprise, c'est-à-dire à lui permettre de déduire de son revenu imposable les salaires et les charges sociales[466]. Il est nécessaire, continuent-ils, tout ensemble de reconnaître de nouvelles richesses, de créer de nouveaux services et d'inventer les nouveaux emplois qui y correspondent[467].

Nous devons prendre la mesure de ces propositions et reconnaître les risques qu'elles comportent. Passons sur les inégalités qui se développeront nécessairement si les services à la personne, appuyés sur des échanges de temps inégaux et sur des investissements initiaux différents[468] dans l'éducation, sont préférés aux services collectifs ; passons également sur les risques de régression que cette dernière solution comporte — les relations de dépendance personnelle venant remplacer la relation au pouvoir anonyme et la relation entre deux personnes venant rendre inutile tout droit du travail[469]. Ce qui importe véritablement est ailleurs. La logique qui sous-tend le développement d'une société de services est la mise en valeur de tout ce qui existe : ressources naturelles, capacités naturelles, relations sociales. N'importe quoi peut être mis en valeur : il suffit qu'il se trouve quelqu'un pour l'estimer utile. L'ensemble des relations sociales n'échappe pas à cette logique, comme le montre un examen de ce que recouvre le champ des services dits à la personne. Il s'agit, en effet, d'activités qui étaient autrefois prises en charge par la cellule familiale ou la solidarité de voisinage : production domestique, garde d'enfants, garde des personnes âgées, courses, cuisine, ménage... Parce que les femmes ont rejoint massivement le marché du travail et que la structure familiale s'est modifiée, ces activités sont en passe d'entrer sur le marché et, de proche en proche, toutes les relations sociales pourraient ainsi faire l'objet d'une marchandisation. On entend dire aujourd'hui qu'une des manières de reconnaître de nouvelles richesses et de créer des emplois serait, par exemple, de considérer la garde de parents âgés par leurs propres enfants comme une activité sociale et de la faire, par conséquent, financer par l'ensemble de la collectivité...

Qu'est-ce qu'une société de services ? Une société dans laquelle l'essentiel de l'activité prend la forme du « service » et non plus celle de la transformation d'une matière ; dans laquelle l'activité ne va plus nécessairement de pair ni avec la notion de production ni avec celle d'effort. Dans une société de ce type, la différence entre travail et non-travail s'estompe : tout est travail, certes, mais le travail n'est plus ni ennuyeux, ni matériel, ni mesurable ; il est devenu intéressant, voire épanouissant, ou même encore simplement comparable à n'importe quelle autre activité. La formation qualifiante suivie pour se préparer à l'exercice d'un nouveau métier, la garde d'enfants rémunérée par la collectivité, en quoi seront-elles du travail ? Voilà une thèse de plus en plus répandue aujourd'hui : la distinction entre le travail et les autres activités est désormais dépassée.

C'est là que nos sociétés se révèlent, paradoxalement, mais profondément marxiennes : tout est travail, l'emploi est mort, vive l'activité [470]. Car chez Marx également la société se manifestait sous la forme du service et la distinction entre travail et loisir avait disparu. La seule différence avec la société rêvée par Marx est que nous avons conservé un caractère marchand à nos échanges, sans considérer pour autant que cela empêchera notre société d'être parfaitement conviviale et épanouissante. Comme Marx, notre société croit que la plus haute forme de manifestation de l'homme, c'est le travail, que toute activité est appelée à devenir travail. D'où la détermination de ce livre à critiquer les pensées qui confondent, comme Marx, la manière historiquement déterminée dont l'homme a mis en valeur le monde depuis deux siècles et ce que les Allemands ont appelé culture. La première n'est qu'une partie de la seconde. Par conséquent, considérer l'effort créateur, la contrainte, la douleur de la mise en forme, la réflexion, l'écriture, la politique comme du travail ; dire qu'il faut sauvegarder le travail au nom d'une certaine idée de l'homme comme être capable d'effort et de création ; affirmer que si l'on sort du travail, on retombe dans les rapports privés[471], c'est commettre une grave faute historique. La commettent tous ceux qui considèrent que l'emploi ou le travail salarié ne sont qu'une des formes que peut prendre le travail parce que celui-ci recouvre un champ beaucoup plus vaste. Il ne s'agit pas là que d'un problème de mots. Confondre culture et travail, c'est oublier que la vie est aussi action, et pas seulement production, c'est faire courir le risque à nos sociétés de ne concevoir la vie humaine que comme une exhaustion de soi. Ainsi s'explique d'ailleurs l'idée de pleine activité, présentée aujourd'hui comme la solution au problème du chômage. Si tout le monde ne peut accéder à l'emploi, mais que tous doivent pourtant avoir droit au travail, il suffit d'élargir le champ de ce qui est reconnu comme travail, nous dit-on. Après avoir réduit théoriquement la culture (ou la formation de soi) au travail — en particulier au travers de Marx — la logique de nos sociétés est désormais de faire prendre réellement à toutes les activités la forme du travail.

Cette confusion est trop pesante et trop grave : nous devrions cesser d'appeler travail ce « je-ne-sais-quoi » censé être notre essence, et bien plutôt nous demander par quel autre moyen nous pourrions permettre aux individus d'avoir accès à la sociabilité, l'utilité sociale, l'intégration, toutes choses que le travail a pu et pourra encore sans doute donner, mais certainement plus de manière exclusive. Le problème n'est donc pas de donner la forme travail à des activités de plus en plus nombreuses, mais au contraire de réduire l'emprise du travail pour permettre à des activités aux logiques radicalement différentes, sources d'autonomie et de coopération véritables, de se développer. Désenchanter le travail, le décharger des attentes trop fortes que nous avions placées en lui[472], et donc le considérer dans sa vérité, commence par un changement radical de nos représentations et des termes mêmes que nous employons. C'est à cette condition que nous pourrons, d'une part, libérer un espace véritablement public où s'exerceront les capacités humaines dans leur pluralité et, d'autre part, réorganiser le travail.

Libérer l'espace public

Contrairement à ce qu'affirment certains auteurs, le travail et ses à-côtés occupent la majeure partie de la vie éveillée (au moins pour la population qui dispose d'un emploi) ou bien empêchent ceux qui n'en disposent pas d'un possible investissement dans une autre sphère, par manque de revenus et de statut. La réduction de la place du travail dans nos vies, qui devrait se traduire par une diminution du temps de travail individuel, est la condition sine qua non pour que se développe, à côté de la production, d'autres modes de sociabilité, d'autres moyens d'expression, d'autres manières pour les individus d'acquérir une identité ou de participer à la gestion collective, bref, un véritable espace public. L'autolimitation consciente du domaine réservé à la production et au travail[473] doit permettre un rééquilibrage entre les deux sphères de la production et de ce que Habermas appelle l'interaction, et qui est fondamentalement le domaine de la *praxis*, que celle-ci soit d'ordre individuel ou collectif. Mettre une limite au développement de la rationalité instrumentale et de l'économie, construire les lieux où pourra se développer un véritable apprentissage de la vie publique, investir dans le choix des modalités concrètes et l'exercice d'une nouvelle citoyenneté, voilà ce que devraient permettre la réduction du temps individuel consacré au travail et l'augmentation du temps social consacré aux activités qui sont, de fait, des activités politiques, les seules qui peuvent vraiment structurer un tissu social, si l'on excepte la parenté et l'amitié. Le défi lancé à l'Etat aujourd'hui n'est donc pas de consacrer plusieurs centaines de milliards de francs à occuper les personnes, à les indemniser ou à leur proposer des stages dont une grande partie sont inefficaces, mais à parvenir à trouver les moyens de susciter des regroupements et des associations capables de prendre en charge certains intérêts et de donner aux individus l'envie de s'y consacrer, de susciter chez eux le désir d'autonomie et de liberté. C'est une solution à la Tocqueville, dans la mesure où sa réussite est conditionnée par le développement de la passion de la chose publique.

Revoir l'organisation du travail

Cesser de sacraliser le travail devrait également nous permettre de le considérer simplement dans sa fonction de distribution des richesses et nous donner enfin l'occasion de nous interroger sur celle-ci. Si nous ne voulons pas modifier la manière dont est réparti le travail entre les individus aujourd'hui, c'est bien parce qu'il constitue le principal moyen de distribution des revenus, des statuts, de la protection et des positions sociales : revoir la manière dont est partagé le travail conduit à repenser la répartition de l'ensemble des biens sociaux. Mais est-il légitime que le travail continue à exercer cette fonction de distribution des richesses alors qu'il se réduit de fait, alors que nous souhaitons sa réduction, alors que le progrès technique continuera de réduire son volume[474] ? Est-il normal que sa fonction demeure la même alors que le processus d'entrée et de sortie du marché du travail n'est ni contrôlé ni régulé, mais qu'il résulte des arbitrages d'acteurs privés dont l'impératif n'est en aucune façon l'emploi, mais la production ou leur propre développement ? Est-il légitime qu'une société riche laisse ainsi la répartition de l'ensemble des biens sociaux s'opérer d'une manière « naturelle », sauvage et aléatoire ? Et surtout qu'elle se refuse à considérer le travail comme un bien tout à fait particulier, dont la répartition et la fluctuation doivent être régulées, puisqu'il ouvre à tous les autres ? Une société soucieuse de son bien commun et de sa cohésion sociale, soyons-en sûrs, procéderait autrement. Elle considérerait le travail, les revenus, les statuts et les avantages jusque-là liés au travail comme autant de biens qui doivent être répartis entre ses membres, et dont la bonne répartition est constitutive du bien commun lui-même. Elle refuserait d'avaliser simplement la répartition des richesses issues d'une évolution arbitraire, où l'un des membres a eu la malchance de se trouver dans telle entreprise, dans telle région et d'avoir exercé tel métier, tandis que tel autre y a échappé. Le hasard peut-il être au principe de nos sociétés modernes ?

On voit bien que le véritable problème de nos sociétés n'est en aucune façon la pénurie de travail, mais le fait que nous manquions d'un « mode convaincant de partage [475] ». Celui-ci s'effectue aujourd'hui dans notre pays « naturellement », par l'exclusion du marché du travail des personnes les plus âgées ou les plus fragiles, l'existence de sas de plus en plus longs précédant l'entrée des jeunes sur le marché du travail et une forte sélectivité de celui-ci : notre partage s'opère par déversement dans la catégorie du chômage. On voit bien également que la société dont nous parlons refuserait de chercher des critères naturels sur lesquels indexer la distribution des biens sociaux : elle ne croirait pas au droit naturel, mais ne croirait pas non plus qu'il suffit de fermer les yeux pour choisir les principes de distribution. Elle ne pourrait donc compter que sur elle-même, sur sa capacité à expliciter, à débattre, à trouver des compromis, à surmonter des conflits, cela à partir d'une connaissance fine des revenus, des avantages, des positions existantes. Elle déciderait certainement de trois règles : garantir un accès égal au travail ; viser à un partage acceptable de l'ensemble travail, revenus, statuts, protections ; accepter d'autres moyens de distribution du revenu que le seul travail.

Garantir un accès égal au travail n'est pas contradictoire, bien au contraire, avec le rééquilibrage de nos activités entre des sphères différentes, ni avec une réduction du temps de travail. Parce qu'il reste encore nécessaire, parce qu'il demeure encore un moyen de distribuer les revenus et un facteur de production, le travail est un bien, en même temps qu'un devoir, comme l'indique la Constitution ; il est donc nécessaire de permettre à tous d'y participer, au même titre qu'à tout autre droit ou devoir social. C'est même parce que c'est lui qui continue, aujourd'hui, à ouvrir l'accès aux autres bien sociaux, y compris à la liberté réelle, qu'il doit absolument être réparti, même si cela semble dans un premier temps source d'inefficacité, même si cela paraît coûter plus cher, même si cela demande de puissants investissements. Ceux-ci seraient nécessaires pour mettre en place une ingénierie sociale capable de préciser comment les individus et les entreprises doivent composer pour permettre à la fois une réduction des temps individuels de travail et un accès de tous à celui-ci. Il s'agit bien évidemment d'une opération délicate, car les capacités des personnes et les besoins des entreprises ne sont pas homogènes et les formations existantes pas toujours adéquates. Mais l'on peut tout à fait imaginer que l'argent actuellement consacré à la redistribution et à la réparation des dégâts sociaux soit plutôt investi dans cette ingénierie de la répartition, dans l'aide à la prévention du licenciement et à l'adaptation permanente des qualifications, bref, dans la mise en œuvre d'un partage du travail lui-même.

L'idée même d'un possible partage est de nos jours considérée avec suspicion par une partie des responsables politiques et administratifs qui doutent de l'efficacité d'une telle mesure sur la réduction du chômage (il reste des gains de productivité en réserve), craignent la non-réversibilité d'une telle mesure ou son caractère « malthusien », ou encore souhaitent laisser la « machine économique » réaliser ses adaptations propres[476]. Mais, nonobstant les effets que de telles mesures pourraient malgré tout avoir sur le chômage[477], on voit bien que la question du « partage » ou de la « répartition » du travail n'est en aucune manière une question économique. Elle met en jeu notre conception de la société : ou bien celle-ci privilégie sa propre cohésion et la liberté concrète des citoyens et considère le travail comme un bien premier — en soi, et parce qu'il ouvre à l'ensemble des autres biens sociaux —, et alors elle doit précéder les évolutions naturelles, donc arbitraires, et organiser la répartition permanente des gains de temps et de productivité entre tous les individus ; ou bien elle laisse faire, ne considère pas le travail comme un bien premier et laisse les hiérarchies sociales, les rentes et les inégalités s'instituer à partir du « partage » naturel du travail. Rawls incarne cette seconde école de pensée et, en ceci, il est bien le penseur de l'Etat-providence, puisque, pour lui, le travail ne fait pas partie des biens premiers qui doivent être partagés également[478]. En refusant de faire effort pour trouver les règles de ce partage, on court le risque de voir se propager les deux maux que l'on promet à notre société, le chômage (c'est-à-dire une société coupée en deux) ou la pauvreté (c'est-à-dire une société présentant certes un continuum, mais avec de très fortes inégalités et une grande masse de la population vivant au-dessous du seuil de pauvreté)[479]. Seul un tel effort préviendra également le développement, à côté d'un secteur concurrentiel moderne, d'un « quart secteur » qui occuperait les populations exclues du premier cercle en leur confiant des activités d'intérêt général peu rémunérées, sans que l'on sache sur quelles bases telle ou telle partie de la population, tenue pour socialement handicapée, serait affectée à ce secteur.

Une telle ambition nécessite de forts mécanismes de régulation, c'est-à-dire la capacité de la société à se fixer des objectifs, à définir, de manière prévisionnelle, dans quelle mesure elle aura recours au progrès technique, comment les gains de productivité seront répartis entre temps, emplois et salaires, comment les différents chocs internes ou externes se traduiront par un partage régulier... Elle nécessite donc des accords entre des acteurs capables de prendre des engagements sur l'avenir, des études prospectives et rétrospectives solides et l'élaboration de mécanismes de régulation sociale forts ; ce qui suppose que les entreprises acceptent de poursuivre d'autres intérêts que les leurs, mais également qu'elles inscrivent leur action dans une société dont les buts ne sont pas exclusivement économiques. On peut, à ce propos, se demander si la capacité de la société allemande à passer des accords globaux (emplois/salaires/temps) sur plusieurs années, qui permettent une répartition programmée des gains et des pertes issus de la production, ou encore le maintien d'un système de médecine libéral, mais infiniment plus régulé que le nôtre, n'a pas un rapport avec le caractère beaucoup plus communautaire de sa culture.

Le travail n'est pas le seul bien que cette société communautaire partagerait de façon acceptable (et non pas équitable). Elle souhaiterait également que les ensembles constitués par travail, revenus, statuts et protection fassent l'objet d'une répartition régulée, qui ne laisse pas place à de trop grandes différences, préférant au modèle américain — où le travail détermine totalement le statut, la protection sociale et les avantages, et où la répartition est extrême-ment lâche — un modèle où domine le rapprochement des conditions. Là encore, cela nécessite une régulation sociale qui ne soit pas assimilée à un contrôle et qui soit acceptée par l'ensemble de la société. Cela suppose donc que l'existence d'organismes publiant les revenus, leur disper-sion, les inégalités soit considérée comme normale et susceptible d'accroître la cohésion sociale [480]. Enfin, une telle société souhaiterait que le travail ne reste pas l'unique canal de distribution des richesses et des avantages sociaux. Il ne s'agirait certes pas d'accepter l'idée d'une allocation universelle [481], c'est-à-dire d'une allocation généralement assez faible (en théorie, environ 1 500 francs), distribuée à tout le monde et censée donner à tous le choix de travailler ou de ne pas travailler. Une telle solution, comme celle d'un secteur spécialisé, non seulement transforme les bénéficiaires en assistés, mais les désigne également comme socialement inadaptés et risque de constituer un prétexte au développement effréné d'un secteur dit concurrentiel. Dans la mesure où l'accès au travail est garanti à tous, il est préférable d'éviter cette solution et de faire en sorte, en revanche, qu'une partie des richesses issues de la production aille directement financer des services publics ouverts à tous, comme les services de garde d'enfants, les hôpitaux, des services de santé de proximité, des associations renouvelées ayant pris en charge certaines compétences... Ainsi cette société, dotée d'une conception de la « liberté communautaire » et attentive à sa cohésion, ferait-elle sienne une philosophie de la répartition volontaire des risques et des biens sociaux qui se substituerait à la manière « naturelle » dont ils sont actuellement répartis. Cette philosophie s'appuierait sur l'idée que chacun, dès l'instant de sa naissance et tout au long de sa vie sociale, est susceptible d'être confronté exactement aux mêmes risques sociaux, contre lesquels il lui est inutile de vouloir s'assurer seul, car il se retirerait ainsi de la communauté sociale : la reconnaissance du partage de certains risques et de certains biens fait éminemment partie du lien social.

Une telle réduction de la place du travail, même contrôlée, comporte à l'évidence des risques. Quatre en particulier doivent être mentionnés. Le premier, c'est que l'espace ainsi libéré soit l'occasion du développement de formes de domination ou de subordination naturelles que l'on croyait disparues, par exemple que la diminution du temps de travail ne s'opère pas également entre les catégories socioprofessionnelles ou les sexes, mais soit par exemple l'occasion d'un retour des femmes au foyer, alors même que celles-ci ont gagné leur émancipation par le travail, et que cette raison n'est sans doute pas étrangère au fait qu'elles y sont plus attachées que quiconque aujourd'hui. Les formes de partage et les modalités selon lesquelles ce dernier pourrait s'opérer ne sont donc pas anodines. L'enjeu est de réussir à dépasser cette étape historique du « tout travail » sans cependant retomber dans des formes régressives dont le travail nous avait en partie libérés. Le second risque, c'est que l'espace libéré, loin d'être réenchanté, soit au contraire l'occasion de multiplier des comportements de surconsommation, de frustration ou de repli sur la sphère individuelle et de favoriser le désintérêt vis-à-vis de l'action ou de la responsabilité collective, qui, après tout, seront en effet non marchandes, et donc peu intéressantes pour des individus habitués à la rationalité limitée. Tout l'enjeu est donc bien de parvenir à faire de cet espace un espace public, sans bien évidemment y contraindre quiconque, en suscitant l'envie d'une telle participation, et sans, bien entendu, que les activités individuelles soient condamnées[482]. Il y a évidemment là aussi toute une réflexion à mener sur l'articulation des temps privés et des temps sociaux, mais également sur ce que recouvre, en particulier en matière d'activités individuelles ou collectives, le terme de loisir, employé par toute une école de pensée dans les années 1960 et 1970[483]. La question principale est ici de savoir si nous sommes prêts à une « société de liberté[484] », si nous sommes disposés à nous passer de cette logique effrénée de développement, si nous serons capables d'investir aussi puissamment nos énergies utopiques, donc notre peur métaphysique, sur d'autres systèmes et si ceux-ci n'entraîneront pas des formes d'aliénation pires que celles que nous avons connues avec le travail.

Le troisième risque, c'est qu'un fort désinvestissement du travail aboutisse à ce que l'on ne tienne plus aucun compte des conditions réelles de travail et de production, c'est-à-dire qu'il n'y ait plus aucune raison d'améliorer les conditions de travail ou de rechercher une toujours plus grande cogestion de l'entreprise, puisque le travail sera considéré plutôt comme une obligation sociale que comme un possible lieu d'épanouissement et l'entreprise comme un simple lieu de production. De la même façon, et c'est le quatrième risque qu'il nous semble nécessaire de prendre en considération, le désenchantement du travail pourrait freiner les incitations à allonger les formations, à élever le niveau de formation du pays, et donc son potentiel de compétitivité, d'autant plus qu'une partie des rémunérations ne seront plus individuelles.

A cet ensemble d'incertitudes bien réelles, une seule réponse peut être apportée : notre capacité à enchanter d'autres espaces que celui de la production. En formulant cette réponse, nous n'en appelons ni à une nouvelle utopie des Temps postmodernes ni à un « retour aux sources », et donc à la politique, au rassemblement sur l'agora ou à la démocratie directe. Nous espérons plutôt le développement, à côté du travail, d'autres activités, collectives ou individuelles, de manière à ce que chacun devienne, comme le souhaitait Marx, multiactif. Marx avait parfaitement compris à son époque l'enjeu que recouvre aujourd'hui l'expression de « pleine activité ». Dans l'esprit de ceux qui l'utilisent, elle signifie le plus souvent qu'à côté de la population qui dispose d'un emploi il faut offrir à celle qui en est exclue un possible accès à une activité qui, sans être de l'emploi, y ressemble... Ainsi la pleine activité de la société recouvrira-t-elle des réalités différentes : emplois classiques pour les uns, activités « nouvelles » pour les autres, les deux relevant de la catégorie générale du travail. Nous pensons au contraire avec Marx que la notion de pleine activité doit s'appliquer non pas à la société dans son ensemble, mais à chaque individu, chacun disposant à la fois d'un temps d'emploi et d'un temps consacré à d'autres activités qui ne seraient ni de l'emploi ni du travail [485] Car, plus encore que de revenus ou de statut, c'est de temps qu'il s'agit, et Smith n'était sans doute pas si loin de la vérité lorsqu'il assimilait temps et travail. Mais, en contribuant à homogénéiser la notion et à en faire un concept univoque, il a également considérablement gommé, non pas tant la diversité des travaux concrets que le rapport extrêmement diversifié au temps auquel ouvrent les différents types de travail. Chaque type de travail, de statut, de contrat, de position sociale implique un accès propre au temps : rationné pour les uns, totalement dépendant pour les autres, identique au mouvement même de leur vie pour d'autres encore. Parce que son utilisation nous conduit à deux erreurs majeures — croire que le champ du travail est plus large que celui de l'emploi et croire qu'il est perçu de manière identique par chacun —, nous ne devrions plus aujourd'hui employer le terme « travail » que de manière très prudente. Désormais, il signifie trop et ne nous est plus utile. Il cache, derrière son apparente unité, des rapports différents au temps, et particulièrement au temps autonome, c'est-à-dire au temps libre, au sens aristotélicien : libre pour de belles actions, source de richesses au même titre que la production. Sans doute est-ce un nouveau rapport au temps, valeur individuelle et collective majeure, que le desserrement de la contrainte du travail devrait permettre pour l'ensemble des individus, un temps dont la maîtrise et l'organisation redeviendraient, après plusieurs siècles d'éclipse, un art essentiel.

NOTES

1. « Les faits que nous avons étudiés sont tous, qu'on nous permette l'expression, des faits sociaux totaux ou, si l'on veut — mais nous aimons moins le mot — généraux : c'est-à-dire qu'ils mettent en branle, dans certains cas, la totalité de la société et de ses institutions (potlatch, clans affrontés, tribus se visitant, etc.) et, dans d'autres cas, seulement un très grand nombre d'institutions... » M. Mauss, *Sociologie et Anthropologie*, IIᵉ partie : « Essai sur le don. Forme et raison de l'échange dans les sociétés archaïques », PUF, coll. « Quadrige », 1989, p. 275.

2. A part A. Gorz en France, en particulier *Métamorphoses du travail. Quête du sens*, Galilée, 1988 ; J.-M. Vincent, *Critique du travail*, PUF, coll. « Pratiques théoriques », 1987, ou certains auteurs qui se sont intéressés épisodiquement à l'histoire du travail (voir par exemple A. Cotta, *L'Homme au travail*, Fayard, 1987), les auteurs sont surtout allemands et correspondent à des disciplines croisées — philosophie, sociologie, sciences sociales — qui sont regroupées sous l'appellation « sciences de la société » et qui n'ont pas d'équivalent en France.

3. « J'appelle " idéologie " l'ensemble des idées et des valeurs communes dans une société. Comme il y a dans le monde moderne un ensemble d'idées et de valeurs qui est commun à de nombreuses sociétés, pays ou nations, nous parlerons d'une " idéologie moderne " en contraste avec l'idéologie de telle société traditionnelle », L. Dumont, *Homo aequalis I, Genèse et épanouissement de l'idéologie économique*, Gallimard, 1985, p. 16. L. Dumont emploie ici le terme d'idéologie dans son sens le plus tardif. Voir note 6 *infra*.

4. Sciences de la nature et sciences de l'esprit se sont opposées, quant à leur méthode, à leur objet et à leur légitimité respectives, à plusieurs reprises, en particulier entre 1880 et 1914, puis du milieu des années 1950 au milieu des années 1960. Il s'agit de savoir quel est le statut des sciences

de l'esprit vis-à-vis des sciences de la nature. Voir, pour ces controverses, W. Dilthey, *Introduction à l'étude des sciences humaines. Essai sur le fondement qu'on pourrait donner à l'étude de la société et de l'histoire*, PUF, 1942 ; M. Weber, *Essai sur la théorie de la science*, Plon, 1965, et, pour le XXᵉ siècle et la querelle du positivisme (entre Adorno et Popper, puis Habermas et Albert), *De Vienne à Francfort. La querelle des sciences sociales*, Editions Complexe, 1979.

5. Dès 1892, Frege, dans un article célèbre, propose que la valeur de vérité constitue la référence des assertions et des énoncés, qui ont par ailleurs un sens. Les *Principia mathematica* de Russell et Whitehead marquent le début du positivisme logique. La caractéristique majeure des auteurs qui se situent dans cette lignée, c'est d'éliminer du discours les phrases sans sens, comme celles dont est truffée la métaphysique, disent-ils. Comme l'exprime lapidairement A. Ayer dans *Truth, Language and Logic* (1936) : « Un énoncé est littéralement doté de sens si, et seulement si, il est vérifiable de manière analytique ou empirique. » Pour l'histoire de cette période, voir P. Jacob, *De Vienne à Cambridge*, Gallimard, 1980, et M. Canto-Sperber, *La Philosophie morale britannique*, PUF, 1994.

6. La notion a considérablement évolué depuis les « idéologues », dont Destutt de Tracy (1754-1836), Cabanis ou Volney, pour lesquels l'idéologie est la théorie de la constitution des idées à partir des sens, en passant par le moment marxien où l'idéologie est la représentation — fausse — que la société se fait d'elle-même : « Si, dans toute idéologie, les hommes et leur condition apparaissent sens dessus dessous comme dans une *camera obscura*, ce phénomène découle de leur procès de vie historique, tout comme l'inversion des objets sur la rétine provient de leur processus de vie directement physique », Marx, *L'Idéologie allemande*, in *Œuvres*, tome III, Gallimard, coll. « La Pléiade », 1982, p. 1056.

7. Voir la *Lettre sur l'humanisme*, écrite en 1946 par Heidegger pour se démarquer de l'existentialisme français et de l'utilisation qui était faite de sa philosophie en France, par Sartre notamment. Heidegger, *Lettre sur l'humanisme*, Aubier, 1989.

8. L'école de Francfort est le nom donné à ce courant de pensée qui a rassemblé, de 1923, date de la création d'un Institut de recherches sociales à Francfort, à la fin des années 1970, des auteurs allant de Adorno et Horheimer à Habermas, en passant par Marcuse, Fromm et Benjamin. Ils ont pour caractéristique commune d'être les héritiers critiques du marxisme et de revendiquer une approche non pas métaphysique mais critique des problèmes sociaux et politiques. Voir J.-M. Vincent, *La Théorie critique de l'école de Francfort*, Galilée, 1976 ; P.-L. Assoun, *L'Ecole de Francfort*, PUF, coll. « Que sais-je ? », 1990, pour une bibliographie plus complète.

9. Par exemple les ouvrages de L. Dumont, assez lus dans ce milieu.

10. « Ose savoir », c'est le grand défi que Kant lance à l'homme. Selon Kant, l'homme est sorti de sa minorité, de l'obscurantisme, de la croyance

aveugle en l'autorité ; il doit désormais se comporter en individu majeur en se conduisant selon sa raison. Voir E. Kant, *Réponse à la question : Qu'est-ce que les Lumières ?*, GF-Flammarion, 1992.

11. Sur toutes les questions traitant des politiques de l'emploi et de la protection sociale, on pourra consulter pour plus de détails : M.-Th. Join-Lambert, A. Bolot-Gittler, C. Daniel, D. Lenoir, D. Méda, *Politiques sociales*, FNSP/Dalloz, 1994.

12. Les catégories à travers lesquelles sont appréhendés travail et non-travail n'ont pas été considérablement modifiées depuis la fin du XIXe siècle. Voir N. Baverez, R. Salais, B. Reynaud, *L'Invention du chômage*, Paris, PUF, 1986.

13. 12,6 % de la population active, 3,3 millions de personnes officiellement, 5 millions si l'on compte toutes les personnes à la recherche d'un emploi, sorties du marché du travail, en formation, en contrats très précaires.

14. On consultera, pour avoir une idée des différents auteurs qui défendent depuis quelques années des positions assez proches sur le travail, les ouvrages et articles suivants : A. Supiot, *Critique du droit du travail*, PUF, 1994 (livre remarquable dont il sera fréquemment question ici) ; A. Supiot, « Le travail, liberté partagée », in *Droit social*, octobre 1993 et la réponse, D. Méda, « Travail et politiques sociales », in *Droit social*, avril 1994 ; C. Dubar, *La Socialisation*, PUF, 1991 ; une série d'articles dans la revue *Projet* n° 236, intitulée *Le Travail à sa place* et dans la revue *Esprit* n° 204, août-septembre 1994, en particulier ceux consacrés à « La France et son chômage, le partage du travail dans l'impasse » ; le rapport de l'Institut du travail intitulé *Les Attitudes devant le travail*, septembre 1993.

15. Le Centre des jeunes dirigeants est une association de dirigeants d'entreprises qui a souvent pris des positions avancées en matière sociale. La citation est extraite d'un texte intitulé « L'illusion du plein emploi », publié dans le numéro de janvier 1994 de la revue *Futuribles*.

16. H. Bartoli, économiste et humaniste chrétien, a écrit en particulier deux ouvrages très lus à l'époque : *Science économique et travail*, Dalloz, 1957, dont est extraite la présente citation, p. 49, et *La Doctrine économique et sociale de Karl Marx*, Seuil, 1947.

17. Voir principalement J. Lacroix, *Personne et amour*, Seuil, 1956, et « La notion du travail », in XXIXes Journées universitaires catholiques, Lyon, 1942 ; R. P. Chenu : « L'*Homo œconomicus* et le chrétien », in *Économie et humanisme*, mai-juin 1945, et *La Théologie au XIIe siècle*, Paris, 1957 ; E. Mounier, *Le Personnalisme*, Seuil, 1949 ; J. Vialatoux, « La signification humaine du travail », in *Bulletin des sociétés catholiques de Lyon*, juillet-décembre 1948, et H. Bartoli, *Science économique et travail, op. cit.*, chapitre II, « Le travail catégorie finalisante ». Voir également la lettre encyclique *Laborem exercens* du souverain pontife Jean-Paul II, 1981, publiée in *Jean-Paul II parle des questions sociales*, Livre de Poche, 1994.

18. *Par exemple :* « *Un être n'est un être authentique, c'est-à-dire un être libre, que dans la mesure où il fait un effort laborieux.* » (*R. Ruyer, cité par Bartoli.*)

19. « *Le travail arrache l'homme à l'extériorité, il pénètre d'humanité la nature. Jailli de la nécessité, il réalise l'œuvre de la liberté et affirme notre puissance.* [...] *L'acte ontologique du travail ne peut s'effectuer qu'en transcendant les bornes de l'environnement animal vers la totalité du monde humain : le travail est l'acte ontologique constituant du monde.* [...] *Le travail, c'est la vérité de l'idéalisme et du matérialisme, c'est l'homme au principe de la matière et c'est la conscience émergeant du vide vers la plénitude de la joie* », Vuillemin, *L'Etre et le travail*, PUF, 1949.

20. A. Supiot, *Critique du droit du travail*, *op. cit.*, p. 3.

21. Y. Schwarz, *Expérience et connaissance du travail*, Messidor-Editions sociales, 1988 ; du même auteur, *Travail et philosophie, convocations mutuelles*, Octares Editions, 1992 ; et articles du même auteur, dans les n°s 10 et 16 de *Futur antérieur*, consacrés au travail ; J. Bidet, auteur en particulier de *Que faire du* Capital *?*, Méridiens Klincksieck, 1985, et de *Marx et le marché : essai sur la modernité*, PUF, 1990, et codirecteur de la revue *Actuel Marx*. Voir aussi « Le travail fait époque », in *Politis*, n° 7, p. 75 ; J.-M. Vincent, *op. cit.*, et codirecteur de la revue *Futur antérieur*, déjà citée.

22. In *Politis*, n° 7, *op. cit.*, p. 75.

23. *Science économique et travail*, *op. cit.*, p. 51 et 52.

24. Le *Traité de sociologie du travail*, de G. Friedmann et P. Naville, A. Colin, 1972, qui a formé des générations de sociologues, commence ainsi : « Le travail est le trait spécifique de l'espèce humaine. L'homme est un animal social essentiellement occupé de travail. Le travail est le commun dénominateur et la condition de toute vie humaine en société. » Les auteurs se réfèrent à Bergson pour indiquer que le travail humain consiste à créer de l'utilité et à Mayo, pour qui « l'homme, animal social et essentiellement occupé par le travail, ne peut s'exprimer et s'épanouir que dans la collectivité où il exerce son activité professionnelle ». Le titre de l'ouvrage de Sainsaulieu est également significatif : dans *L'Identité au travail*, FNSP, 1977, il écrit : « S'il y a des identités collectives, c'est que les individus ont en commun une même logique d'acteur dans les positions sociales qu'ils occupent. » Voir en particulier p. 318 à 341.

25. « Nos sociétés ont instauré de nouvelles formes de sociabilité en inventant des solutions techniques à leurs problèmes d'organisation. [...] Dès le début des années soixante, l'organisation était ainsi clairement désignée comme lieu d'implication très forte des individus dans un milieu humain complexe. La scène des rapports de travail habituellement envisagée sous le double angle des rapports fonctionnels de production et des rapports collectifs de lutte sociale acquérait ainsi une troisième dimension : celle des échanges humains quotidiens de production, où le fonctionnel, l'interpersonnel et le collectif pouvaient, en se mêlant,

contribuer à donner une nouvelle signification au monde du travail », *ibid.*

26. C. Dejours, « Entre souffrance et réappropriation, le sens du travail », in *Politis*, n° 7, p. 23. On lira aussi du même auteur, *Travail : usure mentale. De la psychopathologie à la psychodynamique du travail*, Bayard, 1993.

27. H. Bartoli, *Science économique et travail, op. cit.*, p. 53 et 54.

28. *Ibid.*, p. 55.

29. « Le travail humain porte en lui la double exigence d'un épanouissement de la personne et de la communauté et d'une spiritualisation de la nature, mais il est l'occasion d'aliénations sans cesse renaissantes. [...] L'appropriation privée des moyens de production et la présence d'hommes sans aucun avoir, la séparation du capital et du travail rendue inéluctable par la nécessité de la possession de gros capitaux pour le lancement d'une grosse affaire en temps de révolution industrielle, entraînent la double apparition d'une classe vendeuse et d'une classe acheteuse de travail. Le travail est ainsi ravalé au rang d'une marchandise objet de trafic », écrit Bartoli dans le même chapitre.

30. Habermas, *Le Discours philosophique de la modernité*, Gallimard, 1988, p. 97.

31. C. Offe, « Le travail comme catégorie de la sociologie », in *Les Temps modernes*, 1985, n° 466, p. 2058 à 2095. Voir aussi, du même auteur, plusieurs articles dans le cahier spécial n° 24 de la *Kölner Zeitschrift für Soziologie und Sozialpsychologie*, 1982, et un ouvrage codirigé par C. Offe, *Arbeitszeitpolitik, Formen und Folgen einer Neuverteilung der Arbeitszeit*, Campus, 1982.

32. R. Dahrendorf, « Im Entschwinden der Arbeitsgesellschaft », *Merkur*, n° 8, 1980.

33. B. Guggenberger, *Wenn uns die Arbeit ausgeht* [Quand le travail vient à manquer], Hanser, 1988.

34. P. Descola, cité par M.-N. Chamoux, « Sociétés avec et sans concept de travail : remarques anthropologiques », in *Actes du colloque interdisciplinaire « Travail : recherche et prospective »*, Pirrtem-CNRS, Lyon, décembre 1992, Groupe transversal « concept de travail », p. 21, document ronéoté. Publié depuis dans la revue *Sociologie du travail*, hors-série, 1994.

35. M. Sahlins, *Age de pierre, âge d'abondance*, Gallimard, 1976, et *Au cœur des sociétés : raison utilitaire et raison culturelle*, Gallimard, 1991.

36. On lira également de P. Clastres *La Société contre l'Etat*, Ed. de Minuit, 1986, en particulier le chapitre XI.

37. B. Malinowski, *Les Argonautes du Pacifique occidental*, Gallimard, coll. « Tel », 1989, p. 177.

38. *Ibid.*, p. 118.

39. *Ibid.*

40. M. Sahlins, « L'Economie tribale », in M. Godelier, *Un domaine*

contesté, l'anthropologie économique, recueil de textes, Mouton, 1974, p 245.

41. « Les hommes rivalisent entre eux à qui ira le plus vite, à qui fera la meilleure besogne, soulèvera le plus de fardeaux pour amener au jardin de gros piquets ou transporter des ignames récoltées. [...] En pratique donc, le jardinier ne tire aucun bénéfice personnel, au sens utilitaire, de sa récolte, mais la qualité et la quantité de sa production lui valent des éloges et une réputation qui lui sont décernés d'une manière directe et solennelle. [...] Chacun dans sa propre parcelle expose le fruit de son travail à l'œil critique des groupes qui défilent devant les jardins, admirant, comparant et vantant les meilleurs résultats », in B. Malinowski, *op. cit.*, p. 118.

42. *Ibid.*, p. 119.

43. Aristote, *Métaphysique*, A, 2, 982b, Vrin, 1986. Quelques lignes plus haut, Aristote écrit : « Ainsi donc, si ce fut bien pour échapper à l'ignorance que les premiers philosophes se livrèrent à la philosophie, c'est qu'évidemment ils poursuivaient le savoir en vue de la seule connaissance, et non pour une fin utilitaire. [...] De même que nous appelons libre celui qui est à lui-même sa fin et n'existe pas pour un autre, ainsi cette science est aussi la seule de toutes les sciences qui soit une discipline libérale, puisque seule elle est à elle-même sa propre fin. »

44. En particulier dans la *République*, livres III, IV, V.

45. Aristote, *La Politique*, livre I, chapitres III, IV, V, VI, Vrin, 1982.

46. *Ibid.*, livre VIII, chapitre II.

47. *Ibid.*, livre III, chapitre V.

48. Platon, *Protagoras*, 320c-322d, GF-Flammarion, 1967.

49. *Ibid.*

50. « La vie de loisir a en elle-même le plaisir et le bonheur de la vie bienheureuse. Mais cela n'appartient pas à ceux qui ont une vie laborieuse, mais à ceux qui ont une vie de loisir, car l'homme laborieux accomplit son labeur en vue de quelque fin qu'il ne possède pas, mais le bonheur est une fin qui ne s'accompagne pas de peine, mais de plaisir », Aristote, *La Politique*, *op. cit.*, livre VIII, chapitre III.

51. Ainsi Archimède s'est-il servi de certaines de ses inventions pour défendre sa patrie et non pas pour produire avec un effort moindre. Voir P.-M. Schuhl, *Machinisme et philosophie*, PUF, 1947.

52. Sur toute cette période on pourra consulter les nombreux ouvrages de P. Vidal- Naquet et J.-P. Vernant, en particulier *Travail et esclavage en Grèce ancienne*, Editions Complexe, 1988 ; *Mythe et Pensée chez les Grecs*, Maspero-La Découverte, 1985 ; *Mythe et société en Grèce ancienne*, Maspero-La Découverte, 1974 ; voir aussi Hannah Arendt, *Condition de l'homme moderne*, Calmann-Lévy, coll. « Agora », 1988. Voir également les nombreux ouvrages de M. I. Finley, dont *Economie et société en Grèce ancienne*, La Découverte, 1984, et *Le Monde d'Ulysse*, Seuil, coll. « Points », 1990. On pourra compléter par H. Wallon, *Histoire de*

l'esclavage dans l'Antiquité, R. Laffont, coll. « Bouquins », 1988, et Rostovtseff, *Histoire économique et sociale du monde hellénistique* Robert Laffont, coll. « Bouquins », 1989. Voir également les articles du *Journal de psychologie normale et pathologique*, années 1947, 1948 et 1955, en particulier l'article d'A. Aymard, « L'idée de travail dans la Grèce archaïque », 1948.

53. Cicéron, *De Officiis*.

54. Voir la discussion qui suit l'article d'A. Aymard cité in *Journal de psychologie normale et pathologique, op. cit.*, 1948.

55. Sur toute cette partie, voir J. Le Goff, *Pour un autre Moyen Age. Temps, travail et culture en Occident*, Gallimard, coll. « Tel », 1991.

56. Genèse, III, 19, traduction L. Segond, Société biblique française.

57. *Ibid.*, II, 2.

58. Saint Paul, IIe Epître aux Thessaloniciens, 3, 10.

59. *Ibid.*, III, 11-12.

60. Saint Augustin écrit ainsi dans les *Confessions* : « Mais tout cela était presque le néant, étant encore complètement informe, et pourtant cela était apte à recevoir une forme [...] Quant à cette terre même, votre œuvre, elle n'était qu'une matière informe, étant invisible, chaotique et les ténèbres régnant sur l'abîme. C'est de cette terre invisible, chaotique, de cette masse informe, de ce presque néant, que vous deviez former tout ce par quoi subsiste et ne subsiste pas ce monde muable », livre 12, chapitre VIII.

61. « Nous vous exhortons, frères, [...] à mettre votre honneur à vivre tranquilles, à vous occuper de vos propres affaires, et à travailler de vos mains, comme nous vous l'avons recommandé, en sorte que vous vous conduisiez honnêtement envers ceux du dehors, et que vous n'ayez besoin de personne », IIe Thess., *op. cit.*, IV, 11-12.

62. Voir E. Delaruelle, « Le travail dans les règles monastiques occidentales du IVe au IXe siècle », in *Journal de psychologie..., op. cit.*, 1948. Les citations de saint Augustin sont extraites de la lettre CCXL, appelée Règle de saint Augustin et du *De opere monachorum*, que nous n'avons pas directement consultés.

63. Règle de saint Benoît, chapitre XLVIII, in *Journal de psychologie, op. cit.*

64. Un des ouvrages essentiels pour mieux comprendre le rôle de la notion d'œuvres dans les religions catholique et protestante est évidemment *L'Ethique protestante et l'esprit du capitalisme* de Weber, Presses-Pocket, coll. « Agora », 1990. Sur le rapport au temps qui va s'inverser, voir le texte de Benjamin Franklin cité par Weber p. 44, et sur les œuvres tout le chapitre II : « Le Dieu du calvinisme réclamait non pas des bonnes œuvres isolées, mais une vie tout entière de bonnes œuvres érigées en système », p. 134.

65. J. Le Goff, *op. cit.*

66. Voir « Métiers licites et métiers illicites dans l'Occident médiéval », in *Pour un autre Moyen Age, op. cit.*, p. 92.

67. *Ibid.*, p. 96.

68. *Cf.* G. Duby, *Les Trois Ordres ou l'imaginaire du féodalisme*, Gallimard, 1978.

69. Saint Thomas, *Somme théologique*, question 77.

70. Malgré tout, le travail ne fait pas l'objet d'une valorisation. Voir l'interprétation que donne Weber de saint Thomas dans *L'Ethique protestante...*, *op. cit.*, p. 192 : « Pour lui, ce n'est que *naturali ratione* que le travail est nécessaire à la subsistance de l'individu et de la communauté...[La prescription] est valable pour l'espèce, non pour l'individu. » Surtout, l'idée de développer ses capacités, par exemple intellectuelles, pour les vendre, demeure inconcevable.

71. Il n'en reste pas moins que le principe *Deo placere vix potest* est considéré comme ayant force de loi, de même que les paroles de saint Thomas qualifiant de *turpitudo* la recherche du profit.

72. F. Brunot, *Histoire de la langue française*, tome VI, Ire partie, fascicule I, p. 1349.

73. L. Febvre, « Travail : évolution d'un mot et d'une idée », in *Journal de psychologie...*, *op. cit.*, 1948, p. 19-28.

74. *Ibid.* Pour toute cette partie, voir également, I. Meyerson, « Le travail, fonction psychologique », in *Journal de psychologie* ..., *op. cit.*, 1955, p. 3-17.

75. A. Smith, *Recherches sur les causes de la richesse des nations*, GF-Flammarion, 1991.

76. B. Mandeville, *La Fable des Abeilles, ou les vices privés font le bien public*, publié en 1714, Vrin, 1974.

77. B. Franklin, *Advice to a Young Tradesman*, cité in Weber, *L'Ethique protestante et l'esprit du capitalisme*, Presses-Pocket, coll. « Agora », 1990, p. 46.

78. *Cf.* C. Larrère, *L'Invention de l'économie au XVIIIe siècle*, PUF, 1992. Voir p. 36 et suivantes.

79. Th. Malthus, *Principes d'économie politique considérés sous le rapport de leur application pratique*, Calmann-Lévy, coll. « Perspectives économiques », 1969.

80. J.-B. Say, *Traité d'économie politique*, Calmann-Lévy, coll. « Perspectives économiques », 1972.

81. Le terme « physiocrates » désigne un ensemble d'auteurs essentiellement français, dont Quesnay (1694-1774), Le Mercier de la Rivière (1721-1793), Turgot (1727-1781), Dupont de Nemours (1739-1817). Ils considèrent que seule la terre est productive, que seule la nature (*physis*) est capable de créer de la valeur, du surplus. L'industrie et le commerce sont, quant à eux, non productifs. Pour une analyse de leurs idées, voir C. Larrère, *L'Invention de l'économie au XVIIIe siècle*, *op. cit.*

82. La manufacture d'épingles est prise comme l'exemple type du lieu

où s'exerce à plein la division du travail. Un ouvrier, « quelque adroit qu'il fût », pourrait peut-être à peine faire une épingle toute sa journée s'il était seul alors qu'à dix, et si chacun ne s'occupe que d'une opération particulière, chacun parvient à en faire quatre mille huit cents. *Cf. Recherches..., op. cit.*, p. 72.

83. *Ibid., op. cit.*, p. 100.

84. *Ibid.*, p. 102.

85. *Ibid.*, p. 75.

86. *Ibid.*, p. 73.

87. « ... qui ne se fixe ou ne se réalise sur aucun objet, sur aucune chose qu'on puisse vendre ensuite [...] ses services périssant à l'instant même où il les rend », *ibid.*, p. 418.

88. *Principes..., op. cit.*, p. 5.

89. « Il est évident que nous ne pouvons aborder, sous le point de vue pratique, aucune discussion sur l'accroissement relatif de la richesse chez les différentes nations si nous n'avons un moyen quelconque, quelque imparfait qu'il soit, d'évaluer la somme de cet accroissement », *ibid*.

90. *Ibid*, p. 13 ; c'est nous qui soulignons.

91. *Ibid.*, p. 14.

92. Locke, *Traité du gouvernement civil*, chapitre v, « De la propriété des choses », § 27, GF-Flammarion, 1992, p. 163. Le *Traité du Gouvernement civil* a été publié en 1690.

93. « Tout ce qu'il a tiré de l'état de nature, par sa peine et son industrie, appartient à lui seul », *ibid*

94. « La plus sacrée et la plus inviolable de toutes les propriétés est celle de son propre travail, écrit Smith, parce qu'elle est la source originaire de toutes les autres propriétés. Le patrimoine du pauvre est dans sa force et dans l'adresse de ses mains », *Recherches..., op. cit* p. 198.

95. « Dans cet état primitif qui précède l'appropriation des terres et l'accumulation des capitaux, le produit entier du travail appartient à l'ouvrier. Il n'y a ni propriétaire ni maître avec qui il doive partager [...] Mais cet état primitif, dans lequel l'ouvrier jouissait de tout le produit de son propre travail, ne put pas durer au-delà de l'époque où furent introduites l'appropriation des terres et l'accumulation des capitaux », *ibid.*, p. 135-136.

96. Et qui apparaissait d'ailleurs comme tel à un auteur comme Polanyi ; voir *La Grande Transformation*, Gallimard, 1983 . « *Labor* est le terme technique qui désigne les êtres humains du moment qu'ils ne sont pas employeurs mais employés », p. 111, et Weber, *Histoire économique, esquisse d'une histoire universelle de l'économie et de la société*, Gallimard, 1991, en particulier le chapitre ix, « La naissance du capitalisme moderne », § 1 : concepts et présupposés du capitalisme.

97. Pour distinguer les différentes formes d'utilisation de la main-

d'œuvre en vigueur de la fin du Moyen Age à la Révolution industrielle, voir Weber, *Histoire économique...*, *op. cit.*, en particulier le chapitre II.

98. Voir ce que G.H. Camerlynck dit de Pothier dans *Le Contrat de travail*, Dalloz, 1982, et cette affirmation de Polanyi dans *La Grande Transformation*, *op. cit.*, p. 242 : « Dans l'avènement du marché du travail, le droit coutumier a joué en gros un rôle positif. Ce sont les juristes, non les économistes, qui ont été les premiers à énoncer avec force la théorie du travail marchandise. »

99. *Le Traité du contrat de louage* date de 1764.

100. Voir G.H. Camerlynck, *Le Contrat de travail*, *op. cit.*, chapitre I p. 3 : « Le contrat de louage de services chez Pothier ».

101. La loi Le Chapelier, qui date, elle, du 14 juin 1791, interdit toute coalition en s'inspirant ainsi très fortement de la condamnation que Rousseau avait portée contre les associations dans le *Contrat social* (livre II, chapitre III, 1762). Le rapporteur de la loi Le Chapelier indique : « Il faut remonter au principe que c'est aux conventions libres d'individu à individu de fixer la journée de travail pour chaque ouvrier, à l'ouvrier de maintenir la convention qui a été faite avec celui qui l'occupe. Quant au salaire, seules les conventions libres et individuelles peuvent le fixer. »

102. « Les conventions légalement formées tiennent lieu de loi à ceux qui les ont faites », Code civil, article 1134.

103. « C'est par la convention qui se fait habituellement entre ces deux personnes, dont l'intérêt n'est nullement le même, que se détermine le taux commun des salaires. Les ouvriers désirent gagner le plus possible ; les maîtres, donner le moins qu'ils peuvent ; les premiers sont disposés à se concerter pour élever les salaires, les seconds pour les abaisser. Il n'est pas difficile de prévoir lequel des deux partis, dans toutes les circonstances ordinaires, doit avoir l'avantage dans le débat et imposer forcément à l'autre toutes ses conditions ; les maîtres, étant en plus grand nombre, peuvent se concerter plus aisément ; et de plus, la loi les autorise à se concerter entre eux, ou du moins ne leur interdit pas, tandis qu'elle l'interdit aux ouvriers... », *Recherches...*, *op. cit.*, p. 137.

104. Weber est d'ailleurs extrêmement prudent : il ne prétend pas « déduire » un phénomène historique d'une transformation des représentations. Voir *L'Ethique protestante...*, *op. cit.*, p. 103-104.

105. Weber s'attarde sur la notion de *Beruf*, qui signifie en allemand à la fois métier, tâche et vocation et qui a pris ce sens avec Luther. Le fait que le travail a été soudainement perçu comme une vocation, un devoir imposé par Dieu, « n'est pas un produit de la nature. Il ne peut être suscité uniquement par de hauts ou de bas salaires. C'est le résultat d'un long, d'un persévérant processus d'éducation. » Weber tente de retrouver les grandes étapes qui ont conduit de la condamnation de l'ici-bas à sa valorisation. Voir en particulier p. 95 et suivantes et p. 123 et suivantes de l'*Ethique protestante...*

106. C'est cette condamnation qui explique en particulier les hésita-

tions de Malthus au début de ses *Principes d'économie politique* : tous les moralistes, dit-il, nous ont bien enseigné qu'il fallait préférer la vertu à la richesse. Si la vertu constitue la richesse, pourquoi la fuir, etc. ? *Cf.* p. 11 et suivantes.

107. A. Hirschman, *Les Passions et les intérêts*, PUF, coll. « Sociologies », 1980, p. 15.

108. Montesquieu, *L'Esprit des lois*, introduction.

109. L. Dumont, *Homo aequalis*, *op. cit.*

110. Voir *Méditations métaphysiques*, GF-Flammarion, 1979, et *Les Principes de la philosophie*, Vrin, 1970.

111. Voir en particulier les *Pensées*, et, dans celles-ci, Ire partie (« L'homme sans Dieu »), chapitre I (« La place de l'homme dans la nature : les deux infinis ») et chapitre II (« Misère de l'homme »), Le Livre de poche, 1962.

112. Descartes, *Discours de la méthode*.

113. F. Bacon, *Du progrès et de la promotion des savoirs*, Gallimard, coll. « Tel », 1991 ; *La Nouvelle Atlantide*, GF-Flammarion, à paraître.

114. Voir sur ce point les commentaires de H. Achterhuis dans « La responsabilité entre la crainte et l'utopie », in *Hans Jonas, Nature et responsabilité*, Vrin, 1993. Cet auteur interprète la transmutation de la peur en enthousiasme à cette époque par la croyance subite dans les vertus du progrès et de la production : « La situation de rareté toujours menaçante où chacun se bat pour posséder les quelques biens disponibles pourrait être résolue par la production de plus de biens », *op. cit.*, p. 43.

115. Saint Paul, Épître aux Romains, XIII, 1, 2, 5.

116. Hobbes écrit ses œuvres politiques entre 1640 et 1670. Voir *Le Citoyen ou les fondements de la politique*, GF-Flammarion, 1982, et le *Léviathan*, Sirey, 1971. Il faut également prendre en compte les travaux de l'école moderne du droit naturel, machine de guerre contre la conception classique du droit naturel. Grotius, Pufendorf, Burlamaqui en sont les principaux représentants. On trouvera une analyse de ces pensées dans R. Derathé, *Rousseau et la science politique de son temps*, Vrin, 1988. Les représentants de l'école moderne du droit naturel imaginent comme Hobbes une généalogie qui leur permet de distinguer un avant et un après, mais ils se « donnent », à la différence de Hobbes, la sociabilité. Grotius et Pufendorf, en particulier, déduisent l'état civil de la sociabilité naturelle aux hommes. Ce avec quoi Hobbes, et plus tard Rousseau, rompent. *Cf.* C. Larrère, *L'Invention de l'économie...*, *op. cit.*

117. C'est l'interprétation qu'en donne en particulier Hegel, voir *infra* chapitre IX.

118. Il s'agit d'une autre manière de présenter le principe de raison : grâce à sa raison, l'individu trouve en lui-même le principe qui lui donne son unité, qui peut guider ses actions et les expliquer.

119. Les théoriciens du contrat sont légion : Grotius, Pufendorf, Burlamaqui, Hobbes, Locke, Rousseau sont les plus connus

120. Les théories du contrat admettent de nombreuses variantes. Voir R. Derathé, *Rousseau et la science politique de son temps, op. cit.*, et Rousseau, *Contrat social, op. cit.*, I, VI.

121. A. Smith, *Recherches..., op. cit.*, p. 82.

122. *Cf. Métaphysique* : λ, 7, 1072a 25-30 et 1072b 10-15, Vrin, 1986, p. 680.

123. A. Smith, *Recherches..., op. cit.*, p. 79.

124. P. Rosanvallon, *Le Libéralisme économique. Histoire de l'idée de marché*, Seuil, coll. « Points », 1989, et L. Dumont, *Homo aequalis, op. cit.*, et *Essais sur l'individualisme*, Seuil, 1991.

125. P. Rosanvallon, *Le Libéralisme économique, op. cit.*, p. II-III : « La naissance du libéralisme économique [...] doit d'abord être comprise comme une réponse aux problèmes non résolus par les théoriciens politiques du contrat social [...] C'est le marché (économique) et non pas le contrat (politique) qui est le vrai régulateur de la société. » Rosanvallon explique ainsi que la régulation économique, caractérisée par l'automaticité des relations, succède aux explications plus politiques, qui auraient échoué. Nous ne partageons pas cette thèse. Il nous semble au contraire que les deux solutions vont continuer de se développer ensemble, ou du moins qu'il existe deux solutions parfaitement envisageables du même problème, et qui présentent des caractéristiques différentes. C'est parce qu'il ne fait pas cette différence que Rosanvallon se prive de mettre en évidence la considérable originalité de la pensée allemande du XIXᵉ siècle, en particulier celle de Hegel. Nous y reviendrons.

126. Comité de mendicité de la Constituante, 1790, *Premier rapport*.

127. Voir aussi M.-A. Barthe, « Pauvretés et État-providence », in *Revue française des affaires sociales*, nº 3, juillet 1991.

128. *Encyclopédie*, article « Travail », tome XVI, col. 567b, 1765.

129. Sur ce bouleversement conceptuel, et en particulier sur le brutal changement de signification que subit le terme de travail dans les quinze premières années du XIXᵉ siècle, on pourra consulter I. Meyerson, « Le travail, fonction psychologique », *art. cit.*, p. 7 · « C'est au cours du XIXᵉ siècle — siècle d'une vie industrielle et sociale dense — que l'image psychologique du travail tel que nous le connaissons va se dessiner et se préciser. »

130. L'idéalisme allemand n'est pas une école au sens propre, c'est un moment de l'histoire philosophique allemande, qui commence avec Kant et se termine avec les successeurs de Hegel. On parle à propos de la philosophie kantienne d'idéalisme transcendantal, car Kant démontre que notre connaissance des objets ne consiste pas en une réception passive mais en une construction dont nous sommes partie prenante à travers les formes *a priori* de la sensibilité et de l'entendement. Voir article « Kant », in *Gradus philosophique*, L. Jaffro, M. Labrune éd., GF-Flammarion, 1994.

131. « De l'Absolu, il faut dire qu'il est essentiellement résultat, c'est-

à-dire qu'il est à la fin seulement ce qu'il est en vérité. [...] L'Esprit n'est jamais en repos, mais il est toujours emporté dans un mouvement continuellement progressif. [...] La substance est essentiellement sujet, c'est ce qui est exprimé dans la représentation qui annonce l'Absolu comme Esprit : seul le spirituel est effectif », Hegel, *Phénoménologie de l'esprit*, traduction J. Hyppolite, Aubier, 1941, p. 18-19.

132. *Ibid.*, p. 12.

133. Il y a dans les philosophies de Fichte, Schelling et Hegel une véritable volonté de réduire (au sens de « faire disparaître ») la nature, pour que rien ne résiste à la formidable puissance de l'Esprit, esprit de Dieu et esprit humain. C'est au même moment que Goethe parle de « l'esprit qui toujours nie ». On pourra voir en particulier la *Philosophie de la nature* de Schelling. L'idée fondamentale est bien qu'il est incompréhensible que « quelque chose », appelé la nature, puisse être, avoir été et continuer à être différent de et définitivement étranger à Dieu, qui est Esprit.

134. Hegel, *La Philosophie de l'esprit, 1805*, PUF, 1982.

135. *Ibid.*, p. 32 « Travail, instrument, ruse », et p. 53.

136. Sur la première période de Hegel, voir P. Chamley, « La doctrine économique de Hegel et la conception hégélienne du travail », in *Hegel-Studien*, 1965, et, du même auteur, *Economie politique et philosophie chez Steuart et Hegel*, Dalloz, 1963. De Hegel, voir *Phénoménologie..., op. cit.* ; *Précis de l'Encyclopédie des sciences philosophiques*, Vrin, 1970 ; *Principes de la philosophie du droit*, Vrin, 1982. Voir aussi J. Hyppolite, *Introduction à la philosophie de l'histoire de Hegel*, Seuil, coll. « Points », 1983 ; K. Papaioannou, *Hegel*, Presses-Pocket, coll. « Agora », 1987 ; E. Weil, *Hegel et l'Etat*, Vrin, 1974.

137. *Principes de la philosophie..., op. cit.*, § 198, p. 224.

138. *Ibid.*, § 245, traduction J. Hyppolite, in *Introduction..., op. cit.*, p. 121.

139. *Principes de la philosophie..., op. cit.*, § 198 : « de plus, l'abstraction de la façon de produire rend le travail de plus en plus mécanique et offre aussi finalement à l'homme la possibilité de s'en éloigner et de se faire remplacer par la machine », p. 224.

140. C'est ce que montre la structure même de l'*Encyclopédie des sciences philosophiques*, manuel qui comprend l'ensemble du système philosophique de Hegel et qui se présente en trois parties : la logique, la philosophie de la nature et la philosophie de l'esprit. Cette dernière présente elle-même trois moments : l'esprit subjectif, l'esprit objectif, l'esprit absolu. Le travail abstrait et industriel appartient au moment de l'esprit objectif : l'Esprit s'est incarné dans des formes particulières et prend la forme de la moralité sociale, d'abord dans la famille, puis dans la société civile, et enfin dans l'Etat. Mais dans son moment le plus pur et le plus haut, lorsqu'il est esprit absolu, l'Esprit s'exprime par l'art, la religion et la philosophie.

141. Marx, *Ebauche d'une critique de l'économie politique*, « communisme et propriété », in *Œuvres, Economie*, Gallimard, coll. « La Pléiade », tome II, 1979, p. 89.

142. « Ce communisme est un naturalisme achevé, et comme tel un humanisme ; en tant qu'humanisme achevé, il est un naturalisme. Il est la vraie solution du conflit de l'homme avec la nature, de l'homme avec l'homme », *op. cit.*, p. 79.

143. Voir toute la page 61 de *Ebauche...*, *op. cit.*, sur le travail aliéné et les fonctions animales.

144. *Ibid.*, p. 62.

145. *Ibid.*, p. 126.

146. C'est exactement ici que s'opère le retournement majeur : Marx se saisit du concept hégélien de travail, au sens de travail de l'Esprit, mais l'applique à l'homme : « Le seul travail que Hegel connaisse et reconnaisse, c'est le travail abstrait de l'Esprit », *Ibid.*, p. 126. Marx s'empare de ce concept de travail et fait de l'homme, de chaque homme, son sujet.

147. Marx, « Notes de lecture », in *Economie et philosophie, Œuvres, Economie*, tome II, *op. cit.*, p. 22.

148. Il y aurait là, si P. Chamley a raison, une sorte de régression de Marx vis-à-vis de l'avancée conceptuelle de Hegel. Il semble bien en effet que Hegel, qui a lu très tôt Locke, reprenne de celui-ci une conception énergétique et dynamique du travail (l'homme met quelque chose de lui-même dans l'objet), ce qui est au fondement des hésitations de Smith et du choix de Ricardo pour la valeur-travail. Mais Hegel abandonnera, d'après P. Chamley, cette conception, et passera rapidement à cette autre idée fondamentale selon laquelle ce qui importe dans le travail n'est pas ce que l'homme met de lui-même dans l'objet, mais le fait que l'homme travaille pour obtenir de la reconnaissance, à travers l'échange.

149. « Notes de lecture », in *Economie et philosophie, op. cit.*, § 17, « Le travail lucratif », p. 27.

150. *Ebauche d'une critique...*, *op. cit.*, p. 63-64.

151. « Travail forcé, il n'est pas la satisfaction d'un besoin, mais seulement un moyen de satisfaire des besoins en dehors du travail. [...] On en vient donc à ce résultat que l'homme n'a de spontanéité que dans ses fonctions animales : le manger, le boire, la procréation [...] et que dans ses fonctions humaines, il ne se sent plus qu'animalité ; ce qui est animal devient humain, et ce qui est humain devient animal », *ibid.*, p. 61.

152. C'est la critique fondamentale de Marx contre l'économie politique : elle fait semblant de considérer comme naturel ce qui n'est qu'historique ; *cf.*, par exemple, *Economie et philosophie, op. cit.*, p. 37, 44, 56, 67, 71, etc.

153. *Ibid.*, p. 72.

154. Marx, *Principes d'une critique de l'économie politique*, « Le travail comme sacrifice et le travail libre », in *Œuvres, Economie*, tome II, *op. cit.*, p. 289.

155. « Considérer le travail simplement comme un sacrifice, donc comme source de valeur, comme prix payé par les choses et donnant du prix aux choses suivant qu'elles coûtent plus ou moins de travail, c'est s'en tenir à une définition purement négative. [...] Le travail est une activité positive, créatrice », *ibid.*, p. 291-292.

156. *Ibid.*, p. 305, commenté par Habermas dans « L'idée d'une théorie de la connaissance » in *Connaissance et intérêt*, Gallimard, coll. « Tel », 1991, p. 82.

157. *Principes d'une critique de l'économie..., op. cit.*, p. 303.

158. *Ibid.*, p. 310. On lira avec profit les pages qui précédent et, notamment, p. 306 : « La réduction du temps de travail nécessaire permettra le libre épanouissement de l'individu. En effet, grâce aux loisirs et aux moyens mis à la portée de tous, la réduction au minimum du travail social nécessaire favorisera le développement artistique, scientifique, etc., de chacun. »

159. Marx et Engels, *Critique des programmes de Gotha et d'Erfurt*, Editions sociales, 1981.

160. *Ibid.*, p. 154.

161. *Ibid.*, p. 32.

162. *Principes d'une critique de l'économie..., op. cit.*, p. 311.

163. *Ibid.*, p. 308.

164. *Le Capital*, livre III, Conclusion, in *Œuvres, Economie*, tome II, *op. cit.*, p. 1487.

165. A. de Laborde, *De l'esprit d'association dans tous les intérêts de la communauté*, Paris, 1818, p. 3-4, cité in I. Meyerson, « Le travail, fonction psychologique », *art. cit.*

166. « L'industrie comprend ainsi tous les genres du bien-être, elle réunit également tous les moyens de l'obtenir ; tout est de son domaine et participe à ses avantages. [...] On pourrait la définir par l'intelligence, la sagacité dans le travail, la simplification dans la main-d'œuvre, la hardiesse dans les entreprises, le génie d'utilité de la société », *ibid.*, p. 5.

167. *Ibid.*, p. 9.

168. « L'obligation est imposée à chacun de donner constamment à ses forces personnelles une direction utile à l'humanité. Les bras du pauvre continueront à nourrir le riche, mais le riche reçoit commandement de faire travailler sa cervelle et si sa cervelle n'est pas propre au travail, il sera bien obligé de faire travailler ses bras », Saint-Simon, *Lettres d'un habitant de Genève à ses contemporains*, Pereire, 1925, p. 41, cité in J. Dautry, « La notion de travail chez Saint-Simon et Fourier », *Journal de psychologie..., op. cit.*, 1955, p. 64.

169. Saint-Simon, *Introduction aux travaux scientifiques du XIXᵉ siècle*, cité in J. Dautry, art. cit., p. 65.

170. *Ibid.*, p. 67.

171. « Le travail est d'ordre moral et humain, donné dans la conscience, avant même que la nécessité l'impose. En conséquence, il est libre

de sa nature, d'une liberté positive et intérieure, et c'est en raison de cette liberté intérieure qu'il a le droit de revendiquer sa liberté extérieure, en d'autres termes, la destruction de tous les empêchements, obstacles et entraves que peuvent lui susciter le gouvernement et le privilège », écrit Proudhon in *Œuvres complètes*, Bouglé-Moysset, 1932, tome VIII, 3, p. 89, cité in I. Meyerson, « Le travail, fonction psychologique », *art. cit.*, p. 90. Que Proudhon ait beaucoup étudié ou non Hegel, en particulier par l'intermédiaire de Grün (voir P. Haubtmann, *Proudhon, Marx et la pensée allemande*, PUG, 1981, p. 59 et suivantes), le résultat est que les deux penseurs tiennent à peu près le même discours, ou du moins que le schème du travail de l'Esprit chez Hegel est désormais également celui de Proudhon : « L'intelligence humaine fait son début dans la spontanéité de son industrie et c'est en se contemplant elle-même dans son œuvre qu'elle se trouve » (I. Meyerson, *art. cit.*, p. 11). L'homme, créateur à travers le travail (« Le travail, un et identique dans son plan, est infini dans ses applications, comme la création elle-même »), détient ainsi un pouvoir presque magique de transfiguration du monde, dans quoi il trouve son bonheur : « Je me demande pourquoi la vie entière du travailleur ne serait pas une réjouissance perpétuelle, une procession triomphale. »

172. Marx a insisté à de nombreuses reprises, en bon élève de Hegel, sur le caractère à la fois négatif et positif du travail abstrait moderne : « La dissolution de tous les produits et de toutes les activités en valeurs d'échange suppose la décomposition de tous les rapports de dépendance personnels figés (historiques) au sein de la production [...] Dans la valeur d'échange, la relation sociale des personnes entre elles est transformée en un rapport social des choses, le pouvoir des personnes en un pouvoir des choses... », *Principes d'une critique de l'économie..., op. cit.*, p. 208-209.

173. Ces trois passions mécanisantes doivent être convenablement mélangées pour former des séries équilibrées. La papillonne, c'est le besoin de variété périodique, situations contrastées, incidents piquants... La cabaliste est la manie de l'intrigue. La composite, la plus romantique des passions, crée les accords d'enthousiasme (*cf.* chapitre v). C'est à condition de savoir bien combiner ces passions que le travail pourra devenir attrayant.

174. C. Fourier, *Le Nouveau Monde industriel et sociétaire ou invention du procédé d'industrie attrayante et naturelle distribuée en séries passionnées*, Flammarion, 1973.

175. *Ibid.*, p. 37.

176. Sur ces évolutions majeures, voir H. Hatzfeld, *Du paupérisme à la Sécurité sociale*, PUN, 1989, et A. Soboul, « Problèmes de travail en l'an II », in *Journal de psychologie..., op. cit.*, 1955, p. 39-58. Voir également F. Tanghe, *Le Droit au travail entre histoire et utopie, 1789-1848-1989 : de la répression de la mendicité à l'allocation universelle*,

Publications Fac. univ. St-Louis, 1989. Voir, du même auteur, « Le droit du travail en 1848 », in *Le Droit au travail*, Institut des sciences du travail, dossier n° 13, Université catholique de Louvain, novembre 1991.

177. Turgot, cité par Tanghe, *op. cit.*, p. 47.

178. *Rapport sur l'organisation générale des secours publics*, présenté à l'Assemblée nationale le 13 juin 1792, Bibliothèque nationale, p. 9.

179. L. Blanc, cité par Tanghe, *op. cit.*, p. 61.

180. « Le droit considéré de façon abstraite est ce qui, depuis 1789, tient le peuple abusé. [...] Le droit, stérilement et pompeusement proclamé dans les chartes, n'a servi qu'à masquer ce que l'inauguration d'un régime individualiste avait d'injuste », *ibid.*, p. 64.

181. « Par le droit au travail, on crée en même temps un droit et une obligation. On suppose un contrat entre l'individu et la société, aux termes duquel la société devrait l'existence à chacun de ses membres, contrat non synallagmatique et qui n'engagerait qu'une des parties », L. Faucher, in J. Garnier éd., *Le Droit au travail à l'Assemblée nationale, Recueil complet de tous les discours prononcés dans cette mémorable discussion*, Paris, Guillaumin, 1848, p. 344-345

182. « Tandis que l'Etat devrait fournir aux individus, sur leur demande, les moyens de travailler, il ne serait pas armé du pouvoir de les contraindre à chercher dans le travail leur subsistance habituelle. On proclamerait ainsi la supériorité de la force, du droit personnel sur le droit social. L'individu deviendrait le maître, le tyran, et la société, le serviteur, l'esclave. [...] Le droit au travail est une servitude que l'on impose à la communauté tout entière, dans l'intérêt de quelques-uns », *ibid.*

183. *Ibid.*, p. 345-346.

184. Lamartine, *ibid.*, p. 286-287.

185. L. Faucher, *ibid.*, p. 350 ; L. Wolowski, *ibid.*, p. 360.

186. Cette ligne sépare les anciens tenants du travail-nécessité, conçu comme moyen de subvenir aux besoins, de ceux qui ont déjà assimilé l'idée que le travail est la plus haute manière pour un individu de se réaliser. « Le premier droit de l'homme est le droit de vivre. Ce droit en implique un autre, celui de l'entier développement et du complet exercice des facultés physiques, morales et intellectuelles de l'homme ; c'est ce droit qui constitue la liberté », Manifeste des sociétés secrètes, in *1848 : la révolution démocratique et sociale*, Editions d'histoire sociale, 1984.

187. L. Wolowski, in J. Garnier éd., *Le droit au travail à l'Assemblée...*, *op. cit.*, p. 365.

188. Proudhon, *Mémoires sur la propriété*, Premier mémoire, p. 215-217, in *Œuvres complètes*, Nouvelle Edition Rivière.

189. *Ibid.*

190. L. Blanc, *Le Socialisme, Droit au travail. Réponse à M. Thiers*, Paris, Bureau du Nouveau monde, 1849, p. 45-46.

191. Cité par J.-M. Humillière, *Louis Blanc*, Les Editions ouvrières, 1982, p. 75.

192. Habermas, « La crise de l'Etat-providence », in *Ecrits politiques. Culture, droit, histoire*, Cerf, 1990, p. 109-110. Cette phrase doit être replacée dans son contexte : Habermas écrit quelques lignes plus haut : « Quant aux énergies utopiques, elles ne se sont pas absolument retirées de la conscience historique. C'est bien plutôt une certaine utopie qui est arrivée à sa fin, celle qui dans le passé s'était cristallisée autour du potentiel qui résidait dans la société du travail. »

193. Pour les horaires et les conditions de travail, voir les très nombreux rapports officiels et enquêtes de l'époque, en particulier celle du Dr Villermé, cité in M.-Th. Join-Lambert, *Politiques sociales, op. cit.* ; Engels, *La Situation de la classe laborieuse en Angleterre*, Editions sociales, 1975 ; voir égalᵗment J. Le Goff, *Du silence à la parole*, Calligrammes-La Digitale, 1985.

194. En cela. le xIxᵉ siècle socialiste est très ricardien. Dans *Des principes de l'économie politique et de l'impôt*, GF-Flammarion, 1993, Ricardo écrit. dès le chapitre I, que « la valeur d'une marchandise dépend de la quantité relative de travail nécessaire à sa production ». Un grand nombre de socialistes reprendront ces thèses pour revendiquer en particulier que tout le revenu issu de la production revienne aux travailleurs.

195. Ce vocabulaire religieux (il s'agit de l'opération par laquelle le pain et le vin se transforment en corps et sang de Jésus-Christ, dans la liturgie catholique) est assez bien adapté ici, nous semble-t-il.

196. La Iʳᵉ Internationale (ou Association internationale des travailleurs) a été fondée à Londres en 1864. On en trouvera les statuts dans *La Critique des programmes de Gotha et d'Erfurt, op. cit.* La IIᵉ Internationale rassemble des courants et des partis très divers, marxistes, libertaires, syndicalistes, proudhoniens.

197. Le programme d'Eisenach, marxiste (1869), est celui du Parti ouvrier social-démocrate : « Le Parti ouvrier social-démocrate poursuit l'établissement de l'Etat populaire libre. »

198. E. Bernstein (1850-1932) adhère en 1872 à l'Internationale ouvrière. Exilé en Suisse à cause des lois antisocialistes, il dirige avec Kautsky le *Sozial Democrat* et adhère au marxisme. A Londres, il devient le secrétaire d'Engels. En 1899, il écrit *Socialisme théorique et social-démocratie pratique*.

199. E. Bernstein, *Les Présupposés du socialisme*, Seuil, 1974.

200. Seule exception à cet unanimisme, la critique radicale de Lafargue, marxiste et guesdiste farouche, en 1883, dans *Le Droit à la paresse, réfutation du droit au travail de 1848* ; mais elle n'est pas représentative de la pensée marxiste ni de la pensée sociale-démocrate. Lafargue ouvre ainsi son ouvrage : « Une étrange folie possède les classes ouvrières des nations où règne la civilisation capitaliste. Cette folie traîne à sa suite des misères individuelles et sociales qui, depuis deux siècles, torturent la triste humanité. Cette folie est l'amour du travail, la passion moribonde du

travail, poussée jusqu'à l'épuisement des forces vitales de l'individu et de sa progéniture. Au lieu de réagir contre cette aberration mentale, les prêtres, les économistes, les moralistes, ont sacro-sanctifié le travail », *Le Droit à la paresse*, Climats, 1992, p. 17.

201. Sur la mise en place des lois de protection sociale et les rapports de celle-ci avec le travail, voir M.-Th. Join-Lambert, *Politiques sociales, op. cit.*, p. 255-490.

202. « Le socialisme vulgaire a hérité des économistes bourgeois l'habitude de considérer et de traiter la répartition comme une chose indépendante du mode de production et de représenter pour cette raison le socialisme comme tournant essentiellement autour de la répartition », Marx et Engels, *Critique des programmes de Gotha et d'Erfurt, op. cit.*, p. 33.

203. Il s'agit là d'une configuration totalement aliénée, dans le schéma marxien par exemple : le travail n'est pas voulu pour lui-même, mais pour autre chose.

204. En particulier au travers du vote des premières lois sociales, *cf.* M.-Th. Join-Lambert, *Politiques sociales, op. cit.*

205. Habermas, « La crise de l'Etat-providence », in *Ecrits politiques, op. cit.*, p. 113.

206. « Il lui faut intervenir dans le système économique en ayant en vue, tout à la fois, d'entretenir la croissance capitaliste, d'aplanir les crises, mais aussi de garantir non seulement les emplois, mais encore la compétitivité internationale des entreprises, de sorte que des surplus soient dégagés qui puissent être redistribués, sans que soient découragés les investisseurs privés. [...] Il faut pour accéder au compromis que suppose l'Etat-social, et pour parvenir à la pacification de l'antagonisme de classe, que le pouvoir d'Etat, légitimé démocratiquement, se constitue en préservateur et en dompteur du processus « naturel » de croissance du capitalisme », *ibid.*, p. 112.

207. « Les nouvelles valeurs et la notion d'accomplissement ; réflexion de philosophie sociale sur l'avenir du travail et des loisirs ». H. Lenk, OCDE, in *Forum de l'OCDE sur l'avenir*, 1994.

208. D. Mothé, « Le mythe du temps libéré », in *Esprit*, n° 204, 1994.

209. P. Boisard, « Partage du travail : les pièges d'une idée simple », in *Esprit*, n° 204, 1994.

210. D. Mothé, « Le mythe du temps libéré », *art. cit.*

211. « Le technicien, le chercheur, l'universitaire, le charpentier peuvent procéder à des calculs pendant leur temps de loisir, sur la plage, dans leur lit. Ils peuvent travailler dans n'importe quel lieu. Que peut faire la diminution du temps légal de travail sur ces activités intellectuelles invisibles ? », D. Mothé, *ibid.*

212. Elles sont aujourd'hui très peu nombreuses : à part quelques sondages, on dispose des enquêtes du CREDOC sur les aspirations des Français Cette enquête annuelle n'analyse néanmoins pas les représenta-

tions en tant que telles. On dispose également de quelques enquêtes citées in H. Riffault, *Les Valeurs des Français*, PUF, 1994, chapitre sur le travail, ou in Lenk, *Forum de l'OCDE, op. cit.* Mais les représentations (le travail est-il considéré comme épanouissant ? contraignant ? pourquoi ?) en tant que telles sont mal connues. Voir, par une entrée différente, *Souffrances et précarités au travail. Paroles de médecins du travail*, Syros, 1994.

213. Weber, *Histoire économique..., op. cit.,* Gallimard, 1991, p. 296 : « Une exploitation capitaliste rationnelle est une exploitation dotée d'un compte de capital, c'est-à-dire une entreprise lucrative qui contrôle sa rentabilité de manière chiffrée au moyen de la comptabilité moderne et de l'établissement d'un bilan. »

214. Weber renoue ainsi avec ce qu'il avait démontré dans *L'Ethique protestante et l'esprit du capitalisme*. Il cite B. Franklin (*cf.* Acte I) : « Tiens un compte exact de tes dépenses et de tes revenus », et ajoute que l'esprit du capitalisme fait à chacun un devoir d'augmenter son capital, ceci étant supposé une fin en soi, p. 46-47.

215. *Histoire économique..., op. cit.,* p. 297.

216. K. Polanyi, *La Grande Transformation, op. cit.*, p. 107. Polanyi nous permet de nous étonner à nouveau devant ce qui aujourd'hui ne provoque plus l'étonnement. Il écrit par exemple (p. 70) : « En fait, la production mécanique, dans une société commerciale, suppose tout bonnement la transformation de la substance naturelle et humaine de la société en marchandises. »

217. En particulier, *Réflexions sur les causes de la liberté et de l'oppression sociale*, Gallimard, coll. « Idées », 1955, et *La Condition ouvrière*, Gallimard, coll. « Espoir », 1951.

218. G. Friedmann, *Où va le travail humain ?*, Gallimard, coll. « Idées », 1978.

219. T. Di Ciaula, *Tuta blu* (bleu de travail), Federop et Actes Sud, 1982.

220. S Weil, *La Condition ouvrière, op. cit.* Trois lettres à Mme Albertine Thévenon, 1934-1935, p. 18-19.

221. S. Weil, *Réflexions..., op. cit.*, p. 13. Simone Weil fait certainement allusion aux *Principes d'une critique de l'économie politique, op. cit.*, où Marx explique que « la tendance à créer un marché mondial est incluse dans le concept même de capital », p. 258 et suivantes

222. *Cf.* G.H. Camerlynck, *Le Contrat de travail, op. cit.*, p. 52.

223. A. Supiot, *Critique du droit..., op. cit.,* p. 98.

224. « Cette contradiction entre autonomie de la volonté et subordination de la volonté aboutit à ce que le salarié est à la fois appréhendé dans l'entreprise comme sujet et comme objet du contrat », *ibid.*, p. 123. Pour l'analyse du droit collectif, voir chapitre III, particulièrement p. 133 et suivantes.

225. On lira la passionnante analyse de G.H. Camerlynck, in *Le*

Contrat de travail, op. cit., qui explique comment P. Durand et une tradition française institutionnaliste ont tenté d'introduire la conception allemande, p. 14-27. Voir également chapitre VII du présent ouvrage.

226. A. Supiot, *Critique du droit...*, *op. cit.*, p. 165.

227. Que penser par ailleurs de cette affirmation : « Comme le travailleur indépendant, le salarié a le droit d'arbitrer entre les périodes qu'il consacre à sa vie de travail et celles qu'il consacre à sa formation ou sa vie sociale, il est juge du danger que présente une situation de travail, il peut jouir d'une réelle liberté dans l'accomplissement de la tâche pour laquelle on le paie... », *ibid.*, p. 169 ? Qui peut se reconnaître dans ces lignes aujourd'hui ?

228. Le statut s'oppose au contrat : le statut est ce qui détermine les droits et obligations des personnes concernées par celui-ci (par exemple statut des fonctionnaires, statut des directeurs d'hôpitaux...).

229. A. Supiot écrit que « cette relation prétendument égalitaire entre employeurs et salariés est [...] manifestement inégalitaire », mais que « l'édification du droit français peut se lire tout entière comme une tentative d'englobement du principe d'égalité concrète dans un cadre juridique dominé par le principe d'égalité formelle ». Donc : subordination ne signifie pas inégalité... *Critique du droit...*, *op. cit.*, p.133-136. A. Supiot se réfère à L. Dumont pour cette démonstration...

230. « La dernière forme de servitude que prend l'activité humaine — travail salarié d'un côté et capital de l'autre... », *Principes d'une critique de l'économie...*, *op. cit.*, p. 272.

231. « Le recrutement des forces de travail pour la nouvelle forme de production telle qu'elle se développe en Angleterre à partir du XVIIIe siècle [...] s'effectue d'abord par des moyens coercitifs très incisifs [...] L'expropriation des petits paysans dépendants par de plus gros fermiers a contribué à [...] créer en excédent une population qui tombait sous le coup du travail forcé. Quiconque ne se rendait pas spontanément était expédié dans un établissement de travail où régnait une discipline de fer ; celui qui quittait son emploi sans un certificat à décharge délivré par le maître était susceptible d'être considéré comme vagabond ; aucun aperçu de travail accordé au chômeur, autre que sous la ferme contrainte de devoir se rendre dans un établissement de travail », Weber, *Histoire économique...*, *op. cit.*, p. 326.

232. *La Grande Transformation*, *op. cit.*, *passim* dans les chapitres VI, VII et VIII ; *cf.* surtout le rôle de la faim dans le chapitre X et dans le chapitre XIV : « Le dernier stade a été atteint avec l'application de « la sanction naturelle », la faim. Pour pouvoir la déclencher, il était nécessaire de liquider la société organique, qui refusait de laisser l'individu mourir de faim », p. 222.

233. Voir les deux ouvrages cités. Dans *La Condition ouvrière*, Simone Weil parle de ses « camarades d'esclavage » (p. 159, « Lettre à un ingénieur directeur d'usine », juin 1936). Voir également ce qu'elle dit de

l'oppression sociale : « Cette contrainte inévitable ne mérite d'être nommée oppression que dans la mesure où, du fait qu'elle provoque une séparation entre ceux qui l'exercent et ceux qui la subissent, elle met les seconds à discrétion des premiers et fait ainsi peser jusqu'à l'écrasement physique et moral la pression de ceux qui commandent sur ceux qui exécutent », *Réflexions...*, *op. cit.*, p. 39. (*Cf.* aussi p. 77, 83, 129, 139, 143).

234. *Réflexions...*, *op. cit.*, p. 79.

235. Habermas, « La crise de l'Etat-providence », in *op. cit.*, p. 113.

236. Hannah Arendt, *Condition de l'homme moderne, op. cit.*

237. *Ibid.*, Prologue, p. 37

238. Heidegger, « Contribution à la question de l'Etre », in *Questions I*, Gallimard, 1982.

239. E. Jünger, *Le Travailleur*, Christian Bourgois, 1993.

240. « Contribution... », *op. cit.*, p. 206.

241. *Ibid.*, p. 217.

242. C'est l'un des grands « messages « de la philosophie heideggerienne. Sur ce point, voir « La question de la technique », in *Essais et Conférences*, Gallimard, 1973.

243. M. Heidegger interrogé par le journal *Der Spiegel*, in *Réponses et questions sur l'histoire et la politique,* Mercure de France, 1988, p. 44 et 50.

244. Heidegger, « La question de la technique », *op. cit.*, p. 20.

245. Heidegger, *Lettre sur l'humanisme, op. cit.*

246. Entretien avec *Der Spiegel, op. cit.*, p. 61.

247. M. Horkheimer, Th. Adorno, *La Dialectique de la raison*, Gallimard, coll. « Tel », 1983.

248. *Ibid.*, Introduction, p. 13.

249. Le véritable titre du livre est d'ailleurs *Dialectique de l'Aufklärung*

250. *Ibid.*, p. 23.

251. *Ibid.*, p. 27.

252. *Ibid.*

253. *Ibid.*, p. 58. Simone Weil ne dit pas autre chose : « Il semble que l'homme ne puisse parvenir à alléger le joug des nécessités naturelles sans alourdir d'autant celui de l'oppression sociale, comme par le jeu d'un mystérieux équilibre », *Réflexions...*, *op. cit.*, p. 77.

254. Horkheimer, Adorno, *Dialectique..., op. cit.*, p. 44.

255. « A l'époque actuelle [...], ce n'est pas dans les sciences de la nature, fondées sur les mathématiques présentées comme Logos éternel, que l'homme peut apprendre à se connaître lui-même, c'est dans une théorie critique de la société telle qu'elle est, inspirée et dominée par le souci d'établir un ordre conforme à la raison », in Horkheimer, *Théorie critique*, Payot, 1978.

256. Marx, *L'Idéologie allemande*, cité et traduit par Habermas in « La crise de l'Etat-providence », *Ecrits politiques... op. cit.*, p. 110.

257. A. Gorz, *Adieu au prolétariat*, Galilée, 1980, et, plus récemment, *Métamorphoses du travail..., op. cit*

258. Simone Weil l'avait parfaitement compris et c'est pour cette raison qu'elle reprenait à son compte la critique marxienne tout en refusant ses conséquences, trop optimistes à son goût : « La complète subordination de l'ouvrier à l'entreprise et à ceux qui la dirigent repose sur la structure de l'usine et non sur le régime de la propriété », in Simone Weil, *Réflexions...*, *op. cit.*, p. 16.

259. Habermas, « La crise de l'Etat-providence », in *Ecrits politiques...*, *op. cit.*, p. 110.

260. L'une et l'autre ouvrent en effet leur principal ouvrage sur le travail (*Réflexions...*, *op. cit.*, et *Condition de l'homme moderne, op. cit.*) par une critique de Marx.

261. Les livres d'Y. Schwarz et Y. Clos en particulier, donnent parfois l'impression d'une sorte de renouveau de la pensée stoïcienne. Une partie de leur démonstration consiste en effet à montrer comment, dans l'acte le plus contraint et le plus déterminé, une part évidente de liberté et de créativité subsiste : dans l'acte de travail, disent-ils, sont convoqués les traditions, les savoir-faire, mais aussi toute l'habileté personnelle de chaque travailleur. Dans le travail se détermine donc une approche particulièrement riche d'ouverture au monde et aux autres. Ce qui est mis en évidence par ces auteurs, c'est donc la nécessité de l'initiative du sujet humain à la source de toute formalisation. Mais en disant que dans l'acte le plus déterminé, c'est-à-dire même au cœur du pire taylorisme, le sujet garde sa créativité, ne risque-t-on pas, d'une certaine manière, de justifier celui-ci ?

262. « Pour Gorz, la libération du travail ne peut résider que dans la libération de l'industrialisme, dans l'alternative éthique radicale du capitalisme. Redonner son sens au travail signifie pour Gorz chercher du sens dans le non-travail. [...] Mais comment Gorz peut-il ne pas comprendre que c'est à partir de la profondeur de l'insertion de la force de travail dans le capital que tout futur prendra forme [...] et qu'il vaut mieux rester sur le terrain que nous offre le marxisme : celui de la critique du travail ? [...] Ne faut-il pas lutter contre l'hétéronomie du travail et utiliser cette lutte comme instrument contre l'autonomie du capital ? », J.-M. Vincent, T. Negri, « Paradoxes autour du travail », in *Futur antérieur*, n° 10, p. 6-8.

263. H. Kern, M. Schumann, *La Fin de la division du travail ? La rationalisation dans la production industrielle*, Ed. de la Maison des sciences de l'homme, Paris, 1989 : « Jusqu'à présent, toutes les formes que prenait la rationalisation capitaliste reposaient sur un principe de base qui concevait le travail vivant comme une barrière s'opposant à la production. [...] Le credo des nouveaux modèles de production devient maintenant : la qualification et la maîtrise professionnelle de l'ouvrier constituent des capacités productives qu'il s'agit d'utiliser de manière accrue », p. 8-9.

264. C'est la grande critique d'Hannah Arendt : « Dans une humanité

complètement socialisée, qui n'aurait d'autre but que d'entretenir le processus vital — et c'est l'idéal nullement utopique, hélas ! qui guide les théories de Marx — il ne resterait aucune distinction entre travail et œuvre ; toute œuvre serait devenue travail », *Condition..., op. cit.*, p. 134.

265. On se souvient de l'image qu'emploie Marx dans les *Manuscrits de 44* : « Nos productions seraient autant de miroirs où nos êtres rayonneraient l'un vers l'autre. »

266. La *Monadologie* est l'œuvre maîtresse de Leibniz. Pour celui-ci, le monde est composé de monades qui s'expriment les unes les autres à l'infini : si l'on déroule chaque monade, pourtant totalement différente de toutes les autres, on trouve le monde entier. C'est en quelque sorte l'unicité de son point de vue, la manière unique dont elle exprime toute les autres qui fait la singularité de chacune.

267. Aristote, *Les Economiques*, I, 1343a, Vrin, 1993 : « L'Economique et la Politique diffèrent non seulement dans la mesure où diffèrent elles-mêmes une société domestique et une cité (car ce sont là les objets respectifs de ces disciplines), mais encore en ce que la Politique est l'art du gouvernement de plusieurs et l'Economique celui de l'administration d'un seul. »

268. « La *polis* se distinguait de la famille en ce qu'elle ne connaissait que des égaux, tandis que la famille était le siège de la plus rigoureuse inégalité », Hannah Arendt, *Condition de l'homme moderne, op. cit.*, p. 70.

269. Concernant cette analyse voir Hannah Arendt, *ibid.*

270. Tel est, étymologiquement, le sens d'« économie » : l'administration du domaine.

271. Hannah Arendt, *Condition..., op. cit.*, p. 66. Hannah Arendt écrit aussi (p. 71) : « Depuis l'accession de la société, autrement dit du ménage (*oikia*) ou des activités économiques, au domaine public, l'économie et tous les problèmes relevant jadis de la sphère familiale sont devenus des préoccupations " collectives ". »

272. Hegel, *Système de la vie éthique*, Payot, 1976.

273. Voir les ouvrages de P. Chamley cités dans le chapitre IV dont *Economie politique et philosophie chez Steuart et Hegel, op. cit.*

274. Hegel, *Principes de la philosophie du droit, op. cit.*, § 183.

275. *Ibid.*, § 258.

276. *Le Droit naturel*, Gallimard, coll. « Idées », 1972.

277. Habermas, « Travail et interaction, Remarques sur la philosophie de l'esprit de Hegel à Iena », in *La Technique et la science comme « idéologie »*, Denoël, 1973. Voir aussi *Connaissance et intérêt, op. cit.*, chapitre II, et *Après Marx*, Fayard, 1985.

278. Voir par exemple les ouvrages de R. Sainsaulieu déjà cités ou le plus récent ouvrage de C. Dubar, *La Socialisation, op. cit.*

279. E. Durkheim, *La Division sociale du travail*, PUF, coll. « Quadrige », 1991.

280. A. Supiot, *Critique du droit...*, *op. cit.*, p. 31.

281. Voir les nombreuses études de B. Reynaud, en particulier *Le Salaire, la règle, et le marché*, Christian Bourgois, 1991, et *Théorie des salaires*, La Découverte, 1993.

282. Il s'agit de l'agrément ou du désagrément des emplois en eux-mêmes, de la facilité avec laquelle on peut les apprendre ou de la difficulté et de la dépense qu'ils exigent pour cela, de l'occupation constante qu'ils procurent ou des interruptions auxquelles ils sont exposés, du plus ou moins de confiance dont il faut que soient investis ceux qui les exercent, et enfin de la probabilité ou de l'improbabilité d'y réussir. Voir Smith, *Recherches...*, *op. cit.*, chapitre X, section I.

283. Sur ces points, voir Hatzfeld, *op. cit.*, et M.-Th. Join-Lambert, *Politique sociales*, *op. cit.*

284. *Ibid.*

285. « L'entreprise est en passe de prendre rang parmi les grandes institutions de notre époque, après l'Eglise, l'Armée, la justice, l'Ecole, la commune, l'Université », écrit R. Sainsaulieu (dir.) in *L'Entreprise, une affaire de société*, Presses de la FNSP, 1990.

286. *Cf.* D. Flouzat, *Economie contemporaine*, PUF, 1981, p. 148 : « L'entreprise apparaît ainsi comme un processus qui consomme certains facteurs de production (terre, capital, travail) pour les transformer en produits vendables. »

287. L'idée est que le travail humain n'est pas qu'un coût et que le travail peut constituer un apport de productivité majeur : la formation, la qualification, la motivation, la confiance constituent des atouts majeurs pour l'entreprise et une source d'augmentation de la productivité. On remarquera d'ailleurs le paradoxe qui consiste à ne prendre en considération le travail humain que lorsqu'il est traité comme du capital... Ainsi se réaliserait, d'une manière détournée, la prédiction de Marx, pour qui le destin du capitalisme est que tout travail devienne du capital. Voir *Principes d'une critique de l'économie...*, *op. cit.*, le chapitre intitulé : « Le travailleur devant l'automation ». Marx écrit en particulier : « Ainsi, toutes les forces du travail sont transposées en forces du capital. »

288. Conformément à la théorie contractuelle de l'entreprise : « Par contrat, le propriétaire se procure la main-d'œuvre dont il a besoin. Dans les limites fixées par le droit du travail, le chef dirige comme il l'entend », écrit P. Sudreau, in *La Réforme de l'entreprise*, La Documentation française, 1975. L'entreprise n'est que la somme des contrats individuels de travail.

289. *Cf.* H. Bartoli, *Science économique et travail, op. cit.*, p. 227 : « Il ne suffit pas d'établir des comités d'entreprise pour que la participation des travailleurs à la gestion des entreprises soit acquise. Trop faibles pour pouvoir limiter effectivement l'autocratie patronale et technocratique, n'ayant pratiquement pas de pouvoir de décision en matière économique, soumis à trop de manœuvres de la part des conseils d'administration, mal

informés de la marche de l'entreprise, les comités d'entreprise se sont révélés incapables de modifier la nature de l'entreprise. Elle est demeurée de style et de procédé capitalistes. [...] Les comités d'entreprise ne pouvaient pas devenir les organes d'une vraie démocratie industrielle. »

290. Voir le rapport Bruhnes, *Choisir l'emploi*, Commissariat général du Plan, La Documentation française, 1993.

291. H. Bartoli, *Science économique et travail, op. cit*, p. 54. Il ajoute : « Maintes fois il a été dit que l'appropriation privée des moyens de production constitue l'un des moyens indispensables à la défense des valeurs de la propriété personnelle. Longtemps on a jugé préférable l'appropriation privée, parce que, disait-on, elle stimule l'ardeur au travail, garantit l'ordre social, pousse l'homme à mieux comprendre l'excellence de l'état social et à s'y dévouer. [. .] Dans le capitalisme, ces justifications s'estompent. [...] Ce n'est pas le corporatisme, simple masque au régime de l'argent, qui se trouve appelé par l'exigence d'une gestion commune des moyens de production, mais bien une économie du travail. [...] Le droit à la liberté du travail est le droit de travailler dans une économie dotée d'organisations juridiques positives, celles que requiert le droit naturel du travail humain, non le droit d'œuvrer dans une économie anarchique, sans lois, sans institutions sociales. Le droit du travail est un droit social. La liberté du travail dont parlent les libéraux n'en est que la caricature. »

292. P. Durand, cité par G.H. Camerlynck, in *Le Contrat de travail, op. cit.*, p. 17.

293. A. Supiot, *Critique du droit, op. cit.*, p. 16.

294. Voir chapitre IX.

295. *Privatrecht*, volume I, 1895, p. 116-117. Sur Gierke, voir L. Dumont, *Essais sur l'individualisme, op. cit.*, et G. Gurvitch, *L'Idée du droit social, notion et système du droit social*, Sirey, 1932.

296. A. Supiot, *Critique du droit, op. cit.*, p. 18.

297. G.H. Camerlynck, *Le Contrat de travail, op. cit.*, p. 17.

298. « Le contrat de travail lui-même, qu'on nous présente comme le fait juridique primaire et irréductible, n'est qu'un fait secondaire et dérivé. A y regarder de près en effet, il implique, outre un commencement de division du travail, une organisation sociale relativement complexe et suffisamment stable pour que des individus puissent envisager en sécurité l'avenir dans un acte de prévision. [...] A côté des contrats, où les ouvriers interviennent comme parties, il y a l'institution organique dont ils deviennent membres : membres solidaires dont la collaboration active et intelligente à une œuvre commune et la soumission à une même discipline font de véritables associés », Thèse de E. Gounot, Lyon, 1910, citée par G.H. Camerlynck, in *Le Contrat de travail, op. cit.*, p. 15.

299. G.H. Camerlynck, *Rapport de synthèse établi pour le compte de la CECA*, 1964, p. 147.

300. « Il est certes normal d'insister sur le caractère personnel du lien

obligatoire, sur l'*intuitus personae* qui préside parfois à la formation de ce lien et sur certaines obligations accessoires en découlant. Mais le *vinculum juris* reste essentiellement un lien d'obligation traditionnel, tel qu'on le rencontre dans les contrats d'échange », *ibid.*

301. *Ibid.*, p. 148.

302. Voir le chapitre IX.

303. « Depuis que l'économie politique est devenue la simple exposition des lois qui président à l'économie des sociétés, les véritables hommes d'Etat ont compris que son étude ne pouvait leur être indifférente. On a été obligé de consulter cette science pour prévoir les suites d'une opération, comme on consulte les lois de la dynamique et de l'hydraulique, lorsqu'on veut construire avec succès un pont ou une écluse », cité par F. Fourquet, *Richesse et puissance, une généalogie de la valeur*, La Découverte, 1989, chapitre XVII, « La naissance de la science économique ». Cet ouvrage magistral analyse l'économie dans sa dimension « politique » et conceptuelle. Je remercie Christine Afriat d'avoir attiré mon attention sur lui.

304. A. Cournot, *Traité de l'enchaînement des idées fondamentales*, 1911.

305. L. Walras, *Principes d'une théorie mathématique de l'échange*, mémoire lu à l'Académie des sciences morales et politiques les 16 et 23 août 1873.

306. L. Walras, *Eléments d'économie pure*, Paris, F. Pichon, 1900.

307. *Ibid.*, p. 27.

308. *Ibid.*

309. C. Larrère, *L'Invention de l'économie...*, *op. cit.* Voir le chapitre I, « Droit naturel et sociabilité ».

310. J. Bentham, *An Introduction to the Principles of Morals and Legislation*, 1789, in *The Works of Jeremy Bentham*, John Browning ed., Edinburgh, W. Tait, 1838, I, I, 2, p. 1.

311. J. Stuart Mill, *Autobiography*, 1873, cité in M. Canto-Sperber, *La Philosophie...*, *op. cit.*, p. 19.

312. J. Stuart Mill, *L'Utilitarisme*, Flammarion, coll. « Champs », 1993, p. 54.

313. W. S. Jevons est considéré comme l'autre grand théoricien de l'école néoclassique. Mais alors que L. Walras fait partie de l'école de Lausanne (qu'il a fondée), Jevons (1835-1882) appartient à l'école anglaise.

314. Ce type d'analyse, que l'on a appelé la révolution marginaliste, est appliqué par les néoclassiques à de très nombreux domaines. Voir les *Principes d'économie politique* de A. Marshall pour sa description. Marshall donne l'exemple des mûres : une personne cueille des mûres pour les manger. Cette action lui donne du plaisir pendant un moment. Mais, après en avoir mangé une certaine quantité, le désir diminue et la fatigue s'accroît. « Lorsque le désir de se récréer et son éloignement pour

le travail de cueillir des mûres contrebalancent le désir de manger, l'équilibre est atteint. »

315. L. Walras, *Eléments d'économie pure, op. cit.*

316. L'œuvre de Nietzsche n'est qu'un long développement de cette idée : les valeurs, écrit par exemple Nietzsche, sont « le résultat de certaines perspectives d'utilité bien définies, destinées à maintenir et à fortifier certaines formes de domination humaine » (*Volonté de puissance*, Gallimard, 1947, tome I, livre II, § 58, p. 218.). Il n'y a pas une vérité unique que nous pourrions atteindre, mais un pluralisme des points de vue qui correspond au pluralisme foncier du monde lui-même. On lira sur ce point J. Granier, *Le Problème de la vérité dans la philosophie de Nietzsche*, Seuil, 1966.

317. Elle est composée de personnages comme C. Menger (1840-1921), E. Böhm-Bawerk (1851-1914), F. von Hayek.

318. F. von Hayek, *Scientisme et sciences sociales*, Presses-Pocket, coll. « Agora », 1986, p. 54.

319. Voir en particulier *Droit, législation, liberté*, où cette approche est particulièrement développée, avec la notion des ordres construits ou fabriqués (*taxis*) et des ordres spontanés ou mûris (*kosmos*), PUF, 1985.

320. Walras est connu pour avoir trouvé le théorème de l'équilibre général, c'est-à-dire démontré qu'il existait une solution au système d'équations représentant les relations d'échange sur le marché ou les marchés (des produits, des facteurs de production et de la monnaie), ou encore qu'il existe un système de prix qui permet d'atteindre un état d'équilibre stable, et donc une autorégulation de l'activité économique.

321. L'école de Vienne ira encore plus loin dans cette manière de considérer qu'il existe un ordre naturel : il y a, profondément inscrit dans la pensée libérale, l'idée qu'il existe un ordre naturel ; y « toucher » reviendrait à ouvrir la boîte de Pandore... Cette idée trouve une expression presque caricaturale chez Hayek, lorsqu'il explique que jamais aucun ordre construit ne parviendra à égaler la précision et la justesse de l'ordre naturel. *Cf. Droit, législation, liberté, op. cit.*

322. Comme l'écrit F. Fourquet, in *Richesse et puissance, op. cit.*, p. 262. : « L'habit d'économiste revêt donc un observateur comme un autre. Tous les économistes classiques ont eu une intuition primordiale sur un ordre de priorité. Les catégories comptables ou économiques n'ont été que les moyens intellectuels pour traduire et communiquer cette intuition dans un langage codifié d'apparence scientifique. Ce qui les conduit, c'est un critère sur la nature de la bonne utilité. [...] L'idéal historique opère le partage entre le bon grain productif et l'ivraie improductive. »

323. Ainsi doit-on comprendre le fait que c'est la production d'objets matériels devant être vendus qui est valorisée.

324. Sur le rapport entre le concept de nation et l'économie, voir F. Fourquet, *Richesse et puissance, op. cit.*

325. Il suffit de relire Malthus : dès le début de sa recherche, c'est

l'échange qui est au centre de la question. Il ne s'agit que de savoir si l'échange doit porter sur des objets matériels ou immatériels.

326. Pour cela, il est nécessaire de postuler une harmonie des intérêts telle que, lorsque je poursuis mon intérêt, soit je poursuis en même temps celui des autres (fusion des intérêts, grâce à la bienveillance, par exemple), soit le bien des autres en résulte conformément à l'ordre naturel (identité naturelle des intérêts, la main invisible), soit le bien de tous en résulte par une construction (identification artificielle des intérêts, *cf.* J. Bentham). Pour toutes ces questions, voir E. Halévy, *La Formation du radicalisme philosophique*, Felix Alcan, 1903, épuisé, à paraître aux PUF, coll. « Philosophie morale », et en particulier le premier volume : *La Jeunesse de Bentham*.

327. Voir sur ces questions A. Sen, *Ethique et économie*, PUF, 1994 ; J.-P. Dupuy, *Le Sacrifice et l'envie*, Calmann-Lévy, 1992 ; Ph. Van Parijs, *Qu'est-ce qu'une société juste?*, Seuil, 1991 ; S. C. Kolm, *Philosophie de l'économie*, Seuil, 1985 ; et, évidemment, J. Rawls, *Théorie de la justice*, Seuil, 1987, en particulier le chapitre V, consacré à l'utilitarisme.

328. Ou encore plus simplement : « si, et seulement si, il est impossible d'accroître l'utilité d'une personne sans réduire celle d'une autre personne », A. Sen, *Ethique et économie, op. cit*, p. 32.

329. Le Produit intérieur brut se calcule en additionnant les valeurs ajoutées par toutes les branches, c'est-à-dire en additionnant les valeurs des biens et services de chaque branche, dont ont été retranchées les valeurs des consommations intermédiaires.

330. Le SECN a élargi le concept de production adopté dans l'ancien système (1976) : la production était considérée comme l'ensemble des biens et services échangés sur un marché ou susceptibles de s'y échanger. Ainsi l'apport des administrations était-il exclu puisque les services qu'elles rendent ne font en général pas l'objet d'une vente. On continue néanmoins de distinguer entre le PIB marchand et le PIB non marchand. Mais, comme les prestations correspondant à des fonctions collectives, le plus souvent prises en charge par des administrations, ne sont pas marchandes, elles sont mesurées par les dépenses qu'elles représentent : salaires et consommations intermédiaires. Dans cette mesure, les services rendus par les administrations sont conçus comme n'étant à l'origine d'aucun enrichissement pour la collectivité. La même activité, en revanche, si elle était exercée par une entreprise privée et était vendue pour une valeur supérieure à son coût de revient, ce qui est habituellement le cas, serait considérée comme ayant enrichi la collectivité de cette différence. Bien qu'étant à l'origine d'une dépense totale plus grande (coût de revient plus valeur ajoutée), l'activité privée est donc considérée comme enrichissant la collectivité, mais ce n'est pas le cas de la prestation réalisée par l'administration.

331. La production est « l'activité économique socialement organisée qui consiste à créer des biens et services s'échangeant habituellement sur

le marché et/ou obtenus à partir de facteurs de production s'échangeant sur le marché », Système élargi de comptabilité nationale.

332. *Cf.* A. Chadeau, A. Fouquet, « Peut-on mesurer le travail domestique ? », in *Economie et statistiques*, n° 136, septembre 1981. L'étude avait montré que les Français consacraient plus de temps au travail domestique qu'au travail rémunéré.

333. A.C. Pigou, *L'Economie du bien-être,* 1920.

334. Comme lorsque par exemple nous consommons des ressources naturelles non reproductibles ou très longues à reproduire et que nous n'établissons pas de bilan entre cette disparition et la production d'une richesse, ou que nous transformons des relations sociales denses en services marchands. « Le PIB est l'agrégat le plus utilisé pour comparer la croissance des économies nationales. Or, sa signification reste limitée, car il ne représente pas le gain économique net réalisé dans le processus de production, puisqu'il peut être obtenu par usure du capital existant. [...] L'agrégat le plus apte à mesurer le bien-être semble donc être le produit national net, mais celui-ci n'intègre pas tous les éléments permettant une évaluation précise des gains nets d'utilité. Certains éléments ne font pas l'objet de comptabilisation alors qu'ils augmentent l'utilité globale, il en est ainsi des services gratuits de l'économie domestique. Plus importants encore, les inconvénients, nés des nuisances de la société industrielle, ne figurent pas en général dans les tableaux comptables comme flux négatifs. Bien plus, quand les désutilités externes qui accompagnent la croissance sont comptabilisées, elles ne sont retenues que par le biais des dépenses de reconstitution partielle de l'environnement et sont considérées comme un accroissement du produit », D. Flouzat, *Economie contemporaine*, PUF, 1981, tome I, p. 70.

335. Système élargi de comptabilité nationale, base 1980, Méthodes, collections de l'Insee, C. 140-141, juin 1987, et O. Arkhipoff, *Peut-on mesurer le bien-être national?*, collections de l'Insee, C. 41, mars 1976.

336. Malthus, *Principes...*, *op. cit.*, p. 26.

337. S. C. Kolm, *Philosophie de l'économie*, *op. cit.*, p. 250.

338. Les douze pages que consacre Malthus à la recherche de ce qu'est la richesse sont extraordinaires. Tous les arguments de l'époque en faveur d'une conception extensive de la richesse sont examinés. Il écrit : « Tout savoir, fruit d'une éducation soignée ou de talents supérieurs, aurait le droit d'être compris dans cette estimation de la richesse [...] Pour ce qui regarde les objets immatériels, la difficulté paraît être insurmontable. Où pourrait-on s'en procurer un *inventaire*? Ou comment pourrait-on en dresser un de la quantité, de la qualité de cette immense masse de savoir et de talents réservée à l'usage et à la consommation personnels de ceux qui les possèdent, aussi bien qu'à celle de leurs amis ? En supposant même qu'il fût possible de faire un tel inventaire, comment pourrions-nous arriver à obtenir une évaluation, même approximative, des articles qu'elle pourrait contenir ? », *Principes...*, *op. cit.*, p. 3-14.

339. La prise en compte de l'échange mutuellement avantageux comme source essentielle de richesses a certes constitué un « progrès » par rapport à la conception exclusivement patrimoniale, au sens de possessions de terres, de biens meubles... et est allée de pair avec l'émergence de l'individu. Mais aujourd'hui, de même que nous avons à dépasser le stade de la reconnaissance de l'individu, nous devons inventer une conception de la richesse qui prenne en compte l'échange mais ajoute cette dimension patrimoniale : richesses des individus ne faisant pas nécessairement l'objet d'un échange, patrimoine collectif.

340. « C'est le capital qu'on emploie en vue de retirer un profit qui met en mouvement la plus grande partie du travail utile d'une société », *Recherches...*, *op. cit.*, p. 335.

341. A. Smith, *Ibid.*, p. 334-335.

342. Malthus, Principes..., *op. cit.*, chapitre I.

343. Dans *Philosophie de l'économie, op. cit,* S.C. Kolm explique que le PNB a été inventé en période de guerre et d'après-guerre, c'est-à-dire à un moment, en effet, où l'essentiel était de recommencer à produire : « Cet indice a été inventé pour réaliser la politique keynésienne, calculé d'abord en Angleterre pendant la guerre par Stone et Meade (l'inventeur de l'expression « produit national brut ») comme arme secrète pour l'organisation de l'effort de défense, puis aux Etats-Unis et dans les autres pays (en France vers 1951). Son objectif initial était de raisonner sur l'activité et la production économiques de sous-emploi. Il a ensuite été utilisé pour mesurer les capacités de production globales et leur croissance » (p. 250). Voir plus généralement le chapitre XII : « La pensée économique bouleverse le monde : le vol d'Icare du keynésianisme ».

344. A. Sen, *Ethique et économie, op. cit.*, p. 32.

345. J. Rawls, *Théorie de la justice, op. cit.*, chap. V.

346. E. Halévy, « Les principes de la distribution des richesses », in *Revue de métaphysique et de morale*, 1906, p. 545-595. Je remercie Jean Saglio d'avoir attiré mon attention sur ce texte.

347. R. Aron, *Dix-Huit Leçons sur la société industrielle*, leçon VI, « Les types de société industrielle », Gallimard, coll. « Folio », 1986, p 127. Il écrit aussi, p. 83 : « Il n'y a pas de preuve que l'organisation la plus efficace pour augmenter le plus vite possible la quantité de ressources collectives soit simultanément l'organisation qui répartisse le plus équitablement les biens disponibles. En termes abstraits, une économie efficace n'est pas nécessairement une économie juste. »

348. A. Marshall, dans les *Principes d'économie politique, op. cit.*, 1890, analyse la manière dont les différentes classes sociales investissent de manière différente dans l'éducation de leurs enfants : « Le placement de capitaux en vue de l'éducation et du premier apprentissage des ouvriers en Angleterre est limité par les ressources des parents dans les divers rangs de la société. »

349 *Cf.* M.-Th. Join-Lambert, *Politiques sociales, op. cit.*

350. En matière d'assurance-maladie, par exemple, toutes les cotisations, qui sont proportionnelles aux salaires (et non pas aux risques des individus), sont mutualisées, versées dans un même fond qui sert au financement des soins de tous, donc selon les besoins de chacun. La logique est d'ailleurs un peu celle du « De chacun selon ses facultés à chacun selon ses besoins ».

351. Il est obligatoire, dès lors que l'on travaille ou que l'on se trouve dans un certain nombre de situations qui se rapprochent artificiellement de la condition de travailleur, de cotiser à un régime de sécurité sociale, pour l'employeur et pour le salarié. La protection ne dépend donc pas du bon vouloir ou de l'épargne du salarié. Ceci constitue le meilleur moyen pour que toutes les personnes soient couvertes et pour que l'accès à la protection sociale ne dépende pas du niveau de ressources. *Cf.* M.-Th. Join-Lambert, *Politiques sociales, op. cit.*, p. 270 et suivantes.

352. P. Veyne, *Comment on écrit l'histoire*, Seuil, coll. « Points », 1979.

353. A. Sen, *Éthique et économie, op. cit.*, p. 10.

354. L. Robbins, *Essai sur la nature et la signification de la science économique*, Médicis, 1947, cité in M. Godelier, *Rationalité et irrationalité en économie*, Maspero, 1966, p. 19. Cette définition est très célèbre parce qu'elle sera reprise par toute une tradition : L. von Mises, P. Samuelson, R. Burling...

355. M. Herskovitz, E. LeClair, R. Burling, R. Salisbury, H. Schneider, cités in M. Godelier, *Rationalité..., op. cit.*, et surtout in M. Godelier, *Un domaine contesté..., op. cit.*

356. *Ibid.*, p. XI.

357. R. Burling, « Théories de la maximisation et anthropologie économique », in M. Godelier, *Un domaine contesté... op.cit*, p. 113.

358. E. LeClair Jr, « Théorie économique et anthropologie économique », in *Un domaine contesté..., op. cit.*, p. 124-126. C'est nous qui soulignons

359. *Cf.* ci-dessus, note 354 concernant L. Robbins.

360. « Il n'y a pas de techniques ni de buts économiques spécifiques. C'est seulement la relation entre des fins et des moyens qui est économique. [...] Si tout comportement impliquant une allocation de moyens est économique, alors la relation d'une mère à son bébé est également une relation économique, ou plutôt a un aspect économique, tout autant que la relation d'un employeur avec son ouvrier salarié », R. Burling, in M. Godelier, *Rationalité..., op. cit.*, p 19.

361. O. Lange, *Économie politique*, PUF, 1962, cité in M. Godelier, *Rationalité..., op. cit.*, p. 24.

362. K. Polanyi, « L'économie en tant que procès institutionnalisé », traduit in M. Godelier, *Un domaine contesté..., op. cit.*, p. 53-54.

363. « La méthode ainsi que le contenu de la théorie économique sont issus de deux caractéristiques fondamentales de l'Angleterre du XIXe

siècle : la production industrielle en usines et le marché. En tant que principe d'intégration de toute l'économie, l'échange marchand oblige ses participants à se conformer à des règles très spéciales. Chacun tire sa subsistance de la vente de quelque chose sur le marché. [...] Il faudrait souligner que c'est l'organisation marchande qui oblige ses participants à rechercher le gain matériel personnel », G. Dalton, « Théorie économique et société primitive », traduit in M. Godelier, *Un domaine contesté...*, *op. cit.*, p. 183.

364. Sur la notion de besoin, voir les extraits et les textes de W. Moore (p. 193), J. Boecke (p. 241), M. Sahlins (p. 243), in M. Godelier, *Un domaine contesté...*, *op. cit.* « Dans une économie domestique, la motivation économique n'agit pas continuellement ; c'est pourquoi les gens ne travaillent pas continuellement. En somme, il y a deux voies vers la satisfaction, vers la réduction de l'écart entre fins et moyens : produire beaucoup ou désirer peu. Orientée comme elle l'est vers une modeste production des moyens de subsistance, l'économie domestique choisit la seconde solution, la voie du Zen. Les besoins, disons-nous, sont limités. Leur activité économique ne se fragmente pas en un troupeau galopant de désirs aiguillonnés par un sentiment continu d'inadéquation (c'est-à-dire par une rareté des moyens) », M. Sahlins, « L'économie tribale », traduit in M. Godelier, *Un domaine contesté...*, *op. cit.*, p. 243.

365. Voir les textes cités dans M. Godelier, *Un domaine contesté...*, *op. cit.*, p. 183-212 : « Les hypothèses paramétriques de l'analyse économique d'autrefois étaient présentées comme des faits physiques. Les lois de l'économie marchande que l'on en dérivait prenaient de ce fait valeur de lois de la nature. Les processus économiques semblaient répondre à des lois physiques particulières, distinctes des conventions sociales. L'approche économistique qui séparait l'économie de la société et créait un corps d'analyse théorique de l'industrialisme marchand trouva une expression plus raffinée vers la fin du XIXᵉ siècle dans les travaux de Jevons, Menger, Clark et Marshall. [...] La nécessité institutionnelle pour les individus de poursuivre leur intérêt privé matériel au sein d'une économie marchande se refléta idéologiquement sous la forme de généralisations portées sur la nature de l'" homme " dans la société. »

366. Voir l'article de M. Sahlins cité in M. Godelier, *Un domaine contesté...*, *op. cit.*, en particulier p. 236 et suivantes. « Ce qui, dans la sagesse conventionnelle de la science économique, constitue des facteurs exogènes ou non économiques représente, dans la réalité tribale, l'organisation même du processus économique. L'anthropologie économique ne peut les concevoir comme extérieurs, comme empiétant de quelque part à l'extérieur sur le domaine de l'économie. Ils sont l'économie, ils sont des éléments fondamentaux du calcul économique et de toute analyse véritable qu'on peut en faire. A ce sujet, on

pourrait dire en général ce qu'Evans-Pritchard disait à propos des Nuer :
" on ne peut traiter des rapports économiques des Nuer en soi, car ils font
toujours partie des rapports sociaux directs de type général ". »

367. C'est cette tradition qui a été nommée institutionnalisme et dont
se réclament aujourd'hui non seulement des juristes, mais aussi des
sociologues, dont l'idée maîtresse consiste à dire que le marché n'existe
pas tout seul et ne régit pas la société, mais que c'est au contraire un
ensemble d'institutions, produit spécifiquement humain, culturel et social,
qui régit celle-ci et le marché. C'est l'institution qui est première.

368. E. Halévy, « Les principes de la distribution des richesses », *art.
cit.* C'est nous qui soulignons.

369. *La Science économique en France*, ouvrage collectif, La Découverte, 1989. La citation est extraite de l'introduction de M. Guillaume,
« Le sommeil paradoxal de l'économie politique », p. 5.

370. O. Lange, *Economie politique*, cité in M. Godelier, *Rationalité...*,
op. cit., p. 26.

371. M. Allais, « Fondements d'une théorie positive des choix compor-
tant un risque », cité in M. Godelier, *Rationalité...*, *op. cit.*, p. 43.

372. A. d'Autume, in *La Science économique en France*, *op. cit.*, p. 17.

373. Lors d'une émission qui faisait dialoguer, sur Arte, A. Gorz et le
commissaire général au Plan, J.-B. de Foucault, cet argument avait été
mis en évidence. A A. Gorz expliquant que l'on pouvait envisager de
renoncer à une augmentation aveugle de la production, J.-B. de Foucault
répondait : « Mais il reste tant de besoins insatisfaits »... Il oubliait, bien
sûr, de dire qui exprimait ces besoins et si l'augmentation de la production
avait bien pour but de satisfaire ces besoins-là.

374. Ce n'est pas *que* dans les sociétés socialistes qu'il est conçu comme
un producteur, ce n'est pas *que* dans les sociétés capitalistes qu'il est conçu
comme un consommateur ; c'est l'image moderne de l'homme.

375. Habermas, « La crise de l'Etat providence », in *Ecrits politiques*,
op. cit., p. 115-116.

376. Il ne faut pas oublier que Keynes a commencé à être écouté
lorsqu'on s'est aperçu qu'il pouvait y avoir un équilibre de sous-emploi, et
donc une anomalie majeure de la régulation, laquelle présuppose le plein
emploi.

377. M. Guillaume, in *La Science économique en France*, *op. cit.*, p. 6.

378. C'est le processus que met bien en évidence P. Rosanvallon dans
La Crise de l'Etat-providence, *op. cit.*, et qu'il fait remonter à la
Révolution française : l'Etat dissout les corps intermédiaires pour n'avoir
plus en face de lui que des individus dispersés, qui n'ont pas le droit de se
coaliser et en face desquels l'Etat apparaît tout puissant. Sur ce point,
démontré de manière très concrète et passionnante, *cf.* A.M Guillemard,
Le Déclin du social, PUF, 1986.

379. Habermas, *La Technique et la science comme « idéologie »*, *op.
cit.*, p. 40.

380. La fameuse technostructure dont Galbraith décrit la puissance à côté des propriétaires des entreprises.

381. Prononcée en 1919 et rassemblée avec une autre (« Le métier et la vocation de savant ») sous le titre général *Le Savant et le politique*, qui manque la signification essentielle du propos. On se réfère ici à l'édition de poche, M. Weber, *Le Savant et le politique*, 10/18, 1971.

382. M. Weber, *L'Ethique protestante* ..., *op. cit.*, p. 81-104.

383. M. Weber, *Le Savant et le politique*, *op. cit.*, p. 121 et 123.

384. « La comptabilité nationale fut conçue en France à l'image de celle de l'entreprise. Les anciens économistes, même Smith, avaient en tête de diriger la nation productive comme une entreprise, un capital à gérer et à faire grandir », F. Fourquet, *La Richesse et la puissance, op. cit.*, p. 267.

385. J. Rawls, *Théorie de la justice, op. cit.*, p. 40 et 43. Rawls rappelle plus loin (p. 175) que le concept de rationalité est celui qui est bien connu dans la théorie du choix rationnel : l'individu rationnel est celui qui a un ensemble cohérent de préférences face aux options disponibles. Il hiérarchise ces options selon la façon dont elles réalisent ses buts. Cet individu ne souffre ni de l'envie, ni de l'humiliation, ni de la jalousie.

386. *Ibid.*, *op. cit.*, p. 30.

387. R. Burling, « Théories de la maximisation et anthropologie économique », cité in Godelier, *Un domaine contesté..., op. cit.*, p. 110.

388. *Cf.* la fin du chapitre III du présent ouvrage.

389. Les théories politiques du contrat se sont révélées impuissantes à fonder une société conçue autrement que comme un agrégat. Hobbes et Rousseau parviennent néanmoins à donner une unité organique à la société qu'ils décrivent, le premier grâce à la quantité de pouvoir que les individus transfèrent au souverain, le second grâce au caractère presque sacré du pacte qui transforme d'un coup la multitude en corps : « Et nous recevons en *corps* chaque membre comme partie indivisible du tout [...] A l'instant [...], cet acte d'association produit un *corps* moral et collectif [...], lequel reçoit de ce même acte son unité, son moi commun, sa vie et sa volonté » (*Contrat social* livre I, chapitre IV ; c'est nous qui soulignons). Mais cette transmutation initiale est tout aussi miraculeuse que celle qui permet de passer de la multiplicité des volontés particulières à la volonté générale (*cf. Contrat social*, livre II, chapitre III). Malgré les nombreuses explications convaincantes qui ont été données de ces deux opérations (*cf.* R. Derathé, *Rousseau et la science politique de son temps, op. cit.*, A. Philonenko, *Jean-Jacques Rousseau et la pensée du malheur*, Vrin, 1984), on ne peut nier que la pensée de Rousseau demeure aporétique, en raison de son point de départ individualiste, ainsi que le met en évidence l'intervention du législateur (*Contrat social*, livre II, chapitre VII). Il nous semble qu'en revanche Hegel évite cette impasse parce que son point de départ est situé dans l'histoire et dans la société

390. Comme c'est le cas chez Rousseau.

391. C'est parce qu'il croit que l'homme n'est pas essentiellement, originellement et exclusivement producteur, mais aussi un être parlant (*homo loquax*), que Habermas a consacré une grande partie de sa philosophie à la communication et à l'herméneutique. Il s'intéresse non seulement à la manière dont les signes renvoient au sens, mais également à la façon dont une communauté peut voir son rapport à son histoire ou à elle-même obscurci, et au fait qu'elle a besoin, pour se parler, de s'accorder sur un certain nombre de règles qui permettent l'exercice même de la parole.

392. C'est encore une fois le schème de l'équilibre qui domine, « équilibre adéquat entre des revendications concurrentes », *Théorie de la justice, op. cit.*, p. 36. Ce schème est évidemment profondément économique. La notion même de voile d'ignorance (et de justice procédurale) renvoie à l'économie, comme le montre cette référence à Hayek, cité par J.-P. Dupuy dans *Le Sacrifice et l'envie, op. cit.*, p. 227 : « C'est seulement parce que nous ne pouvons prédire le résultat effectif de l'adoption d'une règle déterminée que nous pouvons admettre l'hypothèse qu'elle augmentera les chances de tous également. Que ce soit l'ignorance du résultat futur qui rend possible l'accord sur les règles [...], c'est ce que reconnaît la pratique fréquente qui consiste à rendre délibérément imprévisible un résultat, afin de rendre possible l'accord sur une procédure... »

393. J. Rawls, *Théorie de la justice, op. cit.*, p. 38. C'est nous qui soulignons.

394. « Parmi toutes les conceptions traditionnelles, je crois que c'est celle du contrat qui se rapproche le mieux de nos jugements bien pesés sur la justice et qui constitue la base morale qui convient le mieux à une société démocratique », écrit Rawls, *ibid.*, p. 20.

395. « La justice sociale est l'application du principe de prudence rationnelle à une conception du bien-être du groupe considéré comme un agrégat », *ibid.*, p. 50.

396. C'est parce qu'il proposait une synthèse tellement délicate que Rawls a été introduit et surtout très commenté en France, en particulier après la publication d'un rapport du CERC, en 1989, montrant que les inégalités avaient fortement augmenté en France dans les années 1980 (*Les Revenus des Français, le tournant des années 80*, Documents du CERC, n° 94). Rawls fut opportunément cité dans un document de travail du Commissariat général du Plan intitulé *Inégalités 90*, l'année suivante, pour illustrer le fait que certaines inégalités étaient tout à fait supportables, alors que d'autres ne l'étaient pas : « Des réflexions théoriques récentes, pouvait-on lire dans ce document, permettent de porter un regard nouveau sur les inégalités : considérée avant la crise comme un bien en soi, la réduction des inégalités apparaît aujourd'hui comme une question plus complexe. » Toutes les inégalités ne doivent pas être combattues, bien au contraire. Sur l'introduction de Rawls en France et

les diverses interprétations dont il a été l'objet, on pourra lire B. Théret, « Le " Rawlsisme " à la française », le marché contre l'égalité démocratique ? », in *Futur antérieur*, n° 8, hiver 1991, et Y. Roucaute, « Rawls en France », in *L'Evolution de la philosophie du droit en Allemagne et en France depuis la fin de la Seconde Guerre mondiale*, PUF, 1991. Ce dernier écrit, p. 213 : « C'est l'époque où l'on commence à croire, sur fond de ruine des dérivés du léninisme, que Rawls pourrait être un atout non négligeable pour penser dans le " libéralisme " devenu hégémonique, mais à gauche. » Il poursuit, p. 223 : « Les intellectuels " de gauche " n'acceptaient pas avant 1982 une théorie qui légitimait l'inégalité sociale, marquée du sceau du lieu culturel de sa production (nord-américaine) ; les libéraux français voyaient dans le principe de différence celui de la redistribution, et donc l'interventionnisme de l'Etat. [...] D'où le succès : la référence à Rawls n'est guère dissociable d'une double crise qui coïncide en quelques années. »

397. Sur tous ces auteurs, on pourra lire J.-P. Dupuy, Ph. Van Parijs, A. Sen, déjà cités, et aussi J.-F. Kervegan, « Y a-t-il une philosophie libérale ? Remarques sur les œuvres de J. Rawls et F. von Hayek », in *Rue Descartes*, n° 3, 1992, ainsi que *Individu et justice sociale, autour de John Rawls*, Seuil, coll. « Points », 1988.

398. F. von Hayek, *Droit, législation, liberté*, tome I, PUF, 1986, chapitre v.

399. K. Polanyi, *La Grande Transformation, op. cit.*, chapitre v. Dans ce chapitre, ainsi que dans les deux précédents, Polanyi met bien en évidence que c'est ce schème autorégulateur qui caractérise l'économie. Il écrit, p. 88 : « La société est gérée en tant qu'auxiliaire du marché. [...] Au lieu que l'économie soit encastrée dans les relations sociales, ce sont les relations sociales qui sont encastrées dans le système économique. »

400. P. Batifoulier, L. Cordonnier, Y. Zenou « Le don contre-don, approche économique et approche de la sociologie », in *Revue économique*, septembre 1992 ; B. Reynaud, *Théorie des salaires, op. cit.*, et *Le Salaire, la règle et le marché, op. cit.*

401. *Ibid.*

402. Voir les ouvrages de J. Elster, *Leibniz et la formation de l'esprit capitaliste*, Aubier, 1975 ; *Karl Marx, une interprétation analytique*, PUF, 1989 ; et la revue *Actuel Marx*, n° 7 : « Le marxisme analytique anglo-saxon ».

403. Pour une bibliographie et une analyse de l'institutionnalisme américain, voir L. Bazzoli, T. Kirat, M.-C. Villeval, « Contrat et institutions dans la relation salariale : pour un renouveau institutionnaliste », in *Travail et Emploi*, n° 58, 1994. Sur J.R. Commons, voir note ronéotée, L. Bazzoli, « La création négociée et pragmatique de règles. Apport de l'analyse institutionnaliste de J.R. Commons et enjeux d'une action collective régulatrice du rapport salarial », avril 1993.

404. Voir par exemple M. Lallement, « Théorie des jeux et équilibres sociaux », in *Revue du Mauss*, n° 4, second semestre 1994.

405. A. Sen, *Ethique et économie, op. cit.*, voir tout le chapitre II, « Jugements sur l'économie et philosophie morale ». A. Sen écrit, p. 45 : « Par conséquent, puisque la thèse de l'utilité en tant que seule source de valeur repose sur l'assimilation de l'utilité et du bien-être, on peut la critiquer pour deux raisons : 1. parce que le bien-être n'est pas la seule valeur ; 2. parce que l'utilité ne représente pas correctement le bien-être. »

406. F. Fourquet, *Richesse et puissance, op. cit.*, p. 261.

407. Il s'agit là d'une formule bien connue de Jean Bodin.

408. « Il est de l'intérêt public de corriger par une bienfaisance réfléchie les maux résultant des mauvaises institutions qui ont maintenu et propagé la pauvreté », Comité de mendicité de la Constituante, *Quatrième rapport*, 1790. Voir aussi M.-A. Barthe, « Pauvretés et Etat-providence », *art. cit.*

409. Le rapport de la Commission de l'assistance et de la prévoyance publique, rédigé par A. Thiers en 1850, est un bon exemple de cette doctrine officielle. Par exemple : « Il importe que cette vertu [la bienfaisance], quand elle devient, de particulière, collective, de vertu privée, vertu publique, conserve son caractère de vertu, c'est-à-dire reste volontaire, spontanée, libre enfin de faire ou de ne pas faire, car autrement elle cesserait d'être une vertu pour devenir une contrainte. » Voir aussi M.-Th. Join-Lambert, *Politiques sociales, op. cit.*, p. 258-270.

410. E. Durkheim, *La Division sociale du travail, op. cit.*

411. Et, en particulier, évidemment les « déchirements » de notre système de protection sociale entre deux conceptions, l'une relevant de l'assurance et l'autre de la solidarité, *cf.* M.-Th. Join-Lambert, *Politiques sociales, op. cit.*, p. 255.

412. P. Laroque nous a confirmé qu'il s'agissait bien, en 1945, de mettre en place un véritable système de sécurité sociale couvrant la totalité de la population. Voir des extraits de l'exposé des motifs de l'ordonnance du 4 octobre 1945, in M.-Th. Join-Lambert, *Politiques sociales, op. cit.*, p. 276. On y lit notamment : « Le problème qui se pose alors est celui d'une redistribution du revenu national destinée à prélever sur le revenu des individus favorisés les sommes nécessaires pour compléter les ressources des travailleurs ou des familles défavorisées. [...] Envisagée sous cet angle, la sécurité sociale obligatoire appelle l'aménagement d'une vaste organisation d'entraide obligatoire. »

413. P. Rosanvallon, *La Crise de l'Etat-providence, op. cit.*

414. L'opposition *Gesellschaft/Gemeinschaft* a été analysée par F. Tönnies in *Communauté et société. Catégories fondamentales de la société pure*, Retz, 1977. Voir aussi L. Dumont, *Essais sur l'individualisme, op. cit.*

415. Kant, *Idée d'une histoire universelle du point de vue cosmopoliti-*

que, opuscule écrit en 1784, repris avec une série d'autres textes dans *Opuscules sur l'histoire*, GF-Flammarion, 1990. L'expression « insociable sociabilité » est utilisée par Kant ; elle désigne l'inclination des hommes à entrer en société, « qui est cependant doublée d'une répulsion générale à le faire, menaçant constamment de désagréger cette société ».

416. Aristote, *La Politique, op. cit.*, livre I, chapitre I, 1252a. Aristote ajoute dans le livre I, chapitre II, 1252b-1253a : « Enfin, la communauté formée de plusieurs villages est la cité au plein sens du mot. [...] Ainsi formée au début pour satisfaire les seuls besoins vitaux, elle existe pour permettre de bien vivre. C'est pourquoi toute cité est un fait de nature. [...] La cité est au nombre des réalités qui existent naturellement, et l'homme est par nature un animal politique. Et celui qui est sans cité, naturellement et non par suite des circonstances, est ou un être dégradé ou au-dessus de l'humanité. » On se reportera également aux analyses de E. Benveniste consacrées à la différence entre la cité grecque et la *civitas* romaine : la *polis* grecque est première et fonde la relation d'appartenance qui définit le citoyen ; la *civitas* romaine est seconde par rapport aux citoyens, c'est la totalité additive des *cives*. Elle apparaît donc comme une sommation, écrit Benveniste, et elle réalise une vaste mutualité. E. Benveniste, *Problèmes de linguistique générale*, tome II, Gallimard, coll. « Tel », 1974, chapitre XX, p. 272-280.

417. Voir sur ce point les nombreuses analyses d'I. Berlin, *Eloge de la liberté*, Presses-Pocket, 1990 ; *Le Bois tordu de l'humanité*, Albin Michel, 1992, et *A contre-courant. Essais sur l'histoire des idées*, Albin Michel, 1988.

418. En 1985, J. Rawls précisait sa pensée, écrivant : « [La justice politique] doit tenir compte d'une diversité de doctrines et de la pluralité des conceptions du bien qui s'affrontent et qui sont effectivement incommensurables entre elles, soutenues par les membres des sociétés démocratiques existantes », in *Individu et justice sociale, op. cit.*, p. 281.

419. Sur cette interprétation, et pour la contredire, voir en particulier sur Hegel, E. Weil, *Hegel et l'Etat, op. cit.* ; et sur Marx, la préface de M. Rubel aux *Œuvres* de Marx, Gallimard, coll. « La Pléiade », *op. cit.* ; son ouvrage, *Karl Marx, essai de biographie intellectuelle*, Rivière, 1971 ; et M. Henry, *Marx,* 2 tomes, Gallimard, 1976. Ces derniers distinguent fortement la pensée de Marx du marxisme.

420. Les exemples sont multiples. Parmi les plus fameux, on retiendra les ouvrages de F. von Hayek, et plus encore ceux de K. Popper, en particulier *La Société ouverte et ses ennemis*, Seuil, 1979, dans lequel Popper fait de Hegel l'ancêtre du totalitarisme. Mais, d'une manière plus générale, une très grande partie des travaux philosophico-logiques anglosaxons sont destinés, depuis le début du XXᵉ siècle, à démontrer l'inanité des propos de la métaphysique allemande.

421. Dans ses *Essais sur l'individualisme*, L. Dumont propose un lexique dans lequel on peut lire qu' « on désigne comme holiste une

idéologie qui valorise la totalité sociale et néglige ou subordonne l'individu humain ». Or, toute la thèse de L. Dumont consiste à dire qu'une société qui n'est pas conçue comme une agrégation est holiste, donc opprime l'individu... L. Dumont développe dans cet ouvrage comme dans d'autres une interprétation de Hegel qui passe à côté de l'apport véritable de celui-ci, et qui le confond avec la grande masse des « holistes ». Voir en particulier « Genèses II », in *Essais sur l'individualisme, op. cit.*, où L. Dumont interprète les tentatives allemandes exclusivement comme une renaissance de l'*universitas*.

422. L. Dumont, *Homo aequalis, op. cit.*, p. 134. Nous nous appuyons largement sur ce livre, car c'est, nous semble-t-il, l'un des mieux connus des responsables politiques et administratifs. C'est un classique qui constitue pour beaucoup un bon résumé de la théorie politique actuelle et dont se sont également inspirés un certain nombre d'essayistes.

423. *Théorie de la justice, op. cit.*, p. 53.

424. *Ibid.*, p. 92.

425. *Ibid.* Rawls écrit également que les institutions les plus importantes sont : la protection légale de la liberté de pensée et de conscience, l'existence de marchés concurrentiels ; la propriété privée des moyens de production et la famille monogamique en sont des exemples (*ibid.*, p. 33).

426. J.-P. Dupuy, *Le Sacrifice et l'envie, op. cit.*

427. Toute la philosophie hégélienne du droit est une critique de l'idée de contrat, de même que de l'individualisme et du droit abstrait sur lesquels cette idée se fonde : la volonté pleinement autonome et l'individu du droit romain ou de la philosophie du XVIIIᵉ siècle ne sont que des abstractions. Il n'y a d'individu que pleinement incarné dans une société, de volonté que déjà à l'œuvre dans le monde, de contrat que dans la société.

428. Hegel, *Précis de l'Encyclopédie des sciences philosophiques*, Vrin, 1970, § 495. Voir aussi *Principes de la philosophie du droit, op. cit.*, § 75 et l'article de G. Planty-Bonjour, « Majesté de l'Etat et dignité de la personne selon Hegel », in *L'Evolution de la philosophie du droit..., op. cit.*, p. 7.

429. Hegel, *Principes de la philosophie..., op. cit.*, § 258.

430. *Cf.* A. Wellmer, « Modèles de la liberté dans le monde moderne », in *Critique*, juin-juillet 1989, p. 506 et suivantes.

431. En ce qui concerne Hegel, les exemples sont innombrables. On retiendra : « Le droit de la particularité du sujet à trouver sa satisfaction ou, ce qui revient au même, le droit de la liberté subjective constitue le point critique et central qui marque la différence entre les Temps modernes et l'Antiquité », *Principes de la philosophie..., op. cit.*, § 124 ; ou encore : « Il faut évaluer comme quelque chose de grand le fait qu'aujourd'hui l'homme en tant qu'homme est considéré comme titulaire de droits en sorte que l'être humain est quelque chose de supérieur à son statut. Chez les Israélites, avaient des droits, seulement les Hébreux, chez

les Grecs, seulement les Grecs libres, chez les Romains seulement les Romains et ils avaient des droits dans leur qualité d'Hébreux, de Grecs, de Romains, non en leur qualité d'hommes en tant que tels. Mais à présent, comme source du droit, sont en vigueur les principes universels, et ainsi dans le monde a commencé une nouvelle époque », cité par G. Planty-Bonjour, « Majesté de l'Etat... », *art. cit.*.

432. C'est ce que tend à démontrer toute la philosophie de Hegel : non seulement l'individu abstrait que décrivent les philosophies individualistes ou l'économie du XVIIIe siècle n'existe pas, l'individu n'existe qu'incarné dans une communauté, une langue, un territoire, des institutions politiques, mais, de plus, l'Etat est ce qui respecte infiniment l'individu : « Le principe des Etats modernes a cette force et cette profondeur prodigieuse de permettre au principe de la subjectivité de s'accomplir au point de devenir l'extrême autonome de la particularité personnelle et de le ramener en même temps dans l'unité substantielle, et ainsi de conserver en lui-même cette unité substantielle », *Principes de la philosophie..., op. cit.*, § 260.

433. Tocqueville dépasse, lui aussi, l'étape de la liberté négative comme seul principe et tente de la concilier avec l'idée d'une communauté politique. C'est pour cette raison que sa conception fait place à l'idée d'un bien commun et d'individus discutant et débattant de la conception de ce bien commun : « La liberté négative telle qu'elle s'incarne dans les structures de la société civile est ici transformée dans la liberté positive ou rationnelle de citoyens qui agissent ensemble ; cette liberté positive ou rationnelle revient à une forme de restauration de ces liens communautaires entre les individus dont l'absence définit leur existence en tant que propriétaires indépendants. [...] La liberté seule [peut] retirer les citoyens de l'isolement dans lequel l'indépendance même de leur condition les fait vivre, pour les contraindre à se rapprocher les uns des autres. [...] Elle les réunit chaque jour par la nécessité de s'entendre, de se persuader, et de se complaire mutuellement dans la pratique d'affaires communes. [...] Seule elle fournit à l'ambition des objets plus grands que l'acquisition des richesses », *L'Ancien régime et la Révolution*, GF-Flammarion, 1988, p. 94-95.

434. I. Berlin, *Eloge de la liberté, op. cit.*, p. 50.

435. Les spécialistes de Hegel ont montré depuis longtemps les confusions sur lesquelles s'appuyaient certaines lectures de Hegel : il est bien au contraire, le penseur antinationaliste par excellence. Il est également le concepteur de l'Etat moderne, un Etat fortement centralisé dans son administration, largement décentralisé en ce qui concerne les intérêts économiques, avec un corps de fonctionnaires de métier, sans religion d'Etat. On lira sur tous ces points, outre les ouvrages déjà cités de J. Hippolyte, K. Papaionnou et E. Weil, une série d'articles dans les *Cahiers internationaux de sociologie*, 1948, dont celui de J. Hippolyte, « La conception hégélienne de l'Etat et sa critique par Marx ».

436. Voir Marx, *Critique de la philosophie politique de Hegel,* écrit en 1843 et publié dans le tome I de La Pléiade, qui est un commentaire acéré des *Principes de la philosophie du droit* de Hegel et dont le nœud est précisément l'articulation entre société civile et Etat. La critique de Marx est extrêmement pertinente : elle montre que, chez Hegel, les individus, même s'ils sont reconnus, ne participent pas réellement à la détermination des objectifs de l'Etat, que les ordres intermédiaires ne servent qu'à peu de chose et que la société civile n'a aucun moyen de se protéger des débordements de l'Etat (voir en particulier p. 943). Mais Marx, de ce fait, en déduit qu'il faut supprimer l'Etat, et non le réformer.

437. C'est la Nation qui, dans le préambule de la Constitution de 1946, assure à l'individu et à la famille les conditions nécessaires à leur développement, garantit à l'enfant, à la mère et au vieux travailleur la protection sociale, le repos et les loisirs, proclame la solidarité et l'égalité de tous les Français devant les charges...

438. Dans cette tradition, on compte P. Rosanvallon, avec *La Crise de l'Etat-providence, op. cit.,* mais aussi I. Illich, qui critique l'Etat au nom des valeurs d'usage ou du domaine vernaculaire ; voir en particulier *Le Travail fantôme,* Seuil, 1981 ; *Le Chômage créateur,* Seuil, 1977 ; *Libérer l'avenir,* Seuil, coll. « Points », 1971 ; *La Convivialité,* Seuil, 1975 ; mais aussi le « premier » Habermas, par exemple *La Technique et la science comme « idéologie »,* Gallimard, 1973. La quatrième de couverture de *La Crise de l'Etat-providence* indiquait ainsi : « Cet essai se propose de substituer une triple dynamique de la socialisation, de la décentralisation et de l'autonomisation à la logique classique de l'étatisation du social. »

439. Sur le développement des inégalités dans notre pays, voir en particulier Documents du CERC, *Les Français et leurs revenus, le tournant des années 80,* n° 94, La Documentation française et le rapport *Santé 2010,* atelier « Les inégalités devant la santé », La Documentation française, 1993.

440. C'est l'idée développée depuis trente ans par Habermas et reprise des Lumières : accroître l'espace public, qui est le seul espace réellement politique. Sur ce point, voir la thèse de J.-M. Ferry, *Habermas. L'éthique de la communication,* PUF, 1987, et ce que J.-M. Ferry dit des premiers travaux de Habermas consacrés à cette notion.

441. L'expression est de Habermas, « La crise de l'Etat-providence », in *Ecrits politiques, op. cit.,* p. 120. Habermas précisait auparavant qu'il n'y avait pas de solution de rechange perceptible à l'Etat social.

442. Voir J.-L. Nancy, *La Communauté désœuvrée,* Christian Bourgois, 1990.

443. « Le projet de la modernité est le projet d'une telle réconciliation entre la liberté négative et la liberté communautaire. Il faut dire contre Marx et contre Hegel que ce projet est un projet en marche, sans solutions définitives. [..] Contre le libéralisme, il faut dire que, sans la réalisation d'une liberté communautaire et rationnelle, et donc d'une forme démo-

cratique de vie éthique, la liberté négative ne peut devenir qu'une caricature ou qu'un cauchemar », A. Wellmer, « Modèles de la liberté dans le monde moderne », *art. cit.* C'est une des grandes idées de Hannah Arendt que de penser que la sphère de l'action politique est son propre contenu ; autrement dit, c'est en débattant du bien social que l'on fait le lien social ; *cf. Essai sur la révolution*, Gallimard, 1967.

444. Il ne s'agit évidemment pas de ne plus tenir compte des contraintes que nous impose notre intégration dans un système d'échanges mondiaux et dans leurs institutions, mais de revoir progressivement la place que tient l'économie dans nos sociétés modernes et de renverser le rapport économie/politique en discutant des critères de richesses considérés, du contenu de la croissance, du périmètre pris en compte pour le calcul de la rentabilité... Il ne s'agit pas de « rêver » ou de prendre nos désirs pour des réalités, mais de redonner à l'économie sa place : celle d'une technique qui fait des calculs et propose différentes solutions, en affichant ses critères, et dont les résultats et les hypothèses de travail sont ensuite soumis à discussion.

445. Et donc d'engager une véritable réforme de notre comptabilité nationale : de la soumettre à discussion et à examen, de ne pas laisser les économistes décider de ce qui est ou n'est pas une richesse pour la société.

446. Dans *Le Désenchantement du monde*, Gallimard, 1985, M. Gauchet explique que le rôle de l'État est désormais de s'adapter totalement aux souhaits des citoyens : « L'État démocratique — bureaucratique — progresse à la mesure de son renoncement même à toute vue prescriptive de l'avenir et de l'accentuation de son ouverture représentative à la multiplicité mouvante des aspirations et des initiatives de ses administrés », p. 262. C'est sans doute avoir là une idée insuffisante de la fonction de l'État. La fonction de médiation ne peut se réduire à une fonction de reflet.

447. La liste de tous les éléments que devrait publier l'État (comptes certifiés, analyses des revenus et de leurs écarts, analyses des dépenses publiques avec des comptabilités analytiques intégrées, etc.) serait fixée dans une loi d'un caractère particulier. Le rôle de l'État en matière de « publicité » est essentiel : publier selon une périodicité donnée, et en les rendant accessibles, les données nécessaires au débat social, sur la protection sociale, les différentes structures chargées de la gestion d'un intérêt public ; publier les mêmes données concernant son propre fonctionnement, de manière très précise et sans qu'aucun gouvernement puisse y échapper ; donner des informations sur la structure et l'évolution des revenus et des avantages divers des différentes catégories socioprofessionnelles doit permettre d'améliorer la participation des citoyens au débat public : il n'y a aucune raison que seuls les fonctionnaires spécialisés aient accès à ces informations.

448. L'État n'a pas suffisamment recours à cette procédure. Ainsi par exemple, la loi Debré de 1958 sur les hôpitaux prévoyait que des cliniques

privées pourraient obtenir des concessions de la part de l'Etat, c'est-à-dire prendre en charge un intérêt public, en assurer la gestion, en suivant les objectifs fixés par l'Etat. Au lieu de cela, se sont développés, soit des hôpitaux publics gérés de manière « publique », soit des cliniques privées, dont les obligations étaient (et restent) très peu pesantes et différentes de celles qu'avait à remplir le public : incapacité de l'Etat à fixer des objectifs et à évaluer régulièrement leur réalisation, incapacité des acteurs privés à se plier aux contraintes issues de la prise en charge d'un intérêt public... Qui est responsable ? Un raisonnement identique pourrait être tenu aujourd'hui en ce qui concerne la gestion de la Sécurité sociale : distinguer intérêt public et gestion publique, distinguer responsabilité générale et gestion quotidienne, cela est aujourd'hui essentiel.

449. En particulier de l'ENA, de manière à ce que cette école forme des fonctionnaires et non des hommes politiques.

450. Dans cet ordre d'idée, Habermas écrit : « Les sociétés modernes disposent de trois ressources à partir desquelles elles peuvent subvenir à leurs besoins de régulations : l'argent, le pouvoir et la solidarité. Il serait nécessaire qu'il y ait un rééquilibrage de leurs sphères d'influence », « La crise de l'Etat-providence », in *Ecrits politiques, op. cit.*, p. 122.

451. H. Bartoli, *Science économique et travail, op. cit.*, « Le travail, source de droit », p. 51-54.

452. C'est une notion qui a été répandue en France par la traduction du livre de J. Rawls. Le terme *fairness* est traduit par « équité » et J. Rawls parle de « la théorie de la justice comme équité » (voir p. 29, par exemple).

453. Les sommes dépensées pour permettre aux familles disposant des plus hauts revenus d'utiliser une aide à domicile pour faire garder leurs enfants est évidement proportionnellement beaucoup plus coûteuse qu'une bonne politique d'équipements publics. Les équipements publics ont vu leur développement entravé en France, à la différence par exemple des pays scandinaves, parce qu'ils pèsent sur le budget de l'Etat et obligent à recourir à l'impôt. On préfère les solutions individuelles. Mais, comme on l'a dit, ces services publics ne doivent pas nécessairement être gérés par l'Etat ; leur inscription comptable peut être revue (si ce n'est que cela...) ; enfin, le tabou pesant sur l'impôt devrait faire aujourd'hui l'objet d'une pédagogie active : l'impôt sert à financer des fonctions collectives, il faut donc, et il suffit, qu'il soit bien utilisé. Pour cela, il reste à fixer des règles d'information et à améliorer la participation des citoyens au choix des priorités et à la connaissance de ce à quoi l'argent public a été employé.

454. Voir le numéro spécial de la revue *Droit social*, n° 3, mars 1990, sur ce thème, et B. Théret, « Le " rawlsisme " à la française », *art. cit.*

455. La régression à l'infini à laquelle se livre Rawls (*Théorie de la justice, op. cit.*, p. 30 et suivantes) est la suivante · — une situation est équitable parce qu'elle a été choisie dans des conditions équitables. Cette

procédure aboutit, en fait, à un résultat semblable à celui d'un tirage au sort. Ce qui est évident, c'est qu'ordre naturel ou tirage au sort reviennent au même : il s'agit d'éviter à tout prix le choix et la discussion, ainsi que la constitution d'un intérêt commun.

456. Le terme a été popularisé par Weber, qui utilise la formule « désenchantement du monde » à de nombreuses reprises dans son œuvre. Le terme « *entzaubern* », qui signifie désensorceler, désenchanter, briser le charme, était utilisé dans le corpus romantique, en particulier par Goethe pour désigner le résultat de l'Aufklärung. Les Lumières, l'utilisation de la raison ont vidé le monde de ses forces magiques et mystérieuses, ont ôté la dimension énigmatique du monde pour le soumettre aux sèches catégories de l'entendement.

457. M. Weber, *L'Ethique protestante...*, *op. cit.*, p. 117. Voir aussi C. Colliot-Thélène, *Max Weber et l'histoire*, PUF, coll. « Philosophies », 1990, p. 52 et suivantes.

458. Habermas, « La crise de l'Etat-providence », in *Ecrits politiques, op. cit.*, p. 110 ; voir aussi C. Offe, « Le travail comme catégorie de la sociologie », *art. cit.* : « Le fait de travailler en lui-même, ne peut guère être pris comme point de départ de la formation de groupes culturels, organisationnels et politiques », et B. Guggenberger, qui, dans *Wenn uns die Arbeit ausgeht, op. cit*, p. 94, parle d'« *anachronistische Arbeitszentralität* » c'est-à-dire de « l'anachronique centralité du travail ». Il écrit aussi : « Le travail manque à la société du travail. »

459. Qu'il s'agisse de Nietzsche, de Weber, de Freud, de Hannah Arendt, de Benjamin, de Bloch, de Habermas, de Hans Jonas, mais aussi de Heidegger. L'école de Francfort, au carrefour des héritages marxistes, freudiens et heideggeriens, avait tenté de donner à la philosophie une telle ambition : celle d'être une philosophie sociale, appuyée sur des études sociologiques et statistiques et capable de déboucher sur une pratique.

460. Voir en particulier *Généalogie de la morale*. Pour comprendre l'entreprise généalogique qui caractérise la pensée de Nietzsche, voir, de J. Granier, *Le Problème de la vérité dans la philosophie de Nietzsche, op. cit.*, en particulier les chapitres II et III sur les notions de généalogie et de critique.

461. « Nous avons l'art pour ne pas mourir de la vérité », écrit Nietzsche, qui décrit l'art comme un voile jeté sur la vérité. Créer, c'est voiler la vérité de la nature. L'art est la catégorie générale sous laquelle Nietzsche comprend toutes les formes que prend la faculté artiste, la faculté de créer de l'homme : l'art, c'est l'activité plastique de la volonté de puissance. « Identité de nature entre le conquérant, le législateur et l'artiste — la même façon de se traduire dans la matière, la plus extrême énergie. [...] Transformer le monde, afin de pouvoir tolérer d'y vivre, voilà l'instinct moteur », in *Volonté de puissance*, tome II, livre IV, § 118, cité par J. Granier, *Le Problème de la vérité dans la philosophie de*

Nietzsche, op. cit., p. 524. On lira également le *Nietzsche* de Heidegger, Gallimard, 1980, qui illustre parfaitement ceci.

462. H. Achterhuis, « La responsabilité entre la crainte et l'utopie », in *Hans Jonas, Nature et responsabilité, op. cit.*, p. 44. Voir aussi, du même auteur, « La critique du modèle industriel comme histoire de la rareté », in *Revue philosophique de Louvain*, 1989, n° 81, p. 47-62.

463. Telle est la genèse de la « civilisation » que présentent Nietzsche ou Freud.

464. Certes, nous n'en sommes pas au point où l'ensemble des apprentissages éducatifs devront être déterminés par leur capacité à rendre les facultés humaines totalement disponibles pour le système productif (ce qui n'est pas grave, nous rétorquera-t-on, puisque le système productif est productif de tout, y compris des besoins humains les plus élevés...) et où les résultats issus des recherches en sciences cognitives seront utilisés à grande échelle pour rendre cette opération la plus rentable possible, mais nous sommes sur la bonne voie...

465. Voir l'ensemble des travaux réalisés par le CNAM au moment de son bicentenaire, en particulier le colloque « Changement technique, mondialisation, emploi — où allons nous ? », 17 et 18 novembre 1994, et, dans celui-ci, le support écrit intitulé « Une nouvelle dynamique pour l'emploi », dont l'ambition est le retour au plein emploi. Voir aussi Banque Indosuez, *Conjoncture mensuelle*, novembre 1994, n° 59, « Le chômage : idées fausses et vraie solution ».

466. *Ibid.*

467. Club de Rome, note d'O. Giarini, " Some Considerations on the Future of Work. Redefining Productive Work ", OCDE-Scénario-Emploi, juin 1994.

468. La logique d'un tel développement, c'est que le temps d'un cadre est infiniment plus précieux que le temps d'une personne qui a fait trois ans ou cinq ans de moins d'études, ou dont la qualification est inférieure. Le cadre préfère donc consacrer un dixième ou un vingtième du salaire qu'il gagne en un mois à payer une personne à disposition chez lui. Les deux temps de ces deux personnes n'ont pas la même valeur, et pourtant l'échange est considéré comme égal. Dès lors, on conçoit que l'investissement initial importe énormément. L'éducation apparaît comme un investissement qui rapportera vingt ans plus tard.

469. L'idée d'une société de serviteurs, d'une néo-domesticité a été développée par A. Gorz à de nombreuses reprises. Elle paraît absolument évidente, sauf si l'on continue à considérer que les personnes disposant de moyens financiers font un cadeau aux personnes moins qualifiées en leur « donnant » un travail.

470. M. Godet, *Le Grand Mensonge : l'emploi est mort, vive l'activité !*, Fixot, 1994.

471. Voir C. Dejours, « Entre souffrance et réappropriation, le sens du travail », *art. cit.*

472. « Il serait vain d'essayer de construire une cohésion vitale, en tant qu'unité subjectivement significative, en partant de la sphère du travail. [...] Discontinuité dans la biographie de travail et part de temps de travail diminuée sur l'ensemble de la vie auront probablement pour effet de transformer le travail en fait parmi d'autres et de relativiser sa fonction comme point de repère pour l'identité personnelle et sociale », C. Offe, « Le travail comme catégorie de la sociologie », *art. cit.*

473. Expression de Habermas qui se situe dans la droite ligne du « La vie est action, non production » d'Aristote, in *La Politique, op. cit.*, livre I, chapitre IV, 1254a. Voir également le commentaire de cette expression par G. Markus (philosophe de l'école de Budapest), « *Praxis* et *poeisis* : au-delà de la dichotomie », in *Actuel Marx*, n° 10, 1991.

474. Les avis sur ce point sont très partagés : certains soutiennent que le progrès technique va contribuer, au moins dans un premier temps, à supprimer de très nombreux emplois (voir le colloque du CNAM cité, et un numéro spécial de *Futuribles*, consacré à l'allocation universelle et au partage du travail, n° 184, février 1994, « Pour ou contre le revenu minimum, l'allocation universelle, le revenu d'existence ? »). Des industriels affirment que 40 % des emplois seraient en Allemagne susceptibles d'être supprimés dès aujourd'hui, sans compter les réserves de productivité dans les services non marchands ; sur ce dernier point, voir l'article de B. Bruhnes, « Le travail réinventé », in *La France au-delà du siècle*, L'Aube, D.A.T.A.R., 1994.

475. B. Guggenberger, *Wenn uns die Arbeit ausgeht, op. cit.*, p. 123.

476. Selon la théorie économique classique, le chômage doit se résorber dans la mesure où les personnes qui se trouvent brutalement déqualifiées doivent peu à peu se porter vers les nouveaux secteurs créateurs de produits et demandeurs de main-d'œuvre. C'est la thèse de Sauvy, dite « du déversement ».

477. Un certain nombre d'études macroéconomiques ont montré qu'une réduction du chômage était possible si certaines conditions étaient réalisées, comme une légère baisse des salaires, un remaniement de l'organisation du travail, le caractère massif de la réduction. Voir les études de l'OFCE et l'intervention de P. Artus, in actes du colloque « Les réductions du temps de travail », CGP-DARES, Documentation française, 1995.

478. Il proposera au contraire une allocation universelle.

479. Actuellement un certain nombre d'auteurs soutiennent que l'importance de notre chômage vient de la surprotection qui est accordée à ceux qui ont un statut protecteur et, d'une manière générale, à ceux qui ont un emploi et dont les salaires ont augmenté. Parmi eux, certains ont développé l'idée que la diminution des statuts protecteurs accordés aux salariés (baisse du SMIC, contrats précaires, « petits boulots » très peu rémunérés, qui consisterait en une autre forme de partage) développerait une pauvreté à l'américaine, c'est-à-dire tout un pan de la population

vivant d'expédients. Dans les deux cas, la société est fortement segmentée et dans les deux cas aussi, la possession d'un travail permet de doubler la mise : plus le travail est intéressant, bien payé, responsabilisant, etc., plus la protection et les avantages attachés sont grands.

480. Sur le nombre de personnes en situation « fragile » aujourd'hui, voir Documents du CERC (Centre d'études des revenus et des coûts), *Précarité et risque d'exclusion en France*, n° 109, La Documentation française, troisième trimestre 1993 : « Au total, le nombre de personnes (y compris conjoints et enfants) qui échappent à la pauvreté ou à la précarité grâce aux différents mécanismes de notre protection sociale est aujourd'hui probablement de l'ordre de 12 à 13 millions. » Il faut néanmoins considérer ces chiffres avec précaution, car toute une partie de la fragilité ainsi mise en évidence n'est pas mesurée objectivement, mais ressentie subjectivement.

481. De très nombreuses analyses ont été consacrées à l'allocation universelle depuis quelques années. On pourra en particulier consulter ∨ Bresson, *L'Après-salariat*, Economica, 1984 ; un numéro spécial de la *Revue Nouvelle*, « L'allocation universelle », avril 1985 ; « Garantir le revenu, une des solutions à l'exclusion », in *Transversales Science Culture*, mai 1992, n° 3 ; « Allocation universelle et plein emploi, l'inéluctable alliance », in Ph. Van Parijs, *Reflets et perspectives de la vie économique*, Bruxelles, 1994 ; et *Futuribles, op. cit.*, février 94, n° 184.

482. Dans les années 1970, une partie des critiques contre le travail se faisaient du point de vue de la dignité de l'individu et au nom de celui-ci. Habermas, A. Gorz, Illich imaginaient la libération du travail aussi comme un retour à l'individu. Habermas et A. Gorz sont largement revenus sur ce point de vue depuis.

483. Voir les ouvrages de J. Dumazedier, W. Grossin et l'ensemble des réflexions sur le temps libre en 1980, qui n'ont pas abouti après la mise en place éphémère d'un ministère du même nom.

484. B. Guggenberger pose cette question et intitule l'un des chapitres de son livre : « La paresse des actifs ». « Le problème, écrit-il, ce n'est pas l'ennui, c'est notre impatience, notre incapacité à rester tranquilles. » C'est nous qui traduisons.

485. A combien d'heures doit être fixé le temps de travail de chacun ? Il s'agit d'une question qui a occupé beaucoup d'esprits. M. Johada se demande aussi : « De combien de travail l'homme a-t-il besoin ? », « Braucht das Mensch die Arbeit » [L'homme a-t-il besoin du travail], in F. Niess, *Leben Wir um zu arbeiten ? Die Arbeitswelt im Umbruch*, Köln, 1984. B. Guggenberger pose la même question dans *Wenn uns die Arbeit ausgeht, op. cit.*

TABLE

CHAMPS-FLAMMARION

SCIENCES

HISTOIRE

SCIENCES HUMAINES

ART

CINÉMA

BIOGRAPHIES

Achevé d'imprimer en septembre 2004
sur les presses de l'imprimerie Maury Eurolivres
45300 Manchecourt

N° d'Éditeur : FH140015.
Dépôt légal : février 1998.
N° d'Imprimeur : 04/09/109538.

Imprimé en France

∫